AMERICAN COURAGE, AMERICAN CARNAGE

7TH INFANTRY CHRONICLES

ALSO BY JOHN C. MCMANUS

The Americans at D-Day:
The American Experience at the Normandy Invasion

The Americans at Normandy:
The Summer of 1944–The American War
from the Normandy Beaches to Falaise

The Deadly Brotherhood:
The American Combat Soldier in World War II

Deadly Sky:
The American Combat Airman in World War II

Alamo in the Ardennes:
The Untold Story of the American Soldiers
Who Made the Defense of Bastogne Possible

U.S. Military History for Dummies

The 7th Infantry Regiment:
Combat in an Age of Terror; the Korean War Through the Present
(Also in the 7th Infantry Series)

American Courage, American Carnage

7th Infantry Chronicles

The 7th Infantry Regiment's Combat Experience, 1812 through World War II

John C. McManus

A Tom Doherty Associates Book
New York

AMERICAN COURAGE, AMERICAN CARNAGE:
7TH INFANTRY CHRONICLES

Copyright © 2009 by John C. McManus

Maps © 2009 by Rick Britton

A Forge Book
Published by Tom Doherty Associates, LLC
175 Fifth Avenue
New York, NY 10010

www.tor-forge.com

Forge® is a registered trademark of Tom Doherty Associates, LLC.

ISBN-13: 978-0-7653-2012-4
ISBN-10: 0-7653-2012-6

First Edition: June 2009

Printed in the United States of America

0   9   8   7   6   5   4   3   2   1

To Nancy, love of my life. I hope I did justice to your great idea. . . .

To Cottonbalers past, present, and future. . . .

Coat of Arms
Seventh United States Infantry

EXPLANATION

The crosssed rifles and the cotton bale above the shield commemorate the Battle of New Orleans, 1815, when cotton bales were used as breastworks.

The field piece on top of the mound recalls the action at Cerro Gordo, Mexico, 1847, when members of the Seventh carried the heights, dragging a field piece with them.

The wall represents the famous stone wall on Marye's Heights, Battle of Fredericksburg, 1862, behind which the Confederates were posted.

The seven diagonal stripes on the bottom of the shield are for World War I, representing three major engagements and four minor engagements.

The Croix de Guerre with star was awarded by the French Government for service in World War I.

The motto, *Volens et Potens,* means "Willing and Able."

I am the Infantry — Queen of Battle!
For two centuries I have kept our Nation safe,
purchasing freedom with my blood.
To tyrants, I am the day of reckoning;
to the oppressed, the hope for the future.
Where the fighting is thick, there am I . . .
I am the Infantry!
FOLLOW ME!

FROM THE CREDO
OF THE INFANTRY BRANCH,
UNITED STATES ARMY INFANTRY CENTER,
FORT BENNING, GEORGIA

CONTENTS

LIST OF MAPS

✦

ACKNOWLEDGMENTS

THIS BOOK IS THE SECOND IN A TWO-VOLUME HISTORY OF the 7th Infantry Regiment. Those of you who read the first book, *The 7th Infantry Regiment: Combat in an Age of Terror; the Korean War Through the Present,* know that the series was actually my wife Nancy's idea. One night at dinner she wondered if there was any infantry unit that had fought in all of America's wars from the Revolution to the present. This question so piqued my curiosity that I spent hours researching for answers that night. I found that no unit could claim a direct, continuous link dating back to the Revolution, but some had been in service since the early nineteenth century. Among those older regiments the history of one, the 7th Infantry, clearly stood out. For instance, among the oldest regiments in the U.S. Army, the 7th is the only unit that has fought in every nineteenth- and twentieth-century war. The 7th has the most battle streamers of any unit in the Army and the second-most Medal of Honor recipients. Hour after hour, as I dug around for more information on the 7th during that sleepless night, I realized that the unit's story is a remarkable journey through the history of America's conflicts. I decided that its story must be told.

In the months and years that followed, I dedicated myself to researching and writing the history of the 7th Infantry. Eventually, with some prompting from Bob Gleason, the executive editor at Forge, I formed the opinion that the best way to tell this extensive tale was over the course of two volumes. I covered the modern phase of the regiment's history in the aforementioned book. This book, then, is a prequel; it fills in the rest of the story as the 7th Infantry evolved from a fledgling frontier force in the early nineteenth century to a full-blown twentieth-century combat outfit, fighting world wars with thousands of soldiers serving in its ranks.

Neither this book, nor the one that preceded it, is a standard unit history, whose tendency is sometimes to glamorize the past or chronicle minutiae. My focus is different. My purpose is to write an objective, graphic, combat history of the 7th, not to discuss the regiment's every move or establish its exact lineage for army researchers. I have never served in the 7th. I am only its historian.

My objective here is the same as in the previous volume: to take you on a journey through the past, so that it springs to life for you. Imagine if you could hop into a time machine, go back, and experience history. You could see what these soldiers faced, what combat looked like, sounded like, smelled like, felt like. My aim is to give you that kind of vicarious experience through prose. My hope is that you'll be able to envision these soldiers as flesh-and-blood human beings, people who loved, hated, fought, cried, and bled. Who were they? Where did they come from? Why did they serve? How and why did they fight? I address all of these questions. Their story tells us much about American history and perhaps even our own lives.

There is no way I could have written this book without the help of a great many dedicated people. I conducted research at many archives and would like to thank the archival staffs and select individuals who proved particularly helpful. Tim Reeves at the Kansas City branch of the National Archives helped me find the information I needed from the microfilm rolls containing nineteenth-century enlistment information. Mitch Yokkelson and many others at the National Archives in Washington, D.C., and College Park, Maryland, helped guide me to a treasure trove of sources on the regiment's history. Rich Baker, David Keough, and Richard Sommers at the United States Army Military History Institute in Carlisle, Pennsylvania, are professionals in every sense of that word. They helped me get the most out of a tangled web of sources in the extensive USAMHI holdings. The staff at the Center for the Study of War and Society at the University of Tennessee, particularly Cynthia Tinker, was nice enough to send me a taped copy of an interview with a 7th Infantry rifle platoon leader in World War II. John Doerner at the White Swan Library, Little Bighorn Battlefield National Monument, in Crow Agency, Montana, cheerfully sent me copies of memoirs, diaries, and letters written by 7th infantrymen who participated in the Sioux War of 1876. Later, he facilitated a research visit to his fascinating library, helping me in every way possible. Sharon Small, curator of the Little Bighorn Museum, went the extra mile to find 7th Infantry photographs from the Sioux War. At the Big Hole National Battlefield Library in Wisdom, Montana, Mandy Wick and several other park rangers were kind enough to give me complete access to the 7th Infantry's files, many of which were chock-full of remarkable information. My good friend Kevin Hymel, an excellent military historian and all-around good guy, knows photo archives like the back of his hand. On multiple occasions, he opened his D.C.-area home to me, helped find many of the pictures in this book, and served as a perfect sounding board.

Closer to home, the library staff at the Missouri University of Science and Technology, especially Jean Eisenman and Scott Peterson, did terrific work in obtaining books and other materials for me through interlibrary loan. The university and, in particular, my Department of History and Political Science provided me with much-appreciated travel funds for my research. I would like to thank all of my colleagues in the history department for their support: Wayne Bledsoe, Michael Meagher, Tseggai Isaac, Lawrence Christenson, Don Oster, Harry Eisenman, Jack Ridley, Shannon Fogg, Michael Bruening, Jeff Schramm, Diana Ahmad, Petra DeWitt, and Pat Huber. I owe a special debt to Larry Gragg, Russ Buhite, and Tom Fleming, three outstanding mentors who have influenced me immensely. All of them are great historians and, more important, great people.

Thanks go to my editors at Forge Books, Eric Raab, Melissa Frain, and Bob Gleason, for their patience and insight. I especially appreciate Bob's input on how best to tell the story of the 7th in two volumes. I want to thank my agent, Ted Chichak, for finding an excellent home for this amazing story and also for his steady guidance. Rick Britton, a cartographer with great artistic talent, produced the maps for this and the other volume. I'd like to thank Rick for his dedication and his decency as a human being.

I wish to single out several key individuals whose help has been instrumental in the writing of this book. Without their generous input, this Story of America's Combat Experience, as told through the history of the 7th Infantry Regiment, would never have gotten off the ground.

David Jones, Rick Rhoades, and Fred Long of the 7th Infantry Regiment Association were all quite receptive to the idea of this book. They pointed me in the right direction, introduced me to many people, and gave me a great many sources. The reenactors of the 7th Infantry Living History Association know more about the regiment and its soldiers in the nineteenth century than any other single group or source. Friendly and accessible, they embraced this modern historian and made the nineteenth-century chapters feasible. Robert Paul Wettemann penned an excellent thesis on the history of the 7th Infantry in the antebellum period. He also happily answered many questions about his work. Chris Kimball took the time and trouble to send me copies of newspaper accounts, letters, and papers dealing with the 7th Infantry in the Seminole Wars. He is an expert in this area. I thank Chris for his assistance. Kevin Young, a font of Mexican War knowledge, gave me copies of valuable 7th Infantry letters as well as many useful Mexican War accounts without which that chapter could not have been written. Gary Kurutz was nice enough to share valuable Mexican War–era letters with me. My greatest debt of gratitude in this category goes to the redoubtable Steve Abolt, the foremost authority on the 7th Infantry in the nineteenth century and the commander of Company A, 7th Regiment, U.S.I. Living History Association. Steve took a great leap of faith in lending me some of his prized possessions—back issues of his newsletter, *The Cottonbale,* so that I could make copies of relevant information. Steve also sent me plenty of other valuable information, and he was quite generous with his time and knowledge in our conversations. I am deeply appreciative of his help.

The twentieth-century chapters also benefited from the help of some unselfish, knowledgeable people. Sandy Dechert was kind enough to send me several chapters of her biography of her grandfather Bob Dechert. Tom Millea typed up his father's World War I diary and sent me a copy. Ed Dojutrek and Jim Drury of the 3rd Infantry Division Association provided help in finding back issues of their association newsletters. Ed, in particular, put me in touch with Mrs. Cornelia Carswell Serota, who allowed me access to her mother Emma Dickson's World War I remembrances. For that, I thank her.

In relation to World War II, Steve Mazak provided me with an informative retrospective look at the combat experiences of his greatuncle in the 7th Infantry. Veterans such as Russ Cloer and Russell Sutton made sure I had as much information on their combat experiences as I desired. I want to single out four very special 7th Infantry veterans of World War II for their incredible generosity and enthusiasm for this project. Isadore Valenti authored an excellent memoir of his time as a combat medic in the 7th Infantry but also, in several conversations, related plenty of important details. Earl Reitan did something he did not have to do: he gave me an advance copy of his manuscript about his experiences and those of his buddies in the regiment in World War II. He also wrote a terrific paper on the Battle of Utweiler, probably the most dispiriting episode in the Second World War for the 7th Infantry. Sherman Pratt holds a special place in my heart. He is a historian himself and, in that capacity, guided me to many key sources on the regiment's history, especially in World War II and Korea. Like Steve Abolt, Sherm kindly trusted me with his back issues of *The Cottonbaler*, the veterans' association newsletter for those who have served in the 7th's modern wars. Sherm also gave me plenty of moral support, in addition to writing a powerful, descriptive memoir of his time in the regiment in World War II. I will be forever thankful to him. Bob Appel provided me with much valuable information, including a copy of his book, *The Outdoor Kids of Company B, 7th Infantry Regiment, Third Division, U.S. Army*.

I wish to thank all Cottonbalers, living and dead, for their service in this remarkable organization. The Cottonbalers' history is, I believe, synonymous with the story of America's combat experience.

As always, my greatest debt is to my friends and family. I want to thank Mike Chopp, Mark Williams, Joe Carcagno, Dave Cohen, Ron Kurtz, Chris Anderson, the Vincent brothers, John Villier, Ed Laughlin, John Anderson, Thad O'Donnell, Bob Kaemmerlen, Steve Kutheis, and Sean Roarty, among others, for being true friends at all times. My in-laws, the Woody family, including Doug, David, Ruth, and Nelson, have extended enduring kindness and kinship to me. The same goes for Nancy and Charlie. Thanks to my siblings, Nancy and Mike, for tolerating a workaholic brother. Thanks also to my nieces and nephews for their love and youthful energy. My parents, Michael and Mary Jane, have my greatest respect and appreciation for the wonderful life they've given me. Hopefully this book will honor them in some way. My greatest word of appreciation, of course, goes to my loving wife, Nancy. She inspired this series, which has impacted our lives in so many ways. She assisted with many research details, especially with regard to photographs, and functioned as my alter ego. The research and writing for this two-volume series absorbed my life for several years. Nancy understood, every step of the way, what it means to pursue one's passion. The word "thanks" does not convey the gratitude I feel.

JOHN C. MCMANUS
St. Louis, Missouri

AMERICAN COURAGE, AMERICAN CARNAGE

7TH INFANTRY CHRONICLES

The Beginning of the Regiment

The Battle of New Orleans

OFFICIALLY, AND DIRECTLY, THE 7TH INFANTRY CAME INTO existence on January 11, 1812, when the United States, after years of tension over neutrality rights, began preparing for imminent hostilities with Great Britain. At that time Congress authorized the raising of several infantry regiments for the coming war. Fair enough, but unfortunately, the story of the 7th's lineage is far more complicated than those simple facts might indicate. To begin with, a unit called the 7th Infantry Regiment existed as early as 1798, when the country endured a war scare with France and Congress passed a law briefly raising the strength of the tiny Regular Army. That version of the 7th Regiment existed for two years and was then disbanded. Then, in 1808, Congress revived it, partially due to the recruiting efforts of a young officer named Zachary Taylor, who would later become president of the United States. Portions of this 7th Infantry fought at such battles as Tippecanoe in 1811 and Fort Harrison in 1812. Later the whole regiment fought at the Battle of New Orleans in 1815.

So why the confusion? In May 1815, after the war with Britain, Congress, in a decision that would befuddle and vex future generations of military unit genealogists, ordered that the 7th consolidate with the 3rd and 44th Infantry Regiments to form the 1st Infantry Regiment, which still exists today. Three other regiments, the 8th, 24th, and 39th, were organized into a *new* version of the 7th Infantry Regiment. The oldest of these vanishing regiments, the 8th, had been founded on January 11, 1812, which accounts for the "birth" date mentioned earlier. This reorganization might have made sense to a Congress concerned primarily with downsizing the Army, but it played hell with unit integrity and traditions for many years to come.

For decades the Army cared little for such nostalgia, until General George B. McClellan in 1862 began the practice of allowing units to fly battle and campaign streamers with their colors. McClellan was a poor fighting general, but he intuitively understood how to build soldier morale. He correctly believed that emphasizing a unit's proud lineage would contribute to pride, discipline, and combat effectiveness. The 1862 version of the 7th Infantry Regiment naturally included New Orleans amid its battle streamers. By this time the unit had built a proud heritage, handed down through generations of antebellum soldiers, and that heritage began at New Orleans because soldiers from the old 7th Infantry Regiment had fought tenaciously there. The regiment even acquired a nickname as a result of its key role in this battle—the Cottonbalers. Supposedly, the soldiers of the old 7th fought the British from behind bales of cotton that had been hauled to their positions from New Orleans warehouses. Although this is probably not true—British cannonballs would have easily set such cotton bales afire—the name stuck and fostered a spirit of identity and pride among the soldiers who served in the "new" 7th Regiment born during the reorganization of 1815.

For most of the nineteenth century the Army allowed the 7th Infantry to include New Orleans among its battle streamers, even though technically this post-1815 version of the 7th had not fought there, since it was the product of what had been three other regiments not involved in the battle. In 1895 the War Department decided to address the innumerable lineage problems created by the 1815 reorganization. As a result, the War Department stripped the 7th of its New Orleans streamer. Then, in 1896, the War Department reversed itself. But, fourteen years later, it reversed itself again, ruling that New Orleans could not be counted among the 7th's battles. For several years this view prevailed, and with war in Europe on the horizon, no one much cared. After the war, though, 7th Regiment officers voiced furious opposition to this policy. For one thing, the city of New Orleans had in 1919 adopted the 7th as "Louisiana's Own." For another, the unit's nickname and much of its heritage stemmed from its central role in the Battle of New Orleans. One officer summed up the general attitude nicely: "It is not believed that the War Department in doing this realized how deep was the feeling in the 7th Infantry because of this action. In some of our old Infantry regiments . . . the esprit de corps and regimental traditions built around old battles have been more or less broken up." The War Department relented in 1923 and issued a compromise. The 7th would receive credit for New Orleans (and other smaller engagements in which the "old" 7th participated) but would trace its birth to 1812 instead of 1798. This was a wise decision. After all, what difference did it really make that the actual officers and men who served at New Orleans finished their postwar careers as members of the 1st Infantry Regiment? Most of them left the Army within months of the battle anyway. Direct lineage notwithstanding, logic would dictate that those who fought under the colors of a unit called the 7th Regiment in early 1815 would share a common heritage with soldiers of a unit with the same name and colors, no matter the year. As a result, the modern 7th Infantry can rightfully and officially trace its heritage to the Battle of New Orleans, and this is where the combat history of the unit can begin.[1]

At New Orleans the Cottonbalers fought their first battle as a cohesive regiment, but previously, groups of them had been involved in fighting the battles of Tippecanoe and Fort Harrison. The latter is particularly interesting because in the first year of the War of 1812 Taylor commanded a motley assortment of sick and hungry 7th infantrymen at this fort near present-day Terre Haute, Indiana. A group of several hundred Native Americans, under the leadership of the famous chief Tecumseh, attacked the tiny fort on September 4. At the outset of the war, Tecumseh had allied himself with Britain, mainly because of his antipathy to American settlers who were steadily but surely encroaching westward into present-day Ohio, Indiana, and Michigan. When Tecumseh's troops arrived at Fort Harrison, they shot at the fort and set fire to one of its blockhouses. The flames spread with alarming speed and provoked anguished screams from several women and children who had taken refuge within the dubious security of the fort. Unnerved by the fear of the civilians, the soldiers wavered in carrying out Taylor's orders to man their posts and shoot back at the Indians. Like any good commander, Taylor sprang to action and set an immediate example for his troops: "I saw that by throwing off part of the roof that joined the blockhouse that was on fire, and keeping the end perfectly wet, the whole row of buildings might be saved, and leave only an entrance of 18 to 20 feet for the Indians to enter after the blockhouse was consumed. A temporary breastwork might be erected to prevent their entering there. I convinced the men that this could be done, and it appeared to inspire them with new life, and never did the men act with more firmness and desperation."[2] Eventually the men put out the fires, plugged the gap in blockhouses, and hunkered down in safety while Tecumseh's men ineffectually shot arrows and musket balls at the fort. The chief withdrew his soldiers out of range of the fort's guns, and before he could mount a new attack, a U.S. Army relief force arrived at Fort Harrison. Tecumseh's forces slipped away to fight again elsewhere, and Taylor became a war hero.[3]

THE FIRST TWO YEARS OF THE WAR OF 1812 FEATURED American offensives, generally aimed at Canada. Knowing that the British were preoccupied with battling Napoleon Bonaparte's French Army in Europe, American leaders were determined to hit the British swiftly and effectively before their superior military power and resources could come into play in the Western Hemisphere. It didn't work. The amateurish American offensives failed miserably. By 1814 the British had defeated Napoleon and could now send a vast armada and army westward to deal with the contentious, outgunned Americans. The British planned a three-pronged offensive: one out of Canada aimed at Lake Champlain and the Hudson valley, one in the Chesapeake states aimed at Washington, D.C., and Baltimore, and the third aimed at the southern coast of America, primarily the port cities of Mobile and New Orleans. They went one for three. The northern prong failed in the face of American naval strength on the waters of upstate New York. The Chesapeake prong succeeded. Here the British defeated a force of pitifully led and trained American militia forces at the Battle of Bladensburg. They waltzed into Washington and burned the President's Mansion, the Capitol, and other government buildings, but rain put out the fires before destruction was complete. Their southern prong failed, though, partially because of the 7th Infantry Regiment.

Throughout much of 1814, General Andrew Jackson, in command of American forces in the 7th Military District, which covered the southern coast, warily watched for British movements in his area. The year before, he had led a successful campaign against the Creek nation in present-day Florida and Alabama, depriving the British of a natural ally in their coming offensive. Nonetheless, a British officer reported to his superiors that the Creeks were ready and willing to fight Jackson's forces again. The British sent soldiers and supplies to Pensacola and set up a base, under the approving eyes of Spanish authorities who weakly controlled northern Florida. Fully informed of these British moves, Jackson attacked Pensacola and ejected the British. But most of their strength was still at sea, bearing down on Mobile and perhaps New Orleans. The latter city had come under American control roughly ten years before as a result of the Louisiana Purchase. In early December 1814, Jackson hurried his small force back to New Orleans. Previously he had believed Mobile would be the main target, but intelligence sources now told him that a British amphibious force of about six thousand troops was planning to invade Louisiana and capture New Orleans.[4]

He immediately set to work strengthening his defenses near the city and along the rivers, swamps, and deltas south of New Orleans. The 7th Infantry constituted a vital component of those defenses. Eight companies of the unit arrived in New Orleans in early 1814 and endured garrison duty for most of the year. Two companies were dispatched to Fort St. Philip, a strongpoint on the lower mouth of the Mississippi River. For the other six companies in New Orleans, disease was rife, life was stark, and discipline was harsh. Many soldiers could not resist the temptations of liquor, women, and trouble in New Orleans. This led to a sharp rise in court-martials. One sergeant was charged with "being drunk when sergeant of the police on the evening of the 17th [of January]. He plead not guilty. The court finds the prisoner guilty and sentences him to be reduced to ranks." Another noncommissioned officer, a Corporal Hall, did something even worse. One night in early April 1814, he brought a prostitute, "an indian squaw known by the name of 'toky,'" with him into the guardhouse of which he was in command. He was charged with shameful conduct. "Remaining or lying apart from the members of the guard with the said prostitute and not suffering any candle, or other light in the guardhouse during the time in the evening." The court-martial found Hall guilty. His night of carnal fun cost him his stripes.

Regular privates who were found guilty in such proceedings fared much worse. For instance, one private received twelve slaps with a paddle for "neglect of duty." Apparently he left a water-collecting detail and wandered off into the city. Another man got six slaps for drunkenness on duty. Every now and then an enlisted man was accused of petty thievery or a violent crime. For example, on November 11, 1814, Corporal Wood Long and Privates Henry Helm and John Archer were charged with improper conduct for assaulting a citizen in town. "While some of them held him [the citizen] others attempted to force from him his watch, and in the act broke it, on or about 8th November 1814. To which charge they generally plead not guilty. The court finds the prisoner John Archer guilty as charged and sentences him to receive ten slaps with a paddle, and acquits Corporal Wood Long and Henry Helm."[5] Actually, Archer was lucky he didn't get worse because the twenty-year-old laborer from Sevier County, Tennessee, had constantly gotten himself in trouble for a range of offenses, including drunkenness and absence without leave, ever since joining the regiment this summer before.[6]

Most of the men of the regiment did not come from cities, and they had a hard time meshing with the population of New Orleans, who found the soldiers' rough-hewn habits to be outside the boundaries of "acceptable society." Particularly distasteful was the soldiers' tendency to urinate in public—everywhere and anywhere. The typical 7th infantryman saw no reason not to relieve himself wherever and whenever the need arose, no matter who happened to be around. When it came to bathing, the soldiers often stripped naked and washed themselves in the Mississippi River. The local New Orleans belles who witnessed this brand of hygiene maintenance complained loudly to the regiment's officers, who dutifully issued an order to stop bathing naked in the river. One suspects that the practices of public bathing and urination did not end completely, though.[7]

The men who populated the regiment on the eve of the Battle of New Orleans were mostly frontiersmen and southerners with little patience for social niceties or high society. One company was composed almost entirely of shoemakers and farmers from Virginia, North Carolina, and Tennessee.[8] The other companies were made up mostly of farmers, laborers, artisans, and seamen who came from backgrounds on the margins of respectability in American life. While not quite poor and destitute, neither were they educated or financially well off. Some had been recruited by Taylor a few years before the war. Others were recruited from around the New Orleans area in the months leading up to the battle. Some signed up during the war for patriotic reasons or because their lives had been disrupted by the war. A few were immigrants from Ireland, England, or Sweden. Most likely, the combatants of the 7th were all white, since the U.S. Army did not permit blacks in regular units. The lone exception to this color line was Jordan Noble, a musician from Georgia who sounded the call to arms for the regiment on January 8, 1815, and was apparently held in fairly high esteem, given the racial mores of the time.[9] Collectively, the men of the 7th got into plenty of mischief. If they wanted something (usually liquor), they went after it, regardless of the consequences. They could be a handful to discipline and train in a garrison setting, but they were tough fighters when battle called.[10]

That call came on December 23, 1814, at place called Villeré's Plantation. By this time the British had overwhelmed a small force of American gunboats on Lake Borgne, east of New Orleans, and landed a force of about fifteen hundred soldiers at Bayou Bienvenu (which ironically means "welcome" in French) about twenty miles southeast of New Orleans. More would follow later. For now, though, this group began a cautious northward advance in the direction of New Orleans since they were not entirely sure what lay in front of them. They captured a few prisoners who told them Jackson had anywhere between eighteen and twenty thousand men at his disposal (truthfully, he had about five thousand), and this information caused them to sit tight and wait for reinforcements. This delay was a break for Jackson because his army was badly disorganized and his defenses incomplete. What's more, he had little idea of the disposition and strength of the British because they had destroyed or captured many of his gunboats along the lakes and bayous below New Orleans.

On the twenty-third, Jackson sent a reconnaissance force out to gather information. His chief engineer, a French soldier named Arsène Lacarrière Latour, served as the eyes and ears of this party. Latour and his group proceeded in the direction of Lake Borgne until they encountered several people hurrying back to New Orleans. They told Latour that the British had captured Villeré's Plantation along with a small force and were setting up a headquarters there. One officer immediately rode back to inform Jackson of this information while Latour stuck around and observed the British force. "I approached within rifle-shot of those troops, and judged that their number must amount to sixteen or eighteen hundred men. It was then half past one P.M., and within twenty-five minutes after, general Jackson was informed of the enemy's position."[11] When Jackson was told of the British force, he smashed his fist on a table and exclaimed, "By the Eternal, they shall not sleep on our soil. We must fight them tonight. I will smash them, so help me God!"[12]

He decided to launch a night attack, and one of the units tabbed for this attack was the 7th. He planned to take a force of two thousand soldiers south from the city and assault the British positions with the support of two ships, the USS *Carolina* and the USS *Louisiana*. The latter vessel, however, never made it to the scene of battle. As the late-afternoon shadows grew longer, the men of the 7th crept silently into position, almost to within five hundred yards of the unsuspecting British who were busy setting up camp and cooking dinner. At this point their commander, General John Keane, had no idea Jackson knew of the British landing, though some of his soldiers had noticed the *Carolina* sailing down the river and dropping anchor immediately to their left in the nearby Mississippi River. Some of these redcoats even waved at the *Carolina* before returning to the chore of looting the Villeré plantation house and slave quarters.

In the meantime, the Americans waited in the trees near a house owned by Denis de la Ronde, who commanded a local militia unit. The 7th Regiment huddled together quietly and waited with the rest of the Americans. They checked their muskets, adjusted their uncomfortable blue tunics, and fought off the chill of an early winter's evening. The minutes seemed like hours. After a while, complete darkness descended. All was quiet, except for the distant voices of the British and the current of the river somewhere off to the right. Then, finally, after this interminable wait, they heard a massive boom from the guns of the *Carolina*. According to a British officer, the ship raked the British camp for about ten minutes. "Flash, flash, flash came from the river, the roar of cannon followed, and the light of her own broadside displayed to us an enemy's vessel at anchor near the opposite bank [of the river], and pouring a perfect shower of grape and round shot, into the camp."[13] The British soldiers immediately scattered amid the angry buzzing of grapeshot that wounded some of them. They hurriedly extinguished their campfires and hastened to organize themselves into some semblance of a fighting formation.

Finally, Jackson gave the order to advance. The plan called for eight hundred dragoons and militiamen on his left flank, under the command of General John Coffee, to advance about one thousand yards, with the edge of a swamp on their left, and then pinch to the right in an effort to force the British toward the river. The rest of his force, a mixture of artillerymen, marines, local volunteers, "free men of color," Choctaw Indians, and army regulars, was to move forward and engage the enemy's main strength. The 7th led the way. Its lead company ran ahead about two hundred yards and began taking fire from a British outpost of eighty men. Both sides exchanged blisteringly accurate shots until the 7th drove the British troops back to a makeshift defensive line in a ditch behind a small fence. Troops of the 7th covered their artillery brethren as they ran their guns up a levee road along the river. At this point the battle degenerated into a confused melee. A blanket of fog settled over the area, reducing visibility to practically nothing. Both armies got mixed up. Friends shot at friends. Enemies slashed and bayoneted enemies. Jackson's two artillery pieces roared unevenly at shapes in the night. At various times, the British came close to capturing the guns only to be repulsed. Jackson himself rallied the gun crews, as well as nearby marines and 7th infantrymen who threatened to falter. The enemy was no more than fifteen or twenty yards away. Somewhere in this vortex, a British officer struck down and killed Captain Michael McClelland, a well-regarded company commander from Ohio.[14]

On the left flank of Jackson's army, Coffee brushed through British pickets but then ran into trouble when he encountered the enemy's main camp. After several minutes of seesaw fighting, in which some of his men captured a group of British troops before being captured themselves, Coffee ordered a withdrawal. After about two hours of fighting, the battle started to die down, and Jackson, with the British threatening to overrun his artillery—not to mention the confusion engendered by the fog—decided to fall back to reorganize his forces. Confused troops still sniped at one another in the dark, but the real fighting was over. The "night attack" or "first Battle of New Orleans," as some historians call it, had ended in a tactical draw. The British took 277 casualties; the Americans, 213. The 7th lost seven killed and twenty-eight wounded, significantly higher casualties than it would take in the more famous engagement fought two weeks later, when the 7th lost two killed and one wounded.[15] Among the wounded was Josiah Leach, a rare bird in that he was commissioned from the ranks at a time when that almost never happened. A Massachusetts native, Leach had joined the Army in 1811 and ascended the enlisted ranks until he received a slot as a junior officer in the fall of 1814, probably for obeying orders, showing good soldierly discipline, and natural leadership ability. In the December 23 fighting he more than justified the confidence his superiors obviously had in him. He took a nasty wound in the side, but according to a report filed by Jackson's adjutant not long after the war, Leach "refused to leave the Army until compelled the next day from extreme severe pain, but returned in time to perform in all the subsequent engagements."[16]

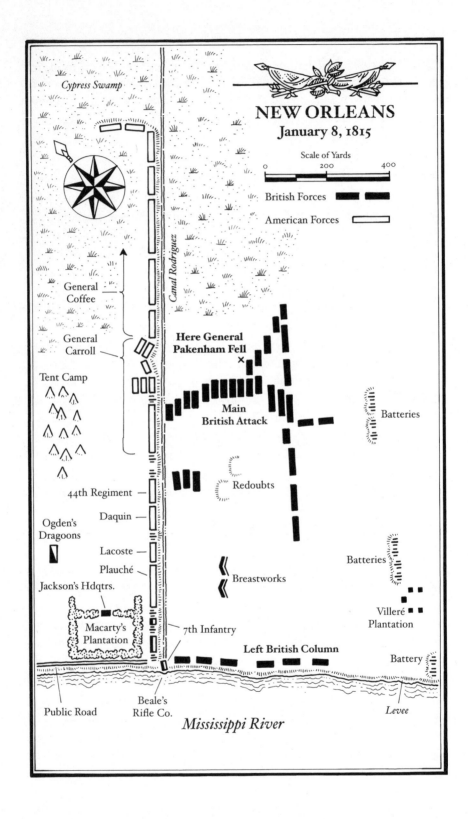

NEW ORLEANS
January 8, 1815

Scale of Yards

0   200   400

British Forces

American Forces

Cypress Swamp

General Coffee

General Carroll

Tent Camp

44th Regiment

Daquin

Ogden's Dragoons

Lacoste

Plauché

Jackson's Hdqtrs.

Macarty's Plantation

Public Road

Beale's Rifle Co.

7th Infantry

Canal Rodriguez

Here General Pakenham Fell
×

Main British Attack

Redoubts

Breastworks

Left British Column

Batteries

Batteries

Villeré Plantation

Battery

Levee

Mississippi River

In the wake of the Villeré Plantation fight Jackson hoped to attack again in the morning, but once he found out that British reinforcements were on the way, he withdrew his army north, behind the Rodriguez Canal, and began to fortify the area known as the Chalmette Plantation. As he did so, he sent a small party out to cut the levee between the enemy and him. This had the effect of creating a small flood that impeded the British long enough to buy time for Jackson's men to construct extensive positions behind the Rodriguez Canal. Under the watchful eye of Latour, the soldiers dug and scraped positions for themselves and their artillery, creating a formidable mud bank that became known as Line Jackson. On Christmas Day, General Sir Edward Pakenham, the overall British commander, arrived with the rest of his army. Surveying the tactical situation, Pakenham, whose brother-in-law was the famous Duke of Wellington, thought it might be best to load his troops back on ships and find a better place to invade and capture New Orleans. For many years after the battle, a story circulated that the British naval commander, Admiral Alexander Cochrane, shamed Pakenham into a straightforward advance by exclaiming that if Pakenham's soldiers shrank from the task of assaulting Line Jackson, his sailors would push forward and rout the "Dirty Shirt" Americans and then march into New Orleans while Pakenham's men "bring up the baggage." This is nonsense.[17] In reality, Pakenham's staff officers convinced him that his force was powerful enough, and Jackson's army weak enough, that a frontal attack could prevail. At heart, the British officers did not believe that a ragtag army made up primarily of militia and backwoodsmen would stand and fight against the scarlet might of well-trained British soldiers.

On December 28, those soldiers tried a reconnaissance in force and had to fall back amid devastating artillery barrages. In the days that followed, the British landed fourteen guns—ten "eighteen pounders" and four "twenty-four pounders"—from Lake Borgne and dragged them arduously to positions overlooking Line Jackson. On New Year's Day they opened up on Jackson's positions in an effort to destroy the American guns and their dug-in positions. But the British got the worst of that encounter. The American artillerymen found their targets with an alarming degree of accuracy. Pakenham ordered that his guns be moved out of range, but not before some incurred extensive damage. For the next week Pakenham sat tight and waited to be reinforced by three more regiments comprising about 2,000 soldiers. In the meantime,

500 Louisiana volunteers and 2,250 Kentucky militiamen reinforced Jackson. Still, he was content to remain on the defensive because he knew he was outnumbered and that some of his troops and commanders were not reliable. The campaign reached a climax on January 8, when Pakenham opted for an all-out assault on Line Jackson. In spite of the earlier fighting, it is this engagement that is generally referred to as the Battle of New Orleans.

On this day, the 7th Regiment, with an operational strength of around four hundred men, found itself at the extreme right of Line Jackson, immediately along the riverbank, in a position that spanned about 150 yards of the line. For more than a week the men had alternately sweated and shivered as they dug and improved their muddy positions. They were constantly pelted with rain, which gave their coats and trousers a musty, sweaty odor. Almost no one had a clean uniform. White wool trousers that had once looked flashy on parade in New Orleans were now spattered with rust-colored earth. Blue coats were smudged and unkempt. The men took small comfort in their standard army rations—salted pork, bread, and whiskey.[18]

On the night of January 7, groups of British soldiers went forward into the muck to dig artillery positions for the next day's attacks. Others went forward, in the dark, with the job of providing cover fire for the emplacements once they were completed. At 4:00 A.M. the rest of the British forces quietly moved into their assault positions. Their skirmishers (a nineteenth-century term roughly correlating to the modern term "point men") were within two hundred yards of Line Jackson, which stretched for roughly one mile, west to east, from the river to a cypress swamp.

All through the night the Americans heard digging and hammering noises. "We distinctly heard men at work in the enemy's different batteries," Latour recalled; "the strokes of hammers gave 'note of preparation,' and resounded even within our lines; and our outposts informed us that the enemy was re-establishing his batteries. In our camp all was composure; the officers were ordered to direct their subalterns to be ready on the first signal. Half the troops passed the night behind the breastwork, relieving each other occasionally. Everyone waited for day with anxiety and impatience, but with calm intrepidity; expecting to be vigorously attacked, and knowing that the enemy had then from twelve to fifteen thousand bayonets to bring into action, besides two thousand sailors and some marines."[19]

The morning was chilly and misty. The mist afforded the stealthy British some semblance of concealment in spite of their bright red uniforms. All at once, a British rocket sizzled through the early-morning fog. A chorus of voices shouted three cheers. This was the signal to move forward. Immediately British artillery opened up on the American batteries. The British plan was actually quite ingenious. While the artillery kept the American guns busy, the infantry would move forward in two waves. On their right flank, near the cypress swamp, the main infantry force, augmented by ladders and fascines, was to advance on the edge of Line Jackson. On the British left flank, along a levee road next to the river, light infantry would advance in columns, overwhelm American outposts, and breach the ramparts of Line Jackson. The two forces would act as pincers that would trap a confused, reeling American Army. It did not quite work out that way.

Far from being distracted or put out of action, American artillery raked the enemy columns. Cannonballs flew back and forth in every direction. British balls slammed into ramparts. American balls slammed into bodies. Still, the British troops advanced closer and closer. Everyone could see them clearly now, including the men of the 7th Regiment. The 7th was covering the first three batteries of artillery along the western edge of the American line. Some of the men could practically spit in the river. It so happened that the British column attack along the levee road clashed with the advance elements of the 7th. The soldiers of this advance element occupied a redoubt located several feet in front of the main line, south of the Rodriguez Canal, on the extreme west flank, right next to the river. The purpose of this position was twofold: first, it afforded a nice observation post; second, it allowed American troops to fire into the flanks of any British troops who assaulted the main ramparts. Unfortunately, these very advantages also made the redoubt vulnerable. The men in the redoubt had a nice view of British activity—most would have said far too good a view!—and clear fields of fire, but like any observation post detached from a main defensive line, the redoubt was inadequate in the face of a stronger enemy force. In fact, Jackson himself expressed misgivings about the usefulness of the redoubt. Two days earlier, when it was constructed, he told his engineers, "That will give us trouble!"[20]

He was right. Although most of the Americans out ahead of the main line were clustered together in small outposts, the redoubt provided them with no special comfort or protection when they scrambled away from the British and headed for the redoubt. The British simply pursued them and entered the redoubt themselves. This was a bad situation for the men of Lieutenant Andrew Ross's company of the 7th Infantry. Two of them, a sergeant and a corporal, were killed immediately. The sergeant was killed by the British officer in command of the assault, Colonel Robert Rennie. Fighting desperately, but awkwardly, in wet, hand-to-hand bayonet struggles, the company's survivors either were captured or fell steadily back toward the main line.

As the British cleared the redoubt, they now had a real chance to breach the American line. The redcoats rushed into the American breastworks, led by Rennie, who screamed, "The day is ours!" He was brave, but he was wrong. At this point the British troops, most of whom hailed from the West Indies, were staggered by a volley of shots from the American line they hoped to breach. Immediately behind the redoubt, eyeball-to-eyeball with the British, was a small company of thirty Louisiana riflemen. The British tried to shield themselves with some of the 7th infantrymen they had captured in and around the redoubt. This tactic failed. From the west bank of the river, cannons roared. Worse, the Louisiana riflemen poured steady fire into the British along with the two American batteries to their left. Along with that came the concentrated muskets of the rest of the 7th Infantry. This concentration of firepower, coming from the front and the side, ripped into the British troops. Some of them were hit several times and fell backward; some had heads blown off; others caught musket balls in bellies or limbs. A shot tore part of Rennie's calf off, but he kept going. Then he took a mortal shot just above the eyebrow, probably the work of one of the Louisiana riflemen. The 7th Infantry, with bayonets fixed, charged the British in a major counterattack. In no time, the British survivors turned and ran back down the levee road. But that didn't guarantee them safety. American artillery hurled grapeshot at them, and several fleeing British soldiers were hit. They fell and writhed in agony with terrible wounds caused by the stinging metal of the grapeshot, a weapon designed more for wounding than killing.[21]

In the meantime, some 7th infantrymen stood behind their parapets and sniped at the retreating enemy soldiers. Others pursued the British until they were too far away. Here and there an enemy soldier fell, but the unit's role in the battle was mostly done. On the opposite side of Line Jackson the British attack failed in an even bigger slaughter. Pakenham was killed, as were several of his key officers. An attack on the west bank of the river was more successful but ultimately for naught. For all intents and purposes the great battle was over by midmorning, an almost absurdly short amount of time given the many months of buildup, tension, and preparation.

The soldiers of the 7th, with gunpowder-streaked faces, smoking muzzles, and muddy coats, surveyed an awful scene of slaughter on the fields beyond their ramparts. "The whole plain on the left, as also the side of the river, from the road to the edge of the water, was covered with British soldiers who had fallen," one soldier recalled. "What might perhaps appear incredible . . . is that a space of ground, extending from the ditch of our lines to that on which the enemy drew up his troops, two hundred and fifty yards in length, by about two hundred in breadth, was literally covered with men, either dead or severely wounded. The artillery of our lines kept up a fire against the enemy's batteries and troops until two o'clock in the afternoon. The enemy's loss . . . was immense, considering the short duration of the contest, the ground, and the respective number of the contending forces."[22]

Indeed, it was a slaughter. British casualties numbered about twenty-four hundred while the Americans lost seventy men, thirteen of whom were killed. Burial details from both sides worked together in the days ahead to dispose of the dead. The wounded were carried to nearby homes that had been turned into makeshift hospitals. The level of ghastliness and suffering there is beyond imagination. One British captain remembered hearing the piteous cries of his wounded soldiers and seeing "a basket nearly full of legs severed from these fine fellows."[23] The British Army retreated from the scene of the battle, boarded ships, and left. Andrew Jackson and the United States had won a great victory, securing the Gulf Coast and New Orleans for America as well as awakening a strong sense of identity and nationalism in the new country. Ironically, the climactic battle was fought after American and British negotiators had concluded a peace treaty in Ghent, Belgium, on Christmas Eve in 1814. But on that fateful day in early January 1815 no one knew anything about the peace treaty. The American soldiers only knew that their country had been invaded and they must fight. They proved that they could defeat the best troops in the world, who fought on behalf of the strongest nation in the world. They also proved the lethal efficiency of applied and concentrated firepower, a blend of technology, policy, and tactics that would prove to be the cornerstone of the American way of war.

But that was the big picture. Of far more importance to the men of the 7th was that a collection of laborers, farmers, artisans, and frontiersmen had won a great victory. They had also won for themselves an enduring nickname — the Cottonbalers.

2

"Thirty Years of Peace"

The Life of the Soldier in the Antebellum Years

BETWEEN THE YEARS 1815 AND 1845 THE REGIMENT SAW
little combat, at least compared with later points in its history. Most of
the fighting during that thirty-year period took place during the Second Seminole War between 1839 and 1842. However, the unit was also
involved in the First Seminole War, which broke out soon after hostilities with Britain came to an end. In the days leading up to these hostilities, the War Department downsized and reorganized the Army,
ordering the 7th Regiment to Fort Scott, Georgia, on the Apalachicola
River. Fort Scott was located in the extreme southwestern portion of
Georgia, fairly close to present-day Tallahassee. At the time this was the
southern border of the United States. Spain still nominally owned most
of Florida, but, in practice, northern Florida was under the control of a
mixed bag of Native American tribes usually referred to as Seminoles.
The Seminoles were a collection of tribes—most of whom originated
elsewhere in the Southeast—who steadily migrated to Florida in reaction to the influx of Europeans and, later, Americans in the Western
Hemisphere.

In 1816, when the 7th Regiment arrived at Fort Scott, the border between the United States and Seminole Florida was tense. The Seminoles resented the incursion of white American settlers on what used
to be tribal lands. The Americans resented the haven Florida provided
to escaped slaves—some of whom found themselves subjected again to
slavery at the hands of Native American masters—as well as the constant threat presented by armed bands of Seminoles. The Cottonbalers'
task in this volatile mix, in addition to protecting the borders of the
United States, was to keep Indians and whites from killing one another.
The American commander on the scene, General Edmund P. Gaines,

was particularly concerned with preventing Native Americans and whites from infringing on one another's land. He refused to protect white squatters on Indian lands, but he was also quite determined to find and punish any Seminoles responsible for killing Americans. Seminole chiefs refused to turn over those responsible for such killings. Some even refused to recognize the so-called Jackson Treaty borders. This treaty included land Andrew Jackson won from various tribes in his victorious campaign in the Southeast during the War of 1812. The United States believed that its borders and sovereignty were at stake, and the Seminoles felt the same way. This was only the first of many times the Cottonbalers would be affected by turf wars between their country's government and Native American tribes.

In 1817, the chief of Fowltown, a Seminole settlement located about fourteen miles due east of Fort Scott, proved himself to be particularly obstinate in his defiance to the Jackson Treaty. In November, Gaines decided that he could no longer tolerate this kind of resistance from the chief. The general ordered Brevet Major David Twiggs of the 7th Infantry to take a force of 250 soldiers to Fowltown and remove the Seminoles from the village. Twiggs was a Georgian with a long military career ahead of him. He had fought in the War of 1812 with the 8th Infantry Regiment. After the war he left the Army for six months only to come back as a captain with the 7th Regiment. Dedicated, intense, cruel but not without a sense of humor, Twiggs led his troops eastward through the Georgia wilderness.[1] He was actually a captain but had attained the brevet, or honorary, rank of major. The awarding of brevet ranks was a common practice in the nineteenth century. The government, ever parsimonious in its salaries and military appropriations, could ill afford to promote officers quickly. So, quite often, a good officer would hold a permanent rank, and the accompanying pay, in addition to the honorary brevet rank, which amounted to little more than a pat on the head. So, Twiggs drew a captain's pay even as he often carried out the duties of a major.

When he and his soldiers reached Fowltown, the Indians had fled. Shortly after, Gaines ordered the town destroyed. He hoped to terrify the Seminoles into submission, but he miscalculated. In a cycle of bloodshed, destruction, and revenge that would repeat itself throughout the entire history of the Seminole Wars, the Native Americans struck back with horrifying ferocity. On November 30, a group of soldiers, under the command of Richard W. Scott of the 7th Infantry, embarked on a supply run along the Apalachicola bound for a nearby military post. They brought fresh clothing back with them along with the wives and children of some Cottonbalers, but most of them never made it back to Fort Scott. A powerful force of five hundred Indians ambushed them on the river. Scott's people didn't have a chance. With characteristic speed and ruthlessness, the Seminoles descended on them and hacked many of them—women included—to pieces. The Seminoles swung children by their heels, bashing their skulls against the boats. Only six soldiers escaped. No firsthand accounts survive from this one-sided engagement (massacre, really).

Suffice to say the American response was swift and just as ruthless. Freshly arrived in the Southeast, General Andrew Jackson unleashed a campaign of crop destruction and village burning in northern Florida. He even executed two Britons who he believed were responsible for fomenting the Seminoles' violent behavior. Strangely, the Seminoles did next to nothing in response. The same could not be said of Jackson. Using a mixed force of Creek tribesmen, U.S. Army regulars, and volunteers, he crushed the Seminoles, many of whom fled south.

The Spanish merely sat back and watched this American force invade their colony. Once again Jackson, in his own inimitable way, had achieved decisive results for the United States. Peace came in 1818, and the next year Spain ceded control of Florida to the United States in the Adams-Onis Treaty. In the years to come, the American government attempted to confine the Seminoles to 4 million acres of second-rate land, sowing the seeds of future conflict as the Seminoles inevitably chafed under these new restrictions. In addition, they clashed with whites, Creeks, and free blacks over slaves. All this would eventually lead to combat involving Cottonbalers.[2]

But, for now, the unit settled down and garrisoned the southern borders again. The regiment spread out between Forts Scott and Gadsden. For the soldiers, life was just one step above dismal. They existed at the margins of American life. Posts such as Scott and Gadsden were far away from the population centers of the growing country. Most Americans knew little and cared even less about the Regular Army. These attitudes reflected traditional American distrust of professional military forces. The average American believed that local and state militia could provide for the country's security far less expensively and far less dangerously to the citizenry than could professional forces. Anyone who chose the military as a career was suspect. These views represented a continuing conundrum in American life, one that has never fully been resolved. It boils down to this: when an American looks at the professional soldier, he asks himself, "Is that soldier a danger to my liberty or the protector of it?" In the early nineteenth century most Americans would have viewed the professional soldier as a danger and not a protector.

All of this meant that the Army was at the back of the line when it came to such tangible concerns as the federal budget or such subjective concerns as public esteem. Consequently, few cared if American soldiers lived in privation and squalor in sparsely settled, disease-ridden areas. After all, anyone who was enough of an outcast to join the Army deserved what he got, at least in the view of many of those who took the time to ponder such issues. So, what kind of men endured such scorn and adversity to serve their country? Some theorized that they were the "scum of the population of the older states, or of the worthless German, Irish, English immigrants." But if the 7th Infantry Regiment is any indication, this was not true. In fact, the vast majority of those who enlisted between 1815 and 1830 were native born, including 96 percent of recruits in 1826. Most Cottonbalers during those years were skilled artisans, farmers, and laborers from middle states such as New York, New Jersey, and Pennsylvania. In the context of American society, these were respectable origins. Some of these men signed up in reaction to economic downturns in 1819 and 1820, but most were motivated by adventure, restlessness, or personal problems. Upon enlistment, they signed up for a five-year hitch and received a sixteen-dollar bounty. The recruiting officer then moved them through the military pipeline, with minimal training, until they reached their assigned unit.[3]

Those assigned to the 7th experienced the full range of disease and misery that south Georgia offered. The regiment's surgeon, Thomas Lawson, wrote about the pestilential nature of Fort Scott: "As soon as the cold weather commenced . . . all diseases exhibited new complications and more fatal results . . . for days, for weeks, nay longer, would one of these poor creatures stagger under the burden of intermittent fever, dropsy, and scurvy combined when the diarrhea also coming on him, he necessarily sank under the accumulated weight of the disease."[4]

The experiences of Charles Martin Gray tell us much about the spartan lives of 7th Infantry soldiers during this time period. In 1868 Gray published one of the few known accounts from an enlisted soldier who served in the early nineteenth century. A South Carolinian born in

1800, Gray dreamed of soldiering from the earliest days of his childhood. He tried to enlist during the War of 1812, but he was too young. Later he ran off and tried again only to be foiled by his father. Finally, at the age of nineteen he successfully enlisted in the 7th. Twiggs signed him up. It was the beginning of an adversarial, headmaster–student type of relationship. Not long after he enlisted, Gray witnessed the kind of ruthless discipline Twiggs routinely enforced. A musician left camp for a few hours without proper authorization. When he came back, Twiggs made the man strip: "[Twiggs] then pulled off his own coat, rolled up his sleeves, and inflicted upon his bare back, with a horse whip, twenty-five lashes, which made the blood spout and trickle down his manly form, and that scarred the skin at every stroke. At another time, for some small offense, he sentenced one of his command to pitch straws against the wind, for four or five hours without intermission. The wind was blowing a gale, and the penalty was that he should receive *one lash* for every straw he failed to produce. At the end of this delightful exercise . . . he found himself minus many a straw, and crowned with many a stripe, for he was compelled to pitch the straws as high in the air, as his strength, and the boisterous elements would allow, and an unrelenting Orderly was present to report minutely every failure either of his strength or his skill."[5]

These were not isolated events. Officers meted out punishment and favor with almost total impunity. Enlisted men had few, if any, individual rights. In extreme cases, punishments led to death. Gray witnessed one such incident at Fort Scott. The commander of I Company, an unpopular officer from Virginia named Granville Leftwich, had a female friend in camp. She asked the cook, a man named Stevens, for some of the soup he was preparing for his company's meal that night. Thinking that he should not dispense food that rightfully belonged to the company, he gave her a "courteous, but decided refusal." When Leftwich found out about this, he practically went berserk. He ordered Stevens to be "stripped, tied up, and lashed by the drummer boy whilst he deliberately smoked out three Havanna [*sic*] Cigars. This surpassed in severity all the acts of petty tyranny I was ever called upon to witness. Stevens . . . suffered more than death from the infliction, for if he was about to faint, and nature was giving away under the terrible scourging, he was stimulated with brandy to enable him to endure a little more, and I hesitate not to say that his Captain deserved, not a soldier's death, but to be hanged like a felon." This cruel-hearted murder earned

Leftwich no approbation except for "the disgust of all of the generous-minded officers, and . . . the utter dismay of the privates." Leftwich died in 1824 of unknown causes.[6]

Enlisted men had little recourse in the face of such authoritarian disregard. Any resistance they posed had to be confined to minor high jinks or tricks, lest they receive swift and brutal punishment. Ever imaginative, Gray found a relatively benign way to harass Lieutenant Richard Wash, a fellow South Carolinian whom he loathed. On patrol one day, the unit had to cross the Colomochee Creek. An incident soon happened that signified the times. Army custom allowed each officer to pick a soldier to haul him across the water, the elitist presumption being that officers should not get wet and dirty like enlisted men. Wash chose Gray, and the latter looked upon his selection as a golden opportunity to humiliate Wash. Gray feigned enthusiasm for carrying the lieutenant across the creek, but then "I began to reel and stagger under the weight that oppressed me, but recovering proceeded mildly forward until, when making the very middle of the swollen current, I stumbled . . . and fell in the waters and . . . disengaged myself entirely from any superincumbent load. The gallant Lieutenant, to his great discomfiture, and to the inordinate merriment of all the men and officers present, was thus compelled to struggle alone . . . while his rich and gaudy uniform was soiled and begrimed with the mud, and rent in shreds by the rocks."

Enlisted men, of course, were not entirely blameless. They could be unruly, mischievous, and undisciplined, provoking the officers to dispense corporal punishment. But the harshness of such punishment sometimes bordered on cruelty and criminality. Few Americans knew this climate existed in their armed forces, and, truthfully, few would have cared had they known.

Initially, Gray excelled in his soldierly bearing, drilling, and discipline, so much so that he was promoted to sergeant. But over time, as the desolate nature of army life on the margins got to him, and as his peers exerted influence on him, he began to get into his share of trouble. In fact, it is fair to say he was a hell-raiser. One day at Fort Scott he and his buddy George Riley, who had once served in the British Army, conceived of a brilliant scam to acquire free alcohol. Amid the boredom, degradation, and near hopelessness of antebellum army life, alcohol constituted an obsession for soldiers. Many of them would do anything to escape from the drudgery for a few hours and put on a good buzz. Alcohol consumption became so acute that the Army banned its issuance to enlisted men. By the time Gray joined the unit, the only way to procure alcohol was from sutlers, unsavory merchants who set up shop near army camps and sold supplies and alcohol to soldiers.

On the day in question, Gray and Riley were part of a supply party that traveled, under the command of Twiggs, from Fort Scott to Fort Gadsden. Gray and his buddy desperately wanted to wet their collective whistles, but they had no money (soldiers were paid pittance wages and the disbursement of their money was often unreliable and haphazard). So they ingeniously figured out a way to cheat the sutler, whom they loathed. Riley gave Gray a deep-pocketed overcoat and the scam began. Gray went to the sutler, handed him an empty bottle, and asked him to fill it with whiskey. The sutler obliged and demanded payment. "Poor soldier as I was, I had no money, and beg[ged] for a little credit. The hard-hearted Sutler having had many such applications made to him before, peremptorily refused the credit and demanded the bottle of Whiskey to be returned." With a quick slight of hand, Gray produced a bottle of water he had stored in one of the pockets in his overcoat. He watched in disguised bemusement as the sutler poured the water into the cask of whiskey. Gray took the empty bottle back from him, and left. Word of the successful scam spread like wildfire among Gray's enlisted comrades. Many of them succeeded in doing the same thing (the dim-witted sutler must have wondered why the 7th had so many penniless soldiers in its ranks).

Gray took particular delight not necessarily in besting the sutler but in deceiving Twiggs. "For on observing me on my return from the direction of the Sutler's, he called me to him, and ordered me to display my bottle. With all the consciousness of innocence, or rather of an instant acquittal, I handed him the bottle, when he immediately excused me, uttering at the same time the direst imprecation of what he [would] have done, had it only contained Whiskey." Twiggs never found out what had happened, but the local sutlers did. In a rare display of amiability they merely laughed it off.

Like many soldiers, Gray did not simply indulge in a sip or two on the occasions he successfully acquired whiskey. He drank to get roaring drunk. One day this almost cost him his life. He was on detached duty with a small group of soldiers. Their job was to meet up with a batch of recruits who had made the long sea journey from Governors Island, New York, to the southern coast. The recruits did not arrive for several days. In the meantime Gray's group, under the benevolent command of a lieutenant who had once been an enlisted man, whiled away the time swimming and playing. The lieutenant even allowed his men to procure whiskey. Gray proceeded to get drunk, dive into the waters of a nearby lagoon, and challenge an alligator to a fight. Man and beast parried for a time, until Gray bordered on exhaustion. He decided to get out of the water, but the alligator had other ideas. "The wicked animal that hitherto appeared to avoid me, turned upon me as if actually to mock my distress, or to murder me outright. Never were the muscles of a human being so taxed to save their master, as well from a watery grave as from the maw of a voracious monster." Gray got away, but he never forgot how quickly drunkenness gave way to stone-cold fear. Nor did he forget the alligator's face: "His image was ever afterwards so indelibly impressed upon my mind as not only to give me an aversion to the name of alligator itself, but to all prize fighting, and even to dear whiskey also, the instigator of this foolish feat in me."

Not that he stopped drinking. In late 1821 he and most of the 7th moved from the Southeast to points west. They got on boats and traveled to New Orleans and then up the Mississippi River and west near what was then America's western border with Mexico. They skulked around in the vicinity of Natchitoches, Louisiana, looking for a good place to build a frontier fort. Soon disease swept through the ranks, claiming soldiers, laundresses, and "camp followers" alike such as "Mrs. Glenn, an old . . . 'Vivandiere' of the army, whose exuberant spirits, fun and frolic had enabled the soldiers to while away many a tedious hours." Gaines arrived, observed the wretched health of the garrison, and ordered them to move west along the "Mexican Road" to build what became known as Fort Jesup. Here they worked for several weeks under the supervision of Zachary Taylor, who was now a colonel and had recently been detailed back to the 7th. Gray himself now got sick, but, true to form, he parlayed his sickness into another whiskey scam. His weak stomach led Dr. Lawson to put Gray on a special milk diet. After a few days, he started to feel better, at least enough to conceive of a new scam. Lawson sent him to a local camp follower for his milk and armed him with a coffeepot that Gray fiddled with so that it could hold both whiskey and milk separately. He succeeded in smuggling his whiskey back into camp and rejoined a work party to which he belonged. "And lo! In about an hour's time, the whole working party were drunk—some shouting and laughing—some cursing—some reeling and some stretched insensible upon the yard, so that the idea of work had quite vanished from their minds. They were all as much elevated above the drudgery to which they had been assigned."

Taylor heard the carousing and immediately investigated. He quickly saw that the work party was drunk but wondered where they had gotten their whiskey. Then it hit him—Gray's coffeepot. Taylor inspected it, found the remnants of whiskey, and ordered that Gray be taken into custody and court-martialed. The next day the court found him guilty and sentenced him to wear the coffeepot "strapped upon me, to do police duty in the Garrison, in that plight, for one month. For the time being I thought that I had been made a soberer, a wiser, and a better man. I . . . resolved in my heart to change my habits."

This resolution did not last. Gray cleaned up his act, worked hard for a while, but then got in trouble again. He asked Taylor for a recreation pass "since I had worked faithfully for several weeks, and finished my task to the entire satisfaction of the inspector." Taylor graciously agreed and signed the pass. It read: "Permit Private Gray . . . to leave the Fort until Retreat." But Gray could not resist adding "and to purchase a gallon of whiskey from the Sutler." Gray, Riley, and others bought the liquor, went to a nearby lake, and had a great time. When they got back to camp, they affected sober dispositions and tiptoed to their quarters. But Taylor caught them and confronted Gray with the forged pass. A wave of horror coursed through Gray and he didn't know what to do. "But Taylor, storming at me, demanded whether I could not read my own writing. I . . . finally swallowed the bitter pill." The "bitter pill" consisted of sawing planks, almost nonstop, for one week. This was tough punishment, but it was just. Twiggs probably would have whipped Gray to within an inch of his life, but Taylor, more even tempered and judicious, did not operate that way. Part of him understood and sympathized with enlisted men, even troublesome soldiers like Gray.

In ten years (1819–29) with the unit, Gray saw very little combat. The notable exception was a minor skirmish that took place between a detachment of forty Cottonbalers and some Comanche Indians who posed a danger to white settlers near Fort Towson in present-day southern Oklahoma. Gray was part of this tiny detachment that left Fort Jesup and traveled for eight days along rough trails and roads to Towson. They patrolled the area and found the offending Native Americans along with a shocking scene. "The Indians were drunk and unwary. The evening, and the day before, they had killed all the settlers—men, women and children—within the vicinity of the Fort. They had erected in the centre of their camp a long pole, on which was strung forty-five scalps, of men, women and children. Around this, they were singing and dancing, with savage glee, while their meat and corn were being cooked in several large pots that were on the fire boiling." Gray and the other soldiers became enraged. Somehow they recognized several of the scalps as belonging to people they once knew, including a young woman some of them had courted. They crept to within sixty yards of the Indians and leveled their weapons. "Forty muskets were discharged right into the thick crowd of the drunken frolicking Indians, and with a shout, and fixed bayonets, the whites charged upon them." In sheer panic the Comanche ran away. "Our men had killed nine of them outright, at the first fire, and the number of wounded they could not tell, for the miserable cowards flew through the plains." Gray ordinarily sympathized with Native Americans as peaceful, honorable people, but the apparent bloodthirstiness of this particular group still incited passionate condemnation from him decades later: "Only an hour before . . . they were boasting of their exploits, in taking the lives of helpless women and children, but when they came to be confronted with men, having arms in their hands, their mean sneaking souls, betook them to panic, and to utter rout and confusion."

Gray served two enlistments and left the Army in 1829. He went home to South Carolina—his parents did not recognize him—and muddled about for many years as a drunkard and troublemaker, before settling down with a wife, family, and career. He even served for a time as a color-bearer for the 7th South Carolina Infantry Regiment in the early days of the Civil War.[7]

THE 7TH REGIMENT WAS PROFOUNDLY AFFECTED BY ONE of the most controversial laws in American history, the Indian Removal Act of 1830. This act witnessed the removal of approximately sixty thousand Cherokee, Choctaw, Creek, Chickasaw, and Seminole Indians from their homes in the Southeast to inferior lands west of the Mississippi River (especially present-day Oklahoma). The mostly forcible relocation of these "five civilized tribes" has, rightfully, drawn sharp criticism from historians. The Jackson administration, which largely masterminded this law, experienced resistance from political opponents who felt that such relocations were unfair, immoral, or at least not the proper solution to the Native American "problem" in the Southeast. The Cottonbalers largely spent the years 1830–42 dealing with the residual effects of the Indian Removal Act.

The 7th spent most of the 1830s dispersed in and around Fort Gibson near present-day Muskogee, Oklahoma. With the arrival in the area of thousands of Native Americans, the 7th saw its duties change from simple road and fort building to officiating. Rival tribes made war on each other. White settlers infringed on Indian lands. Smugglers sold whiskey, weapons, and trinkets to Indians. The area, generally known as Indian Territory, was a mess of conflicting tribes, peoples, and policies. Rarely was the unit ever concentrated together in one place. Cottonbalers instead spread far and wide around Indian Territory to enforce government policies.

Fort Gibson, the central base, was a desolate breeding ground for such diseases as cholera, smallpox, pneumonia, and dysentery. In 1834 alone, sixty-eight soldiers from the 7th died. In a typical year, close to fifty died. George Catlin, a frontier artist at Gibson during this time, recalled hearing the "mournful sound of 'Roslin Castle' with muffled drums, passing six or eight times a day under my window, to the burying ground."[8] The place was little more than a ramshackle collection of buildings in a depression surrounded by gradual hills. Officers lived in small two-man cabins on a hill overlooking camp. Enlisted men lived in crowded, rotting barracks. The men sweated through stifling heat in the summer and shivered amid blustery cold in the winter. The Army could hardly have chosen a less hospitable site.[9]

Fort Gibson posed a challenge to everyday survival. Men constantly had to mend their buildings, cut firewood, and draw whatever clean water they could. This left them with little time for drilling and combat training. Captain Joseph Phillips, a West Pointer who served with the 7th at Fort Gibson, was so outraged by the conditions that he wrote to Alexander Macomb, the commanding general of the Army: "We are losing our best men here, in consequence of this incessant labor, who go off to other stations to enlist, to avoid these toilsome duties. In fact, I have almost come to the conclusion that the troops of this post, instead of being enlisted as soldiers to perform military duty, are received into the service to become only 'hewers of wood and drawers of water.'" In another letter he addressed the disease problem: "Ought not the deaths of officers and soldiers who have fallen victims to the diseases of this climate be considered a sufficient sacrifice?" He went on to note that close to three hundred soldiers (from various units) had died at Gibson during the previous two years.[10]

Phillips might very well have been the writer of an angry, innuendo-laced letter written under the alias "Arkansas" to the *Army and Navy Chronicle* in 1835, the same year he wrote to Macomb. Arkansas addressed his communication to the editor of the paper and wondered why the 7th had not been rotated to a different, and healthier, post: "It is natural we should feel some curiosity to know the motive for keeping this regiment so long in one position, particularly when its location has neither health nor society to recommend it. Can it be that the regiment has been stationed principally on the Arkansas frontier for fifteen years for the purpose of gratifying the pecuniary advancement of some of its higher officers? The chief of the regiment has a plantation on the Arkansas river, and has frequently expressed his unwillingness to be removed from the country!" The chief in question was Brevet Brigadier General Mathew Arbuckle, who served as commander of the regiment for over three decades but never actually led it in combat, not an unusual occurrence in the early nineteenth century. Officers routinely took leaves of absence to attend to personal affairs. Arbuckle's command responsibilities often included more soldiers than his own regiment. Arkansas concluded his letter with a plea to the Army's leadership to alleviate the awful conditions at Gibson. He pleaded that "for the health and safety of those men who have devoted their lives to their country's service, [they] be furnished with good and comfortable barracks, instead of the decayed and miserable log cabins in which they have been, and still are quartered."

In a subsequent issue of *Army and Navy Chronicle,* another anonymous officer blasted Arkansas for implying that the financial interests of the regiment's leadership led to its employment in lousy, inhospitable country. Even so, this officer, who referred to himself as "Neosho," conceded that "the seventh regiment . . . has long and faithfully stood as a wall of defence to the Arkansas frontier. It has served not merely as a sentinel on the outworks of civilization, but it has annually and without noise, showed itself a force among the predatory bands of the prairies, averting the evils of savage warfare, and opening a way for the introduction of the arts and comforts of rural life." Ultimately, Neosho agreed with Arkansas's aims, if not all of his reasoning: "I would say with 'Arkansas' that this regiment has acquired a right to choose itself a station from among those occupied by this arm of service."[11]

These letters had no effect. The 7th stayed at Gibson, and the days and years passed with the usual misery, disease, and privation. Humor helped the soldiers cope with the drudgery of their lives and provided them with a healthier distraction than alcohol consumption. Every now and then something hilarious happened. During the summer of 1837, Arbuckle allowed half the regiment to escape the stifling heat of the barracks and set up camp on the cooler high ground around the fort. The only drawback for the lucky campers was that they had to haul their water from the fort's well several hundred yards and up to the high ground.

Arbuckle tried to solve this problem by detailing two guardhouse prisoners to dig a well in the camp area. For a few days these two men dug industriously, until their hole was deep enough to shield them from sight. Each day, before heading back to the fort, the duo reported their progress to the officer of the day, who dutifully recorded the information. An officer who served at Fort Gibson related what happened next: "At first, the report would be two or three feet, then a foot or ten inches; and so it went during the winter, the officer merely inquiring of the prisoners, who . . . worked without a guard, how many feet or inches they had advanced toward the centre of the earth. The summer of 1838 arrived, without the prisoners having reached water, and the troops expressed to the General their preference to remain in the Fort, rather than to be obliged to drag the water up the hill. The good old General acceded to their request, but ordered the prisoners to push their work and get to water before the summer had reached the dog days. Time passed, and the summer had drawn to a close, when one bright October day it occurred to the General that the prisoners must have reached the level of the river-bottom . . . and it was very strange that they had not come to water. So he called his Aide-de-Camp and requested him to examine the guard-reports, and see how deep the well was. The Aide-de-Camp . . . informed the astonished General that, according to his daily reports . . . the well was *four hundred and sixty-five feet and nine inches deep*."

General Arbuckle blew a gasket. He shouted for the officer of the day and ordered him to check on the prisoners. He and a corporal went to the well and the officer lowered himself inside: "When at the depth of fifteen feet he landed on flat rock, which covered what he soon found out was the bottom of the well, upon which the two prisoners were seated face to face, with a pack of cards between them, a-playing *'Old Sledge.'* " Thanks to the neglect of the aging Arbuckle and his distracted officers, the two prisoners had enjoyed a nice vacation for almost a year and a half. They dug deep enough to carve a shelter for themselves that was cool in the summer and warm in the winter. They even ate meals there and played thousands of card games.[12] The two well diggers were probably very popular with their comrades for successfully putting one over on the "Old Man" and his officers.

THE REGIMENT EXPERIENCED A BIT OF EXCITEMENT IN 1836 when war broke out in nearby Texas. The Texans were fighting Mexico for independence, and the U.S. government sympathized with the Texans since most of them originally came from the United States. Some in the U.S. government worried that Native Americans would cross the border from the United States into Texas and fight against the Texans. Accordingly, in early May General Gaines ordered several companies of the 7th to leave Fort Gibson and disperse among Forts Jesup and Towson, closer to Texas. Getting from Gibson to these forts was no small feat. The soldiers had to march through prairies and oak woods with little support beyond their own awkward supply wagons. Significantly understrength, each company numbered somewhere between twenty and thirty men. The column consisted of the Cottonbalers, plus some dragoons (cavalrymen) and militia.

Lieutenant William Mather, an 1823 graduate of West Point, helped lead this motley expedition. Before leaving Fort Gibson, Mather had written a letter of resignation from the Army. But the regiment's new mission put his resignation in limbo, and he did not know when he would see his young wife and two children again. He settled in, hoped for the best, and contented himself with writing descriptive letters to his wife. He wrote one such letter just a few days into the expedition, when the column reached Fort Coffee, a small post located about fifty-five miles southwest of Gibson. By necessity, the men ignored regulations and adapted to the wild countryside. "You would laugh if you could see our detachment going on such duty & in this part of the country; they have left their uniform & everyone wears such clothing as he chooses only he must wear flannel shirts & have two blankets. The men carry all their things in their knapsacks, everyone wears a cotton haversack, tin cup & knife in addition to their ordinary equipment. My own costume will give you some idea of the officer's appearance. My hat is a broad brimmed gray felt six inches broad to keep off the hot sun, a brown short frock coat filled with pockets like a sportman's coat, rifle in hand, bullet pouch, canteen for water slung over my shoulder, a waist belt with a tomahawk & knife attached to it & pistol stuck into it, gray woolen pantaloons & thick cowskin boots. The whole detachment puts me in mind of so many Indians rather than of civilized men."[13]

This ragged force pressed on, heading in a southerly direction toward Fort Towson. Within ten days they reached Towson and set up a camp. Mather observed the surrounding terrain with the keen interest of an amateur geologist: "Iron ore abound in some of the prairies where small streams had washed away the soft rock so as to expose that and the ore. Salt licks are seen everywhere on the prairies as well as buffalo wallows and stamping grounds. The wallows are mud holes made by buffalo wallowing as pigs do in the mire and the stamping grounds cover many acres." The soldiers had no inkling of the situation in Texas and even less idea what they were supposed to be doing. "We came here with the expectation that we might have some active service but we know no more about it than we did at Gibson. Reports come in from all directions that Santa Anna has been taken by the Texians [sic]. If so we shall probably have nothing to do but return. We may be here a week or a year. We are within 6 miles of the Mexican frontier of Texas but all around is perfectly quiet."[14]

It stayed that way, at least for the 7th. The Texans won a victory at the Battle of San Jacinto, and this turned around what had previously shaped up as a losing fight for them. Even so, Gaines worried about the stability of the American border with Texas. On July 10, as a precaution against any remaining bands of Indians with aggressive intentions, he ordered six companies of the 7th, along with dragoons, to occupy Nacogdoches, Texas. This incursion into Nacogdoches, which Mexico considered its territory, led the Mexicans to break off diplomatic relations with the United States. In fact, the occupation of Nacogdoches was only the beginning of a long dispute between the two countries over the status of Texas and the southwestern boundaries of the United States. But, at the moment, none of that really mattered to the Cottonbalers (although it sure would a decade later). They stayed in Nacogdoches for four months, until Arbuckle, who inherited command from Gaines in October, ordered them back to Fort Gibson.[15]

EVEN AS THE UNITED STATES WORRIED ABOUT TROUBLE along its border with Texas, a much bigger problem was brewing in Florida. In 1834, Osceola, a charismatic, courageous chief of mixed white-Indian lineage, succeeded in uniting and mobilizing the amorphous collection of tribes and renegade bands whom whites usually called "Seminoles." For fifteen years, since the signing of the Adams-Onis Treaty, white settlers had been migrating to Florida. As they did so, some infringed on Seminole lands, and vice versa. The government hoped to persuade these remaining Seminoles to migrate westward, like the other "civilized" tribes had done earlier in the decade. The tension between whites and Seminoles boiled over into violence on December 28, 1835, when a group of Seminoles trapped and annihilated a force of 108 soldiers under the command of Major Francis Dade. Most historians view the Dade massacre as the beginning of the Second Seminole War. Initially, this war did not go well for the United States. By the fall of 1836, even as the Cottonbalers sat around in Nacogdoches, the Seminoles consolidated their control over most of northern Florida. Osceola got sick, but leadership soon passed to a succession of Seminole commanders with colorful names such as Wildcat, Alligator, Jumper, and Billy Bowlegs.

For three years the U.S. Army fought this tenacious foe in a guerrilla war. Both sides committed atrocities and used "dirty tricks." For instance, on the one hand, one American commander, General Thomas Jesup, took to seizing key Seminole leaders during truce negotiations. On the other hand, Jesup also used benevolence to further his goals. He realized that several hundred blacks were providing crucial support to the Seminoles, so he offered them a deal. If they joined the American forces, they would gain their freedom. As a result, blacks abandoned the Seminoles in droves and served as crucial guides and intelligence collectors for American troops in Florida.

None of this involved the 7th Infantry until the spring of 1839 when it received orders for northern Florida. The regiment was about to spend three dismal years in Florida fighting a frustrating war against an elusive, dangerous foe. In all, thirty Cottonbalers would be killed in combat, while ninety more fell to the deadliest enemy of all—disease. These casualties, suffered mostly in obscurity, dwarfed those incurred in the famous Battle of New Orleans.

The first year was the worst for sickness. The swamps and rivers of Florida teemed with strange organisms and diseases. The hot climate sapped a man's strength even more than harsh Fort Gibson. An officer who was there recalled that "the prevailing disease was dysentery, caused by being obliged to drink the turbid water from stagnant pools, and aggravated by the long continued and unvaried heat of summer. The troops sunk under the debility arising from exposure to noonday suns, constant rains, cool nights, turbid water, and the heavy marches through the deep sands." By contrast, the Seminoles moved more smoothly through this inhospitable land. "Every hammock [a stand or copse of hardwoods] and swamp was to them a citadel, to which and from which they could retreat with wonderful facility. Regardless of food or the climate, time or distance, they moved from one part of the country to the other, in parties of five and ten; while the soldier, dependent upon supplies, and sinking under a tropical sun, could only hear of his foe by depredations committed in the section of country over which he *scouted* the day before."[16]

Besides dysentery, a litany of other diseases killed soldiers, including yellow fever, dropsy, malaria, typhoid, catarrhus, and "congestive fever." Foolish accidents accounted for other deaths. Private Augustus Kohl drowned while going for a swim in a pond in the late summer of 1839. Early in 1840, falling timber killed Private George Shields. About a month later, Private John Walsh fell from his horse, hit his head, and died.[17] The combination of accidents, disease, and an invisible, bloodthirsty enemy must have made Florida seem like a swampy hell for the Cottonbalers, the kind of place where death could claim you at any moment and in a demoralizing variety of ways. Florida must have seemed especially alien to those men who came from other lands such as Ireland, England, and Germany. By the Second Seminole War the ranks of the 7th included more foreign-born troops than ever before, most of whom thought of themselves as professional soldiers. During these years, foreign-born men comprised about half the strength of the regiment. Most likely they had a tough time finding good employment in the midst of a bad economy in the late 1830s and enlisted in the Army for basic food and shelter.[18]

The Cottonbalers did most of their fighting in 1840. Using small forts and camps as a base of operations, they patrolled the surrounding territory in the hopes of finding and destroying hostile tribesmen. In practice, the soldiers were little more than sitting ducks. Usually the Indians owned the initiative. The enemy chose where and when he would fight and on what terms. This meant that even as soldiers died from camp diseases, they also got killed in small, lightning-quick skirmishes. Examples abound. Seminoles shot and killed Private Jeremiah Austin on August 13, 1840, while he escorted a doctor to Fort Micanopy, the 7th's main base in northern Florida. That very same month, Private David Finney got separated from his comrades outside Micanopy. Seminoles captured him, tortured him, and killed him. Another soldier, Sergeant Isaac Hogins, met his death while in command of a small group hoping to set an ambush for the enemy. Private Hugh Kelly was "shot through the body while on a scout [patrol] . . . by an Indian, on whom he was rushing." Kelly's patrol startled the Indian, who attempted to flee. Before he took off, he fired his weapon and hit Kelly at close range. Even so, Kelly "fired and charged upon the Indian and wounded him more or less with his fire." Kelly's lieutenant then administered the coup de grâce on the trapped Seminole. Kelly may or may not have known of his adversary's death. He himself died about two hours after the skirmish.[19] And so it went, day after day, month after month.

Every now and again, the 7th fought a larger engagement. Generally these fights did not turn out positively for the regiment. The first of these battles occurred on April 28, 1840. On that day Captain Gabriel Rains, a North Carolinian and 1822 graduate of West Point, led a sixteen-man patrol from his A Company on a scouting mission out of Fort King, the southernmost base for the 7th. The regiment was dispersed in a triangle pattern from Fort King in the south northward to Forts Drane and Micanopy and east to Fort Brooks, an area that covers much of the ground between present-day Gainesville and Ocala.

On this spring day Rains led his small group into a local hammock located about two miles away from Fort King. The night before, Rains had set up several booby traps—consisting of exploding shells under a blanket—in the hammock, in response to several small-scale incidents in which Seminoles had killed individual soldiers. During the night the men had heard an explosion, and now Rains wished to investigate his handiwork. He estimated the hammock to be about 100 yards wide and 140 yards long. Pine and palmetto woods surrounded it, and the men warily eyed the trees, knowing that Seminoles could easily be concealed among them.

The woods around this hammock were so thick that the men could only search them by getting down on their hands and knees and crawling. Rains did not like this one bit but knew it had to be done. The soldiers found no bodies, just blood, pony tracks, and fragments of clothing. Still, Rains could not shake the feeling that danger lurked close by, especially when two scout dogs started barking furiously: "I ordered the men to ascertain the cause and was proceeding myself . . . through the bushes . . . when the men in front shouted 'Indians,' raised their guns and fired simultaneously with the enemy who were concealed, prostrate, in the undergrowth."

The enemy fire was withering. Bullets hit several soldiers with an ugly "thwack" sound. Rains took cover and quickly surveyed the situation. Confused soldiers were rushing around and yelling to one another. Rains screamed at them, "Clear the hammock; each man take his tree and give the enemy a fair fight!" Without any hesitation they followed him into the trees. They no sooner got there than Rains saw his first sergeant behind a tree. The sergeant, George H. Smith, stared at his captain with glassy eyes. "'Captain, I am Killed,'" he said, "with blood running from his mouth & nose." Smith had been hit four times, and he died in a matter of moments.

Rains and his men took the trees and began taking fire from the side and behind. Out of the corner of his eye, Rains saw a large force of painted Seminoles, probably somewhere between fifty and one hundred, rush along the western flank, between the soldiers and Fort King in an attempt to surround them. "With the enemy in front, on our right and left and extending their line behind us, keeping up an incessant firing & yelling, our numbers reduced to eleven or twelve, I perceived that our retreat through the enemy's line to Fort King, or destruction was inevitable." He ordered his men to fix bayonets, stand up, charge through the enemy lines, and run as fast as they could back to Fort King.

They sprinted through the hammock, slashed their way through several Indians, and ran for their lives. Now the Seminoles concentrated their entire fire on the backs of the retreating soldiers. Rains realized that he would have to return fire to slow down the Indians, who were now pursuing the soldiers. The soldiers found cover in another stand of trees and shot at the Indians. This slowed down the enemy while Rains hung back to rally his men and direct fire. As he did so, a musket ball found him. "Feeling faint from loss of blood I informed the soldiers of my condition when they ran to me and Corporal Bedford by my side fired and killed a distinguished chief on our right flank." Three other men grabbed Rains and carried him back to the fort. As they ran, one of the men, Private Taylor, got hit in the shoulder. Staggered by the loss of their chief, the Seminoles held up and then contented themselves with shadowing the soldiers from a safe distance. The entire fight lasted about an hour and cost the 7th Regiment Sergeant Smith and two privates killed along with several other men wounded. Rains estimated Indian losses at four killed and an unknown number of wounded.

He was a good and conscientious officer, but he did not get all of his men back to the fort. Two of his soldiers got left behind as they lay wounded in the hammock. They found hiding places and watched as the Indians carried their dead away and left. They counted ninety-three "warriors," several African-Americans, twenty "squaws," and four dead men. Some members of this large force threatened the fort but were scattered by howitzer fire. They moved on to points unknown. Rains spent several weeks in bed recuperating, but he lived.[20]

A few weeks after Rains and his men fought for their lives in this brief engagement, another group of 7th Regiment soldiers, based to the south at Fort Micanopy, clashed with an enemy force. On May 19, 1840, four soldiers from the 2nd Infantry Regiment were hauling a supply wagon from Micanopy to nearby Wacahoota. Seminoles ambushed them, killing everyone except their lieutenant, who was wounded but escaped to Micanopy to report this incident to the fort's commander, Lieutenant James S. Sanderson of the 7th. Sanderson was a well-respected officer because of his experience and his humble origins. He joined the unit as a private in 1825 and earned a commission in 1838, a rare accomplishment in the nineteenth century. When the wounded officer told Sanderson about the ambush, he listened intently and decided to get some payback.

He organized a patrol (numbering somewhere between thirteen and eighteen men) and led it out into the wilderness beyond the fort's shaky ramparts. The patrol took three bloodhounds with them and began tracking their way to the Indian position. After a short time, someone noticed smoke in the distance. Like bees to honey, Sanderson and his soldiers advanced in the direction of the smoke. An experienced soldier like Sanderson should have realized that the smoke was a Seminole trap, because they almost always built small campfires to evade detection. These ostentatious fires should have set off alarm bells in Sanderson's mind, but they didn't. This mistake cost him his life.

As he and his troops approached the smoke, an aggressive force of fifty or sixty Seminoles surrounded them and attacked. These were the same enemy troops who had ambushed the 2nd Infantry soldiers. They were smart, tough, and committed to the total destruction of Sanderson's force. Reacting to the ambush, Sanderson's troops formed a little perimeter, but their situation bordered on the hopeless. Enemy shots ripped into several men. Sanderson knew he had no choice but to order a charge in hopes of breaking through and escaping. He leveled his gaze at his terrified men and bellowed the order. They rose up as one and charged the Seminole positions. In response, enemy muskets crackled, spewing a solid wall of musket balls that immediately tore through Sanderson and his remaining soldiers. They never had a chance. Almost all of them were killed, even the bloodhounds and their handler.

The Indians didn't linger long. They descended on the dead soldiers, mutilated their bodies—they cut off some of Sanderson's fingers and stuck them in his mouth—and moved on. A few wounded soldiers managed to survive, including a private who died several months later from the effects of his wounds and a sergeant major named Francis Carroll who fought like a tiger that day until he got wounded and then managed to hide from the Seminoles while they policed up the battlefield. Carroll subsequently received the rarest of honors for an enlisted man. He had a fort named after him. He and the other lucky survivors were rescued on May 20 by a group of American soldiers who heard about the ambush and hustled to the scene.[21] By any measure the Seminoles won this fight, know as the Battle of Bridgewater, decisively. They virtually annihilated the 2nd Infantry supply group and then baited the 7th Regiment troops into another, costlier, ambush.

As the summer unfolded, the Cottonbalers' sector calmed down a bit. Still, that didn't mean the soldiers sat around and relaxed. They engaged in backbreaking labor, building roads and bridges. They destroyed Indian camps and crops and disrupted Indian rituals and movement. In their spare time, they strengthened their fort, cutting logs, digging ditches, and tending gardens. These gardens provided necessary sustenance to the soldiers, especially those at Micanopy. They grew various vegetables and fruits, setting an example for future settlers about what kinds of crops could successfully be grown in the region. The soldiers even raised their own hogs and cattle. The men soon learned how to deal with what had been an unfamiliar climate and the disease rate dropped to the point where the Army actually built a hospital at Micanopy.

Life settled into a routine of sorts—wake up, eat, drill, work on a construction detail, patrol, tend cattle or gardens, eat, go to sleep, and then wake up and do it again. Naturally the soldiers attempted to spice up the monotony of Florida duty any way they could. That meant finding alcohol. The official army policy forbade enlisted consumption of liquor on post, but that barely deterred those with an unquenchable thirst. In a time-honored pattern that still exists today in such places as Phenix City, Alabama, and Fayetteville, North Carolina, seedy grog shops soon sprouted up around the Army's military posts in Florida. Officers did what they could to shut these places down. One of them reported from Micanopy to the adjutant general in Washington that "this post has long been annoyed by a great number of grog shops and tippling houses. One of the worst of them, kept by Francis Bray a discharged soldier, had his liquor destroyed and his family removed from the post. This act has met my approbation as one indispensably necessary to the discipline and efficiency of this garrison."[22]

Truthfully, though, officers were fighting a losing battle. Civilian sutlers could operate with virtual impunity. If an officer harassed them, they could simply pack up and find another location, which the enlisted men would quickly find. Frankly, sutlers were not the problem. The real problem stemmed from the "demand" side: in other words, from the simple fact that so many soldiers—including many officers—wanted to buy whiskey and get drunk. The experiences of Captain Washington Seawell, who commanded Micanopy for a time, typify the hopeless fight against alcohol consumption. Try as he might, he could not keep sutlers away from the fort. Nor could he keep his men out of grog shops. Totally exasperated, he wrote to the adjutant general: "The traffic of whiskey to the soldiers at this post is carried on to a great extent by some of the citizens in this vicinity. I have used every endeavor to put a stop to this traffic, but without success, or any prospect of it. It seems that these citizens consider it greatly to their interest to carry it on; far more so than they consider the presence of troops necessary for the purpose of protection against Indian depredations." Violence inevitably resulted from all this drinking. Seawell reported that one of his musicians killed a sergeant for "taking from him two bottles of whiskey, which he had procured . . . and was . . . introducing to the garrison."[23]

The situation got even worse. At one point, Lieutenant Colonel Bennet Riley, one of the Army's best officers, inspected Micanopy and wrote a scathing report to his commanding officer: "I have never seen men in such a state since I have been in the Army; there were ninety-nine in the sick report and about 50 or 60 men in the guard house. Some of the companies had only eight [men] on parade and others had fifteen . . . some of which were drunk at the time, and others had all the appearance of having very recently been drunk. I saw very few sober men during inspection. The officers . . . say that nothing under the sun can remedy the evil. I considered it dangerous to go out after night." Riley recommended that the post be disbanded immediately.[24]

That didn't happen. Instead life went on as before. The drinking situation improved slightly but not completely. One cannot help but wonder if excess drinking affected the unit's performance in combat. Perhaps it was even a factor in the last major battle the 7th fought in this war. On December 28 elements of the regiment fought the Seminoles at Martin's Point, about four miles from Fort Micanopy. On this day, a group of thirteen mounted Cottonbalers set off from Micanopy bound for Fort Wacahoota. They had someone special with them, Mrs. Alexander Montgomery, the brand-new bride of one of the regiment's lieutenants. In the nineteenth century, officers sometimes brought their wives and families with them to military posts, no matter how distant. Enlisted men tended to be single, but those who were married rarely enjoyed the same privilege. This lack of feminine companionship only added to the desolate nature of enlisted life on the frontier and no doubt exacerbated the pervasive thirst for alcohol.

That aside, the men relished the chance to escort Mrs. Montgomery to Wacahoota. They took a supply wagon and five mules with them. The trails they used had been scouted for months and, the soldiers thought, swept clear of any Seminole presence. The soldiers rode their horses at a slow trot on this crisp winter morning and scanned the surrounding terrain for any sign of enemy troops. They had covered about four miles, reaching a hammock called Martin's Point, when Lieutenant Nevil Hopson, a young West Pointer, spotted something out of place. "I saw an Indian in the edge of the hammock and reported to Lieutenant [Walter] Sherwood [the commander of the force] there were Indians on our right. While pointing them out to him I saw from 15 to 20 others squatting about behind the trees near the road just in front of us. Lieut. Sherwood jumped from his horse and ordered the men to dismount." The Seminoles opened fire. The mounted soldiers were terribly vulnerable. In their saddles, they made wonderful targets for the concealed Seminoles.

As the soldiers dodged musket balls and scrambled off their mounts, Hopson and Sherwood argued about what to do with Mrs. Montgomery. Sherwood wanted to dismount her and hide her in the supply wagon. Hopson, for some reason, thought she would be safer on her horse. Sherwood finally ordered Hopson to put her in the wagon. No sooner did Hopson do this than he bumped into a wounded man. The Seminoles had fired "six or eight" volleys, prompting three or four other men to run for cover about one hundred yards down the road. Sherwood, fighting for his life with what remained of his detachment, hollered at Hopson to retrieve the men down the road. "I mounted my horse," Hopson recalled, "and carried them back, and while going back we saw some Indians running down towards the hammock, and others [along] the road. This seemed to encourage the men very much and there was a general shout among them 'they are running!'"[25]

The men were wrong. The Indians were closing in for the kill. Even as Hopson was rallying the men down the road, the Seminoles scored hits on Sherwood, Sergeant Major Carroll (of Bridgewater fame), two privates, and Mrs. Montgomery. The officer's wife got hit in the right rear shoulder blade as she attempted to hide in the wagon. The ball ripped through her body and exited out of her right breast, killing her quickly. Sherwood, Carroll, and Private Lansing Burlingham fought hand to hand with the Indians for a short time. Sherwood inflicted mortal wounds on one of the enemy troops in a desperate struggle. He and the others were wounded and in bad shape, though, and they couldn't last long. Seminoles killed Sherwood and Carroll. Burlingham managed to hang on and protect Mrs. Montgomery's body "from the merciless barbarities of the savages, who gathered around her, determined to gratify their diabolical revenge" in the confusion of the slaughter. The term "gratify their diabolical revenge" is probably nineteenth-century-speak for necrophilial rape. The Indians did not stick around for long. They knew that Martin's Point was close to Micanopy and that they could expect an agitated, powerful response from the fort's garrison. They scalped a few dead bodies and took off.

Within hours soldiers from Micanopy, including Lieutenant Montgomery, arrived at Martin's Point. Amazingly, Burlingham was still alive, although just barely so. He lay near Mrs. Montgomery and watched as the devastated lieutenant examined his wife's body. Very close to death, Burlingham summoned the strength to speak: "Lieutenant, I fought for her as long as I could, but they were too strong for me." He paused a second and his eyes glazed. "I did my duty." A second later he died, in the kind of scene usually reserved for the imaginations of melodramatic Hollywood scriptwriters. In this case, the scene was all too real and all too tragic. Five Cottonbalers lay dead alongside Mrs. Montgomery.

Various detachments scrambled to action around the 7th's area of operations, but to no avail. They found no Indians and got no payback. Weeks later the secretary of war ordered an investigation and criticized the deceased Lieutenant Sherwood for not following standard operating procedures. Sherwood failed to adhere to a regulation that prescribed a thirty-man minimum for patrols (that probably wouldn't have made much difference) and disobeyed orders by mounting all of his soldiers. Obviously, none of this hindsight could bring back the dead.[26]

This disaster notwithstanding, the Second Seminole War was winding down. The Indians won plenty of tactical victories, but they were losing strategically. The Army harassed their camps, their supply lines, and their way of life. In a sense, battles were beside the point. The Army could win simply by uprooting the Seminoles and forcing them to live a migrant life. This would inevitably disrupt and destroy what the Seminoles fought for—stable homes on stable land free of outside interference. The moment the U.S. government decided to commit its resources to bring about change in the status quo in Florida, the Seminoles were well on the path of defeat, even though they managed to win many tactical victories through guerrilla warfare. These victories essentially meant nothing in the face of such daunting strategic odds. This pattern of Native American tactical prowess and strategic weakness would repeat itself time and again during the so-called Indian Wars of the nineteenth century.

In the case of Florida in the early 1840s, slowly but surely the combination of internal dissension, white settlers, the U.S. Army, local diseases, and warfare eroded the will and capacity of the Seminoles to resist. Gradually they died off or submitted to the dictates of the U.S. government, surrendering peacefully for migration or relocating within Florida to wherever the government wished them to live. By the summer of 1842, only a few hundred Seminoles had not surrendered to the government. The army commander in Florida, General William Worth, declared the war over. An ugly internecine conflict had ended and with it one of the darker chapters in American history.

The 7th Regiment, like every other military organization, merely served as an instrument of the government's policy, for well or ill. The unit received orders in July 1842 to pack up and leave Florida. The companies scattered among military posts along the Gulf of Mexico and the men spent their days as "hewers of wood and drawers of water" on various construction and maintenance details. Within three years, though, they were back in combat, this time against their southern neighbors, the Mexicans. In this coming war they would record their finest combat achievements of the nineteenth century, starting at a place called Fort Brown.

3

Assault Troops Without Peer

The Mexican War

THE ORDERS CAME DURING THE SUMMER OF 1845: proceed to Texas and join General Zachary Taylor's "Army of Observation" near Corpus Christi. One by one, the ten companies that composed the 7th Infantry Regiment answered the call. They had been scattered throughout the South and the West, and now, for the first time since 1832, they would serve together at the same location. They journeyed aboard steamboats and wagons and on foot. In September they encamped south of Corpus Christi along the Gulf Coast beaches.

Farther to the south, across the Rio Grande, their potential enemies, the Mexicans, camped and waited. Relations between the United States and Mexico had steadily deteriorated since the Texas war for independence. American sympathy for the Texans during that war and the outright occupation of Nacogdoches still rankled in Mexico. Now, ten years later, another issue threatened to lead to war—annexation. Independent Texas, which Mexico still thought of as its own territory, wished to become part of the United States. The question of Texas annexation divided Americans, not necessarily out of concern for Mexico's sovereignty but because of the delicate balance that existed in the mid-1840s between slave and free states. Slavery existed in Texas, and that state's entry into the Union could tip congressional balance in favor of slave states. In spite of this fractious sentiment among Americans, James K. Polk of Tennessee narrowly won the presidency in 1844 on a plank favoring annexation and expansion. Polk, like many other Americans, believed in the concept of Manifest Destiny: the notion that God had bequeathed the continent to Americans so that they might establish an empire of liberty from coast to coast.

Upon taking office in 1845, Polk intended to dramatically expand the borders of his country to include such present-day states as Oregon, California, Arizona, and Texas. He would attempt to do this diplomatically, but if that did not succeed, he would accomplish it militarily. In 1845 his administration endorsed the annexation of Texas and sent troops into the new state. At the same time, his envoys offered Mexico $35 million for the land Polk desired. The Mexicans rebuffed him. They had internal problems of their own. Their government was weak and unstable. Some Mexicans favored accommodation with the United States, but most did not. They realized that Texas was long gone, but they could not agree with the Americans as to where Mexico ended and Texas began. Mexico believed the border to be at the Nueces River, while the United States thought of the Rio Grande as the rightful boundary. Upon entering Texas, Taylor's army bivouacked south of the Nueces but north of the Rio Grande, and the Mexicans derided his troops as an "army of occupation." The situation cried out for sober, reasonable negotiations. But neither side was in the mood for such statesmanlike discourse, seeming to prefer war instead.

So the Cottonbalers and the rest of their army brethren trekked to Texas in 1845 to provide a "show of force" to a country that refused to be intimidated. Throughout late August and early September, the 7th Infantry set up camp, settled in along the beaches of southeast Texas, and waited for the Mexicans to acquiesce to Polk's entreaties. The soldiers sweltered, baked, and cursed in the late-summer heat. The hot weather and miserable conditions affected everyone, even officers like young Lieutenant Napoleon Jackson Tecumseh Dana, an 1842 graduate of West Point and the son of an army officer who also had attended that school. Dana's family traced its roots to early-seventeenth-century Massachusetts and counted notable chemists, clergymen, poets, and novelists among its ranks. Napoleon (named after the obvious) was born in 1822 at an army fort in New Hampshire and entered the military academy at the age of sixteen in 1838. Upon graduation four years later, he joined the 7th as a newly minted second lieutenant.

Two years after that he married a woman named Susan Sandford. During the war he faithfully wrote to her and, in the process, recorded a rich skein of details on the 7th's experiences. In early September, as he and the regiment struggled to establish a livable camp, he wrote to Sue and described the amazing, inescapable, filth: "This is the dirtiest place, I believe, I was ever in. It is almost impossible to keep clean, although the bay is just behind our tents where we can bathe whenever we wish. If

I sit down to read or to write, I get my face, hands, eyes, papers all full of sand, sticks, etc. There is a constant wind blowing from the sea. As for clothes, I do not pretend to keep them clean." Nor did he and the other soldiers eat particularly well. He and a fellow officer dined on "coffee, boiled ham, pickles, and hard biscuit. At supper hard biscuit and coffee. We have no lobscouse [naval stew with meat and vegetables], and we have no potatoes, and no gloves to wipe our plates with. We sit on two boxes and eat off a chest." The enlisted men probably ate even worse.

The situation hadn't changed much by early October when he reported to Sue that "there are millions of flies about here. They won't let us sleep in the daytime, [they] cover the walls of the tents at night, fly into our noses and mouths, get into our eatables on their passage from the plate to the mouth. There is at least one fly in every cup of coffee we drink. Our boiled ham today was covered with dead ones, which had drowned in the fat after it was put on the table. Whilst I am writing they dirty all over the paper. Then this is a mighty thriving country for cockroaches too. Their eggs have bred most plentiful. Our clothes, papers, coats, trunks, and everything is full."

A week later the heat gave way to torrential rains, which left the camp an oozing, muddy, sticky mess. "It is another rainy day, all is damp and wet and everything feels nasty. The guard mounted in a driving rain, a guard of two hundred men. This is the kind of weather which makes the bane of a soldier's life. The sentinel, wet to the skin, has still to tread his miry post and even when relieved has but to sit still for his clothes to dry on him. The ground on which the soldier sleeps is wet, his tent is wet, his blanket is wet, his clothes are wet. The rain extinguishes the fires, and he is obliged to wait until the sun comes out to dry his disagreeable, uncomfortable property. In addition to this his meals are irregular and only half-prepared. If it rains hard he gets no coffee, so that he is obliged to take cold comfort, and if he can get a little whiskey he is apt to raise spirits by artificial means."[1]

Not surprisingly, diseases thrived amid such conditions. Historian Thomas Irey claimed that, statistically at least, the Mexican War was the deadliest in American history because the mortality rate among those who served was close to 11 percent. The vast majority of those who expired met their ends from sickness rather than battle, at a rate of about ten to one. The usual killers were responsible—dysentery, malaria, yellow fever, smallpox, and cholera. At any given time in the fall of 1845, sickness claimed between 10 and 15 percent of Taylor's army.

Dozens died. Those who survived might have wished they were dead. They writhed on their cots, fought fever, and filled their chamber pots with diarrhea. This miserable set of circumstances resulted from several facts: the United States was unprepared for war; the logistical architects of the war did a pathetic job of supplying their armies and caring for them; the soldiers themselves, especially nonregulars, failed to observe basic hygiene methods such as separating sewage water and drinking water, and medical science still festered in the dark ages. Even the best doctors had no inkling of the link between microorganisms, hygiene, and contagious diseases.

Established Regular Army units generally experienced the lowest disease rates in the Army because of their relative discipline, cleanliness, and professionalism when compared with "volunteers," militiamen from the various states who had little or no idea of how to set up a camp or maintain any semblance of cleanliness. Old Regular Army units (established before the war) lost 76 men out of every 1,000, as compared with 103 in the volunteers, appalling rates by more modern standards but nonetheless the best rates in the Army during the war.[2] One volunteer officer had nothing but praise for the way the regulars set up their camp. "The tent of every officer and private was pitched in its proper place, so that knowing a man's rank and company, his quarters could be almost as easily found as any number in the streets of our principal cities. In front of the camp was a vast and well smoothed parade-ground; along the edge of which was a row of fading fires at which breakfast had just been prepared. Here . . . was Mars himself; in repose, yet armed . . . and ready for action."[3]

For all its combat success in the coming war, the 7th did not quite measure up to the camp standards witnessed by this volunteer officer. The regiment lost 226 men to disease or accident during the war (as opposed to 46 in combat), more than any other established regiment.[4] In all, more than 10 percent of the regiment's men died of disease. Those who joined the unit later in the war, under duration of the war enlistment contracts, were particularly hard hit, dying at a rate of almost 20 percent.[5] In other words, if you were a Cottonbaler in the Mexican War, the greatest danger to your life did not come from enemy ordnance but rather from microorganisms, lousy food, lousy water, lousy shelter, or lousy medical care.

AS 1845 CAME TO AN END, THE COTTONBALERS CONTINued to sit and wallow while politicians in Washington and Mexico City planned and schemed. In early February 1846, Polk decided to turn up the pressure on the Mexicans. He ordered Taylor to pack up his army and move south, as far as the northern side of the Rio Grande. Because of logistical difficulties, Taylor did not get his army to the river until March 28. Once there, his soldiers began to fortify a camp near present-day Brownsville, Texas. Across the river, in Matamoros, a Mexican army of five thousand soldiers warily watched the Americans. The two sides could easily see each other. In fact, Dana even claimed that the opposing troops could talk to each other across the narrow river.

The Mexicans made use of these intimate circumstances, launching a propaganda campaign designed to incite American soldiers to desert. The Mexicans believed that most U.S. Army regulars were emigrants from Catholic nations and would have no great desire to make war on fellow Catholics. They were not far wrong about the origination of many regulars (more on that later), if not always the fighting disposition. The Mexican commanders, General Pedro de Ampudia and General Mariano Arista, issued heartfelt pleas to the American soldiers, denouncing the lawlessness of the Polk government, promising land, good treatment, and religious camaraderie. The Mexicans even attempted to entice desertion by posting colorfully dressed, sultry Mexican women along the river who called out to the Americans and urged them to cross the river. For some reason, the Mexican commanders believed the 7th Regiment to be especially vulnerable. They convinced themselves that the entire regiment would, with a little prodding, lay down its arms and come over to the Mexican side.[6]

By and large, these Mexican efforts amounted to little, although some soldiers did steal away. The problem of desertion was significant enough, though, that Taylor had to post guards along the river with orders to shoot anyone who tried to cross. On April 11 Dana heard about what happened to a small group that attempted to desert. "Four men attempting to swim the river to desert have been shot by our guards. One belonged to the Seventh. Three were killed and sank, and one was wounded. Good men are always placed on the picket guards and show the deserters no mercy. Those who were killed called out loudly for mercy, but the more they cried, the more the pickets fired. They [the deserters] were . . . shot all to pieces." The ill-fated group Dana described suffered the wrath of their fellow soldiers, who considered them infamous scoundrels and traitors. Other, luckier, deserters succeeded in escaping and some of them joined the famous Saint Patrick's Battalion, a group of expatriate American soldiers who fought for Mexico. Nonetheless, American desertion rates during the war hovered around 8 percent, not substantially different from peacetime rates.

Day by day, the tension along the river multiplied. Dana and his soldiers camped in plowed fields near the river, fought mud and insects, and watched Mexican sentries. The soldiers grew increasingly restless for action. On the twenty-first, Dana wrote that they were "anxious for the fray. If we come to the fight our men will fight well and no mistake, when we commence we expect to see some tall walking on the other side [of the river]." They were experiencing an emotion that would be quite familiar to later generations of Cottonbalers, namely, the desire to get on with the task at hand, get it done, and get home. The soldiers could only stand so much digging, fortifying, guarding, and waiting. To their way of thinking, the war had to start eventually, and they would much rather it begin sooner than later. But in late April, they were still working twelve-hour days cutting down trees, digging earthworks, camping in mud, and eyeballing the Mexicans.

On April 23 the Mexican government announced that a state of defensive war existed between the two nations, but the first real fighting happened two days later, when a force of U.S. dragoons clashed with Mexican troops not far from where the 7th was encamped. The Mexicans got the better of this fight, killing five dragoons and capturing another forty-seven. As Dana put it, "the dogs of war are now indeed let loose."[7] Polk heard about the fighting within two weeks and succeeded in securing a declaration of war from Congress. By that time, though, significant fighting had already taken place above the Rio Grande.

In late April, Taylor sent out scouts who clashed here and there with Mexican troops. He also took a good look at the state of his army and realized that it needed more supplies, reinforcements, and ammunition. The general quickly surmised that he had to strengthen his main supply base at Point Isabel (now known as Port Isabel), located twenty-eight miles to the northeast on the Gulf of Mexico. He collected most of his army, over two thousand men, and set off on May 1. Whom did he leave behind to defend his fort along the Rio Grande? Primarily the Cottonbalers, along with several batteries of artillerymen from the 2nd and 3rd Artillery Regiments, some of whom served under a young officer named Braxton Bragg.

The fort's garrison now numbered 560 enlisted men and forty officers. Taylor designated Major Jacob Brown commander of this force.

The troops liked Brown, a man who came up through the ranks in the War of 1812 and earned a commission due to battlefield bravery. Born in Vermont in 1788, Brown was no young man at age fifty-eight, but he commanded respect from all who knew him. In effect, he replaced Lieutenant Colonel William Hoffman, an imperious commanding officer who had died in late November.[8] Late on the afternoon of the first, Taylor's force left. The men of the 7th stood and watched them leave, forlornly wishing them luck. Each and every man earnestly hoped he would see them again—and soon.

The Mexicans now made their move, crossing the river in force and splitting their army. One group shadowed Taylor while the other besieged the fort. For two days and nights, the garrison worked desperately to strengthen the fort that, in Brown's estimation, was nowhere near strong enough. The infantrymen worked on their bastions— digging, smoothing, and siting positions—while the artillerymen placed their guns along the sides and corners of the fort where they could hope for interlocking fields of fire. "The location of the fort was in a bend of the winding Rio Grande," wrote one historian. "The fort was a star shaped earthwork. The location of the fort commanded the river both upstream and downstream. It was also exposed to the fire of Mexican batteries directly across the river in Matamoros. Three of the bastions commanded the aforementioned town. The perimeter of the fort was eight hundred yards. Its walls were nine feet high, fifteen feet thick at the base. The work was also surrounded by a ditch to the depth of twelve feet."[9]

One 7th Regiment officer estimated that the garrison's defenses numbered 373 infantrymen from his unit, ninety-one artillerymen, six independent dragoons, and ninety-three "inefficient" (in other words, sick) soldiers from other regiments. In addition, the fort included twenty-five sutlers and civilians among its numbers. The civilian ranks included several laundresses, women who took care of sewing, clothing, and mess duties for the 7th Regiment.[10]

Early in the morning on Sunday, the third, the Mexican batteries in Matamoros opened up on the fort. Dana had just woken up and was in the process of washing when he heard shooting: "Their shot and shells began to whistle over our heads in rapid succession. They fired away powder and copper balls as if they cost nothing and they had plenty of ammunition. We were all at our arms in a moment and the artillerists at their guns, and soon our big guns began to pay them back in their own coin with interest. Our shot told on them very severely, as our artillery was much heavier and better than theirs. In the first eight shots we silenced their nearest battery. Having dismounted their heaviest cannon, we could see pieces of the carriage fly into the air, and what men they had in that battery who were not killed or wounded were obliged to abandon it."[11] According to another regimental officer, this direct hit happened twenty-three minutes after the Mexicans opened fire. The American ball hit the Mexican cannon "directly in the muzzle, and knocked it, head back and stomach into the air about 20 feet, and it was accompanied by legs, hands and arms. Seven Mexican officers were wounded, and eight privates who were round their piece killed." Farther down the line, another soldier could "sometimes hear the shot crashing through the houses [in Matamoros]."[12] Already, one of the U.S. Army's greatest advantages in this war, better artillery, had come into play. Immediately before the war, American artillery had undergone a renaissance of sorts, and its array of field guns, siege guns, heavy mortars, and howitzers was among the finest and most effective in the world because of superior range and killing power.[13]

Unfortunately, the Americans did not have much ammunition and their guns could only be so effective against well-entrenched and -concealed Mexican cannons. After several hours of back-and-forth shooting, the Americans had expended half of their 350 shots, so Brown decided to conserve his ammunition. The Mexicans had no such concerns. They poured fire into the fort all day long, somewhere between twelve and thirteen hundred shots according to the estimates of several American officers.

However, the enemy realized very little return for this investment. During that entire day, they killed one man, a luckless sergeant named Horace B. Weigart who was killed during the first half hour's exchange of fire. Weigart was standing on a banquette, or parapet, observing the enemy when "a grapeshot struck him in the chin, came out of the back of his head, and he fell on his face down the banquette, dead." Another sergeant stared in horror at the bloody pulp that used to be Weigart's head and, clearly in shock, confused Weigart with another soldier. With a trembling voice, the sergeant cried out to his company commander, "Shea is killed, sir!" But the real Shea, very much alive, stood up and called out to the captain, "No, sir, I ain't!" A group of men hauled Weigart's blood-dripping body off the parapet and carried it, under fire, to the fort's makeshift hospital tent. The detail plopped Weigart's body on a bed amid dozens of sick men around the tent. Less than an hour later, one soldier recalled, "a bomb shell was thrown through the top of the tent, lit near the bed, burst and blew the dead man's head off without injury to anyone else." As Dana said, it was "as if they had a special spite against that particular man."[14]

Now someone noticed that the American flag was not flying outside the fort. The Mexican attack had come immediately after reveille, while Brown conferred with his officers. Accounts conflict as to whether the regiment had not yet had a chance to raise the flag or it had been shot away in the bombardment.[15] Brown asked for volunteers to leave the relative safety of the fort, negotiate the one-hundred-yard distance to the flagpole, and hoist the national colors. Lieutenant Earl Van Dorn, a West Pointer and future Confederate general, eagerly volunteered. A moment later, he took an assistant with him and set off: "I dodged several bomb-shells which threatened to fall on my head. I skipped out of the way of a rolling howitzer ball; and stooping . . . a cannon ball passed over my head which would have cut me in two—musket balls flew around me at one time like a thousand humming-birds. The only wound I received was a scratch on the ankle in dodging a shell."[16] Van Dorn and the other man successfully raised the flag while dodging enemy fire like children eluding intermittent raindrops. As the officer, Van Dorn got the accolades for this feat of bravery. The assistant's name has been lost to posterity.

THE SOLDIERS KNEW THEY HAD LITTLE CHOICE BUT TO hunker down, let the Mexicans expend their ordnance, and hope that Taylor's forces returned to rescue them. Ingenious and steadfast, the Cottonbalers devised ways to protect themselves amid the hail of shot and shell that came their way. "We went to work to throw up a kind of temporary bomb proof shelter," a soldier remembered, "by taking our barrels of pork, laying sticks of wood across them, and throwing up six feet of earth upon that. These we built at points in the fort where they would be convenient for the men; and when we saw the smoke from [enemy] guns, everyone would fall from the parapet, and 'hole.' When we would see a shell coming we would fall upon the ground, as the explosion generally takes place upwards."[17] In this way, the troops protected themselves during several days of bombardment.

Even so, they could ill afford to sit around. At night, the troops removed barriers from outside the fort so that potential attackers could not sneak up unseen. During the day, the men improved their "holes" and kept a sharp eye out for any sign of an enemy attack. The Mexicans now began to harass the fort's defenders with musketry. "This fire was extremely annoying to us, as the balls, although spent, fell all around us, being thrown from a gun called by the Mexicans 'escopettes,' (a short gun carrying a ball nearly as large as a grape shot) and which, being elevated, throw the balls a considerable distance. This fire continued about an hour, but served to keep us on the alert all night."[18] Grapeshot, a form of artillery ammunition, consisted of several tiers of iron balls held together by plates, rings, and an iron bolt, thus taking on the appearance of grapes. This weapon could cause great casualties among dense concentrations of troops. The Mexican escopettes shot a firearm version of grapeshot. Clearly, though, these shots were not effective from a distance of four hundred yards, so the Mexicans undoubtedly hoped only to harass the fort's garrison and deprive the troops of much-needed sleep. In this they succeeded.

On Monday the fourth, and Tuesday, the fifth, the Mexicans continued to pound the fort, with little effect. In addition, they probed and scouted the fort's defenses, so much so that Brown decided to send out a patrol to sniff out the enemy and ascertain his intentions. First Lieutenant Charles Hanson, a veteran of the Seminole Wars, volunteered to lead this dangerous patrol. He took the dragoons and a few infantrymen, left the fort, and nosed around for a while late in the morning of the fifth. Hanson's party stayed out for an hour and returned safely. He reported that the Mexicans were in the process of setting up a battery at a crossroads eight hundred yards north of the fort. He also observed enemy troops taking up positions in the same fields the 7th had occupied just a week before. Were they preparing for an assault? No one knew.

The troops dozed and rested a bit on a fairly quiet night, but at dawn on the sixth the Mexicans once again laid down an intensive barrage on the fort. For about an hour, round shots (traditional cannonballs), mortar shots, and shells peppered the American positions. The shells posed the most dangerous threat because they burst and threw the most shrapnel, a technique that would eventually make artillery the most effective killer on the battlefield. The early-morning barrage fell heavily on the interior of the fort, tearing several tents apart and wounding many horses. The Americans responded with one of their eighteen-pound artillery pieces (a cannon that fired an eighteen-pound ball, shell, or canister) and the Mexicans then opened up with several other guns that had previously been hidden. Not long after this, groups of Mexican infantry crept into a ravine outside the fort and fired their muskets, but with no effect. The American infantrymen did not even return fire for fear of giving away their positions. But the artillerymen responded. Bragg's battery fired canister rounds—metal cans filled with musket balls—into the ravine and killed several of the Mexican soldiers.

Then something awful happened. Late in the morning the Mexicans hit a very valuable target—Major Brown. He got hit while making the rounds of the fort, checking on various positions, making sure his soldiers were OK. An eyewitness described what happened to the major. "He stood for a moment to give some directions to some of the soldiers who were busily employed at one of the bomb-proofs. Every instant the men engaged in dodging to avoid the ball and bursting shell. One of the latter . . . struck in the parapet." Brown, perhaps not as quick as the younger men around him, failed to dodge the shell, and it smashed into his right leg, just above the knee. "His right leg had been shot off, exhibiting the torn muscle and jagged bones to the pained sight of his command. Although suffering the most excruciating tortures, he remained perfectly calm, and said to those who were sympathetically standing about him, 'Men, go to your duties, stand by your posts; I am but one among you.'" A group of soldiers, under heavy fire, took him to the hospital tent: "While suffering under the operation of having his leg amputated above the knee, which was most skillfully done, he congratulated his country that the misfortune had befallen him, and not been meted out to a younger man."

After the amputation, Brown was moved to the powder magazine because the surgeons worried about the safety of the hospital tent, which had been hit many times by enemy shells. No one had yet been hurt, but they figured there was no sense taking chances with the life of the commanding officer. But the dank, stifling powder magazine was no place for a fifty-eight-year-old man who had just endured the trauma of an amputation. Brown fought fever and extreme pain for three days and died at two in the afternoon on the ninth of May. The 7th Regiment had lost a beloved commander, and the grief-stricken Cottonbalers soon dubbed their besieged home Fort Brown. Someday the town of Brownsville, Texas, would also take its name in honor of this remarkable officer.[19]

Captain Edgar S. Hawkins, another older officer from the 7th, assumed command of the fort when Brown got wounded. The new commanding officer immediately found himself confronted with an important decision. As afternoon shadows boded the approach of evening, somebody noticed white flags flying from two old buildings several hundred yards from the rear of the fort. The Mexicans wanted to talk. Hawkins recalled: "Two officers advanced and were met by two officers of my command [Captain Washington Seawell and First Lieutenant Forbes Britton], who brought me the document marked: A, signed by Gen. Arista, allowing me one hour to reply." It was a surrender demand. "This document being considered one of great importance, I deemed it necessary to convoke a council consisting of all the company commanders in my command, and laid it before them. They unanimously concurred with me in the reply." In the memory of one officer who was part of the council, "The vote of the youngest member was taken first, and so on throughout. This was the unanimous vote: 'Defend the place to the death.' "[20]

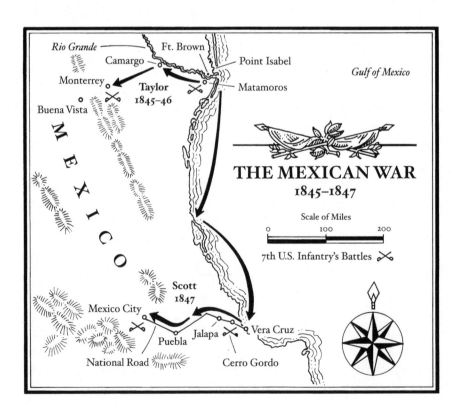

Rio Grande ——— Ft. Brown

Camargo

Point Isabel

Gulf of Mexico

Monterrey

Taylor ✗

1845–46

Matamoros

Buena Vista

M E X I C O

THE MEXICAN WAR
1845–1847

Scale of Miles

0   100   200

7th U.S. Infantry's Battles ✗

Scott
1847

Mexico City

Jalapa ✗ Vera Cruz

Puebla

National Road

Cerro Gordo

Taylor had given orders to that effect several days before, but Hawkins and his men had no clue where Taylor's army was or when it would be back. In his surrender proposal, Arista tried to paint a bleak picture of the situation, emphasizing the strength and size of his army, as well as the fact that he had cut the fort off from any resupply. In truth, the Mexican commander had badly miscalculated the amount of damage his guns had inflicted. The garrison was still strong enough, and self-sufficient enough, to hold out indefinitely against a siege or an assault. Basically, Hawkins told the Mexicans to go to hell, nearly one hundred years before General Anthony McAuliffe conveyed a similar response to the Germans at Bastogne.

When the Mexican commander received this unwelcome reply, he ordered his gun crews to resume firing with everything they had. In the words of one anonymous soldier, "It just rained balls, but in the midst of all the storm, the Star Spangled Banner still floated on our breastworks, at the point where they directed their strongest efforts. The fire was kept up all night, while their musketry played on us from the rear, at the distance of five hundred yards."[21] The surrender ultimatum and the musketry convinced the American soldiers that the enemy planned to carry out an assault that very night. According to Dana, the men actually welcomed this prospect. They had little but contempt for the Mexicans (partially because of condescending racial views toward the darker-skinned enemy) and were spoiling for a fight after helplessly enduring days of pounding. "Our men were delighted, in the highest spirits, and highly incensed at the idea of a surrender to those 'niggerly rascals.' All put their arms in the best order and made up their minds to shoot as many Mexicans as each man could." The enemy never came. In fact, the bombardment died down after dark and the occupants of Fort Brown actually passed a reasonably quiet night.

The next day at dawn the Mexican shelling resumed. It continued on and off for the next couple of days and inflicted a few casualties, most notably a private who lost his arm. Far less important, the 7th Regiment band lost most of its instruments when a shell hit the tent in which they were stored. Bragg's battery lost a caisson and a few horses got killed, but the enemy bombardment inflicted little damage. Even as the enemy shells fell like hail, the laundresses remained at their posts and shuttled food and coffee to men who could not leave their positions. One woman, Sarah Borginnis, whom the men nicknamed "Great Western," demonstrated particular bravery in constantly ministering to the culinary needs of the soldiers, even preparing a bean soup concoction the men especially enjoyed. "Thus did she continue to discharge her duties," an officer recalled, "during the [time] that the enemy kept up an incessant cannonade and bombardment. She was ever to be found at her post; her meals were always ready."

For many decades, the United States frowned on the idea of women in the military, much less in combat, but somehow women like Borginnis found a way to carve out a niche for themselves in the Army of the early nineteenth century. Still, that role had to conform to societal ideas about the proper place of a woman. She had to be subservient, supporting, and she must primarily concern herself with taking care of domestic chores like cooking and cleaning. Moreover, the same officer who lauded the bravery of Great Western found it necessary to vouch for her proper feminine "respectability" in such a predominantly male environment. "She is probably as celebrated for her personal appearance as she is for her needs. With an erect and majestic carriage, she glories in a height—six feet—which fully entitles her to a place in the grenadiers [usually the best-conditioned and most athletic soldiers]. But her reputation, the dearest of all things to a woman, is what she prides herself on. The tongue of slander has never yet dared to attack her well earned and sustained character."[22] Regardless of prevalent gender roles, she and her colleagues dodged shells every bit the same as the men.

Close calls abounded in dodging those shells, as Dana described in a letter to his wife. "[Shells] fell everywhere amongst us and burst in all directions in crowds of men. A kind . . . Providence kept us safe. A shell burst at the feet of Corporal Van Voorhies, another rolled over a man's back, and another between a man's legs whilst he was eating dinner, and although they all burst, they hurt no one. A shot went through Captain Hawkins' tent just over his head when he was eating breakfast, two through Mr. Page's tent, a shell and a grapeshot through mine. In fact tents were nipped in every direction. We all the time husbanded our ammunition for an assault, and only now and then threw a few eighteen-pound shot where we saw men, and we killed and wounded at least twenty of them. One of our shot passed through a house in the town and killed two poor women."[23]

What accounted for these incredible near misses? Probably not Divine Providence, as Dana thought, but instead the inaccuracy and antiquated nature of Mexican artillery. Their balls, shells, and grapeshot did not have the same intensity and killing power as the more modern U.S. artillery. Because of the depth of the American fortifications, the Mexican artillerymen had to get lucky in order to hit someone. Their ordnance did not have the power to destroy the embrasures, parapets, ramparts, and holes that sheltered the Americans, so they had to hope they could peg American soldiers in the open, and the kind of ball and shell projectiles the Mexicans shot at the fort rarely scored those kinds of hits.

On the afternoon of the eighth, the Fort Brown garrison heard more cannon shots. Business as usual? Well, not quite. These shots were in the distance, probably about eight or nine miles away. They could mean only one thing. Taylor was close, and in the middle of a fight as well. Morale soared, even though the Mexicans continued their bombardment of Fort Brown. "The excitement in our command cannot be described," recollected a 7th Regiment officer, "We now well knew that the attention of the main body of the [enemy] army was diverted from us."[24]

What the men heard was the Battle of Palo Alto, a sharp engagement that saw Taylor's outnumbered army drive the Mexicans from the field. Fort Brown's beleaguered garrison could only wait, hold out longer, and hope for good news. As Hawkins related, that good news came in the late afternoon. "A little before sunset, a Mexican came running in with a white flag. He stated that our forces had come in contact with those of the enemy; had driven them back; that he was . . . in charge of the picket guards fired on by our batteries; that while they were burying the dead and carrying off the wounded he effected his escape. The excitement in our command . . . was intense. We passed a very quiet night—the troops on alert at their guns."[25]

The Mexicans retreated to a series of heights north of Fort Brown called Resaca de la Palma and dug in their heels for another scuffle with Taylor's men. Barely pausing for breath, Taylor hurled his army at them and defeated them again. This time they retreated in disarray. At Fort Brown, the men heard the crashing of muskets and the boom of cannon that indicated battle. This time the sounds were even closer—probably about four miles away—than the day before. In the meantime, the Mexicans in Matamoros kept hurling shells, balls, and mortar shots at Fort Brown. As usual, they splashed mud around, ripped up tents, and caused tension but did not kill or harm anyone.

Then, late in the day, the fire steadily slacked off, allowing the

Americans to emerge from their holes and brave a few looks outside the fort. They could scarcely believe their eyes. To the north and the west, hundreds of broken, panicked Mexican soldiers were retreating, trying to make it to the Rio Grande as fast as they could. From a tiny spot somewhere within the muddy, messy fort, Robert Pruyn, a twelve-year-old drummer boy who had recently run away from home in Harlem to join the 7th, watched the broken Mexicans. Immediately he felt a tangible sense of glee. "We could see across the plain . . . the broken groups of peon soldiers, dogtrotting in their haste to get to the river, and then hundreds and thousands of them in wild panic. Tall-hatted officers galloped away from their men and swam the river. The privates threw away their guns, abandoned their blanket rolls, dodged and twisted their way through the bushes to the shelter of the river bank. Then our men came into view, companies of Texas Rangers shooting down the fugitives, and finally the Regular infantry and the rumbling guns."[26]

Not far away, Lieutenant Dana practically jumped for joy at the sight of the Mexican retreat. "There they went, a perfect rout. Horse and foot had thrown away their arms and fled like the wind, trying to strike the river at the nearest points, where they would plunge in to swim over. Many were drowned. They were wild with fright. Our fellows were perfect devils. The heat and excitement of the battle and the flush of one of the most astounding and brilliant victories on record had made them terrible in wreaking vengeance on these savage peoples. All who did not throw down their arms and ask for quarter were cut down without any hesitation." Soon Taylor's troops got to the fort, ending the one-week siege. "They swung their hats over their heads to tell of their victory. They were the first friends we had seen for eight days." Fort Brown's exhausted but exhilarated defenders could no longer contain their euphoria. "Five hundred of our brave fellows mounted the parapets, threw their caps in the air, and gave them such cheers as made Matamoros ring from the faubourg to the square. You might have heard the cheers two miles. Those shouts told the enemy what had happened on this side of the river. The effect was instantaneous. Their guns immediately ceased to fire upon us, and disheartened, disgusted, and appalled, they slunked from their batteries into the town."[27]

Filthy and disheveled, their eyes red with fatigue, the Cottonbalers summoned the energy to welcome their liberators to their battered home. Those liberators had tremendous respect for the men of the garrison and what they had weathered. Captain William Seaton Henry, who served with Taylor's forces at Palo Alto and Resaca de la Palma, said: "I would rather have fought twenty battles than have passed through the bombardment of Fort Brown."[28]

The 7th Infantry and its comrades had endured more than a week of pounding and privation and had lost two killed and thirteen wounded. American soldiers, by that point in their history, had never really been besieged and pressured in the same manner as Fort Brown's garrison. The soldiers at Fort Brown took understandable pride in their resolve and the fact that they had held off a numerically superior, better-supplied enemy for a significant length of time. Even so, the siege of Fort Brown has remained a fairly obscure event in American history, although it can be haltingly, if not necessarily favorably, compared to Bastogne and Khe Sanh.

By the next day, the joy of relief gave way to the aftermath of battle as the Cottonbalers helped take care of Taylor's wounded. Pruyn went to the hospital tent and helped out as much as he could. "All night long our surgeons worked by lantern light, and we boys carried bandages and medicines. It was rough work. There were no anesthetics. Legs and arms were cut off while men writhed and groaned and screamed with pain. And outside the carpenters' hammers rang all night building coffins for the dead. The horror of it burned itself pretty deep into my brain."[29] Little wonder, considering Pruyn was a mere adolescent witnessing the horrible detritus of war. In the next war, though, he served as an officer in the Confederate Army. Dana also witnessed the shocking results of Palo Alto and Resaca de la Palma and quickly grew tired of the "sight of ghastly wounds, the agony of death, its look in every shape, the groans of the expiring and the cries of excruciating pain, the smell of blood and putrid human flesh and the polluted atmosphere."

IN SPITE OF HIS BIG VICTORIES, TAYLOR WAS NOT ABLE TO move on Matamoros because he did not have the necessary pontoon equipment to safely cross the river. As it turned out, this really did not matter. The remnants of the Mexican Army opposite Taylor were in no shape to fight another battle. General Arista sent an officer with a white flag across the river. He proposed a truce, in which both sides would simply settle down and wait for their respective governments to negotiate an end to the war. Taylor quickly refused. He had no intention of allowing the Mexicans time to refurbish their army, not while he held the cards. He told the Mexicans that hostilities would continue and that he fully intended to cross the river and occupy Matamoros. In response, their army quickly evacuated the town even as the civil authorities invited Taylor into the town. This kind of Mexican ambivalence would continue for much of the rest of the war. Americans would find themselves welcomed like long-lost brothers by some Mexicans while others exhibited open hostility, or fought tenaciously in the uniform of their country, or harassed the gringo invaders with guerrilla warfare tactics.

Beginning on May 19, the Army, including the 7th Regiment, crossed the Rio Grande via ferries and occupied Matamoros. The soldiers conducted a systematic search and found large quantities of abandoned ammunition, weapons, and various caches of pens, desks, and clothing. The Mexicans also left most of their wounded, about three hundred in all. Given his inherent prejudices against Mexicans, it is not surprising that Dana was not impressed with the town or its inhabitants: "It is a mean, dirty-looking place. It is full of fleas and dirt. The better class of people and all the decent women have left. The women there now are as dark as mulattoes and dirtier and more filthy than Indian squaws. Our ugliest camp woman is better looking than any Mexican woman I have seen. They dress very lightly, show a good part of their legs and titties, both mighty nasty-looking sights. They pick the lice out of each other's heads."[30]

Luckily for Dana's sensibilities, the regiment did not stay in Matamoros for very long. Now that Taylor had invaded Mexico itself, he planned to capture Monterrey, the largest city in northern Mexico and a key crossroads at the foot of the Sierra Madre mountains. The general knew that even though he might not face much Mexican opposition, he could not hope to march his army directly from Matamoros to Monterrey, because the route lacked water. Therefore he decided to move his army west along the Rio Grande to Camargo, 120 miles away. Once there, he would use Camargo as a supply base and, when ready, march his six-thousand-man army south on Monterrey.

On July 6, 1846, the 7th Regiment set out for Camargo. Three companies boarded antiquated steamboats and the rest went by foot. The steamboat pilots had a tough time navigating an unfamiliar river, and they made tortuous progress. They got about halfway to Camargo and could go no farther, so everyone got off their boats and set off in the scorching heat and muddy river deltas for Camargo. The regiment did most of its marching by night in an effort to minimize the soldiers' exposure to the harsh Mexican sun. In spite of that sensible policy, men still suffered terribly from the elements. At least one man died of sunstroke. Dana told his wife that "the heat was intolerable, and we suffered much there on account of it. It was impossible to get under a good shade, and the perspiration oozed from every pore. In addition to this, all the water we had to use was very warm and did not refresh us in the least. My dear wife, those who have never tried marching under a blazing sun have yet to learn the real suffering consequent upon excess of heat. It was like marching in a oven. The men suffered greatly. Several of them gave out, and the doctor was obliged to direct them to get into . . . wagons. Your hero, dearest, was the only officer left on foot." Dana prided himself on slogging alongside his men, sharing their privation and their misery. Late in the afternoon, he lost the sole out of one of his shoes, but still he kept going.

They drank muddy water and arduously squished their way through waist-deep mud holes caused by the river's flooding: "The sun was absolutely like a blaze of fire, and it was impossible to stand under it." After the sun set, the troops collapsed in exhaustion and slept for several hours until reveille bugles sounded at two in the morning. Several more hours of tough marching lay ahead. They finally got to Camargo at 7:00 A.M. on July 15 and met up with the two advance companies of the regiment that had gotten there the day before. "We had marched forty-five miles in three marches in fifty hours, and that in the middle of one of the hottest months."[31]

The Cottonbalers set up camp in the town's main plaza and spent the rest of July and most of August in Camargo, a town of about two thousand inhabitants who had been fairly decimated by the incessant flooding along the length of the Rio Grande that summer. The soldiers prepared as best they could for the coming battle and spent much of their free time singing the regiment's theme song, an upbeat ditty called "The Girl I Left Behind Me."

Taylor arrived in Camargo, reconstituted his army, received replacements, and accepted whatever meager supplies the War Department sent him. Many of his new men were volunteers from the various states who served under radically different terms than regulars like the men of the 7th. Some volunteer regiments served for three months, some for six months, and some for one year. The men in these regiments served alongside friends and neighbors and often received nice enlistment bonuses, land, and pensions for their soldierly troubles. They were militiamen, citizen soldiers who joined up for adventure, glory, patriotism, and, in some cases, sheer lust for troublemaking.

They represented the best and worst aspects of the American way of war. On the positive side, they were self-motivated, idealistic, literate, and democratic in outlook, more or less reflecting middle-class America in the mid-nineteenth-century. On the negative side, they were undisciplined, unprofessional, often poorly armed, and, worse, quite smug in their belief that military discipline and training did not apply to them. They looked down on the regular soldiers, whom they thought of as mindless robots, foreign hirelings, or, at best, degraded simpletons. A clear and sometimes unbridgeable difference existed between the volunteers, militiamen who inherited the hallowed role of revolutionary-era minutemen, and the regulars, who were the inheritors of the professionalism of the Continental Army.

The United States has never completely resolved or eliminated this chasm between part-time, citizen soldiers and full-time professionals. In the Mexican War era, the divide between volunteer and regular had more to do with class differences than anything else. Middle-class, native-born volunteer soldiers viewed regulars, often foreign born or hailing from occupations on the margins of respectability, as social inferiors. In addition, the volunteers thought of the regulars as somehow un-American because of their discipline and ingrained obedience to authority. For their part, the regulars often viewed the volunteers as poor, slovenly soldiers who had no idea how to set up camp, much less fight battles.

In late August, Taylor was finally ready to move, but not before a tough summer of drilling and preparing for the Cottonbalers. Pruyn, the drummer boy, decreed that "we were not ready to fight the first battles [at Palo Alto and at Resaca de la Palma]. We won them because the Mexicans were not disciplined. Our little force of Regulars was. Then we had to sit down and toil through the summer, drilling, waiting for wagon trains, for provisions, for almost everything that is needed by an army—and while we did that, the Mexicans built up an army down at Monterrey. We boys got bronzed and hardened."[32]

On August 19, the 2nd Brigade—including the 7th Regiment, under the command of Brigadier General William Worth—left Camargo and moved in the direction of Cerralvo, which lay seventy-five miles to the south. In the days to follow, the rest of the Army followed suit, bringing along everything it would need in the weeks ahead. "Every eight men have one pack mule, and every three officers ditto." Dana reported. "These are to carry tents, poles, baggage, cooking utensils, and everything. Our mess has purchased a pack horse to carry our messing things, for it is quite impossible for us to get along with one mule to carry everything. And the farther we go, the rougher will be our life. We will live like real soldiers on nothing but hard fare to eat, hard ground to walk on, only blankets to sleep on, and lots of watchfulness."

The first few days of the march were reasonably pleasant, but then the weather turned hotter and the men endured numerous frustrating delays, waiting for their baggage. The only saving grace was the food. The men feasted on eggs, chicken, mutton, and milk purchased from local farmers. The Army's inefficient supply system had forced them to learn how to fend for themselves. "We have mills along for grinding corn. Wherever we can find plenty of corn, we can subsist our troops on cornbread and beef and will not have to transport the immense amount of bread, pork, and forage which we are now obliged to carry."[33]

Once the column got going again, they made fairly good progress, reaching Punta Aguada by August 29 and Cerralvo by the eighth of September. Along the way, the typical line of march featured "our Texas Rangers and the dragoons in the vanguard, and other Texans covering our flanks and great creaking boxes of provisions and water and ammunition behind the plodding infantry and the rear guard."[34] The men shuffled along, kicking up great clouds of dust during dry weather and fighting their way through sticky pools of mud in wet weather. The one constant the men noticed was the rocks that dotted the primitive road and prevented any kind of comfortable footing.

The regiment spent several days in Cerralvo while the rest of the Army caught up with Worth's division. In all, Taylor's forces in Cerralvo numbered six thousand men, half of whom were regulars. They milled around the town, artillerymen in their red-striped trousers, infantrymen in their sky blue trousers and coats, cavalrymen in their fancier, darker blue garb, all of them enjoying the cool air that portended higher ground and mountains. Some of them even swore they could smell the Sierra Madres, somewhere unseen in the distance. The Army had eighteen pieces of artillery, one mortar, and about twelve hundred horses.

Taylor sent out a reconnaissance force consisting of scouts who called themselves "pioneers," a squadron of dragoons, and a company of Texas Rangers. These men moved cautiously down the southerly road, scouting what lay ahead and preparing the road for the main force. By September 17, the Army was closing in on Marin, a town that lay roughly halfway between Cerralvo and Monterrey. Here they began to see the Sierra Madres in all their splendor, seemingly touching the sky with their craggy, rocky peaks, so vivid and "more grand and picturesque than any mountains I have seen," Dana said, "and I have seen the highest ones in our country." Monterrey grew closer by the minute and, with it, more combat.

The troops needed only to look at the deserted villages they now entered to realize how close they were to Monterrey. Mexican troops had driven the inhabitants from their homes to keep them from trading with the approaching Americans. Some of these refugees crowded into Monterrey and some migrated farther to the south.

On September 19, Taylor's army moved into position just to the north of Monterrey. His cavalry scouted the land ahead and, in the words of the best history of the war, the cavalrymen saw "one broad plain . . . with Spanish dahlias, and curious trees and plants . . . on all sides. Every few miles a stream of cool, sparkling water leaped across the road. Farther on, lilac mountain rose above lilac mountain and purple range looked over purple range until the crowning peaks touched the firmament. Grapes, figs and pomegranates delighted the eye, and, as an officer quoted to himself, 'the air was heavy with the sighs of orange groves.'"

And then there was the town, fortified to the hilt by General Ampudia. Situated literally at the foot of the mountains, between steep, high spurs, the Santa Catarina River in the south and a series of low ridges in the north, Monterrey was ideal for defenders. From west to east, the town stretched for about a mile. The western end featured steep foothills augmented by redoubts. The southern end of town had a rough, high riverbank and many fortified buildings, along with barricaded streets. The main roads from the north emptied into the eastern part of town, and the Mexicans fortified this area with barricades, breastworks (shallow trenches with log protection), embrasures, ditches, and redoubts. The buildings here were protected by sandbags, rubble, and stone parapets.

An old cathedral stood in the middle of the town, almost like a beacon. The Mexicans concentrated most of their heavy artillery and a garrison of four hundred men south of Monterrey, on heights that afforded a panoramic view of the city and truly guarded its approaches. From those hills, the Mexicans could pour fire on every approach to Monterrey. The most imposing of these heights was Independence Hill, a mountainous protrusion dominated by an unfinished castle known as the Bishop's Palace. Needless to say, Mexican engineers turned the palace into a formidable fortress. Just south of the river lay another significant height called Federation Hill.[35] The 7th Infantry would get to know practically every inch of this hill.

The American soldiers thought of Monterrey as a Central American Gibraltar, but it had two fatal flaws: not enough defenders and not enough good leadership. Instead of guarding the approaches to the key hills southwest of town and massing his artillery on those hills, Ampudia spread his defenders throughout Monterrey and its outskirts in fortified buildings and along earthworks. He would have been better advised to fortify the valleys between the strategically located hills and concentrate his forces on top of those hills, since they really held the entire key to taking Monterrey. Literally, he who controlled the high ground behind the city controlled the city.

Realizing this, Taylor decided to send Worth's 2nd Division around the city, the right flank, with the intention of capturing the high ground, cutting the Saltillo Road, the enemy's main supply route to the south, and neutralizing Mexican gun positions. This was a bold, almost desperate plan, but two superb officers, Major Joseph Mansfield, the chief engineer, and Captain William G. Williams, the highest-ranking topographical officer, reconnoitered the route and assured Taylor that such an attack could succeed. In fact, the successful scouting mission of Mansfield and Williams served as a harbinger of sorts. Throughout this war, junior engineering and topographical officers consistently performed brilliantly in determining feasible attack routes and gathering useful, valuable information for American commanders. Captain Robert E. Lee and Lieutenant Pierre Beauregard were two of the most famous of these young officers.

Like everyone else in Worth's 2nd Division, the Cottonbalers camped at Walnut Springs, just outside of Monterrey, and waited for orders. Early on Sunday afternoon the twentieth, a bugle sounded. This was the signal to pack up and move out. The men scrambled to action, stamping out fires, putting on coats, gathering up meager belongings, and trotting into formation by company. Word of the unit's mission soon filtered down and spread among the men. Some of them stared at the heights and swallowed hard. This would not be easy. As the assault force prepared to move out, the rest of the Army gathered around and stared at them in silence. Dana remembered them "strung along the road as we passed, looking with curiosity at what they considered the forlorn hope. The volunteers wanted to see how men looked who were marching out to battle."

The column, consisting of two thousand men, made for quite a sight. Four hundred mounted Texas Rangers led the way. Behind them trudged the infantrymen in their sky blue uniforms, followed by artillery caissons and crews in dark blue with red-striped trousers (hence the nickname "redleg" for artillerymen). Near the front of the column, General Worth rode his horse with ramrod-straight posture. An energetic, restless man, he had waited his entire life for this opportunity. He intended to capture the Saltillo Road, all of the hills, and more.

Somewhere in the middle of this small but potent force, the Cottonbalers trudged anonymously forward. They walked through cornfields for several hours and several miles. Near sunset, they heard the sounds of a skirmish. The Texans had run into enemy cavalry. In a few minutes the shooting died down, but the Mexicans hurled a couple of rounds randomly from the direction of the Bishop's Palace. The troops had covered about six miles and were not far away from the Saltillo Road.

Someone felt a raindrop and then another and another. A second later, rain poured out of the sky in pelting torrents. Soon the rain was so heavy that the soldiers could barely see three feet in front of them. Still they kept going, even though they were now soaked to the skin from the cold, unrelenting rain. In a later age, rain like this posed little threat to the proper function of weapons, but not in 1846. The flintlock muskets used by most Cottonbalers could be quite vulnerable to malfunction in rain. In loading their weapons, soldiers had to prime the firing pan and the muzzle of their muskets with gunpowder, and driving rain could make the powder wet and useless, rendering the musket unable to fire. On that wet Sunday evening in 1846, the regiment's soldiers cursed quietly to themselves about the rain, the cold, and the slippery ground, even as they wondered if they would be asked to assault the Mexican-controlled hills under cover of darkness.

They wouldn't. Early in the evening they were ordered to halt. "There on the wet ground on a hillside with no cover, wet clothes, on a cold and cheerless night, no supplies, and as dark as pitch," Dana remembered, "we lay on our arms with nothing but our coats. That was the most cheerless, unhappy night I ever spent." Because the Mexicans were only a few hundred yards away, Dana and his men had no choice but to lie there all night and deal with the miserable conditions. Very few men got any sleep. They shivered and scrunched into fetal positions in an effort to keep warm. Dana languidly commented: "It was impossible for us to take that rest which was necessary to . . . invigorate us for the fatigues which tomorrow was to bring forth."

Sometime during the night the rain tapered off and, at dawn, the soldiers roused themselves and prepared to move out. They welcomed the prospect of a clear day, but that did not make anyone less wet. Everyone was still dealing with the residual effects of the previous night's rainstorm—wet, muddy trousers, coats heavy with moisture, smelly, rotting shoes, muskets dark with wetness. The officers made sure that their troops had enough dry powder and shot safely tucked away in their cartridge boxes. They would need it on this day.

Around 6:00 A.M. the column moved out, again with the Texans in the lead, along the Topo road, a tiny route that led into the larger Saltillo Road. Half an hour later, they started taking artillery fire from the rear of the Bishop's Palace. The enemy rounds screamed overhead and slammed into the surrounding countryside, doing almost no damage to the column. The Americans kept going. Before long the Rangers closed to within two hundred yards of the Saltillo Road. The Mexicans, incredibly passive to this point, attacked the Texans with a force of two to three hundred ostentatiously uniformed cavalrymen. They hit the Rangers with a determined fury, slashing and shooting. Worth immediately ordered the infantry to assume "line of battle" formations. "Line of battle" referred to the practice of forming infantry into boxlike alignments, each box usually consisting of two lines, under the close supervision of an officer who gave commands in such a way as to maximize the formation's firepower and maneuvering. The Cottonbalers ran as fast as they could along the road until they were within range of the enemy; then they set up in line of battle formations, firing as quickly and uniformly as they could.

The fighting did not last long. The considerable weight of Worth's infantry firepower, in addition to several of his artillery pieces, broke the Mexican attack. The enemy troops steadily retreated, having lost over one hundred men killed or wounded, against a dozen American casualties. Just like that, the vital Saltillo Road lay wide open and Worth quickly captured it. Dana and the other Cottonbalers fully expected a vigorous counterattack: "Here we remained for a half an hour or so, thinking that this cavalry regiment was only the advanced guard and the enemy would be out in force to fight us in order to keep secure its line of retreat."

But again the Mexicans reverted to passivity. They contented themselves with an inaccurate bombardment of round shot from the batteries on Independence Hill. In response, the Americans simply moved out of range. The 7th Regiment stacked arms and relaxed. Some caught up on the sleep they had missed out on the night before. Others, like Dana, ate lunch. His "gourmet" fare included bologna sausage accompanied by hard bread. Soon after this meal, Dana heard the stentorian voice of Captain Dixon Miles, who had assumed command of the regiment after Fort Brown. "Pick up your muskets and prepare to move out!"

Worth had a new job for the 7th. The regiment had inherited the task of reinforcing an attack on Federation Hill. At around noon, Worth had ordered an artillery officer, Captain C. F. Smith, to take four artillery and five dismounted Texan companies and assault the hill. They were having a tough time doing so, and Worth decided to reinforce them with the 7th Regiment.

The troops grabbed their muskets, formed into companies, and set off at a run through cornfields and sugarcane until they got to a river that they quickly recognized as the Santa Catarina. The river at this spot lay directly below the hill they wished to capture. To this point, they had only been subjected to a couple of inaccurate grapeshot rounds fired from a battery on Federation Hill. That changed when they hit the river. The current was waist high and swift. Worse, the men had trouble crossing because of the presence of millions of loose, slippery stones that coated the river bottom. Grapeshot burst around the soldiers but somehow hit no one.

Then, Dana wrote, the Mexican infantry joined the fight: "We put into the river, and the depression being too great for them to use their cannon any longer, the infantry rose, about five hundred of them, and poured in their lead as fast as they could send it. They were high up the side of a steep hill and we were right under them in the water. Their bullets showered on us literally like hail. They struck the water all around us, between us, before and behind, everywhere. It appeared impossible that we could escape being shot. That was . . . the hottest fire I have seen, and I have seen it pretty warm. Several men stumbled and fell in the water around me. I thought they were shot, but no, they got up again and laughed. Our blood was now getting up, we were excited. We all hallooed and yelled, but I tell you we made tracks to get under cover of the rocks at the foot of the hill. Well, we got under cover and would you believe it? Not one man was hit in crossing that river."

They lay under cover and waited for Smith's men to make a move up the hill. So eager were the Cottonbalers to keep going that officers actually had to restrain their men from charging aimlessly up the hill. Finally the order came to take the hill. The 7th Infantry, along with two hundred Texans, stood up and charged. "We raised a tremendous shot, and up the hill we went with a rush, the Texans ahead of us like devils. Terror soon found way to the hearts of the foe. On we came like an irresistible wave. Nothing could stop us, and the enemy saw that if they remained at their post, they would soon feel again the American steel." The American soldiers were practically in a frenzy, the kind of berserk, adrenaline-induced courage that sometimes takes hold of good troops in combat.

The enemy fire slackened as Mexican infantrymen and artillerymen abandoned their positions and began to retreat. "When we were on top of the hill, we saw right before us and a little lower than we their second height." This was another part of Federation Hill called El Soldado (Soldier) Fort. "There was a stone fort on it and the top of the hill was covered with large tents. They commenced playing upon us immediately with another nine-pounder from this place. We were flushed with victory. A tremendous shouting and yelling was raised and all cried out, 'Forward!' We rushed again like a torrent on the enemy. The effect was the same. We routed them from their fort. They fled like good fellows, scarcely stopping to look behind once, and left in our hands two heights, two brass nines [artillery pieces], and a very large amount of ammunition. We placed our colors on the hills and cheered like real Americans."

Truly the Americans had won a great victory. At very little cost, they captured one of the key positions in the entire Mexican defense system. Once the Cottonbalers and their cohorts got into the position of going toe-to-toe with Mexican infantry the battle was decided. Clearly the Mexicans hoped to lay back, dig into positions on top of the hill, and depend on their artillery to keep the Americans at bay. But, in a recurring pattern, their artillery was not effective enough to break up an American assault. Their infantry did not have the same fighting spirit so omnipresent in the American foot sloggers and proved no match at close quarters. Accordingly, once the Cottonbalers safely climbed the hill, they completely destroyed the capacity of the Mexicans to resist.

As the sun set on September 21, the 7th Infantry found itself perched atop Federation Hill. The rest of the assault force had been withdrawn in the expectation of attacking nearby Independence Hill and the Bishop's Palace the next day. For the rest of the day Mexican artillery lobbed shells at Federation Hill. The Cottonbalers found cover wherever they could and took the fire. Dana took charge of one of the captured nine pounders and returned fire. As if on cue, heavy rains fell again, almost at the same time as the day before. If anything, tonight the rain fell even more heavily, in overwhelming torrents, so much so that small rivers of rainwater flowed down the hill. The men had no blankets and many of them had not eaten in over a day. They had little choice but to find a hole or a nook and try to get a little sleep. They shivered, tossed and turned, and wallowed in their hydrated filth.

In the middle of the night, Worth collected the rest of his division and prepared for the assault on Independence Hill. By morning they were in position. From his spot atop Federation Hill, Dana was awake and on duty at his gun and he heard the assault force before he saw them: "Cheer succeeded cheer in perfect roars, yell succeeded yell, and these were followed by the heavy fire of musketry and the din of arms. I immediately opened on the enemy with my cannon and kept up a fire as fast as we could load. The sides of that hill were very steep and the hill very high." In hand-to-hand fighting, the Americans captured the hill and raised the American flag amid cheers on the hill and the surrounding valleys.

Now, among the key hill positions southwest of Monterrey, only the Bishop's Palace remained in Mexican hands. A garrison of 250 soldiers held the palace, and they remained under cover behind the building's thick stone walls. Three companies of the 7th received orders to leave Federation Hill and support the coming assault. Their job was to post themselves at the bottom of Independence, make sure no one reinforced the palace, and, while they were at it, make plenty of noise in an effort to confuse the enemy. Worth ordered the assault, but twice his troops were repulsed. Chagrined, he now knew that he needed artillery fire and plenty of it. The palace did have a significant vulnerability in the fact that it had no roof and no properly barricaded windows. Naturally the American artillerymen took advantage of this weakness, hurling howitzer shells through the windows. Dana's nine pounder also took its toll. "The first shot I threw went right in among them inside their fort, and the effect of the howitzer was terrible. It was evident they could not stand this long."

Indeed they could not. Reinforced by Mexican cavalry from the city, the garrison sallied forth from their fortress with the intention of attacking and destroying the American force that had tried to gain the palace. In so doing, the enemy soldiers ran right into an ambush, and Dana saw the whole debacle clearly from his perch. "This was just what we wanted, a perfect godsend for us. When the cavalry had advanced halfway up the hill and the infantry began to rattle their musketry, our twelve hundred fellows rose with a shout and rushed on to meet them, and you never saw such a surprised set of fellows in this world as were those lancers to see so many soldiers rise . . . out of the rocks. Our fellows rushed on and poured in their fire whilst I threw cannon shot among them. They turned their horses' tails and struck off like quarter racers for the city, leaving some twenty or thirty of their fellows on the ground. Our men then took off after the infantry." In a matter of minutes, the Americans captured the palace and turned its guns on the city. So, by 4:00 P.M. the Americans possessed the Saltillo Road and all of the key heights southwest of Monterrey along with several captured guns. Exhausted, the soldiers slept soundly that night.

Meanwhile, at the opposite end of town, the rest of the army had not met with such great success. They succeeded in capturing several batteries in front of the city, but at the cost of between three and four hundred casualties. These losses ground them to a halt while Worth's division engaged in its heroics. On the morning of the twenty-third, he had received no orders from Taylor, so, on his own initiative, he ordered his men to descend on the city later in the day. He wanted to capture the town before the Mexicans could send reinforcements from Saltillo.

Thus began the final assault on Monterrey. Worth first ordered that one of the guns captured at Soldado be moved farther east where it commanded more of the city. The fire from this gun drove the Mexicans from their positions bordering the river and in the western suburbs. At 10:00 A.M. the 7th Infantry left its redoubt atop Federation Hill, and shortly after it joined the rest of Worth's division in its assault. The men emitted Rebel yell–like guttural screams. At first the attack went very well, as the troops brushed through the evacuated portions of Monterrey. The men could see the Mexicans retreating and they expected yet another rout, but it was not to be.

All of a sudden the attackers, pouring enthusiastically down six major streets, hit the center of Mexican resistance. "The tops of the
houses were filled with Mexicans," Dana explained, "and they poured
their bullets like hail upon us in the streets." In a matter of seconds
three Cottonbalers got hit, one of them mortally. The others dived and
scrambled for whatever shelter they could find. Soldiers rarely experienced this kind of urban combat in the mid-nineteenth century. No
one in the unit had any kind of real training in house-to-house fighting.
This type of combat inevitably caused high casualties and demanded
close coordination among assault troops. To wit, the unit took almost
all of its casualties in the Battle of Monterrey during this phase.

The men found themselves confronted with two choices: go up to the
roof and get the enemy or infiltrate underneath him. In terms of the
latter, they would run into the Mexican-controlled buildings "and
then, making a small hole in a wall that divided two dwellings, they
would drop through it a six-inch shell with a three-seconds fuse lighted,
and throw themselves flat. Results followed promptly. The aperture
was then enlarged; and crawling through, they repeated the operation."
This tactic was remarkably similar to one used by World War II–era
Cottonbalers who sometimes attacked their enemies in urban settings
by blowing holes in the walls of buildings and outflanking them.

Dana's group dealt with the Mexicans differently. They built ladders
and, covered by infantrymen and artillery pieces in the street, climbed
the makeshift ladders and attacked the Mexicans point-blank. This was
dangerous, time-consuming, and quite difficult, considering that their
muskets were almost five feet long, weighed ten pounds, and took almost half a minute to load—and that in the most ideal conditions. All
throughout the day, the men arduously worked their way from fortified
house to fortified house: "The enemy fought very obstinately here, and
we had to fight them by inches and advance upon them from house to
house. They fired with great accuracy, too, and wherever they saw a
man they threw their bullets thick and very close." At one point during
one such assault, Dana glanced sideways at one of his men. The soldier
rose up slightly on a rooftop to take a shot at a Mexican soldier. Before
he could pull the trigger, a musket ball smashed into his right eye,
ripped through his brain, and took much of the back of his head off.
One of Dana's friends and fellow officers, a West Pointer and captain
named Richard Gatlin, also got surprised by a round. He was luckier,
though. His musket ball caught him in the arm and he survived. Gatlin,

who lost a brother to the Seminoles in 1835, went on to serve as a general in the Confederate Army.

The Mexicans fought hard, but they eventually died off or were forced to retreat toward the city center. Lieutenant Franklin Gardner of the 7th led a group of soldiers, armed with ladders and pickaxes, after them in a dangerous, courageous assault. As he did so, the Mexicans turned and fired, in conjunction with other enemy troops in buildings near the city center. Their rounds blistered Gardner's people, who screamed and scattered around the buildings. Nearly everyone was hit, including a quartermaster sergeant named Henry. Eventually, other Cottonbalers joined Gardner and helped return fire against the Mexicans and drive them from the buildings.

By nightfall the Mexicans had been pushed back into the city's main plaza. Most of their men holed up in a cathedral known as the citadel. The Americans wheeled up mortars and artillery and lobbed shells at the citadel and its environs. The pyrotechnics of this barrage impressed Dana, who watched in awe along with his filthy, dust-covered men: "Soon after dark our mortar began to fire and threw these very large shells, each weighing over a hundred pounds, all night. The shells all burst beautifully right in the plaza, scattering death and devastation on all sides and making them tremble lest one should go into the cathedral where they had all their powder and blow them sky high."

The Mexicans probably could have held out longer in the city center—after all, they had partially rebuffed Taylor's attacks—but they had had enough. Early in the morning on the twenty-fourth, they sent an envoy to Taylor in hopes of negotiating some kind of settlement. Taylor initially demanded unconditional surrender, but the Mexicans demurred. The two sides negotiated for a couple hours, until Taylor lost patience and issued an ultimatum. He demanded that the citadel be given up immediately, that within a week Mexican troops, with their arms and six of their cannons, should leave town, retreat to Saltillo, return any prisoners taken, and cede much of the land north of that town to the U.S. Army. In return he offered them an eight-week truce and the promise that, before the Mexican evacuation, the Americans would only remain in the town for hospital and storage purposes. They quickly took the deal.[36]

Over the next few days, the Mexican soldiers left town. As they did so, the American victors watched them leave. At first glance, the Mexicans looked like the winners. They were cleaner and better uniformed.

The American soldiers were dirty, greasy, stubble chinned, dull eyed, and, in the words of one soldier, "as dirty as they could be without becoming real estate." But, on closer examination, maybe that contrast sheds light on why the Americans won so decisively. The Mexicans passively sat back on their hills and in their forts and waited for the Americans to come to them. By contrast, the Americans marched, sweated, and dug their way to advantageous attack positions. Exposed to the elements, they eschewed material comfort and performed with an élan the Mexicans did not possess. That's why the Americans won, and after the battle it showed on the faces of both victor and vanquished.

WITH THE BATTLE OF MONTERREY OVER, THE COTTON-balers would not hear another shot fired in battle for six months. The regiment moved into two of the largest houses in town and made themselves comfortable. They gorged on oranges and other fruit and enjoyed a life of comparative luxury. For fun, they wandered down to the river and watched Mexican women bathe naked. This idyllic life lasted until December 13, when the unit left Monterrey on yet another muddy, chilly, exhausting march. Most of them had hoped to be heading north by this time, but instead they were bound for Tampico, a port city on Mexico's eastern coast.

Throughout the fall of 1846, many soldiers held out hope that the Mexican and American governments would make peace on America's terms, but that did not happen. The Mexicans stubbornly and defiantly elected to keep fighting. In response to this intransigence, Polk and his general-in-chief, Winfield Scott, decided to capture Mexico City and then dictate peace terms. Instead of reinforcing Taylor and ordering him to proceed overland and capture the Mexican capital from the north, they devised a plan for an amphibious invasion of Mexico's east coast at the city of Veracruz. The president also decided to feed Taylor some humble pie. Polk stripped him of most of his army, including the 7th Regiment, and placed these soldiers under Scott, who would command the invasion. The victories at Palo Alto, Resaca de la Palma, Fort Brown, and Monterrey had turned Taylor into a war hero and a potent political rival. What's more, Taylor was a Whig and had no love for and nothing good to say about Polk's Democratic administration. For his part, Scott viewed Taylor as an amateurish commander whose lax discipline threatened the effectiveness and morale of the Army.

All of this political intrigue meant that the Cottonbalers would now board ships and engage in their first amphibious assault. In late February 1847, after waiting around in Tampico for several weeks, the men finally boarded ships and began what would prove to be an uncomfortable, possibly even miserable, voyage. For nearly two weeks, the troops spent most of their time "rolling and pitching and tossing . . . like chips at sea" and fighting the resulting seasickness. At last Veracruz appeared on the horizon.

While the big guns of the town kept the American ships at a safe distance, Scott and his commanders conferred on the best place to land, finally deciding on a point three miles south of the town. The general had organized his army into three divisions: the 3rd Division of volunteers under General Robert Patterson, the 1st Division of regulars under Worth, and, last, the one to which the 7th Infantry belonged, the 2nd Division of regulars commanded by Cottonbaler alumnus David Twiggs. This rough-hewn general had not mellowed with age. In the coming campaign, he often hankered for frontal assaults, even in the face of overwhelming enemy defensive systems, and without any modicum of common sense. Dana described Twiggs as "somewhat advanced in years; of a large body; full, round, red face; heavy whiskers and moustachios [sic]; but these are all white, or nearly so."[37]

On March 9, a beautiful and clear day, Scott gave the go-ahead for the first major amphibious landing in the history of the U.S. Army. Worth's division went in first. As gunboats and larger ships bombarded the beach, Worth's men transferred from their miserable transports to surfboats, the nineteenth-century equivalent of Higgins boats. Each surfboat held between fifty and eighty soldiers. Sailors on either side of each surfboat rowed toward the shore. Seeing this, the American soldiers waiting their turn farther out to sea emitted a thunderous cheer that could be heard for miles on a westerly sea breeze. The roaring died down a bit when the surfboats neared the beach. Mexican cavalry appeared on the dunes Worth's men hoped to capture. An instant later, the American gunboats opened up on them, and the enemy horsemen had no choice but to scatter inland away from the accurate shots. In the meantime, aboard the surfboats "the oars of the straining sailors flashed. Muskets—not loaded but with fixed bayonets—glittered. Regimental colors floated at the stern of each boat. Suddenly one of the boats darted ahead and ground on a [sand] bar about one hundred yards from the shore. Out leaped Worth; his officers followed him; and the whole brigade were instantly in the breaking ground-swell, holding aloft their muskets and cartridge-boxes."[38]

Incredibly, they encountered no resistance. Greatly excited, they charged over the dunes and set up positions inland, raising their muskets in triumph and cheering wildly. The chorus of voices offshore soon joined them. Next the volunteers landed without incident and, by nightfall, Twiggs's division, including the Cottonbalers. The Mexicans did nothing to stop them, preferring instead to hunker down behind the formidable walls of Veracruz and hurl a few inaccurate shells at the Americans. This was inexcusable. Had the Mexicans vigorously resisted the landing, they might have had a chance to rebuff Scott's army, which was not properly supplied, trained, or prepared for a vigorously opposed amphibious landing. But, in a familiar pattern, the Mexicans remained passive, ceding the initiative to the Americans. In the campaign ahead, they continued this shameful pattern, and it cost them dearly.

In the days after the successful landing, Scott's men encircled Veracruz and cut it off from the interior of Mexico. The general commanded an army that numbered slightly under ten thousand soldiers and he knew his resources were limited. Instead of ordering his men to assault the bristling guns and defensive positions of Veracruz, he opted for a siege. The American line, called Camp Washington by the troops, formed a seven-mile semicircle around the city.

The 7th Infantry occupied a position near the extreme northeast of this line, almost above the city, in sandy, gritty soil. Dana wrote to his wife on March 18 that "we have no tents, no baggage yet, and for nine days I have been rolling in the sand with nothing but my cloak and sometimes in the rain. We have nothing but what we carry on our backs, and in addition to my cloak I have to carry about with me a haversack with four days' provisions and canteen of water. Our guard duty is very hard, and we have to constantly be on the alert to preventing the enemy from communicating to or from the city. The duty is more tedious and harassing than dangerous. It is evident that the enemy are very weak in the city. They dare not show themselves beyond the walls. They have made several attempts within the last few days to communicate their situation to friends outside, but we have intercepted all their letters."

The siege soon got worse for the Mexicans when Captain Lee and his fellow engineers set up ideal positions from which American heavy guns, recently landed from the ships amid arduous labor, pounded the city. Mexican return fire did little damage to the well-sited and dug-in American gun positions. Scott even arranged for naval guns to be brought ashore and set up around the perimeter. Accomplishing this job meant more backbreaking labor for the small collection of artillerymen and marines who did it. They dragged the guns into positions, dug pits for them, and exhaustively placed the cannons at the proper angles, to Lee's satisfaction. The results of this herculean effort more than offset the sweat and exhaustion of the soldiers, because the guns proved highly effective.

Infantrymen like Dana either helped with the digging or kept a close eye on the Mexicans in the city. On the twenty-fifth of March he told his wife that the "poor city is in a bad fix, a constant stream of shot and shells pouring into it all the time, day and night. They still continue to return fire . . . but with little effect. We are merely lookers-on. We have as yet no fighting to do. We are out here in the sand beyond the reach of the city . . . and we can see all that is going on from the top of our little hillocks without being exposed at all. It is true we are in an uncomfortable fix still, having no tents and no baggage. We have had storms of wind and sand for a great part of the time, but we have had but little rain. This is the most sandy place I have ever seen, nothing but sand hills to be seen as far as the eye can reach, and when the wind blows we are almost buried alive."[39] The soldiers went through their daily routines, ate their salt pork and their hard bread, and waited for the Mexicans to capitulate.

The bombardment continued, creating a ghastly scene of destruction, as one historian described: "Crashing roofs; burning houses; flying pavements, doors, windows and furniture blocking the streets; a pandemonium of confused and frightful sounds; domes and steeples threatening to fall; the earth quaking; crowds of screaming women; terrible wounds and sudden deaths."[40]

In late March, the Mexicans in the city began to realize that they could expect no help from the interior of their country. Bands of guerrillas roamed about, harassing the Americans, but they could not hope to break through enemy lines and into the city. The garrison of Veracruz knew it was doomed and opted to surrender on March 28.

The next day the Americans moved into the city and Dana could scarcely believe the destruction. "The damage done to the city by our shot and shells is immense. The lower half of the city is almost ruined. Whole blocks of buildings are so shattered . . . that it will cost as much to repair them as it would to rebuild them. Our immense shells would fall through the tops of houses, go through both stories, and then bursting would shatter the whole house, throw down walls, and blow two or three rooms into one. Doors and windows are blown to pieces all over the city. One of their splendid churches is ruined. Several ten-inch shells fell in among the altars, and a number of forty-two-pounder shot went through it."[41] The infantrymen of the 7th proved to be merely interested onlookers in this fight. They took no casualties. Artillery won at Veracruz, liberally spiced with Mexican miscalculation and incompetence.

With Veracruz safely in hand, Scott now resolved to push inland to the west with the ultimate goal of capturing Mexico City. He still had major supply problems, mainly inadequate food, transportation, and ammunition. But he knew that the longer he stayed in Veracruz, the more vulnerable his troops would be to *el vomito,* the yellow fever season. Accordingly, on April 8 he ordered Twiggs to take his division, move west along the national highway, and proceed eighty miles to Jalapa, a town located on higher elevation, out of the fever zone. This movement order once again put the 7th Infantry at the vanguard of the Army.

Twiggs had about twenty-six hundred men, including several artillery pieces, and a couple squadrons of dragoons who scouted and screened the movement of the main force. At first the march proved to be a nightmare. The road consisted of little more than packed sand, and the soldiers, walking in columns, quickly found themselves sinking and thrashing in the sand. To make matters worse, the weather grew hotter. Clear skies allowed the sun to beat down on their necks. Soon they started throwing away equipment and collapsing by the side of the road. Hundreds fell by the wayside, including dozens of Cottonbalers. When the unit reached its halting place for the night, nearly two-thirds of the men had not made it.

Clearly Twiggs had to make changes. He began marching his troops at night, and that helped. Better still, the sandy road gave way to an actual paved highway. The men moved forward with greater ease now and even found time to take in the surrounding sights of cactus, palm trees, rolling prairies, and hills. Everyone noticed that the farther west they traveled, the higher the ground got. In fact, this was ideal ground for defenders and the Mexicans made use of it, fortifying a series of hills and passes near Cerro Gordo, a tiny hamlet about twenty miles east of Jalapa.

The soldiers who manned those fortifications belonged to an entirely new army raised by General Antonio López de Santa Anna, the charismatic, vengeful commander who had so vigorously opposed the Texans a decade earlier. Santa Anna had lived in exile before this war, but he came back home at the behest of Polk, who mistakenly believed that the Mexican general would establish a government in Mexico City friendly to American designs. Rarely has an American president misread an individual or a situation so badly. Far from friendly, Santa Anna was an implacable enemy of the United States, for whose inhabitants he had nothing but malice and contempt.

Quick-tempered and brilliant, Santa Anna won power in Mexico through his presence and strong will. Late in 1846 he rebuilt the Mexican Army, in spite of the country's impending bankruptcy. In late February 1847 he unleashed this new force on General Taylor's defanged army in northern Mexico at the Battle of Buena Vista. Santa Anna enjoyed greater numbers and better supply, but Taylor still beat him with nothing more than a collection of a few thousand volunteers, augmented by a handful of regulars. As at Veracruz, artillery proved to be the determining factor at Buena Vista. Santa Anna reluctantly retreated with the remnant of his army and decided to concentrate on thwarting Scott's expedition.

To that end, the Mexican general-dictator ordered his commanders to fortify the foothills and mountains east of Jalapa with artillery and entrenched infantry. Twiggs made first contact with cavalrymen from this new army on April 11. In the wake of this skirmish, American scouts reconnoitered the hills around Cerro Gordo and found them to be strongly defended. Impulsive and hotheaded as always, Twiggs on the twelfth ordered his entire division to forge straight down the road into the teeth of the Mexican defenses. This should have been a disaster. Twiggs's men were being asked to walk down a road in full view of an enemy who commanded hills on all sides of the road. No matter what the qualitative difference between Mexican and American soldiers, the Mexicans could not help shooting down the Americans like proverbial fish in a barrel. But instead of allowing Twiggs's entire division into the kill zone before opening fire, the Mexicans shot too soon and allowed most of the Americans, including the 7th Infantry at the back of the column, to escape unharmed.

Furious, Scott now arrived on the scene and ordered the Army to hold fast while his engineers searched for a viable assault route. For

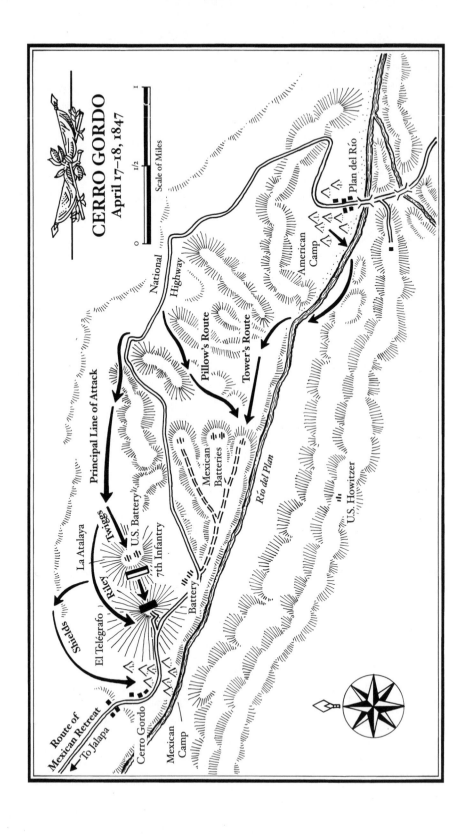

CERRO GORDO
April 17–18, 1847

Scale of Miles

National

Highway

American Camp

Plan del Río

Pillow's Route

Tower's Route

Río del Plan

U.S. Howitzer

Mexican Batteries

Principal Line of Attack

La Atalaya

Twiggs

Riley

U.S. Battery

7th Infantry

Battery

Shields

El Telégrafo

Route of Mexican Retreat

←To Jalapa

Cerro Gordo

Mexican Camp

about three days, they poked and skulked around the ravines and high ground immediately north of the road, in search of a trail or path that the Army could use to outflank the enemy force. Lee assumed command of these intrepid engineer-scouts. He himself experienced a hair-raising expedition that saw him hide behind a log, some thirty yards from unsuspecting Mexican soldiers, for the better part of the day on April 15. He managed to make it back to camp that night, dusty, dirty, and tired, but with an idea of how to outflank the Mexicans.

Lee believed that two hills, both immediately north of the road, comprised the key to the entire Mexican defensive line. At the point where Santa Anna hoped to spring his trap, the national highway sloped gradually southward directly into a series of ridges and then one dominant hill, about five hundred feet high, called Telegraph Hill. One American officer described Telegraph as "towering high above all the other summits . . . crowned with a tower from which floated the Mexican ensign; around the summit of the mountain was formed a breastwork for 5,000 infantry, and between this and the tower . . . was planted a battery of artillery." The north side of Telegraph Hill sloped into a craggy ravine strewn with thickets and lined by a crude trail that, if taken far enough, eventually led to the national highway. A few hundred yards to the northeast lay another hill, not quite as steep, called Atalaya. Lee's trail was located between Telegraph and Atalaya. He found that the Mexicans had made the error of lightly covering Atalaya with one gun and twenty-five men.

An ingenious plan soon took shape as a result of the intelligence Lee collected. The volunteer 3rd Division would march down the highway retracing the exact path trod by Twiggs. They would simulate a major attack on the Mexican defenses, exactly where Santa Anna expected them. But, unbeknownst to him, the bulk of the army, both Twiggs's and Worth's divisions, would veer off the road and head directly west. Twiggs would be in the lead. From here one group of his would capture Atalaya and turn its gun on Telegraph Hill, thus achieving what is called enfilade, or flanking, fire. At the same time, American artillerymen would drag their guns to the top of Atalaya and add to its enfilade fire. Meanwhile, the main force of Americans would follow Lee's trail, which the engineers were busily improving. The main force would essentially hug Telegraph Hill even as they skirted its main defenses. Hoping to remain out of sight, they would infiltrate around the hill. Some Americans would then attack the hill's defenders from behind while others took off for the highway in an effort to head off an enemy retreat.

Soon after first light on the seventeenth, Twiggs and his men went forward on the national highway. At the appointed place, they veered off the road and began to use the trail the engineers had improvised. In spite of the work of those indefatigable men, Twiggs and his command experienced slow going. They covered about one and a half miles in two hours, working their way through craggy rocks, thickets, oaks, and uneven ground. All the while, they moved as silently as they could, sweating and cursing under their collective breath. By late morning they could see the stone fort and its Mexican flag atop menacing Telegraph, maybe seven hundred yards in the distance. They had arrived at Atalaya.

Twiggs wanted this hill and he wanted it quickly, so he ordered Lieutenant Gardner, of Monterrey fame, to detach his company, seize the hill, and observe the enemy from its crest. Gardner's soldiers left the column and spread out in skirmish formation as they moved toward the hill. He and his men ran straight into a group of Mexican cavalrymen headed for the hill themselves. Unbeknownst to Twiggs, Mexican soldiers on Atalaya had spotted his forces and alerted their comrades on Telegraph of the enemy threat. In response, Santa Anna had ordered that the hill be reinforced.

Taken by surprise, Gardner's people did the best they could. He hollered at them to deploy and fire. They did so and their musket balls stopped the Mexican cavalry. In a matter of moments, American cavalry and artillerymen came to the rescue and helped drive the enemy soldiers away. Once the enemy reinforcements were repulsed, the Americans took Atalaya without much trouble. The 7th Infantry assaulted the left slope of the hill and, that night, helped occupy this new American possession.

The engineers were now more confident than ever that Telegraph could be taken from the north and the Americans planned to launch their attack in the morning. During the night, artillerymen dragged their weapons to the top of Atalaya. This job required the help of nearly five hundred men. An artillery officer explained how the men got each of the guns to the top of the hill: "A fire was kindled at the foot of the mountain. Five hundred men manned the drag ropes of the 24-pounder at about 9 o'clock, reliefs of 500 men each following in the rear of the gun, to take the places of the first detachment when their strength should be exhausted. Such a time of hard, grinding toil . . . as then followed for six successive hours I hope never again to look upon, much less take part in." Many soldiers collapsed from exhaustion or thirst. Their work was not done when they finally dragged the guns to the hill's summit, because they then had to dig them in and properly site them with only the light from tiny campfires guiding them.[42] By morning they had the guns in position to provide invaluable fire support for the coming infantry assault.

Many of the 7th infantrymen helped drag the guns up the hill until they fell into an exhausted sleep at the summit of Atalaya. They would need the rest. The next day, April 18, the decisive day of this battle, they helped carry out the main assault on Telegraph Hill. After an artillery duel, troops under Colonel Bennet Riley and General James Shields, using Lee as a guide, began moving west along the improvised trail, right under the noses of the Mexicans on Telegraph. The enemy saw them and opened fire. Santa Anna still thought the main American assault would come on his right flank, along the national highway, but he had nonetheless reinforced Telegraph, just in case. His fresh troops joined with his veterans and inflicted significant damage on Riley and Shields. Still those commanders kept their men moving in the direction of the road.

At this point, Twiggs ordered his old unit into the battle. The 7th Infantry, in conjunction with the 3rd Infantry on the left, supported by the 1st Artillery on Atalaya, would assault Telegraph and capture it. When the order came, the Cottonbalers were lying under cover just behind the crest of the hill watching Mexican grapeshot shriek over their heads. Now they had to leave the safety of their cover and advance, but they never hesitated. They fixed bayonets, stood up, and trotted down the slope of Atalaya.

The regiment had a new commander now, Lieutenant Colonel Joseph Plympton, a veteran soldier from Massachusetts. In his official report, he recounted the moment when the regiment left cover and advanced. "The regiment charged with cheers, passing the crest of this height [Atalaya], and ascending under a raking fire of grape and canister, and a heavy fire of musketry on my right and extending towards the left and front."[43] In an instant, the Mexican grapeshot, canister shot, and musket balls peppered them and "the front [rank] melted like snowflakes." Bright red blood splattered all over light blue uniforms as men got hit. Still the unwounded kept going. They reached the ravine and began ascending Telegraph. About sixty yards up, they ran into an enemy force behind stone breastworks. "We literally fought our way foot by foot till within 50 yards of the enemy's works from which we were separated by a brush fence," Captain John Henshaw, a Cotton-baler officer, later wrote. The Mexicans fired desperately and several American soldiers went down, but the Cottonbalers fired back and kept running until they were within the breastworks. Slashing, bayo-neting, and clubbing, they captured the position, leaving many dead en-emy soldiers in their wake.

Now the hill's rocky, steep slopes became the main enemy, making progress difficult and exhausting. Most of the Mexican soldiers were ensconced near the summit of the hill, and some members of the 7th Infantry had little trouble finding good cover amid ridge crests, dips, and swales. "Here a little time was taken for rest, and then forward pressed the troops, helping themselves up the slope, over craggy rocks and loose stones, and through the chaparral by catching at bushes and trees." Others were not so fortunate. "Very different proved the clear part of the hill, where small trees, bushes and thorny cactus lay spread with tops pointing down. Here progress was slow and concealment im-possible. But with deliberate fearlessness, the men plodded firmly on, firing at will, strong in that mutual confidence which gives a charge its force. Here and there, one [man] was struck down; here and there, breathless and exhausted, one dropped; but no flinching could be seen."[44]

As the men neared the crest of the hill, the battle approached its cli-max. Truly in a frenzy, officers screamed at their men to charge the summit and take it. The 7th Infantry became a military tidal wave, sweeping away all in its path. They flung themselves up the hill and right at the breastworks guarding the fort. The Mexicans poured as much fire into them as they could, but the assault continued. The scene of confusion, motion, and carnage can scarcely be imagined. In crazed fashion, groups of American soldiers ran as fast as they could, straight up the hill, right at the Mexicans. Musket balls zinged through the air, most missing but some splattering against men's heads, torsos, arms, and legs. The enemy fire would stagger the Cottonbalers for a few sec-onds and then, inevitably, the survivors would keep going, moving closer and closer to the enemy. One soldier compared the enemy fire to hail-stones. "The shots fell around us, cutting down the low bushes, and passing through the clothes of some, cutting down others. You can imagine my feelings. They fired on us briskly cutting down one after another; but still we pushed on, excited and maddened to a complete frenzy—that madness insensible to fatigue or even fear."[45]

In the midst of this firestorm, Dana's luck ran out. Crazed and berserk like everyone else, he was leading a cluster of troops toward the Mexican breastworks when a shot ripped through the side of his right thigh. He went down in a heap and lay helplessly on the battlefield while his men pressed on. Those who saw him get hit feared the worst, but in the heat of the moment they could do nothing for him, and he was left for dead on the hill.

The assault continued, reaching its climactic phase. To this point, the Mexicans had fought fairly well, but they were not prepared for the intensity or spirit of the American troops. When the U.S. soldiers got in among the breastworks and began clubbing and bayoneting the Mexicans, the enemy soldiers finally broke and ran. In the words of a 1st Artillery Regiment soldier who found himself in among the Cottonbalers during the final routing of the enemy: "Mexican infantry . . . threw down their muskets and scampered in the utmost confusion down the opposite side of the hill. Several of the enemy's guns were manned and fired on the retreating enemy, a disordered mass running with panic speed down the hill and along the road to Jalapa."[46]

American soldiers, led by a sergeant from the 7th named Henry, surged into the fort, hauled the Mexican flag down, and raised the colors of the United States in its place. With Telegraph Hill now in American hands, the battle turned into a rout. Those Mexicans who had retreated from the hill mixed with others who were advancing down the road from Jalapa, sowing confusion and panic. The victorious Americans atop Telegraph made the enemy predicament worse by pouring fire from captured guns into their ranks. Once American troops under Riley and Shields successfully negotiated the valley north of Telegraph and reached the highway, the Mexicans no longer had any chance of winning the battle. They turned tail and fled west on the road as far as their legs could carry them.

Cerro Gordo was perhaps the most impressive victory to this point in the war. Outnumbered and in the face of a well-fortified enemy, Scott's army had prevailed because of superior military professionalism and, most of all, the incredible bravery and fighting spirit of the American soldiers, including those who populated the ranks of the 7th. The Mexicans lost thousands of weapons, including many artillery pieces, and about 1,200 men killed and wounded along with 3,000 captured. The Americans lost 417 men, 64 of whom were killed.[47]

One of those American casualties, Lieutenant Dana, clung to life, bleeding and alone, on Telegraph Hill for a day and a half before an American stretcher team found him. They took him to a makeshift hospital, where he received medical care from a reasonably competent surgeon named Adam McLaren. At first McLaren thought Dana might die, but he changed his prognosis after the lieutenant responded well to medical treatment. One of Dana's officer friends wrote to Sue that "his wound threatened at first to be very serious . . . but the ball passed through without injuring vitally any of the internal parts. Everybody . . . is sure he will soon be well and so far recovered as to be able to go home and be placed in your loving care. So console yourself and be not distressed and all will be well." A few days later, Dana was strong enough to write to Sue himself, from a hospital bed in Jalapa, which Scott's army occupied bloodlessly in the wake of Cerro Gordo. "My wound is fast recovering, as fast as possible, and soon I hope the doctor will allow me to take the road to Veracruz. Once there I can easily get to you. I lie here on a comfortable cot, dearest one, all day, reading, eating oranges . . . and thinking of my darling ones at home and laying plans for our happy future. In the morning the doctor comes about eight o'clock to dress my wound and congratulate me on its fair appearance."

Of course, medical care wasn't exactly the best in Jalapa in 1847, and as was so common at that time, Dana's wound got infected. For several days he fought fever and chills, to the point where his hands shook badly. But Dana was young and strong and he fought off the infection until he felt well enough to be sent on recruiting duty in New York. He took a brevet promotion to captain with him. The gunshot wound did not completely heal for many months, but Dana survived the war and went on to enjoy a long military career. He fought on the Union side in the Civil War and left the Army after the war for a business career.[48]

ON THEIR WAY TO JALAPA, AMERICAN SOLDIERS GAZED upon a scene of awful carnage and suffering. "Mexicans lay dead in every direction," a war correspondent wrote, "some resting up against trees, others with legs and arms extended, and occasionally a lancer laying with his arm upon the charger that received his death wound from the same volley which ended the career of his rider. Some of the [soldiers] passing through would occasionally halt to view the features of the deceased."[49]

In spite of his enormous victory at Cerro Gordo, Scott found himself in no position to advance on Mexico City. In mid-May his army made it as far as Puebla, a city of eighty thousand people and the second largest in Mexico. Santa Anna had retreated back to the Mexican capital and, once there, he busily refurbished his army and intrigued night and day to keep power and build resistance to Scott's army of invaders.

Meanwhile, Scott had many problems. Close to 20 percent of his army was down with disease and sickness. Moreover, the enlistments of thousands of volunteers expired in June. Once they were gone, his army would dwindle to, at most, seven thousand effectives. He had supply headaches too. Not only did the government fail to send him adequate sustenance for his campaign, but the highway route back to Veracruz, the natural supply artery, proved to be quite untenable, because of distance, inadequate transportation, manpower, and harassment from guerrillas.

The general had no choice but to settle in, live off the land, and wait for reinforcements. He wisely cultivated good relations with local farmers and ranchers, and this helped his supply situation immeasurably. Scott won many Mexicans over to his side by paying for food instead of plundering it. After all, his army was but a tiny force far away from home in the middle of a nation of millions. Seeing before them a nice source of income and an army that sometimes ruled with more benevolence and input than their own government, some Mexicans formed a positive view of Scott's army and its soldiers, especially the disciplined regulars.

The Cottonbalers spent the summer of 1847 resting and replenishing their ranks. The unit, understrength from the outset, had already taken dozens of casualties in this war. It had fought most of its battles with only six companies. In an effort to build up the Army, the government passed a law creating ten new infantry regiments and encouraging more enlistments in existing outfits like the 7th. These new regulars fleshed out the four other companies after Cerro Gordo and enlisted under different terms than their veteran comrades. The new men received twelve-dollar bounties, the possibility of land and bonuses for a year's service, and the option of enlisting only for the duration of the war.

Understandably, the demographics for these new regulars differed from the veterans'. By the time of the Mexican war, foreign-born soldiers comprised anywhere between 40 and 50 percent of the Army. Most of these emigrants hailed from Ireland, Germany, or Britain. The 7th Infantry reflected this trend. Of those who joined between 1842 and 1844, 44 percent were foreign born, most from Ireland or Germany. They enlisted for five years and generally hailed from farmer, laborer, or artisan backgrounds. In 1846 and early 1847, about 60 percent of the recruits came from overseas, but the new men who joined the unit in the summer of 1847 were mostly native born. These men, numbering 534 in all, joined the unit in response to government enticements. Patriotic and a bit more ambitious than the veterans, they eschewed societal prejudice against the Regular Army in exchange for the possibility of land, money, pensions, and perhaps limited combat service. The volunteer regiments, raised state by state, still offered recruits better money and perks, but the new recruiting law somewhat evened the playing field for the regulars.

To sum up, the typical Cottonbaler before Cerro Gordo was foreign born and hailed from an "outsider" background. He saw the Army as an opportunity for betterment or for making inroads in a new country. Often scorned by native-born Americans and, in the case of the Irish, unable to find employment because of prejudice, he turned to the Army as a way to feed and clothe himself. After Cerro Gordo the composition of the unit changed. The majority of the replacements originated from native-born, fairly respectable backgrounds in the northern part of the country (owing to the location of recruiting officers). So the regiment featured a mix of backgrounds and occupations by the late summer of 1847 and, correspondingly, for the climactic battles of the war in August and September. The veterans still led the way in combat, though. For instance, all but three Cottonbalers killed in action in the war were five-year enlistees.[50]

IN THE MIDDLE OF AUGUST, SCOTT ORDERED HIS ARMY TO move in the direction of Mexico City. He believed that as long as he did not get drawn into a terribly costly battle, he could capture the enemy capital with his rebuilt army of ten thousand soldiers, two divisions of which, as before, were composed of regulars. Santa Anna had managed to piece together an army of close to twenty-five thousand troops, many of whom were raw recruits. The Mexican commander deployed his forces in a ring around Mexico City and fully expected, once again, the Americans to attack at the obvious place. In this case, that obvious place lay immediately east of town. That locality featured rolling terrain and roads directly into the city.

Once again, Scott did not oblige the expectations of his adversary. He ordered his resourceful engineers to find a feasible, cost-effective way into Mexico City. Lee and Beauregard obliged him. At that time, Mexico City sat astride the national highway going east to west through the city as well as several smaller roads emptying into town from the south. Lake Texcoco presented a natural boundary to anyone approaching from the east and the north. The national highway ran south of Texcoco, and anyone proceeding toward the town by that route would have to go straight into El Peñon, a hill complex on which Santa Anna placed many of his guns and soldiers. Scott had no intention of pursuing this approach. Veering to the south, the only other practicable route, presented problems of its own. For one thing, the road ran between two lakes (Xochimilco and Chalco) and wound to the west until the tiny town of San Agustín. At San Agustín, the road turned north over a river crossing at Churubusco and then on to the city. West of this portion of the road lay the Pedregal, a lava bed, "which looked as if a raging sea of molten rock had instantly congealed, had then been filled by the storms of centuries with fissures, caves, jagged points and lurking pitfalls, and finally had been decorated with occasional stunted trees and clumps of bushes."

Superstitious locals believed that demons inhabited this place. Mexican generals thought it impassable. Lee and his retinue proved both of them wrong. The inventive engineering captain found a mule trail running west to east across the Pedregal until it ended at a small crossroads called Padierna. Lee felt that his engineers could improve the road enough to accommodate a portion of the Army. Scott now developed another ingenious plan. He ordered Worth's division to keep the Mexicans busy in front of El Peñon, where they expected the Americans. At the same time, Twiggs's 2nd Division and Patterson's 3rd would swing southwest on Lee's road and across the Pedregal if need be. From here they would capture Padierna and move north in the direction of the city.

On August 19 Scott set his plan in motion. Worth's regulars moved north in the direction of San Agustin and another town called San Antonio. While the Mexicans fixated on his soldiers, the main force moved west along Lee's makeshift road. Twiggs's division took the lead.

Colonel Bennet Riley led the division's point brigade, composed of the 2nd Infantry Regiment, the 7th Infantry Regiment, and the 4th Artillery Regiment, into the Pedregal. All day long they picked, hacked, cut, and stumbled their way through the lava field. Mexican artillery and cavalry periodically harassed them. Other than that, the enemy remained quiet.

Late in the afternoon, clouds obscured the sun and portended the creeping darkness that would shield the Americans. Sometime after dark, the 7th Infantry emerged from the lava field, negotiated its way across a wet ravine, skirmishing here and there with stray groups of Mexican soldiers, and occupied an Indian village directly along a north–south road that led to Mexico City. They had strong enemy forces to the south of them at Padierna and to the north of them at San Angel. Then the rain started. With each passing minute it fell harder and harder, soaking the soldiers, dripping down their backs and into their flintlocks. They huddled in makeshift circles, lay down in the mud, and waited for orders.

The soldiers spent a wet, miserable night—few slept—and received orders to attack south after daylight. Just after 3:00 A.M. they moved out, in the lead of a two-brigade effort designed to attack the flank of the Mexican force near Padierna. Onward they stumbled in the darkness, muttering and slipping. The night was so dark that the soldiers found it difficult to keep track of one another. Slowly but surely they inched down the road for several hundred yards and then veered to their right (west) and swung around the Mexican defenders, who occupied high ground near Padierna. Finally, at just after 6:00 A.M. they were in position. The order came to move out.

The enemy had no clue they were about to be attacked. The Americans emerged from a slight ravine that had afforded them cover during their approach. The battle did not last long, as one soldier recounted. "The enemy did not perceive us until we had pushed on to the most serious obstacle in our progress . . . a deep barranca containing about two feet of water. As we got over that we saw a devil of a hubbub in their camp, the men running to arms, the mounting of horses. Just before getting to the top of the hill, down the other side of which was the enemy's camp, we halted for a minute for the men to close up. Here we received a volley from the enemy's Infantry thrown hastily out to oppose us. We did not return a shot but stood up as if they were throwing apples instead of lead at us. We marched toward them under heavy fire of musketry, for some twenty or thirty yards, then halted, and deployed column. When we had deployed into line of battle, we gave them a volley, and then made a head long rush, the enemy could not stand this more than twenty minutes. They then broke. We pursued with relentless ferocity."

As at Cerro Gordo, the Cottonbalers plunged into their hapless enemy, scattering them like seagulls on a beach. The fighting was brief. The Mexicans quickly ran away in a northerly direction up the road or surrendered. The 7th Infantry concentrated on the latter, taking prisoners at will, whooping and hollering in victory. Once again the Americans had inflicted a humiliating defeat on their opponents. The Americans called this battle Contreras and the Mexicans Padierna. The Yanks lost about eighty-three men while the enemy lost almost seven hundred killed, eight hundred captured, and two irreplaceable cannons. In an added bonus for the Americans, the enemy soldiers who managed to escape up the road imported their panic to their countrymen manning strong defenses at San Angel. Santa Anna, seeing the west wing of his army in the process of disintegration, ordered a tactical retreat to the north.[51]

Exhilarating as Contreras was, it did exact a price from the 7th Infantry. Captain Richard H. Ross, who had been cited for gallantry at Monterrey and would be again as a result of this battle, got wounded and would see no more combat in this war. Worse, Captain Charles Hanson, commander of the Fort Brown reconnaissance patrol and one of Dana's good friends—Hanson wrote to Sue after Dana's wounding— was killed at Contreras. By all accounts, Hanson was a fine officer. One of his colleagues wrote later that Hanson's death "was lamented by all who knew him; the regimental, brigade and division commanders referred to him in their reports in the most befitting and complimentary terms, and of him the general-in-chief says, 'He was not more distinguished for gallantry than for modesty, morals, and piety.' "[52]

Even as American soldiers won decisively at Contreras, another battle was shaping up at Churubusco, where Worth's division and the rest of Twiggs's division pushed north. Churubusco, located a few miles south of Mexico City, was a collection of houses and a bridge across a river by that same name. Worth's division advanced due north along the road and straight at Churubusco, while the leading troops of Twiggs's division came from the west after the fight at Contreras. The Cottonbalers played a support role in this battle. After the excitement of

Contreras, they steadily moved up the road past the Indian village and took a quick right, just shy of San Angel. This route took them through the northern edge of the Pedregal. They gingerly worked their way through a maze of boulders and brambles and, as they did so, they could hear the sounds of gunfire in the distance. Soon they exited the Pedregal and moved back on a road heading northeast toward the sound of the shooting.

Word filtered down that the regiment should turn left off the road, into a cornfield. Some of the men got separated from one another amid the tall stalks, some of which stood six feet high. For a few minutes each man concentrated on the three feet in front of him, hacking and pushing his way through the gangly stalks. Within a few minutes most of the soldiers emerged from the field and formed into companies, but the sight that greeted them did not bode well. Dead ahead stood a formidable stone-walled building surrounded by flooded ditches—somebody said it was a convent—that would obviously have to be captured before anyone could entertain notions of reaching the river. The convent sat astride an access road that led a couple hundred yards toward the river and the Churubusco bridgehead. Immediately to the east, within and among the buildings of this tiny village, Worth's people were fighting for their lives.

Here at the convent, the Cottonbalers watched and provided fire support as the 2nd Infantry, just in front of them, attacked the western side of the building. A hail of fire erupted from behind the walls of the convent and immediately a dozen 2nd Infantry soldiers went down, including one of their officers. The Americans tried to fire back, but smoke began to obscure the building. They had no choice but to take cover in dips and swales and, in the case of a few, behind the bodies of their dead comrades and return fire as best they could. Of course, loading and firing a smoothbore musket from a prone position was, at best, a difficult undertaking, so, for a time, the volume of firepower from the American positions tapered off significantly, until the men began spotting their targets through the smoke and sniping at the Mexicans.

A couple of times the enemy attempted attacks only to be repulsed by American musket fire. Gradually, enemy resistance slackened as American troops made bloody progress to the east in Churubusco and captured the bridge. The Americans gathered the 2nd and 3rd Infantry Regiments for an assault on the convent. The 1st Artillery and the 7th Infantry would provide fire support. Over the course of a couple of hours, the Mexicans within the convent had been exhausted by pressure from east and west. They fought valiantly but could not stop the American attack. By late afternoon, the 2nd and 3rd Infantry had overrun the convent and planted their colors along its ramparts. The Battle of Churubusco ended as the sun set on that August 20. The Mexicans retreated a few miles north, to the gates of the city, and the Americans wearily crossed the Churubusco River. The ferocity and tenacity of Mexican resistance stunned the Americans, who incurred close to a thousand casualties in the battle. The Mexicans probably lost six times that number, and the Americans captured several guns along with much-needed ammunition, but that wasn't the point.

Scott's tiny army could ill afford massive casualties. His command was in a similar position to that of the Spanish explorer Hernando Cortés, whose tiny group of conquistadors had trod over this same path in the face of overwhelmingly superior numbers centuries before. Scott knew that extensive casualties would cripple his army and rob it of its aura of invincibility. Like a snake charmer, he had to rely on the hypnotic effect his victories over numerically superior Mexican armies produced in the local population. Costly battles like Churubusco threatened to pierce the hypnosis. He could not afford to give Santa Anna an opportunity to rally the Mexican government and the enormous population of Mexico City in opposition to the American invaders. What's more, he wanted to finish this campaign as soon as possible.

This consideration probably influenced his decision to agree to an armistice with the Mexicans. Scott viewed this armistice as simply the first step in a general cessation of hostilities and the surrender of the city. Instead, it turned out to be nothing of the kind. Santa Anna and the Mexican negotiators merely paid lip service to capitulation while they rebuilt their forces south of the city. At heart, they believed they could still win by turning Scott back at the gates of Mexico City. Plus, they needed the rest provided by the armistice more than did Scott's battered, but victorious, army.

The tainted armistice lasted for two weeks, until Scott deduced the enemy's true intentions and decided he had to storm his way into the city. All this time, the 7th Regiment tried to find adequate shelter and food. By now replacements and veterans had mixed together to form a cohesive unit, albeit one that would not be put to extensive use in the fighting ahead. On September 8 Scott renewed his offensive. This time

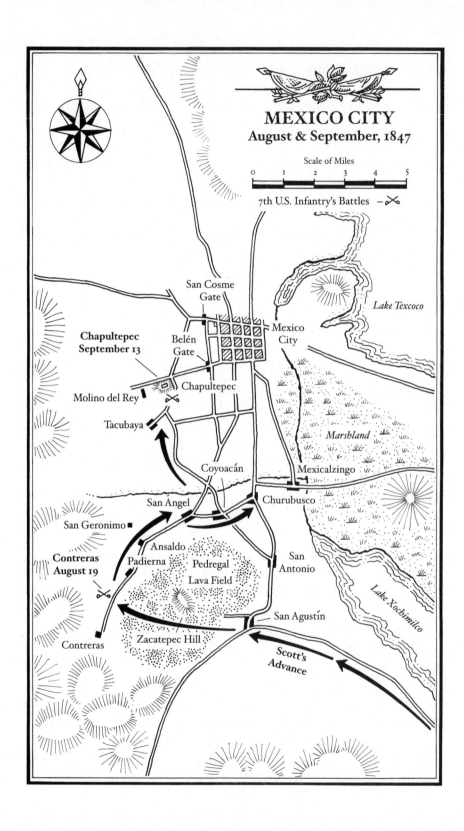

MEXICO CITY
August & September, 1847

Scale of Miles

0 1 2 3 4 5

7th U.S. Infantry's Battles —✂

San Cosme
Gate

Lake Texcoco

**Chapultepec
September 13**

Belén
Gate

Mexico
City

Chapultepec

Molino del Rey

Tacubaya

Marshland

Coyoacán

Mexicalzingo

San Ángel

Churubusco

San Geronimo

Ansaldo

**Contreras
August 19**

Padierna

Pedregal
Lava Field

San
Antonio

Lake Xochimilco

San Agustín

Contreras

Zacatepec Hill

*Scott's
Advance*

he sent Worth's division to capture Molino del Rey, a complex of buildings, including an armory and a flour mill, that led directly to Chapultepec, a castle that proved to be the gateway of the southwestern approach to the city, directly along the route Scott hoped to exploit.

Worth's men ran into a buzz saw at Molino del Rey (King's Mill). The Americans walked through cornfields, groves, and open, marshy ground straight into the guns of Mexicans holed up in the buildings. Predictably, Mexican fire took a terrific toll on Worth's men. All day long they struggled and fought their way into the complex of buildings, finally prevailing as evening approached. Sometime in the late afternoon, the Cottonbalers were called in to help out Worth's division, but by then the battle was well in hand, so the unit did not see any extensive fighting at Molino del Rey. Like Churubusco, Molino del Rey proved to be a bloody victory for the Americans, costing them 124 dead and 582 wounded. Everyone in the Army knew that the generals had made a mistake in attacking Molino del Rey. Worth and Scott, who had no love for each other, pointed fingers of blame at each other. A melancholy mood settled over the Army as soldiers mourned their dead comrades. The men of the 7th sympathized with their countrymen who bore the brunt of Molino del Rey but, more than anything, were pleased they had not been tapped for such an ill-fated attack.

Fiasco or not, the attack at Molino del Rey forced the Mexicans to retreat again. Most of their survivors hightailed it for the gates of the city. Now the castle of Chapultepec presented the greatest, and final, obstacle for the Americans. For several days Scott's principal engineers and subordinate commanders scouted avenues of approach to Mexico City, and inevitably each axis of advance depended on capturing Chapultepec. Located at the confluence of several roads, most of which led another three-quarters of a mile to the city's southwestern gates, Chapultepec towered on high ground (about 150 feet), dwarfing and dominating the surrounding plains. The Mexicans had surrounded the castle, home to the nation's military academy, with a dizzying array of infantry entrenchments, guns, and buried mines. Inside, they had reinforced the great fort's walls with sandbags and planks in an effort to withstand American heavy artillery. The defenders themselves were a stalwart group, a combination of Mexican Army regulars and military academy cadets whose patriotism and thirst for military glory knew little bounds.

Scott's soldiers had warily eyed Chapultepec ever since they got within sight of it in late August, knowing deep in their hearts that the day would probably come when this place would have to be taken by assault. Scott reluctantly came to the same conclusion on the night of September 12. That day his artillery worked over Chapultepec and inflicted significant damage, but nowhere near enough to entice the Mexicans within to capitulate. The aging American general sighed heavily and ordered an assault for the next morning, knowing full well that if this attack failed he might yet lose the war.

Thus, as the sun rose on September 13, 1847, the immediate fate of Scott's army rested on the shoulders of the infantrymen who would carry out the assault. In other words, the campaign and perhaps the outcome of the war depended on the infantry, specifically the assaulting parties who would breach the walls with ladders, overwhelm the enemy, and capture the fort. For this daunting mission, Scott's subordinate commanders chose a mixture of volunteers from state regiments and hard-core, experienced regular outfits. These two groups were organized into two distinct assault forces, one volunteer and one regular.

The latter group included about fifty Cottonbalers. These men, whose ranks included Captain Gabriel Paul and Lieutenant Levi Gantt—both fine officers—volunteered their services on the night of the twelfth in response to a call for volunteers. In an effort to entice the men, the generals offered brevets for the officers, commissions to the sergeants, promotions for corporals, and financial incentives for privates. On this mission, the soldiers would serve under Captain Silas Casey of the 2nd Infantry, who commanded the Regular Army portion of the Chapultepec assault force. The rest of the 7th Regiment, along with the other soldiers of Riley's brigade, was ordered to make noise and demonstrate in front of the city's southern gates, the object being to divert Mexican attention from the attack on Chapultepec.

After dawn on the thirteenth, American artillery hurled shot after shot at Chapultepec and the defenses around it. The shells plowed up ground, smashed through parapets, and even breached the walls of the fort here and there. At 8:00 A.M. Scott decided that the artillery had softened up the fort sufficiently for the two assault groups to move in. The state volunteers approached from the western, back end of the fort, while Casey's group went in from the front (southeast). At the order to move out, Casey's men stood up and peered intently at their commander. Casey glanced at them and uttered a word familiar to generations of infantrymen: "Forward." A junior officer who watched them move out described what happened next. "They moved down the road towards Chapultepec at a 'double quick' . . . and for 600 yards were exposed to a raking fire from the Castle, but were partially concealed from view, and protected from the fire of the batteries near the road by several adobe houses on the left of it, and by rows of maguey growing along the edge of the ditch. Beyond the houses showers of grape came from the guns of the batteries on the left of the road, passing among and over the men, causing a few casualties, and the hostile musketry opened, knocking over a few men. Two hundred yards beyond the adobe houses the road made a slight bend to the left; 200 yards beyond this were the two Mexican batteries; and in advance of the bend a short distance was a ditch, eight or ten feet deep and nine or twelve feet wide. Here the stormers were brought to a halt, as the ditch could not be passed. Between the road and the wall surrounding Chapultepec the ground was intersected by ditches covered with water, and on the right of the road there was a ditch, but beyond it the surface was dry, though it might have been unsafe for the stormers, weak in numbers, to have made a sweep around in that direction."

Casey was pinned down and did not know what to do. The wet, muddy, slimy ditch in which he and his men took shelter provided little cover against Mexican artillery and musket fire. The men listened to the enemy lead, gritted their collective teeth, and hoped nothing would hit them. General John Quitman, a volunteer officer whom Scott had anointed as overall commander of the southeast assault group, soon arrived on the scene and gave orders to "turn off to the left at right angles to the road and move against the Castle through an opening visible in the surrounding wall." As the soldiers carried out this order, Casey got hit. In no condition to lead the men any farther, he turned around and headed for the rear, ceding tactical command to Captain Paul of the 7th. At almost the same time Casey got wounded, the Mexicans scored a hit on another officer, Gantt. A Mexican sniper shot Gantt as he listened to an order from Casey, killing Gantt instantly. His lifeless body collapsed and crumpled by the side of the road.

The Americans now succeeded in placing two artillery pieces on the road in a perfect position to support the assault. These guns, under the command of Lieutenant Henry Jackson Hunt, provided terrific fire support. They broke and scattered many of the Mexican soldiers guarding the approaches to the fort and cleared the way for the infantry. Now, as one soldier recalled, the battle reached a climax. "We dashed forward along the road and drove the Mexicans before us with great slaughter. The other storming party [the state volunteers] had in the meanwhile gained the height from the opposite side and when we entered the enemy's advanced works, the Stars and Stripes were flying from the highest point of the Castle. The havoc among the Mexicans was now horrible in the extreme. Pent up between two fires they had but one way to escape and all crowded toward it like a flock of sheep. I saw dozens hanging from the walls and creeping through holes made for the passage of water & whilst in this position were shot down without making the least resistance. Our men were shouting give no quarters 'to the treacherous scoundrels' and as far as I could observe none was asked by the Mexicans."[53]

The members of the storming party rushed around shooting as many enemy soldiers as they could. Soon more artillery fired at the retreating enemy and added to their casualties. Then the rest of Worth's division advanced into the grounds of Chapultepec, adding to the catastrophe for the enemy. The Mexicans tried a few halfhearted counterattacks, but the battle was over. They ran as fast as they could for the city, closely pursued by Worth's men, who entered the city soon after.

Another day's fighting lay ahead in Mexico City, but not for the Cottonbalers. Their war was over. Gantt proved to be the final fatality and he was sorely missed.[54] Indeed, the drummer boy Pruyn never forgot the sight of "the dead face of the young lieutenant of our regiment who had always looked after me, as he lay by the roadside, after Chapultepec, and we marched into the City of Mexico."[55] The regiment participated in the occupation of Mexico City while the politicians hammered out peace terms that would finally be concluded in February 1848 with the Treaty of Guadalupe Hidalgo. The treaty ceded enormous portions of territory to the victorious United States, including present-day California, Arizona, New Mexico, Texas, and portions of several other states, such as Colorado and Utah.

By any measure no unit contributed more toward this victory than the 7th Infantry Regiment. The outfit fought from the beginning of the war until its end and played a major role in the war's greatest victories—Fort Brown, Matamoros, Monterrey, Cerro Gordo, Contreras, and Chapultepec. Disciplined and well-led, the Cottonbalers proved to be exceptional assault troops in a war that hinged on effective and well-timed attacks. Rarely in the annals of warfare can one find so many examples of successful attacks carried out by numerically inferior assault forces. Nearly every time the Cottonbalers moved forward in this war, across the deadly space of ground combat, they were outnumbered, yet they always prevailed. Why? Better weapons, better commanders, better equipment, and better fighting spirit. American victory in the Mexican War stood for the triumph of quality over quantity. The achievements of the Cottonbalers merely exemplified this larger trend.

In June 1848, a few months after ratification of the Treaty of Guadalupe Hidalgo, the regiment received orders to go home. After two and a half years away from home, the weary veterans were only too happy to oblige. They headed back to the United States, eventually bound for their old stomping grounds in and around Fort Gibson, Oklahoma. Most of the soldiers wanted to leave foreign places, faces, and names far behind them and return to the comfortable routine of frontier garrison duty. For over a decade they and their successors, as they wished, saw no more foreign places. Instead, when they were called into battle once again in 1861, the enemy who faced them was all too familiar. The Cottonbalers would find themselves leveling their weapons not at foreigners in a strange land but at fellow Americans on American soil.

4

Reclaimed Honor

The Civil War

AFTER THE MEXICAN WAR THE 7TH REGIMENT SETTLED back into its old routine of frontier duty. The unit served a stint in Florida between 1848 and 1850 when Seminole troubles ignited again. After that the Cottonbalers returned to the Fort Gibson area, split up into companies, scattered around like seeds in the wind, and built roads and small forts. In 1858–59 the U.S. government ordered the regiment to join much of the rest of the Regular Army in an expedition to Mormon territory in Utah. Relations between the government and the Mormons, never good, had steadily worsened, mainly because of philosophical differences over such issues as polygamy. President James Buchanan sent troops in response to real and imagined Mormon violence against non-Mormon settlers who hoped to live in Utah.

All of these pre–Civil War pursuits had one thing in common for the Cottonbalers—they resulted in practically no combat of any kind. The regiment saw no significant action against the Seminoles or any other Native American peoples in the 1850s, nor did the soldiers have to do any fighting against the Mormons. The Mormon Expedition was almost entirely bloodless for the Army. The 7th Regiment lost a few soldiers to disease and crime and even one from suicide, but no blue-clad soldiers lost their lives from Mormon bullets.[1]

No longer needed in quiet Utah, the Cottonbalers in May 1860 packed up their baggage and headed east, bound for New Mexico, a territory won a dozen years earlier from Mexico as a result of the Treaty of Guadalupe Hidalgo. The 7th Regiment's mission in New Mexico consisted of guarding settlers and miners from local Indian tribes, primarily Navajos and various subtribes of Apaches. By late August most of the troops had reached New Mexico, after an exhausting march of more than a thousand miles. The ten companies of the 7th split up and manned a slew of rudimentary forts up and down the Rio Grande, which runs north–south through New Mexico. For instance, Companies F, D, and K went to Fort Craig, located about halfway between Albuquerque and Las Cruces. A and E Companies went to Albuquerque. The soldiers spent their days patrolling and escorting wagon trains to and from various locales. Usually this was boring, monotonous work, carried out along dusty trails, over steep mountain passes, and in broiling heat.

Every now and then the troops got into a skirmish with small groups of Indians. On September 24, 1860, a private named Strothman got wounded in a brief fight with Navajo Indians while escorting a wagon train of supplies. A few months later, Indians attacked a group of Cottonbalers while they stopped to drink water from a spring and wounded Sergeant Daniel Robinson.

The most serious altercation occurred with Apaches, not Navajos. In October 1860, Indian raiders attacked a local ranch, stole some oxen, and kidnapped the rancher's six-year-old stepson. The rancher went to Fort Buchanan, north of Las Cruces, and appealed to Lieutenant Colonel Pitcairn Morrison for help. Morrison, the commander of the fort, counted two companies of the 7th among his forces. The rancher mistakenly thought the Indian assailants hailed from a group of Apaches (known as Chiricahuas) who owed allegiance to the famous chief Cochise. Morrison foolishly accepted this story at face value and, in January 1861, ordered a raw young lieutenant named George Bascom to mount a company on mules, ride to the Apache camp, and demand the return of the boy and the property.

On February 4, Bascom and his people reached Apache Pass, home to the Chiricahuas. There they confronted Cochise, accused him of kidnapping, and demanded he produce the boy and the rancher's property. Cochise had no idea what Bascom was talking about. Thinking Cochise was lying, the impatient and inexperienced Bascom ordered his soldiers to take several of Cochise's Indians hostage. The two sides started shooting at each other and everyone took cover. Bascom made off with five hostages. Cochise escaped and, in retaliation, took hostages of his own among white travelers. This debacle of mistaken identity quickly spiraled out of control when Bascom hanged several of Cochise's relatives even as the chief executed his white prisoners. Nothing positive came out of this incident, which became known as the Bascom affair. In fact, it led to twenty-five years of poisonous relations between the government and the Chiricahua Apaches.[2]

Perhaps as a result of the Bascom affair, Indians stepped up their raiding efforts against government property and ranchers in the spring of 1861, resulting in the deaths of three Cottonbalers: Private Robert Crawford, of A Company on May 22, 1861, Private Thomas Drieskell of C Company on June 22, 1861, and another C Company man, Private George Talbott, on May 16, 1861. The latter two men served under Bascom. According to a letter written by Bascom, Talbott met his death while "in pursuit of property stolen by [Indians] from the Government herd [of sheep and cattle]." Apparently Talbott was no rookie, having seen combat in Mexico. "Pvt. Talbott was an old soldier and by his distinguished services in the War with Mexico obtained a certificate of merit from President [Millard] Fillmore."[3]

Stuck in an inhospitable, alien land with complicated internal issues most of them knew nothing about, the Cottonbalers were ill prepared for this kind of glorified police work. As tensions with Native Americans increased, some of the soldiers grew jumpy and nervous while out on patrols. This led to mishaps like the accidental shooting of Private Henry Buckley of Bascom's C Company. On the night of May 4, 1861, while on convoy and patrol duty, Buckley stood watch near a supply wagon. At about nine o'clock that night someone shot him in the ass.

Buckley claimed that, just before he was shot, he heard the cry of Indians: "I rose up and while in a stooping position received the charge of a gun in my back—. The man who was on post and myself had always been the best of friends ever since we left Governor's Island, N.Y." That man was Private John Carrigue. He also claimed to have heard Indians. He even said that he saw a mysterious Indian fire a weapon. "I . . . saw an Indian squatted between two mules. I stepped back and gave the alarm. As soon as I hollered, he [the Indian] jumped out from the mules and I fired at him. I saw the flash of his rifle but cannot say that I heard the report. My gun was loaded with buck ball." The "Indian" Carrigue saw squatting between two mules was probably Buckley. Nearby, Private Charles Smith heard someone yelling about Indians but didn't see any of them. Suspicious, the next day he investigated the scene of the mishap. "We looked over the spot for tracks of Indians. The ground was soft and had Indians been there, they would have left tracks, but there were none." For good reason, because no Indians were anywhere near C Company's position that night.

Instead, Carrigue accidentally shot his buddy Buckley. Scared and worried about the ubiquitous Native Americans who had been harassing their unit, the two men conjured up images of enemies in the darkness. Instead of investigating what they believed they saw, they screamed a warning to the rest of the camp about Indians. Worse, Carrigue carelessly discharged his weapon with Buckley in front of him, thus hitting him in the posterior. The doctor who worked on Buckley testified that the gunshot wound was "evidently inflicted from a short distance, and with an arm heavily charged. The whole charge passed through with the exception of one buck shot which I found and removed." The closeness of the shooting, the direction of the shooting and the evidence of buckshot provided incontrovertible proof as to what really happened. The board of officers that investigated the shooting concluded that "Pvt Henry Buckley . . . was accidentally shot by Pvt John Carrigue. In the opinion of the Board . . . Pvt Carrigue . . . fired at what he thought was an Indian. The Board attach no blame to . . . Pvt Carrigue."[4] The board made the wise and proper decision. The phantom Indian notwithstanding, they understood the jumpiness that existed among their soldiers and knew that friendly fire incidents like this one happen, in spite of the best efforts of officers, even marginal ones like Bascom.

IN THE FRANKEST TERMS, THE SOLDIERS WHO POPULATED the regiment at this time were hardly perfect. They had lived on the frontiers, at the margins of American life, for too long. They existed almost completely outside the mainstream of American society. They lived their lives at rudimentary dusty, filthy camps and forts, transient, rootless, forgotten. They carried out a lousy, tough job no one else wanted to do. They came from backgrounds that most "respectable" Americans thought of as beneath contempt or even recognition. Some of them could not read or write. Most of them had little education and almost no property to speak of. Plain and simple, they were outsiders, anonymous drifters who lived a regimented, colorless existence and sometimes put their lives on the line for a society that mostly ignored them.

They also dealt with the typical nineteenth-century American view of soldiers. Many Americans on the eve of the Civil War still viewed professional soldiers with suspicion and contempt. They thought of soldiers as people who did not want to work at an honest job, people who simply copped out of real life so that they could live off the government. In addition, the typical native-born American had little in common with the regular soldier who wore the country's uniform. By 1860, the foreign born absolutely dominated the ranks of the Regular Army. A total of 2,342 men joined the 7th Infantry between 1849 and 1860. Less than one-quarter of these men were born in the United States. The vast majority of the enlistees were Irish or German immigrants, most of whom came from impoverished backgrounds in their own countries. Safe to say, they did not trod on many welcome mats in America. Irish immigrants in particular found themselves shunned, scorned, and excluded from an increasingly tight job market in the late 1850s. Many of them joined the Army out of sheer desperation.[5]

As soldiers, these immigrants were a mixed bag. Some found a home in the Army and thrived in the Army's structured world of discipline. Others behaved like unruly schoolchildren and found themselves constantly in trouble. Both types were ill prepared for the ordeal that awaited them.

In the summer of 1861, the regiment's officers began to worry less and less about Native Americans and more and more about Southern Americans. The officers knew about Fort Sumter but did not really know what might happen next or what exactly Washington expected them to do. Adding to this confusion, several of the regiment's Southern-born officers resigned their commissions and left Federal service to join the Confederate Army. These men could not just declare their sympathy with the South and leave in peace. Anyone doing so would be seized and incarcerated as a prisoner of war. As a result, those men with Confederate sympathies had to play a waiting game, lying low, doing their duty, until they saw a chance to safely bolt. Naturally, this created a climate of suspicion and intrigue among the leadership of the regiment as men questioned one another's loyalty to the United States and wondered if their previously trusted friends were Rebels in blue clothing.

Robert Rice Garland, a young captain and company commander, was one such Rebel in blue clothing. When his native Virginia seceded in April 1861 Garland decided he would join the Confederacy, but he knew he had to bide his time. He continued to serve in the regiment throughout the summer of 1861, affecting the pose of a loyal officer. In August, he saw a chance to get away and took off for nearby Texas, all the while "pursued by mounted men four days & nights without getting out of the saddle." He made it to Texas and joined the Confederate Army, eventually rising to the rank of colonel. He commanded the 6th Texas Infantry and spent his war fighting Yankees in the west, though he hankered to get back to his native Virginia and join General Robert E. Lee's Army of Northern Virginia.[6]

Although most of the 7th Regiment's officers did not choose the path of rebellion, there is little doubt that the atmosphere of suspicion and doubt that pervaded the leadership of the unit in the summer of 1861 could not help but erode its effectiveness, even though very few enlisted soldiers went over to the Confederacy. Foreign-born and hailing mostly from the Northeast, the outfit's rank and file had no ties with the South and very little, if any, sympathy for its cause. The native-born men in the unit came mostly from the Northern states and, like their immigrant comrades, thought of Confederates as traitors.[7]

THE MAN WITH THE TASK OF HOLDING THE 7TH REGIMENT together in the face of this impending war between North and South was Isaac Lynde, an aged West Pointer and infantry officer from Vermont. Lynde graduated in 1827 near the bottom of his class. He spent the next thirty-four years serving in a succession of undistinguished, anonymous posts in the stultifying, dead-end atmosphere of the antebellum army. In 1861 he was a fifty-six-year-old major. By all rights he should have been enjoying a quiet retirement by then, but in the Army of that time officers routinely served their entire adult lives and received only standard promotions. The result of this policy was a strangely mixed officer corps of fuzzy-cheeked lieutenants fresh out of West Point and grizzle-bearded, silver-haired old dinosaurs still performing the duties of field-grade officers.

For the men of the 7th Regiment, the policy meant that their immediate fate would be in the hands of Lynde, an officer way out of his depth. In mid-June Colonel Edward Canby, the commander of the Department of New Mexico, ordered Lynde to assume command of Fort Fillmore, located on the east side of the Rio Grande, four miles from Mesilla near present-day Las Cruces. Seven companies of the 7th Infantry, along with three companies of mounted rifles, were concentrated at Fillmore, a rudimentary and indefensible place without proper earthworks, artillery, or sustenance. Fillmore's significance lay in its geographic location forty miles up the Rio Grande from El Paso, Texas. The fort would be the first target for any prospective enemy force in the area, and it would also serve as the natural destination for U.S. forces moving east out of Arizona Territory. Canby warned Lynde of a possible Confederate invasion from Texas and ordered him to prepare defenses and recruit volunteers from the indigenous population.

Lynde arrived at Fort Fillmore in the first week of July and found himself confronted with a difficult situation. The men had almost no horses because local secessionists had stolen them. Mesilla seethed with secessionist sentiment. Apache raiders plagued the fort, plundering its food, hay, and livestock. The troops had not been paid in quite some time and were none too happy about it, and, of course, their officers, as previously mentioned, buzzed with intrigue. To make matters worse, Lynde had to figure out what to do with the families of the fort's garrison, since some of the soldiers had wives and children with them and these dependents could not be properly cared for or fed.

All of this would have taxed the energies of a good and resourceful officer, much less the gray-haired, gray-bearded, quiet, and kind-hearted Lynde. The major felt that the fort, located in a valley and surrounded by high ground, was poorly situated for defense—he was right—but he took few steps to improve the fighting readiness of his command. In the words of the fort's surgeon, Lynde made "no effort to put the command in fighting trim . . . no measures taken . . . against surprise."

Trouble soon resulted. As Canby had feared, the Confederates invaded New Mexico and headed straight for Fort Fillmore. Incredibly, Lynde made no effort to scout the surrounding terrain in anticipation of such an invasion; nor did he post guards outside the fort. This negligence should very well have cost the fort's garrison dearly, but Lynde got lucky. On the night of July 24, a force of 258 Confederate soldiers, Texans under the command of Lieutenant Colonel John Baylor, camped undetected six hundred yards from the fort, with the intention of attacking in the morning.

Sometime during the night, one of the Texan soldiers—a former regular—began to contemplate his loyalty to the new Confederacy. The man decided that he could not turn his back on the United States, so he slipped out of camp and headed for the fort. Once at the fort, he told Lynde all about Baylor's attack plan. Lynde listened attentively and then contented himself with placing the fort's garrison on full alert, specifically by ordering the garrison's drummers to loudly sound the alert call. Naturally, the Confederates heard the sound of these drums. Baylor wrote that "the long-roll was distinctly heard, which apprised us that our approach was known to the enemy." Baylor wisely called off the attack and ordered his men to occupy friendly Mesilla.[8]

Of all Lynde's command screwups, this one might have been the worst. Armed with crucial information about his enemy's intentions, strength, and plans, he held all the cards on the night of the twenty-fourth. Instead of playing the hand out and pursuing victory, he folded. He should have set an ambush for Baylor's troops. Had Lynde sprung such an ambush, the unsuspecting Rebels almost certainly would have been defeated by a fully alerted and prepared force of U.S. regulars. But he foolishly sounded the alert drums, producing so much noise that it could not fail to tip off the Confederates that their attack had been compromised.

After a quiet night, Lynde finally grew a bit more aggressive. He decided to pursue Baylor's force into Mesilla on the twenty-fifth and capture the town. Leaving behind one infantry company and the band to guard Fort Fillmore, Lynde set off with the rest of the fort's garrison late in the afternoon. In all, he had six companies—one acting as artillery—along with dragoons, numbering, in total, 380 soldiers. When they got within sight of Mesilla, Lynde sent his adjutant, Lieutenant Edward J. Brooks, into the town under a flag of truce to speak to the Texans and demand that they surrender Mesilla. The Confederate officers—no doubt snickering to themselves at Lynde's presumptuousness—replied laconically: "If you want the town, come and take it." Upon receiving this negative reply, Lynde ordered an attack: "I moved the [artillery] battery forward and fired two shells at long range, but they burst in the air short of the object. The command continued to advance slowly towards the outskirts of the town, while the battery, which had to be moved by hand, was working through the heavy sand. From a corn field and a house on the right we received a heavy fire of musketry, wounding 2 officers and 4 men and killing 3 men. As night was coming on, and the fields and houses on both sides of the road were filled with men, and the howitzers useless, owing to the difficulty of moving through the sand, I decided to withdraw my force and return to my post."[9]

The soldiers charged four separate times, but to no avail. The pro-Confederate *Mesilla Times* claimed that Lynde maliciously fired artillery shells into the town heedless of the presence of women and children: "They . . . commenced firing bombs and grape into a town crowded with women and children, without having in accordance with an invariable rule of civilized warfare given notice to remove the women and children to a place of safety." Fort Fillmore's surgeon, J. Cooper McKee, leveled the same accusation. "Lieut. [Francis] Crilly was ordered to fire shells into the town full of women and children; indeed, I heard Lynde order Crilly to fire a shell at a group of women, children, and unarmed men . . . and a shell was so fired; luckily it fell short, and no harm was done." McKee felt nothing but contempt for Lynde and his charge is certainly serious, but one must still wonder why the noncombatants had not left Mesilla. All day long they knew a Yankee force was heading in their direction, and they must certainly have realized the town would come under fire, especially after the Confederate refusal to surrender. Luckily, no one got hurt.[10]

After calling off his amateurish and poorly planned attack, Lynde set about the task of returning to the fort. Most of his casualties occurred among the dragoons and mounted riflemen who had advanced to within seventy yards of the Confederates. As these unfortunate men gathered their wounded and dead and retreated, the main force fired at them, but no one was hit. Dispirited, Lynde's command trudged wearily through sandy, uneven soil back to Fillmore.

That night the major heard that the Confederate force would soon be augmented by artillery. Believing that they could set up these guns on the high ground around the fort and bombard his troops at will, Lynde decided he could no longer hold Fillmore and ordered an immediate evacuation. He planned to march his men northeast to Fort Stanton by way of San Augustine Springs in the mountains, but not before destroying anything of value at Fort Fillmore, including "much valuable property and munitions of war," according to the *Mesilla Times;* "muskets, clothing, a blacksmith's shop, bakery and one of the Quartermaster's store rooms had been completely burned down. The Hospital stores, medicines and furniture were most completely broken up, and nearly all the arms and a great quantity of ammunition destroyed."

Confusion, defeat, and chaos reigned among the garrison. Orders passed by word of mouth rather than through the chain of command. A postwar newspaper account claimed that amid this state of veritable military anarchy, some of the soldiers found their way into the medicinal stores of liquor: "As the soldiers appraised the situation, abandonment of a military post under orders was one thing, but abandonment of high class liquor was a much more serious matter, one that required consideration and reflection. The soldiers met the situation sensibly, and in the beginning, with discretion. First one trooper, then another, and then many, took a moderate swig of the soon-to-be-abandoned liquor, then each helped himself to a drink that seemed more appropriate to the occasion. One sergeant of the 'old army' decided that a drop of brandy, or perhaps two or more, on the road to Fort Stanton might be eminently fitting under the circumstances. Pouring water out of his canteen, he replaced it with liquor. Others . . . substituted liquor for water in their canteens."[11] If this is true, then McKee failed to mention it in his report, as did the rabidly anti-Yankee *Mesilla Times,* which would normally have relished the chance to use such a story to embarrass the enemy. McKee's silence on this issue may not be terribly surprising considering the fact that he was responsible for the hospital's medicinal liquor. But the newspaper's silence is more difficult to explain, given its pro-Confederate agenda. The whole truth will probably never be known.

However, alcohol consumption almost certainly played some part in the debacle that soon befell the 7th Infantry. The troops left Fort Fillmore in the early-morning hours of July 27 and proceeded several miles without many problems. But when the sun rose and waves of heat began shimmering off the featureless desert terrain, the problems began. "The day became intensely hot," Lynde wrote, "and soon after the men . . . began to show signs of fatigue." To make matters worse, he did not know the route at all, and the distance to the nearest water proved to be greater than he thought. He watched in consternation as his foot soldiers began falling out and collapsing in exhausted heaps, overcome with heat prostration. Feeling that he must do something to alleviate the suffering of his soldiers, Lynde decided to forge ahead with his mounted troops to the nearest spring, retrieve water, and bring it back. Although commendable, this decision meant splitting his forces, in alien country, in the presence of an enemy whose whereabouts were unknown.

The Confederates made him pay for this strategic error. Unbeknownst to Lynde, the enemy knew all about his northerly movement. Colonel Baylor's men were busily trying to catch up with and intercept the crowded and confused Yankee column of soldiers, horses, baggage, artillery pieces, women, and children. Soon the Rebels began coming upon the pitiful, hopeless stragglers lying by the side of the dusty road. One Texan, Hank Smith, wrote after the war about the experience of capturing dehydrated and helpless Cottonbalers: "We began to overtake the infantry scattered along the road in little bunches of ten or twenty. On demand of their surrender they dropped their guns, but we made them march on until we had about one hundred of them. We would stack the guns and take all the ammunition from them. We found some of the [artillery] guns loaded with whiskey and a good portion of the soldiers drunk and begging for water."[12] The Confederates treated their prisoners well, giving them water and allowing them to rest. Smith's allegation of alcohol use is much more believable than the newspaper account because it comes from an eyewitness and also because it goes a long way toward explaining why many of the soldiers were so quickly overcome by the heat.

Even as a substantial portion of his command evaporated like water into desert sand, Lynde arrived at the water hole (at San Augustin Springs) in which he had invested such high hopes. "I found the supply of water so small as to be insufficient for my command. After procuring all the water that could be transported by the men with me I started back to the main body. After riding some distance I became so much exhausted that I could not sit upon my horse, and the command proceeded without me . . . and I returned to the Springs." Simply put, Lynde was too old to soldier in the blistering heat of a New Mexico summer. Like many of his men scattered far behind him along the line of march, he sat in dizzy confusion, drinking water and trying to stay cool.

This was the background for the most ignominious and disgraceful incident in the entire proud history of the 7th Infantry Regiment. As Lynde rested at San Augustin Springs, Captain Alfred Gibbs, a cavalry officer, caught up with him and told him about the Confederate force threatening the rear of his column. "Major Lynde asked what force I had, and I replied 70 men, all told. He said that there were two companies of infantry on rear guard . . . and that would be sufficient." But Gibbs, whose troops had gone without water while he strenuously tried to catch up with Lynde's column, had seen the poor state of the rear-guard infantry. They were "under the bushes by the side of the road; over 150 men were lying, unable to rise or to carry their muskets, and useless and disorganized in every way. This was the rear guard. Major Lynde had not seen it for several hours." Gibbs galloped to the rear and deployed his men along with whatever remnants of the infantry he could muster, in an effort to slow the Rebel advance. He also sent word to Lynde about the disintegration of his rear guard. Lynde sent a reply ordering Gibbs to protect the wagons, if possible, and then fall back to a camp he had begun to set up near the head of the column at San Augustín Springs.

The Confederates had reached the makeshift camp and were quickly preparing to attack it, even as Lynde hastily tried to mount some kind of defense. But there would be no fighting on this day. At some point during the time his remaining troops rushed into formation to defend against the Confederate attack, Lynde lost his nerve: "Under the circumstances I considered our case hopeless; that it was worse than useless to resist; that honor did not demand the sacrifice of blood after the terrible suffering that our troops had already undergone, and then that sacrifice would be totally useless." He sent word to Baylor that he wanted to talk and, after a short parley, agreed to the Confederate commander's terms. Lynde never consulted his officers before making this sweeping decision. Not surprisingly, they voiced intense opposition to the surrender, so much so that the Confederate commander asked Lynde, "Who's in charge here?" Lynde assured Baylor that he was in charge and that his decision would be carried out. The regimental officers, turning away in angry disgust, decided that they could still salvage some semblance of honor. They removed the regiment's colors from its staff, tore them up, and distributed the pieces among themselves, so that the colors would not fall into enemy hands.

The enlisted men were not especially pleased either. "To see old soldiers and strong men weep like children," McKee wrote, "men who had faced the battle's storm of the Mexican war, is a sight that I hope I may never again be present at. A braver and truer command could not be found than that which has in this case been made victim of cowardice and imbecility." McKee's last sentence can be classified as hyperbole, but the bitter disgust and shame he and others felt in the wake of the surrender was all too real. "I am unable to express to you the deep grief, mortification, and pain I, with the other officers, have endured from this cowardly surrender of a brave and true command to an inferior force of the enemy, without having one word to say or firing a single shot."

In his official report, Lynde attempted to justify the surrender: "Surrounded by open or secret enemies, no reliable information could be obtained, and disaffection prevailing even in my own command, to what extent it was impossible to ascertain . . . my position has been one of great difficulty, and has ended in the misfortune of surrendering my command to the enemy. The Texan troops acted with great kindness to our men, exerting themselves in carrying water to the famishing ones in the rear; yet it was two days before the infantry could move from the camp, and then only by the assistance of their captors."[13]

In the days ahead, the Confederates paroled their captives and sent them to Las Cruces. From there they would head north and sit out the war until they had been officially "exchanged" with Confederate prisoners heading south, a common practice during the early days of the Civil War.

In the months ahead, Lynde took flak from all quarters. Newspaper editorials assailed his surrender as shameful and disgraceful. The officers of the 7th Regiment successfully lobbied the War Department for a court-martial. Many misguidedly accused Lynde of being a traitor. He was not a traitor, just incompetent, cowardly, and ineffective. He had no business occupying such a position of responsibility, and, in the final analysis, his actions were inexcusable. At every turn during his time in charge of Fort Fillmore and its garrison, he showed himself to be incapable, indecisive, and, more than anything else, passive. By any measure he must be regarded as one of the worst officers in the history of the regiment.

In late 1861 the War Department stripped him of his rank and drummed him out of the Army. Five years later, in response to a petition from Lynde and some of his friends, the government restored him to the rank of major and allowed him to retire. He died in obscurity twenty years later.[14]

WHEN THE DUST SETTLED, OVER FOUR HUNDRED SOL-diers, most of them members of the 7th Infantry, were paroled. A tiny few defected to the Confederacy. Seven companies of the regiment, along with the band, would be out of action until they could be exchanged. Three other companies, C, H, and F, did not surrender. They had been at Fort Buchanan in Arizona Territory on their way into New Mexico when Lynde surrendered. In fact, they passed the parolees on the way to their common destination—Fort Craig.[15] These three unsullied companies would spend the entire war separate from their regimental brothers. They stayed in New Mexico and fought against Rebels and Indians.

Meanwhile, the other seven companies made their way north. They hiked three hundred miles through desolate country to Fort Union, in the northeast corner of New Mexico. Once there, they were put to work improving the fort's defenses. They hacked and dug and sweated in the heat, working four-hour shifts. On their down time, they sometimes got into trouble at the nearby village of Loma Parda. This tiny little burg featured a dance hall, a bar, and a scattered few tiny buildings that could accommodate one bed and one prostitute.

Some soldiers could not resist absconding from the mind-numbing work at the fort and losing themselves in the revelry of Loma Parda for a few days. Officers apprehended these men and court-martialed them. One such unfortunate, Private Michael Patton, wrote in his own defense: "I went to Loma Parda for my overcoat, which I had left there. A few of my friends asked if I would like to have something to drink. I said yes. I got into a house where I thought my overcoat was and got a drink. I didn't know anything for ten hours. When I woke up, my money was gone. Then I started home." No word on whether Patton ever found the overcoat for which he claimed to be searching. Private Patrick McKenney was convicted of being absent without leave for five days. He claimed he stayed away that long because he "had the D.T.s." McKenney, Patton, and several other miscreants were sentenced to three months' hard labor, each with an iron ball and chain attached to his left ankle.

In late September the seven paroled companies received orders to go to Jefferson Barracks in St. Louis. During this long march, the regiment experienced several more alcohol-related incidents, including one episode when a sergeant chugged down whiskey until he reached a fighting level of belligerence. He became upset with a mouthy private and decked him. Another night, a soldier got drunk on guard duty and fired his weapon at imaginary Confederate raiders. The regiment reported in at Jefferson Barracks on November 5, 1861, and the next few weeks saw several more alcohol-related court-martials. In January they moved on and manned defensive positions along the Great Lakes.

The New Mexico companies also wrestled with alcohol troubles. Sergeant Thomas Breen got drunk one night while in charge of a detail guarding an artillery battery. He was initially reduced to the ranks, but his sentence was later remitted because he had been a good soldier for most of his career. From time to time, various privates ran afoul of the military justice system by hitting the sauce on duty or wandering off in search of a good time. These men were convicted of various charges and sentenced to hard labor with a ball and chain, a new punishment to supplant the now outlawed corporal punishment that had been so prevalent in the antebellum Army.[16]

In spite of these occasional discipline problems, the New Mexico Cottonbalers were good soldiers, and they proved it in one of the far western theater's most significant battles at Valverde in February 1862. With the loss of Fort Fillmore and the subsequent abandonment of Fort Stanton, Union men found themselves in trouble in New Mexico. The Confederates marshaled their resources and moved north, sending the territory into a veritable panic. Colonel Canby husbanded what forces he could amass in this forgotten theater of war. His army consisted of 3,810 men, a foundation of regulars leavened by several regiments of volunteers from New Mexico and Colorado. These volunteer regiments varied in quality from decent to awful.

On February 16, 1862, a similar-sized Confederate army under the command of General John Sibley advanced to within one mile of Fort Craig. For nearly a week the two sides shadowboxed as each commander tried to maneuver the other into fighting on favorable ground in favorable conditions. Nothing more serious than cavalry skirmishes happened until the armies finally clashed in a bloody struggle on the twenty-first, near a ford called Valverde, east of the Rio Grande. Early that morning, Sibley moved part of his army toward Fort Craig, located six miles south of Valverde and on the west side of the river. As the diversionary force executed this demonstration, the main force moved north, straight at Valverde, in an attempt to draw the Federals away from the fort and pin them against the river.

Upon seeing the Rebels heading in this direction, Canby dispatched Colonel Benjamin Roberts with various companies of regular infantry, including one from the 7th under Captain Charles H. Ingraham, several companies of cavalry, and a few companies of volunteers he trusted. Their orders were to prevent the Confederates from reaching the ford and crossing the river. When they reached the ford, they found the Confederates already there. Shooting started as the Union troops forded the river, walking step-by-step through armpit-depth water and a strong current. Artillery covered them as they did so. At all costs, Roberts wished to control a vital *bosque,* or small wooded area, near the east bank of the river, and the battle became a contest over this key terrain.

Like the rest of their comrades, the Cottonbalers splashed across the Rio Grande, rifles held high, and charged into the woods. Their uniforms, consisting of the famous Union dark blue coat and light blue trousers, were soaked and heavy, their shoes caked with mud. They watched, through clouds of smoke, as dismounted cavalry ran ahead and drove the remaining enemy from the woods. The fire slackened for a few minutes, but then the enemy came back, in greater numbers. The soldiers took up positions behind and around the *bosque*'s trees and opened fire. From across the river, artillery batteries went to work on the enemy soldiers, creating a tremendous crescendo of sound, confusion, and death. "The ground shakes and trembles," wrote a cavalry trooper, "the roar shuts out all sounds beyond, and shells go shrieking into the woods to cut trees short off, to mow great swaths in the undergrowth, to hurl and scatter mangled men."[17]

For several hours the battle continued in this manner. Union and Confederate artillery dueled; cavalry charged; infantry supported. The Cottonbalers manned their section of the Union line and poured steady fire into whatever distorted enemy shapes they could see through all the gunpowder smoke. At noon the fighting died down, as the enemy retreated and reorganized north of the Federal positions. The Rebels tried a flanking move across the river, but Roberts countered that threat by sending several hundred regulars (excluding the Cottonbalers) and a reliable volunteer regiment under the command of none other than Kit Carson. This mixed force crushed the Rebel attack and sent them reeling back across the river.

Roberts now felt secure enough to move his artillery to the east side and place it along the right (south) and left (north) of his line. Facing east, his forces were anchored by infantry in the extreme north, several pieces of artillery under Captain Alexander McRae, more infantry south of him, and, on the extreme south of the line, another battery under Lieutenant Robert Hall. Roberts placed the Cottonbalers on the left near McRae. In the meantime, the Confederates withdrew their army out of range of the guns, behind the protection of a sand ridge paralleling the river.

The soldiers now had a chance to rest a bit, eat something, and replenish their cartridges with supplies of ammunition recently brought across the river. The battle had not been costly, as yet, but it had been tiring, since the men had been marching, wading, or shooting for the better part of a day. Tired and nearly spent, the men gnawed on hardtack biscuits and counted their remaining cartridges. Some of them optimistically predicted that the day's fighting was over.

They were wrong. A few minutes after 3:00 P.M. the battle reached a climax when the enemy launched a major attack with practically everything they had. Confederate forces struck on both flanks of the Union Army in a two-pronged attack. On the right they emerged from over the ridge and bore down on Hall's section of the line. At that exact moment the Union forces in that sector had been preparing to push skirmishers ahead in a probe on the enemy positions, so they were ready for the enemy attack. Even so, Canby, who had arrived about half an hour earlier and assumed command, sent reinforcements to the right, including Ingraham's H Company. Once again, the shooting began, and it soon reached deafening levels. The Northern soldiers advanced and then held steady in the face of the enemy attack. Not far away, a cavalry officer watched the whole thing unfold: "In their front the Texan lancers, which had been moved forward, were forming for a charge; gay in gaudy trappings and the little flag pendent from their arms. Just as the formation had been perfected, down upon the infantry charged the lancers, riding in the wild abandon of the movement. We waited for the volleys of our troops; but steadfast and stern they stood, not a gun fired, until it seemed as if . . . our fellows would be ridden down by the impetus of the horses upon them. Not a movement, not a sound, save the yells of the advancing lancers." The Union soldiers, including the Cottonbalers, finally began "pouring a withering fire into the face—horse and man—of the charging troop. Down, down they went, like grain before the reaper's scythe; great swaths are mowed among their ranks. Out of that gay and gallant squadron that rode so bravely down, scarce a fourth rode back to tell the doleful story of that charge."[18]

The infantry merely held their ground and kept firing as quickly as they could. The enemy soon had even bigger problems, as another officer recalled: "Just then Lieutenant Hall dropped a shell in the midst of them, and so increased the panic which the enemy had just received from our volley of small arms that he retreated entirely out of sight."[19]

The enemy attack on the right had been stopped in its tracks, but the left was a different story. Here the Confederates made a desperate charge, supported by artillery in an effort to neutralize McRae's artillery and break the Union line, which was partially manned by Companies C and F of the 7th Regiment. Canby later wrote about the bloodcurdling moment when the enemy attacked: "At this moment a formidable storming party, supported by several infantry columns and four pieces of artillery, the whole estimated at more than 1,000 men, suddenly made its appearance from behind the sand ridge, and moved rapidly upon McRae's battery."

The enemy artillery fire ripped through men and horses while Rebel infantry ran forward screaming at the top of their lungs. On they came, filled with "wild ardor and determination," in the words of one Yankee. Faced with the terrifying determination of the enemy infantry and the buzzing butchery of their artillery, many of the New Mexican volunteers decided that Valverde was no place to be. They broke and ran across the river, screaming and crying, sowing panic in whatever troops they encountered. This was Canby's worst nightmare. He had little confidence in most of his volunteer units, and the frightened flight of his New Mexicans meant that a few hundred regulars, along with a few steadfast Colorado volunteers, were left to deal with the brunt of the entire enemy assault. McRae's battery was the vortex of this fierce and uneven struggle.

"The [Confederate] storming party proper was deployed as skirmishers, enveloping the left, front, and a part of the right of the battery by a circular segment nearly half a mile in length," Canby wrote. "Armed with double-barreled fowling-pieces and revolvers, and converging as they approached, a rapid and destructive fire was poured into the battery. From the moment that it made its appearance the storming party was met by a terrible fire of grape and double canister from the battery and of musketry from its infantry support."[20]

The Rebels staggered and paused, but a moment later, in the present-tense recollection of one Union soldier, they came back with renewed fury: "They and we are firing grape and canister as rapidly as guns can be loaded and discharged. The second charge is preparing; men gather for the rush, and at us they come, and again, with double-shotted [sic] guns, we drive them back. In the first and second charge and the canister firing which preceded it, certainly one-half the men and two-thirds the horses were killed or *hors de combat*. We hadn't long to wait for the coup de main. Through the smoke we see a swarm of men. It is not a battle line, but a mob desperate enough to bathe their bayonets in the flame of guns. Onward, rushing through the fire poured upon them, with maddened determination. The guns leap from the ground almost as they are depressed on the foe. On they came—no hesitation before the sweeping fire poured into them—the discharge which picks live men from off their feet and hurls them back bleeding and dead. Cannon wheels are blocked by bodies jammed in between the spokes."[21]

Eventually numbers told and the Confederate attackers overwhelmed their enemies. Here and there hand-to-hand fights raged. Half of McRae's artillerymen were dead or wounded. The captain fought magnificently until he too got killed in a face-to-face pistol confrontation with a Confederate officer. The infantry units were also decimated and on the verge of collapse. Union reinforcements stabilized the situation somewhat late in the day, but Canby, whose horse had been shot out from under him, soon decided that he must retreat. Bit by bit, he delicately withdrew his exhausted forces to the west bank of the river: "The ammunition wagons, a disabled gun, and all the material except the captured battery [of McRae] and a part of the arms of the killed and wounded, were safely passed over." Canby withdrew his forces to Fort Craig, and for the next two days the armies dealt with their dead and wounded under a flag of truce.[22]

The Battle of Valverde was a costly Confederate victory. Each side suffered between 250 and 300 casualties (accounts differ). The Cottonbalers lost more men in this battle than in any other in the Civil War: sixty-two in all, nineteen killed, thirty-nine wounded, and four missing. Among the dead was Lieutenant Bascom, who lost his life fighting with C Company near McRae's battery. In fact, C and F Companies suffered most of the regiment's casualties in this battle because these were the two companies involved in repelling the bloody late-afternoon Confederate assault on the left of the Union line.[23]

The Confederates failed to follow up their victory with the complete destruction of Union forces in New Mexico. Instead, over the next couple years, a campaign of maneuver and skirmish ensued, one in which the Union ultimately prevailed. During that time, the 7th Regiment was involved in several other skirmishes in New Mexico, but none bigger or more costly than Valverde.

THE REGIMENT'S TROOPS IN THE EAST WHILED AWAY MOST of 1862 in forts along the Canadian border watching out for Confederate infiltrators and Fenian raiders. Nothing of consequence happened. This duty served as a kind of limbo for the 7th Regiment until the unit could recover from its terrible disgrace at San Augustin Springs. K Company was disbanded for lack of manpower and the regiment's strength concentrated into the other six companies: A, B, D, E, G, and I. Together, these companies numbered 219 men. David Hancock, an 1854 West Point graduate and capable captain who had served with the regiment for eight years, took command of the six companies.[24] On September 30, he found out that the regiment had been officially exchanged. Moreover, his superiors ordered him to immediately join the Army of the Potomac, which had just won a costly victory at Antietam and was in the process of pushing south.

On October 31 the Cottonbalers caught up with the Army at Sandy Hook, Maryland, directly across the Potomac River from Harpers Ferry. The unit was assigned to a division composed of fellow regulars under the overall charge of General George Sykes, a gruff, tough, no-nonsense commander. Sykes's men were in camp on the thirty-first, resting and cooking, when they noticed a blue column approaching down the road from the north. They watched intently as a weary-looking officer brought the column to a halt in parade ground manner and then reported his unit's presence to the commanding general. The 7th Infantry had arrived.

Shortly after, the Army of the Potomac was on the move. Its general, George B. McClellan, was trying to maneuver his forces between Richmond and Lee's Army of Northern Virginia. McClellan ordered Sykes to push south and capture Snicker's Gap in Virginia, and his forces took the gap and the mountain pass uneventfully on the night of the second. Sykes now wasted no time in putting his new arrivals from the 7th to use. On November 3 he ordered them to go on a reconnaissance in force south down the road to Snicker's Ferry, which crossed the neighboring Shenandoah River. The 1st Massachusetts Cavalry led the way, followed by the 6th and 7th Infantry Regiments and, behind them, the 14th Infantry. Bundled up to keep warm amid chilly temperatures and raging winds, the column moved south, the river and wooded meadows to their right.

Before long the cavalry clashed with Confederate cavalry in a stand of woods to the right of the road. This attracted the leading numbers of infantry, including the 7th, who helped chase the enemy horsemen to the river. When the Northerners approached the riverbank, the world suddenly erupted. Rebel artillery and rifle fire from ridges and houses across the river boomed and crackled, the sound echoing off nearby mountains. From their windows and barriers the enemy fired at the bluecoats who spread out and took cover in the woods. The Cottonbalers spread out, found cover among the trees and autumn leaves of the forest, and exchanged long-range shots with the Southerners.

The unit watched in stunned silence as dozens of 14th Infantry soldiers ran past them in a suicidal charge toward the riverbank. These men were the victims of a command mishap. The regiment's commander, Captain John O'Connell, had halted his men in a copse of trees near the road when he saw a group of staff officers galloping down the road: "I called for orders, and was answered, 'Move forward.' I did so." He and his men walked into a death trap on the bank of the river. Their charge convinced the Rebels that they were trying to force the river and attack the houses, so every Rebel gun concentrated on the unfortunate men of the 14th. After a few minutes of seeing his men torn up by Rebel fire, O'Connell ordered a withdrawal. No one ever found out who gave the foolish order (needless to say, its author was not anxious to come forward and claim his deed). O'Connell would later say, in reference to the ill-fated charge, "I would take the 14th to the gates of Hell, but I would like to have a chance to whip the devil when I got there."

The regulars withdrew back to the road and then into camp. They lost five killed and twenty-six wounded, most from the 14th Infantry, in the inconclusive Battle of Snicker's Gap. Many of the wounded got hit by flying stones that inflicted shrapnel-type wounds typical of a later age. The 7th Regiment took no casualties.[25]

The same, unfortunately, could not be said for its next battle. After Snicker's Gap, the regiment camped near Warrenton, Virginia, for a couple weeks. During this time, President Abraham Lincoln relieved McClellan from command in favor of General Ambrose Burnside, a muttonchopped, amiable man suited for divisional or corps command but certainly not army command.

Day after day, in the crisp fall weather, the Cottonbalers drilled, giving the appearance of "sky blue walls," in the view of one author, "moving and pivoting across the parade ground bundled in their heavy greatcoats." Gone were the forlorn yet slightly happy-go-lucky, whiskey-soaked days of frontier duty. This was now serious business. The battle fought two months earlier at Antietam had been, to that point, the bloodiest single day in American history. The Antietam casualty numbers alone totaled more than all previous American wars combined. Both sides in this war wanted to score a knockout blow before year's end. The stakes were now very high: emancipation for the slaves, foreign recognition for the South, and the survival of Lincoln's total-war policies. Most believed the East would be the decisive theater of the war and that the next battle could decide the conflict's outcome.

On November 17 the men of the entire Regular Division rose before dawn and prepared to move out. Burnside planned to cross the Rappahannock River at Fredericksburg and threaten Lee's eastern flank. The day started out sunny and pleasant and the men marched in high spirits accompanied by regimental bands playing such tunes as "Garry Owen," "Paddy O'Toole," and of course "The Girl I Left Behind Me." Late in the day clouds rolled in and spit rain on the regulars. The men camped in the mud that night, cursing the cold rain and longing for their old camp, with its modest shelter of squad tents. For several more days after this they marched south over muddy, slick roads until they reached Falmouth on the north side of the Rappahannock about a mile from Fredericksburg. The quality of the shelter improved at Falmouth. The soldiers lived in crude log cabins covered with shelter half roofs. Some enterprising men built mud and stone fireplaces with barrels for chimneys.

The Army stayed here for nearly three weeks. Thanksgiving came and went. The holiday did not mean as much to the regulars as it did to the state volunteers who received packages from their families. The men who populated the 7th, and most of the other regular outfits, often did not have such family ties. They were usually loners and the Army was their home.

Heavy snow fell and the weather grew colder. Still the regiment endured the same old camp routine and waited for orders. They finally came on the eleventh of December. In the predawn darkness of that morning a dispatcher raced into camp with orders to pack knapsacks, prepare weapons, and fill haversacks with three days' cooked rations. In a flurry of movement the men roused themselves and prepared to go. In the distance they could hear cannons firing. They hunched under their overcoats, put one foot in front of the other, and tried to keep warm. After so many months of waiting and stewing, the Cottonbalers were eager for battle. Most of them did not consider Snicker's Gap to have been a serious engagement, but they knew that the next battle could be the most important of the war. Many of the soldiers wanted to reclaim their unit's lost honor.

As it turned out, they would have to wait a little longer. For the better part of two days they bivouacked under the cover of ravines outside of Falmouth. Finally, at 4:00 P.M. on the thirteenth of December they left their bivouac area and marched with the rest of the division across the Rappahannock on a pontoon bridge, into Fredericksburg. As they

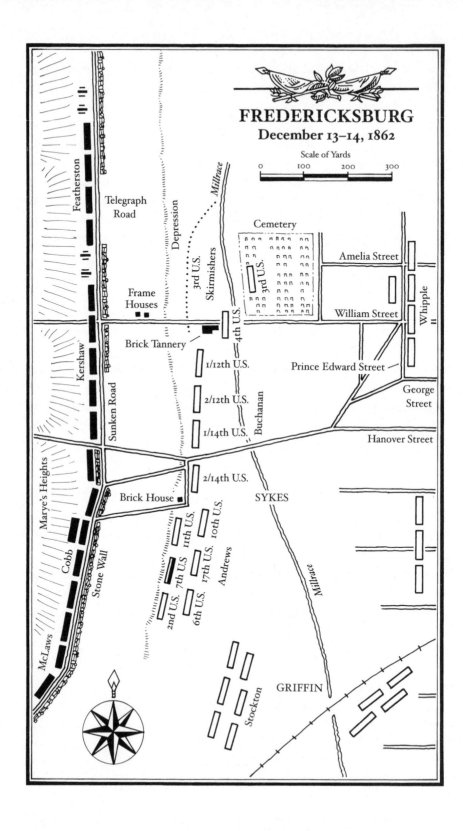

FREDERICKSBURG
December 13–14, 1862

Scale of Yards

0   100   200   300

Featherston

Telegraph
Road

Depression

Millrace

Cemetery

3rd U.S.
Skirmishers

3rd U.S.

Amelia Street

Whipple

Frame
Houses

William Street

4th U.S.

Brick Tannery

Kershaw

1/12th U.S.

Prince Edward Street

Sunken Road

2/12th U.S.

Buchanan

George
Street

1/14th U.S.

Hanover Street

Marye's Heights

2/14th U.S.

Brick House

SYKES

Cobb

2nd U.S.

7th U.S.

11th U.S.

17th U.S.

10th U.S.

Stone Wall

6th U.S.

Andrews

McLaws

Stockton

Millrace

GRIFFIN

crossed, stray shells landed here and there and the men could hear a terrific din coming from the heights above the town. They did not know it, but the hours leading up to their crossing had been a nightmare for the Army of the Potomac. Lee had detected Burnside's intentions and fortified a natural defensive area consisting of ridges, slopes, and stone walls immediately west of the town. For a time Lee contested the town, which lay astride the river, as well as the Yankee river crossing, but his true intention was to force Burnside into attacking his defenses or retreating back across the river. Frankly, Lee expected Burnside to order the latter course of action, but Burnside foolishly chose the former. He ordered his army to advance through the town and attack straight uphill into Lee's formidable defenses.

Throughout the day on the thirteenth, wave after wave of courageous bluecoats threw themselves at the enemy lines. The Confederates cut them down in staggering numbers. They zeroed in on every inch of the open, sloping ground in front of them and slashed the Yankee attackers with everything in their arsenal—grapeshot, canister, rifles, pistols, and cavalry. The predictable result of Burnside's foolish assault plan was abject slaughter. Thousands of Yankees got caught in a hellish kill zone. Rebel lead scythed through them, tearing off arms, heads, and legs, ripping up torsos, spraying blood and gristle everywhere. Once men went in they could not get out. Anyone who moved, wounded or unwounded, drew fire.

The Cottonbalers could hear the din of this hopeless battle—booming, crackling, and screaming—as they picked their way along Hanover Street on the north side of the town. They reached the edge of town and soon saw the remnants of the hopeless attacks. Wounded and freezing men, with terror in their eyes and screams emitting from their throats, steadily filtered past them and back into the town. In the fading light of late afternoon, the regular troops looked at the hillsides and saw thousands of bodies, covering the earth like a blue blanket. Soon an awful realization dawned on the men: they were next!

They now peered intently at the ground their superiors had ordered them to capture. From left to right along a distance of some fifteen hundred yards, Confederate soldiers, clad in an array of gray and brown uniforms, were barely visible behind a continuous stone wall. Between the town and the wall, open ground sloped for roughly three hundred yards, over an area called Marye's Heights. The gentle rise and old stone wall would have made a picturesque scene in peacetime, but on this winter day it provoked nothing but fear and trepidation in those who had to carry out the assault.

The Regular Division was split up into two brigades. The 7th Regiment served in the 2nd Brigade, along with the 1st, 2nd, 6th, 10th, 11th, 17th, and 19th Infantry Regiments. In the impending attack, the 2nd Brigade would veer to the left of a battered but prominent brick house. The Cottonbalers would advance in the front rank of the brigade between the 2nd Regiment on the left and the 11th Regiment on the right.

At just after 5:00 P.M. the order came to move out. The men formed into their ranks and the air rang with the clinking of bayonets onto rifle muzzles. No one talked or laughed. A deathly silence hung in the air, save for shouts here and there from sergeants closing up the ranks. Men glanced at one another and swallowed hard. Many shivered, either from the cold or from raw fear. In a few moments they left the relative safety of the town and advanced with muskets shouldered, closer by the second to the Confederates and the deadly killing ground of Marye's Heights. Within a hundred yards they came upon a deep drainage ditch (participants estimated that the ditch was ten feet deep and five feet wide, with roughly four feet of icy water at its bottom). Under the circumstances most of them welcomed the presence of the ditch because it offered cover.

They slid down the banks of the ditch and settled into the cold water. Many of them were shivering violently now. The water soaked through their pants and shoes and made the bottoms of their blue coats wet and stiff. Knapsacks and cartridge boxes got wet, but the men made sure to keep their rifles above the water. One by one they clambered out of the water and up the far side of the ditch and collapsed into prone positions along the lip of this indentation. Now they had a panoramic view of the sloping plain the generals expected them to conquer. The sight that greeted their eyes defied description. Yard by yard along the span of Marye's Heights, blue-clad bodies lay in every conceivable position of death and dismemberment, like bloody rag dolls. But these weren't rag dolls. They were human beings who had had hopes, dreams, and fears.

Confederate firepower had turned them into pulpy hamburger. Here and there a head with no body lay, eyes staring into oblivion, along with an endless series of horrors: torsos full of holes, mangled legs with no bodies, mangled legs with similarly mangled bodies, pristine-looking bodies with some mysterious source of death, eyes opened or closed, hands stretching from bodies that had been blown onto their backs, the hands forever reaching for the heavens, dead men with parts of their heads blown away, probably by grapeshot, untucked shirttails ripped loose by the trauma of invading lead, revealing white bellies with gray, ropy guts protruding from crimson wounds, lifeless heaps with broken limbs pointing in crazy directions.

Maybe even worse than the dead were the wounded. In various states of helplessness and trauma, they lay everywhere on the hill, moaning, praying, screaming, cursing, and begging. Men with bullet holes in their faces crawled gingerly away from the wall. Others with bloody uniforms cried for water or their mothers. Most could do nothing but lie still and pretend to be dead for fear of drawing enemy fire. They stared back at the regulars with beseeching eyes that might as well have roared, "Help me! Oh God, please help me!" Confederate ordnance still buzzed around, periodically hitting the living and the dead.

With parched throats and slack jaws, the Cottonbalers stared at this Dante-esque scene and dreaded with every fiber of their being the order to attack. Mercifully, the word came down that the attack had been called off. The generals believed that the wounded and dead must be retrieved before any fresh troops could make it up the hill. Those lucky men on the hill who were still unhurt hoped to withdraw under the cover of darkness.

The postponement of the attack had the effect of a reprieve from the governor for a condemned man. The men of the 7th had to be careful to keep their heads down, but they were not in much immediate danger as long as they hunkered down in the ditch. In this cold and uncomfortable bedroom, they caught a few hours of fitful sleep after the sun set. Sometime after 11:00 P.M., with the front having considerably quieted down, the 2nd Brigade received orders to leave the cover of the ditch and advance up the hill. Their mission was to cover the men withdrawing quietly from Marye's Heights.

The regiment shook off its sleep, climbed out of its ditch, and moved out along Hanover Street, which extended, if one could make it that far, all the way to the wall and beyond. As originally planned, they veered left off the road and into the fields where so many nameless soldiers had died that day. In the inky darkness they could barely make out the shapes of withdrawing men who walked by wordlessly, deep in shock. Various Cottonbalers tripped over dead bodies—men and horses—then cursed softly and moved on. When they reached the brick house, a bizarre sight greeted their eyes, as one soldier recalled: "Inside sat a woman, gaunt and hard featured, with crazy hair and a forlorn face, still sitting by a smoking candle, though it was nearly two hours past midnight. But what woman could sleep . . . alone in a house between two hostile armies—two corpses laying across her doorsteps, and within, almost at her feet, four more! So with wild eyes and face lighted by her smoky candle, she stared across the dead barrier into the darkness outside with the look of one who heard and saw not and to whom all sounds were a terror."[26]

They walked past the house and took up prone positions in a nearby depression that afforded about a foot of defilade cover, some eighty yards from the stone wall. Here they untied their knapsacks and spread their wet blankets along the cold ground. Many of the soldiers used dead men as pillows. Many others could not sleep. All they could think about was the prospect of assaulting the wall in the morning. They wondered if this miserable night would be the last they would ever experience.

Morning finally came, and with it a thick blanket of fog over the entire battlefield. As the sun rose at their backs and began to burn away the fog, the men noticed a fresh set of horrors in front of them near the wall. During the night the Confederates, desperate for warm clothes, had stripped the Union dead of their uniforms. The pasty, blood-spattered skin of the dead contrasted sharply with the grass on which they lay. Violent death had afforded the ghastly heaps of dead men no dignity yesterday when clothed, much less today when naked. No one could think of himself ending up this way, as a raw piece of discarded meat, stripped of identity and humanity, naked and inert, like a piece of debris left to rot.

Beyond the dead bodies the men saw the Confederates behind their wall, moving about with impunity, cooking, laughing, talking, and cleaning their weapons. The Union men felt cut off from their army, almost like prisoners. Being this close to the enemy was surreal, fostering an absurd sort of intimacy. A few seconds later, the Confederates opened fire, almost as if they had punched a time clock and started work for the day.

Each man scrunched down into the dubious cover of the tiny depression and made himself as small a target as possible. The fire grew steadier and thicker by the moment, pinning the men down completely. Anyone who moved or exposed himself in any way got shot. The soldiers could do little else besides lie still and listen to bullets whistling a foot, or less, above their prone forms. Those with strong stomachs maneuvered dead bodies in front of themselves to use as cover. They could hear and feel bullets smack into the naked dead. The order came down to hold fire as long as the Confederates did not attack. The brass did not want to provoke a larger engagement, and the Rebels merely contented themselves with their grisly target practice.

The regulars were on their own. They could not go forward or back. They were trapped in this hellish no-man's-land, not quite exposed to the enemy but not quite safe either. As long as daylight lasted, no one could safely go anywhere. Disciplined and dedicated, they made the most of this awful situation. "After two or three hours of this experience," an officer later wrote, "we became somewhat accustomed to almost anything that savors of routine—and learned with considerable exactness the limit inside which we might move with safety, and limit also of endurable constraint. All this would have been ludicrous but for the actual suffering inflicted upon so many. Men were mortally hit, and there was no chance to bind up their wounds; they were almost as far beyond our help as if they had been miles away. A little was accomplished for their relief by passing canteens from hand to hand, keeping them close to the ground out of sight. It was sad to hear the cries fade away to low moans, and then to silence, without a chance to help." Here and there men would jump up and run to fetch some tobacco. Most were cut down brutally. A brand-new officer, with a baby face and a full head of flaming red hair, raised his head for a quick look at the enemy. With stunning swiftness a bullet tore through his brain and he sunk down in death, blood running from his head onto his folded hands. Others got hit too: "Next a leg or arm was shattered as it became exposed in shifting from the wearisomeness of our position."

The men settled into a tense routine of frozen stiffness. Some read fragments of newspapers or took naps; others took to writing down or vocally reporting the casualties. Hour after miserable hour dragged by, the only relief coming from the sun, which provided some semblance of warmth. The officers worried that Confederate artillerymen would take an interest in the pinned-down soldiers, but they never did. The opposite was true of Union stretcher bearers. When these brave medics tried to retrieve the wounded, the enemy unmercifully shot them down. The regulars screamed in anger and wanted badly to shoot back at the Rebels, but their officers wisely restrained them.

The afternoon wore on and, as it did, some of the men took to peering at the sun, almost willing it to set. They understood that only darkness would bring liberation from this tour of duty as shooting gallery targets. Mercifully, once the sun began to set, it did so quickly. When darkness set in, the entire Regular Division stood as one and, releasing an entire day's worth of pent-up frustration, emptied their rifles at the Rebel lines. The Confederates answered in kind, but they did not hit anyone. The Union troops moved away and out of range as quickly as possible. To their surprise, other Northern soldiers tagged along with them. "With our line also rose a few men from the ghastly pile of yesterday's dead, who hobbled up on muskets used as crutches. These poor fellows had bound up their own wounds. Their cheerfulness grew into hilarity and merriment as they found themselves clear, at last, from the dead, and facing toward home. Poor fellows! Their joy was more touching than their sufferings."

The troops shuffled away into the night, but their losses were not far from their minds: "In our own [2nd] brigade we had lost nearly 150 men out of a present for duty strength of 1,000 men. This would have been a fair average loss in any ordinary battle, but we had suffered it as we lay on the ground inactive, without the excitement and dash of battle and without the chance to reply; a strain upon nerves and physical endurance which we afterward remembered as severer than more fatal fields."

They made their way through the dark and back into town. "We marched past the courthouse—past churches, schools, bank buildings, private houses—all lighted for hospital purposes, and all in use. Even the door-yards had their litter-beds, and were well filled with wounded men, and the dead were laid in rows for burial. The hospital lights and camp-fires in the streets, and the smoldering ruins of burned buildings, with the mixture of lawless rioting of the demoralized stragglers, and the suffering and death in the hospitals, gave the sacked and gutted town the look of pandemonium."[27]

They wandered around and then bivouacked that night in the city. The next day they ate and utilized the city's water pumps to wash away their battle filth. Happy to be alive, they scouted and scrounged their way around town and waited for further orders. For a time, Burnside contemplated ordering more attacks—even leading them himself—but his officers dissuaded him from this silly idea. Sad and dispirited, he ordered the Army to leave Fredericksburg and retreat back into camp near Falmouth, having absorbed one of its greatest defeats of the entire war.[28]

The Cottonbalers lost two men killed, twenty-six wounded, and nine missing in this battle (the latter group probably mistakenly wandered into Confederate lines and got taken prisoner on the night of the thirteenth).[29] In spite of these losses and the bitter defeat of this ill-conceived engagement, Fredericksburg served as a redemption for the unit. The men had fought with great bravery and determination. They had been asked to hold fast under fire in the wake of a terrible defeat, immediately within and around the torn bodies of the dead and wounded. The unit never wavered. It stood shoulder to shoulder with other regulars and more than held its own in the face of awful circumstances. On Christmas Day, the regiment received a present for its bravery on the battlefield. The War Department awarded the unit a new set of colors—never since relinquished—in a stirring ceremony. Hancock proudly led the unit on parade, with the new colors flying high. To this day the regimental crest of the 7th includes a rendering of the stone wall at Fredericksburg.

DESPITE THE DISASTER AT FREDERICKSBURG, BURNSIDE remained in command of the Army of the Potomac. He still hoped to flank Lee and draw him into a decisive battle. To that end, Burnside ordered the army to leave its Falmouth camping ground and cross the Rappahannock farther upstream in an effort to outflank Lee in his Fredericksburg winter quarters. The Southern commander knew all about Burnside's plans, though, and skillfully parried every move. For five days in late January, the Army of the Potomac, including the Cottonbalers, marched around muddy, soggy, sticky Virginia roads. A steady winter drizzle fell upon the men, soaking their greatcoats, trickling down their backs, saturating their rifles. Temperatures dropped and the rain turned to stinging sleet, battering the ruddy faces of the soldiers. Finally, on January 25, having accomplished nothing but misery and sickness for his troops, Burnside ordered his army back into camp for the rest of the winter at Falmouth. The soldiers called this fruitless foray "The Mud March." Lincoln had finally had enough. He sacked Burnside and replaced him with General Joe Hooker, who had a reputation as a bluff talker, hard drinker, and tough fighter who instilled good morale and fighting spirit in his soldiers.

DURING THESE DEMORALIZING DAYS FOR THE NORTHERN army, the 7th nearly had a command change of its own. Hancock was a competent officer, but he had an alcohol problem. He warmed himself during the Mud March by nipping at his flask any chance he got. Hancock undoubtedly was not alone in this indulgence, but many of his junior officers thought that he seemed a bit out of control: overtly drunk, staggering a little, and slurring his words ever so imperceptibly. Back in camp they muttered their disapproval to one another and agreed to keep an eye on their captain.

The whole incident probably would have blown over—this kind of thing was fairly common during the Civil War—except for the presence of a new regimental officer who had just arrived from the west. Captain Gurden Chapin, a West Pointer, had joined the regiment as a second lieutenant in 1851. He served in the outfit for ten years before being dismissed from the Army for unknown reasons—perhaps loyalty issues?—in August 1861. He managed to get himself reinstated three months later and, for a time, commanded the three companies that escaped captivity in New Mexico. He fought honorably with the New Mexico contingent and transferred east in early 1863.[30]

Chapin was senior to Hancock by three years, so he naturally assumed command of the regiment. Upon hearing of Hancock's drunkenness, and loath to have Hancock serving as his second in command, Chapin decided to court-martial him. Chapin garnered the support of several regimental officers, most notably Captain Charles Stivers, who shaped up as third in command. Strangely, Chapin preferred his charges directly to the adjutant general instead of going through brigade or divisional channels, as was customary. In his letter, Chapin claimed that during the Mud March, Hancock "was drunk & conducted himself in such a manner as to expose his condition to the officers and men. I . . . assumed command on the 26th of January, and I was informed that I came just in time, for some of the officers were determined not to go into action under a drunken commander, & the men had lost all respect for him, & all confidence in him. I think the regiment and the service would benefit by his dismissal, as Capt. Hancock's character is fully established, & there seems to be no hope of reform."

The adjutant general did not react well to Chapin's charges, nor did

Hooker, who wondered, in a prickly response, why this wasn't being handled at the regimental or brigade level. "Capt. Chapin will be called upon for an explanation of his non-observance in this instance, of the regulations governing the subject of military correspondence." Hooker ordered the matter to be settled at the brigade level. This put Hancock's fate in hands of Major George Andrews, commander of the 2nd Brigade. Andrews smelled a rat. He thought that Chapin and Stivers were conspiring to get rid of Hancock for their own purposes. Andrews quickly dismissed the charges, and his immediate superior, General Sykes, concurred. Realizing that, in the aftermath of this bitter and petty incident, Chapin and Hancock could not productively serve together, Andrews and Sykes effectively chose Hancock over his accuser. They transferred Chapin out of the regiment and restored Hancock to command. In the final estimation, Hancock deserved to keep his command, but he was clearly wrong to have drunk excessively in front of his men and in a potential combat situation.[31]

THE COMBINATION OF BATTLE CASUALTIES AT FREDER-icksburg and sickness from the Mud March significantly reduced the ranks of the 7th Infantry. During the early months of 1863, Hancock eliminated D and G Companies and consolidated all of his survivors into four remaining companies: A, B, E, and I. Replacements were almost nonexistent. For the entire year of 1862, the Old Army regiments (1st through 10th) recruited a grand total of 138 men, of whom only a few went to the 7th.[32] Casualties, desertion, and disease had taken a heavy toll on the Northern armies, but none more so than the regular regiments, which could not hope to compete with state volunteer regiments for an ever-shrinking pool of recruits.

Those who joined state volunteer outfits — the units that comprised the overwhelming majority of the U.S. Army in the Civil War — enjoyed the advantage of substantial enlistment bonuses, pensions, and sometimes land. Moreover, they fought among neighbors, family, and friends, under the umbrella of prestigious state organizations. Naturally that gave them a nice support system as they faced the rigors of battle. The regulars were offered no such amenities. The enlistment bounty was smaller, the pay lesser, and the term of enlistment usually longer. Unless a man signed up with a friend or two, he joined a unit full of strangers. As before, the Regular Army still primarily appealed to the rootless, the penniless, and the disenfranchised among the white population.

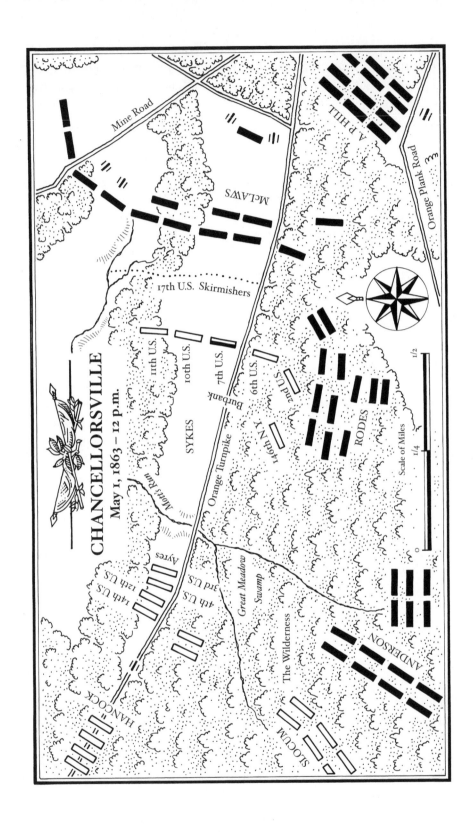

CHANCELLORSVILLE
May 1, 1863 – 12 p.m.

Mine Road

McLAWS

17th U.S. Skirmishers

A. P. HILL

Orange Plank Road

11th U.S.

10th U.S.

7th U.S.

SYKES

Burbank

6th U.S.

2nd U.S.

149th N.Y.

RODES

Mott's Run

Orange Turnpike

Ayres

14th U.S.

12th U.S.

3rd U.S.

4th U.S.

ANDERSON

Great Meadow Swamp

The Wilderness

HANCOCK

SLOCUM

Scale of Miles

1/2

1/4

Adding to the problem, officers sometimes transferred from the regulars to volunteer units, receiving higher rank and greater prestige. Enlisted men deserted from regular regiments, assumed civilian identities, and enlisted in state units.

All of this meant that as the crucial campaigns of 1863 approached, the 7th Regiment and its sister units in the Regular Division could not begin to replenish their losses. They would have to fight with what they had and hope for the best. Most companies had somewhere around forty soldiers, but some were down to twenty men. The units may have been understrength, but they soldiered on through the tough winter months of 1863. Day after day they could be seen drilling, practicing battle formations, cooking, cleaning, and serving on picket duty.

In late April, the Army received its marching orders. Hooker planned a feint on Fredericksburg in the east even as the main portion of his army, including the regulars, crossed the Rappahannock and Rapidan rivers and flanked Lee in the west, through a wooded area known locally as the Wilderness. On the morning of April 27, the Regular Division left its camp at Falmouth. Each man took eight days' rations—mostly bacon and hardtack—along with sixty rounds of ammunition. Two days later they crossed the Rappahannock at Kelly's Ford. The next day they splashed their way across the Rapidan at Ely's Ford. The river was about four feet deep and a steady rain fell as the men crossed. It seemed to the men as if the minute they left camp they got wet!

At the moment the sun rose on May 1, Hooker's plan was working quite nicely. He had maneuvered more than three corps' worth of soldiers behind Lee. The Northern general now turned his army east at a tiny crossroads called Chancellorsville. Here his troops moved through the Wilderness along the Orange Turnpike, straight into the rising sun. Hooker placed the Regular Division in the lead on the dusty road, flanked by the XII Corps under General Henry Slocum in the Wilderness on the right.

Sykes, in turn, ordered the 2nd Brigade to take the lead. This meant that the Cottonbalers now helped lead the entire vanguard of the Army of the Potomac as it attempted to close the noose around Lee's neck. During the final minutes of that morning, the soldiers marched up the road, warily eyeing the terrain ahead of them. They knew that they could clash with the enemy at any moment. Tension, stemming from not knowing where and when contact would happen, pervaded the ranks. Yard by yard they advanced. The day grew warmer and some of them sweated beneath their dark blue wool coats.

At almost high noon, they ran into something. In the distance, about a quarter mile ahead, they could see Confederate troops coming out of the woods. These men belonged to a Virginia brigade that was busy chasing Union cavalry skirmishers. The new 2nd Regular Brigade commander, Colonel Sidney Burbank, immediately ordered his soldiers to fan out on either side of the road. The 7th Regiment went left, taking up fighting formations in a gentle, rolling meadow just along the road. The 17th Infantry ran ahead and took up positions as skirmishers screening the whole brigade. Behind them the Cottonbalers, shoulder to shoulder with two other regiments on their left, went straight at the enemy. In the process they captured several prisoners.

They swept ahead for a few hundred yards. Here enemy fire grew thicker. The Confederates took cover behind trees and in shallow valleys and sniped at the regulars. The Yankees returned the fire. This had the makings of a toe-to-toe fight. Bullets whipped around with impunity. The regiment remained in place near the crest of a small hill. The men stood in formation, loading and firing at will. Their rifles were still loaded through the muzzle, but the flintlock priming pan had given way to a percussion cap that made for significantly smoother loading and firing. In a fight like this a soldier stood with his musket resting against one foot, removed a cartridge from a cartridge box on his hip, tore open the cartridge, poured its powder and ball into the muzzle of the rifle, rammed the ball in place, replaced his rammer, retrieved a percussion cap, put it in place, aimed, and fired.

This created a wall of firepower when properly trained soldiers fired at will or in unison. So, the Cottonbalers, standing on that piece of ground along the Orange Turnpike, were a formidable fighting force, though small in number. Fifteen minutes went by, then half an hour. To this point, the regulars had gotten the better of the fight, and they continued to do so in the Cottonbaler sector, in spite of casualties. A Rebel bullet slammed into the regimental color-bearer. He slumped and crumpled to the ground. Immediately Corporal Stephen C. Neil, of E Company, rushed to the color-bearer and pried the colors away from him. Neil proudly waved the flag, and the rest of the regiment cheered. All Civil War regiments placed a high priority on keeping their colors flying during battle, especially the 7th, which had seen its emblem disgraced and was determined to prevent that from ever happening again.

Undoubtedly this motivation played a part in Neil's exuberance to keep the colors flying. Congress awarded him the Medal of Honor for this act (no disrespect for Neil's bravery, but standards for the awarding of this supreme honor were much lower in the nineteenth century).

Although the regulars were holding their ground nicely, they did not have much support along their flanks. Union reinforcements had not been able to push through the woods on the right and the hills on the left and take up positions alongside the regulars, who found themselves dealing with an increasing number of Rebel reinforcements, especially in the woods to the right of the Orange Turnpike. General Sykes knew his men were fighting quite well, but he worried about what might happen if the weight of numbers began to tell and the Confederates collapsed his flanks.[33]

Even as Sykes ruminated, Hooker made one of the war's most infamous decisions. His lead division, the regulars, was certainly in a vulnerable spot, but he had thousands of reinforcements to bring up in support. In a big-picture sense, he had Lee in a bad position. The Confederate general had detected Hooker's plan and was frantically moving troops westward to meet the threat to his rear, but that would take time. This meant that Lee did not have much help to give the troops who were in action against the regulars. Now was the moment for Hooker to go forward with everything he had, crush Lee's vanguard, and push eastward to intercept Lee's reinforcements. Instead Hooker got spooked by the sight of Confederate resistance to the regulars. "Fighting Joe" ordered the regulars to withdraw down the turnpike so that the Army could prepare positions around Chancellorsville and wait for Lee. This negated Hooker's advantage of position, numbers, supply, and maneuver, not to mention initiative, and, in effect, it lost the Battle of Chancellorsville for the Union.

When the men of the 7th heard the withdrawal order they were surprised and disappointed. They had suffered two killed and nine wounded but had plenty of fight left.[34] One soldier recalled that when the order came "there was heard cursing and grumbling . . . not at being ordered into danger, but at being ordered out. All knew too well that again somebody had blundered." The soldiers trudged angrily down the turnpike and then took up positions along the road, facing the woods. The regiment spent a sleepless night on picket duty, in close proximity to the Rebels, covering Union troop movements. "The woods were on fire throughout the length of the picket line, and when night fell, soon after the sentinels were posted, the burning branches and falling limbs made the scene almost appalling; at intervals the enemy would approach our line and fire at random; nobody was hurt, but a more agreeable way of passing the night can be easily imagined."[35]

The next day, of course, General Stonewall Jackson pulled off his famous flank attack on the luckless Union XI Corps, bringing Hooker's army to the brink of disaster. The 7th Infantry did not take a major role in any of the remaining fighting, though. Hancock explained their post–May 1 activities in his official report: "We took our new position next morning, and protected ourselves by abatis. We were moved again near dusk to the support of Sickles corps [in reaction to Jackson's attack]; were not engaged, and took a new position again during the night, which we strongly fortified in the morning, and remained there without being engaged until our final retreat on the morning of the 6th. In retreating there was much confusion, owing to the mixing of the troops on the road, which it was a moral impossibility to prevent, and the very many conflicting and contradictory orders received from the different staff officers, not only from brigade but division and corps headquarters."[36]

Outnumbered more than two to one, Lee nonetheless thrashed Hooker at Chancellorsville. Hooker ceded the initiative to the Confederate general and Lee used that mistake to deadly effect. For five days, his forces attacked and demoralized Hooker's army, until the Union general finally ordered a withdrawal north across the Rappahannock. He selected the regulars as the rear guard.

The men took up positions south of the river and kept watch for a Confederate attack. If the enemy chose to do so, the regulars could be in trouble, outnumbered and pinned against the river. Late on the afternoon of the fifth, a torrential downpour doused the soldiers. Muddy, wet, tired, and disgusted, they bided their time while the rest of the army crossed pontoon bridges across the river. A couple hours after midnight, they left their positions and headed for the river. Behind them, ever so imperceptibly, they could hear Rebel scouts picking their way through empty Union camps. The sounds faded as the Cottonbalers marched, slipping and sliding along roads that had been trampled into pulp by thousands of feet. By morning they had finally crossed the river. They tromped wearily to Falmouth and collapsed in their makeshift log huts.

The Army of the Potomac had suffered yet another disaster under yet another hapless commander. The soldiers felt little but contempt for their senior generals, along with a sense of deep pride in their own ability to fight on in the face of such incompetent leadership. Help was on the way, though. Lincoln replaced Hooker in favor of General George Meade, a cautious but competent commander.

IN THE MEANTIME, THE 7TH REGIMENT AND THE REST OF the Regular Division spent a month in camp, finally receiving the order to move out on June 4. Lee had conceived of yet another bold strategy. He now planned to invade the North in hopes of defeating the Union armies and forcing an end to the war on the Confederacy's terms. The Regular Division marched to Benson's Mills in pleasant early-summer weather. Here they kept a watch on the confluence of the Rapidan and Rappahannock rivers, in hopes of spotting Lee's northbound army and perhaps hindering it. After a week of this benign duty, they left Benson's Mills and marched north in a driving rainstorm. They arrived at Manassas Junction on the fifteenth and camped out on the old battlefield, right next to the graves of those killed the previous two summers. The rains washed away soil, exposing the macabre sight of decomposed arms and legs sticking out of the ground. Sergeants detailed men to dig new graves for these unfortunate souls.

The regulars did not stay long. After a day or two at Manassas, they headed due north into Maryland as Union commanders realized Lee's army had crossed the Potomac River and was rapidly moving north. Now the weather turned hot and many soldiers collapsed from exhaustion along the steamy roads. Eventually those who did not fall out camped at Aldie and waited for more orders. On the twenty-sixth of June, they moved out again in pursuit of Lee. "The Reveille sounded at the unearthly hour of 2 A.M. and the march [began] at 4," an officer wrote in a letter to his mother. "We made a huge march that day pushing up rapidly toward Leesburg crossing Goose Creek which was waist deep and quite wide, the bridge being destroyed long ago. Leesburg was shady and small, quiet and obscure, and the darkies welcomed us with enthusiasm, women and boys . . . men and babies cheered the Union and 'blessed' us—the soldiers . . . never ceased to wave their arms and caps and rags; the white people looked sallow and cadaverous, sour and billious, and womankind mostly put on its unloveliest cast of countenance." The troops crossed the Potomac River. "Then we marched seven miles further that day, making about twenty-four in all, which in the slippery, clayey, cloggy condition of the roads, was quite prodigious for the loaded men."³⁷

For a few days they rested in camp around Frederick, Maryland. On the twenty-ninth, with their batteries slightly recharged, they set out again. They continued to move north, in broiling heat, through Maryland farmland, on the thirtieth, camping at Union Mills three miles south of the Pennsylvania border. The next day they crossed the border and headed for a town called Gettysburg. Fragmentary reports indicated that Union troops under General John Buford had clashed with major enemy forces just northwest of the town. All day long the

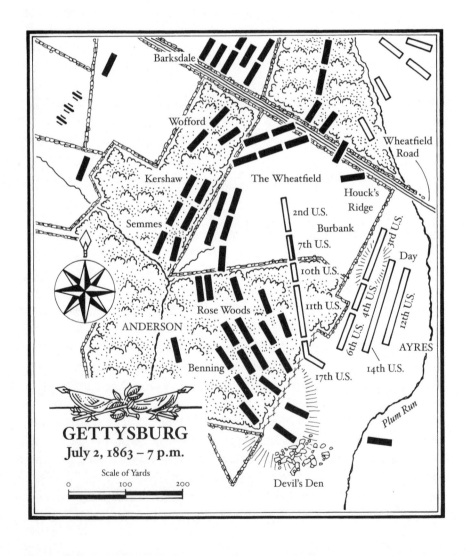

GETTYSBURG

July 2, 1863 – 7 p.m.

Cottonbalers hiked down Hanover Road, choking on dust and sweating profusely. Everyone's uniform smelled gamey—a mixture of sweat, body odor, and moisture. Exhausted, they collapsed into slumber at midnight at an improvised bivouac near Bonneauville, four miles east of Gettysburg. Reveille sounded at 3:00 A.M. on July 2 and the men slowly roused themselves and prepared for what would be a fateful day.

By midmorning they had arrived at Power's Hill in the Federal center. Meade chose to stand them down and use them as a reserve. The men took advantage of this welcome inactivity by spreading out in fields and meadows below Power's Hill. Some slept. Some played cards. Some ate. Some speculated on the thunderous noises of battle they heard in the distance. Most were grateful for the opportunity to rest in nice terrain, in spite of the hot sun overhead that baked and sunburned them.

The stand-down was too good to last. Sometime near 5:00 P.M., Meade found a job for the regulars. Seeing high ground and the Emmitsburg Road, General Dan Sickles, commander of III Corps, had rashly pushed his troops ahead of the main Union line. This jeopardized the entire Union left, which was anchored at two hills called Round Top and Little Round Top. Even as Sickles ordered his corps forward, they ran into a Confederate attack designed to unhinge the Union left. Not only did this mean Sickles's people were in deep trouble, it also meant that the Rebels might be able to capture the hills and flank the whole Union Army. Meade could not allow this to happen. He ordered the regulars to get up and get ready for battle.

The men disassembled their musket stacks, checked to make sure their weapons were clean and ready, and slung their knapsacks. Here and there soldiers stamped out cooking fires. The officers hurried everyone along, not even bothering with the usual line of march. Soon they gave the order to double-time. The regulars ran across fields and hopped fences. They panted and sweated but kept running, heading toward an unknown destination. Burbank began to worry that the men would exhaust themselves before they met the Rebels, so he ordered them to slow down a bit. They came within sight of Little Round Top and could see that a Rebel assault had been bitterly repelled there. Forming into a line of battle at nearby Round Top, they began to push westward, the late-afternoon sun directly in their eyes.

They could already hear Rebel cannon and musket fire as they pushed through a marshy area known as the Plum Run. Some of the men could see Southern skirmishers—mostly Texans and Georgians as it turned out—in the woods ahead. Adrenaline pumping, they began to forge ahead at the double quick, straight at the Rebels in the woods: "At this we all cheered and broke into a run toward the enemy, who were firing at us from the cover [of] a stone wall a short distance in our front, and from the Devil's Den on our left flank. Our cheers were in the nature of shrieks."[38] The enemy soldiers gave way, firing as they retreated. Bullets smacked into slender trees, and a few bodies too. The Union soldiers had to watch their collective step, because the woods sloped downhill. One look away could mean turning a foot on a root or thicket and falling into the tangled bramble. Inevitably, the soldiers had to slow down as they gingerly made their way through the woods. Their eyes bulged with fear and excitement. Their throats were already parched. Vines and branches whipped against any exposed skin. A low stone wall came into view. This was where the Rebels had taken cover moments earlier. The men instinctively made a beeline for the relative safety of the wall.

Here they lay down and took cover, brushing briars off themselves and pausing to drink from canteens, their faces sweaty and red. Peering beyond the wall, they gazed on the ugly face of battle itself—shattered fences, shattered trees, dead men, swirling smoke, and bloody pasture cows lying in various stages of decomposition. Just ahead of them was an extensive wheat field, filled with dead and dying Union soldiers, the detritus of Sickles's failed maneuver. Men in blue were still running around this wheat field, seemingly in confusion and chaos. To the left of the Cottonbalers was Rose Woods. The men could see Union and Confederate soldiers exchanging close-range shots at each other in and around these woods.

For several minutes the Cottonbalers lay behind the stone wall, the 10th U.S. on their left and the 2nd U.S. on their right. As long as the men kept their heads down, the fire wasn't too bad. Just as many of them caught their breath, the regiment and its two partners received orders to get moving. "The Seventh was . . . ordered to cross the fence and wheel to the left," Captain Hancock later wrote, "and form in a line perpendicular to the original direction and advance in the woods. This was immediately done, at the same time relieving a brigade already there. Our firing to the front then was slight, as no enemy was apparently visible in that direction." Rifles at the ready, they moved into the Wheatfield, over a spur called Houck's Ridge (which probably accounted for the slight fire Hancock mentioned), around and past the dead forms of Union soldiers who had tried to capture this ground earlier in the day. In spite of the violence around them, the disciplined regulars maintained a perfect line of battle formation. Retreating soldiers from the 148th Pennsylvania and the 5th New Hampshire headed in the other direction, right through the small lines of regulars. These brave men had fought their hearts out in Rose Woods and had eventually given way in the face of strong Confederate forces.

The regulars then stood and fired into the woods, repelling small groups of Southern skirmishers. For a few minutes this part of the battlefield hung in limbo, as the men ran out of targets and waited for reinforcements to arrive before they could push into Rose Woods. Then, in the blink of an eye, the situation changed. While the Cottonbalers and their comrades stood facing Rose Woods, they began to take heavy fire from their right, out of the other side of the Wheatfield. Confederate soldiers sweeping down both sides of the Wheatfield Road had flanked the regulars. The blue-coated soldiers, standing in perfect battle formations, across an open field, made ideal targets for the enemy infantry. Major Arthur Lee of the 2nd Infantry remembered this awful moment: "Three lines of the enemy, elevated one above the other on the slope to our right, poured in a most destructive fire, almost decimating my regiment and cutting off the color-staff, causing the colors to fall into the hands of the color-bearer." Lee himself got hit in the leg and his horse took a bullet too.

Most of the initial Confederate volleys slammed into the 2nd, since that unit was on the extreme right of the Union position in the Wheatfield. The 7th saw a few of its men get hit, but not as badly as the 2nd, whose bulk had acted as a kind of awkward shield for the 7th. This could not last, though, and Burbank knew it. He realized that he had to get his men out of the Wheatfield—fast. He hollered above the din of battle and ordered a steady, measured retreat. The men immediately turned back in the direction from whence they had come and marched as if on parade. Almost no one broke and ran. The three regiments simply marched away in formation even as Rebel bullets assailed them.

According to Hancock, the Cottonbalers grumbled at the order to retreat, but they obeyed it. There was really no other option but to get out of the Wheatfield, because four brigades of Georgians were closing in for the kill, screaming and hollering, their "Rebel yells," sending chills down the spines of many who could hear them above the roar of the shooting. The Georgians were pressing forward eagerly, almost wildly, in anticipation of surrounding and cutting off the proud regulars. This pursuit did not keep them from pouring withering fire into the ranks of their enemies. Much of that fire found its way into the ranks of the 7th, and casualties mounted. "While retiring, the fire of the enemy became very destructive," Hancock recalled, "and after recrossing the stone fence and over the open field, became frightful, we receiving there a fire from three different directions."[39]

One by one, soldiers got hit. Minié balls ripped through their jackets, tearing clothing and skin; blood spattered on the wounded and the unwounded alike. Some men fell down as they got hit, but most kept moving. Others turned and fired and then closed ranks again. The discipline of these soldiers during this retreat was incredible, the bravery beyond question. The woods provided little surcease for the embattled troops, as one soldier wrote nearly two decades after the war: "The few hundred yards to the foot of Little Round Top, already strewn with our disabled comrades, became a veritable charnel house, and every step was marked by ghastly lines of dead and wounded. Our merciless foes from their vantage ground . . . poured volley after volley, their sharpshooters picking off with unerring aim many a valuable officer and gallant color bearer."[40]

As they emerged from the woods and marched across the Plum Run valley, entire companies were dissolving in a matter of minutes. The list of Cottonbalers killed during this phase of the battle was extensive. Private John Ashton was turning to fire a shot when a bullet smashed into the left portion of his chest. He died five days later. Lieutenant Richard Crawford got hit in the left arm while leading his soldiers through the woods. The bullet shattered his arm, prompting a painful amputation. He died several months later of the effects of this amputation. Private William Curtis felt a minié ball crash through his back and pass through his lung. Blood filled his entire chest cavity and he collapsed into unconsciousness. Within two weeks he was dead. Private Thomas Lawlave also got shot in the back during the retreat. He lasted two more days. Private William Mason took a bullet in the head, destroying most of his brain. First Lieutenant Wesley Miller, the highest-ranking member of the 7th to die at Gettysburg, got hit by a Rebel sharpshooter and died instantly. Minute by awful minute, more soldiers added their names to this grisly roll call.[41]

Just as it seemed as if the regular regiments might be annihilated in the marshy mud of the Plum Run, a division of Pennsylvanians pushed into the woods behind the backs of the regulars. The Pennsylvanians fought almost face-to-face with the Rebels. The enemy now had other problems to worry about instead of pursuing the regulars. This bought the Cottonbalers and their comrades enough time to make it back to the relative safety of Little Round Top where Federal artillery had dug in. For the Cottonbalers, the Battle of Gettysburg was over.[42]

Out of a battle strength of 116 men, the regiment lost 12 killed, 45 wounded, and 2 missing. Only two other regiments in the entire Regular Division suffered a higher casualty rate than the staggering 50 percent the 7th Regiment suffered.[43] Fredericksburg and Chancellorsville had already whittled the unit down to a perilously lean fighting force, but Gettysburg finished it as an effective combat organization for the rest of the Civil War. The hard-core veterans of the regiment, the professionals who had experienced the surrender in New Mexico, the humiliating year of parole duty, along with the major battles in the East, had been decimated. Men with this kind of fighting spirit could not be replaced, especially in the midst of a declining pool of quality manpower in the North. The government's decision to raise most of the Army through state regiments doomed regular regiments to a perishable existence. In effect, this meant that units like the 7th went into combat with all the manpower they could expect to have and that any ensuing losses could not be replaced.

The 7th participated in Meade's halfhearted pursuit of Lee after Gettysburg. They tromped into Maryland and Virginia with no consequence except the endurance of more heat, more rain, and more sore feet. On August 14 they received orders to go back north to New York City, the site of bloody draft riots the previous month. Worried about the possibility of more such riots, the Lincoln government sent several regiments of regulars to New York. There they would maintain order and perhaps recruit back to strength. Thus the 7th Regiment left the Army of the Potomac, never to return, marched to Alexandria, Virginia, boarded ships, and sailed for New York. In spite of the fact that most of the surviving members of the unit traced some sort of immigrant heritage—something they had in common with most of the rioters—the soldiers had little, if any, sympathy for the rioters. They felt the typical soldier's contempt for those reluctant to serve and, what's more, abhorred chaos, indiscipline, and mindless destruction of life and property. They had seen enough war-related destruction to last a lifetime and thus had no sympathy for those who destroyed in spite of secure circumstances.

The soldiers arrived in New York on the twentieth of August. By then the city had mostly settled down and loyal citizens could now walk the streets without fear. Even so, they were glad to see the regulars, as one of the soldiers recalled: "Marching up the 'Bowery,' I think all of us felt proud of our brown faces and dirty, ragged clothes. We knew, that as soldiers, we were 'the real thing,' and the cheering crowds on the sidewalks seemed to think so, too. The march through the city ended at Madison Square, where we camped, staying there quite a long time."[44]

The regiment remained in New York for two years, split up among various harbor forts such as Fort Lafayette, Fort Schuyler, and Fort Hamilton. Chapin came back and commanded the scattered forces for several months until he got promoted and transferred to the 14th Infantry in May 1864. Major Henry D. Wallen, a West Pointer who had also presided over the three companies out west, replaced Chapin. Wallen had grown sick and tired in the difficult western forts he oversaw and he lobbied to be transferred in a letter to the assistant adjutant general: "I am suffering from hemorrhoids and an accumulation of mucous [sic] in the urine. I have been quite ill at different times, so much so as to be confined to my bed, and I find that the . . . water is a constant aggravation to these complaints." The adjutant general complied and arranged for him to assume command in New York.[45]

If he was looking for an exciting command situation, he came to the wrong place. The regiment did little else in New York besides recruit marginal men, stand guard, drill, and wait for an end to the war. For a brief moment in late October 1864 it looked like the Cottonbalers would be sent back to the Army of the Potomac to shore up General Ulysses S. Grant's manpower situation in the Petersburg siege. But Secretary of War Edwin Stanton, intensely worried about the potentially explosive political situation in New York in the days leading up to the presidential election of 1864, persuaded Grant to leave the 7th Regiment in New York.[46]

The unit settled into a quiet lethargy. With the exception of the post–World War II era, this process tended to happen in the 7th Regiment. During peacetime or idle days, the regiment's morale and its quality of manpower would decline. Conversely, when the outfit was called upon to serve in combat, its morale generally rose and the quality of its manpower, in terms of fighting readiness, bravery, and behavior, improved. Perhaps this is just another way of saying that the men of the regiment were similar to soldiers in most combat outfits—better in battle than in garrison.

Wallen did not get much trouble from his veterans. Most of them were too tired, or too wracked from the effect of wounds, to make much trouble.[47] The recruits were another story. Most of them came from the margins of New York City. They probably chose to join the regulars for one of two reasons: to avoid the draft or to avoid combat. Drafted soldiers had no control over their destination in the Army. Men who joined volunteer regiments received terrific incentives (especially by this time in the war), but those regiments often had the nasty habit of ending up in bloody battles. In that context, regular regiments like the 7th were probably the best military alternative for the transitory laboring male population of New York.

Naturally these men did not make good soldier material. Take, for example, the case of Adam Horhall, who deserted from Fort Schuyler in June 1864. After being apprehended, Horhall wrote a statement explaining his actions: "I enlisted in [the] Reg. 29th March 1864. I received $400.00. On the 1st of June 1864 I obtained a pass to expire at 6 o'clk on same day to purchase a pair of shoes. I went to New York, there was invited to drink, by two parties. I drank with them, after being urged some time, a glass of ale. Soon after drinking this ale, I became unconscious & when I returned to consciousness, I was on a train near Rochester, N.Y. & robbed of nearly all my money. I went from there to Lockport, N.Y. [his hometown] to let my Brother know that I had enlisted. I did not see him and was about to take care to return to the Regt. when I was arrested." A likely story, if one believes in the profitability of the proverbial swampland in Alaska. In his statement, Horhall actually claimed to have drunk poison ale that drugged him while he mysteriously ended up on a train bound for his hometown, his enlistment bounty evaporated like early-morning dew! Unfortunately, the records do not mention what kind of punishment he received.[48]

In another typical case, Private John Brady, a musician in E Company, disappeared from the unit sometime on September 15. Soldiers apprehended him in Brooklyn and put him in jail. Brady enlisted the support of his political ward captain, who wrote that Brady had only been "fishing off the Fort & the tide drifted the boat to the opposite shore & he was arrested there." The officers did not buy this story. In a court-martial decision they found Brady guilty and sentenced him to "make good time lost by desertion, and to forfeit the U.S. $14.00 per month of his monthly pay for twelve months, and to be confined at hard labor under charge of the guard for the same period, wearing a 24 pound ball attached to his left leg by a suitable chain. The Court is lenient on account of the prisoner's youth (about seventeen years)."[49] Perhaps they were not as lenient with Horhall.

While Brady made off in a fishing boat, other men found ways to escape shallow forts like Lafayette. In August 1864 Wallen wrote to Lieutenant John Jackson, commander of I Company and a Danish immigrant. In the letter, Wallen warned Jackson about an ingenious way men had found to successfully desert: "From a deserter just returned I find that the men who escape from the Fort and the service do so by wading around the pickets at low tide. I have to request that you will have more pickets driven, so that the depth of water will be *six feet* at extreme low tide. We have lost eighteen men within the last month and this after great expense incurred by the government in getting them here."[50]

Deserting was a relatively simple proposition, then, because the unit was stationed in a major metropolitan area. If a man could make it from his harbor fort into the city, he stood a fairly good chance of melting into the population or moving on to points unknown, unless he was unlucky like Brady and Horhall.

The regiment languished in New York until May 1865, when the fighting finally came to an end. Lee had surrendered at Appomattox the month before and Richmond had fallen soon thereafter. In the weeks since, John Wilkes Booth had assassinated Lincoln and the last Confederate guerrillas had slowly laid down their arms. The Army of the Potomac marched in Washington in a grand victory parade, but the 7th Regiment did not participate. Instead, the 7th Regiment boarded the steamer *Fulton* and sailed south, first to Hilton Head, South Carolina, and then to Florida, ending up eventually at St. Augustine on the east coast.

Here they dealt with heat, disease, and a hostile population. "The command now numbers . . . 289 men and three officers—absent forty privates," wrote the new commander, Colonel John T. Sprague, a consummate professional. "The men are in good health, the sick forty privates are on Tybee island. The command is now on Anastasia island, opposite this post, as a precautionary measure, but in a few days, if no disease appears, it will be placed . . . at this post, together with other companies of the regiment where a camp of instruction will be formed.

The absence of so many officers from the regiment is seriously felt [many were on leaves of absence]. It is my most earnest desire that the absent officers be ordered to join without delay. The sickness of the regiment, its scattered condition . . . the arrival of recruits . . . renders it necessary that a course of instruction should be commenced immediately."[51]

In Florida they occupied the South and attempted to carry out the victorious Washington government's reconstruction policies. The Civil War was over. This bloodiest of all American conflicts had begun ignominiously for the 7th Infantry, but it had ended, in a combat sense, with the incredible bravery and stolid discipline the unit displayed at Gettysburg. Sadly, the regiment's days of fighting fellow Americans were not over, though. A few years after the end of the Civil War, the soldiers of the 7th found themselves in combat again, half a continent away in a place that many Americans called "the last frontier."

5

Instruments of Manifest Destiny

The Final Frontier Years

By its very nature the U.S. Army is the manifesta-
tion of the will of the government it serves. For good or ill, the Army
carries out the policies of its government. The late nineteenth century
saw the culmination of a process that began the moment Christopher
Columbus set foot on dry land in the Western Hemisphere. In Columbus's wake thousands and then millions of Europeans and Africans
came to the New World and made lives for themselves. As they did so,
they inevitably collided with the indigenous population, collectively
known as American Indians or Native Americans. The immigrants
from the Old World had developed immune systems with heightened
resistance, and so the ravages of smallpox and some other diseases were
less severe for them. The Indians, however, had never been exposed to
these Old World diseases, and their immune systems were not primed
to resist them, a situation that led to catastrophic epidemics. This,
more than anything else, led to the decline in Native American civi-
lizations.

As the United States expanded westward throughout the nineteenth
century, it conflicted and negotiated with the dizzying array of Native
American tribes and nations that existed across the continent. In spite
of excellent fighting skills and bravery, Indians usually proved to be no
match for the bustling, prosperous nation that hungered for control of
the entire continent. White Americans overwhelmed the declining
Indians with numbers, wealth, firepower, and determination.

During the final phase of westward expansion, 1865–91, the U.S. government was generally of two minds regarding Indians. On the one
hand, policy makers genuinely hoped the Native Americans could enjoy peace and prosperity, that they could blend in and find a rightful,

secure place in the growing country. On the other hand, the government cared most about manifest destiny—the widely held belief among non-native Americans that God had bequeathed the continent to the United States because of its unique values of democracy and freedom and that they were obligated to extend the benefits of their civilization from coast to coast.

The Army thus found itself enforcing policies designed to incorporate these two divergent aims. The United States by 1865 had successfully extended its reach to such places as Texas, California, Colorado, Oregon, New Mexico, and Washington. The 1870s and 1880s saw the country exert final control over the last quadrant of the country, lands that had heretofore remained relatively untouched—primarily Montana, Wyoming, and the Dakotas. The 7th Infantry Regiment became intimately involved in the clash of cultures that took place there.

After the Civil War, the regiment at first served in Florida, enforcing the victorious Washington government's Reconstruction policies. Over the course of four years, the soldiers patrolled and adjudicated in the tense atmosphere of the postwar South. Radical Republicans in Congress hoped to bring some semblance of racial equality to the states of the former Confederacy. Southern whites opposed this policy, sometimes bitterly and violently. In Jacksonville, Florida, the Cottonbalers found themselves caught up in this racial enmity. White locals heaped abuse on the Yankees, whom they saw as cruel conquerors. Nor were blacks any more hospitable. They expected the northern soldiers to openly side with them and protect them, only to experience racism from both the soldiers and the convening government authorities responsible for Reconstruction.

As a result, the average Cottonbaler found himself unwelcome among both whites and blacks. This ugly situation boiled over into violence between white soldiers and black civilians on February 22, 1869. Many of the soldiers and local African-Americans liked to frequent the same brothel close to the regiment's camp. Over time the combination of alcohol consumption and vice led to nasty exchanges between the soldiers and black patrons. Soon groups of African-Americans took to hiding outside the brothel, ambushing soldiers, and beating them up as they drunkenly made their way back to camp. In reaction to this, the regiment began to send out patrols in search of the assailants.

Colonel John Sprague, the regiment's commander, related what happened on the evening of the twenty-second: "[A] patrol . . . was fired upon by a band of armed negroes, secreted in the bushes, without a warning. One of the patrol was mortally wounded and died the next day. The soldiers under Captain [Charles] Rawn . . . assembled and pursued the negroes, and followed them into the city, where an indiscriminate firing took place, both by negroes and soldiers, when one colored man was killed. The affair has been greatly exaggerated . . . arising from political prejudice, and the natural antipathy here to the vigilant exertion of the military."

Indeed a riot almost broke out among the black community. Black political leaders demanded that Rawn be brought to justice. Instead he received a fine for breaking the peace. The white population of the town offered to pay his fine entirely. Clearly they liked the idea of Yankee soldiers and blacks shooting at each other. Sprague naturally defended Rawn. The colonel claimed that a mob of one hundred African-American men had been planning to attack the army camp on the twenty-second and that Rawn's actions saved the camp from this attack. Whether this contention is true or not, it is clear that Rawn did little more than react to a very real threat to his soldiers. Given the hostile environment in which the regiment found itself, it is a wonder that other, more serious, incidents did not take place. "The military in this quarter are surrounded by enemies," Sprague wrote, "and unless encouraged, even sustained, their exertions will be futile. Cattle and hogs are shot down at the white man's door, and the colored man, as well as the lawless white assassins, or robbers, roams at large, gun in hand, in utter defiance of any authority."[1]

In short, the situation was a complete mess and there was little the soldiers could do about it. Nearly everyone, white and black, hated the troops, and the feeling was very mutual. In 1869 the regiment enthusiastically received orders to proceed west to Montana Territory. One can only imagine the joy the soldiers must have felt at receiving the news of their deliverance from the boiling kettle of race hatred in Jacksonville.

Ironically, in the West they found themselves in the middle of more racial tension. The government had established a series of forts along the river systems of Montana and had enacted a reservation policy for the local Indians, primarily members of tribes known to whites as Sioux and Crow. The government provided a modest amount of food, clothing, and shelter for those tribes that remained on the reservation land the government had mostly chosen for them. In addition, Washington pledged to protect them from the incursions of unscrupulous furriers, traders, and whiskey hawkers. The Crows enjoyed friendly relations with the government and considered whites to be good friends. They lived peacefully on their reservation, run by an agency administered under the control of the Department of the Interior. The Sioux, bitter enemies of the Crows, were another matter. Warlike, defiant, and proud, the Sioux chafed at the unwelcome presence on their traditional lands of the U.S. government and its retinue of soldiers and settlers.

By 1871 the 7th Regiment had scattered among various forts in Montana. The main headquarters was located at Fort Shaw, about fifteen miles west of present-day Great Falls. The numbers of the 7th had been augmented by consolidation with the 36th Infantry Regiment, which now ceased to exist. In the fall of 1871, the headquarters contingent at Fort Shaw received word that a renegade band of whiskey and ammunition traders had come down from Canada and encroached on Indian lands. The traders were of mixed Indian and white heritage (brusquely called half-breeds by nineteenth-century soldiers and Native Americans alike).

Government policy forbade this kind of illicit commerce, so two companies of Cottonbalers, B and H, were dispatched from Fort Shaw to put it to an end. This small force served under the capable command of Captain Henry B. Freeman, an experienced officer. Freeman was born in Ohio in 1837 to parents with New England roots. From his earliest age he dreamed of soldiering. At the tender age of fifteen, he joined the 10th Infantry and served with that unit until his sergeant discovered he had lied about his age and sent him home. The onset of the Civil War afforded a grown-up Freeman plenty of opportunity for martial life. He served with bravery and distinction, even earning the Medal of Honor. At the Battle of Chickamauga he was captured, and he spent the rest of the war in Libby Prison, a crowded warehouse jail for Union officers in the Confederate capital of Richmond. Freeman repeatedly tried to escape the misery of Libby—one time he got outside the walls only to be caught—until he finally got away for good and made his way to General William T. Sherman's forces on February 14, 1865. After the war, Freeman married, fathered two sons, and decided to make a career of the Army.[2]

On October 20 Freeman and his troops left Fort Shaw and headed northeast in the direction of the traders' camp near Fort Belknap. On November 2 they found the camp and quickly destroyed it. "The surprise of the camp was complete," Freeman wrote. "No resistance was offered at any stage of our proceedings. I . . . had all the Half-Breeds brought in and explained to them as clearly as I could . . . that they were there in violation of our laws, had been selling the Indians liquor and ammunition and purchasing stolen property from them . . . that they, the Half-Breeds, had done this for a long time, but it would no longer be permitted and they must leave the country at once." The traders professed ignorance of the laws, apologized, and eventually moved on.

The two companies remained in place for a couple weeks to make sure the traders complied and then left on November 16. The troops had, as yet, faced no real danger during this mission, but that soon changed on the journey back to Fort Shaw. One of the soldiers' greatest enemies, nature, reared its ugly head on the twenty-fourth. During the morning hours of that day, the men marched uneventfully in windy, but temperate, weather. Around noon everything changed. Suddenly the temperature dropped radically—Freeman estimated that it fell twenty degrees in one hour—and a huge snowstorm raged, accompanied by piercing winds. Freeman's men were not prepared for this kind of inclement weather. They did not have adequate clothing or footgear, and they were still miles away from Fort Shaw.[3]

The men went through agony in the swirling storm. "The howling wind drove the coarse snow, as hard and cutting as grains of sand, straight into our faces," one soldier recalled, "in a few minutes all land marks were obscured. Some men cried and begged to be permitted to lie down and die. Cries that feet, hands and parts of the face were freezing were heard on all sides."[4] Sergeant William Molchert, a German emigrant who had made B Company his home since 1870, told of how badly the cold affected one of his NCO colleagues: "I very well recollect the case of [Sergeant] Pearein of my company who ran ahead of the company to keep warm, laid frozen on the ground when we got up to him. He lost both feet and hands."[5] The men had no choice but to keep moving and hope for the best, finally reaching Fort Shaw the next day. Over half the men suffered frozen body parts, and almost twenty had to have feet, toes, or hands amputated.[6]

THE NEXT FEW YEARS SAW THE ODD SKIRMISH HERE AND there, but mostly the regiment went about its usual garrison routine—building roads and forts, surveying land, or patrolling. Once more, the Army had undergone an extensive demobilization after the Civil War.

Companies numbered anywhere between twenty-five and fifty men, and the Army was expected to act exclusively as a continental force, policing the final frontiers of America. The Civil War, and its resultant universal military experience for American males, had had an impact on the way Americans viewed the military, though. Most Americans still frowned on the notion of spending their lives in the Army, but they better understood those who chose to do so and even afforded them a kind of grudging respect. In a general sense there was now a better comprehension of soldiers and their travails, if only because so many Americans had lived that life themselves during the war years.

Probably for these reasons, the composition of the Army, and correspondingly the 7th Regiment, changed a bit during the immediate post–Civil War period. Emigrants from England, Ireland, and Germany still accounted for almost half the strength of the outfit, but native-born Americans—almost all of them from northern states—entered the ranks in growing numbers. The foreign-born joined the Army for the reasons they always had, namely, disassociation with their new country, along with limited economic and social opportunities. The native-born soldiers were mostly farm boys and small-town kids longing for excitement and adventure in the overpublicized West. Upon joining the Army they signed up for five-year hitches and made thirteen dollars a month. The officers were almost all veterans of the Civil War. Some predated the war. Others joined the Army at the war's start and ended up choosing a career in the service because they liked soldiering. A few were green second lieutenants fresh out of West Point, but not many. In total, the officers during the final frontier period proved to be one of the most experienced and sagacious groups in the history of the regiment.[7]

One author conducted an extensive investigation into the composition of K Company's enlisted ranks during this period in the regiment's history. He found that, of twenty-three enlisted men, eleven were reenlistees, five were Civil War veterans, and nine were foreign-born. The men ranged in height from five-three to five-nine and weighed between 130 and 150 pounds. They had a wide range of complexions from ruddy to dark or fair, and their eye and hair color was the usual mix among the white population of the time. They ranged in age from seventeen to forty-four years old. Many had no education, but those who did tended to serve in positions of responsibility.[8]

Life for these men generally consisted of rigid, dull routine. They woke early in the morning and drilled, built, worked, and cleaned until night. Breakfast consisted of hash or stew accompanied by hard bread and coffee. The lunch menu featured stringy beef, salt pork, bacon, maybe a few potatoes, and more coffee. The men often augmented their standard rations by cultivating gardens.

Naturally those who sought adventure and heroic immortality in the annals of western lore grew disenchanted with this dronelike existence. Some deserted, but most hung on and finished their enlistments, marrying and settling in the West. However, every now and then adventure beckoned. Such was the case in the summer of 1876 when relations between the U.S. government and the Sioux deteriorated. The 7th Regiment received orders to leave Fort Shaw and participate in a punitive campaign against the Sioux, a prospect most of the soldiers warmly welcomed, not because of any particular grudge against the Sioux but as a departure from the monotony of fort life.

The seeds of this campaign had been sown years earlier with the Treaty of 1868, which had established a large Sioux reservation in Dakota Territory. Some of the Sioux settled on this reservation while others, under the notable leadership of Sitting Bull and Crazy Horse, resisted the treaty and settled farther west in Montana in an area bordered by the Powder River. After discovery of gold in the Black Hills of the Sioux reservation in Dakota in 1874, the U.S. government tried to negotiate the purchase of the hills with the Sioux. This purchase attempt failed largely because of the recalcitrance of nontreaty chiefs such as Sitting Bull and Crazy Horse. These men felt abject contempt for whites, whom they considered avaricious and untrustworthy. The government tried to get tough with them and curtail their independence in 1875 by ordering them to report to their reservation's administrative agencies by January 31, 1876. If they did not report, they would risk war with the United States. Predictably, they failed to report, so the Department of the Interior formally turned the matter over to the War Department in February 1876. This meant war.

The Army estimated that the hostile Indians numbered no more than a few hundred. This would be a quick and easy victory—or so the brass thought. The commanders planned a three-pronged advance on the Sioux, who they believed were hiding out in eastern Montana or northern Wyoming. One column, eventually under the command of Brigadier General Alfred Terry, would advance westward from the Dakotas into Montana. Another, under Brigadier General George Crook, would move northward from Wyoming toward the Yellowstone River in Montana. The third column, under Colonel John Gibbon, consisted of the Cottonbalers and elements of the 2nd Cavalry Regiment. This force would move eastward and link up with Terry coming from the east. The generals hoped these three prongs would pin down the hostile Indians and force them to do battle or surrender. This hope proved to be far more difficult in implementation than in theory.

On March 17, 1876, Companies A, B, E, H, I, and K of the 7th Regiment left Fort Shaw and proceeded south in a terrible snowstorm and subzero temperatures. Eugene Geant, an adventure-seeking private in H Company, kept a journal of his experiences in the Sioux campaign: "There was about a foot of snow . . . and we marched 8 miles the first day. The marching is bad and we are all tired as we get into camp. It is cold. We have to shovel the snow away to pitch our tents, and build big fires to dry the ground. As soon as we had our supper each man took off his shoes and greased them for the next day. The worst is the snow will penetrate through the leather of the shoes, and the shoes are too low, allowing the snow to get in at the top."[9] Another soldier, Lieutenant William L. English, a Civil War veteran who had made a career in the Army after the war, also kept a journal in which he commented on the soul-trying conditions: "Heavy and cold wind all day in our faces. [Lieutenant Frederick] Kendrick and Dr. Hart frozen in delicate place. Severest march I ever made. Good deal of drunkenness among the men."[10]

In the days ahead they pressed on, in spite of the horrendous weather, hoping to reach Fort Ellis to the southeast as soon as possible. There they would link up with the 2nd Cavalry and more Cottonbalers, including Gibbon. Along the way the weather soon took its toll. Two men deserted, taking off for nearby Helena, only to be apprehended and returned to their companies. The commander of the expeditionary force, Captain Rawn of Reconstruction fame, experienced terrible snow blindness, so much so that he had to cede command to Freeman, the next officer in line on the pecking order. Rawn was not alone in his affliction. Many other soldiers struggled with the blinding glare created by the sun's rays bouncing off fields of white snow. "The loss of sight comes on with a feeling such as is created by smoke in the eyes," wrote one officer, "that, if the case is a severe one, soon increases into the most intense burning pain. The eyes cannot bear the light and the eyeballs seem to roll in liquid fire with a grating feeling as though in contact with particles of sand. [Snow blindness] is mainly brought on by the exposure of the eyes to the glare of the sun upon the snow, but is accelerated and aggravated by high wind and flying snow."[11]

Freeman and his charges made it to Fort Ellis on March 28. So far they had traveled 190 miles. Here they met up with Gibbon and his forces, including E Company of the 7th, which had experienced its own hellish march 180 miles from Fort Baker through snow and cold. For a few days, the men laid up in camp as their commanders decided what to do next. Gibbon resolved to follow the north side of the Yellowstone River east until he joined hands with Terry in eastern Montana.[12]

Like the other officers, Gibbon could boast a wealth of military experience. In fact, he was unquestionably one of the best officers in the U.S. Army at that time. A consummate professional, Gibbon graduated from West Point in 1847 and served at the tail end of the Seminole Wars. For a time he became an artillery instructor at West Point, but he really hit his stride during the Civil War when he commanded the famous Iron Brigade and then ascended all the way to corps command and a brevet rank of two-star general. He fought bravely in some of the war's biggest battles, including Antietam, Fredericksburg, Gettysburg, Spotsylvania, and Petersburg. Several times he was decorated for gallant and meritorious service. After the war he served as colonel of the 36th Infantry until that organization was melded with the 7th in 1869 and Gibbon took over command of the Cottonbalers, succeeding Sprague. By 1876 Gibbon was serving in two capacities: as commanding officer of the 7th Regiment, of which he was colonel, and as commander of the District of Western Montana. In the latter post he functioned as a brevet general (his soldiers often called him General Gibbon even though his actual rank was colonel).[13] This profusion of responsibilities and titles was not at all uncommon in the nineteenth-century Army, especially in the wake of the Civil War, when many regular officers had served as generals in state volunteer units only to revert to their permanent Regular Army ranks after the conflict.

Not surprisingly, Gibbon's men almost universally respected him as a fine officer and combat leader. The lone exception seems to have been the 2nd Cavalry's surgeon, Dr. Holmes Offley Paulding, who thought Gibbon appallingly neglectful of medical matters.[14] The good doctor was in the minority, though. Gibbon's officers and men had confidence in his leadership.

In early April, Gibbon's redoubled force began moving according to his plan—eastward along the north shore of the Yellowstone. The river bent in many different directions, meaning the soldiers had to cross it at shallow points, occasionally even several times a day. They would take off their shoes and socks, plunge into the cold water, and forge ahead as quickly as possible. They braved yet another snowstorm and then muddy, wet roads when the weather warmed up slightly. From April 9 through 12 they got a chance to stay in camp for a few days while Gibbon attempted to persuade the Crows to join his forces as scouts.

The story of Gibbon's recruiting pitch presents an interesting clash of cultures. He wanted twenty-five Crows to serve as guides. This practice was quite common during the so-called Indian Wars. The U.S. Army often made use of Native Americans from one tribe while the Army made war on that tribe's enemies. These scouts formally enlisted into the Army (usually for three to six months) and were paid like regular soldiers, even though they were not always treated as such. They often wore red armbands or headbands, along with some kind of amalgamation of the standard blue tunic and trouser uniform of the nineteenth-century Army.

One of the regimental officers witnessed Gibbon's sales pitch: "'I have come down here to make war on the Sioux,' the colonel said. 'The Sioux are your enemy and ours. For a long while they have been killing white men and killing Crows. I am going to punish the Sioux for making war upon the white man. If the Crows want to make war upon the Sioux, now is their time. If they want to drive them from their country and prevent them from sending war parties into their country to murder their men, now is their time. White men and red men make war in a different way. The white man goes through the country with his head down and sees nothing. The red man keeps his eyes open and can see better than a white man. Now, I want some young warriors of the Crow tribe to go along with me, who will use their eyes and tell me what they see.' "[15]

The pep talk went over like the proverbial lead balloon and Gibbon was astonished, as he himself later recalled: "Somewhat to my surprise the proposition did not appear to be favorably received, and when an Indian does not want to do a thing he resembles a white man a good deal, and has a thousand and one excellent reasons why he should not do it. [The Crows] listened in silence to the interpreter as he translated . . . what I said. The talk was received in silence, followed by a very earnest discussion amongst themselves, after which two of the principal chiefs, Iron Bull and Blackfoot, replied."[16]

Blackfoot came forward, shook hands with Gibbon, and spoke: "'The white people want us to assist them. I do not know the ways of the whites, my people do not know their ways. All other Indian tribes do evil to the whites, but I and my people hold fast to them with love. I have something to say to you and the Great Father [president]. We are not given enough flour and beef. You ask for some of our young men. If they go, it is their right, but if they are unwilling to go, I can not compel them.'"[17] This was the Native American version of a concept familiar to whites: we'll take it under advisement. Even the Crows, who enjoyed friendly relations with whites, did not fully trust them.

The council broke up and Gibbon, completely nonplussed, contemplated the prospect of going into Sioux territory with no scouts. As it turned out, he need not have worried. What he witnessed at the council was a generational divide among the Crows. The older men had no desire to accompany Gibbon's forces and make war on the Sioux. The younger men felt different. Some of them hungered for revenge on their enemies. Others felt their honor demanded that they go. The morning after the council, twenty-five Crows came forward and volunteered their services in a simple ritual. Gibbon was thrilled: "All the volunteers were paraded, and an officer presented to each in succession a hunting knife, on the point of which each one gravely placed the tip of his forefinger and the deed was done. They thus became United States soldiers for three months, and were to receive soldier's pay, rations, and clothing."[18]

Gibbon immediately placed his new charges under the command of a dashing young officer named James H. Bradley. Born in Sandusky, Ohio, in May 1844, Bradley served in the Civil War, enlisting in the 14th Ohio at the age of seventeen. He completed his term of enlistment in that outfit and then enlisted in the 45th Ohio, with which he finished the war after many western theater battles. He spent half a year in a Confederate prisoner-of-war camp and fought at such battles as Kennesaw Mountain, Jonesboro, Franklin, and Nashville. Bradley secured a regular commission after the war, eventually ending up in the 7th Infantry in late 1871. He wedded Mary Beech, the daughter of an Atlanta physician, and had two daughters with her.

Lithe and strong, Bradley was an excellent horseman who betrayed no fear to his men. He was the type of man who could not sit still, busying himself with whatever duties he could find. He rarely harassed his men, preferring instead to lead by example. In short, he was a good officer, courageous, resourceful, energetic, and thoughtful. His men thought highly of him, and his superiors had confidence in him. Bradley earned a reputation as someone who knew how to scout and reconnoiter, and this is probably why Gibbon chose him as commander of the newly recruited Crows. Throughout the Sioux campaign, Bradley spent much time away from the main column, functioning, like any good scout, as the eyes and ears of Gibbon's command.

Thoughtful and scholarly, Bradley kept a diary that stands as the best single document on the 7th Regiment's role in the Sioux campaign of 1876. Tremendously excited to be appointed scout commander, Bradley described his Crow allies: "The warriors are mostly young men of less than thirty years of age, but two are veterans of middle age and two more, old men over sixty, who are expected to do little service beyond giving the young fellows the benefit of their encouragement and advice. They furnish their own arms, all carrying good breech-loaders except two, one of whom has a revolver and the other a bow and arrows."

Gibbon's forces now numbered close to 450 men, including six companies of the 7th Infantry under Captain Freeman, along with four companies of the 2nd Cavalry. They were supported by a twelve-pound "Napoléon" gun and two Gatling guns. Transportation consisted of horses for officers and cavalrymen and thirty-six wagons for the infantrymen. Actually, many of the infantrymen walked, because wagon space was at a premium, since wagons were used for supplies (logistics were a constant headache in the remote areas of Montana).

Day after day that spring, Gibbon's force marched east, scouting for Sioux, camping, and dealing with the elements. One day Bradley and his scouts found markings left behind by none other than Captain William Clark of Lewis and Clark fame. The men immediately set about making their own inscriptions on the soft sandstone near where they found Clark's message (which read: "Wm. Clark, July 25, 1806"). Bradley commented that "it still appears as distinctly as when graven there seventy years ago." Then Bradley noticed a cavalryman writing too close to Clark's precious scrawl: "A cavalry vandal today disfigured the inscription by carving his own name over the letter 'K,' for which he deserves to be pilloried."[19] Bradley claimed that when rebuked, the man professed complete ignorance of the Lewis and Clark expedition. One can only imagine the erudite young officer shaking his head in abject disgust.

In the middle of May, Bradley's scouts began to pick up signs of

Sioux, the most prominent of which were large herds of buffalo. Bradley knew that where there were large numbers of buffalo there were often Sioux. After a harrowing scouting mission of several days in the vicinity of the Tongue River, one that saw his force sneak up to within seeing distance of a large Sioux village, Bradley's men rode back to the main column and related what they had seen. Gibbon immediately made preparations to sneak up on the village and attack it.

His scouts had achieved the most difficult accomplishment in the Indian Wars of the upper plains — finding the hostile tribes. Usually the hostile Indians ran rings around the heavily laden army columns as they thrashed about ostentatiously in land they did not know. The Native Americans knew the terrain, the weather patterns, the trails, the water sources, and the tendencies of their enemies. That meant the Native Americans could usually choose battle on their own terms. The situation was roughly analogous to the daunting task a later generation of Cottonbalers faced in trying to find an elusive enemy in the jungles and rice paddies of Vietnam.

Thus Gibbon knew he could not afford to let this opportunity slip away. If he was to have any chance of surprising the Sioux, he had to find a way for his whole force to cross the Tongue River. "Now the wagons, covered with infantrymen, start in," he related, "and as they approach the deepest part some of the smaller mules barely have their backs above the water, but still they struggle on. The mules struggle and plunge, fall down and get up again, the drivers, outsiders and men shout out their loudest yells to encourage the frantic animals, and at last the long line of wagons reaches the opposite shore, water pouring from every crack in the wagon bodies, which makes us hope that the bottom layer of each load is bacon rather than 'hardtack' and bedding. Our dripping teams are given a short rest, mounted officers and men pour the water from their boots."[20]

In the end the crossing was a dismal failure. Gibbon could not get all of his troops successfully across the Tongue. For over four hours they tried to cross. Surprisingly, the biggest problem was getting the cavalry across, not the ponderous infantry. Private Geant watched the debacle unfold: "Four day's rations were issued to the command and three days [sic] to be carried by pack mules. Each man was to carry 100 rounds of ammunition, one blanket or a great coat. Our mounted detachment [of infantry] crossed the river, swimming their horses and holding on by the mane or tail. The cavalry were to follow, but were unable to cross their horses, and, after drowning five horses, they gave up the attempt. The expedition had to be given up."[21] As it turned out, the Sioux village contained many of those who later massacred Lieutenant Colonel George Custer's troops at Little Bighorn. Whether this would have been prevented if Gibbon could have pulled off his attack will never be known.

A week later, Gibbon's men found out, in horrifying fashion, that the Sioux knew of their presence. Three men left camp to go hunting, something fairly routine, but in this case the men went without permission. They paid a steep price for their unauthorized expedition. Captain Freeman described in his journal what happened: "Shots were heard on the bluffs [above the camp], and in a few moments it transpired that two cavalrymen . . . and a citizen teamster named Quinn had gone out hunting without permission and, attracted by a pony, had been surrounded and killed. [Paulding] with Cav. escort went out and brought the bodies in, but one was scalped, a soldier. One of them had a butcher knife fixed in either side of the head. The men had been shot from above and at close range. The bodies were filled with bullets."[22]

Dr. Paulding recorded a more detailed, if grislier, report on the fate of the three men: "The citizen teamster, Quin[n], and Reyhmeyer of Co. H, 2nd [Cavalry], lay together and Stoker the other H Co. man had crossed the ridge about 75 yds. And was shot from behind and rolled down followed by the Indians who scalped him and drove two knives into his brain, above and below his left ear, out of his face, and shot him full of bullet holes. Reyhmeyer had his head mashed in with the butt of a gun and all the bodies were riddled with balls and mutilated. The wounds were inflicted . . . both before and after death. Each man having received several, each one of which alone would have been mortal." Lieutenant John F. McBlain, a cavalry officer who helped Paulding retrieve the bodies, summed up the experience mournfully: "The sight of them was one not soon to be forgotten."[23]

The soldiers now began to spot large numbers of Indians in the area, especially on the bluffs near where the three men had been killed. With the enemy so close, Gibbon ordered new security precautions. "Every morning," Geant wrote, "the whole command turns out at 2 o'clock, and forms a skirmish line around and 500 yards from camp, remaining there until broad daylight." In Lieutenant McBlain's view, the camp was now "arranged nicely for defensive purposes. The soldierly instincts of the commander [Gibbon] appreciated the necessity for constant vigilance and preparation. The wagon train was in an almost circular corral, around which were camped the six companies of infantry; at the open or entrance side of the [horse] corral was camped the four troops of cavalry."[24] All of this enhanced security, but it did not do any damage to the enemy.

In early June, the column dealt with more inclement weather, this time a bizarre snowstorm that dumped nearly a foot of snow on the cold, shivering soldiers. Food supplies ran low and the men subsisted on half rations for a few days. The frustration of being toyed with by an elusive enemy, along with the half rations, the desolate surroundings, and the harsh weather, all led to tension among the soldiers, especially the officers. At an officers' gathering in late May, Bradley and Captain William Logan, an Irish-born officer who had been commissioned out of the ranks during the Civil War, got into a silly, rum-induced argument over the veracity of Bradley's scouting reports. Freeman felt that Bradley "made an ass of himself," and Paulding wrote that Logan behaved with utter "foolishness."[25] Interestingly enough, Bradley never mentioned the altercation in his diary. Nothing ever came of the spat.

Of course Freeman himself was not immune to such steam-blowing rows with fellow officers. For over two months, ever since the unit had left Fort Shaw, Freeman had found himself becoming increasingly irritated with Captain James Sanno, a West Point graduate whose service with the regiment dated back to the summer of 1863. Sanno daily complained about the rotten roads and weather, annoying the no-nonsense Freeman, who could not see the point in such carping. He grew to dislike Sanno with a steady intensity and finally lost patience with what he considered to be Sanno's insubordinate manner. Freeman charged Sanno with insubordination, but Gibbon later persuaded him to drop the charges and return Sanno to duty.[26]

Deeper into June the campaign finally came to a climax when the Gibbon, Terry, and Custer columns were finally able to coordinate and communicate better than before (Crook had been turned back on June 17 because of a sharp and costly fight with the Indians known as the Battle of Rosebud). The brass now believed that the main Sioux camp was in the Little Bighorn valley. They decided to close in for the kill. In the most basic sense, the plan called for Custer's 7th Cavalry to pressure the Sioux from the south, flushing the Indians like quail straight into Terry and Gibbon approaching from the north along the Yellowstone River. Gibbon and his men watched Custer's troops leave camp in the early afternoon of June 22. Mounted on their horses, flying their guidons, the troopers made for a splendid sight. Gibbon remembered sharing a special moment with Custer before he left: "As he turned to leave us I made some pleasant remark, warning him against being greedy, and with a . . . wave of his hand he called back, 'No, I will not,' and rode off after his command. Little did we think we had seen him for the last time."[27]

The fate of Custer and his men is so well-known that it requires no retelling here. After Custer left camp, the Cottonbalers spent several days carrying out their part of the plan. They marched in searing heat over difficult country, short of water. "It was a rough country, over hills and ravines," Geant recalled. "I was awfully thirsty . . . my lips and tongue being parched and chapped. The commanding officer sent a party of cavalry ahead with all of the canteens they could carry, to bring water back to the infantry." Geant received a welcome drink of water only to faint from the heat. He soon felt better, at least until he and the other men got rained on and were forced to camp in sticky mud.[28]

On the same day Geant scribbled in his journal, Bradley also found time to relate the situation as he saw it: "We are now fairly en route to the Indian village, which is supposed to be on the Little Big Horn. It is undoubtedly a large one, and should Custer's command and ours unite, we, too, will have a large force numbering all told about one thousand men, armed with the splendid breech-loading Springfield rifles and carbines, caliber forty-five."[29] Indeed, those Springfields were formidable weapons in the hands of the well-trained Cottonbalers. This modified rifle afforded greater firepower than ever before. The soldier loaded single shots into the breech, not the muzzle, and there was no longer any need for a percussion cap. By most estimates a decent rifleman could squeeze off twelve shots per minute.

On the twenty-fifth, of course, Custer met with his fabled disaster. Captain Freeman cryptically recounted the activities of the 7th Regiment that day: "Left Camp at 5 AM, moved 2 ½ miles up Tullock [Fork], took to hills and crossed to Big Horn. Marched 19 miles through dry, rough country. Very hot. No water. Men played out when we reached river. Halted 2 hours. Crows . . . brought in word that there was a large village on the [Little Bighorn]. Rained all night. Slept against a (tree) trunk."[30] The next day featured more of the same, only now the men began to see ominous signs of Custer's demise, the most notable of which was the testimony of three of his Crow scouts who had managed to escape the massacre. "They reported that Custer had attacked the village and had been annihilated," Captain Walter Clifford, commander of E Company, 7th Infantry, recorded in his personal diary. The Crows claimed that "soldiers were shot down like buffalo." Their panicked stories sowed terror among Bradley's Crow scouts, many of whom urged the white men not to go on. Several of the Crows deserted.

From his vantage point in the column, Lieutenant English watched all of this with dismay and, like many other officers that day, clung to the vain hope that the Crows were mistaken: "This news I was sorry to hear and tried to argue myself into the belief that it was not true. We marched on however and at two o'clock P.M. forded the Little Big Horn about four miles above its mouth. Inspection of arms was had and ammunition carefully examined, and every man provided with sixty rounds." The soldiers fully expected to be attacked at nightfall: "We halted and formed a square, expecting they would attack us, and slept on our arms that night in position, but no attack was made and the night passed quietly."[31]

As the sun rose to greet another steamy day, the soldiers tensely prepared to resume their march, breakfasting on bacon, hardtack, and coffee. They moved out along a crude trail, their heads craning and their eyes straining for any sign of the Sioux. They could sense the presence of the enemy out there somewhere, and the feeling was eerie. Some of the soldiers glimpsed strange smoke signals in the distance and even shapes and forms they supposed to be men. Late in the morning they found an abandoned Indian village with tepee poles, pots, kettles, robes, and other clothing. They also found several dead Sioux and a bloody shirt belonging to one of Custer's officers.

Not long after this portentous discovery, they sighted men on a ridge some two or three miles away. At first, they could not figure out if these men were Indians or cavalry. Almost involuntarily the column began to move faster, as if no one could stand another minute of the tension of not knowing who was on the ridge. Then someone called out, "They are white men!" Sure enough, it was the 7th Cavalry, or at least the remnants of it under Major Marcus Reno. They were overjoyed to see Gibbon's men because they could not have held out much longer in the event of more Indian attacks. Reno's men had no idea of Custer's whereabouts or disposition, because they had spent much of the last thirty-six hours fighting for their lives against waves of Sioux warriors. Gibbon saw the evidence of this desperate fight: "Dead horses and mules were lying about in every direction, and in one little depression on the other slope of the main divide I counted forty-eight dead animals. Here and there, these had evidently been made use of as breastworks, and along the top of the ridge holes and rifle-pits extended, connecting the two lines [of soldiers]. On the far side of the ridge, the ground gradually fell away in lower ridges, behind which the Indians had sheltered themselves and their ponies during the fight."[32] Reno's men had also made use of hardtack boxes as cover. His group had lost fifty-six killed and fifty-nine wounded and could well have been annihilated if not for the timely arrival of the Cottonbalers and their comrades.

All this time, Bradley's troops had been operating two or three miles to the left and ahead of the main column, on the opposite side of the river, scouting for any sign of Custer or the Sioux. For much of the morning they could see small parties of Indians in the hills and underbrush ahead, apparently keeping a wary eye on them. Even as he kept close watch on the retreating Sioux, Bradley scouted the terrain. All at once, he smelled a powerful stench, an odor very familiar to him from his service in the Civil War. At the same time, he saw something out of the corner of his eye. A horse, reeking with the sickly waft of death, was lying on its back, legs straight up, not more than a few feet from Bradley. He stared at the horse for a second and then peered at the ground beyond the dead animal, really seeing the terrain for the first time. The sight that greeted his eyes made him shudder, and for a moment he felt as if he might pass out. Then he collected himself and called for a runner.

BACK AT THE MAIN COLUMN, GENERAL TERRY AND COLOnel Gibbon watched as a lone horseman, Bradley's runner (Private Henry Rice from H Company), rode across the river and up to them. Rice's face was pale and flushed and his voice trembled as he spoke: "I have a very sad report to make. I have counted one-hundred-ninety-seven bodies lying on the hills!" Horror-stricken, everyone stared at Private Rice for a few seconds. "White men?" Terry asked. "Yes, white men." Rice nodded in reply. Terry and Gibbon exchanged worried looks. They now knew that the Crows' reports were correct. Custer had met disaster; the only question was to what degree.

By now, Bradley knew all too well. He and his men picked over the battlefield, identifying what bodies they could, looking for survivors, searching the bodies of dead cavalry troopers and Indians. Bradley found the body of Custer and claimed that although the flamboyant officer had been stripped, his body had not been mutilated. Nor did it show signs of any particular trauma or violent death. The same could not be said of many others. Soon the main column reached the battlefield, and Gibbon saw firsthand the grisly remnants of what had happened there. "I came upon the body of a soldier lying on his face near a dead horse. He was stripped, his scalp gone, his head beaten in, and his body filled with bullet-holes and arrows. Close by was another body, also close to a dead horse, lying, like the other, on its face, but partially clothed, and this was recognized by one of our officers as the body of Captain [Donald] McIntosh."

At a distance, the stripped bodies of Custer's men had resembled nothing so much as white boulders. Up close, they were truly ghastly to behold. "The men . . . were . . . scalped and horribly mutilated," one soldier recalled. "There the bodies lay, mostly naked, and scattered over a field maybe half a mile square." As Captain Clifford surveyed the battlefield and saw the terrible aftermath of violent death, torture, and mutilation, waves of nausea simmered in his gut: "It is sickening to look at the stripped bodies. Here a hand gone, and here a foot or a head . . . gashes cut in all parts of the body; eyes gouged out, noses and ears cut off, and skulls crushed in." Another officer recalled that "eyes had been torn from their sockets, and hands . . . and arms, legs, and noses had been wrenched off. Many had their flesh cut in strips the entire length of their bodies, and there were others whose limbs were closely perforated with bullets, showing that the torture had been inflicted while the wretched victims were still alive."

Rather than allow his men to simply stand around the grassy slopes of the battle area, gawking at these horrible sights, Colonel Gibbon immediately set them about the task of cleaning up: "The command was placed in camp here, and details at once set to work to haul away the dead horses and bury the men, both of which were already becoming offensive."[33]

This work was gruesome. The soldiers had to pull arrows out of their dead comrades and, in the case of many, struggle to identify them. Many of the bodies had swollen to twice their normal size, the faces blackened from accelerated decay in the heat. The bodies oozed with noxious gases and liquids. Some were missing scalps. Some of the faces had been beaten so thoroughly as to be unrecognizable. All of the bodies stank beyond belief. The odor was unearthly, death personified. The steamy heat naturally made the stench even worse. For hours the men dug and scraped, laying the dead soldiers into shallow graves.

Other work details dealt with Reno's wounded, most of whom were lying on the same hot, dusty hill where they had made their determined stand against the Indians. Now they had no shelter and little medical care. Gibbon ordered them moved down to his camp in a fairly cool area near a creek bed. There the wounded waited and suffered, mostly in silence as Dr. Paulding did everything in his power to save their lives and make them comfortable. In Lieutenant McBlain's memory, the doctor was "here, there and everywhere . . . [alleviating] the suffering of those whose wounds were necessarily fatal, and who had lain out in the hot June sun for two days and a half." Paulding spent most of his time, though, helping "those whose wounds were less serious or painful" and could thus be saved.

Flies were attracted by the preponderance of dead flesh in the area. They descended on the wounded, eating away at their sores and pus. They inundated the dead and swarmed around the camp. "The repulsive . . . green flies that have been feasting on the swollen bodies of the dead, are attracted to the camp fires by the smell of cooking meat," a revolted Captain Clifford wrote. "They come in such swarms that a persevering swing of the tree branch is necessary to keep them from settling on the food. An instant's cessation of the motion of the branch and they pounce down upon the morsel that is being conveyed to the mouth. They crawl over the neck and face, into eyes and ears, under the sleeves with a greedy eagerness." The captain and many other men lost their appetites.

Meanwhile, the toughness of the wounded cavalrymen deeply impressed Gibbon: "I have seen in the course of my military life many wounded men, but I never saw any who endured suffering, privations, and the fatigue of travel, more patiently and cheerfully than those brave fellows of the Seventh Cavalry."[34] Predictably, the unwounded survivors of the 7th Cavalry were deeply infused with melancholy. Private Homer Coon, a Cottonbaler from G Company, watched the cavalrymen closely as they sat in stunned silence around camp: "Men . . . would sit in front of their dog tents with drawn faces thinking of their loved ones at home. It looked that way to me." The mournful mood affected everyone. A somber, brooding silence infused the whole camp. "We miss the laughing gaiety that usually attends a body of soldiery even on the battlefield," Captain Clifford commented. "Sorrow hangs like a pall over our every thought. Every sound comes to us in a muffled monotone."[35]

On the evening of the twenty-eighth, the Cottonbalers, along with surviving cavalrymen, attempted to carry the wounded by hand and by horse to the mouth of the Little Bighorn, where a steamboat waited. In the darkness, over thick terrain, with an unknown number of enemy perhaps lurking in the vicinity, the going was arduous. "We carried the wounded on litters on our shoulders," Private Geant recalled, "but we had to give it up. The distance was too great and we were all played out, so we went into camp at 2 a.m. I . . . dropped behind a sage brush and fell asleep."[36] They had covered only four and a half miles.

Everyone realized that a better way of transporting the wounded had to be devised. First Lieutenant Gustavus Doane of the 2nd Cavalry took charge and supervised the building of improvised litters. Freeman described them: "The litters were made of two poles 16 feet long, a crossbar 4 feet from either end, a lacing of rawhide [skinned from dead horses] between the bars upon which the wounded were laid. The ends of the long poles in front and rear of the crossbars made shafts into which the mules were put, and sling rope passed over the saddles. Each mule was led by a man on foot while two others walked at either side of the litter to steady it."[37]

Doane's ingenuity made the wounded a bit more comfortable, but the fact that they were moved in pitch-darkness still made for extreme difficulties, as Geant related: "We were lost half the time, one part of the command running against the other and challenging each other." The soldiers were extremely anxious that the Sioux would sneak up and attack at any moment: "It was very skittish work, sometimes the men being excited and thinking there were Indians in the vicinity. I believe that if one man had fired a shot one part of the command would have blazed into the other, thinking they were Indians. We arrived at the river at 3 O'Clock A.M. and transferred the wounded to the steamer. It was a trying night. I would never like to pass another like it. It was dark, there were no roads, the mules were unruly, the wounded were groaning and we were tired to death."[38] Like the previous night, the men collapsed into an exhausted sleep.

After resting near the river for a couple days, the Cottonbalers began searching for the Native American tribes that had wreaked such havoc on Custer. In the process the Cottonbalers sought to make contact with General Crook's column, which was thought to be approaching from the southwest. Gibbon attempted to order the Crows to leave camp and find Crook. They refused. Next a civilian teamster offered to do this dangerous job for the princely sum of fifteen hundred dollars. Gibbon scoffed and told him he would pay six hundred dollars — take it or leave it. On the night of July 4 the teamster left, but he wasn't gone long. He returned four days later, minus his rifle and equipment, claiming that he had narrowly escaped being caught by the Indians, proving once again that money cannot buy courage. Three Cottonbalers, Privates James Bell, William Evans, and Benjamin Stewart of E Company, now volunteered to do the job for nothing. They left on July 9, made it to Crook, and returned on the twenty-fifth. For this harrowing runner duty through country controlled by hostile Sioux they received national publicity and Medals of Honor.

For the rest of the summer, the 7th Regiment participated in the vain search for the Sioux, logging many more Montana miles and plenty more privation. The war between the U.S. government and the nontreaty Sioux, specifically Sitting Bull and Crazy Horse, continued in the years ahead, but it would not involve the Cottonbalers. The unit finally got back to Fort Shaw on October 6 having logged about seventeen hundred miles of marching during the summer.[39]

THE ONLY SIZABLE BATTLE THE 7TH REGIMENT FOUGHT during the entire post–Civil War period of Indian conflict occurred in the summer of 1877. The men of the regiment had served as pursuers, saviors, medics, and undertakers during the Sioux campaign of 1876, but the next summer saw them function as bona fide combatants. The adversary this time was the Nez Percé tribe, whose grievances with Uncle Sam sprouted from deep roots. In 1863 they had signed a treaty with the government that shrank their reservation from what the government had originally awarded them in 1855. They had done so under pressure from both the government and settlers who hungered for gold that had been discovered in the mountainous areas of Nez Percé land. Those who signed the treaty settled along Idaho's Clearwater River, but as with the Sioux, there were many Nez Percés who did not sign the treaty and lived wherever they pleased in Oregon, Washington, and portions of Montana. In the early 1870s, as more settlers moved into the areas populated by nontreaty Nez Percés, they lobbied the government to remove the Indians to the established reservation in Idaho. At first the government refused. President Ulysses S. Grant even set aside much of the Wallowa Valley, home to a charismatic nontreaty chief named Joseph, as a reservation for his people.

The trouble started when the Grant government rescinded this order after vociferous pressure from Oregonians. This waffling naturally infuriated the nontreaty chiefs, and they debated among themselves what to do about it. After fierce debate, they decided to stay in place and do whatever they could to live in peace with the whites. This wise decision did nothing to defuse tension between young Indians (who burned at the injustice of the government's flip-flop) and white settlers, who cared little for the Indians or their ways.

In the fall of 1876 the government tried to buy the land from the nontreaty Nez Percés, but these tumultuous negotiations went nowhere. The chiefs tried to explain their religious ties to the land they occupied, but these explanations fell on deaf ears, even among government commissioners who felt great sympathy and respect for the Native Americans. The government essentially gave them two choices: sell or be forcibly removed to the Idaho reservation. In early June 1877 they finally decided to move. The chiefs who made this decision could not control all of their people, especially young men angered at their forcible removal from tribal lands and imbued with hatred for whites. This festering tension sparked violence on June 13–14 when a group of young Native American men, fortified with liquid courage, killed four white settlers who were known for treating Indians poorly.

In spite of the best efforts of cooler heads on both sides, these dogs of war, once unleashed, could not be contained. The area spiraled into violence. On one occasion seventeen whiskey-sodden Nez Percés killed fifteen settlers over the course of two bloody days. General Oliver Howard, a devout Christian and idealist, who thought of himself as the Indians' friend, began to gather infantry and cavalry forces to track down, punish, and properly relocate the renegade nontreaty bands of Nez Percés. Howard's vision was to capture wayward Native Americans, give them proper schooling, convert them to Christianity, and blend them into American society as humanely as possible. Nonetheless, throughout June and July his troops, augmented by local volunteers, fought several pitched battles with the Indians. The Nez Percés generally got the better of these struggles. They now hoped to leave Idaho, enter Montana, lie low for a while in lands controlled by their friends the Crows, and then bide their time until passions cooled enough for them to return to their homeland. The Nez Percés did not quite comprehend that they would still be fugitives in Montana. They did not understand that Montana and Idaho were of one mind, full of people who shared a collective identity as U.S. citizens under the government in Washington, D.C.[40]

None of this involved the Cottonbalers until the Nez Percés began moving east, into Montana. Here the Native Americans planned to make a right turn and follow the Bitterroot valley south. It just so happened that the Army was in the process of establishing a small post—to be named Fort Missoula for the town it guarded—in the exact path of the Indians. Companies A and I of the 7th Infantry had been there since late June building the post. Their commander, the ubiquitous Captain Rawn, heard in July that the Nez Percé tribesmen and women were heading his way, and immediately set to work preparing a defensive position. One of the soldiers under Rawn's command, Sergeant Charles N. Loynes, described the hurried preparations: "We at once commenced to fortify our camp as best we could, by throwing up rifle pits, cutting away the brush that would shelter the Indians, and piling up the sacks of grain in such a position as to give protection to the wives and children of officers and the laundresses of the companies."[41]

But the Indians were not coming straight at the camp. Their path would take them seven miles south through the natural thoroughfare of the area, a mountain pass named the Lolo trail (the soldiers called it Lou Lou). Knowing this, Rawn organized a mixed force of about one hundred regulars and local volunteers to intercept them. "My intentions were to compel the Indians to surrender their arms and ammunition," wrote Rawn, "and to dispute their passage, by force of arms, into Bitter Root Valley."[42] The Nez Percés soon arrived. Sergeant Loynes went along with Rawn's force and recalled that "we soon arrived at the entrance to the pass . . . and with our skirmish lines thrown out in front and on flank, we advanced to meet the Indians." Nez Percé skirmishers opened fire on them, and ineffective shooting took place for a few minutes back and forth. The Cottonbalers took cover and then began felling trees to set up breastworks. Late in the afternoon a drizzling rain began and seemingly washed away the civilian volunteers, most of whom decided that the job of dealing with about five hundred armed Nez Percés was best left to the soldiers.

For two days a stalemate reigned, as Rawn negotiated with the major Nez Percé chiefs—Joseph, Looking Glass, and White Bird. The Indians offered to give up their ammunition in return for safe passage through Lolo. Rawn refused, telling them that they had to surrender all arms and ammunition. The Indians promised to talk among themselves and get back to Rawn with an answer. As the Cottonbalers and the volunteers who remained in camp tensely waited behind their improvised breastworks for an attack or a surrender—whichever came first—the Native Americans quietly escaped.

Leaving behind a few fighters to hold the attention of Rawn's men, the main group—warriors, women, and children—climbed up a ravine and, using slopes and ridges out of Rawn's line of sight and effecting an almost complete circle around the soldiers, escaped. Rawn vainly pursued them, but they were long gone. In newspaper editorials he drew a significant amount of criticism for allowing them to escape, but in fairness to Rawn, there was little he could have done, outside of accomplishing the annihilation of his outnumbered and outgunned command, to impede the Nez Percés. His best hope would have been to delay them long enough for reinforcements to arrive, probably in the form of General Howard's troops pursuing from the west. Rawn did the best he could under the circumstances. In Loynes's estimation "a better officer never lived. That body of Indians could, if they wanted to, walk right over us." Moreover, Loynes claimed that the Nez Percés possessed more personal firepower "with weapons better than the soldiers had. We had single breech loaders." Many of the Indians had repeating carbines.[43]

Thus the migrant Nez Percés successfully entered the Bitterroot valley in late July. Here and there they trampled some crops, damaged some property, and stole some items, but generally they kept to themselves. Some settlers even befriended the Nez Percés and traded with them when they made it clear that they came in peace. In the meantime, Colonel Gibbon assembled Companies D, F, G, and K of the 7th Infantry at Fort Shaw and headed for Fort Missoula, where he combined with A and I companies on August 3. This force consisted of fifteen officers and 146 enlisted men (the companies were pitifully understrength, typical fare for the peacetime Army), along with about forty civilian volunteers and a twelve-pound howitzer. Rawn had been shadowing the Indians as they headed south in the Bitterroot valley, so Gibbon, unlike the summer before, at least had some inkling of the direction his quarry was headed.

For several days they pursued the Indians, who moved about twelve to fourteen miles per day through country they knew fairly well. According to Sergeant Loynes, the soldiers had a tougher time negotiating the difficult terrain: "We followed the Indians for five days, passing over the roughest country imaginable. In places the trail was so steep that the mules were detached from the army wagons, and with ropes were drawn up the steep sides." In the valley, the soldiers passed numerous unscathed small towns that had seen the Nez Percés only a day or two before. "They did not do very much damage," Private Coon of G Company reported, "except that the crops were trampled down by their ponies as they had about 1,000. They killed none of the settlers."[44]

The ambitious Lieutenant Bradley reported to Gibbon and proposed a plan. A cavalryman trapped in an infantry officer's body, Bradley suggested to Gibbon that he take a group of scouts, ride ahead, and act as the eyes and ears of the command. Bradley wanted to carry out a night scout, find the one thousand ponies Coon had mentioned, and stampede them just before dawn. In this way, Bradley could immobilize the migrating Nez Percé village while Gibbon's infantry closed in on them for the kill. Gibbon granted permission and Bradley set off on August 7 with a force of sixty mounted infantrymen and a few civilian volunteers. Bradley found the Indian village, but it was farther away than he had estimated and he sent word of this back to Gibbon, whose men were busily sweating and humping their way through thick mountain terrain.

Bradley's troops found hiding places a few miles from the Indian camp and waited for Gibbon's infantry to reach them. Worried that Bradley's men would soon be discovered and knowing that he was within striking distance of the village, Gibbon moved with as much haste as possible, but the wagons and camp equipment necessary to keep an infantry force properly supplied deep in the wilderness greatly slowed him down. "As our impatience to get forward increased," Gibbon said, "the difficulties of the route seemed to redouble. Again and again we recrossed the creek into the 'glades' on each side, struggling through thick timber and in places swampy flats, in which our wagon wheels sunk to the hub."[45] Finally, late in the afternoon, Gibbon decided to leave his supply wagons behind, tell his men to carry only the essentials for battle, and move forward as quickly as they could to link up with Bradley.

They found Bradley's men, still five miles shy of the Nez Percé camp, just before sunset on the evening of the eighth. For a few hours they rested and waited for the supply wagons to catch up with them, which they did after darkness, affording the opportunity for one last meal of hardtack and water. Bradley had found a trail that led straight to the Indian camp, in the Big Hole basin, a stretch of low, marshy ground near a glorified creek called the Big Hole River. Gibbon planned to line his soldiers up single file, proceed down the trail in the darkness, set up ambush positions around the camp, and attack at dawn. Again the men were only to carry what they would use in battle—rifles, ninety to one hundred rounds of ammunition, and maybe a few canteens. The wagon guards would drag the howitzer and spare ammunition to the ambush site at dawn and provide whatever fire support the coming battle required. All animals, except those belonging to Gibbon and a few other officers, would stay behind in a hastily improvised corral near Placer Creek.

At eleven o'clock they set out, with Bradley's men leading the way. The force now consisted of 149 soldiers and thirty-five civilian volunteers, each of them keeping as quiet as possible. The night was moonless, clear, starry, and cool. The soldiers, stumbling here and there, becoming separated from one another every now and then, made their way through alternating pinewoods and marshlands for three miles. Most of them, at some point, stepped into muck that reached the tops of their inadequate shoes. Each man simply concentrated on keeping sight of the person ahead of him and moving wherever the column was supposed to go. Soon they came to foothills overlooking the small valley that gently led to the Big Hole River. Gibbon was astounded that the Indians had not posted scouts and skirmishers along this route, but he wondered if perhaps the Nez Percés planned this strange omission as some kind of trap. Actually, this was an uncharacteristic oversight for the wily and formidable enemy.

Slowly but steadily the soldiers walked in the dead of night and emerged from the foothills, with the river to their right. All of a sudden, they saw campfires in the distance, across the river. Some men could even make out the silhouettes of tepees. For a split second, they recoiled at the sight of "moving bodies directly in our path on the sidehill." This was only a Nez Percé horse herd. The horses gently neighed and dogs in the village barked a bit, but these noises did not alert the Indians. Relieved, the soldiers gingerly moved into ambush positions two hundred yards away from the camp. A little later, Private Patrick

Fallon of I Company did something stupid that risked the lives of the entire 7th Regiment. "[He] could not resist an inclination to smoke, so he lighted a match for that purpose," Loynes related, "but soon discovered that he had made a mistake." A nearby officer quickly extinguished the match and undoubtedly rebuked Fallon in manner, if not in speech. Even so, Gibbon thought that Fallon should have been "shot on the spot or knocked over with the butt of a musket." The need for absolute silence spared Fallon from such a draconian fate.

For at least two hours, the Cottonbalers waited in the scrub brush and watched the village, their mouths dry, their hearts pounding with anticipation. In spite of the darkness, Loynes could see activity in the village: "Now and then a tepee would flash . . . with light, as perhaps someone in it would throw a stick on the fire, for the nights were chilly there." Lieutenant Charles Woodruff, Gibbon's adjutant, remembered hearing "the cry of a wakeful child, and the gentle crooning of its mother as she hushed it to sleep."[46] The soldiers lay in ambush positions, shivered in their summer uniforms, and tried to suppress coughs and sneezes, all the while impatiently waiting for the first streaks of dawn and the command to attack.

Their commander was just as impatient. He knew he had achieved something exceedingly rare for an infantry unit in the Indian Wars. He had found an entire Indian village and maneuvered his troops into position for an ambush against a completely unsuspecting foe: "The most wonderful thing to me was that we had gotten into the very presence of the Indians without discovery. We were in precisely the position I desired. We were between the Indians and a large part of their herd."

For Gibbon, the question now was how to parlay this advantageous situation into accomplishing his mission of apprehending the nontreaty Nez Percés. Gibbon still planned to stampede the horses at dawn, but his civilian guide, Henry Bostwick, a man of considerable experience among Native Americans, talked Gibbon out of it, arguing that the Nez Percés would not leave their horses unguarded. Colonel Gibbon knew he did not have enough men to surround the village and capture its several hundred occupants, so he instead opted for a surprise attack, a standard army tactic—albeit one of questionable morality—against wayward Native American villages. Of course, at this point, the element of surprise was his greatest asset against an enemy that outnumbered him. The best way to take advantage of that asset, and protect the lives of his own soldiers, was to attack. Because the Nez Percés were separated from most of their horses, Gibbon felt he could launch his swift attack, keep the Indians from getting away, stun them into submission, and then simply round them up peacefully, thus limiting the bloodshed. Such are the moral vagaries of command deliberations. Having made his decision, Gibbon whispered orders for his men: "When you hear the first shot, fire three quick volleys and charge the village."

At 4:00 A.M. the men crept forward, even as the sun was about to rise to the east. On the extreme left, Bradley led with his mixed force of soldiers and civilian volunteers. In the middle Captain Sanno's K Company pressed ahead, while Captain Richard Comba's D Company did the same on the right. All three of these strike forces were moving from west to east. Following close behind, Company G, under Captain George Browning, A Company, under Captain Logan, F Company, under Captain Constant Williams, and I Company, under Captain Rawn, remained in reserve. All along the thin skirmish line, the men could smell the swampy mix of river and mud around them as they duck-walked and crawled through the underbrush as quietly as they possibly

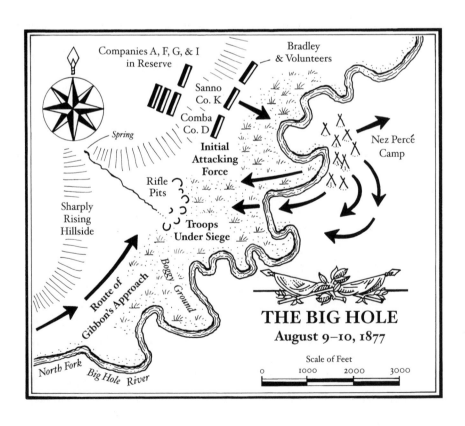

could. Their senses were sharp with the adrenaline of anticipated combat. They reached the bottomland near the river and found it was inundated with stagnant pools of waist-deep water. Ever so quietly, they sloshed through the water, approaching the river. Insects buzzed everywhere. The men could not so much as slap at mosquitoes for fear of making too much noise.

Up ahead, some fifty yards away, beyond the river's shabby beard of scrub brush, willow clumps, and reeds, the troops could see the Nez Percé tepees in the dim half light. Private Coon never forgot the feeling of watching the Indians going about their business, totally oblivious to the imminent danger they faced: "We were but a short distance from their tepees and could plainly see the squaws, running with lighted sticks, getting their fires going for the morning breakfast." Coon looked to his left and clearly saw Bradley and his troops approaching a cluster of Nez Percé ponies.[47]

The lieutenant and his men eagerly pressed forward, their trouser cuffs fluttering against the reeds of the muddy marsh ground just shy of the river. All at once, they saw a tribesman on a horse, literally right in front of them, heading for the main herd. He did not see the troops until he was within a few yards of them. "He then put spurs to his horse and attempted to ride through our lines," one of the civilian volunteers recalled. Several of the volunteers raised their rifles and shot him. The man, known to his fellow Nez Percés as Wetistokaith, fell dead.

Upon hearing the shooting, the Cottonbalers immediately stood up and opened fire on the village. With bloodcurdling screams, Comba's men and Sanno's men ran forward, straight across the river, while Logan's men charged in from the right. "I gave the order to Charge," Captain Comba wrote. "The men obeying promptly, and with a loud cheer we were in instant fighting in the enemy camp. 'K' Company on the left took up the charge. Both companies entering the camp at about the same time."

A couple hundred yards away, Colonel Gibbon was perched atop his horse, watching the chaotic attack unfold: "The men, rushing forward with a shout, plunged into the stream and climbed up the opposite bank, shooting down startled Indians as they rushed from their tents pell-mell, men, women, and children together. Many of the Indians broke at once for the brush, and sheltering themselves behind the creek bank, opened fire on the troops as they came into the open ground."

Seemingly in a matter of minutes, the reserve companies charged in, right behind the lead units. Sergeant Loynes, with I Company, ran into the fight with a cluster of soldiers from his unit. They were soon part of an intimate, bloody struggle: "We rushed to the water's edge, everyone seeming to want to get to the opposite side first. So into the water we leaped, not knowing its depth . . . through it and into the camp of the Indians, we followed with a yell that would do credit to the Indians themselves. We will never forget . . . how we fought with those savages, kill or be killed, no time to load our rifles, with the butts and muzzles of our guns, we struck right and left. The shouts of soldiers, the war whoops of the Indians, the screeching of the squaws, who with Winchesters [repeating carbines] in their hands were as much to be feared as the bucks. I remember a young buck . . . about 12 or 14 years old . . . with a Hatchet rushing at Sergeant [Mildon] Wilson who was on my right." Wilson clubbed the teenager with the butt of his rifle. Soon, Loynes had a close call of his own. "My rifle . . . was empty—as a Buck raised his rifle to fire at me, Lieutenant [Joshua] Jacobs shot at him. *He saved my life.*"

Though surprised, the Indians rallied quickly and, in Lieutenant Woodruff's memory, fought desperately: "Men, white and red, women and boys, all take place in the fight, which is actually hand to hand, a regular melee, rifles and revolvers in full play, men are powder burned, so close are they to death dealing guns, the dingy lodges are lighted up by the constant discharge, the ground is covered with the dead and dying, the morning air laden with smoke and riven by cheers, savage yells, shrieks, curses, groans."[48]

Actually, it was sickening in the extreme. In this kind of combat, everyone from the baby who had been born the previous evening to the most wrinkled elder tribesman was a target. This could not be helped. It was a logical by-product of Gibbon's attack order. The resulting action took place at close quarters, with little time for thought or circumspection. There was only time for quick reaction, and some women, as Loynes mentioned, wielded weapons. The soldiers had no desire to kill women or children—truthfully, the thought of it nauseated them—but that did not mean it did not happen. The men fired wildly, indiscriminately, even irresponsibly. They fired into tepees and all over the camp. They fired at anything that moved. Some Indians were forced into the water and tried to hide underneath their blankets, holding their breath in the hope that the soldiers would pass them by. The troops merely paused a second, drew a bead, and killed them. The bodies of these unfortunates floated down the river, the blood from bullet wounds turning the water pink in places.

The air was hazy and unhealthy with gunpowder smoke now, and the troops could not see much beyond twenty or thirty yards. They pressed into the middle of the camp and shot up as many tepees as they could. With every passing minute they took casualties. "Soldiers were constantly falling," Loynes said, "and we soon discovered they were being hit by shots coming from the tepees, occupied by Indians who had not time to get away, or had retreated into them at the first attack. It was necessary to get them out at once. To do so, three or four soldiers would throw a lariat over the top of the tepee and with others on the opposite side, lying on the ground with rifles ready, the tepee would be pulled over, exposing an Indian who, of course, with his last shot, at so close a distance, would kill or wound a soldier."[49]

In fact, the fighting in and around the tepees accounted for most of the casualties among Nez Percé women and children. One soldier shot a two-year-old child through the hip. When the baby's mother ran to save him, the soldier shot her through the back, the bullet coming out through her breast. One young Indian boy recalled seeing a woman shot near the stream and she "pitched into the water and I saw her struggling. She floated by us and [my] mother caught and drew the body to her. She placed the dying woman's head on a sandbar just out of the water. She was soon dead." A second later, soldiers appeared on the opposite side of the bank and pointed their weapons right at him and his mother. The mother screamed, "Women! Only women!!" The soldiers lowered their weapons and left. Not far away the new mother who had given birth the night before lay dead, along with the woman who had served as her nurse. In the mother's lifeless arms the baby lay in repose—killed by the initial three-shot volley the troops had fired before they charged. Loynes saw a similar scene. "A squaw was . . . lying on her back, dead, with wide open eyes staring heavenward, an infant upon her bare breast, alive, and crying as it painfully waved its little arm, which had been shattered by a bullet. It was probably hit when we sent three volleys into the camp before charging."

In some tepees women and youngsters resisted mightily. Private Charles Alberts charged into one such shelter and found himself surrounded by women and children advancing on him with knives and hatchets. Grabbing his rifle by the barrel, he swung it indiscriminately until he finally escaped the tepee. Private George Leher ran past another tepee and got hit in the head by a spent bullet. Stunned, he lay unconscious until awakened by a squaw who was dragging him by the foot. He managed to grab a rifle and shoot her.[50]

The village melee lasted about twenty minutes until many of the Indians fled north in the direction of Chief White Bird's portion of the camp, roughly astride Bradley's position. Quite a few others—particularly warriors—retreated west, under cover of trees, onto high ground, and east into the foliage. Once the Indians had fled, the troops set about the task of destroying the part of the village they had just captured. After absorbing the initial surprise attack, the surviving Indians were in the process of rallying. Many of the Cottonbalers could clearly hear the Nez Percé chiefs (alternately identified as Chief Joseph, White Bird, or Looking Glass) screaming emotionally and imploringly at their men. The Native American voices fairly dripped with grief and outrage over the deaths of so many of their women and children.

BY THIS TIME LIEUTENANT BRADLEY WAS DEAD. HIS attack ran into what turned out to be the strength of the Nez Percé positions and it went nowhere. Completely ignorant of this, he forged ahead courageously, panting a bit, urging his men to follow. When he was just on the verge of entering a thicket that looked like an ideal defensive position, one of his men warned him, "Hold on, Lieutenant; don't go in there. It's certain death!" He kept going, almost as if he hadn't heard the warning. A millisecond later an Indian rose up, leveled his weapon at Bradley, and blew him away from point-blank range. The lieutenant pitched backward and fell in a bloody heap, killed instantly. Private Philo O. Hurlburt of K Company shot the Indian who killed Bradley, while other troops shot several more. Bradley, the scholar, the aspiring author—he planned to publish his diary from the 1876 summer campaign—the young father of two little girls, was gone forever. "No regiment ever had a more fearless or better officer," Loynes commented. "We all knew him to be a splendid officer and a very brave and humane man. Lieut. Bradley was all that a good man and officer could be."[51]

Bradley's counterpart in the frivolous, prideful spat of the summer before, Captain Logan, also lay dead by now, shot to death by a squaw at the western edge of the village, near Chief Joseph's tepee. Logan's long gray hair flapped in the summer breeze. Ironically, only moments before his death he had been exhorting his men not to shoot women and children. Logan, strong willed and good-humored, had served twenty-seven years in the Army, earning his commission as a result of his bravery in the Civil War. He also would be sorely missed.[52]

About this time, the battle began to turn in favor of the Native Americans. The Cottonbalers were outnumbered and outgunned, attempting to attack and subdue a brave, resilient enemy. The 7th had already expended its one great weapon in this fight—surprise. With each minute that ticked by, the Indians became stronger and the soldiers weaker.

Even as the soldiers began burning the village, the Indians rallied on the high ground all around their village and opened a deadly fire on the Cottonbalers. Some Indians even shot at the troops from behind. "The Indians were able to pass around our flanks, and take positions in the willows, and the wooded hills in our rear, from which points they kept up a destructive fire on our men," Captain Comba wrote. The troops tried to return fire in kind, but it was an uneven exchange. "It soon became evident," Gibbon wrote in his official report, "that the enemy's sharpshooters, hidden behind trees, rocks, & c., possessed an immense advantage over us." All around him bullets were crackling. Far too many of them were finding their soldier targets, striking flesh with dull thuds.

Gibbon himself had been in the process of crossing the creek on his horse when he realized the volume of fire his men were taking. He dismounted and watched the battle for a second. As he did so, Woodruff told the colonel that his horse's leg had been hit. Gibbon looked down and saw blood running, not just from the horse's leg but his own too: "The same bullet which broke my horse's leg passed through mine. I was more fortunate in the fact that it had not broken the bone." He hobbled a few steps, plunged into the water, and then sat down on the riverbank to wash his wound. With this accomplished, he then made a decision that probably saved many lives: "The only remedy was to take up some position where we would be more on an equality with the enemy." That meant a withdrawal across the river, back to defensible high ground. He ordered Rawn to screen the withdrawal by pushing his I Company soldiers forward as skirmishers. These men fought at close quarters with the Indians and covered the retreat of the entire command.[53]

The rest of the men maintained the best discipline they could. Facing the enemy, they retreated backward across the stream. Some began to run, but an officer, probably Gibbon, yelled, "Don't run, men, or I will stay right here alone." This had the desired effect. In disciplined clumps, the soldiers splashed across the river, waded through the marshland, and ascended the high ground, into the trees, all the while under a withering fire.

As the rearguard force, Sergeant Loynes and his I Company comrades were the last to leave the burning remnants of the Nez Percé village. This made them ideal targets for Nez Percé sharpshooters who, by now, were deployed in every direction, some on high ground, mostly behind trees or embankments. "With faces toward the exultant savages, we gradually fell back. As we did so . . . our wounded would clutch at our legs and beg not to be left behind." In one such instance, Loynes saw a Nez Percé bullet shatter the knee of Private Herman Broetz, a twenty-three-year-old German emigrant. Private Broetz reached out and grabbed another soldier's rifle, hanging on for dear life. But Broetz soon lost his grip and lay down to die. Not far away, Loynes was with two other soldiers, Sergeant Michael Hogan and Corporal Daniel McCaffery. Captain Rawn hustled past, saying, "Get right out of here!"

Loynes and the two other NCOs were following behind the captain when, just as they were about to cross the river, a bullet smashed into McCaffery's chest: "He fell forward, and with his right hand on the ground, his left on his chest where he was hit."

Terrified and in pain, McCaffery screamed, "Don't leave me here!"

"We won't!" Loynes replied. He and Hogan leaned over, grabbed McCaffery, and lifted him up. Hogan took McCaffery's left arm, Loynes his right. The three of them stumbled forward: "We had gone about two steps when Sgt. Hogan put his hand to his breast and fell forward." The Irish-born sergeant was probably dead before he hit the ground. McCaffery too went down in a lifeless heap. All alone now, Sergeant Loynes felt a tug at his sleeve and glanced down at his arm. A bullet had narrowly missed him, passing through his shirt and coat—an inch in either direction and his arm would have been shattered. He looked across the river to the right and saw several armed Indians. One in particular was leaning out from behind a tree, shooting at him. This Nez Percé fighter was so close—probably no more than thirty yards away—that Loynes could clearly see his face: "I can see him in my mind now—with his dark hair hanging down in front of his ears—and black eyes." Loynes raised his rifle and fired: "If I hit him anywhere, I did not know it." Nor did he have time to find out. "Bullets were singing by my ears. I leeped [sic] into the river—got acrossed into the Alders [marshes], and started to find the command." By following footprints and listening to the sounds of friendly firing, he found the rest of the outfit about a quarter mile from the south end of the village, on high ground, in an acre of shaded pine forest. Loynes saw that the soldiers had gotten almost all of their wounded out of the village, but the dead were another matter. Most of them were left behind, and ended up stripped and looted.[54]

The Indians warily worked their way around the new Cottonbaler position, taking potshots whenever they could. The Cottonbalers, fighting for their lives now, hurriedly dug improvised rifle pits with anything they could—knives, spoons, mess kits, and trowel bayonets. The Indians soon laid down a withering volume of fire on them, and this fire motivated the soldiers to work even faster. "One man would scrape up the dirt, while every second man would continue to fire," Loynes explained. Gibbon maintained that the return fire took a deadly toll on the tribesmen. "The Indians crawled up as closely as they dared to come, and with yells of encouragement urged each other on; but our men met them with a bold front, and our fire, as we afterward learned by the blood and dead Indians [we] found, punished them severely."[55]

The diggers made the kind of rapid progress that only self-preservation can stimulate. Those who used trowel bayonets seemed to dig especially fast. The Army soon phased this odd piece of equipment out of service, but on that hot August day, when the Cottonbalers faced extinction, it helped save their lives. The trowel bayonet was a pyramid-shaped dagger, fourteen and a half inches long and three and a half inches wide. The thing looked more like a hand shovel than a bayonet. Upon seeing the trowel bayonet for the first time, one commentator wisecracked that "some genius seeking to transform a soldier into a jack of spades has given him a shovel to wear on the end of his gun."[56] But, on this day, in this situation, the trowel proved to be a godsend. Indeed, Captain Comba later wrote to an army equipment board in favor of keeping it in service: "They were . . . used by my company as intrenching tools, giving great satisfaction. The men . . . under a heavy fire from the enemy, placed themselves under cover in an incredibly short space of time and a little later by an organized effort quite a formidable breastwork was constructed making the position comparitively [sic] secure."[57]

The resourceful enemy soon adjusted their tactics in an effort to keep pouring murderous fire on the soldiers. Bullets thudded into flesh with alarming frequency. "The Indians were getting up in the trees," Private Coon recounted, "to pick us off as we were on a slope of about

45 degrees. They were quite successful in this as they got about seven of us, including Lieut. English . . . before we found the sniper. He was finally located and dropped from his perch by Sergeant [John] Abbot of the Ordnance." English had been hit in the back, the bullet lodging in his abdomen. He "fell backward with a cry." This young lieutenant—another of the many Bighorn diarists—eventually died from his wound, and Coon never quite got over his officer's untimely death. "He had been married but a year and was the father of a baby that he never did get home to see."[58]

For a brief moment, the soldiers perked up at the sound of the howitzer firing somewhere behind them. Perhaps this weapon could drive the Indians away. But the makeshift gun crew only fired two shots before the Indians subdued them in a vicious close-quarter fight that killed Corporal Robert E. Sale and wounded two sergeants. Two privates on the gun crew fled at the first sign of danger and didn't stop until they had put nearly one hundred miles between themselves and the battlefield. The Native Americans who captured the gun could not get it to work and abandoned it, missing out on a golden opportunity to destroy the remnants of Gibbon's force.

The battle now settled down into a stalemate. Nez Percé fighters kept up a steady volume of fire on the entrenched Cottonbalers, who returned fire at whatever targets they could find. Periodically the rifle fire would slacken, and when it did the soldiers heard unearthly sounds coming from the village, a kind of "wail of mingled grief, rage, and horror . . . when the Indians returned to it and recognized their slaughtered warriors, women and children," Gibbon said. Mixed with this primal scream of collective grief were the cries of seven wounded soldiers who had been left in the village. "I can never forget the cries of our helpless wounded when they [the Nez Percés] . . . finished them," Loynes wrote five decades later. "It rang in my ears for a long time." Infused with grief and outrage over the attack on their village, the Indians killed the wounded troops with swift impunity.

Here and there, brave but foolhardy Indians made suicidal charges on the entrenchments. One mounted Nez Percé rode out of the trees, leveled his weapon, and shot Sergeant Edward Page, killing him instantly. A moment later, when the mounted man tried to repeat his exploit, the soldier next to Page shot and killed him. The Indian fell off his horse, dead before he hit the ground. The horse galloped back into the trees. Another Nez Percé charged on foot at the soldiers. This man, named Five Wounds, had just found out that his closest friend had been killed and he snapped. Other Indians remembered him crying for a long time and then saying, "This sun, this time, I am going to die. My brother is killed, and I shall go with him." Five Wounds nearly made it to the trench line before being cut down with several bullet wounds.

IN THE SHALLOW TRENCHES, MEN WHO HAD BEEN HIT SUR-veyed their wounds. Private Charles Alberts had been hit in the left breast by one of the snipers. He carefully crawled over to Lieutenant Woodruff and asked if he would live. Woodruff studied the wound and noticed bubbles of air in the flowing blood. These bubbles meant that Alberts had been hit in the lung. Woodruff then looked at Alberts's back and found a small hole where the bullet had exited: "I described the nature of the wound and said, 'Alberts, you have a severe wound, but there is no need of your dying if you have got the nerve to keep up your courage.'" Alberts hung in there and survived. He was lucky. On-the-spot medical care consisted of hastily slapping makeshift bandages (usually pieces of cloth torn from shirttails) over wounds cauterized with heated gunpowder.[59]

Early in the afternoon, Gibbon smelled smoke. He turned and looked in the direction of the village and, sure enough, saw a large volume of smoke blowing toward his positions. The Indians were trying a new tactic. They had set fire to the grass in the woods, in the hopes that the grass would catch the trees on fire, smoke out the Cottonbalers, or simply provide enough concealment to sneak up and attack the soldiers. Somewhere behind the smoke the enemy fighters hollered war cries at the top of their lungs. A collective shudder ran down the spines of the Cottonbalers. They fully expected the Indians to follow up this fire with an all-out attack. Sergeant Loynes and the men around him said a short prayer and waited to die: "We crouched down behind our slight earth work, with rifles loaded and cocked, prepared for what we believed to be our last struggle." Many had visions of ending up like Custer's troops the summer before.

But the attack never came. "Fortunately, the grass was too green to burn rapidly, and before the fire reached any of the dead timber . . . it went out," Gibbon explained.[60] The Indians now contented themselves with keeping the soldiers pinned down with occasional, but uncomfortably accurate, rifle fire. Those soldiers still able to see the village noticed that many of the Nez Percés were busy packing and loading up their animals. Obviously the Nez Percé fighters planned to hold off the soldiers while the rest of the tribe got away. The Cottonbalers had no choice but to remain in place: leaving the trenches meant sure death. Indeed, anyone who raised his head even a few feet risked having it blown off.

The soldiers huddled behind their hastily built earthworks and waited anxiously for nightfall. Gibbon ordered an ammo check and found that his men had expended over nine thousand rounds. He gave orders that ammunition be conserved. Afternoon turned into evening and still the soldiers remained pinned down and besieged. Gunpowder stains streaked their faces like war paint. Their eyes were red and irritated from smoke and their throats parched from inhalation of the same. They had fought all day long in the heat, under the strain of threatened annihilation. The wounded whimpered, groaned, and begged for water. No one had any food. The men had journeyed to the Nez Percé camp with no rations except hardtack, and most of that had dissolved in their knapsacks when they crossed the river. Some men grew so hungry that they carved off pieces of hindquarters from Lieutenant Woodruff's dead, bloated horse and ate the meat raw, since no one could risk starting a fire.

During the night, many of the soldiers, especially the wounded, were nearly crazed with thirst. Gibbon asked for volunteers to crawl to the river and fill canteens. Private Coon assented: "Because this trip for water would involve being open to a cross fire from the Indians on both sides the General [Gibbon] would not order anyone to undertake it. However, Charlie Hines, Ed Welsh and myself finally undertook it. It was not entirely because of the wounded that we volunteered—we were . . . nearly famished ourselves for a drink so we were thinking of ourselves too. Before we started the rest of our comrades poured volley after volley into the bushes lining our side of the stream to drive out any Indians that might be lurking there." He and the two other men grabbed their canteens and started crawling down the slope: "Although it was only about 100 yards it seemed more like 100 miles to me." They got to the river undetected and filled the canteens. That too seemed to take forever. "It seemed as though they would never fill up. The shots began to whistle around us and, as thirsty as I was, would you believe that I actually forgot in my excitement to get a drink for myself." In fact, Coon never got a drink at all. He and the others safely scrambled back to their positions and gave their canteens to the wounded.[61]

In the meantime, Gibbon dispatched runners to get in touch with General Howard and inform him of the 7th's predicament. The colonel also worried about the fate of his supply wagons. He knew his men badly needed food, ammunition, and medical care. The night passed quietly, if uneasily. "The discomforts of that night cannot be . . . exaggerated," Gibbon recalled. "We were all soaked to the waist; we had no covering except pine boughs, and the night was cold enough to freeze the water in the ponds near us." The nighttime minutes dragged by like hours. "It seemed as if daylight would never come," Woodruff wrote. "The nights are cold in the mountains, even in summer, the men have no covering; their clothes have been soaked [while] recrossing the river. More than one-third of the command are killed and wounded; they have no medical attendance, and some of the wounded suffer intensely and their groans are very trying." At dawn on August 10, a courier from Howard, Sergeant Oliver Sutherland of the 1st Cavalry Regiment, rode into the Cottonbaler positions with the joyous news that Howard was on the way. The infantrymen cheered loudly, but their ordeal was not completely finished.[62]

Howard was a day away and the Cottonbalers were still under fire from Indians attempting to cover the flight of their families, including elders. Their fire had slackened, though, so Gibbon thought the situation was safe enough to send Captain George Browning with a patrol of twenty-five men to go back, find the supply wagons, and bring them up. This provided the soldiers with some much-needed food but not exactly a feast. Gibbon also sent a small group to determine the fate of the howitzer and its crew. They found the disabled gun next to the dead body of Sale and discovered that the Indians had captured two thousand rounds of ammunition, most of it for small arms.

The next morning Howard and a small party finally arrived, followed by the rest of his troops the day after. Through weary, almost teary eyes, Loynes watched the relief force, consisting of the 1st Cavalry, the 8th and 21st Infantry Regiments, and Bannock Indian scouts, file into the perimeter: "The Bannocks soon found the dead Indians who were . . . near us . . . and commenced to scalp them. They took the entire scalp from the head, and after carefully washing it, had what they most highly prized. But to us it was not a pleasant sight, considering the state of our empty stomachs, and the air laden with the stench of dead bodies and ponies from the camp below, mingled with burning sage brush, and the ether the surgeons were using."

These surgeons from Howard's command rolled up their sleeves and did whatever they could to help the wounded, many of whom were in bad shape. Private Coon stood silently and sadly watching the doctors: "The doctors of Howard's outfit went to work with a will and fixed them up for a long ride in wagons to Deer Lodge, 90 miles away. Many of the enlisted men had been hit two or three times. The Indians used a flat nosed explosive bullet in their Winchesters which made a frightful wound and caused many of our wounded to die."

The cavalrymen blew their bugles and rode south in hopes of catching the escaped Nez Percés. Meanwhile, Captain Browning and Sergeant Loynes took a small patrol and investigated the abandoned Nez Percé camp. Loynes wrote mournfully of the disposition of the dead: "We found our dead comrades stripped of all their clothing, their bodies swollen to twice their normal size, from the heat of the sun, very few being mutilated. 1st Sergeant [Frederick] Stortz with the glaze of death . . . in his light blue eyes; 1st Sergeant [Robert] Edgeworth, who left two sisters in England, whom he was never more to see; Sergeant Hogan, with a mother in Dayton, Ohio; Sergeants [William] Martin and [Howard] Clark; Corporals McCaffery, [Dominick] O'Connor, [William] Payne, and [Jacob] Eizenhart [sic]; and the many privates. They were buried as best we could at that time, but some few weeks after, a detail was sent to more properly perform that duty. Some of the bodies were found torn up by bears and wolves."[63]

Gibbon took stock of his casualties. They were staggering. In all, he had lost fifty-nine soldiers killed and wounded, roughly one-third of his force. He himself had taken a bullet in the thigh, but he could still walk. Many others could not, though, and they would have to ride or be carried to Deer Lodge. The rickety army supply wagons that served as crude ambulances painfully jolted and jostled the wounded men, so the able-bodied improvised. They took tepee poles from the Indian village, skinned dead ponies, cut the hides into strips, and braided them over the poles, building what they called a travois, a glorified stretcher. In this way, they slowly marched to Deer Lodge, arriving there on the fifteenth. The wounded received decent medical care at this frontier town, but several of them, including Cottonbalers Lieutenant English and Sergeant William Watson, died there. This brought the final 7th Infantry casualty tally for Big Hole to twenty-five dead and thirty-four wounded. The Indians lost between sixty and ninety killed and probably a like number wounded.[64]

Shortly after General Howard had linked up with the 7th Infantry in the pine forest, he and Gibbon sat down on a log, under the shade of tree limbs, for a quiet conversation. Sergeant Loynes overheard them.

"If I had got here sooner," Howard said, "you would never have attacked those Indians." As always, General Howard wanted to round up the Native Americans, not fight them.

Gibbon agreed that this would have been preferable and even possible with the strength his force, combined with Howard's, would have possessed. Yet Gibbon still believed that regardless of whether he had linked up with Howard, the nontreaty Nez Percés would have deserved punishment. "If I had got hold of their chiefs, I would have hung them up on those limbs," Gibbon told General Howard.

In the final analysis, this bloody and unnecessary battle was a draw. Gibbon did not achieve the campaign-ending victory he had hoped for, and the Nez Percés were not able to annihilate the 7th Infantry. One of their men later explained why his tribe left the battlefield after setting the grass afire rather than press the attack: "If we killed one soldier, a thousand could take his place. If we lost one warrior, there was none to take his place." Truly these were the last survivors of an age-old culture and they knew it. So, instead they continued their flight, periodically battling with the Army in Montana, until finally checkmated in the Bear Paw Mountains in early October 1877. Here Chief Joseph, whom whites thought of as the overall leader of the Nez Percé, uttered his famous and poignant words: "Hear me, my chiefs! I am tired. My heart is sick and sad. From where the sun now stands, I will fight no more forever." He and his people were never allowed to return to their traditional land.[65]

The soldiers hardly rejoiced at their country's victory. Most of them sympathized with the Native Americans and held no special grudge against them. Private Coon summed up the general attitude of the soldiers when he wrote that "none of us felt very hostile towards them . . . but our orders were to go after them." Sergeant Loynes agreed: "No doubt the surviving Indians who were there at that time look at it in the same light as we do. It was all wrong—all unnecessary—and of all the Indian tribes, it has always seemed to me that the Nez Perces were superior to all."[66] With these statements, Coon and Loynes unwittingly encapsulated the role of the 7th Infantry in the Indian Wars. Truly, the soldiers were merely instruments of manifest destiny.

Big Hole proved to be the last significant combat the 7th Regiment saw in the Indian Wars. It was the last time the 7th Infantry fought fellow Americans and the last time the men of the unit participated in a battle of any size on the North American continent. The outfit remained in Montana until 1888, when it transferred to Fort Snelling, Minnesota. The regiment participated in a short campaign against hostile Ute Indians in 1889 but saw no real fighting.[67] The long series of wars for control of the North American continent were finally over. From here on out, America's wars, and consequently the Cottonbalers' battles, would be fought on foreign shores. Continentalist America was giving way to internationalist America, and that historic change ushered in a new era of industrial growth, sophistication, and economic expansion for the United States. For the Cottonbalers this tectonic shift in the history of the world meant that the future foresaw many journeys to distant, unseen, exotic battlefields, the first of which lay to the south, in the Caribbean, on the island of Cuba.

6

First Fight on Overseas Shores

The Spanish-American War

IN 1898 THE 7TH INFANTRY REGIMENT, FOR THE FIRST time in its history, fought a battle outside of the North American continent. This was the wave of the future. In fact, from this point forward, the 7th fought all of its battles outside the confines of its home continent. Here is how this new era in the history of the regiment and, by extension, the U.S. Army happened.

In 1895 Cuban nationalists, led by a man named José Martí, began to fight for their independence against Spain, their colonial overseer for close to four hundred years. The Cubans' best hope for success was to fight a guerrilla war against the better armed and supplied Spanish. They harassed Spanish troops and authorities with every means at their disposal—bombs, jungle ambushes, and sniping primarily. In reaction, the Spanish made war on the Cuban people themselves. The Spaniards reasoned that the guerrillas found sustenance, sympathy, and protection among the people, so they instituted a policy that called for detaining much of the civilian population in detention camps. These camps were mostly hellholes, and thousands of Cubans died from poor food, poor shelter, or disease. In addition, the Spanish committed numerous atrocities against the Cuban guerrillas, who responded in kind, leading to an endless cycle of violence and retaliation. Much the same way that swamps combined with mosquitoes produce malaria, guerrilla war inevitably produces such atrocities.

This nasty conflict between Spain and Cuba seemingly grew worse by the year, and soon it aroused international concern, especially from the neighbor to the north—the United States. In major metropolitan newspapers like the *New York World* or national newsmagazines like *Harper's Bazaar,* the American people read numerous hair-raising tales about Spanish atrocities in Cuba. This media onslaught, coupled with the unresolved situation in Cuba, incited a significant amount of anti-Spanish sentiment in the United States. Responding to public opinion, the U.S. government, under President William McKinley, began to lean on Spain to grant Cuba its independence. Worried that such an imperial retreat would spark political upheaval at home, the Spanish government resisted these American entreaties.

The war continued, and relations between the rising power of the New World and the fading power of the Old World grew worse by the day. McKinley, a Civil War veteran who had seen enough carnage to last a lifetime, despised the very notion of war and worked for a diplomatic solution. However, his task became nearly impossible when the USS *Maine,* anchored in Havana Harbor on a show-of-force mission, mysteriously exploded and sank on February 15, 1898, killing 269 American sailors. Public opinion in the United States now overwhelmingly favored war with Spain, because most Americans believed that the Spanish had sunk the *Maine* and should now be punished.

For the Spanish, now facing the very real prospect of a war with the United States, this entire mess could not have come at a worse time, mainly because the 1890s saw the coalescence of two distinct, and powerful, forces in American society. The first such force can be termed the American moralist or crusader instinct. This instinct stemmed from the belief among most Americans in the essential goodness and unique nature of the United States as a representative of justice, democracy, and civilization. As such, the United States bore a responsibility to right wrongs wherever and whenever it could. This responsibility was usually sparked by some dramatic event around which the American people could rally—the sinking of the *Maine* in this case, but future examples spring to mind such as the Zimmerman telegram, unrestricted submarine warfare, Pearl Harbor, the North Korean invasion of South Korea, the Iraqi invasion of Kuwait, and the September 2001 terrorist attacks on the United States itself. Thus when the American people, in modern times, go to war they prefer to do so under the banner of idealism and some kind of moral crusade. In 1898 that crusade necessitated the "liberation" of the Cuban people from their colonial oppressors, something Americans could certainly relate to, having expelled colonial overseers themselves just over one hundred years before.

The second powerful force in the late 1890s was raw imperialism. With Native American tribes now subdued and the continent secured, many Americans began to look overseas to satisfy an expansionist impulse—a kind of overseas manifest destiny. At a time when European imperial powers dominated the majority of the globe, Americans started to hunger for their nation to take its rightful place among the great powers of the earth. After all, wasn't the United States the most industrialized, civilized, modern, and economically powerful country in the world? If so, it must prove its mettle by acquiring an empire, since empires served as veritable trophies, symbols of greatness.

In the case of Cuba, Americans had been interested in the place for years. In fact, during the antebellum period the U.S. government had even tried to buy Cuba from Spain (southerners dreamed of creating a slave empire there). Not that anyone really wanted to colonize Cuba at this late date, but certainly its liberation from Spain would be good for American economic interests.

So the American enthusiasm for war in 1898 can be seen, then, as a convergence of these two forces: the laudable desire to see moral right-ness prevail throughout the world, married with a sheer, avaricious, quest for overseas expansion. Also, by the late 1890s a new generation had come of age, one that had no memory of the Civil War beyond the heroic tales told to them by their fathers and grandfathers. These young men, with little conception of the real horror and tragedy of war, yearned to prove themselves in battle and inscribe their own heroic deeds into history. This glory-seeking mind-set, combined with collective amnesia, unquestionably contributed a great deal to the irresistible lust for war that compelled McKinley to ask Congress for a declaration of war on April 25, 1898. The legislative branch was only too happy to comply, and the United States was now officially at war with Spain.[1]

BY THE LATE 1890S THE COTTONBALERS HAD CHANGED stations many times, finally landing in Fort Logan, Colorado, a nice post with decent barracks and amenities, located roughly twelve miles southwest of Denver. The men spent their days involved in the usual garrison chores—drilling, marksmanship, hauling wood, unloading coal, parading, mess duty, Saturday morning inspections, and so forth. The quality of life had improved significantly from the days of old when men struggled for mere survival at such pestilential places as Fort Gibson. The men ate better than they ever had, consuming a balanced diet of bread, potatoes, fresh meats, beans, onions, fish, fruit, coffee, sugar, and the ever present hardtack. Field rations consisted of canned tomatoes, corned beef, bacon, beans, and hardtack, which would be washed down with coffee. Everyone looked forward to early June each year, when the regiment held an annual field day. On field day, the various companies competed with one another in athletic contests including bike riding (hugely popular in the late nineteenth century), relay races, dashes, high jumps, long jumps, shot putting, and many other track-and-field events. Every now and again, the unit would leave Fort Logan for maneuvers or practice on the rifle range.

The soldiers were solid, disciplined, reliable troops who knew their weapons well and generally took good care of their equipment, since they paid for whatever they lost. The only real deficiency in their training was physical fitness, something the Army did not yet emphasize the way it would by the middle of the twentieth century. Moreover, recruits still received basic training with their regiments rather than in special training outfits. That too would change in the near future.

Officers generally hailed from West Point, and promotions were still few and far between. Consequently, it was not at all unusual for companies to be commanded by forty- or fifty-year-old captains. Colonel Daniel Webster Benham, a grandfatherly Civil War veteran, commanded the regiment.

The men in his charge hailed from many different backgrounds among America's white population (the unit would not be integrated for another half century). On the eve of the Spanish-American War, the foreign-born still accounted for a major chunk of the regiment's ranks, maybe 35–45 percent. These men came from such places as Ireland, Germany, and Austria and had either become citizens or were well on the way to doing so. The native-born majority originated from all over the country (still more northerners than southerners, though) and had worked in such occupations as mining, plumbing, woodworking, clerking, and farming. Aside from these solid working- and lower-middle-class professions, an increasing number of Cottonbalers thought of themselves as career professional soldiers—a harbinger of the future. Those who enlisted in 1898 were almost all native-born, middle-class men motivated by patriotism, if not the prospect of a career in the Army.[2]

Herbert O. Kohr, a native-born, lower-middle-class youth from Ohio, joined the regiment in May 1896 and later penned a perceptive, detailed memoir describing his life as a Cottonbaler. After witnessing the 7th Infantry march smartly by him during a festive parade, probably in Denver, he decided he wanted to be one of them, so he took a train to Fort Logan and told the regiment's sergeant major that he wanted to join the outfit. This began a military career that saw him serve two enlistments of three years each. Lanky and uncoordinated, Kohr struggled at first to learn basic drill procedures. His teacher, an upright, hard-bellied drill sergeant who had trained many raw recruits during his thirty years in the Army, tried to be patient, but he finally lost his temper with Kohr. "Well, you are one of the most awkward monkeys I have ever seen!" Kohr blushed furiously as other soldiers laughed, but eventually he overcame his physical shortcomings and learned to be a good, well-respected soldier.

As the months piled up and he grew more comfortable with his place in the outfit, he keenly observed the men in his E Company. "About half of our company were Americans; the other half was made up of Germans, Irishmen, Englishmen, Welshmen, Norwegians and Swedes. This element of the company seemed to be the most dissatisfied. They grumbled, complained and cursed when things displeased them. Of course some of the Americans did the same thing. There were divisions among the men in the company. Those who drank sought that kind of company among the men of the regiment. Those who liked athletics and exercise mingled together."

For over a year, he lived the life of a 7th infantryman, performing kitchen patrol, learning to shoot a rifle, cleaning his barracks, drilling constantly, perpetrating and being victimized by practical jokes, and participating in a mock battle against the 2nd Cavalry. In early 1898, his steady service earned him a two-month furlough, which he used to earn a little money with the Colorado Fuel and Iron Company. While at work there, he heard about the sinking of the *Maine* and grew excited at the prospect of war with Spain. Returning to the regiment, he found his comrades in the same state of mind.

In the middle of April, orders came to leave Fort Logan. The plan called for the soldiers to leave behind all nonessentials and march to their train. Thousands of well-wishers showed up to say good-bye. "Amid the tears and waving of handkerchiefs, the train pulled away from the platform; many wives and children had looked for the last time on the faces of their loves. We soon . . . steamed into the union depot in Denver. Thousands of people had gathered here on the principal street to bid us farewell." They got off the train and marched a short distance to catch another train. "Excitement ran high, and the streets were strewn with flowers, and crowds cheered as we marched by, many crying out, 'Give it to them, boys!' 'Remember the Maine!'" As their train snaked its way east, they encountered the same kind of large crowds and wild enthusiasm.

On April 24, 1898, they arrived at the Chickamauga battlefield. There they bivouacked and trained for almost three weeks. "Our regiment was placed on war basis and this meant hard work for everyone. Recruits began to arrive and we had much difficulty in drilling these men and preparing them for service." Kohr was promoted to sergeant and ordered to train these new arrivals. "The recruits . . . were principally Americans; most of them from Boston, Philadelphia, Denver and other large cities." These new men, idealistic, patriotic, often wealthy by the standards of the Regular Army, signed up for two-year enlistments or the duration of the war, whichever came first.[3] After a difficult initiation process, a few washed out, but most of them fit in quite nicely and ended up fighting bravely.

Kohr also saw another type of new soldier at the Chickamauga camp—state volunteers, many of whom now called themselves the National Guard. At the outset of the war, the Regular Army numbered only 28,000 men. Obviously, many more soldiers than that would be needed in the coming war. To that end, McKinley and Congress authorized a big buildup in the Regular Army (roughly 80,000) to flesh out newly created regiments or bring old regiments, such as the 7th, to full strength. They did this by filling out twelve full companies in each regiment. These companies were then divided into three battalions. For their part, the volunteers, ultimately about 225,000 strong, served in state regiments set up the same way. The majority of these men never left the United States, languishing instead in unhealthy, filthy army camps in which disease claimed many victims.[4]

On May 12, the 7th Regiment left Chickamauga and boarded a train for Tampa, the main staging port for the impending invasion of Cuba. The Cottonbalers set up their tents along a railroad about two miles west of the city and settled down for a stay that would last a couple weeks. The town turned into a veritable madhouse. "Troops began to arrive at Tampa from all sections and the town seemed alive with soldiers," Kohr wrote. "In every direction could be seen the dotted lines of tents, which were occupied by the regular soldiers. Men from other cities now came here to start gambling places, and other devices to attract the soldiers. Every inducement they could think of was used to drain the soldiers' pocketbooks and in most instances the boys were easy victims. Alligators were sold on nearly every street in the city."

Despite this carnival atmosphere, the troops kept drilling and preparing for war. In a sign of the times, officers vigorously searched Tampa for servants to do their cooking, cleaning, and laundry. In peacetime, they usually hired enlisted soldiers to do these chores—other enlisted men sneered at these hirelings as snitches or "dog robbers"—but no such manpower could be spared in wartime. Now the officers found few takers for the servant jobs and often had to attend to their own chores. Watching this happen, many enlisted men grinned slyly and muttered to themselves, "Welcome to how the other half lives," a reference to a popular book at the time.

In their spare time, many of the enlisted troops gathered on the grounds of the palatial Tampa Bay Hotel, where the officers were staying, and listened to band concerts. Kohr greatly enjoyed these pleasant evenings. "The grounds surrounding the hotel were very beautiful, and it was very pleasant to listen there on moonlight evenings." On the night of June 6, while he and his buddies listened to the sweet music, they heard a bugle call. They looked at one another with excitement in their eyes. The bugler was sounding the general call, which meant that the order had finally been given to take down their tents, clean up their camp, and board trains that would take them into the port of Tampa, where ships waited.

Kohr and the other soldiers scrambled back to camp as fast as they could and dismantled their lodgings with lightning quickness. A rumor was flying around that any unit that did not break camp quickly enough might be left behind because of a lack of transport shipping, and no one wanted to be left behind, stranded in Tampa while everyone else found glory on the shores of Cuba.

The rumor was not true, but the logistical headaches that hatched it were all too real. The U.S. Army was woefully unprepared for an amphibious operation of this magnitude. Tampa did not have enough railroad tracks or cars to carry all the troops, much less the supplies needed to keep them in action. There was a shortage of labor on the docks, which meant that equipment, ammunition, food, and clothing could not be loaded efficiently. The War Department hastily scraped together ships of every description, seaworthy or not, and commissioned workmen to build bunks aboard the ships. This took time and manpower. The whole enterprise, including the coming campaign in

Cuba, was hastily slapped together—amateurish, really—emblematic of a country that aspired to martial greatness but had not yet paid the price, in terms of dollars, professionalism, and preparation, to achieve such a lofty goal.

At the Cottonbalers' camp the soldiers busily struck their tents, burned their garbage, rolled up their packs, and marched to their trains. They jammed aboard coal cars and journeyed the two miles to the port. There they found a chaotic scene, a kind of free-for-all that saw units furiously competing to find and board the limited number of transports. In the words of one observer, the port was not orderly but instead featured "the grim determination of every commanding officer, every overworked quartermaster, to get his regiment on board some particular transport. The docks were piled high with tentage, luggage and commissary supplies, and the sweltering, already-tired soldiery struggled in long, thin, loaded lines, to get their stuff aboard."[5]

The 7th Regiment found itself spread out among three transports: *Comal, D. H. Miller,* and *Iroquois*. After hustling to get to these ships, the soldiers could not exactly relax once aboard. "On our boat there was scarcely room to accommodate one-half of the men who had boarded the vessel," Kohr wrote. "Men were scurrying everywhere, looking for sleeping quarters in every nook and corner. Some had secured hammocks and these were strung up in all parts of the main deck, as there were not enough temporary bunks to accommodate them. I was very fortunate myself as four sergeants from each company were allowed berths off the saloon or dining deck." Even so, he could not escape the stench and noise that emitted from a group of furry four-legged Cottonbalers below him. "On the lower deck were placed three hundred and fifty army mules, which kept up a continual roaring and squealing." The mules were used to transport supplies in Cuba.

Company cooks prepared their meals in the ship's tiny galley, designed to accommodate a crew of about fifty or sixty men. Now it had to feed three hundred soldiers, roughly one-third of the regiment. Plus the ship somehow had to hold these soldiers along with all their equipment and several hundred mules. The meals, in Kohr's wry recollection, were incredibly monotonous, almost tasteless: "Cornbeef, beans, tomatoes, hardtack and coffee one meal; the next, beans, tomatoes, hardtack, coffee and cornbeef; the next, tomatoes, hardtack, coffee, cornbeef and beans."[6]

This armada was the largest ever launched by the United States to that point. It consisted of over sixteen thousand soldiers (most of them Regular Army), nearly four hundred civilian teamsters, packers, and stevedores, twenty-three hundred horses and mules, over two hundred wagons, twenty-six artillery pieces, eight mortars, and four Gatling guns.[7] The 7th Regiment, in tandem with the 12th and 17th Infantry Regiments, comprised the 3rd Brigade of the 2nd Division of the V Corps, with General William R. Shafter in command. Immensely fat at well over three hundred pounds, Shafter was a Civil War and Indian War veteran who had compiled a record of bravery and a reputation as a no-nonsense, strong-willed commander. As it turned out, Cuba's tropical heat melted his resolve and his reputation like a giant mound of butter in an oven.

With his ships barely out of port, Shafter received word from the War Department to turn around and go back to Tampa. The Navy believed that a Spanish cruiser and torpedo boat were operating along the route to Cuba and wanted to hunt down and destroy these enemy ships before they could impede the vulnerable invasion fleet. So, the transports hung a U-turn and went back into port. There Kohr and thousands of others waited and found ways to amuse themselves: "We returned to the dock; the mules were unloaded but our quarters were to be on the boat. Here we spent several days, the boys passing away the time by bathing in the bay or wandering along the shore. We were not allowed passes and were limited to docks and Picnic Island which was a short distance from the main pier. Men covered these places in groups at all hours of the day, telling yarns, playing jokes, and inventing all sorts of schemes to while away the time."

Finally, on June 14 the armada left port again, this time for good. The seas were calm, but the weather grew hotter as the fleet, escorted by several U.S. Navy warships, slowly made its way south. With the warm weather came powerful odors. "The stench which arose from the mule quarters was terrible. These were all loose in the hold, and kept up a continual kicking and squealing," Kohr recalled. The heat, the lousy food, and the cramped, dirty conditions made the soldiers stir-crazy. "The men all became anxious to land, some vowing that they would never again board another transport. The water which had been taken from Port Tampa was warm and scarcely fit to drink. We used salt water for bathing and as we had no salt water soap, had a trying time to keep clean. Our faces became shiny and greasy."[8] As they sailed along the southern coast of Cuba, heavy winds began to scatter the transports.

Kohr's ship got lost for a while, only to be shepherded back to the fleet by a navy gunboat. Then someone spotted land and the spirits of the troops soared.

Infantrymen, as a whole, despise the discomfort and vulnerability of being cooped up on ships, and the Cottonbalers of '98 were no different. In spite of the perils that they knew full well they would face somewhere out there in Cuba's steamy jungles, they could not wait to get off their cramped, smelly ship. Kohr's ship, and dozens of others, dropped anchor in Daiquiri Harbor and the men impatiently waited for orders to debark.

After a day or so of waiting and watching, the orders finally came. The soldiers carefully climbed from their transports into lifeboats. Navy steam launches then towed the lifeboats a mile to shore. The mules enjoyed no such comforts. They were emptied into the sea and swam ashore. The Spanish put up nothing more than token resistance at Daiquiri. Navy gunboats bombarded a few lightly garrisoned blockhouses, forcing their Spanish occupants to surrender or flee. Thus the Cottonbalers moved unmolested from their lifeboats onto piers and inland. Officers formed their men into companies and marched them away from the landing beaches.

In a sense, the landing was quite similar to the one at Veracruz half a century before. If the opposition had put up even mild resistance, the Americans would have taken many casualties. Shafter's amphibious force did not have the kind of fire support, training, and logistical support to assault a skillfully defended beach. In other words, the Yanks were very lucky. American soldiers who came ashore at Daiquiri worried more about keeping their uniforms and weapons dry than anything else.

The primary objective of this campaign was to destroy the Spanish fleet and capture its seaport of Santiago. The U.S. Navy had blockaded Cuba for several weeks now, bottling up a small Spanish naval flotilla in Santiago Harbor. Shafter and his colleagues believed that the capture of Santiago, along with the destruction of Spanish ground forces in the area, would lead to the collapse of Spanish control of Cuba. The Navy wanted to accomplish this objective with a head-on attack at Santiago. The soldiers would capture the port's batteries, opening the way for navy ships to sweep the harbor's channel of mines and then destroy a cornered, and outgunned, Spanish fleet. Shafter had other plans. He did not like the idea of assaulting the enemy's strong points in a head-on attack. Instead he decided to land his troops at the Daiquiri and nearby Siboney beaches, push inland, swing around Santiago, and besiege it by capturing the series of hills that dominated any approach to the town. This plan would bring him into direct combat with an army of at least fifteen thousand Spanish troops, but he saw it as the best option, especially in view of the fact that he expected help from Cuban guerrillas.

The Cottonbalers, grateful to feel solid ground under their feet, milled around outside of the town of Daiquiri and took in their new surroundings. Cuban irregulars, hungry, raggedly dressed, and desperate looking, stared at the Americans. These Cubans, gaunt eyed and listless, looked like they had not eaten in weeks. Their legs and ankles were mere skin and bones. Some of the Cubans carried rifles; others, machetes. The Americans traded knowing looks and murmured comments with one another: so the Spanish atrocity stories were true after all. Some of the men gave rations and whatever else they could spare to the Cubans.

If the people bore the imprint of many hard years of merciless warfare, so did the land. Everything—homes, machinery, boats, trees—lay in a state of disrepair, and none of the surrounding fields showed even the slightest hint of fertility or cultivation. Only coconuts, which lay about in immense piles, betrayed any sign of life. Some of the Cottonbalers helped themselves to the coconuts, gorging themselves on the sweet milk. Later these men experienced terrible nausea and cramps. For the rest of their lives, many of them felt sick at the slightest whiff of coconut.

Late in the afternoon, the men began to move inland on a trail, along slightly rising high ground, surrounded on all sides by palm trees and tropical jungle. For several miles, guided by their Cuban allies, they made slow progress, sweating profusely in the heat. The jungle itself along with their cowboy-style "doughboy" hats provided the only shade. Their uniforms represented the last vestiges of the nineteenth-century Army—blue tunics with light blue trousers, blankets worn around the torso, cartridge belts wrapped belly button high, knapsacks and canteens resting on either hip. Their footgear consisted of typical army campaign shoes, leathery and uncomfortable, encased in canvas leggings that would challenge the mettle of Cottonbalers for the next half century. The rifles that rested on their shoulders were of the latest design. In 1893, the Army transitioned from the old Springfield single-shot weapons (the Cottonbalers used these at Big Hole) to the new Krag-Jørgensen bolt-action, breech-loaded rifle. The Krag, as soldiers called it, fired a five-shot smokeless powder cartridge at distances of up to two miles. The troops liked this new rifle and knew it could hold its own against the best European-made firearms, including the German-manufactured Mauser rifles their Spanish antagonists possessed.[9]

After darkness the unit finally halted near a stream and set up camp for the evening. Soldiers scrambled around looking for firewood. Others pitched their crude pup tents, and not a moment too soon, because rain began to fall in buckets. All night long, in varying degrees, the rain continued. It swept away tents and drenched soldiers. Even those who managed to keep their tents secure could not keep dry, as the rain dripped through little tears and stitches in the tent cloth or ran in rivulets into the tents from outside. Men scratched skin irritated by wetness and poison oak, a nasty combination. One soldier made the mistake of pitching his tent on a massive anthill and received a uniform full of tiny insects and a body full of little red welts for his trouble.

At daylight the rain finally stopped and some of the soldiers succeeded in lighting fires over which they cooked their rations of bacon and hardtack. Soon the order came to move out for Siboney, and they quickly gathered up their sopping-wet tents, blankets, and equipment and marched back into thick jungle. The heat was almost too much for the soldiers. The jungle was so thick that officers had to dismount from their horses. Land crabs, measuring a foot across, their joints cracking and squeaking, scuttled away at the sound of the soldiers' approach. Flies and mosquitoes buzzed around, making a general nuisance of themselves.

The march dragged on forever, sapping the soldiers of energy and vitality. Late in the day, they camped at a destroyed fruit plantation. The owner had apparently been loyal to the cause of Cuban independence, and the Spanish authorities punished him by ruining his land. No one knew what had happened to the owner—probably dead or in a detention camp.

As the troops set up their tents and settled in for what they hoped would be a dry night, they noticed a messenger enter camp at full gallop. He handed a note to General Adna Chaffee, the 3rd Brigade commander and one of the best combat leaders in the entire Army. A moment later, the brigade bugler sounded the call to arms. Immediately everyone scrambled into formation. Apparently, a division of dismounted cavalry under the command of hard-charging Major General Joseph Wheeler, a former Confederate officer, had run into trouble at Las Guasimas, a key stretch of high ground along the road to Santiago. Upon landing at Siboney, Wheeler had pushed his division toward Las Guasimas at breakneck speed. The old Rebel knew that the Spaniards could turn the place into a formidable fortress.[10]

Now he and his men needed help from the infantry. The Cotton-balers and their brigade brethren from the 12th and 17th Regiments moved out quickly along jungle trails, passing Siboney and moving west. They could hear shooting in the distance. Somewhere among this swarm of soldiers, Kohr ran eagerly toward what he hoped might be his first fight: "There were Cubans along the trail we were now following, cutting poles and brush to fill in the swamps so our column could pass over. Our men were endeavoring to keep together in the line of march, some who were almost breathless throwing away knapsacks and other articles so as to be able to keep up with the brigade which was now on the run. Our companies kept together in good order. The firing now became plainer and our brigade halted for a short rest; men cut open tomato cans and drank as much of the contents as they could, passing the remainder to other boys so as to be relieved of a part of their burden. The bugle once more sounded forward and our column started on double time, our commander leading on horseback. The firing had almost ceased now but we rushed on, some of the men tumbling out of the line, overcome by heat. The trail now became narrow and our companies proceeded in twos."[11] They reached a small stream that flowed between two steep hills, and the bugler sounded a halt. The cavalry no longer needed help.

The Spanish had retreated from Las Guasimas. In so doing, they had ceded precious ground to the United States, opening the gateway for an advance on Santiago from whichever direction the Americans chose. The battle cost the Spanish ten killed and twenty-five wounded, while the Americans lost sixteen dead and fifty-two wounded, many from Teddy Roosevelt's famous Rough Riders and the all-black 10th Cavalry Regiment.[12]

After a short halt, Kohr and the other infantrymen advanced past the field hospitals where many of the cavalry troops lay badly wounded. Doctors dressed and bandaged wounds while mangled soldiers moaned and screamed. Some men walked around in a stupor, completely overcome by the heat, dehydrated and raving incoherently. Kohr and his buddies climbed the high ground of Las Guasimas and then spread out along the plain just beyond this high ground. In the distance they could see Santiago about eight miles away. Already the Spanish were busy building a ring of fortifications around the town, mainly along the hills and villages to the north and east of the city—San Juan, Kettle, El Caney.

For nearly a week the Cottonbalers camped and stood guard in the valleys east of Santiago as General Shafter established his headquarters nearby and pondered his next move. Mule trains supplied the infantry troops with rations and ammunition, but trails had to be cut and roads built to accommodate transportation wagons and artillery. Cuban troops hacked away at the jungle while U.S. engineers felled trees and built corduroy roads. Rain turned the ground into muck, making their jobs that much tougher.

SHAFTER, SUFFERING TERRIBLY FROM HEAT EXHAUSTION, decided to launch an attack as soon as possible. He was worried about the possibility that Spanish reinforcements would soon augment Santiago's ten thousand defenders. The general decided on a two-pronged attack. In the north, two artillery batteries and General Henry Lawton's 2nd Division, which included the 7th Regiment, would attack the fortified village of El Caney, overwhelm its defenders, and capture the water station that supplied Santiago. As soon as Lawton engaged El Caney, the left side of Shafter's corps, including Wheeler's cavalrymen and another infantry division, would push forward along the main trail against the San Juan heights directly to the east of Santiago. Lawton, having easily taken El Caney, would then wheel left, link up with the rest of the army, and join a final push on Santiago the next day. Shafter's plan was a bit risky, because he possessed little artillery and naval gun support was almost nonexistent. But the Spanish played right into his beefy hands by spreading their troops thinly all around Santiago rather than concentrating them at likely attack points like San Juan and El Caney.

Even so, the coming battle proved to be very difficult for the American soldiers. The Cottonbalers received word to leave their camp at four o'clock on the afternoon of June 30. For several hours, first in the twilight and then in the darkness, they walked quietly along a muddy trail that had been cut the day before. Sometime during the night they stopped and bivouacked, stacking their rifles and lying down next to them. They were so close to the Spanish that no one talked above a whisper. Over the course of the night, the only disturbance came from a lost mule wandering around in the dark. It bellowed and roared, waking up several of the men, who charged for their rifles in the belief that the Spanish had found their camp. Then someone called out softly, "Hold on there! It's only a blamed mule." The soldiers settled down and went back to sleep, although some threatened to cut the mule's throat.

Just after three in the morning, officers and sergeants crept from position to position softly waking the men. They shook cobwebs of sleep from their heads and prepared for a day of battle. All of them knew that this day would bring fighting and dying. No one could imagine that he might be killed. It was always the other guy who might get it. The men gathered their blankets and knapsacks and sat down for one last meal. Kohr remembered the quiet introspection among the men as they ate and then left their bivouac for battle. "We . . . ate our hardtack and cold tomatoes and were soon in line, following a narrow trail single file. We were soon strung out for miles. We crossed over hills, through small valleys and across small streams. Light in the east became stronger, and we could now distinguish large trees on the hills." No one said a word. Each man simply concentrated on putting one foot in front of the other.[13]

They emerged from the trail and stealthily deployed along the reverse slope of a grassy ridge overlooking the north side of El Caney, the 12th Infantry on the left, the 7th in the middle, and the 17th on the right. The wind swept through the tall grass, tickling their cheeks and ears. General Chaffee had personally reconnoitered the trail and the entire battlefield before them. From their prone positions they could see the village and the entire enemy defensive system. The village consisted of "thatched and tiled roofs half hidden by the large shade-trees that we afterward learned to dread as the lurking-places of sharpshooters," wrote one man. "In the village itself profound quiet reigned, and there was no sign of life beyond a few thin wisps of smoke that curled from the cottage chimneys. Beyond lay the fertile valley with a few cattle grazing, and around us on three sides arose, tier upon tier, the beautiful Maestra Mountains. To our left stretched the thick green jungle, with its rippling bamboo-groves and clumps of royal palm." Just in front of the village, he could see the Spanish fortifications. "At the southeast corner [of El Caney] is a steep conical hill, one hundred feet high, crowned by an old-fashioned but strong stone fort, which forms a prominent feature in the landscape and commands the whole village and its approaches. This fort was extensively loop-holed, and was further strengthened by a steep rifle-trench outside on the south and east sides. At intervals around the rest of the village were some half dozen smaller block-houses, connected by short lengths of trenches with [barbed] wire entanglements in front. Above the little bastion flapped lazily the red and yellow flag of Spain, and lounging outside the gateway was a group of soldiers in their light blue pajama uniforms and white straw hats. If they were aware of our presence they seemed remarkably indifferent to it."[14]

At 6:35 A.M. the American artillery, located roughly one mile west of the Cottonbalers, opened up on the Spanish positions. The barrage from these four guns was pathetically ineffective, but no matter. The infantry sprang into action. Like everyone else around him, Kohr clutched his Krag, jumped to his feet, and raced forward: "The long, thin blue line of men crossing the hills and twisting around through the valleys must have resembled a huge snake making its way over the sur-

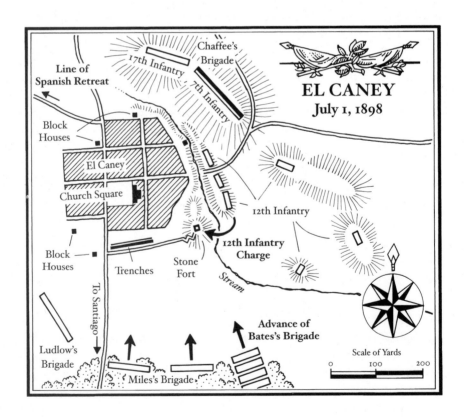

face. We could hear the sharp crack of small arms mingled with the continuous roar of the artillery . . . as we descended the slope of the ridge, our line advanced in full range of a block house, which was located across a small ravine on the hillside to our right. As we came in view their bullets began clipping the leaves around us, but we continued our march paying no heed to this."[15]

That soon changed. The volume of Spanish rifle fire increased to deadly proportions. An enemy bullet smashed into a soldier near Kohr, shattering his ankle and leaving an ugly, jagged wound. The enemy fire, combined with the heat, soon took a toll, and the men stopped for a second. Squatting in hiding places within the tall grass, they threw away their blanket rolls, knapsacks, and rations. Then they took off their blue tunics and rolled up their sleeves. Clad now in only their shirt-sleeves, trousers, and doughboy hats, they embodied the notion of light infantry.

Freed from their personal encumbrances, they pressed forward again, this time a bit more cautiously, bent over in the hopes of making smaller targets. For several long moments they advanced, up and down a steep grade, through a small stream, and into a gully where many American wounded had collected. Bullets whizzed around angrily, smacking and slapping here and there into the flesh of unlucky men. Those who were hit barely cried out. They simply groaned and fell down. The soldiers could not pause to help them or the attack would lose momentum. Officers hollered above the din to keep moving and the troops slowly walked, at a crouch, up a gradual slope through a pineapple field until finally the enemy fire grew so thick that they had to take cover along a grassy ridge, some four hundred yards in front of the Spanish positions.

The enemy had only rifles with which to oppose the attack but used them well. The volume of fire defied belief. Shot after shot zinged through the Cottonbaler ranks. Seemingly no place was safe. The 7th Regiment had unknowingly advanced right into the thickest field of enemy fire. James Burton, a *Harper's Weekly* photographer assigned to the regiment, took cover like everyone else. "Within five minutes we were in the midst of a heavy shower of bullets from the Mauser rifles of the Spanish, and between two fires—one from a small block-house on our right, the other from the strong stone block-house at El Caney, immediately in front of us."[16]

The Cottonbalers were now pinned down. They lay prone, cowering along their grassy ridge and frantically searching for targets. The grass provided a bit of concealment, but it also tickled and sliced at exposed arms and faces. Men had to force themselves to ignore ants and other insects crawling over and around them.

Not far away from Burton, Sergeant Kohr and his men staked out a small hiding spot just behind the slope of the ridge. "Directly in front of us were two or three blockhouses; the dirt was thrown up in front of these ten or fifteen feet high; in front of that were intrenchments. We were ordered to fire at will." The noise of the shooting was so loud that men had to scream in one another's ears to be heard. "We could see nothing to fire at, except buildings and blockhouses, for no Spaniards were in sight. The two other brigades of our division were attacking on our left, continuing nearly opposite from where we were. We stuck to the top of the hill, the Seventeenth Infantry to our right."[17] Private William Knipes, like many other men in the 7th Regiment, tried to survive as he moved across this death ground in front of El Caney. "The bullets were tearing around us on all sides. I felt two of them ping across my belt. [It] was a death pit. We were mowed down like sheep."[18] Within seconds he got hit six times, but he kept going until a bullet tore through his neck. His buddies carried him, grievously wounded, to safety and he managed to survive.

SHAFTER'S ATTACK WAS FALTERING BADLY. HE HAD EXpected the Spanish to quickly retreat from El Caney at the first sight of the American attack, but it wasn't happening. Instead, they had fortified the town and settled in for a tough fight. With little or no hope of more fire support or reinforcements, the success or failure of the El Caney assault, and perhaps the entire Santiago campaign, rested upon the sweaty, overburdened shoulders of the pinned-down infantrymen of Lawton's division. Could they find a way to move forward and capture the formidable blockhouses and rifle pits that defended the village?

For several hours during the late morning and early afternoon of July 1, the answer seemed to be negative. No one along the line could make any headway. Any forward movement brought death from Spanish sharpshooters concealed in trees, cottages, and blockhouses. "They knew every range perfectly and picked off our men with distressing accuracy if they showed as much as a head," commented one man, "if one didn't actually 'eat grass,' one kept remarkably close to it." Seven skirmishers from the 7th Regiment tried to advance beyond the ridge and take up firing positions along some tiny hedges. In a matter of seconds, enemy fire ripped through them. Three of them fell dead instantly. Four others were wounded. They lay on the ground, coughed, and groaned, blood gurgling from bullet holes and exit wounds. With pleading eyes, they looked back to the main line for help, but no one could do anything for them.[19]

Caught in the most dangerous section of the entire battlefield, the Cottonbalers had no choice but to lie still, return fire as best they could, and hope the battle turned. To make matters worse, the sun had risen high in the sky now and the heat of the day grew worse. The sun shone mercilessly on their backs and the men could do nothing but remain in place; better to sweat than to die.

Of course hiding in the grass did not guarantee safety. Far from it. Kohr saw a scene that would almost have been comical if not so grim: "A . . . member of our company . . . was conversing with comrades on both sides of him; the one on the right ceased to talk to him and he remarked to the comrade on the left that he must be asleep. The fire continued and after awhile the one on the left ceased talking also. Later on he found that his two comrades had been killed and he had been lying between them for several hours thinking they were asleep."[20]

Photographer Burton quivered silently among the soldiers and recalled "bullets whistling around . . . on all sides, yet seeing nothing, only hearing them as they rush by, crashing through the leaves and twigs on their deadly errand. I heard several heavy thuds near me, and on looking around me, saw some of our men on the ground, dead or wounded." The volume of fire steadily increased and the men had no choice but to remain in place: "The men stood it without flinching, the fierce sun scorching their backs, and suffering heavy losses from an enemy who was practically invisible and to whom they could not reply effectively." Spanish bullets smashed through bodies like a random, bloody scythe: "Some were killed instantly, and sank with scarcely a groan, some with a curse, and others with the name of God on their lips, whilst most of the wounded swore terribly at the Spaniards. Everyone was brave and patient, some of the wounded having to lie two or three hours before they were attended to, owing to the great lack of surgeons and medical attendants."[21]

As Burton's last sentence indicated, the Medical Corps, like the rest of the Army, was unprepared for this campaign. The Army did not have enough stretcher bearers or doctors to deal with the number of casualties that resulted from the battle. Consequently, some Cottonbalers finally began to drag their wounded comrades back a couple hundred yards to a sunken road relatively immune from enemy fire. Dozens of them lay there in stoic silence waiting for hours to be treated by the scarce number of doctors.

One correspondent moved among the wounded, doing whatever he could for them: "Some of the slightly wounded were tending those who were badly hit, and nothing could have surpassed the unskilled tenderness of these men. I was astonished, too, at their thoughtful consideration. 'Keep well down, sir . . . Them Mausers is flying pretty low, and there's plenty of us here already.' The heat in the little road was intense, there was no shade nor a breath of air, and the wounded lay sweltering in the sun till the head reeled with the rank smell of sweat and saturated flannel. The stench was overpowering and a sudden lull in the battle brought into sickening prominence the angry buzzing of the disturbed flies and the creaking of the land-crabs which waited in the bushes. One man I noticed lying very quiet in a great pool of blood. A comrade with a shattered leg was fanning him with a hat and keeping flies off his face. I sat down beside them, and seeing the man was shot right through the stomach [I] knew there was nothing I could do beyond giving him a little water." He asked the gut-shot man how he was doing and the man replied, " 'Oh! I am doing pretty well, sir.' " The man's buddy wondered if a doctor could be found, but the man with the belly wound said, " 'That's all right, Mick; I guess the doctors have more than they can [handle] looking after them as are badly hurt, and they will be along soon.' " The correspondent marveled at the soldier's quiet courage.[22]

MEANWHILE, BACK ON THE LINE, THE STALEMATE CONTINued. It was early afternoon now and the Cottonbalers still had not been able to move from their sweaty, bloody ridge. Enemy fire still snipped and snicked the grass and bushes and the men continued to endure this nightmarish glorified game of Russian roulette. The soldiers lay motionless, peering intently at the blockhouses and village, searching for targets. Periodically a soldier would find one, rise up quickly, fire his rifle, and then hit the dirt as an angry volley of bullets answered his shot. Sometimes these brave soldiers got hit. A few died instantly. The rest crawled painfully back to the sunken road, their eyes dazed and glazed.

In spite of their tenacity, many of the troops were crazed with thirst.

Frederick M. H. Kendrick, the Civil War and Big Hole veteran, was now a sixty-year-old captain in command of D Company.[23] He called for volunteers to go to a nearby creek and fetch water for the wounded. A young private named McMurphy, alongside a buddy named Grider, crawled forward and volunteered. McMurphy's real name was Fred B. MacPherson, but he had enlisted under the name of McMurphy, perhaps in an effort to shed the stigma of a questionable civilian record. At any rate, the pseudonymed Private Murphy performed bravely on this day: "I thought every step would be the last, as we double timed over the same ground we had taken and then to the creek to fill our canteens, and the bullets spattered all around us from the two block houses and the stone church in El Caney." McMurphy and Grider continued successfully on their mission of mercy and distributed water to the wounded and the thirsty.

As he distributed water, McMurphy encountered Lieutenant Thomas Wansboro, a fresh-faced young officer just a few years out of West Point. Optimistic, pleasant, and irrepressible by nature, Wansboro gave McMurphy a friendly greeting and moved on foot, through thick underbrush, toward the positions held by D and E companies.[24] McMurphy did not know it, but Wansboro was in the process of caring for the wounded. All day long the young lieutenant had risked his life moving from wounded man to wounded man, providing comfort, providing water, helping them back to the collection area if need be. With a distinct sense of awe, one of the war correspondents watched Wansboro's selfless bravery: "Close in front of me a slight and boyish lieutenant compelled my attention by his persistent and reckless gallantry. Whenever a man was hit he would dart to his assistance regardless of the fire that this exposure inevitably drew." In the early afternoon, not long after McMurphy saw Wansboro, the law of averages caught up with the young officer: "Suddenly he sprang to his feet gazing intently into the village, but what he saw we never knew; for he was instantly shot through the heart and fell over backward clutching at the air."

Frustrated and enraged, Wansboro's men screamed and pounded their fists in the dirt. Some of them crawled over to the prostrate lieutenant and dragged him out of danger. They unbuttoned his tunic and looked at the wound, knowing all too well that there was nothing they could do for Wansboro. "You will never see his better," one of the men said. "He fought like a little tiger." The lieutenant struggled to breathe, but his situation was hopeless: "A few convulsive gasps and the poor boy was dead, and as we laid him in a shady spot by the side of the road [his] sergeant reverently drew a handkerchief over his face and said, 'Good-by, Lieutenant, you were a brave little officer, and you died like a true soldier.' "[25]

The regiment had lost one of its best junior officers, the kind who usually die first in combat because of their willingness to court danger, and the kind who can never be replaced. Even so, the men had little time to mourn. Their situation was far too serious for that. By the early afternoon, the attack on the southern sector of El Caney had been reinforced and the soldiers there were making slow, yard-by-yard progress, but for the Cottonbalers nothing had changed. They were still pinned down and taking casualties from enemy Mauser fire. From time to time, General Chaffee appeared, seemingly out of nowhere, field glasses in hand, and directed fire, but that was the extent of what the Cottonbalers could do. "There was no hope of charging," Sergeant Kohr wrote, "as barbed wire entanglements were strung in every direction in front of us, and it was certain death to anyone who attempted to pass over the line of the hill."[26]

Just when it seemed like Lawton's entire division would be stymied at El Caney, the situation changed. Artillery fire from the two small American batteries began to batter and knock down the walls of the stone fort (El Viso), and infantrymen crawled forward far enough to cut holes in the Spanish barbed-wire defenses. The division commander received orders from Shafter to disengage and reinforce the attack at San Juan but knew he could not do that. A withdrawal from El Caney would be disastrous to morale, and he knew he was close to taking the Spanish forts and the village. So at 2:15 P.M. he ordered an assault. The 12th Regiment, located immediately to the left of the Cottonbalers, led the way. The 7th, decimated and still under a murderous cross fire from the blockhouses and the village, stayed put.

The Cottonbalers watched as the men of the 12th rushed forward, running up a ravine and then a hill, right at the Spanish. "They swarmed over the wire fences and the trenches beyond like a hive of angry bees," one man recalled, "and amidst the cheering of the rest of the line drove the enemy helter-skelter over the crest of the hill." Within half an hour, they reached El Viso and overwhelmed the remaining Spanish soldiers. "The men ran about like schoolboys; cheering and waving their hats; the officers were shaking hands and congratulating each other."[27]

Back at the 7th Regiment positions, excitement also reigned. Private

Tomanus of E Company saw the American flag raised over El Viso and, according to Kohr, could not contain himself: "He . . . rose to his knees and began to cheer. A Spanish sharpshooter, from the cupola of his church in El Caney, shot him through the heart. The shot pierced the corner of his wife's photograph, which he carried in the left pocket of his blue army shirt." One week before, Tomanus, the company barber, had had a premonition of death, telling his lieutenant he would not survive the coming battle.

Everyone began to realize that though El Viso had been taken, much fighting remained to be done. Spanish fire kept whistling around the little fortress, hitting men, so the Americans formed skirmish lines behind the remaining walls of the fort and returned fire at the Spanish survivors in blockhouses and the village. Other American soldiers, at the same time, kept up the pressure on the town, and Spanish resistance finally broke. Enemy soldiers streamed out of the northwest end of El Caney, even as American fire cut them down in the streets. By 3:45 P.M. the fighting was over. The Americans had won a costly victory, losing 81 killed and 360 wounded against 411 Spanish casualties.[28] The 7th, pinned down in a cross fire for most of the battle, suffered nearly one-third of the U.S. casualties: thirty-three killed and ninety-nine wounded, over 13 percent of the regiment's strength.[29]

After removing their wounded, replenishing their ammunition, and retrieving their discarded clothing and equipment, the Cottonbalers took stock of the El Caney battlefield. The forts, blockhouses, and rifle pits looked like a sloppy butcher had been at work: "Inside the shattered fort the walls were splashed with blood and a dozen dead and wounded were laid out on the floor, or wedged under the debris. The trench around the fort was a grewsome [sic] sight, floored with dead Spaniards in horribly contorted attitudes and with sightless, staring eyes. Others were littered about the slope, and these were mostly terribly mutilated by shell fire. Those killed in the trenches were all shot through the forehead, and their brains oozed out like white paint from a color-tube."[30] In the very same rifle pits, another man saw a dead Spanish soldier "in a sitting position, his back resting against the end of the pit, his knees raised, the legs being drawn toward the body, his hands flabbily resting by his sides, his head slightly thrown back, exposing to view the white of his eyes, and his partially opened mouth showing his teeth. In his lap rested a straw hat—partially filled with his own brains!"[31]

Kohr and his men explored the town and found the bodies of the

Spanish commander, General Vara del Rey, and several of his officers: "On the general's light blue uniform were three silver stars on each shoulder. A friend of mine began cutting off several of these stars with his pen knife. We told him we would not take these, but he wanted them for souvenirs. They never did him any good, and he died about four weeks later with dysentery."

They encountered a lone die-hard Spanish officer in a blockhouse who would not surrender. The enemy officer fired several shots at Kohr and the others until the Americans poured a massive volume of rifle fire on the blockhouse, wounding the recalcitrant Spanish captain. In spite of his best efforts, he ended up being taken prisoner.

Cubans, half-starved and dressed in rags, wandered around the town, cleaning up the streets. Discarded Spanish flags, rifles, and clothing lay everywhere. The 7th Regiment soldiers set about the task of cleaning up and burying their comrades. As they did so, Kohr's commanding officer, a popular fifty-one-year-old Big Hole veteran named Captain Charles Worden, started behaving strangely. He took a captured Spanish mule and loaded it with as many souvenirs as he could find, even a Mauser rifle that he apparently "tied to the mule's tail." He then wandered off and no one knew his whereabouts for several days until someone found him asleep under a tree, his mule loaded down with every conceivable scrap of loot. Worden was suffering from heat exhaustion and dysentery and could not stand the tropical heat. His superiors quietly removed him from command and eventually he was evacuated back to the United States, where he died two months later.[32]

For two days, half of the regiment, including Kohr's E Company, carried out the arduous task of moving the wounded to field hospitals closer to the coast. They built improvised stretchers out of poles, blankets, and shelter tents and hauled their suffering comrades in terrible heat, along crude trails.

In the meantime, the other half of the regiment, Companies B, D, F, and H, left El Caney at sunset on July 1 and marched all night, in the rain, to reinforce the newly won American positions along the San Juan ridges overlooking Santiago. In an all-day fight that centered around the capture of San Juan and Kettle hills, the rest of Shafter's V Corps, in spite of terrible casualties, took this vital high ground. The fighting here emerged as the most famous of the war, partially because of the key role played by future president Teddy Roosevelt's 1st U.S. Volunteer Cavalry Regiment, better known as the Rough Riders. That night

Shafter, fading terribly in the heat, worried about his thinly held line around Santiago and even pondered withdrawing from his hard-won territory for fear of being attacked by Spanish reinforcements he believed were on the way. So he needed every available man to hold the positions around Santiago and the Cottonbalers of those four companies occupied the right side of his line.

Both sides had entrenched themselves, and the campaign settled down into a stalemate. The Cottonbalers dug in and traded ineffective, but worrisome, shots with the enemy all day long on the second of July. Actually, these trenches were really more like glorified ditches, affording the men enough room to crouch in the dirt, cover most of their bodies, and take up firing positions. The positions were hot, muddy, and smelly, but they were reasonably safe, especially compared with the carnage of El Caney, still fresh in everyone's mind.

The next day the Spanish fleet tried to fight its way out of Santiago Harbor and was annihilated. In effect, this meant that the Spanish in Santiago now had no hope of victory unless rescued by friendly troops from the northwest, an unlikely, if not impossible, prospect. Shafter, ignorant of the fate of the Spanish fleet but having no desire, in view of his terrible losses on July 1, to assault Santiago, called for the Spanish to surrender. He warned that if they did not surrender, he would soon open up a terrific bombardment on the city that could lead to the deaths of many innocent people. The Spanish declined to surrender, but they did agree to a truce while the city was evacuated.

The truce lasted for a week. During that time, refugees streamed out of the city. Kohr and the men of E Company watched these unfortunate souls and felt a deep sense of sadness and pity: "Some carried white bundles of clothing, others furniture of every description; others came in carriages. Thousands made their way to El Caney, which had now been thoroughly cleaned and was in a respectable condition." The refugees taxed an already overwrought American supply system.

Meanwhile, the Cottonbalers and the rest of the Army worked on their trenches: "We were supplied with picks and shovels and set to work digging intrenchments," Kohr wrote. "These intrenchments were drained perfectly dry. Sand bags were filled and it was not long until they were in first-class condition. The Twelfth Infantry was intrenched on our left; the Seventeenth on our right."[33]

Spanish and American officers negotiated and haggled every day during the truce. The Americans wanted a surrender. The Spanish wanted some honorable way, short of surrender, to end the campaign. They could not reach an agreement, and at 4:00 P.M. on the tenth the truce flags were lowered and the firing resumed. American ships, cannons, mortars, and Gatling guns pounded the Spanish positions in and around Santiago.

The Cottonbalers fired a few volleys in the direction of the enemy at a range of about four hundred yards, but mostly the artillery carried the weight of the renewed American offensive. The Spanish hardly responded. The biggest peril for the Americans was a torrential rainstorm that dumped sheets of water on them. They found a way to sleep in their filthy trenches in spite of water up to their knees. Lightning crackled in the distance and the wind blew rain in every direction. No one could even imagine what it would be like to be dry.

Luckily for the Cottonbalers and the rest of the U.S. Army in Cuba, the Spanish were in no shape to keep fighting. They agreed to yet another truce on July 11 and then indicated their desire to surrender on the fourteenth. For the 7th Infantry, the fighting had ended on the eleventh when the 1st Illinois Volunteer Infantry Regiment, newly arrived in country, replaced them in the trenches. As the negotiations continued, the 7th received orders to dig entrenchments along a different stretch of the line about four miles to the right of their original spot, in a swamp near a railroad. Here they toiled for a few days, dealing with more rain and plenty of heat, dreading the onset of the yellow fever season. On the afternoon of the seventeenth, a messenger informed them that the Spanish had formally surrendered. Two days later the 7th triumphantly left their trenches "amid the playing of bands and cheering of soldiers." They watched as the American flag was raised over Santiago.

THE FIGHTING WAS OVER BUT NOT THE DYING. DISEASE and climate-related problems decimated the survivors of El Caney. "We marched to the top of a long ridge, where we went into camp," Kohr wrote. "We now received large quantities of fresh beef and an abundant supply of rations. Large tents were brought out from Santiago and new khaki uniforms [the U.S. Army's standard dress for the next half century] were furnished to us. The camp was in good condition, but sickness still increased. Our regiment's loss was three and four each day. Many of the men had fever, others malaria."[34] Many others had dysentery or were suffering from sunstroke. For many weeks the soldiers suffered in this tropical hell and wondered when the War Department would finally send them home.

Medical science had progressed since the rudimentary days of the Civil War, but not far enough. The United States still lost more men to disease in the Spanish-American War than combat. Among the Cottonbalers no one wanted to go to the hospital because rumors abounded about the awful treatment there.

To make matters worse, the Commissary Department sometimes issued rotten food to the 7th Regiment. Captain Kendrick wrote an extensive report to the inspector general in Washington about the problems his men encountered with bad food: "The first refrigerated beef issued to Company D, 7th Infantry was to the best of my recollection about July 24th, 1898 while in camp near Cubitas. The first four issues appeared to be good although immediately after a number of my men were taken with dysentery. About August 8th the fresh beef . . . had a peculiar odor and a bad appearance. I inspected the beef and declined to receive it fearing that as the men's stomachs were weak it might create disease. For three days in succession this was the case." He brought the problem to the attention of his regimental commander Lieutenant Colonel Gilbert Carpenter, who had assumed command from the aged Benham. Carpenter ordered Kendrick to bury the rotten meat.

Kendrick also commented on the food his D Company Cottonbalers ate during the Santiago campaign: "Referring to the canned roast beef it was on June 7th, 1898 issued as part of the travel ration on the transport 'Iroquois' for use between Tampa, Fla and Daiquiri, Cuba. It was labeled McNeil and Libby and was tasteless and nauseating. Many of my men would not touch it after the first meal. The next issue was about June 28th and was only consumed by men who were hungry. A great deal of it was thrown away. I tried it myself. It tasted as if the extract had been boiled out of it. I tried it several times uncooked and it was nauseating. I then tried it cooked and seasoned with salt and pepper and it was unpalatable. While in the trenches before Santiago . . . I thought the sickness of my men . . . was traceable to the canned beef and I told them to that effect. When leaving Santiago, part of the travel ration consisted of the canned roast beef which the men refused to eat and it was thrown away upon arrival at Montauk Point, NY. The other parts of the ration, bacon, canned corn beef and hard bread were good."[35]

On August 20, Companies B, C, E, G, H, and I, along with the band

and headquarters, boarded ships, followed by the rest of the regiment the next day. The miserable journey to Montauk on Long Island lasted about a week. Basically there were now three types of Cottonbalers: those who were sick, those who had been sick, and those who were going to be sick. Dysentery, malaria, and yellow fever raged among the men, and seasickness, combined with disgusting food, did not exactly help matters.

Sergeant Kohr fit the first category. Debilitated with fever, he remembered nothing of the boat ride home until he was carried off the ship at Montauk Point and into a waiting hospital bed. He spent a week there and improved to the point where the Army sent him home to Ohio for convalescent leave. He recuperated and after two months at home returned to the regiment, where he served out the rest of his enlistment. In 1899 he was discharged and spent a few days as a civilian before reenlisting, this time in the engineers. He served another three-year enlistment, including tours of duty in the Philippines and China, before leaving the Army for good. A year and a half later, he suffered a horrible accident while laying water mains in Iowa. He and the other workmen used dynamite to excavate the frozen Iowa soil, and one day they set a charge that seemed to be a dud. Kohr figured that the dynamite needed a new blasting cap or maybe a new fuse, and he picked up the explosives for a closer look. The dynamite exploded, tearing off his right arm, blowing out his eyes, and fracturing his jaw. He recovered but spent the rest of his sight-impaired life as a traveling pencil salesman.[36]

After returning home, the other survivors of the 7th Regiment recuperated from the bevy of tropical diseases that plagued them. After a few months, the regiment was scattered among numerous posts throughout the United States. The Cottonbalers were taking the places of other units that had been dispatched to take care of some new business for Uncle Sam. Upon winning the Spanish-American War, the United States inherited control of the Philippine islands, an extensive archipelago that had been the other major theater of war besides Cuba. The Spanish had controlled the Philippines for many hundreds of years, but no more. The islands now came under the jurisdiction of the victorious United States. McKinley contemplated whether to remain as an imperial overseer or grant the Filipinos their independence. He decided on the former, setting off a costly and atrocity-laced war between the Americans and the Filipinos. Indeed, ten times more Americans would end up dying in this war than in the short-lived conflict with Spain.

At first the Cottonbalers were not involved in this war. Some of the soldiers went to Alaska to guard mining operations against the encroachments of hostile Native American tribes. Others went to the Presidio in San Francisco. But in March 1901 Companies C, D, H, and M boarded transport ships bound for Luzon, the main island of the Philippines. The men who ascended gangways did not know it, but they were part of a historic moment, a kind of turning point, in the regiment's history. For the first time, the unit was being asked to serve outside the Western Hemisphere, a harbinger of things to come and an indicator of the future course of American foreign and military policy.

The four companies of the 7th Regiment served in a garrison function in Luzon for six months before transferring to Samar in October 1901. There they participated in a campaign against insurgents fighting a guerrilla war against U.S. power. Almost no accounts or records of any kind survive from this period of the regiment's history, and the historian can only speculate on the reasons for that gap.[37] The Samar campaign carries with it a reputation for brutality (American soldiers occasionally used torture and detention camps as a weapon against the insurgents here and elsewhere in the islands), but the 7th's role in the campaign is practically anonymous. In fact, the latest histories of the Philippine War make no mention of the 7th at all.[38] Most of the fighting ended by 1902, and the four companies went home that year.

What is certain is that the unit served several tours of duty in the Philippines during the early years of the twentieth century and, alternating between the Pacific and the Presidio back in California, settled down into its usual garrison routine. The next time the men of the regiment fought, their battlefields would not be the steamy jungles of the Pacific but instead the chilly trenches and forests of Europe, completely new battlefields for these American soldiers who would soon find themselves fighting a new and formidable enemy.

7

The Cottonbalers' First Modern War

World War I

THE BROKEN, TORN, DESTROYED LANDSCAPE TOLD THE
story in a way that nothing else could. The shattered rows of trees that
had once been peaceful woods, the muddy, shell-hole-pocked ridges
and plains now generally referred to as "no-man's-land," the deep,
jagged, head-high entrenchments that honeycombed and snaked their
way through what had once been rich farmland, quaint towns, and the
sites of profitable industries, all bore mute testimony to the great and
overarching reality of modern warfare. Firepower ruled the battlefield.
An awesome symphony of horrendously destructive weapons, produced faster and in greater numbers by modern technology and factories, dictated, from this point forward, nearly everything about the
experience of combat.

To be sure, warfare had been heading in this direction for quite some
time, particularly since the middle of the nineteenth century, when improved rifles and artillery reaped an enormous harvest of death among
those who fought the Civil War with the tactics of the Napoleonic era.
The trend toward better small arms and accurate artillery continued
throughout the rest of the nineteenth century, but years of improve-
ments in the grisly art of death culminated in the nightmare of World
War I. Whereas in the past the rifled musket posed the greatest threat
to the life and limb of a soldier, now machine guns and artillery were
the deadliest of all weapons. Three or four machine guns, properly
loaded, positioned, and manned, could wipe out an entire infantry battalion in a matter of minutes. Artillery, firing at greater range and with
greater accuracy, a bevy of deadly fragmentation and gas shells, could
annihilate entire regiments in the right circumstances. The terrible destructiveness of modern weapons turned World War I into a bloody,

hopeless war of stalemate and attrition. Officers who had spent their whole careers preaching the decisiveness of attack and assault now favored the defense.

The lonely infantryman with a rifle in his hands could no longer expect or hope to win—and survive—through sheer guts and fighting spirit. He now had to learn, more than ever before, how to protect himself from the maelstrom of deadly metal that angrily and anonymously spread death like gasoline spreads fire. This was modern war—round-the-clock, firepower dominated, impersonal, and enormously destructive.

The soldiers of the 7th Infantry Regiment had never fought this kind of war until they went to France in 1918. From this point forward, they would never fight a war that did not fit this new mold. During the dark years of World War I, some analysts theorized that the lethality of the twentieth-century battlefield consigned infantry to a garrison and defense role.[1] These theorists (along with their "airpower wins wars alone" descendants) fell prey to exaggeration. Infantrymen could, and would, still carry out an offensive role. However, they now needed increasingly more support to do so. The rest of America's twentieth-century wars would prove both those points. With proper support, training, and management of firepower, American infantrymen continued to accomplish their decisive job of controlling ground and populations.

Thus, in World War I, the Cottonbalers began the difficult process of coping with the deadliness of the modern battlefield. After its hard-fought victory over the Spanish in Cuba in 1898, the regiment reverted to its traditional peacetime garrison role. The 7th served several stints in the Philippines and, when not overseas, settled into a new home at the Presidio in San Francisco. In 1912 it headed east to Fort Leavenworth, and a year later it went to Galveston, Texas. The next year, the regiment participated in the punitive American expedition against Pancho Villa and his cohorts. The 7th landed at Veracruz, just as it had some sixty-seven years before, but this time it saw no action, serving instead in an occupation role. Later that fall, the Cottonbalers returned home and resumed their sedate, staid peacetime duty at various stateside posts.

In the meantime, the United States drifted ever closer to war with Germany, mainly over the question of neutrality rights. When war broke out in Europe in 1914, the United States remained neutral, but over time American sympathies inevitably gravitated toward democratic

Britain and France over imperial Germany. By early 1917, the United States was actively aiding the hard-pressed British and French through bank loans and the sale of munitions. The Germans, hampered by a Royal Navy blockade of their country, sent their submarines into the North Atlantic to cut Britain off from its overseas empire and strangle the kingdom into submission. This brought German submarines into conflict with American ships bound for Britain and France, and when the Germans elected to unleash unrestricted submarine warfare that did not differentiate between belligerent and neutral shipping, American public opinion overwhelmingly favored war with Germany. President Woodrow Wilson, like McKinley, was a bit of a pacifist. He sought to avoid war if at all possible but knew by April 1917 he had little other choice. On the second of that month he asked for and received a declaration of war from Congress.

Unfortunately for Wilson and the Allies, the United States was woefully unprepared for war. The Regular Army consisted of 127,588 soldiers, a pathetically low number for the task ahead. The bloody trench warfare of World War I consumed manpower at a voracious rate. In order to have any impact on a war that could still go either way, the United States would have to build a mass army, comparable in size to those raised during the Civil War, but even larger.

THE MEN WHO MADE UP THE 7TH REGIMENT ON THE EVE of the war were mostly native born and from farming or labor backgrounds. Most of them thought of themselves as professional soldiers. They were disciplined, dedicated, and reasonably well educated—several years of grade school maybe—at a time when a significant minority of the population could not read or write. The officers still came mostly from West Point or the ranks. But once the war started, these hardcore regulars found themselves joined, and eventually outnumbered, by idealistic volunteers from all classes of society as well as lower-middle-class and working-class draftees hailing from all over the country.

The war and its demands eroded the old distinctions between regulars and volunteers that were so prevalent in the nineteenth century. Total war required total mobilization, and that meant enlisting millions of citizen soldiers. The same process had occurred during the Civil War, but in this new era the citizen soldier (whether draftee or volunteer) often served shoulder to shoulder with his Regular Army comrade in mixed units. The War Department, for instance, recognized that the

United States could no longer afford to fight its wars with the amateur-ish approach so prevalent in previous conflicts. Only professionals could improve and modernize this new Army enough to defeat the German Army, which had a reputation of being the best in the world. Training standards were raised. Regular officers found themselves promoted to greater positions of responsibility or transferred to other units to pre-pare and inculcate recruits in the kind of military discipline necessary to survive in battle. Regular noncommissioned officers served as drill sergeants and combat leaders for an entire generation of American fighting men. Other Regular Army sergeants (usually the younger ones) ended up with gold bars on their collars. In the space of a year, the U.S. Army transitioned from a staid, stale organization to a modern mass army geared for twentieth-century ground combat.

So, by the time the 7th Infantry went into battle in 1918, the vast ma-jority of its soldiers were men serving wartime enlistments and not pre-war regulars. In practice, this meant that the unit now reflected a more inclusive cross section of white America than ever before. Indeed, the U.S. Army in 1918 formally abolished the previous distinction it had made among regulars, draftees, and members of the National Guard (the twentieth-century equivalent of the nineteenth-century state vol-unteers and militia).[2] In other words, the Army of the twentieth-century was slowly, but surely, becoming more professional and more demo-cratic, an army heavily influenced and shaped by a rising and increas-ingly authoritative federal government.

THE 7TH REGIMENT SPENT THE SUMMER OF 1917 AT GET-tysburg, on the old battlefield, welcoming and training new recruits. Oddly enough, the regiment bivouacked for much of its time at Gettys-burg on the very same Wheatfield where Cottonbalers had fought and died fifty-four years before. In the fall, the unit moved to Camp Greene, North Carolina, where it continued its training and preparation rou-tine. Here it joined the 3rd Infantry Division, the parent organization to which it would belong for much of the rest of the century. In World War I, the U.S. Army, in an effort to maximize fighting power at the point of attack, organized its infantry divisions into massive quadran-gular units. Each division consisted of four infantry regiments, broken down into brigades containing two regiments apiece. The 7th Regi-ment, along with the 4th, served in the 5th Infantry Brigade in World War I. The other brigade, the 6th, included the 30th and 38th Infantry

Regiments. Each regiment contained three battalions of about twelve hundred men. The rest of the division was fleshed out with artillery and machine-gun battalions in addition to support units. In the 3rd Division each rifle company retained one of its prewar regular officers, but the rest generally came from the Officer Training Camp at Fort Oglethorpe, Georgia. This training camp served the same role that officer candidate schools would for a later generation. In 1917 and 1918, Oglethorpe and other such camps churned out badly needed officers—quickly.

These new leaders prepared their men as best they could for the fight ahead. Droves of new recruits joined the 7th in the latter days of 1917. They suffered through a miserable winter at this crude camp. "It was a tent camp, and the hardships endured there will not be soon forgotten," one officer later wrote. "The winter of 1917–18 was the most severe known in our entire country. It seemed to snow continually all through December and January, and then when a thaw arrived the entire camp was a quagmire, a bright yellow mud that stuck closer than a brother, and seemingly had no end in depth. In most of the tents were small stoves, but the wood used for fuel was green and filled with sap, and it was only after a persistent struggle that a fire could be started that would last any length of time."[3] Northerners who had grown up on tales of the sunny South found themselves sorely disappointed. Newly commissioned Lieutenant Robert Dechert, a native of Philadelphia, looked forward in vain to the prospect of a warm winter. "What a delusion that winter at . . . North Carolina proved to be. The mud in the road [was] so deep that I had to abandon my knee boots in favor of hip rubber boots, in order to cross the road."[4]

After this chilly, muddy winter, the 7th Regiment on March 27, 1918, left Camp Greene, boarded trains, and traveled to New Jersey for deployment overseas. On April 4 and 5, the regiment, over three thousand strong, boarded ships for an uneventful ten-day voyage across the Atlantic. Some men suffered from seasickness and had no desire to eat. Those with an appetite dined on tinned corned beef, salmon, cornmeal mush, and coffee, augmented now and again by French bully beef (despised) and biscuits. On April 15 the men sighted a lighthouse in the distance. The blinking and winking of this lighthouse welcomed the Yanks to Brest, one of the main debarkation ports for the American Expeditionary Force in France.

The men disembarked at Brest and spent a few days there while the officers organized the regiment for a train trip farther inland. On April

18 the Cottonbalers boarded boxcars—the famous French 40 and 8s—and endured a three-day trip to Bricon Station. Thomas G. Millea, a twenty-two-year-old C Company private from South Bend, Indiana, chronicled the train trip in his diary: "4/19/18: 2:00 am. Cookies served to us at station. Spent sleepless night, 40 men per car. 6 am. Rennes, 8 am. Laval, 2 pm at LeMans—got coffee. Light snow falling all morning. 7 pm—crossed Loire river and through Tours. Everybody got hot wine. 4/20/18: Saturday: 7 am. Got coffee. 9 am. Passed through town of Millan. 7 pm. Red Cross served lunch and chocolates at Dijon. 4/21/18: Sunday—4 am—detrained and slept on ground nearby. 6 am—rolled packs. 9 am—started on 10 mile hike. 12 noon, arrived and were assigned to quarters in a priest's house. Rain."[5]

The regiment had arrived in the Autreville area. There it spread out among various towns such as La Villeneuve, Montheries, Braux, Vaudremont, and Vadelaincourt. A young Regular Army junior officer, watching his men march to their new billets, commented that "never in all my experience as a soldier, at home or abroad, have I saw [sic] such a magnificent body of men as was the 7th Infantry when we left Camp Greene for overseas."[6]

Maybe so, but they were still woefully unprepared for the rigors of trench warfare. In order to alleviate that problem, the unit spent six weeks going through a crash course designed and taught by combat-experienced French and British officers. The Allied officers taught the men a great many useful lessons: how to live in the trenches, how to deal with gas attacks and nighttime raids, how to string and cut barbed wire, and how to prepare a trench system. One British instructor intoned, "Love Mother Earth, love Mother Earth, if you want to go home." He urged the Yanks to find cover during attacks, whenever and wherever they could—in shell holes, folds of ground, whatever—and advance in five- and ten-yard rushes.[7]

The Americans also had to learn how to use the wide array of weapons endemic in early-twentieth-century infantry combat. American unpreparedness meant that Yank soldiers had to depend mostly on French- and British-made weapons, such as the hand grenade (usually the British Mills bomb), a powerful weapon in the close quarters of trench fighting. Stokes mortars and one-pounder antipersonnel guns provided on-the-spot fire support. Rifles could now be modified to fire grenades. The French-made Chauchat automatic rifle served as a kind of submachine gun. The 75mm and 155mm artillery pieces on which

American infantry heavily depended were almost all made in France or Britain.

Even the standard rifles were not entirely American manufactured. In the years leading up to the war, the Krag had given way to the 1903 Springfield rifle, a heavy, magazine-loaded, accurate bolt-action weapon that fired a smokeless five-round clip of 30-caliber ammunition. Unfortunately, the Army only possessed six hundred thousand Springfields when America entered the war. Worse, the Springfield had to be assembled by artisans and could not be mass-produced. This meant that the Army could not hope to equip all of its soldiers with its main infantry weapon, obviously an absurd situation. Fortunately for the Americans, the main British infantry rifle, the Lee-Enfield, could be modified to fire American 30-caliber ammunition. This meant that the Lee-Enfield, also a bolt-action weapon, could be mass-produced and modified at American armories to fire U.S. ammunition. So in World War I, the American infantry soldier was just as likely to carry a British Model 1917 Enfield (the name given to the modified rifle) as the Springfield.

The United States did succeed, however, in producing its own machine gun and automatic rifle by the end of the war. The 1917 Browning heavy machine gun went into use by the end of the summer of 1918. Roughly one out of every three American machine-gun crews used this sturdy 30-caliber weapon by the end of the war. The Browning Automatic Rifle, in use by September 1918, proved to be a superb source of firepower for American infantrymen. Soldiers preferred it over the French Chauchat. The Browning Automatic Rifle (or BAR, as it was soon called) weighed sixteen pounds and fired a twenty-round clip, fastened into the underside of the weapon, of 30-caliber bullets as fast as a man could pull the trigger. The BAR worked like a charm, functioning as a kind of light machine gun. It ate ammunition gluttonously and the barrel tended to warp with prolonged firing, but those problems were by-products of success—a weapon that emitted massive firepower. The United States produced eighty-five thousand BARs during World War I, nowhere near enough to satisfy the demand.[8]

American battle uniforms in World War I looked remarkably similar to those worn by the British. For one thing, American soldiers wore the British-style wide-brimmed tin helmet. For another, the Americans' olive-drab khaki uniforms greatly resembled the colors worn by the British. The typical American combat soldier in World War I wore an olive-drab tunic, stiff at the neck, breech-style trousers, and combat shoes with canvas leggings or, preferably, wrappings. Around his waist he fastened his cartridge belt, chock-full of Springfield or Enfield clips. The cartridge belt was fastened to his knapsack, which held not only blankets and personal effects but also his bayonet and entrenching tool, both vital for trench duty. At his throat and sternum he kept his small box-style British gas mask, an essential piece of equipment in World War I. Some soldiers wore overcoats in the trenches in the fall of 1918. Officers wore laced boots that stretched knee-high and Sam Browne belts just above the belly button.[9]

FOR THE COTTONBALERS, APRIL TURNED INTO MAY AND the weeks of training continued. They listened to lectures, ran field problems, dug trenches, and drilled until they were heartily sick of all of it. In the late afternoons and early evenings, with the day's work behind them, they went to the closest town looking for booze, food, and women (and not necessarily in that order). Most did not find any wild times, but they did find nice rest areas and canteens run by the Red Cross or the YMCA. Red Cross and YMCA workers dispensed chocolate, coffee, and tobacco and perhaps offered a sympathetic ear.

One such YMCA worker was Emma Dickson, the young daughter of a Pittsburgh steel tycoon. Born into a life of wealth and privilege, Dickson was nonetheless determined to do her part for the war effort. Against her father's wishes, she traveled to France in 1918. Like many other idealistic upper-crust Americans in World War I, Dickson found an outlet for service in the YMCA. This Christian organization sent small armies of workers to France. These men and women did whatever they could to improve morale among American soldiers. They fixed hot chocolate, prepared special meals, sold candy and cigarettes, ran canteens, and sometimes, in the case of the women, provided a friendly face for homesick young men starved for female companionship.

Dickson spent her entire time in France working with the 7th Regiment. During the weeks of in-country training in the spring of 1918, she got to know dozens of officers and enlisted men in the unit, especially in G and H Companies. Occasionally she had to fend off the advances of lovesick officers, but most of the men understood that Dickson's relationship with them would, and must, remain platonic. Soon she became like a revered sister. On May 19 she wrote to her mother about her interaction with the soldiers: "Every day I walk a mile or more up to the next village where I have entire charge of the canteen. It's in a little, stone house opposite a café. It's the only place for the men to come to write letters, and in the evening the place is usually packed three deep. I sell chocolate and cigarettes, and do my best to cheer them up when they feel low. It amazes me how willing they are to pour out their troubles. They seem . . . hungry for a little sympathy, and I have heard some strange stories and admired many sweethearts' pictures."[10]

Dickson experienced an enormous amount of personal growth in her work, a kind of independence and self-sufficiency most women did not enjoy in the early twentieth century. She formed a strong bond with the Cottonbalers, and that bond impacted the rest of her life. The men considered her to be a part of the unit, not as a combatant but as an esteemed friend. They saw in her all the qualities they believed a woman must possess—dignity, bearing, nurturing kindness, femininity, and sympathy. Far away from their own wives, sweethearts, and mothers, the men found in Dickson, and many others like her, a kind of surrogate feminine ideal in the decidedly vulgar, male-dominated climate of war. A two-minute conversation with a woman like Dickson could repair a lonely man's morale for a week.

Considering what the Cottonbalers were about to experience, the morale boosting of Dickson and others proved invaluable. Toward the end of May, rumors swirled, correctly, as it turned out, that the unit would soon go to the front. After all, the soldiers had not come to France for a vacation. They had come to stop the powerful German Army from defeating the bloodied British and French. In 1918, that defeat was an all too real possibility. With Russia out of the war, the Germans turned their full might on the western front in an effort to capture Paris and defeat the French and British before the Americans could have a decisive impact on the war.

The enemy had begun this race against the clock with a massive offensive in March, followed up by more attacks in April and May. In the process they had succeeded in breaking the trench deadlock. British and French divisions disintegrated and retreated. Most fought ferociously. Some did not. The Germans pushed west and actually threatened Paris by late May. Every day thousands of partially trained Americans, like the Cottonbalers, entered the country. Their supreme commander, General John Pershing, planned to train, equip, and prepare them for combat in his own good time, as an independent American force. The German offensive negated that luxury. American soldiers, ready or not, must be committed to the front, and fast. In addition to using Allied weapons, many Yanks fought under British or French command in the spring and summer of 1918.

On May 30 the 7th Regiment, along with the entire 3rd Division, received orders to prepare for an imminent move to the Rheims-Soissons sector of the front, an area under fierce German attack. The soldiers gathered everything they might need in combat and marched several miles, all night long, to railroad assembly areas in Bricon. In the darkness, Emma Dickson watched them file by in endless rows. She handed out oranges and tried to remain upbeat. But she knew in her heart that these men, her brothers, were being led to the slaughter. The men tried to smile back, but most of them were already dead tired. "Some of the boys are tired from a long march and on edge from lack of sleep, and they're to be thrown at once into the front line!" she wrote in her diary.[11]

Not far away from where Dickson handed out oranges, Private Millea and his buddies shuffled slowly down the streets of Bricon. Someone remembered that it was Decoration Day (what we now call Memorial Day). A gloomy, cynical soldier blurted a question no one wanted to ponder: "Will the folks back home be decorating our graves next Decoration Day?" Everyone glared at him. Early in the morning, as the sun rose, they stopped and ate breakfast. At 8:30 they boarded flatcar trains, and they rode these trains for over a day until they reached Montmirail. At Montmirail they hopped off the trains and started walking. Millea scribbled in his diary that he and the others "hiked about 20 miles, arrived in a small town the Germans had shelled the night before at 12:00 midnight. Weather warm, road dusty, very little water. Hike hard on men. One man fainted from too much Cognac. Spent the night in the woods near an old Inn. Big guns could be plainly heard all night, but we slept just the same."[12]

On his journey, Millea saw dozens of French civilians. In the villages fifteen or twenty miles behind the front they greeted the Americans cheerfully, with cries of *"Vive l'Amérique!"* The Americans responded with grins and waves. Closer to the front these jovial scenes gave way to gloom and fear. French refugees, most of them farmers, streamed west with whatever meager belongings they could carry. Some knelt by the side of the road and prayed for the Americans. The French had seen war firsthand and knew exactly what the Cottonbalers had in store for them. Groups of French soldiers straggled by hollering, *"La guerre est finie."*

Millea did not know it, but his battalion, the 1st, had taken up positions in reserve at Janvier Farm, near the headquarters of the French 20th Infantry Division, which now assumed tactical command over the Cottonbalers. The 7th Regiment was helping to cover a sector of the French line south of the Marne River, west of Rheims, and east of Château-Thierry. The 1st and 2nd Battalions mostly manned reserve positions on either flank of the French. They dug trenches, patrolled, endured a few light shellings, and kept a sharp eye out for the Germans. The regiment took its first casualties when German shells exploded among D Company's field kitchen near lunchtime one afternoon. No one was killed, but several men were wounded. Other than that, this sector remained quiet.

The 3rd Battalion had a slightly tougher assignment, if only because it was closer to the Germans, who were somewhere out there on the other side of the Marne. The 3rd Battalion went straight into the front line on the south bank of the Marne between Sauvigny and Treloup, with Companies L, M, and I in line from left to right and K Company in reserve. The men took over French trenches and got used to the war a little bit. They took turns keeping watch and learned how to sleep and remain under cover in the trenches. Each day and night they patrolled the riverbank, searching for any signs of enemy activity. A stray shell landed near the trenches every now and again, but the biggest enemies were rats and the weather.

The most notable event during this time involved Lieutenant Walter Flannery of H Company. While Flannery led a small patrol along the river one day, one of his men noticed an unusual object across the river. He got Flannery's attention and pointed across the river. Everyone took cover as Flannery studied the object through his binoculars. It was a man in uniform, lying under cover of the riverbank. Flannery's troops whistled to the man and got his attention. The lieutenant asked him what he was doing (probably in English). The man claimed to be a wounded Frenchman who had been left behind by his unit during the recent retreat from the German onslaught. The Americans exchanged skeptical glances. The mysterious man could easily be a German, posing as a Frenchman, hoping to lure the Americans across the river into an ambush.

Flannery didn't think so. "Why would the Germans go to these lengths to ambush us when they could just as easily open fire on us while we're on patrol?" he wondered. His gut feeling told him the guy on the other side of the Marne was legitimate, and Flannery planned to back this hunch up by risking his life to save the man. The young lieutenant ordered his patrol to remain in place while he made arrangements for a platoon of machine guns to take up positions facing the river. At 7:00 P.M., with the sun still high in the sky, he grabbed a rope and plunged into the water. In no time, he swam the river, tied the rope around the wounded man, and safely pulled him back across the river to the American side. Much to everyone's relief, the Germans never even emitted a peep. Plus, the wounded man was indeed French. His army later awarded Flannery the Croix de Guerre with Palms.[13]

On June 11 the 7th Regiment received orders to leave its positions and assemble on the road south of Condé-en-Brie, about three or four miles from the front. The men gathered their stuff and hiked to the road, where they boarded trucks and headed west. The trucks bumped and rumbled along the crude roads for about twenty-five miles until they reached Saacy, a small town on the south bank of the Marne. Still serving under French command, the men hopped off the trucks and waited for orders. The French high command wanted the Cottonbalers to guard six strategic bridges across the winding Marne. The soldiers spent about three days digging trenches and preparing defensive positions.

The regiment's commander, Colonel Thomas Anderson, was a tough, blunt-speaking, hard-bitten Texan who had been commissioned out of the ranks twenty years earlier. He issued orders for defensive preparations: "The mission of this regiment is to prevent the enemy from crossing the MARNE. With this in view, a defensive line has been laid out and is being organized from the MARNE RIVER at NANTEUIL to the MARNE RIVER at GUAMONT. This defensive line will be fully covered by outposts at all times, and will be held in case of attack, by the forces of the Bns. assigned to defend the different sectors."[14]

The mission of the regiment soon changed. Immediately to the left of the Cottonbalers, the Marne changed direction, taking a sharp southerly turn. The Germans had taken advantage of this change of direction by channeling their advance through a heavily wooded former hunting reserve, known locally as Bois de Belleau. Americans called this area Belleau Wood. For nearly two weeks, the 4th Marine Brigade, serving under the auspices of the Army's 2nd Infantry Division, fought alongside their army brethren in and around the woods to blunt the

German offensive. The Marines, motivated and well trained, fought brilliantly, earning themselves—with a little help from their masterful public relations machine—a place in the hearts of the American people. The other troops of the 2nd Division fought just as hard, but they did not get as much of the glory for a battle that would have a decidedly Marine flavor.

By mid-June the 2nd Division bordered on exhaustion. The Germans could still possibly break through the American and French lines and capture Paris. They were only thirty-five miles away and many French government officials were in the process of evacuating the capital. The units at Belleau Wood had, to this point, absorbed massive casualties, sometimes higher than 50 percent. They needed help. The 2nd served under the operational command of the 6th French Army, whose general now chose the 7th Regiment to relieve the Marine sector at Belleau Wood.

Therefore from June 15 to 17 the men of the 7th Regiment left their trenches at Saacy and boarded trucks for the short ride west. The 1st Battalion went in first. The trucks carrying the soldiers of this battalion arrived in the area just before dark and dumped the men off like cargo. As darkness settled around them, the soldiers of the 1st Battalion hiked through unfamiliar terrain in the direction of the front. Somewhere in C Company's ranks, Private Millea concentrated on simply putting one foot in front of the other. The woods were thick, dark, foreboding. Men got tangled in vines and tripped over roots. They slung their rifles but made sure they were loaded and ready. The men kept gas masks within easy reach. One or two breaths of poison gas could burn a man's lungs out. German shells screamed into the woods behind them, exploding in a tangle of trees and dead leaves, slightly wounding two men from D Company. Millea and the others, breathing heavier, hearts pumping now, kept moving as fast as possible in the dark. Through the inky blackness someone managed to spot the Marine trenches. The leathernecks, thrilled to see the soldiers approach, silently left their positions and melted into the woods. As quickly as they could, the Cottonbalers took over the trench positions, and they remained there all night, keeping a keen watch for the enemy and fighting sleep.[15]

The 1st Battalion had successfully relieved the 2nd Battalion of the 5th Marine Regiment and the 2nd Battalion of the 6th Marine Regiment. The next day, the 2nd Battalion of the 7th Infantry took up posi-

tions immediately to the right of the 1st, and the day after that, the 3rd
Battalion slipped into place on their left. The 7th Infantry Regiment
now held a continuous line covering just over two and a half miles from
a point about one thousand meters southwest of Torcy on the left
(north) all the way to the edge of Bouresches on the right (south).[16]

For three days, the sector remained fairly quiet, with the exception
of patrol skirmishes. Men would shoot at one another in the fog and
tangle of the woods and then move on before the shooting turned into
something serious. Private Millea described these first few days in the
Belleau Wood: "6/16/18: Sunday. On guard in the trenches, everything
quiet except for a few shells exploding. Evening, 1 company saw a few
boche and took up firing, the next company took up firing, until all
companies [were] firing, causing the boche to put down a barrage. Sgt.
Owens slightly wounded. Pvt. Brignaugh wounded. Rest of night quiet.

"6/17/18. Monday. Quiet all day. Evening. Boche started a raid, were
driven back, leaving two machine guns, some prisoners, 4 killed. Company B, a few wounded.

"6/18/18: Tuesday. All quiet. Exchange of a few shots in the evening
and one man [was] slightly wounded as he went for water. Rations slim
lately: bacon, bread, [corn] willie."[17]

INDEED, THE SUPPLY SITUATION QUICKLY DETERIORATED
in a bureaucratic snarl caused by the regiment's transfer to another division and another branch of the service. Lieutenant Isham R. Williams,
a platoon leader in C Company, remembered an even worse situation
than Millea described. "All that could be gotten up to the company sector averaged one can of corn beef and one piece of French bread to
every six men. This condition of affairs lasted until June 21. Water was
extremely scarce as the field . . . where water was obtained . . . was constantly under shell fire. Frequent showers aided matters as the men
would catch rain in their shelter halves for drinking. This condition of
affairs caused . . . the men to become weak."[18]

The men quickly grasped the grim and featureless character of life
on the front line. "The men of the 7th lay in foxholes among the hills
and rocks," one junior officer later wrote: "All day and night they were
subjected to a galling fire. It was almost impossible to get food or water
so closely were they watched, but despite all this, every night a detail
came out of the woods and into Lucy, where the rations were distributed and where they could secure water. It was a life and death game,

but the chow details never missed a night, always they were waiting when the ration carts came in, to carry coffee and corn willy back to their comrades in the woods. I have seen them calmly fill dozens of canteens for their buddies when the very earth was rocking with the thunderous explosions of giant shells and flying pieces of steel were zinging through the air."[19]

When the 7th took over this sector, Brigadier General James Harbord, an army officer in command of the 4th Marine Brigade, had told Anderson and his officers that the Germans were strongest at the northern edge of the woods, along a steep ridge where they had deployed an estimated twelve to sixteen machine guns and two hundred soldiers. The Marines attempted to capture this ridge and destroy the machine guns but could not do it. Harbord warned that any German attack would most likely come from that direction. Eventually, he said, the ridge would have to be taken.

The ridge in question lay directly opposite B Company and slightly to the west of C Company. On the evening of the eighteenth, the B Company commander (a man named Burt) issued foolish orders. He told his men to leave the relative security of their trenches and, in the dark, establish new positions on a hill adjacent to the ridge. What he could possibly have hoped to accomplish is beyond the grasp of the historical records, but the result of this insanity was predictable. The B Company soldiers left their trenches and cautiously advanced about fifty yards. The men gripped their rifles tightly and waited for the inevitable German response. They did not have to wait long. Machine guns opened up on them, cutting a bloody swath through the lead troops. Two or three men were killed instantly. Several others got hit and fell, their screams muffled somewhat in the woods. In a couple minutes the officers ordered a retreat. Those men who had not yet been hit slung their rifles, grabbed those who had, and dragged them back to the original trench line. B Company lost five men killed and sixteen wounded in this appallingly incompetent "attack."

Unfortunately, the 1st Battalion's tree-shrouded nightmare was only beginning. Even as B Company engaged in its nocturnal adventure, General Harbord sent attack orders to Lieutenant Colonel Frank Adams, the commanding officer of the 1st. Harbord expected Adams to prepare and implement a morning attack designed to capture the ridge and destroy the German machine guns. Adams hurriedly briefed his company commanders and set up the attack. He selected limited forces for the job at hand: two platoons from D Company and one platoon each from B and C Companies. Actually, instead of selecting an intact platoon, Captain Paul Cartter of C Company chose sixty "volunteers," probably those men he thought of as his best soldiers. In fact, this assault force was so small and so obviously inadequate that one of Cartter's officers thought of it as a "raiding party" and not a full-fledged attack.

Be that as it may, the unlucky chosen few huddled in their jump-off positions and waited for the first streaks of dawn to appear in the eastern sky. No one smoked, talked, or laughed. They just grimly waited, each man alone in his own thoughts, perhaps even hoping the attack would be called off. They had no such luck. Just after four in the morning, they crept forward, stood up, and advanced toward the German positions. "The woods were trackless jungle and there were Germans in trees, behind woodpiles, in ravines, hid in piles of stone," one sergeant wrote. "We had to advance from tree to tree, looking all around. It was like playing Hide & Seek, only if you lost you were out for keeps."[20]

They had gone about as far as the first German trenches when all hell broke loose. German machine-gun and rifle fire swept the area, ripping through tree trunks, branches, and men alike. Wood splinters slashed at men just as often as did bullets. The Cottonbalers, led by Captain Cartter, hit the dirt and tried to crawl forward, but it was no use. They were caught in a cross fire. Enemy machine guns, augmented now by grenades, were dealing out death at a terrifying rate. The Americans could only lie still and return fire as best they could with their rifles and grenades. Many hapless soldiers lay silent and bleeding. Fresh blood ran down their cheeks and torsos. As it did so, their olive-drab uniforms absorbed much of the blood, giving the uniforms a rusty brownish color.

Seeing this, and having narrowly avoided being hit several times, Cartter knew the attack had to be reinforced or abandoned. For some unknown reason, the two D Company platoons had never made it to the jump-off point. Cartter crawled a short distance in the direction of the American lines, collected whatever stragglers he could for a renewed attack, and then found one of the D Company platoons. This motley force ran into the same problems. German machine-gun fire scythed through their ranks, killing and wounding men with impunity. In no time, the new attack died out. The men merely took cover and prayed to remain unscathed.

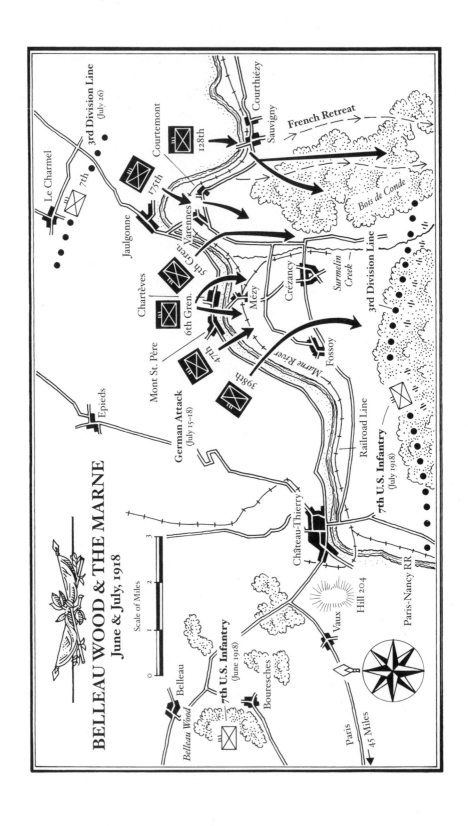

BELLEAU WOOD & THE MARNE
June & July, 1918

Scale of Miles

3rd Division Line (July 26)

French Retreat

Le Charmel

7th

Courtemont

Courthiézy

Sauvigny

128th

175th

Jaulgonne

Varennes

Bois de Conde

5th Gren.

Chartèves

Crézancy

Surmelin Creek

6th Gren.

Mézy

3rd Division Line

Mont St. Père

47th

Fossoy

398th

German Attack (July 15–18)

Marne River

Railroad Line

Epieds

7th U.S. Infantry (July 1918)

Château-Thierry

Hill 204

Vaux

Paris–Nancy RR

7th U.S. Infantry (June 1918)

Boureschs

Belleau

Belleau Wood

Paris

45 Miles

Cartter now knew that he had to retreat before the situation got any worse. He screamed at the men to fall back to the American trenches. They enthusiastically complied, dragging wounded men—many of them screaming in agony—and low-crawled until they were out of the line of fire. Within an hour, the shell-shocked survivors had filtered back to the American trenches. The halfhearted attack had cost the 1st Battalion eleven men killed, forty-five wounded, and seven missing, probably about one-third of the small assault force.[21]

When Adams heard about the failure of the attack, he shook his head in disgust but not in surprise. "The troops under my command were green men; I had been with the battalion for only ten days," he later wrote. "Our line was thinly held—our supports were nil, and our ability to hold our line, should it be attacked in force, doubtful. Laboring under these handicaps, the attack was made, as ordered, and was a failure."[22] Adams relieved one of his company commanders—perhaps the D Company commanding officer who had failed to position his platoons for the attack—for inefficiency.

Not long after the altogether miserable experience of this failed attack, Harbord ordered another one. The general had unilaterally, and somewhat unfairly, formed a poor opinion of the 1st Battalion because of its failure to capture the German-held ridge. Taking into consideration the inexperience of the troops, the strength of the ridge, and the near-complete lack of adequate resources for such an attack, what more could he have expected? No matter. Harbord did not want to be bothered with excuses. He wanted results, anyway, anyhow. On the twentieth of June, he sent Adams a snippy, officious note ordering him to prepare for another attack: "Your battalion will be relieved tomorrow night. Tomorrow morning is the only chance to redeem [its] failure. If you clear the northern half of the BOIS de BELLEAU the credit will belong to the 1st Battalion, 7th Infantry and will be freely given. The Battalion cannot afford to fail again."[23]

With this inspiring pep talk ringing in his ears, Adams set about the task of consulting with his company commanders on the best means of attack. The more he thought about the attack, the more convinced he became that his men must have artillery support. He scouted the German positions himself and talked with many of his officers about his planned artillery request, after which he sent the request to Harbord. The general assented: "You will withdraw your companies to the X line 262.0 [about a kilometer to the rear] beginning at about 11:45 PM carrying out the movement with the utmost secrecy. From 2:00 to 3:15 the artillery will make thorough preparation of part of the Bois de Belleau vacated by your troops. Your troops will attack at 3:15 and capture or destroy the enemy."

Mollified, Adams now met again with his company commanders and issued his final attack orders. Company A would take the lead with B Company slightly to the left and C Company a hundred yards behind, followed by D Company at about the same interval. As the lead troops, A Company needed as many assault weapons as they could carry, so Adams ordered C Company to give all its rifle and hand grenades to A Company.

Just before midnight, the Cottonbalers quietly left their trenches and pulled back to safe positions. There they waited in the darkness, the cool mud under their bellies. Even as the men withdrew, the artillery barrage began. Adams watched as the rounds landed in irregular patterns in the vicinity of the American trench system and his heart sank. "At 2:00 AM, when the artillery was to open barrage fire on the enemy's machine gun position, the increase in the volume of fire was so slight as not to be noticed; from the artillery officer on duty at my P.C. [post of command] I learned that this barrage was being made by 75's and I remarked that 'for all the effect it would have on the enemy position, pea shooters might as well have been used.' "[24]

Adams was right. The artillery bombardment was ineffective and practically useless. Half a mile to the right, in the 2nd Battalion trenches, Captain P. J. Hurley kept waiting for the volume and intensity of the shells falling on the ridge to increase, but to no avail: "I could distinguish no increase in our artillery fire in that sector. If our artillery put down a barrage there, in my opinion, it was not a heavy one, and as . . . I was only about 1½ kilometers from the German position, it would seem that I could hear it if it had been working."[25]

The men of the 1st Battalion assault companies did not see or hear any kind of major barrage either. They could only shake their heads, lament the ineffectiveness of the artillery, and speculate on what kind of horrors awaited them in the German trenches. One man from C Company remembered hearing only "stray shells." The failed artillery barrage was only the first misfortune. At 3:15 A.M. the 1st Battalion Cottonbalers hoisted themselves to their feet (most were carrying full field packs) and walked forward in confused, straggled rows in the pitch-black night. In the confusion of this hastily prepared night attack, B

Company veered too far to the left and became separated from the rest of the battalion. It was lost for the balance of the attack. The commanding officer of this company, no military genius, had misunderstood Adams's verbal orders.

In effect, this meant that the brunt of the assault fell on A and C Companies, because C Company, trailing close behind A, understandably pressed forward into the gap, just to the left of A, where B Company was supposed to have been. First Lieutenant Carl Helm led A Company into its hellish attack that night: "It was . . . dark and cloudy so that one could not see more than 25 feet in either direction clearly. I was afraid my platoons would get lost if they marched in squad columns thru the thick underbrush and woods, so I ordered them to move out in platoon columns until they reached the road at the foot of the knoll we were to attack, and there to extend into skirmish line for the attack. There was no sign of a barrage in front of us nor any indications that it had passed that way. My platoons were followed out by C company. At 4:15 [A.M.] we reached the road at the foot of the German knoll. The first and third platoons, forming the first wave, formed into a skirmish line and upon my order advanced up the hill. After they had gained a distance of some 30 yards I ordered the second and fourth platoons . . . to move forward up the hill. I went with these platoons, in their center."

For a few delicious moments, everything was quiet and Helm wondered if maybe the Germans had abandoned their positions. "Then we were fired upon from all sides and from trees. Machine guns on both our flanks and in our rear opened on us. Firing first commenced on my right flank." The Germans soon added artillery and grenades to their thick machine-gun fire. Helm hollered orders designed to flank the machine-gun positions, but too many men were being hit. The noise was beyond belief. German artillery luckily landed too far to the rear to do much damage, but enemy machine guns, rifles, and grenades reaped a rich harvest. Then a German soldier rose up slightly and threw a grenade at Helm: "I last remember a loud explosion and a flash in front of me. When I regained my senses there was no one left with me." Helm fell victim to concussion, and also shell shock, and was effectively out of the battle. He went back down the hill and attempted to round up men. He succeeded in rallying a few soldiers, but then they got lost and spent the rest of the battle wandering around looking for battalion headquarters.[26]

A Company had blundered into a meat grinder, its soldiers caught in the same cross fire that had decimated the B and C Company platoons in the first attack on this ridge. Lieutenant Williams of C Company, seeing this carnage, could not keep himself from leaving his predetermined attack position to help. "Before I realized what I was doing I had closed on the right of Company 'A' which was not advancing owing to the fire." He and his men found themselves staring down the muzzle of a German machine gun: "As the blazes of the enemy machine gun could be seen just in front of us I concluded that to go back was death and by going forward we could reach the first line at least. With that in view I led my platoon past Lieut Helm. I reached some big rocks about 30 or 40 yds from the blazes of the enemy gun with 15 or 20 men, some of whom belonged to Company 'A.'" In the rock den he saw a courageous lieutenant named Trotter lying under cover with three or four men. Williams and Trotter planned a way to destroy an enemy gun that, even as they talked, was blasting away at the rocks that shielded them. Trotter would assault it from the left and Williams from the right. Trotter didn't make it. The German machine gun stopped him dead in his tracks. He took two slugs in the chest and collapsed in a lifeless heap. His men scrambled for cover.

Williams and his people were not so rash. "My men and I crawled until we got some good shots at the blaze of this gun which we silenced quickly. I had located another gun on my left, but it suddenly ceased firing . . . before we got any decent shots. I hardly think that any of my men could have hit it. While we were crawling around this gun, grenades began to burst just in our rear." Williams thought the grenades came from A Company mistaking them for Germans, but he was wrong. The grenades came from Germans, not A Company: "By now I had three men with me, all the others who followed me being wounded. I was perplexed, my compass had been broken, and I did not know how many times I had changed directions. The wounded lying about showed me the way to the rocks we had first reached. I had the wounded placed behind the rocks. To my left rear I could see more Americans." This was a mixed group of A and C Company troops, including a Lieutenant Paisley, who had taken over effective command of A Company after Helm's wounding.

Paisley and Williams moved more wounded men back to the rocks, but then enemy shells began falling in the area, imperiling the two officers and adding to the woes of the wounded. The two lieutenants took shelter just shy of the German trenches and waited for the barrage to subside. When it did, they set about the task of removing the wounded to the aid station.

Paisley then told Williams a bizarre story about the Germans. He said that as he approached the German trenches, he and his men saw German soldiers in American uniforms and that they even called out in English to the attackers. The Americans were not fooled by this ruse and kept a steady stream of rifle fire at the khaki-clad enemy. Then, all of a sudden, a man in an American uniform sidled up to Paisley and said, "My God! You are not going to fire on your own men out there in front, are you? You are not going to kill your own men?" Paisley whipped out his pistol and shot the man in the face, killing him on the spot. Williams later confirmed the story with other men in Paisley's company and determined that, strange or not, it must have been true (Paisley was killed by a German shell the next day). Colonel Anderson even discussed it in his report to the commanding general of the 2nd Division. Private Millea and many other Cottonbalers, adding to this theater of the surreal, claimed to have seen Germans chained to their machine guns.[27]

Whether these tales were true or not, one fact was beyond dispute: The 1st Battalion attack had failed miserably. Companies D and B took almost no part in the botched assault and, correspondingly, suffered only a few wounded. By contrast, A Company had been ground into pulp, suffering close to 150 casualties, and C Company lost 30 men, mostly from Lieutenant Williams's platoon. He estimated that he lost 24 out of 47 men, and the bitterness of these losses never left him: "With a proper artillery preparation and a carefully planned attack instead of an attack planned and executed in the darkness, the . . . casualties of the 1st Bn., 7th Infantry would not have been in vain."[28]

By 7:30 A.M. the survivors of the failed attack had filtered back to their trenches. The Germans never counterattacked, so the situation settled back down into a stalemate. Belleau Wood, then, proved to be a charnel house for the luckless 1st Battalion. In less than a week it had lost 25 percent of its strength.

ON A BRIGHTER NOTE, THE 3RD BATTALION FARED MUCH better. As previously mentioned, the 3rd Battalion had taken up positions on the extreme left (or northwest) of the 7th Regiment's sector. The battalion commander, Major Jesse Gaston, sent out reconnaissance patrols on the eighteenth and nineteenth of June. These patrols discovered a deep ravine, some twelve hundred yards in front of their positions, that the Germans had left undefended. Accordingly, Gaston received orders to push forward into and through the ravine to a crossroads south of the nearest town, Torcy. He planned his attack even as the men of 1st Battalion bled and died to the south. In fact, Lieutenant Helm's wanderings at one point took him to Gaston's command post. Gaston later stated that Helm was "completely broken up and shellshocked" and that he sat morosely babbling that the two or three men he had with him were "all that was left of [his] Company."

Not much later, Gaston sent the better part of his L and I Companies forward. They negotiated their way through the ravine and made it as far as a crossroads six hundred meters south of Torcy, encountering no resistance, except for intermittent shelling. At this new position, they dug in and waited to be reinforced. They had advanced about a kilometer, a big gain in World War I. On their right, Gaston sent two platoons of M Company to make sure his lead troops did not get cut off. He also wanted to maintain contact with the 1st Battalion on his right. Predictably, they ran into the edge of the German defensive system that had caused 1st Battalion so much strife. "Flares . . . fell . . . and intense artillery fire opened up on the woods which lasted 10 or 15 minutes. There were at least six machine guns flanking the woods at about three hundred meters range." The M Company soldiers retreated and contented themselves with sniping at the Germans.[29]

The Battle of Belleau Wood was over for the 7th Infantry. Beginning on the evening of June 21 and ending just over two days later, the battalions yielded their trenches back to the Marines. In all, the regiment suffered 350 casualties: 51 killed, 265 wounded, and 34 missing, a grisly and costly price for almost no tangible results. The 7th Infantry gained a little ground, held the American line successfully, and afforded the Marines a week's rest off the line, hardly worth the price of so many dead and maimed young men (it's of course debatable whether anything is worth such a price).

Carping between Harbord's Marines and Anderson's Cottonbalers began even before the 7th withdrew from the front. An officer from the 3rd Battalion of the 5th Marines, the unit that relieved the 1st Battalion of the 7th, claimed to have problems with his Cottonbaler guide. The guide was young, obviously scared, and more than ready to leave the front. This soldier moved through the night so fast that the

Marines could not keep up with him. The kid had to stop several times so the leathernecks could catch up. Finally, the officer snarled, "Do I have to shoot you in the ass to slow you down?" The doughboy was anguished. He cried, "Officer, don't shoot me. I got no business here. I only been in the United States Army for five weeks." The marine officer never explained just how this American soldier could only have been in the Army five weeks when his unit had been in France for over two months. Perhaps the guide was a brand-new replacement, but that is doubtful, because, to this point, the 7th Regiment had received very few. Moreover, commanders rarely used inexperienced men as guides, for obvious reasons.

In his official report to the 2nd Division commander, Harbord, something of an honorary marine by now, echoed the critical sentiments of many of his Devil Dogs (as the leathernecks of the 4th Brigade called themselves). Harbord lambasted the "inefficiency of officers of the 7th Inf. and lack of instruction of the men. The 1st Bn. is untrustworthy for first line work at this time. The 2nd Bn. has given satisfaction in the south end of the Bois de Belleau where there has been nothing but watching required of it." He rated the 3rd Battalion slightly higher but still derided the fact that it had "shown no enterprise in carrying out orders for outpost patrols."[30]

Some of Harbord's criticism was fair and some of it was pure nonsense. The 1st Battalion had certainly not done much credit to its reputation in carrying out two botched attacks. Officers did not communicate well with their men. Two company commanders lost their jobs because of inefficiency. Adams did not coordinate the movement of his companies well, resulting in B Company's unproductive walk in the woods while A and C Companies dealt with an entrenched, well-armed enemy. All that being said, it is hard to understand how Harbord could have expected much more from an inexperienced unit being asked to overwhelm a strong enemy position, without proper supply, artillery support, or time for coordinating and planning the assault. So, in many respects, Harbord had only himself to blame for the perceived failures of the 7th Regiment.

The Cottonbaler officers naturally took exception to the Marine charges and grumbled among themselves about the lack of proper supply or leadership from Harbord and his colonels. Gaston, whose men had performed the best, was particularly vociferous in his criticism: "I cannot refrain from taking exception to the statements made by the

Marines against the 7th Infantry. They have not been satisfied with a lot of cheap advertisement in order to glorify their own cause and in addition to making false claims to the press, they tried to besmirch the good name of the 7th Infantry. The Supply . . . of my own Battalion was poor. The Marines are directly responsible for gross inefficiency in supplying my Battalion."[31] Gaston, Colonel Anderson, and other leaders of the regiment also pointed to captured German intelligence reports that lauded the 7th Regiment for its "audacity" and assessed this new American fighting formation as "altogether a good one, whose fighting value will increase with wider experience in warfare."[32]

More than anything, this foolish war of words stemmed, as Gaston's words hint, from the tension that then existed between the Army and the Marines over the national headlines the Marines had earned for their valor at Belleau Wood. The soldiers felt that the Marines had hogged all the credit for themselves (partially true), while the leathernecks believed that they deserved most of that credit because they had done the toughest and most decisive fighting (also partially true). In the final estimation, the 7th Infantry Regiment performed reasonably well at Belleau Wood, given its inexperience and the difficult situation it encountered. To be sure, the unit had vast room for improvement, but the German intelligence report was absolutely correct. The 7th would perform better with more experience.

AFTER BELLEAU WOOD THE REGIMENT SPENT THE REST OF June off the lines, resting and refitting. The survivors tried to force the awful memories of the battle from their minds. The wounded lay in hospitals fighting for their lives. Emma Dickson, the YMCA worker, visited many of them in an effort to help any way she could. These hospital visits were a far cry from dispensing hot chocolate and tobacco. She saw the tragedy and suffering of war firsthand: "I wrote many letters for our . . . soldiers. Some had lost legs, many had serious shrapnel wounds. One with a bullet through his chest dictated a beautiful letter to his wife, so full of tenderness and faith that everything would turn out for 'the best' that my pen could hardly write the words. At all costs we *must* smile in spite of the groans from many beds, the sight of terrible wounds, whole faces gone, screams coming from below as the wounded are taken from the ambulances or into the operating room. Here brave soldiers are dying in agony. Mothers and families at home cannot be here to speak a last word to those who 'go west' [a slang term for dying] or smile to the ones who may pull through. Little wonder that it seems a marvelous privilege to be here in their places to care for their boys, even in so small a way."[33]

The regiment stayed in and around Saacy for nearly a week before boarding trucks on June 29 and moving south to Viels-Maisons and its surrounding towns. The officers moved into houses and the enlisted men into barns and other slightly less comfortable billets. The men got paid, and card games inevitably proliferated like clover after a rainfall. The soldiers hoped for a nice, long rest. "We were in a most beautiful section of France," one soldier later wrote. "The country had not yet been despoiled by war. On every side were fertile fields and green meadows. The hay, recently cut by farmers lay in long winrows [sic] or gathered in huge shocks. Orchards heavy with fruit were on every hand. It was indeed a Paradise to the men of the 7th Infantry in comparison to what they had just come out of, but it was short lived."[34]

After only two wonderful nights at this locale, the regiment received orders to relieve the 38th Infantry of the 3rd Division along the Marne front. "The 38th was to move to the right of the 30th Infantry," the division history explained. "The 3rd Division sector was then to extend from Chierry (on the outskirts of Château-Thierry) on the left to Surmelin Creek on the right, including Blesmes, Fossoy, Mézy and Crezancy. The Fifth Brigade (4th and 7th Infantries) held the left and the Sixth Brigade (30th and 38th Infantries) the right half of the Division sector." The 7th Regiment area extended parallel to the river, straddling the Paris–Metz railroad just opposite Gland, eastward to La Brettonerie Farm, just past Fossoy, and then southward in a gentle curve as far as Gerves Farm. The colonel set up his headquarters several hundred yards behind the lines at Le Rocq Farm.[35]

For two solid weeks, they manned this quiet portion of the line and anticipated a German offensive. Gaston explained the manner in which his 3rd Battalion troops covered the line: "The general scheme of defense is to distribute the troops in depth with a thin line of combat groups along the front at night, withdrawing some (except for observation posts left on the bank) to the railroad line during the day and kept under cover. Combat groups are made up of ½ platoons, each Combat group at night maintains from 3 to 4 observation groups of 2 to 3 men on the edge of the river backed up by small supports of . . . 6 to 10 men." Along the railroad line he posted Stokes mortars and 37mm guns. Machine guns flanked either side of the riverbank.[36]

The Cottonbalers soon began to improve their defensive positions by digging trench systems. The first line of rifle and machine-gun pits extended along the river. As Gaston indicated, troops used these positions to watch for enemy activity. They also served as sally points for patrols along and across the river. Not far behind this first line, a second line snaked along the railroad bank. Riflemen generally covered this shoulder-high trench line of sandbags and firing steps. Behind them was a third line, located along a series of slopes and hills, containing the bulk of the unit's manpower. A fourth line consisted of command dugouts, aid stations, and fire trenches.

Although very few shells fell on the 7th Regiment positions during this time, the men still had to watch for signs of the expected enemy attack, not to mention snipers. A sergeant described life in the trenches: "Each of us has his place in the trench & there are so many men assigned to each dugout and a guard at the entrance for gas duty. If he smells gas, he gives the alarm. In the daytime hardly anybody is in the trenches but only lookouts 50 feet apart. They get relieved every hour. The rest of the boys stay under cover & kill cooties or write home or shoot craps. We never leave go of our rifles and ammunition belts. At 6 p.m. we stand to & every man is at his post till 10 o'clock. Then half the company goes in to the dugouts to rest and the others stay on the watch but at 2 o'clock the whole outfit stands to till daybreak. Every man is on the firing-step in back of sand bags. Gee, how long the night is. The lieut. walks up & down the trenches to see everything is OK and the boys are all in their place. My eyes got sore looking out in No Man's Land. The [barbed-] wire posts & stumps of trees looked like they moved & many a time I [shot] thinking they was Germans. The early morning hours is when a guy's morale is lowest & is when the enemies send over their raiding parties."[37]

"During the day the men of the 7th lay in their shallow fox holes," one officer recalled, "and watched the town of Château-Thierry just to our left, or gazed over beyond the river to where our shells occasionally struck with a muffled roar, throwing great clouds of dust Heavenward. Sometimes during the day the Germans would throw over a few shells and shrapnel toward our front that burst with keen sharp cracks over our heads causing all hands to dive into their dugouts for protection against flying pieces."[38]

Not surprisingly, the trenches were filthy places—muddy, vermin infested, malodorous, and generally unhealthy. The soldiers could not hope to keep clean, only alive. They grew shadow beards and picked lice off one another. Many hunted rats to stave off boredom, and they found plenty of game. For the first several days along the Marne, the Cottonbalers subsisted on foul-tasting tinned French bully beef and bread. Nor did the food situation improve much when the unit's field kitchens arrived in the area. The 3rd Division inspector discussed the thorny problem of feeding the combat men along the regiment's front during those first two weeks of July: "The enemy from the heights across the river could easily observe the front areas and smoke from kitchens was certain to invite a severe shelling. For that reason it was necessary to place the kitchens at some distance from the front line positions where they could not be observed and send the food forward by fatigue details. It was not possible therefore to serve more than one hot meal per day to the front line troops in this sector."[39]

In other words, the poor weather-beaten, beleaguered doughboys at the front—the ones who needed sustenance the most—ate the worst food, in the form of noxious Allied rations. This unfortunate situation compounded itself many times in this war and those to come. The continuous, round-the-clock nature of modern war, as well as the cutting-edge, dangerous job of the infantry, made this unfortunate truism of privation unavoidable. Good, nutritious hot meals usually require secure circumstances. Infantrymen in combat rarely enjoy such circumstances.

For the first two weeks of July, Anderson rotated his companies and battalions in and out of the line, so each formation had at least some short-lived opportunity to leave the trenches and enjoy rest and a hot meal. Several times, though, he received intelligence of an imminent German offensive and placed his troops on full alert in their positions. By the middle of July the attack still had not materialized. Soon that changed.

The Germans were planning one last throw of the dice in their effort to capture Paris and win the war. The series of spring offensives had yielded substantial territorial gains, but at the cost of hundreds of thousands of irreplaceable troops. Germany was running low on manpower and food. The enemy army was weakening each day (even as thousands of fresh American soldiers entered the country every day), but it had enough strength left to throw one more haymaker. The Germans hoped to punch through the Allied lines in the Marne sector, right between the British in the north and the French in the south—straight through the Americans along the river and on to Paris. Just after midnight on July 15, even as Bastille Day revelers partied in Paris, the Germans launched their attack. A total of fifty-two German divisions crashed into thirty-four Allied divisions, nine of which were American. For the Americans, the 3rd Division, especially the 38th and 30th Infantry Regiments, absorbed the brunt of the enemy attack.[40]

The 7th Regiment saw plenty of action too, starting in the early-morning hours of the fifteenth. The front had been unusually quiet all day long on the fourteenth. Then, as that day came to an end, "the Germans seemed to be uneasy," in the memory of one Cottonbaler, "for now they commenced to throw flares and starlights out from their front that dived through the air in long graceful curves, then burst into a full blossom of dazzling light that illuminated the landscape for yards around then suddenly died away."

Bathed in the shadows and flash of these flickering lights, the 2nd Battalion was in the process of relieving the 3rd Battalion in its trenches along the Marne when, quite literally, all hell broke loose. German shells roared in from seemingly every direction and exploded in and around the 3rd Battalion trenches. The enemy attack could not have come at a worse time, because the trenches were packed with men from both battalions. The enemy threw high-explosive, shrapnel, and gas shells at the vulnerable 7th infantrymen.

In a terrifying free-for-all, the men scrambled wildly for cover. Shells exploded at an incredible volume with no slackening in intensity. Rifle pits caved in, as did sandbags. Support logs burst, sending dangerous, hot splinters in every direction. Phone lines were torn up and shattered. Every shell seemed to hit something. The shrapnel flew angrily, searching for flesh. Some shells scored direct hits, disintegrating their victims. Men had legs, arms, and heads blown off. Shell fragments tore through arteries and bones with impunity. The noise assaulted eardrums. Some men found themselves buried in trenches as explosions kicked up and redistributed earth. Poison gas settled over the area, adding to the death and terror. Soldiers had their gas masks shredded by fragments and had no choice but to inhale the gas. Those who were not hit in the first few moments found whatever foxholes, trenches, or shell holes they could, dived in, and cowered. They curled into fetal balls and prayed to God to be spared. They cried and screamed. Still the hellish barrage continued, the explosive and fragmentation shells flashing as they detonated. Some soldiers lost complete control and tried to run away—the exact wrong thing to do. A few got lucky and made it back to the rear, but most got hit. The enemy fire went on for hours during that long night, and the Cottonbalers could only hunker down and hope the shells landed somewhere else.

Supply columns for both battalions were caught on the roads immediately behind the trenches. These unfortunate men never had a chance. "All had been killed or horribly mangled," an anonymous 7th infantryman later wrote, "the entire length of the road, reaching from the Bois de Hesse to Fossoy was one awful destructive sight. Horses and mules literally covered the ground. Some were blown completely away from the wagons, while others had reared and fallen over each other, then fell, twisted and tangled in their heavy harness. Water carts, ration carts and wagons were overturned and lying along the side of the road, while the drivers, their faces burnt black by gas and fumes, were lying beside or upon the fallen animals. This barrage was beyond description. Could it have been painted on canvas, along with the awful loss of life and destruction it caused, it would have put to shame any scene from Dante's inferno." The woods behind the lines had once been quaintly picturesque but no more: "Now [they] had been struck by death, hundreds of trees were lying on the ground, their torn and splintered trunks standing above them. Others had giant limbs torn and twisted, and thrown aside. The ground was burnt and covered with ghastly shell holes, the flowers were dead, the bird's song forever stilled, and in its place the groans and shrieks of wounded and dying men."[41]

Enemy artillery shells also fell at regimental headquarters at Le Rocq Farm as well as Fossoy, at the eastern edge of the regiment's positions. All communications were down. Only runners could carry messages, that is, if they could survive the shelling. French officers serving at 7th Regiment headquarters judged this bombardment to be the worst that they had experienced in four years of war.

Only K Company and one platoon from M Company succeeded in getting safely out of the forward positions. The rest of the 3rd Battalion survivors simply remained in place, mixed together with the 2nd Battalion survivors, manning what remained of the front lines. The artillery fire mercifully tapered off sometime around eight in the morning, then continued intermittently throughout the day. Many of the battered survivors of the 2nd and 3rd Battalions spent the day evacuating the wounded, repairing their trenches, and dodging shells. They held no illusions, though. Everyone knew that the fierce nighttime shelling meant an imminent attack.

Actually, it was already under way. Shortly after dawn the Germans crossed the river on boats and pontoon bridges at Mézy, east of the 3rd Battalion positions. By midmorning they were pouring south, through ripening wheat fields, in the direction of the 30th Infantry and west in the direction of Fossoy and the lead platoons of the 7th Regiment's I and F Companies. Major Gaston had discovered that he no longer had any contact with the 30th Infantry. He worried that the Germans would infiltrate between his 3rd Battalion and the 30th Infantry, which, as it turned out, was exactly what they planned to do. Before he had a chance to do anything about this potential disaster, hundreds of German soldiers attacked the more or less isolated platoons of I and F Companies. The platoon from F Company (2nd Battalion) had been in the process of relieving the platoon from I Company (3rd Battalion) the night before when the shelling began. In the terror and confusion both platoons had, like the rest of their battalions, simply remained in place.

Now, forced by circumstances and geography into this spot along the railroad, they absorbed most of the German offensive in the 7th Regiment's area. Second Lieutenant Edwin Gray commanded the I Company platoon and Second Lieutenant Aubrey Baker the F Company platoon. They and their men watched as the Germans advanced toward them in skirmish formation. A second later the shooting started. Here was a situation where, quite possibly, the fate of an entire regiment rested with a few battle-worn, frightened, exhausted infantrymen, fighting with only their rifles and their resolve, combat at its very essence.

The divisional history told the story of what happened to Gray and Baker's men: "Of the heroism of individual men of these two platoons too little is known. They halted the Germans and died. One automatic rifleman, Clarence Hensley of Company 'I,' fired his Chauchat until ammunition and crew were gone. A broken Chauchat barrel and the bodies of Germans beside his dead body told the story of his last fight. Beyond their position no Germans passed; dead bodies showed the fate of the German who reached this point." The fighting for those few terrible moments on that anonymous battleground must have been singularly desperate, but unfortunately, the story is lost, because nearly everyone engaged that day died. Lieutenant Gray vanished and was listed as missing in action until after the war when he walked into regimental headquarters after several months of captivity in Germany. He left behind no record of his experiences that day except to say that while checking on some of his men he found himself face-to-face with a German machine-gun team that gave him no choice but to surrender.

The incredible courage of these two platoons of Cottonbalers, combined with the stubborn resistance of one other isolated F Company platoon nearby, decimated the enemy assault units and bought valuable time for F Company's commander, Captain Magnus Whitman, to rush reinforcements to the scene. The remnants of his F Company, along with a few refugees from other regimental units, held off the German advance. A Chauchat gunner from F Company, Private Festa, almost single-handedly prevented two boats full of Germans from crossing the river: "With the air filled with dust, and the earth shaking with thunderous explosions, he made his way to the river, and with his automatic rifle opened a severe fire on the Germans who were attempting to cross the Marne. His [ammunition] carrier was killed, but he still held his ground, nor did he retreat until his ammunition was exhausted. He upset two boatloads of German Infantrymen by his fire, causing many to drown, and holding up the crossing for some minutes."[42]

The overarching question now was the location and disposition of the Germans. Clearly their attack had slowed down, but how many more of them were out there in the meadows, trees, and towns and would they be coming back?

In order to find this out, the brigade commander at 1:00 P.M. ordered the 1st Battalion to leave its positions in front of Le Rocq Farm and attack north, through the Bois d'Aigremont, into Fossoy, and all the way to the Marne at Rû Chailly Farm. This route would lead them almost right in front of Whitman's positions. Companies A, B, and C of the 1st Battalion advanced into the trees of the Bois d'Aigremont. To this point, the battalion had been fairly fortunate in dodging the worst of the German pre-attack bombardment, but their luck soon ran out. The three companies had no sooner entered the woods when German artillery rained down on them. Undoubtedly the enemy must have had observers in the woods. The barrage was a slaughter. Shells burst everywhere. Their fragments mixed with tree splinters and lacerated dozens of 1st Battalion soldiers. In a matter of seconds, B Company lost all its officers, including the commanding officer, Captain Newell Fiske, who was killed by shell fragments. In fact, that company ceased to function. The weeping survivors either dug in wherever they could or filtered out of the woods in an effort to get away from the shelling. The other two companies, although bloodied, somehow managed to press on and make it to the Paris–Metz railroad south of Fossoy.

As evening approached, the battle for the 7th now became one of patrolling and reconnoitering. Lieutenant Harold L. White, a platoon leader in M Company, had earned at Belleau Wood a reputation as an outstanding patrol leader. More than anyone else, he was responsible for the 3rd Battalion's success in capturing the ravine and the crossroads south of Torcy. Although he had probably never heard of Lieutenant James Bradley of Little Bighorn and Big Hole fame, White possessed (inherited?) the same passion and talent for scouting and reconnaissance. On the morning of the sixteenth, White led a patrol designed to guide two platoons of A Company into positions at La Brettonerie Farm. In the process he and his men found many of the dead from Baker's and Gray's platoons. At nightfall White's little group went out again to investigate a nearby wood: "I moved my platoon . . . forming two waves on the woods. The first wave hit the woods and pivoted to the left, the second wave moved to the woods, pivoting to the right, combing the woods thoroughly. We found 1 wounded American and 1 wounded German."

Later that same night, White and his troops went out again, even though they had not slept in days. The plan was to investigate Mézy, where the Germans had crossed the Marne the day before. White hoped to find out if the Germans planned any more attacks in the regimental sector. On this cloudy, temperate evening he and his exhausted soldiers—all veterans by now—stealthily walked through a thick stand of woods west of Mézy. They must have looked like little more than ghostly apparitions on that moonless night. "We found two German Maxim guns and 4 packs and brought them in with us. In the immediate front of my position there were four dead Germans and quite a number more toward the river. I found equipment of A Co., of the 30th Infantry scattered over the ground . . . which they had abandoned when they withdrew." In the process he determined that the Germans had withdrawn back across the river. They would not be back.

At daylight on the seventeenth, White and his troops returned to the American lines, where they received orders to go to the rear. White sent his men back with one of his sergeants and then staggered into the 3rd Battalion headquarters, where he dictated a stream-of-consciousness report on his recent experiences. "We have been under heavy shell fire from the Boche ever since the night of the 14th and have had nothing to eat or drink nor have we had any sleep since that time. My men [are] exhausted. All the men in the front line are absolutely exhausted. They . . . won't move back at any cost. Cpl. Brice, Company M accompanied all patrols that were sent out from my platoon and his work was very commendable. One of the German prisoners . . . we captured told me that . . . the 7th Infantry fire that was turned loose on them was so hot that they could not hold their position."[43]

The privation White's men experienced reigned throughout the whole regiment. Between July 14 and 17 most of the men did not sleep. Nor did they have much of anything to eat. Private Homer Wilson of F Company commented that "food rations were terrible at the front [and] we went without food from 7/14/18 to 7/18/18." When they finally did get food they "received canned corn, hardtack, syrup." The nasty food and conditions gave almost everyone diarrhea.[44]

ON THE SEVENTEENTH THE 111TH INFANTRY REGIMENT (Pennsylvania National Guard) relieved the embattled 3rd Battalion and most of the Cottonbalers ate and stood down for a day or two. With the German attack repelled and the Allies now planning a counterattack, Colonel Anderson engaged in a bit of self-congratulation: "Despite the fact that the 7th Infantry was caught in a hellish artillery preparation in the midst of relief, where 2000 men were crowded in woods where intrenchments and dugouts were only intended for 1000, suffering hundreds of casualties . . . owing to exposure and being under enfilade heavy artillery fire, enough to shatter the morale of the most seasoned veterans, this regiment has not only held its ground, which it was to hold at all costs, but it has even taken over ground that was not expected of it. I consider the action of this shell torn and gas attacked regiment most commendable, even deserving of the highest praise."[45]

Without question the 7th performed well at the Marne and added to its proud tradition. The 38th Infantry could boast of even greater exploits. The spear point of the German attack collided with the 38th, especially Captain Jesse Woolridge's G Company, which fended off major assaults and helped bring the enemy offensive to a standstill. The valor of the 38th, in addition to the other regiments that made up the 3rd Division, forever earned that unit the sobriquet "Rock of the Marne."

The division had little time to rest on its laurels. Sensing that the tide had turned (one American general equated the Marne battle with

Gettysburg), the Allied high command now planned to strike back at the Germans by crossing the river and pushing north. For the Cottonbalers, this new offensive meant an attack across the Marne in the vicinity of Mézy. Colonel Anderson scraped together his survivors and whatever green replacements he had on hand and moved his people out of Fossoy and toward the river.

Cottonbaler patrols crossed the Marne in boats in hopes of finding the German positions. On the morning of the twenty-first, Lieutenant Williams, still bravely leading C Company troops, boarded a boat with several men and attempted to cross the river. They had no sooner plunged into the water when two enemy machine guns opened up, riddling the little boat. They ducked their heads and kept rowing forward, even as near misses splashed water on them. Machine-gun bullets made thunking sounds as they hit the wooden boat. Amazingly, none of the bullets found human flesh. When they reached the north bank of the Marne, Williams led his men to a hillside he had previously scouted. This hill afforded good cover. The lieutenant now had to figure out how to get his little patrol back to the south bank. Riddled with many bullet holes, the boat was as good as sunk. Williams knew he was lucky the boat had gotten them this far. After a few minutes of deliberation, he decided what to do.

Handing his weapon to one of his men, he calmly jumped into the water and began swimming to the other side. The Germans opened fire again, but this time they received plenty in return as American machine gunners and automatic riflemen shot at them. Williams made it safely to the south bank, found another boat, and rowed it back across all by himself. He furiously gestured at his men to get in the boat, supervised them as they did so, and then got in. Rowing as fast as their arms could work, they dodged German bullets again and made it back to the American side.

The hot reception Williams's patrol received did not deter Colonel Anderson. Early in the afternoon, he ordered 1st Battalion to board boats and cross the river. Supported by plenty of machine-gun and small-arms fire, they did so and, in the process, drove off the German machine gunners. All four companies of the 1st Battalion spent the night on the north side of the Marne, exchanging desultory fire with the Germans. Anderson pushed the 2nd and 3rd Battalions across in the morning on the twenty-second while the 1st Battalion captured Mont St. Père with no resistance.

The Germans had evacuated this hillside town that overlooked the Marne, but that hardly made the place safe. They knew exactly where the Americans were and they knew the Yanks would take shelter in the dugouts and buildings that, only twenty-four hours before, had had German occupants. In the early afternoon the enemy blasted the place with fragmentation shells. Then the gas shells came flying in. Private Millea, the kid from South Bend, had been fortunate to this point, but now his luck ran out. He failed to deploy his gas mask quickly enough: "[We] got into dugouts while boche shelled the town. 3 pm. Got sick from gas. 5 pm. Started for Hospital." He crossed the Marne and made his way to a rear area hospital, never to return to the regiment.[46]

Quite possibly he crossed paths with Emma Dickson, who was busy providing whatever help she could in a hospital several miles to the rear. "It was a pitiful sight to see the rows of men on stretchers laid out in the courtyard of the hospital—so many of them gassed and suffering terribly. But the worst thing of all is shell shock. One is so powerless to help these poor men who come in with their nerves shattered, trembling and shuddering. In feeding one of them with a spoon, it was all I could manage to hold him steady, his muscles twitched so."

The wounded Cottonbalers kept coming in waves, "some of them frightfully burned with this mustard gas. I don't know which is the worst—the terrible blisters all over their bodies or the burning in their lungs. They all suffer so, and in most cases their eyes are swollen shut. But in spite of it all they are the cheeriest bunch. I can look at these poor men all gory and torn, without turning a hair, and some of them are frightfully burned . . . so that wherever you touch them the skin falls off. As they are taken off the ambulance and laid in the courtyard on litters, I go around with the sergeant and take their names and numbers. So many are only kids nineteen and twenty, but they certainly are plucky. Today I came to one boy who looked specially cheerful and smiling, and I remarked that I was glad he hadn't been badly hurt. He said, 'Sure, I'm cheerful—why not? I only lost one leg, and there's still one left.'"

Two days later, she was dismayed to see two good friends show up in the hospital ward. Both were in awful shape: "Herbert and his chum Bill are both terribly burned with mustard gas, and there is no hope for them, as three quarters of their bodies are raw burns. Herbert asked for a ripe tomato, so I searched the town . . . and finally got one. Of course, he couldn't eat it, but it seemed to comfort him just to look at it. It probably looks cool to his scorched throat." Herbert died the next day.[47]

BACK AT THE FRONT, THE TERRIBLE CARNAGE CONTINUED unabated. The struggle to contain the German onslaught had led to many casualties, but attacking was even more dangerous. For about a week in late July, the 7th Regiment slugged its way from the Marne to the northeast in the direction of Le Charmel, a major German supply depot located some twenty-five miles southwest of Rheims. A fortified castle slightly to the east of the town dominated the approaches to Le Charmel. Whoever wished to capture Le Charmel must capture the castle.

Before the Cottonbalers could do that, though, they had to fight their way through three miles of well-defended German positions. The enemy had not entrenched, but he had machine guns, minenwerfers, and soldiers with which to impede the Americans. The 1st Battalion, led by A and B Companies, attacked the first objective, La Tulerie Farm, about four hundred meters northeast of Mont St. Père. The soldiers cautiously advanced through the woods adjacent to this farm, knowing the enemy was in there somewhere. Sure enough, German machine guns opened fire. The Americans dived for cover and returned fire. In small groups, they maneuvered aggressively, using tree trunks as cover, eventually finding good positions for enfilade fire against the guns. The German gunners wanted no more of this withering fire and raised an improvised white flag, probably made from someone's spare handkerchief. Sixteen enemy soldiers surrendered and twenty-five others had been killed. Unfortunately, the men could not enjoy this triumph for very long. German shells screamed into the woods, killing and wounding many soldiers. Many lay where they were hit, bleeding, crying, and hoping for relief. Others ducked and crawled out of the woods and to the small clump of houses that comprised La Tulerie Farm.

The men of C Company lost a fine leader when shell fragments ripped through Captain Cartter's arms and torso. He had to be evacuated. First Lieutenant Joe Brown now took command of C Company. Later in the day, the 3rd Battalion came up from reserve and relieved the bloodied, battered 1st. On the right the 2nd Battalion had taken La Theodorie Farm, overwhelming several enemy machine-gun nests.

The 3rd and 2nd Battalions slowly advanced several hundred yards on the twenty-fifth until they ran into heavy machine-gun fire from Le Charmel Château, as well as artillery fire from unspotted German guns. Captain Whitman, now commanding the mixture of wary veterans and raw recruits who comprised the 3rd Battalion, had just led his men to a slight valley along the road to Le Charmel when the enemy shooting began: "The enemy opened fire on the Bn with '77's as soon as it came in this open field but the Bn reached the road in good shape and with but few casualties. The advance guard [got] about 200 yards north of Argentol [located almost right in front of the château] when it was opened up on by machine gun fire from the direction of Le Charmel Château. The advance was halted and a platoon despatched with the mission of destroying the machine gun. Almost immediately thereafter other machine guns opened fire and the enemy began a terrific bombardment with high explosives, and gas shells."

The explosives ripped through men randomly, shattering kneecaps, femurs, and humerus bones, tearing into bellies and groins. The gas burned out the lungs of many soldiers. The helpless wounded lay in the grassy valley, many with guts hanging out, pleading for help while their comrades scrambled for cover. Medics did what they could to drag the wounded to safety, but sometimes they got hit too. Whitman finally succeeded in removing his wounded from the kill zone and deployed his decimated companies into a nearby ravine that seemed to be out of the enemy's line of sight. Later Whitman sent out patrols that came back safely, but with disquieting reports about the "presence of a machine gun nest of at least 10 guns covering all approaches to the le Charmel Château." The battalion had suffered at least 20 men killed and 125 wounded and could do little else besides stay put, defend the ravine, and observe enemy activity.[48]

Anderson knew that his regiment had to take the town and the château if it hoped to advance any farther. Built on high ground, the castle dominated the landscape around Le Charmel. This keen observation point probably accounted for the uncanny accuracy of the shelling that had decimated Whitman's 3rd Battalion. The morning after this debacle, the colonel ordered 1st Battalion to capture Le Charmel and the castle. They would be supported by the 4th Infantry on their left and the French on their right.

The Allied soldiers had no sooner begun forming up in the woods for their attack when German artillery and gas rained down upon them. German observers in the château could probably see every last khaki-clad soldier. American artillery, called in by the Philadelphian Lieutenant Dechert, responded, but it did not do nearly enough damage. The 7th Regiment's artillery support from the 10th Field Artillery had been caught in the open a day or two before and slaughtered by German artillery. Now the artillerymen, who set up shop right on the heels of the infantry, barely had enough soldiers to man their guns. Nor did they have observers or proper communication. Dechert was actually a signals officer taking the initiative to string his communication wire through no-man's-land, back to the batteries, and then act as an on-the-spot forward observer. In the process he barely escaped with his life when German shells narrowly missed him, and he earned the Distinguished Service Cross. A graduate of Penn Law School, he later served as general counsel to the Department of Defense during the Eisenhower administration.[49]

Dechert and his little band of artillery did whatever they could to provide support for the infantrymen, but it wasn't enough. In spite of the fact that German artillery exploded among the assault troops, wounding and killing men with each passing second, they still had to move forward into Le Charmel. They hoisted their weapons, steeled themselves, and ran as fast as they could into the southern edge of town. Now enemy machine guns added to their woes. The incredible volume of bullets whistled and ricocheted off buildings. Some men were cut in two. They spent their last moments glimpsing pieces of themselves fly crazily in many directions. The unscathed threw grenades into enemy-held buildings and found whatever cover they could, in or out of the buildings. They cleared the enemy from the south edge of the town but could go no farther because of machine-gun fire from the château. The 1st Battalion was now down to fewer than two hundred men (out of an original strength of over a thousand).

They settled down, tended to their wounded, and waited for help. Lieutenant Brown commanded these battered, filthy, dispirited survivors. That night he sent a runner with a dispatch to headquarters: "We are located in the southernmost buildings in the town of Le Charmel. We are connected with the 4th on our left but the French on our right and the French on the left of the 4th have failed to advance. The town is still occupied by numerous German machine guns and we are flanked with machine guns from the château which remains untaken. We still have with us about 150 men. The rest have been knocked out or strayed. Two officers [are] casualties. It would greatly help if our ... one pounders could be brought in under cover of darkness. The German barrage was quite bad and this town is now being slightly bombarded. We will have a hard time getting much further with our present force."[50]

Luckily for Brown and his men, the Germans elected to withdraw from the town and the château. Perhaps they did not realize the level of tactical advantage they enjoyed over the 7th and its cohorts, or perhaps they were in equally bad shape. Whatever the cause of their retreat, the Cottonbalers more than welcomed it. Anderson set up his regimental headquarters in the château and planned to keep pushing north in tandem with the 4th Infantry. But on the evening of July 29–30, he received word that his regiment would be relieved by troops of the 127th Infantry (32nd Division) that night and sent to the rear for a rest. The exhausted, battle-scarred soldiers of the 7th Regiment gladly complied. They boarded trucks that took them to Viffort. As they did so, many of them undoubtedly thought about their absent comrades. In just under one month on the front lines, the unit lost 189 men killed, 828 wounded, 63 sick, and 112 missing—a whopping total of 1,192 casualties, more than one-third of the regiment's strength. None of the survivors would ever be the same again.

AT VIFFORT THE HOLLOW-EYED VETERANS OF THE MARNE put their nerves back in order with water, clean clothes, and decent food. Anderson left the regiment to become the divisional supply officer. Colonel E. L. Butts, who had served up to now with the 30th, transferred over from that unit and took control of the 7th Regiment. Gaston served as his executive officer. Badly needed replacements arrived, most of whom were idealistic and willing to fight but ill trained and poorly prepared for the ugly realities of the battlefield. The veterans had mixed emotions about them. On the one hand, the veterans knew the regiment badly needed an infusion of manpower after the bloodbaths of the last several weeks. On the other hand, they held out no great hope for the survivability of these fuzzy-cheeked newbies. Along the roads to Viffort, the veterans had seen graves registration details identifying and burying many of their comrades. Most of them wondered how, in this meat-grinder war, they could possibly hope to avoid the same fate.

Between August 15 and 17 the regiment once again was on the move. The men boarded trucks and trains and went to Treveray, where they rested some more and trained their new replacements as best they could. The regiment's strength rose to more than thirty-six hundred men. They stayed at Treveray for two weeks, soaking up every moment of life off the line, knowing it had to end sooner or later.

They were right. During the 7th Infantry's vacation from the line, the war changed. The Allies were now clearly winning. Their armies were pushing the Germans back on all fronts. Privately, the Germans sent out peace feelers in the hopes that they could hang on to most of the territory they had won over the course of four terrible years of war. The Allies refused. The British wanted to decisively defeat the Germans. The French wanted the Germans out of their country. The Americans wanted to establish an independent army and use it to fight their way into Germany itself.

Along those lines, General Pershing and his commanders were planning a massive American offensive in eastern France at Saint-Mihiel, a two-hundred-square-mile German-held bulge that jutted west, in so doing creating a defiant salient in the Allied lines. Pershing planned a pincer-style attack (the French in the north, the Americans in the south) designed to cut off most of the German defenders. From there he would then turn his victorious army east and plunge into Germany to capture Metz. The planners earmarked the 3rd Division to serve as corps reserve in this great offensive.

So on the night of September 4, the newly reconstituted 7th Regiment left Treveray and began marching east, mostly at night, mostly along muddy roads, and mostly in the pouring rain. "On September 4, we started on the concentration marches for the St. Mihiel," one man later wrote. "Those marches formed a new and vivid picture in our minds. The knowledge of a large concentration of troops at any point of the line must be kept secret from the enemy. The American Army was still short of . . . motor transport, and so we marched at night, with never a glimmer of a match or glow of a cigarette. And every night it rained. And every day we lay hidden under cover of some wet woods and cooked our food over smokeless fires. And lacking smokeless fires our food was not cooked at all. Every night we marched along an unknown road through the hushed drizzle of the rain and muffled rumble of the wagons, toward another unknown bivouac, cold, wet and inhospitable before the break of day."

They passed through a mind-numbing series of little towns—Pagny-la-Blanche-Côte, Burey-en-Vaux, Septvigny, Champougny, Montbras, Taillancourt. Here and there men found shelter for a time, but it never lasted: "On the 11th we got our orders, and on the afternoon of the 12th we took up a 'position in readiness' near Bernecourt in support of the St. Mihiel Offensive."[51]

As it turned out, the 7th saw no action in the Saint-Mihiel offensive. The Germans, surprised by the offensive, quickly retreated east to strong positions they had prepared years before. In two days, the Americans inflicted over fifteen thousand casualties on them and eliminated the salient. The 7th Regiment suffered no casualties, which, in the context of World War I, meant that the outfit had done no fighting. The Americans now believed that Metz lay wide open, and many officers wanted to capture it and inflict a war-ending defeat on the Germans.

However, General Ferdinand Foch, Supreme Allied Commander, had other ideas in mind. He envisioned an all-out final Allied offensive on every front from the English Channel to Verdun. The goal was to drive the Germans completely out of France. Essentially, this came down to the French wanting the Germans out of their own country before contemplating an invasion of Germany. He and Pershing bickered over this throughout much of September. Pershing finally had to agree to Foch's plans but did so only with the understanding that the Americans would fight as an independent army, not, as had previously been the case, intermixed in the British and French armies wherever they happened to be needed.

This exercise of sovereignty presented all sorts of logistical headaches as to how exactly Pershing could disengage his growing army, and all its necessary supplies, from the Saint-Mihiel area, move it northwest forty miles, and still be prepared to attack. Consequently, in his plans, Foch assigned the Americans the area closest to Saint-Mihiel, a swath of territory north of Verdun known as the Argonne Forest, crowned at its peak by Sedan, the primary rail hub of the German Army in France. In the impending great offensive, Pershing's army received the job of pushing through the forest, which the Germans had been fortifying over the course of four years, and capturing Sedan. In a twenty-mile corridor, the Americans would have the forest on their left and the Meuse River on their right. For the first ten miles of this corridor, the Germans had constructed three trench lines, each with extensive dugouts, barbed wire, and concrete-reinforced machine-gun posts.[52]

As at Saint-Mihiel, the 3rd Division was not scheduled to lead the offensive. The Cottonbalers spent an entire week in late September hiding in woods near Julvecourt. They tried to drill and stay prepared, but in the memory of one Cottonbaler, they mostly just got wet in the rainy, dripping, leafy, dank forest: "So thick was the canopy of leaves overhead that scarcely a ray of sunshine ever penetrated through it. This of course caused the ground to be wet and soggy. To make conditions worse, it rained continually. At night, the raincoats were laid next to the ground, over these were spread a blanket, then the remaining one was used as a cover. No fires whatever were permitted."

On the night of the twenty-fifth orders came down to move out and head for Montfaucon, one of the first objectives captured during the offensive. Close to the American lines now, they heard the momentous pre-offensive bombardment. After a restless night, they resumed their march. Mercifully, the skies cleared and the day was warm and sunny. Overhead they heard dogfights and even witnessed a German aviator shoot down an Allied observation balloon and then the stricken observer as he attempted to parachute to safety. For three days, even as the great attack began, the Cottonbalers hunkered down in shell holes on a portion of the old Verdun battlefield and waited for orders. By now, no one was clean anymore. Over the course of three weeks the soldiers had been engaged in a glorified camping expedition, living outside in the mud and filth while enduring copious amounts of cold rain.

"The surroundings were desolate and weird," a regimental historian later wrote. "It had been over two years since the French had held these lines. What had once been a beautiful forest was now twisted and broken stumps, standing bare, white and stark in the shadows. Old rusty guns, swords, bits of cloth and bleached bones told the story of that great fight which saved France in 1916."

On the evening of the twenty-ninth, the 7th Infantry left this macabre burial ground and began walking in the direction of the front. "The route . . . was covered with shell holes, trenches and barbed wire. A heavy rain was falling, and the wind was blowing at about 30 miles per hour. The men were in heavy marching order, and wore overcoats. There were no trails or roads to follow. The shell holes were filled with water, and the mud half way to the knees. The men were soon wet through. Whenever a stop was ordered for rest, there was no place to sit down except in the deep mud and mire. Then, too, being wet, and with such a high wind blowing, a few seconds rest chilled one to the very bone. Not a man in the regiment [avoided falling] to the earth a dozen times in that long march, and was pulled up by his buddies, his rifle and clothes covered with mud."

In the morning they camped amid a pockmarked quilt of shell holes and mud just south of Montfaucon: "Blankets were wet, the men were drenched, the [supply] trains were not with us, so there could be no breakfast. Despite all this, the men were cheerful, and munching on hardtack and corn willy, they lay down under their wet tents to get a much needed rest." They had no sooner gotten themselves situated when new movement orders arrived. Grumbling and cursing, they packed up again and walked to the foothills overlooking Montfaucon, a town utterly destroyed in the recent fighting. In the safety of the daylight the Cottonbalers built small fires for brewing coffee and drying out clothes. For several hours on the afternoon of September 30, they stood around chatting. Then word came that the 79th Infantry Division needed help. The entire 3rd Division would now be thrown into the battle.

ONCE AGAIN THEY GRABBED THEIR WEAPONS AND EQUIP-ment and moved out, this time along a road that ran in a northwesterly direction toward the town of Cierges. Father John O'Leary, the Catholic chaplain of the regiment, blessed them as they passed. Ten minutes later many of them were dead.[53]

For a short distance, the regiment walked along the road. Eventually they veered to the right off the road. Before them, fully seven hundred yards away across open fields, lay their immediate objective—the shelter of a cluster of woods known as the Bois de Beuge. The men now had no choice but to go straight across the open fields, right under the noses of the Germans. Enemy artillery covered practically every inch of this ground, but that did not seem to matter. The Cottonbalers lined up single file, at five-yard intervals, and started walking. For a brief and tantalizing moment nothing happened. Then the world exploded:

"The German guns sounded like a steady roll of immense drums, and the air was an inferno of shrieking missles [sic] as shrapnel and high explosive tore great gaps in the earth, and broke into a thousand pieces. Smoke, dust, and deadly fumes filled the air, and it was almost impossible to see the man ahead of you. In front and behind you men fell with a gasp and then lay still, while others, horribly wounded, dragged themselves to some shell hole to seek cover. But despite the . . . terrific fire,

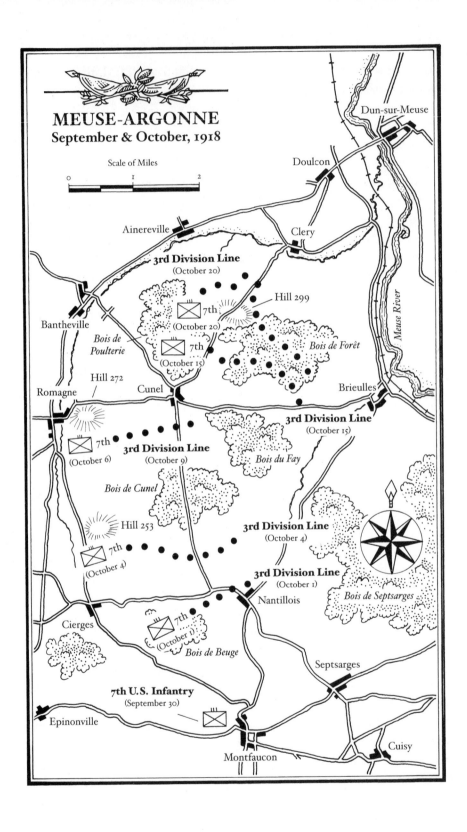

MEUSE-ARGONNE
September & October, 1918

Scale of Miles

0   1   2

Dun-sur-Meuse

Doulcon

Ainereville

Clery

3rd Division Line
(October 20)

Hill 299

7th
(October 20)

Meuse River

Bantheville

*Bois de
Poulterie*

7th
(October 15)

Bois de Forêt

Hill 272

Cunel

Brieulles

Romagne

3rd Division Line
(October 15)

7th
(October 6)

3rd Division Line
(October 9)

Bois du Fay

Bois de Cunel

Hill 253

3rd Division Line
(October 4)

7th
(October 4)

3rd Division Line
(October 1)

Nantillois

Bois de Septsarges

Cierges

7th
(October 1)

Bois de Beuge

Septsarges

7th U.S. Infantry
(September 30)

Epinonville

Cuisy

Montfaucon

the 7th Infantry had accomplished the relief by 6:30 P.M. that evening, but with awful losses."[54]

THIS BITTER EXPERIENCE SERVED AS A HARBINGER, a kind of sardonically fitting introduction to the meat-grinder slaughter of the Argonne Forest campaign.

Upon reaching the Bois de Beuge, the 1st Battalion took up positions at the north edge of those woods and the 2nd Battalion dug in among a clump of trees at the south edge of Bois de Beuge. The 3rd Battalion remained in brigade reserve in a ravine to the southeast of Montfaucon.

After sunset, the 1st Battalion commander, hoping to find concrete information on the location of the German lines, sent a patrol into a small patch of woods just north of Bois de Beuge. Sergeant E. A. Reardon, of B Company, led this small group of about a dozen scared men. Like shadows in the night, they left the American-held woods and skulked into the targeted woods. They never returned. The next day, the 1st Battalion occupied the woods but found no trace of Reardon's men. The sergeant later testified that his patrol ran into an overwhelming number of enemy soldiers. Surprised and flustered, they fought a brief skirmish, during which Reardon was severely wounded and captured, along with most of his men.[55]

For a couple of days little else happened. The 7th Infantry held its positions and weathered enemy artillery and air attacks. The latter hazard proved to be a steady source of consternation and irritation for the Cottonbalers during the Argonne battle. Enemy aircraft operated with seeming impunity, dropping bombs, strafing, and spotting for their artillery.

On the evening of the third, the regiment received orders to attack up the Cierges road and capture the town of Romagne, about two kilometers away. To do this they had to leave their positions and move, in the darkness, to the left in positions formerly occupied by the 125th Infantry (32nd Division). During this movement, the commander of H Company, Captain Branton Kellogg, got lost, wandered into the German lines, and got killed. Days later, someone found his dead, decomposing body a kilometer to the north.

At 5:25 A.M. on October 4 the attack began, with the 2nd Battalion in the lead and 1st Battalion just behind. There was nothing complicated about the assault. The men simply leveled their weapons and ran forward in the face of withering enemy fire. German machine guns and minenwerfers peppered the Cottonbalers. Men fell dead and wounded. Intermittent enemy artillery fire fell here and there. American support consisted of artillery, one pounders, and machine guns. By late morning the men had gained about a kilometer and taken up positions under cover at the foot of Hill 253. The shooting then tapered off and the attack lost momentum.

There the situation stood until late in the afternoon when the officers ordered the men to take Hill 253. In preparation for this attack, the artillery laid down a smoke screen designed to confuse the German defenders and mask the American attack. It did neither. Instead the smoke screen acted as a beacon for German gunners. As the infantrymen formed up for their attack, German artillery and machine-gun fire raked them over, blasting men to pieces. They screamed, shrieked, and groaned. No one could see anything in the smoke. They could only crawl away from the smoke screen in hopes of exiting the kill zone. This fiasco pinned down much of the 1st and 2nd Battalions.

The 3rd Battalion now got into the battle. Led by I and K Companies, this fresh battalion attacked west of the road. As they did so, portions of the other two battalions, in addition to an entire company of machine guns, rallied and attacked on the right. These brave men tried gamely to charge up the hill, but their courage brought them only death and suffering. The Germans at the top of the hill could see their targets well and picked them off at will. Confused clumps of Americans took cover at the bottom of the hill.

The 3rd Battalion, finding the same kind of resistance, maneuvered to the left and occupied the reverse slope of a hill adjacent to 253. Two soldiers from K Company dived onto their bellies and took up firing positions at the crest of this hill. From there they could clearly see a group of Germans forming for a counterattack on the Americans pinned down at the foot of Hill 253. One man had a Springfield and the other had a new BAR. They opened fire and picked off numerous Germans, one after the other, almost shooting gallery style. The throaty bark of the BAR mixed with the roar of the Springfield for several moments. The bullets smashed into several enemy soldiers. Wounded Germans screamed in agony while their comrades took cover and tried to find the source of the fire. A second later, one of their machine-gun crews saw the two Cottonbalers and laid down a burst of fire, killing one of the American riflemen.

For three days, the regiment remained stalled in front of and around

Hill 253, about half a kilometer shy of Romagne. On the fifth, the regimental intelligence officer wrote: "Airplanes continually over our lines locating our positions and directing enemy artillery. Enemy MG fire covers Cierges–Romagne road. There does not seem to be an organized infantry line. Enemy making strong resistance by means of well placed MG and artillery fire. Any night movement of ours on Cierges–Romagne road causes barrage on road. The enemy signal for this fire is one white star breaking into two green stars." Two days later he found out that two battalions of German soldiers defended the hill. American artillery and trench mortars worked them over, but they kept moving around on the top of the hill with no effort at concealment.[56]

On the night of October 7, welcome news spread among the men. That night they would be relieved by the 38th Infantry and go back to Montfaucon in division reserve. The Cottonbalers had been in combat for a week, but it seemed like a year. The mud, the shell fire, the poison gas, the machine guns, the constant contact with the enemy, had all taken their toll. Duty as division reserve, although not exactly a rest, afforded the opportunity to unwind and sleep a little bit.

The stand-down lasted all of two days. On the afternoon of the ninth, the Cottonbalers left their reserve positions and provided support for an attack by soldiers from both the 30th and 38th Regiments, fighting their way north in the direction of Romagne and Cunel. This began several days of agonizing combat for the Cottonbalers.

Hills 253 and 255 had been captured, so now the next hill, 272, had to be taken. Led by K Company and Lieutenant Otto Staehli, the 3rd Battalion brazenly assaulted this hill and routed the exhausted German defenders, who had been under accurate American artillery and machine-gun fire for many days. Staehli skillfully led his men across a machine-gun-swept ravine, using cover wherever they could find it, and into an excellent attack position. One of Staehli's men, Sergeant Dominic Mence, experienced a rather interesting interlude as he and the others waited to attack: "While I was guiding a machine gun, I saw something crawling toward me. It was a German ready to throw a hand grenade. I put him out of action."[57] When Staehli and his troops reached the crest of Hill 272, they swarmed into the German trenches and broke the enemy will to resist. The 7th Regiment captured 128 German soldiers that day. Tragically, Staehli got killed by shell fire as he was dispensing first aid to one of those prisoners.

The capture of Hill 272 unhinged the entire German defensive line before Cunel and the enemy knew it. No sooner had the Americans begun to prepare their positions on 272 than the enemy tried to get it back. They failed. The 7th Infantry's machine-gun company set up withering fields of fire covering every approach to the hill. The gunners spotted a group of Germans massing for an attack, waited until they had came into the open, and scythed them with incredibly destructive fire. The enemy troops fell like rows of tin soldiers. Hill 272 remained in American hands.

But not without cost. For instance, fourteen new lieutenants had joined the 7th Infantry as it returned to the line on October 9. Two days later, three of them were already dead. Ten times as many enlisted men had also been killed, including Color Sergeant George Knieps, the oldest man in the outfit. An enemy shell scored a direct hit on his dugout as he slept. The loss of hundreds of wounded men sapped the strength of each battalion. The chilly, muddy, rainy conditions caused pneumonia and wracking chest colds in many men. Some soldiers suffered from trench foot, a malady of the skin caused by constantly wet feet. Unchecked, trench foot could cause feet to turn a purplish black color. Circulation ended. The skin flaked off in chunks. The foot essentially died, requiring amputation before the decay spread to the rest of the body.

Shell shock and its close cousin, straggling, also eroded the unit's manpower. Straggling lay somewhere between true psychological combat fatigue and outright desertion. "The straggler usually gave as his reason for being absent from his command that he was lost or hungry," an officer explained. "In moving forward at night through woods and across strange country it is not difficult for a man to get lost if he desired to do so. When discovered, stragglers were arrested by the military police and returned to organizations. A favorite hangout for stragglers was their own company kitchen or some other company kitchen. Orders were issued that mess sergeants would feed no man unless he belonged to his own company. This rule forced many men to return to their own company. At one time during the Meuse-Argonne operation the records show that 50% of the [3rd] division were stragglers."[58]

Straggling was a symptom of a larger problem, namely, the abject hopelessness of attacking a fortified enemy for paltry gains, day in and day out, with little prospect of an imminent end. The combat soldiers had no idea that Germany was in a state of near collapse. They only knew that each rotten day on the line they faced tough opposition that killed and wounded an incredible number of American soldiers. Reason dictated that the longer this unwelcome situation continued, the better the chance no one would survive unscathed.

Officers did what they could to round up stragglers but could not hope to corral everyone. Sometimes the officers were stragglers too. In the confused melee of the Argonne, a man could sham and disappear if he wanted to. If the military police apprehended him, they merely sent him back to the front, since units so desperately needed manpower to throw into the voracious maw of battle. In that equation, it made good sense for the ordinary survival-minded soldier to choose his moment and steal away for a time, maybe help carry the wounded to safety, or help with the kitchen, or pose as a runner, anything to get away from the horrors of the front. Only those with the steeliest resolve could resist taking such minivacations when the chance arose.

Thus even though the 7th Infantry had gained some ground and taken some key objectives by mid-October, it was in terrible shape. One captain in the 2nd Battalion reported that "all the men are in very small wet holes and all men have diarhea [*sic*] and a great many have fever. They have no blankets. Artillery fire is very regular." Even Gaston, a tough, serious officer, knew that the Cottonbalers could not take much more bloodshed and terror. Gaston had been promoted to lieutenant colonel and ascended to temporary command of the regiment on October 9 when Butts received transfer orders. On the rainy, cold, dreary morning of the fifteenth, Gaston sent a situation report to the division commander, Major General Beaumont Buck, that dripped with the unmistakable mold of despair: "My troops are spent, their condition is nothing short of complete exhaustion. They have had little rest since 30 Sept. Casualties are very heavy, especially amongst officers. I have only 2nd bn. and MG Co. (less 1 platoon) with me here. 2nd bn. has total of three officers and about 140 men; the MG Co. (less 1 platoon) has 2 officers, 60 men and 7 guns. General situation [is] unchanged. Heavy artillery fire (HE and gas) throughout the night."[59]

If Buck sympathized, his actions did not show it. Even as Gaston penned his desperate note, Buck ordered the 7th Regiment's 3rd Battalion, commanded now by a captain, to carry out an independent mission. The 3rd, supported by a small group of machine gunners, received the job of capturing the Bois de Poulterie, a stand of woods just north of Cunel. They took up positions on the night of the fifteenth and attacked the next morning, in filthy, muddy rain under dark skies. One of their officers, Captain John Madden, later wrote: "Then came a night that was black as sin, and the blinding, cold rain fell. The zero hour was four o'clock, and our chances for life were slim." In terrible close-quarter combat they managed to take most of the woods: "I advanced the men at the zero hour. We won the day at a fearful cost. Over half my men were dead, and I awoke all wrapped in gauze, with a shrapnel wound in my head."[60] Only fifty red-eyed, beleaguered survivors from the 2nd Battalion (out of an original strength of more than a thousand) remained. They were rewarded with orders to attack and capture the next line of woods, the Clair-Chênes, immediately to the north. For this task, they received reinforcements, two companies of the 38th, bringing the number of the attackers to 180 unlucky men. Predictably, the attack went nowhere. The soldiers could only be pushed so far. They had reached their collective limit.

The 7th Regiment remained in an exhausted, shell-shocked state of lethargy for four days after the abortive attack on Clair-Chênes, until a new commanding officer, Colonel William Morrow, took command. General Buck called Morrow and several other officers to his command post on October 19 and ordered an attack to capture Clair-Chênes and Hill 299, right next door to the woods. Buck assigned the 7th (or what now passed for it) the task of capturing the woods. Morrow scraped together everything he had left to carry out this questionable attack. He knew the 2nd Battalion was destroyed, or at least functionally useless. So, he threw everything and everybody from 1st and 3rd Battalions together and formed them into one overstrength company of 301 men, under the tactical command of the valorous Captain Cartter, who had returned from his earlier wounding and somehow managed to survive this long. In addition, Morrow rounded up some other odds and ends: two companies of engineers, one from the 4th Infantry, some machine guns, and a gas and flame unit.

Just after 7:00 A.M. on the twentieth they went forward in two waves. Private William Houghton, one of the engineers, described the experience of assaulting Clair-Chênes Woods on that gloomy morning in 1918: "The captain looked at his watch and motioned to us. You know, I can see him now; he looked so young. 'O.K., men,' he said, 'we've got a job to do—let's go.' We followed him, moving through these woods . . . knocking the branches aside. The next thing we knew we started to hear that damn rat-a-tat-tat of German machine guns. We'd spread ourselves out by this time. Along with the fire I could hear groans and

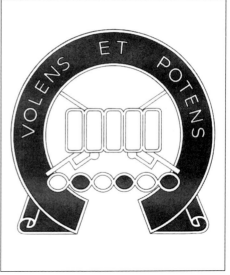

Regimental Colors, Seventh United States Infantry

Regimental Crest, Seventh United States Infantry

A rendering by Derek FitzJames of 7th Infantry soldiers as they appeared in the early nineteenth century, around the time of the Battle of New Orleans. *(Courtesy of Mike Koury)*

One of the earliest known photographs of a Cottonbaler. Lieutenant Napoleon Jackson Tecumseh Dana posed with his wife, Sue, and their young daughter. Dana saw combat in most of the 7th Infantry's battles in the Mexican War. He was wounded at Cerro Gordo. *(United States Army Military History Institute, hereafter known as USAMHI)*

Looking west on Hanover Street as it is today. This is the same route the 7th Infantry took en route to the fighting at Fredericksburg. *(Photograph by the author)*

A worm's eye view of the stone wall at Fredericksburg, roughly at the spot where the 7th Infantry took cover during the battle. *(Photograph by the author)*

Marye's Heights, as a Cottonbaler might have seen it on December 13–14, 1862. *(Photograph by the author)*

East of Chancellorsville today. This is the same spot where the Cottonbalers fought on May 1, 1863. *(Photograph by the author)*

A monument to the 7th Infantry at the Gettysburg battlefield. This marker is located near Round Top, among a row of monuments dedicated to all the U.S. Army regular units that fought with Sykes's division in the battle. *(Photograph by the author)*

A view of the Wheatfield, at the spot where the 7th Infantry fought at Gettysburg. Straight ahead is Rose Woods. *(Photograph by the author)*

The Wheatfield, viewed from behind the wall, at the edge of the woods. The 7th Infantry was right here on the afternoon of July 2, 1863. *(Photograph by the author)*

The headstones of two Cottonbalers who lost their lives at Gettysburg. Private John Keenan, A Company, was KIA at the Wheatfield. He was a twenty-eight-year-old, single laborer. Private William Curtis, A Company, was shot in the back during the retreat; a minié ball tore through one of his lungs. He died of his wounds on July 15, 1863. *(Photograph by the author)*

The headstones of two more Cottonbalers killed at Gettysburg and buried there today. Private Christian Miller, E Company, was shot in the right foot. He died of his wounds on October 11, 1863. Miller was thirty-six and single. Private George Smith, I Company, shot in the right knee, died of his wounds on August 7, 1863. Smith was twenty-five and married. He was an immigrant laborer born in Baden, Germany. *(Photograph by the author)*

This ground-level view affords the best sense of what the Cottonbalers saw on July 2, 1863, at the Wheatfield, Gettysburg. *(Photograph by the author)*

Cottonbalers of the 1870s. Many of these men participated in the Little Bighorn and Big Hole campaigns. Most served enlistments that ranged from three to five years. (*Little Bighorn National Monument Archive*)

Colonel John Gibbon, commander of the 7th Infantry from 1869 to 1885. During the Civil War, Gibbon had earned great distinction as commander of the famous "Iron Brigade." He eventually retired as a general, with a reputation as one of the finest soldiers of his time. (*Little Bighorn National Monument Archive*)

Captain William Logan, commander of Company A, 7th Infantry. Logan was an Irish immigrant who served as an enlisted man during the Civil War. His distinguished combat record earned him an officer's commission and the universal respect of his fellow soldiers. He was killed at the Battle of Big Hole in 1877. *(Little Bighorn National Monument Archive)*

Lieutenant James Bradley, commander of the 7th Infantry's reconnaissance scouts. An Ohio native, Bradley fought in the Civil War and was even a prisoner of war for a time. After the war, he earned an officer's commission, demonstrated a talent for scouting, and was one of the 7th Regiment's most respected commanders. He was killed at the Battle of Big Hole in 1877, leaving behind a young widow and two children. *(Little Bighorn National Monument Archive)*

Cut Ear, one of Lieutenant Bradley's scouts. A member of the Crow tribe, Cut Ear and twenty-four of his fellow tribesmen enlisted in the 7th Infantry in 1876 to fight against the Sioux. Cut Ear and the other scouts were valuable, respected members of the outfit. *(Little Bighorn National Monument Archive)*

Sergeant Charles N. Loynes, of Company I, 7th Infantry. Loynes fought in the Battle of Big Hole and survived to pen some of the most descriptive recollections of what the battle was really like. He lived long enough to see World War II. *(McWhorter Photograph Collection [PC 85, 2-19, MASC, Washington State University Libraries])*

Company E, 7th Infantry, circa 1884. A few years before, many of these men fought at Big Hole and participated in Custer's Little Big Horn campaign. *(National Archives)*

Captain Charles Worden, commander of E Company, at Santiago, his mule piled with loot. A longtime member of the 7th Infantry, he was fifty-one years old in 1898. After El Caney, he loaded up this mule with loot and wandered off alone for several days. Suffering from a severe case of dysentery and heat exhaustion, he was quietly relieved and evacuated. He died two months later. *(National Archives)*

Inspection, summer 1898. *(USAMHI)*

An unidentified 7th Infantry officer in the Santiago campaign. *(USAMHI)*

Camp life in Cuba. In camp, soldiers spent much of their time washing their clothes or playing cards. *(USAMHI)*

The aftermath of El Caney. Cottonbalers man the firing line outside Santiago on July 9, 1898. *(National Archives)*

Sergeant Isadore Valenti, the K Company medic who fought with the regiment from North Africa through Berchtesgaden. *(Isadore Valenti)*

Sicily, 1943. Private Roy Humphrey of Toledo, Ohio, is being given blood plasma by Harvey White of Minneapolis, Minnesota. Humphrey was wounded on August 9, 1943, about a week before the island was secured. He was just one of 480 Cottonbalers who were wounded on Sicily. *(National Archives)*

Troops from the 3rd Battalion march through a muddy street in Belotte, France, on September 14, 1944. The second soldier in line is carrying several K ration meals in the crook of his arm. *(National Archives)*

Vagney, France, where the 7th Infantry fought very hard in October 1944. In this photo, men of D Company are walking across a blown-out bridge on their way to the center of town. *(National Archives)*

Members of I Company move up an alley to screen their movement from German observation as they go toward the outskirts of Vagney. Their mission was to take up positions just outside the town. *(National Archives)*

A Cottonbaler fire team from the 1st Battalion prepares to root out snipers in Guiderkirch, France, on March 15, 1945. *(National Archives)*

Cottonbalers move through the ruins of Guiderkirch. *(National Archives)*

Infantrymen of G Company take cover behind a wall as they move on to the Old City of Nuremberg. The lead man awaits the signal to move forward. *(National Archives)*

The reward after two and a half years of bloody combat. Several Cottonbalers, including two medics, party at Hitler's mountain retreat at Berchtesgaden. The 7th Infantry reached Berchtesgaden at 1558 hours on May 4, 1945, several hours before any other Allied unit. In spite of this fact, the myth still persists that Easy Company, 506th Parachute Infantry, won the race for Berchtesgaden. *(National Archives)*

shouts; obviously men were being hit. I . . . crouched down behind some trees along with a buddy of mine." Even as the shooting continued, Houghton helped evacuate wounded men, including his captain. Eventually, though, German soldiers overwhelmed his little group of lifesavers and captured them.[61]

Meanwhile, Captain Cartter and two platoons had captured three machine guns at the edge of the woods. Some of them got hit, but the soldiers kept advancing, right into the heart of the woods. They captured a few Germans, but other enemy soldiers, hiding no more than ten or twenty yards away, kept shooting. Bullets tore through torsos and heads, sending blood spraying in every direction. Truly in a frenzy now, Cartter and his few remaining soldiers, twelve men, screamed at the top of their lungs and ran right at the German positions. Some of them got hit, but the sheer courage and audacity of this charge broke the Germans. Many of the enemy troops died in this free-for-all. The berserk American soldiers shot them at point-blank range or stabbed them to death with bayonets. At 8:15 A.M. Cartter, his sergeant, and four other men made it to the northern edge of the woods. They had captured the objective, but could they hold it?

For three hours they took cover in a shell hole, losing two more men wounded to German machine-gun fire. The enemy moved around Cartter's flanks, along the western and eastern boundaries of the woods. Realizing this, he decided to take his wounded men and go find the second wave, composed mostly of engineers. The tiny group of soldiers gingerly and painfully made their way through the woods until they came upon some of the engineers. The engineers said that American artillery had pinned them down. So, after all the sacrifices of Cartter's men, the 7th Regiment still could not claim control of Clair-Chênes Woods.

Reports to this effect filtered back to Morrow, and this made him decide to do something fairly unusual for a regimental commander in twentieth-century war. He threw together whatever soldiers he could find, 150 men in all, and personally led another attack into Clair-Chênes. German machine guns and minenwerfers exacted a heavy toll on Morrow's assault force. The story of casualties was, by now, all too familiar: young men destroyed for life, torn and maimed by terribly destructive weapons, serving as mere numbers in the cruel math of industrial war. In spite of severe losses, Morrow and his men reached the northern end of the woods and broke the German will to resist. The Americans captured 112 enemy troops.

Thoroughly spent, the survivors collapsed into shell holes and watched as American machine-gun crews set up positions along the flanks of the woods. But the ordeal was not yet over. Hill 299, located immediately due east of Clair-Chênes, still needed to be taken. Morrow ordered stragglers policed up and then gathered every possible warm body he could muster. The result was an odd mélange of divisional troops—a battalion of the 38th Infantry, a company from the 4th, anyone still breathing from the 7th, plus machine gunners.

They launched their attack on the morning of the twenty-first. Considering the usual meat-grinder nature of the fighting in the Argonne, they captured 299 fairly easily. They overwhelmed a few weary German machine gunners with grenades and rifle fire and reached the crest of the hill. The machine gunners set up positions on the hill. However, these Americans had no sooner taken the hill when Morrow, back in his command dugout, received word from broken, retreating troops left to defend Clair-Chênes that hundreds of German attackers had recaptured these woods, won at such a dear price the day before.

Morrow could not believe his ears. If the Germans recaptured Clair-Chênes, they could easily flank the men on Hill 299 and, most likely, annihilate them. Most disturbingly, he possessed no more reserves—he had thrown everything he had into the Hill 299 attack. Instead of calling for a retreat, he decided to rally his command group, a motley collection of nineteen staff officers, runners, and signalmen, and attack Clair-Chênes. Cautiously, but alertly, they advanced on the woods with Morrow in the lead. They entered the southern edge and kept going, and going, and going. To Morrow's immense relief, they found absolutely no evidence of a German attack. Instead, they only found four frightened enemy soldiers who were more than happy to become prisoners. Morrow and his men quickly pushed on to the well-trod northern edge of Clair-Chênes, where they set up an outpost line. For his outstanding, aggressive leadership on this and the previous day, Morrow earned a Distinguished Service Cross. The division commander, perhaps wanting to shore up morale, actually decorated the colonel three days later while the remnants of the 7th Regiment still manned their thin line.[62]

They remained there another five days after the capture of Hill 299 and Clair-Chênes Woods, but very little fighting took place. As if by mutual agreement, the Germans and Americans contented themselves with an exhausted stalemate. Frankly, neither side could keep going much longer. The Germans had little recourse but to retreat and the Americans no choice but to relieve their battered frontline units with fresh troops.

General Buck informed Morrow on the night of the twenty-seventh that the 7th Regiment would be removed from the line. The soldiers were no longer even capable of the kind of joy this news should have brought. Dispirited, muddy, bloody, shattered mentally, and fatigued almost beyond the limits of human endurance, they turned over their positions to the 61st Infantry Regiment (5th Division) and walked back to the ravine at Montfaucon. On November 1, they boarded trucks that drove them to the rear. The 7th Regiment had seen its last combat in the Great War.

ARGONNE FOREST COST THE 7TH INFANTRY REGIMENT 2,241 casualties: 198 killed, 1,348 wounded, 168 missing, 527 soldiers sick from exposure and exhaustion—all this in a mere twenty-eight days on the line. When the regiment left the front, only four officers remained. Out of fourteen newly commissioned second lieutenants who joined the outfit on October 10, only one remained at the end of the campaign.[63] Argonne was the biggest, costliest battle to that point in American history. Only the Civil War offered any kind of precedent in American military history for this type of bloodletting, but the Cottonbalers, in spite of their long history of combat exploits, could point to no similar experience. They had never experienced a costlier battle than Argonne.

The trucks dropped the surviving Cottonbalers off in Tronville. Emma Dickson watched them shuffle by and she could not help but fight back tears. "There has been a terrible list of casualties in my crowd," she wrote to her sister, "and they have to reorganize and get replacements. I'm hoping and praying that something will happen to bring peace before they are shoved back in the line again. These men have done more than their bit, and I can't bear to think of them going through it again. The horror of it all is more than you can imagine. I've had some very pathetic letters from boys in the hospital. One kid had his leg shot to pieces, and he begged me to send him something sweet. So I sent him a box of sweet crackers."[64]

Ten days after Dickson wrote this letter, her prayers for peace were answered. On November 11, the Allies and the Germans agreed to an armistice, ending the war. Word filtered to the troops in the afternoon.

"In a little French village, we heard rumors of Armistice," Lieutenant Dechert later wrote. "However, we had been fooled by false rumors for several days. Was this story any different?"[65] They soon found out that the armistice was very real: "Cheers arose from the troops." The war was over and the Allies had pulled out a bloody victory. That meant no more machine guns, no more shellings, no more gas attacks, no more killing. All of them would survive the war!

The joy most men felt was, of course, tempered with sorrow. Everyone could conjure up the memory of a buddy who had not lived to see the armistice. Many other men were scarred for life, physically or emotionally. Few of them would look at life the same way again. Even so, most of the Cottonbalers believed and hoped that this war would be the last, that their sons and grandsons would never have to experience the ghastly horrors they had come to know intimately. Future tragedies portended, though. On that emotional, momentous November day, very few, if any, of these valorous veteran soldiers could foresee that their terrible war was little more than a bloody prelude, to the greatest war ever fought.

8

The Greatest War, World War II

Operation Torch Through Rome

ONE HISTORIAN SUCCINCTLY, AND ACCURATELY, CALLED IT the greatest war.[1] It certainly was that. In terms of sheer loss of human life, destructiveness, geopolitical upheaval, and moral crisis, there is World War II and then there is every other war fought in the history of humanity. With the possible exception of the Civil War, there has been no other time in American history when such immensely powerful enemies threatened the continued existence of the republic. Certainly the United States never faced more overtly malevolent enemies than its opponents in World War II. Victory was the only option.

Never were the stakes of war higher or the demands on the nation greater. Victory could only be achieved through total war and total mobilization, the kind of war effort that sparked major changes in every aspect of American life, including within its military. World War II was the last pre-atomic war, the last war fought with a segregated military, the last war in which the Congress formally declared war, the last war that would see American soldiers fight in Europe, and the last war with no significant cultural opposition in America. The war propelled the United States to superpower status. For the Army this meant a new era of copious and complex security commitments, the kind of commitments that could only be upheld by a large, modern, well-equipped, well-trained force.

The Cottonbalers played an integral role in this "greatest war" that changed humanity forever. Within a month of the end of the November 11, 1918, armistice ending World War I, the Cottonbalers marched east and took responsibility for an occupation zone near Andernach in western Germany. For nine months the unit remained in Germany, until the late summer of 1919, when it boarded ships at Brest and sailed for home. The regiment was stationed at Camp Pike, Arkansas, for two years until being transferred to Vancouver Barracks in Washington State (just across the Columbia River from Portland, Oregon), where it stayed until the eve of World War II. At one point during the Vancouver Barracks years, George C. Marshall even served with the regiment.

These peacetime years saw a return to the lethargy of the pre–World War I age. A spirit of isolationism and antimilitarism swept through America in the 1920s and 1930s. Disillusioned by the carnage of the trenches, not to mention the disappointing imperial peace that emerged from the war, the American people began to view involvement in the war as a kind of idealistic mistake that must never be repeated. Many Americans came to view the armed forces themselves as the primary reason for war. In any case, even those who held no special grudge against the military cared little for its readiness or quality. The advantageous geographical isolation of the United States from the other great powers of the world provided America unique security; geographic proximity gave America the breathing space to disarm itself and operate as if no threat to security existed at all. Pacifism, after all, is a luxury afforded only to the secure.

With the prevalence of isolationist sentiments, Congress cut the Army's budget to the bone. Pershing's great army that had helped win World War I was a mere shadow of itself by the 1920s. Only three regular divisions, the 1st, 2nd, and 3rd, remained in service. The 7th Infantry Regiment continued to serve as part of the 3rd Division. Squads and platoons operated at half strength or less. Soldiers, outfitted with surplus, outmoded uniforms, equipment, and weapons, fired their rifles once a year. Very few young men wanted any part of the Army. In public esteem, the Army of the 1920s regressed to where it had been a century before. After all, why would any self-respecting man join the dead-end, passé, stifling army when there were so many good jobs to be had in a booming economy? That attitude modified somewhat during the depression years of the 1930s, when any job that provided shelter and three square meals had to be respected. Even so, the government spent most of its budget on alleviating the suffering of those hurt by the depression. The Army remained an impoverished afterthought, populated by West Point–educated officers who commanded enlisted men hailing from disadvantaged, sometimes criminal, backgrounds.

Even after war broke out in Europe and the United States began to reluctantly prepare for the possibility, if not the inevitability, of war, the lethargy of two decades still hung over the Army, like cobwebs in a basement. Abner Kuperstein, a young ROTC officer fresh out of college, served with the regiment at Vancouver Barracks in 1940: "Peacetime training was slightly augmented, but the Armed Forces still suffered from under-funding and inattention. The Regular Officer Corps was made up primarily of West Point graduates in an Army in which second lieutenants could hope to be captains in 11–15 years, and were almost ready for retirement when they reached the grade of major or lieutenant colonel. Many enlisted men, as well as officers, had joined the Army from the deep south where the Depression had been the worst, and being a soldier was a prized job. There were no black soldiers in the regiment." Nor would there be any until the next war. The Army was still segregated.

As a raw second lieutenant, Kuperstein relied heavily on his sergeants, many of whom had served with the regiment in World War I. "They took me under their wings as gently as they could, protecting me from making too many waves in the established routine of peacetime Army life." In fact, that routine was stultifying. "For the enlisted men, pre-war life was a dull, monotonous, boring and demoralizing routine, made comfortable mainly by the assurance of three meals a day and a place in which to live. Barracks life consisted of reveille, breakfast, calisthenics, close order drill, rifle cleaning, marksmanship instruction, squad tactics, a hike or two, guard duty, KP, latrine duty, gas mask drill, bayonet drill, inspections and retreat parades. We still had WWI-type steel helmets. Rifles were the old WWI 1903 Springfield, bolt-action, single shot .30 caliber. One custom enforced in the mess hall was the necessity to teach new soldiers (mostly farm kids who had never been taught manners at the table) how to ask 'please pass the beans.' "[2]

Sherman Pratt almost perfectly fit the stereotype of the raw southern boy looking for opportunity in the Army that he could not find in depression-era society. Orphaned at age six, he and his sister went to live in North Little Rock, Arkansas, with an aunt, an alcoholic uncle, and their teenage children. These relatives provided the basic necessities of food and shelter for Pratt and his sister, but little else. "Uncle Charlie was unpredictable, absolutely irrational, domineering and terrifying. He was also incoherent and quite unaware of his monstrous behavior. All of which was attributable to his drinking problem."

Pratt weathered this dysfunctional situation and grew into a healthy, normal teenager. But he longed to get away from North Little Rock. In

1939, as war broke out in Europe, he turned seventeen and began mulling exit options. Needless to say, those options were quite limited. College was out of the question; only rich people could afford it (at least in his view). Good jobs were unheard of: "As I looked around town I grew restless and despondent. High school graduates who had finished a year or more before my class were 'gainfully' employed at . . . jobs . . . such as theater ushers at $10 per week, or soda 'jerkers' in the drug stores, sometimes at as much as $15 per week. These 'successful' grads, unlike me, were generally ex-students with impressive academic records. What hope then . . . was there . . . for me in the employment world?"

He looked into the Civilian Conservation Corps, a New Deal agency that employed young men in regimented forestry and park service jobs. The CCC had a three-month waiting list. Pratt checked out the Navy. They had a similar waiting list. Three months seemed like a lifetime to the rail-thin 117-pound Pratt, imbued with the restlessness of youth. He wanted out of North Little Rock sooner rather than later. He no sooner left the Navy recruiting office when he noticed another such office, adorned with colorful, patriotic posters that urged him to join the U.S. Army. Attracted to this place like a bee to honey, Pratt asked the recruiting sergeant if the Army had immediate vacancies. They sure did. He could leave within a week. Pratt joined on the spot and even chose his unit—the 7th Infantry Regiment at Vancouver Barracks.

After a four-day train trip, he and a few other recruits arrived at the post where a sergeant welcomed them on a rainy November morning: "As I looked around me, I saw there were about two to three dozen recruits, all in civilian clothing, some rather neatly dressed, some not. Like me, nearly all had a bewildered expression on their faces and milled about like lambs waiting . . . to be told what to do." In the days and weeks ahead, Pratt and his fellow recruits were trained and indoctrinated the old-fashioned way, as part of their units, a process nineteenth-century Cottonbaler recruits would have recognized. On the eve of the war, this indoctrination changed in favor of a special basic training course for all new inductees, who upon completing such basic training then joined units. This modern, effective, and efficient training system would, from this point forward, be the norm in the Army.

Pratt made the adjustment to army life well, rapidly learning the proverbial right way, wrong way, and army way: "I quickly learned to live by the bugle blown from a megaphone in front of Post headquarters. I was awakened by it at 6 a.m. on drill days with 'first call.' The bugle called us to reveille formation in the dark in front of the barracks in foggy cold, and to eat three times daily with chow call. The bugler's 're-call' signalled the end of the drill day, to be followed a half hour later at 5 p.m. with 'assembly' for the 'retreat' formation and the lowering of the flag on the parade ground." Officers were otherworldly figures. The sergeants ran nearly everything in Pratt's life: "The authority of these NCO's was almost never questioned, and their orders were carried out to the letter." Pratt grew from a scrawny kid into a lean man, the kind who would one day lead soldiers in combat.[3]

IN EARLY 1941, THE REGIMENT MOVED FROM COZY, IDYLLIC Vancouver Barracks to Fort Lewis, Washington. This move, which concentrated the entire 3rd Division together for the first time in years, proved to be the harbinger of a new era. The first wave of draftees netted by the narrowly passed conscription act of the previous year broadened the ranks of the 7th from disadvantaged depression kids to everyman citizen soldiers. The WW I–style helmets gave way to the MI steel pot helmet and plastic liner. Springfields were phased out in favor of the magnificent new MI Garand, the best rifle of World War II, a semiautomatic weapon that could fire an eight-round 30.06-caliber clip accurately and effectively as fast as the rifleman could pull the trigger.

Pearl Harbor accelerated this trend. The staid, isolated, spit-and-polish regiment of the prewar era metamorphosed into a well-trained organization designed to fight a modern war. The same process that had occurred in 1917–18 happened again. Many Regular Army officers and noncommissioned officers (of the younger variety) transferred out of the regiment to serve as leaders and training cadre for a rapidly expanding army. Many others remained with the unit and led it all the way through Europe. Junior officers and enlisted men, hailing from all over the country and all strata of society, provided the bulk of the 7th Infantry's manpower and fighting power. A mass army of young citizen soldiers would be needed to fight this demanding war, and the 7th Infantry reflected that need.

The overwhelming majority of these men would never have spent a day in uniform if not for World War II. Now they were called upon, as many of their fathers had been two decades before, to risk their lives in an effort to win an all-out war between great powers. One such soldier was Robert Maxwell O'Kane, who served with B Company during the war. O'Kane wrote a perceptive, and accurate, description of the typical Cottonbaler in World War II: "He wasn't tall or short; a Southerner or Northerner or Westerner or Easterner; he wasn't Protestant or Catholic, Jewish or Zen Buddhist; he wasn't ugly or handsome, not a Democrat or Republican; not a college boy or a dropout from school; he wasn't loud or quiet; he wasn't happy or sad; he wasn't fearless or frightened. No—he was *all* these. He came from everywhere. He had only recently been playing in the streets of his home town or in the fields of his farm or ranch, or on the beaches of the Atlantic or Pacific. So he found himself . . . in the Army. More specifically, in the Infantry. Here he would meet other young men from everywhere—men he most likely would never have met otherwise. Any differences, for the most part, were soon extinguished." Another soldier echoed this analysis: "Most of the men, officers and enlisted men alike, were draftees or had volunteered to serve 'for the duration.' These were not regular Army career men. They were civilians by nature, (Citizen Soldiers)."[4]

This erosion of differences did not mean that personalities evaporated. Pratt wrote about the typical mixture of character types in his expanding rifle company: "There would be those who were kind, compassionate, cooperative, considerate and eager to please. There would also be some, as in civilian life, who would be troublesome, malicious, evil minded and intent sooner or later on crossing paths with the rules. There would also be the shy introverts, and the . . . boisterous . . . extroverts. There would be the fast and the slow, the quick witted and the dull, the satisfied and the malcontented. Still another category . . . was the guy who seems to have a one track mind oriented almost exclusively on sex. Every military unit has at least one, and maybe more."[5]

In the early months of 1942, just weeks after the Japanese attack on Pearl Harbor, this burgeoning citizen-soldier-dominated 7th Regiment began intensive amphibious training. The military situation by 1942 clearly demanded the need for assaulting hostile beaches. Nazi Germany had conquered most of Europe. Japan was in the process of conquering a vast empire in the Pacific. In order to have any chance of winning this war, the United States would have to get very good at amphibious warfare, the traditional mission of the U.S. Marine Corps. But this small, elite force could not hope to carry out all the invasions the coming war years required. The Army picked up the slack, carrying out the vast majority of amphibious assaults (both Europe and the Pacific) in World War II.

The 7th Infantry Regiment, beginning with its 1942 training, grew into an outstanding amphibious assault force. In fact, in the course of the war the regiment carried out four combat landings, something few, if any, combat organizations, army or Marine, could equal. The unit traveled in January 1942 to San Diego for intensive training. The men practiced loading and unloading their transports. They got used to being at sea. They assaulted mock landing beaches at Monterey near Camp Ord. Paul Nelson was a twenty-two-year-old C Company lieutenant who quickly became a specialist in amphibious warfare. "The 3rd Div. Boat Detachment was activated for training purposes. It was composed of about 5 or 6 officers and about 200 enlisted men. I was . . . Operations Officer of the Boat Detachment. The detachment maintained a fleet of about 40 Higgins boats [specialized shallow-draft landing craft designed to transport combat troops from transport ships to beaches] and a few other assorted craft. Each day selected units from the division would come to the docks, climb down the nets into the boats, and then rendez-vous a few hundred yards offshore to practice landings."[6] Some landing maneuvers went better than others, but through practice and repetition week after week in 1942, the Cottonbalers and their division comrades learned the basics of attacking an enemy-held beach, among the most difficult of all military operations.

During that time, most of the men assumed they were headed for the Pacific. After all, the Japanese were on a rampage out there. Years of tension over the balance of power in Asia and the Pacific had ultimately led to war between Japan and the United States. Japan desired to be the great, dominant power of the Pacific Rim. The United States preferred the maintenance of a delicate balance of power that offset the imperial interests of empires such as Japan, Britain, and France with the aspirations of struggling, but rising, independent Asian nations such as China. Japan decided to aggressively conquer the land and resources it so desperately needed to fulfill its goal of imperial domination. Attacking the unprepared United States was just one aspect of this larger goal of empire building. For six months in 1942, the Japanese won victory after victory. The Dutch East Indies fell to them. Their troops defeated the British at Singapore and the Malayan Peninsula and Burma too. The Japanese invaded and captured the Philippines from the Americans in just under six months. By summertime, they had established an empire that extended from the northern coast of New Guinea to Manchuria.

On its face, this crisis situation seemed to necessitate that all trained American troops be sent to the Pacific. Thousands of islands would need to be captured and thousands of miles of ocean controlled. Plus, the Japanese had struck the first blow, shocking the Americans into the war with the surprise attack on Pearl Harbor. The majority of Americans wanted to crush Japan first and foremost; they wanted to exact revenge against the Japanese for daring to attack the United States of America. So, it seemed logical to most Cottonbalers in 1942 that their amphibious expertise would soon be put to use against the Japanese.

However, President Franklin Roosevelt, along with his British allies and most of his military advisers, envisioned a different strategic blueprint. The United States, from 1939 to 1941, clashed with Germany over the same issues that had led to war in 1917—neutrality rights. Roosevelt grasped the dire threat Nazi Germany posed to the peace and security of not just Europe but also America. He did everything he possibly could to aid Germany's enemies, so much so that the U.S. Navy in 1941 was fighting an undeclared war against German submarines in the Atlantic. Americans ships, serving alongside the Royal Navy, helped keep a vital lifeline open to the United Kingdom.

When the Japanese hit Pearl Harbor, Adolf Hitler decided that his Asian ally had eliminated the only real threat America posed—its Navy. This led him to take the disastrous step of declaring war on the United States. In his mind, the combination of the Japanese Navy and his unshackled submarines unleashing an all-out attack on the U.S. Navy would eliminate American shipping capacity and, in the process, destroy Britain's overseas lifeline. Britain and the United States would then be neutralized while German soldiers systematically conquered the Soviet Union, which Germany had invaded on June 22, 1941. In his heart of hearts, Hitler held little but contempt for the United States and its war-making capacity. He thought of Americans as soft, the products of a mongrel, mixed-race society that exalted such decadent bourgeois values as constitutional, representative government, civil liberties, individuality, and hedonism. A prisoner of his own racism, Hitler denied the prominent role the United States had played in Germany's defeat in 1918.

Roosevelt and his counterpart, British prime minister Winston Churchill, understood all too well that Hitler's Germany could very well make good on Hitler's ultimate aim of conquering the Soviet Union and strangling Great Britain. They knew that of the two major fascist powers, Germany was far more potent than Japan. As such, Germany must be defeated first, even if public opinion in the United States did not feel that way (most Americans loathed the Nazis but held no special grudge against Germany). The Soviet Union, fighting desperately against the bulk of the German Army in 1942, could go under any day. If that happened, the British and Americans would be confronted with a European continent dominated by Germany from the Pyrenees to the Urals. Reentering that continent and defeating Nazi Germany would, in that nightmare scenario, cost a grievous amount of blood and treasure.

The two leaders agreed that Britain and the United States must do whatever they could, as quickly as they could, to help the Soviets in 1942. For his part, Roosevelt wanted American troops in action somewhere in the European theater in 1942 to underscore and legitimize his Germany first policy, especially with midterm elections pending that year. But where would the Anglo-American armies fight? The Americans wanted a cross-Channel attack in France, all the better to drive right into the heart of Germany and end the war. The phrase "easier said than done" comes to mind. American unpreparedness and strong German defenses in France, combined with limited British manpower and resources, consigned such a cross-Channel attack to pipe dream status. The bottom line was this: a cross-Channel attack would only succeed with American leadership—in manpower, tanks, planes, food, equipment, shipping, everything. The United States would not be ready to assume such leadership for another two years.

The British persuaded their American allies (who possessed more impulsive energy than military strength at this point) that a lesser offensive in North Africa made more sense. The British had fought there against Italo-German armies for two years in a seesaw war stretching across the sands of Egypt and Libya. By the fall of 1942, the Germans had driven a deep wedge to El Alamein in British-controlled Egypt. This wedge threatened the Suez Canal, one of Britain's major arteries to its Far East empire. The Germans had supply problems, though, because most of their resources went into the prosecution of their titanic war on the eastern front. They and their Italian allies could go no farther.

The British proposed to launch a major offensive, driving the Italians and Germans out of Egypt and farther west all the way across

Italian-controlled Libya. In the meantime, the Americans would assault selected landing beaches in Morocco and Algeria, countries under the control of the Vichy French government that had surrendered to Germany in 1940. These days, the Vichy government spent most of its time administering and garrisoning French colonies such as Morocco, Algeria, and neighboring Tunisia.

The Vichy French were a mixed lot of fascists and pragmatists. They might or might not fight invading Americans. Secret negotiations might convince them to change sides and yield safe passage to American soldiers, who could then advance on Axis Libya, effectively wedging Italian and German soldiers into a vise. If the Vichy French did fight, then the Americans would defeat them, a far more realistic introductory assignment than taking on well-trained German veterans along the beaches of northern France.

THESE GRAND STRATEGIC AIMS CONSPIRED TO PUNCTURE the Pacific-bound expectations of the Cottonbalers, along with the rest of the Marne division's soldiers. On September 6, 1942, the whole division boarded trains bound for Camp Picket, Virginia. This camp, named after the famous Confederate general, served as a staging area for the 3rd Division. The men did not know it yet, but they would play a major part in the invasion of North Africa. They spent six enjoyable weeks at Camp Pickett. "To our delight, we had no training programs of any significance," Pratt recalled, "and most of our work days were spent inspecting and replacing worn or unserviceable equipment and requisitioning and drawing new equipment." He and the others soon noticed the alacrity with which they received brand-new equipment, along with its combat readiness. They correctly surmised that the next time they boarded ships they would see combat, not training.[7]

On October 23, even as the British unleashed their successful attack at El Alamein, the 3rd Division began loading its ships, an arduous and complex logistical process that taxed the collective energy of the division's leadership and men. Finally, after dark, the loading was finished. "The clatter and hum of winches ceased," the division historian later wrote. "The great gray transports, mysterious in the subdued glare of essential loading lights, stopped taking on inert cargo as the human shipments arrived by train on piers; the doughboys of the 3d Infantry Division. Tired, patient, they waited endless hours, sleeping on the concrete with their heads on their packs until it came their turn to have their names checked on the sailing lists, to mount the gangplank, to seek a bunk in the hot, moist, troop compartments. The dockworkers watched for awhile, then drifted into the night."[8]

The 7th Regiment, numbering well over five thousand soldiers, divided its three battalions onto a like number of ships: the 1st Battalion on *Leonard Wood,* the 2nd Battalion on *Thomas Jefferson,* and the 3rd Battalion aboard *Tasker H. Bliss.* Each battalion contained four companies: three rifle companies and a heavy-weapons company consisting of two machine-gun platoons and one mortar platoon. In addition, every battalion had an antitank company (generally called "Cannon Company"). Sherman Pratt, promoted to sergeant by now because of his reliable character and prewar military experience, served with 3rd Battalion's Cannon Company and sailed aboard the *Bliss.* This ship was nothing more than an old passenger liner that had been hurriedly refitted and repaired for the North Africa invasion: "The musty smells, colored brass, rotten and cracked wood, and layers upon layers of paint on the walls, equipment and pipes stood as mute testimony that this was far from her maiden voyage." In fact, under the strain of its cargo and passengers, the ship began to leak. The *Bliss* took on water faster than its pumps could handle the leaks, forcing the soldiers to form bucket brigades.

The troop compartments, stacked floor to ceiling with bunks, were a nightmare. Men barely had enough room to turn over in their bunks. Privacy was nonexistent: "With five levels of bunks crammed into a vertical space of less than about 12 feet the distance to the next man, up or down, was only about two feet. Many times while lying in my bunk . . . I contemplated in horror the chaos that would erupt if the ship were suddenly torpedoed," Pratt said. German submarines were out there, but the powerful Allied landing fleet, composed of eighty transports, destroyers, and escort carriers, warded them off.

Thankfully, the more immediate concern for the soldiers was the lack of adequate bathroom facilities: "At almost any hour of the day and late into the night, long lines were waiting outside the head stalls by those whose bowels were pleading painfully for the opportunity to be emptied." The ship's crew conceived of a novel, albeit perilous, solution for this uncomfortable situation. They built planks off the main deck, cut holes in the planks, and fastened them in place. This ingenious plan did not work, though. For one thing, soldiers found it very difficult to do their business while staring three or four stories down into the sea.

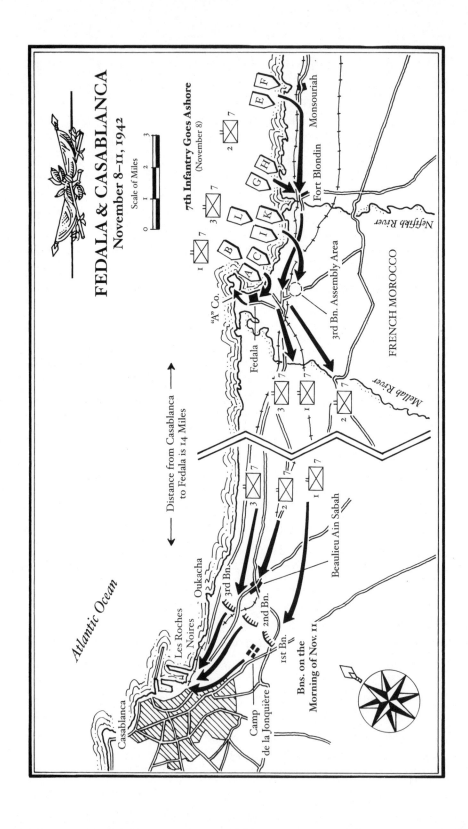

FEDALA & CASABLANCA
November 8–11, 1942

Scale of Miles

0   1   2   3

7th Infantry Goes Ashore
(November 8)

Atlantic Ocean

Casablanca

Les Roches Noires

Oukacha

3rd Bn.

2nd Bn.

1st Bn.

Camp de la Jonquière

Bns. on the Morning of Nov. 11

← Distance from Casablanca to Fedala is 14 Miles →

Fedala

"A" Co.

3rd Bn. Assembly Area

Beaulieu Ain Sabah

Mellab River

Nefifikb River

Fort Blondin

Monsouriah

FRENCH MOROCCO

E F

G H

B L K

A C I K

3rd Bn. Assembly Area

For another, buffeting winds and ocean currents often projected the disgusting waste matter back into the faces and torsos of the troops. The carpenters tore the planks down.

So the Cottonbalers continued as before, crammed into their holds, waiting in impossibly long lines for chow or the head, sitting around doing nothing, speculating on their destination, aching and itching to get the hell off the ship. Finally, on November 7 the men found out where they were going. Senior officers told junior officers who then briefed the enlisted men. In Pratt's recollection, the soldiers crackled with anticipation: "Every eye was on the company commander. The air was tense! 'Men,' our company commander began, 'the 7th Infantry Regiment . . . is to land on the coast of French Morocco. Our regimental objective is, initially, a little Arab town called Fedala, about 17 miles north of Casablanca, and about 25 miles south of Rabat.'" He went on to discuss the rest of the invasion plan. The entire 3rd Division would land in the Fedala area, augmented south and north by the 9th Infantry Division and the 2nd Armored Division. This whole Western Task Force was under the command of General George S. Patton. Two other task forces, primarily American, would assault beaches in Algeria, at Oran and Algiers. The captain did not know yet if the Vichy French would resist the invasion. That depended on how well General Mark Clark's secret negotiations were proceeding. "'In any event, our debarkation will be with the use of the Higgins landing craft on board and we will leave this ship by descending the cargo nets over the sides.'"9

In all, the landing force consisted of 200,000 troops. The 7th Infantry's mission was to capture Fedala, a seaside fishing town of some 16,000 people, along with a prominent cape near the town. French artillery could use that cape to pummel landing beaches on either side of Fedala. After capturing the town and the cape, the 7th was to curve right, going southwest, and capture Casablanca, the namesake of the famous movie. Intelligence estimated that 2,500 colonial soldiers—a battalion of infantry, two troops of cavalry, and assorted artillery—defended the Fedala area. Another 4,325 troops, almost all Senegalese and Moroccan men led by French officers, defended Casablanca.

The commanding officer of the 7th Infantry, Colonel Robert Macon, an energetic, professional southerner, planned to lead with his 1st and 2nd Battalions. The 1st Battalion, commanded by Lieutenant Colonel Roy Moore, would land and then occupy the town and the cape. The 2nd Battalion, under Lieutenant Colonel Raphael Salzman, would leapfrog past the 1st and capture bridges over the Mellah River to the south of Fedala, opening the way for an advance on Casablanca. Major Eugene Cloud's 3rd Battalion, landing one hour later, would advance inland and cut the highways and railroads outside of Fedala. Tanks, artillery, engineers, and antiaircraft troops would support each battalion. H hour was 0445 (between the wars, the military scrapped A.M. and P.M. designations in favor of its modern numerical system).[10]

As darkness descended on the evening of November 7, the invasion force anchored eight miles off the coast of Morocco. Just after midnight the soldiers got word to grab all their equipment, go topside, and board their landing craft. Some men kept asking if any news on a cease-fire had come from the French. "Sorry," they were told. "Nothing doing. We're going and it looks like there'll be resistance." A strange combination of gloom and excitement settled over the men. On the *Bliss,* Sergeant Pratt and his buddies bumped and stumbled around in the darkness topside (blackout conditions were in effect) looking for their debarkation station. When they got there, they looked at the sea and could barely make out the silhouettes of Higgins boats bobbing in the surf. "Some men were grouchy and weary from a sleepless night. Some were . . . on the border of panic and hysteria. All were tense and nervous. A few tried to inject a little humor with a wise crack here or a joke there."

The order came to debark. Gingerly they stepped over the sides and descended, step by precarious step, down the rope ladders. Each one of them was laden with about sixty pounds of equipment, including a rifle strapped over the shoulder. They wore herringbone twill (HBT) trousers and tops, Americans flags prominently displayed on the shoulders, brogan combat boots, canvas leggings, and standard khaki haversacks attached to cartridge belts, from which dangled canteens and bayonets. One soldier near Pratt temporarily lost his grip on the rope. As he frantically grabbed at the rope, his rifle fell, smashing on an unseen landing craft below. A sailor who had nearly been hit by the rifle cursed vigorously. Another man below Pratt froze up with acrophobia. He would not take another downward step. Somebody found a way to pry him loose and get him back on the ship. On the adjacent rope, a soldier completely lost his grip. Pratt could just barely see this unfortunate soldier fall. The man hit his head on the side of a landing craft, went into the water, and sunk like a stone—the first casualty, eventually to be followed by thousands.

Pratt managed to descend the rope and drop the short distance into the rickety Higgins boat. Loaded up now, the boat took off for shore. "We were still about five miles out to sea but were beginning to see the outlines of shore and some buildings coming into view. Gunfire from U.S. Navy cruisers was landing on the beaches and other targets along the coast. Also, fighter planes were strafing inland." The planes came from the Navy and from nearby Gibraltar. The troops huddled together, fought seasickness, tried to keep warm, and waited for the inevitable moment when they must assault a hostile shore.

The Higgins boats used in this invasion were mostly made of plywood and thus did not have the sturdiness of the later steel models that made Allied victory in World War II possible. The hastily constructed wooden boats in which Pratt and the other Cottonbalers rode provided no protection against bullets or shrapnel. Nor did they have ramps. "To leave the vessel upon hitting the beaches, troops were trained to creep forward and 'roll' over the forward rail, and drop into the sand if possible, or at least the shallow surf." Of course that ideal situation depended on the coxswain to maneuver the craft all the way onto the beach—unlikely, to say the least. As it turned out, rough seas and the rocky Moroccan coast shredded these flimsy boats like barbed wire puncturing skin.[11]

In fact, the troops had no sooner boarded their Higgins boats and headed for the coast when everything started to go wrong. Choppy seas, darkness, and confusion led to complete chaos. The naval coxswains who piloted the Higgins boats did not know the coast well, a problem made worse by the lingering darkness as H hour approached. Very few of the first-wave boats landed on their assigned beaches. "Instead they crashed on coral reefs and rocky shores," the regimental history, a remarkable account of the unit's experiences in World War II, recorded. "Men were injured and drowned. Units were broken up and scattered to the winds. Much confusion existed."[12]

In other words, no one had any clue what was going on or what to do except to get off the damned boats and onto dry land. To make matters worse, the sun was rising rapidly and the beleaguered boats began taking some scattered enemy machine-gun and artillery fire from the direction of Fedala. Some boats beached on offshore sandbars, forcing the men to disgorge in throat-high water.

William B. Rosson was a twenty-four-year-old captain serving as regimental S-3, or operations officer. He had graduated from the University of Oregon two years before with an ROTC commission, joined the 7th Regiment, and quickly won the favor of Colonel Macon and other senior officers. Rosson's boat, right in the middle of those carrying the regimental headquarters group, was circling immediately behind the 1st Battalion as daylight approached: "We spent what seemed to be an eternity circling about. I had the uneasy feeling we were off course going into the beach as naval gunfire began. Nonetheless, as dawn broke we could see the overall beach area where our naval gunfire had been directed, could see explosions there and some return firing from the French positions. As we approached the beach, we came under scattered machine gun fire from . . . Fedala. The surf was fairly turbulent and quite a large number of craft had broached. I was amazed . . . to see how many boats had ended up on the beach sideways."[13]

The first wave, Lieutenant Colonel Moore's battalion, began landing at about 0500, fifteen minutes late. They ran and waded ashore, along beaches and reefs a mile east of Fedala. Soaked to the skin, spitting out seawater, and sluggish from carrying so much drenched equipment, they fanned out along the coast. Enemy searchlights probed the area and inaccurate machine-gun fire could be heard coming from Fedala and its environs. Those first-wave men who belonged to A and C Companies took cover in disorganized clumps. A boat carrying C Company's 2nd Platoon smashed against coral rocks, killing Private First Class Roy Wilson. Another boat capsized and the men had to swim to shore. For half an hour these scenes repeated themselves. Boats approached the coast and the vast majority smashed, out of control, into rocks or reefs. Soldiers had to dive underwater to save valuable weapons, like .30-caliber machine guns.

Moore himself landed on rocks offshore at 0530 and spent the better part of half an hour crawling to shore. He scraped together assault groups from A and C Companies and ordered them to head for Fedala. They had not gone long when they saw a platoon of Senegalese soldiers in the distance. Everyone hit the dirt and waited for the colonial troops to get closer. A lieutenant hollered at them to surrender, and having no desire to fight Americans, they readily complied. The men pushed fairly easily into Fedala itself. One platoon surrounded and captured the Hotel Miramar. Another captured nine German Armistice Commission officers who had been staying at the hotel. The biggest problem for the

Americans in the town was navy shelling. Moore sent his executive officer, Captain Everett Duvall, to make contact with the Navy to stop the shooting. To do so, he had to find Brigadier General William Eagles, the assistant division commander, who sent a radio transmission that said, "For God's sake, stop shelling Fedala—you're killing our own men and friendly French groups—the shells are falling all over town—if you stop they will surrender." After twenty more minutes, the shelling finally stopped.

With Fedala firmly in hand, the key now was to capture the Cape, home to coastal artillery guns that had been causing casualties among the troops trying to fight their way ashore through the rough surf. Moore ordered A Company, more or less a cohesive unit now, to attack the gun and its fire control station, which was located in a building on a hill and protected by barbed wire. Four light tanks rumbled into the streets of Fedala to support this attack. The infantrymen spread out and took off running through the town, using buildings and cars as cover. Inaccurate enemy fire, mainly small arms and machine guns, blazed above and to the side of them. Closing to within a couple hundred yards of the fire control station, they skidded and slid into firing positions behind a wall. To get to the station, they would have to cross open ground and deal with barbed wire. Before doing so, they opened up on the station with everything they had. Riflemen fired their eight-round clips as quickly as they could squeeze the trigger, hearing the distinctive "ping" sound as their clips, empty of bullets, popped out of their rifle breeches and clattered on the pavement. A 60mm mortar team scored a direct hit on the station.

Meanwhile, a squad leader, Staff Sergeant Robert Marvin, while being covered by two men, worked his way toward a machine gun. He crept and crawled along the ground for about one hundred yards to the right flank, until he came within submachine gun distance (probably about seventy-five yards). Then, using a small rock as cover, he pointed his Thompson submachine gun and fired a clip of .45-caliber ammunition at the machine gun. The enemy crew quickly hoisted a white flag before Murphy could even reload his weapon.

Murphy had no sooner eliminated the enemy gun when Captain Albert Brown, the A Company commander, gave the order to fix bayonets and charge the fire control station and the gun. Browning Automatic Riflemen covered the men who went forward with Brown. The BAR men showered the enemy positions with clip after clip of deadly slugs.

French gunners returned fire as best they could, especially riflemen firing from upstairs windows in the station. One of the light tanks attempted to move forward and support the infantrymen, but it overturned on the slope of a hill. The assaulting A Company troops, moving bravely into the kill zone, concentrated on cutting their way through the barbed wire and closing with the enemy. They fired their weapons at anything that moved and pitched grenades into the station and its surrounding positions. Five enemy soldiers were blasted apart, killed instantly. The rest had had enough. Company A captured twenty-two prisoners, along with a .50-caliber gun and the three offending coastal artillery pieces. Soon after, eighty enemy soldiers from another gun at the very tip of the cape surrendered. The vital cape was now officially in American hands. Brown's company remained at the scene of its conquest that first night.[14]

THE 2ND BATTALION'S LANDING WAS AN EVEN BIGGER mess than the 1st Battalion's. The first two waves landed five miles east of their assigned beach, near Mansouriah, albeit against no resistance except for the surf and the rocks. They pushed inland and followed the north–south railroad in the direction of Fedala. The third wave, primarily Companies G and H and their support units, came ashore about four miles off-course, near Fort Blondin. This was an enemy strongpoint, containing four large coastal defense guns and infantry, located on a peninsula, firmly astride the main railroad. When G and H Companies came ashore at 0615, American naval vessels were busy shooting up Blondin. The American soldiers had to take cover anywhere they could while the Navy, primarily the cruiser *Brooklyn*, hurled shots at the batteries. "A direct hit was scored on one of the four guns, disabling it and killing several members of the crew," the Navy's official historian wrote. "After about forty-five minutes of firing, another shell hit the fire control station, destroying its stereoscopic range finder. In a bombardment lasting eighty-five minutes, *Brooklyn* fired 757 rounds of 6-inch, culminating at 0742 in two furious minutes of continuous rapid fire."[15]

The soldiers watched the Navy's fireworks and rooted for the enemy guns to be put out of action, but they were not quite finished yet. Even though Blondin was the neighboring 30th Infantry's objective, the 2nd Battalion commander, Salzman, decided to capture it. Covered by friendly mortar fire, his riflemen descended on the batteries from behind, crawling through barbed wire as they did so. The stunned defenders shot at them, but no one was hit. The French garrison, commanded by a chief petty officer who was reluctant to fight Yanks, quickly surrendered.

The 3rd Battalion, most of which came in after the first couple waves, also struggled to get ashore. Only L Company drew the mission of landing at H hour. This company, along with reconnaissance troops, was supposed to land to the left of Fedala, push inland, secure the highway and railroad over the Mellah River, and clear out an adjacent golf course of any enemy troops. That never happened. The transport carrying L Company and the reconnaissance troops got under way late. Then, after circling interminably in the water, they met heavy resistance from intense artillery and .50-caliber machine-gun fire at their assigned beach. After four unsuccessful runs at the beach, the Navy dumped them off, at the L Company commander's behest, on the other side of Fedala. They spent the day chilling out in a cane field. The recon troops went back to the ship.

The rest of the battalion also experienced delays and problems landing. Originally given the mission of reinforcing the 1st Battalion near Fedala, the 3rd Battalion instead landed farther up the coast, almost exactly in the middle of 1st Battalion at Fedala and the 2nd Battalion soldiers who had assaulted Blondin. The 3rd Battalion encountered such heavy fire at its intended beach that it had to land on an adjacent beach. Even there, artillery, mortar, and machine-gun fire ripped into several men, including the regimental chaplain, a Catholic priest and first lieutenant named Clement Falter, who was killed while trying to aid a wounded man. By all accounts, the men loved and respected Falter. In spite of his death, the soldiers of the 3rd Battalion in their hodgepodge groups kept moving inland. The French had the beaches under fire but not the fields and ditches beyond the beaches. So the men settled into the ditches until the firing died down and then moved along the railroad to an assembly area near Fedala.[16]

By the evening of the eighth, the Cottonbalers held a firm foothold in their landing zone. In spite of the terrible landing problems they encountered on that invasion day, they managed to capture most of their objectives and position themselves for a push on Casablanca. The story might have been different had they faced a more determined, less mediocre enemy, but that hardly mattered as the sun set that night and the soldiers dug foxholes and munched on K rations. All that mattered to most of them was that they were still alive. "The long march from the landing points following the difficult landing and the great weight of extra ammunition had taxed the stamina of every man," E Company commander First Lieutenant Lambert Hruska later wrote, "and without exception they were glad to remain in one place long enough to dig slit trenches in position. They were tired, they had sore feet, and many bruises and bumps, but they were in high spirits; they had 'come through,' they were on dry land."[17]

In the morning the drive on Casablanca began. The troops had suffered through a chilly, uncomfortable night. Many of them had spent most of the night stumbling through the darkness to their line of departure for the next day's attack. Their clothes were still wet, and an ocean wind made them shiver. When they reached the line of departure, they could do little except curl up in their wet blankets and try to fetch a little sleep. Colonel Macon ordered the advance to be carried out, roughly along the railroad and the main Casablanca–Rabat highway, with the 3rd Battalion on the right (the ocean to their right), the 2nd Battalion on the left, and most of the 1st Battalion in reserve.

Most of the resistance was in the 3rd Battalion area. Company I, under Captain Clarence H. White, took fire immediately after its soldiers began their advance: "We had no sooner crossed the line of departure when our front lines received small arms fire from rifles and light machine guns. We encountered this fire all day long, but we were able to advance quite rapidly by advancing one platoon and then another. Each platoon assisted the other's advances by flanking fire. The mortars and light machine guns were also used frequently and effectively." This advance was the product of good training. Instead of taking cover and waiting for support, White's men recognized that the resistance they faced, consisting of a few dozen Moroccan spahi cavalrymen, could be defeated with decisive action. Taking care to spread out as much as possible, and working closely with fellow platoons, they laid down cover fire for one another as they advanced—classic American fire and maneuver tactics, used time and again in World War II and thereafter.[18]

The 2nd Battalion, in Lieutenant Hruska's recollection, encountered almost no resistance: "In approach march formation [widely dispersed] . . . the advance continued all morning, over plowed fields, over stone walls and fences, cane brakes, through patches of woods where the enemy could have waited for us; only occasional shots for rear guard patrols were heard."[19] The riflemen and light machine gunners of the lead company certainly welcomed this quiet, unopposed advance, but the men in H Company (heavy weapons), trudging a few hundred yards behind the lead companies, viewed the situation a bit differently. "The heavy weapons had not been employed," H Company commander Captain Gilbert St. Clair wrote, "and that was not altogether a blessing, since the company retained all the ammunition, which was weighing every man down; the soft plowed ground over which the advance was being made, made walking difficult; after several hours, every step seemed a distinct effort; loads had to be reapportioned; the mortar platoon, particularly, found the strength and stamina of every man tested."[20] For good reason, since each of their 81mm mortars, fully assembled, weighed 136 pounds!

At noon the hunchbacked mortarmen and machine gunners of H Company almost had a chance to fire off some of their heavy ammunition. Someone spotted an antiaircraft gun near Sidi Bou Azza, close to the 2nd Battalion's position. But Cannon Company beat H Company to the punch. A platoon of antitank troops set up their gun and delivered such accurate fire on the enemy antiaircraft gun that the crew abandoned their weapon. The battalion moved on.

At 1400 the troops had covered about five and a half miles and were eight and a half miles from Casablanca. Macon ordered his men to halt and dig in. His 7th Regiment was significantly ahead of any other friendly troops and his superiors at division did not want to make them vulnerable to French counterattacks. The Cottonbalers were supposed to remain in place while soldiers from the 15th Infantry moved up and provided support on the left.

The lead troops of the 7th Infantry welcomed the halt. They unhooked their packs (the straps of which often dug into their shoulders), lit cigarettes, took long pulls from their canteens, and ate K-ration meals (which ranged from the breakfast entrée of ham and eggs, to the lunch entrée of concentrated cheese, to the dinner entrées of meat loaf and potatoes or maybe Spam and biscuits). The rest period was short-lived, though, as one soldier in F Company recalled: "The remainder of the day was occupied in . . . digging slit trenches, drawing rations, and then the men prepared for a rest; but artillery fire which seemed aimed at our rear, fell too close for comfort; some of them short, and there were quite a few of them . . . although no casualties were suffered that day; but our rest was, to say the least, not enjoyed. Toward evening the same chill wind which had blown all night, came again; shivering was no inducement to sleep." Nor were the men dry yet. "Our clothes, which had been thoroughly soaked in the landing, had not yet dried completely," Lieutenant Hruska remembered, "and a chill wind came up that made everyone shiver and wish for blankets and heavier clothing." To make matters worse, the soldiers had a tough time penetrating the rough soil of Morocco. "Digging of slit trenches and gun emplacements was really hard work in the rocky surface," Captain James Cruzen of G Company asserted, "however, the whistle of the 75 mm shells which the enemy was throwing in our direction . . . encouraged the work of the digging."[21]

During the night, Macon assembled his battalion commanders at the 2nd Battalion command post and issued new orders. The 2nd and 3rd Battalions, directly supported by the 1st, would attack again in the morning and occupy Casablanca. This meant that the tired men of the 2nd would have to leave their newly dug slit trenches and march in darkness to a jump-off point on the outskirts of Casablanca.

Just after midnight they moved out. Captain St. Clair conveyed the very feel and sense of what the Cottonbalers experienced that night: "Tired men shifted their loads and groaned very quietly; the silence in which the battalion moved was worthy of . . . veterans. Tired legs stretched out, bent backs straightened, deep breaths could be heard; and across the Bled, toward Casablanca, marched the battalion; after a while, we were on the smooth pavement of a highway; in the darkness of that night, with a thin rain coming down persistently, and a chill wind that penetrated to the very bones, no man could but appreciate the smooth walking of a surfaced road, after all the stumbling, shuffling, sinking, on plowed fields, and climbing walls and fences; all the length of the column . . . no sound could be heard other than a low rustling of shoe leather meeting asphalt. But off [to] the front . . . hundreds of dogs howled a continuous alert . . . never quite dying down, gaining in volume occasionally; and periodically, and almost monotonously, the batteries of Ain El Djab roared, accompanied by a great flash; the rush of wind and the scream of the shells passed over our heads; after a while the men forgot to duck. From time to time a new noise could be heard; a man would stumble, fall forward on his face, get up . . . and try to pick up his load again. We . . . reached [Beaulieu] Ain Sebah [their jump-off point] and it was still at least one hour before daylight; we were in the midst of houses, walled gardens, factories, and toward the front as well as on all sides, a few yards away, complete darkness."[22]

An hour before dark, the fighting began. Riflemen from E Company, with orders not to shoot in the darkness but instead fight with grenades and knives, cautiously moved forward along the narrow streets of Beaulieu Ain Sabah, a suburb of Casablanca. Shots rang out. Enemy riflemen and machine gunners had created a roadblock out of abandoned civilian vehicles. They crouched behind these cars and shot at the Americans, who scrambled for cover, skinning arms and knees on the pavement as they did so. Salzman, the battalion commander, happened to be with E Company and saw all this happen. He told Lieutenant Hruska to remain in place until the sun rose while he, Salzman, worked his way over to F Company and ordered a flanking attack on the roadblock, along with other enemy positions he had since found in the buildings of Beaulieu Ain Sabah.

Now the enemy shelling started to get more accurate. High-caliber shells rained down on F Company's hiding places in ditches along the road. One of them exploded close to the company commander, Captain John Casteel, peppering him with deadly shrapnel. He gasped and collapsed into a lifeless heap. The sun was rising and, as it did, the enemy spotters got a better sense of their targets. "Daylight came, and with it a new sound; that of naval guns, which for a while we thought was our own naval gun fire support," Captain Cruzen wrote. "Two . . . warships could be seen close off shore, and they were firing fast . . . their shells came closer and closer to us; they couldn't be ours . . . and they were not. They were enemy warships, adding to the already preponderant artillery fire which the enemy was delivering on us."[23] The day had barely begun, but already most everyone realized that it would be very different from yesterday, when resistance was so light. The French colonials intended to stand fast and defend Casablanca.

Back in front of the roadblock, the pinned-down men of E Company began taking fire, point-blank, from a 75mm artillery piece. In the daylight, they could clearly see the gun, so they opened fire on it with everything they had. Machine gunners poured belt after belt of ammunition at the gun and sprayed the cars for good measure. Riflemen fired measured, aimed shots at anything that seemed to move, while BAR gunners expended clip after clip, primarily at the gun. Expended cartridges tinkled onto the pavement. Once again fire and maneuver prevailed. Hruska's third platoon kept up a steady fire on the French positions, while his first two platoons left cover "to close in to hand grenade range of the field piece." With a scream, he led his two platoons at the enemy gun. The American soldiers chucked grenades everywhere. Many fired as they ran. This combination blew the gun crew apart, but not without cost. Hruska lost one of his platoon leaders and himself got hit by rifle fire.

Everywhere in Beaulieu Ain Sabah, small groups of American assault troops made their way forward as best they could. These men, primarily from F and G Companies, were carrying out Salzman's flanking order. They covered one another and advanced in small bursts, killing enemy riflemen and machine gunners or forcing them to flee. Sometimes machine guns pinned them down. In one instance, a machine gun raked through several American soldiers, hitting most of them in the legs and torso. The wounded men screamed for medics and lay prone in front of the French positions. Mortar and artillery shells exploded uncomfortably close to them. Several medics, demonstrating the kind of bravery typical of American aidmen and corpsmen in this war, rushed forward under fire to drag the wounded men to safety. They dragged the wounded by their boots and shoulder straps, dodging shrapnel and bullets all the way to the safety of the American lines.

The enemy steadily retreated from Beaulieu Ain Sabah. Salzman's envelopment had succeeded in pouring enough fire on the enemy to persuade them to yield ground. The tiring infantrymen of the 2nd Battalion settled down and waited for new orders. As they did so, the 3rd Battalion's lead troops kept moving steadily along the coast. They focused on Point Oukacha, home to several artillery pieces along with two companies of riflemen and machine gunners. A mixed group of American riflemen, mortar crews, heavy machine gunners, antitank gunners, and half-tracks formed up to attack Point Oukacha. By now, the 7th Infantry's supporting artillerymen from the 10th Field Artillery Battalion had landed, set up their guns, and started shooting in support of this attack. This fire support, in tandem with the mortars, half-tracks, and antitank guns, succeeded in forcing the French to keep their heads down as the 3rd Battalion riflemen pressed forward. One platoon captured a phosphate factory on the right at the edge of the point. Other groups drove the French from high ground overlooking the point. This effectively allowed them to hose down the enemy artillerymen with enfilade fire. An enemy ship sailed in and fired several volleys at the Cottonbalers, but no one was hit. Half an hour later, American aircraft attacked the French warship in dive-bombing runs and forced the enemy ship to retreat. The soldiers had succeeded in silencing the guns on Point

Oukacha, but a few snipers remained. Third Battalion troops stayed under cover and exchanged shots with the enemy the rest of the day.

Slightly behind those troops, Sergeant Pratt moved along the relative safety of the coastal road. Like so many others, he had come ashore dazed, drenched, and astray from his planned landing point. Now, two days later, he milled around with the antitank group and observed the locals: "We saw few, if any, French people. The natives we saw mostly were dressed in Arabic or nomadic robes. All the women wore black and covered their faces. Usually [they] stood and watched us indifferently. We saw no hostility or, for that matter, much friendliness. The children were the most forward and quickly learned to ask for chocolate, food or chewing gum."[24]

On the extreme left of his advance, Macon ordered 1st Battalion back into the fray. During the night and early-morning hours, they had marched from Fedala to jump-off positions opposite Camp de la Jonquiere, another suburb of Casablanca. Macon ordered them to capture the suburb, including a key French barracks building. Captain Charles Crall, the commander of B Company, later narrated the way this attack unfolded: "The Company dropped packs and jumped off at 1045, with the 1st and 3rd Platoons abreast in a wide formation. The advance was immediately met with artillery fire. After advancing about three quarters of a mile, the Company Commander held up the attack until 'C' Company, which had been stopped by artillery fire, could move up on the left." He and Herman Wagner, the C Company commander, met and agreed on a joint attack: "The first platoon, on the right, was taken under enemy machine guns and rifle fire, and moved forward behind a knoll. The objective was now 800 yards distant, and the entire Company underwent a devastating mortar and artillery barrage."[25] The enemy fire took its toll among Crall's men. Quite a few of them received shrapnel wounds from the artillery and some got hit by machine-gun fire. The wounded and the healthy took refuge on a nearby walled estate. Crall initially hoped that he could call on tank support, but the tanks earmarked to support him had run out of gas. The attack stalled, and from within the walled estate they exchanged mortar and small-arms shots with the enemy for the rest of the day.

That night, Macon planned an all-out attack on Casablanca for the next morning, but in the early-morning hours of November 11 the French agreed to an armistice. In the morning Macon received orders from Major General Jonathan Anderson, commander of the 3rd Division, to move into Casablanca and not fire unless fired upon. To the relief of nearly everyone, the enemy soldiers did not shoot. They were more than happy to lay down their arms. The 7th Regiment triumphantly entered the town on that day—many were mindful that this was the anniversary of the end of World War I—and enjoyed their victory. Some members of C Company ended up finding a warehouse full of wine casks. They filled their canteen cups from the seemingly bottomless quantities of wine in the casks.[26]

Not everything was fun and games, though. Parts of the city had been destroyed by shell fire from both sides. Sergeant Pratt saw the results: "Smoke poured from a burning and overturned car and the streets were littered with debris. We halted briefly and I looked over at some rubble from a stone wall. In the dust and the grass I saw the arm . . . of a small child, and my stomach twitched. As I gazed down on the little arm and hand, with its fingers curved slightly inward, I could not help but speculate on to whom it once belonged." He moved on, feeling a bit queasy. Then, not much later, he saw something even worse: "There under a small lemon tree lay the body of a very young girl in a blue dress with one arm missing. She was on her back, her little face looking upward. Her mouth and eyes were open. Her dark brown hair was bloody and matted. I . . . saw that the top of her head was blown off and her brains were partially poured out and flowed onto a patch of wet grass." Pratt's stomach turned at the sight of such war-induced tragedy, and he vomited in the grass alongside the body of the little girl.[27]

In addition to the many civilians caught in the cross fire, the 7th Regiment also paid a very real price for its three-day campaign in Morocco. The regiment lost 48 killed in action, 1 who later died of wounds, 4 missing, and 145 wounded.[28] It was only the beginning.

THE CAMPAIGN IN NORTH AFRICA CONTINUED FOR ANother six months, eventually climaxing in Tunisia, but the regiment did not take part in any more of the fighting. The Cottonbalers, along with the rest of the 3rd Division, remained in Morocco. For a couple months, the 7th Regiment bivouacked around Rabat. Then it moved north to guard the border with Spanish Morocco. Allied leaders worried that either the Spanish would enter the war on the German side or, alternatively, the Germans would occupy Spain and use Spanish Morocco to menace Gibraltar and the Allied occupation of Morocco.

Changes in command took place. Major General Lucian K. Truscott, one of the Army's great commanders, took over the 3rd Division. Colonel Macon got promoted to brigadier general, and a new colonel, by the name of Harry Sherman, took over the 7th. Sherman was a forty-nine-year-old West Pointer and World War I veteran from Honeoye, New York. He had served in Panama and, later, the 15th Infantry before coming over to the Cottonbalers. Gruff, competent, and steady, he proved to be an average commander.

Truscott immediately implemented a tough training program designed to make his troops the best, most inexhaustible infantry in the world. The men ran obstacle courses and practiced bayonet training, hand-to-hand combat, and even log tossing. They practiced infantry–artillery coordination, infantry–mortar coordination, simulated battle conditions, and amphibious landings, as well as booby trap and mine detection. Most famously, they engaged in fast road marches that the men took to calling the Truscott Trot. Anyone who couldn't hack it was weeded out and sent to another unit.

The stringent physical conditioning proved to be a challenge for senior-level middle-aged commanders such as Sherman. Lieutenant Kuperstein, now serving as the regimental intelligence officer, remembered one especially fast-paced hike on a warm day and its inevitable effect on the regimental commander: "On a tough training hike (Truscott Trot) Sherman had me along while he was hiking along with one company—mainly to show the troops he was with them—after a while he turned to me with a wry and rare smile and said, 'Well, that's enough for us old guys—this stuff is for younger kids' and got back in his jeep. For the 1st time, it became evident that the type of warfare we were entering required a level of physical standard that only the very young and fit could meet. As the war progressed, battle unit commanders got younger and younger. Up to that time, command was a function of seniority mainly."[29]

Kuperstein was right. This war, like most, belonged to young men. Truscott understood this. He also understood that his division needed to be very well trained and very physically fit to prevail over the formidable German Army. The stateside training of the division had been good enough to defeat half-motivated colonial troops fighting for the dying Vichy government. But it would not be anywhere near adequate for the difficult job ahead.

In the immediate aftermath of the Allied victory in North Africa, that job centered around Sicily, a large Mediterranean island at the toe of the Italian boot. Once again the British had prevailed in the debate over operations for the year 1943. In January 1943, Roosevelt and Churchill met at Casablanca (the 7th Regiment paraded for the president) and decided on the future course of the war. The Allies were still not strong enough for the coveted cross-Channel attack. That being the case, Churchill proposed an assault in July on Germany's weaker partner, Italy. This could be the back door to Hitler's Europe. An invasion of Sicily could serve as a gateway to the Italian mainland, lead to the demise of Italian fascist dictator Benito Mussolini's regime, and, if the campaign went well enough, provide a cheap entry into Germany and the Balkans. In an unfortunate choice of words, Churchill called Italy the "soft underbelly" of Europe. It proved to be anything but, and the Cottonbalers found that out firsthand.

For the 7th Infantry the policy makers' decision to invade Sicily meant that the unit would once again be called upon to assault a hostile beach. To get ready for this demanding job, they trained for amphibious landings almost continuously from March to July. They embarked on and debarked from ships and stormed many practice beaches. In late June, after several of these training exercises, they engaged in a large dress rehearsal for the Sicily operation, after which they confined their activities to speed marches and physical conditioning. Even after all the training, some struggled with the intense heat and dust of July in North Africa. They fainted and medics dragged them off to hospitals. Most found reserves of strength they did not know they had.

Of course, even the strongest of soldiers could not always defend themselves against diseases such as malaria and dysentery. Diarrhea posed the biggest problem. "The prevalence of insects and especially flies resulted in much diarrhea, at times on an almost epidemic scale," Pratt wrote. "Rigid orders went out . . . to company sized units directing that messes be screened, toilets covered, and trash piles sprayed with insecticide. If any unit reported more than six cases of diarrhea in any one day, teams of medical inspectors . . . were immediately dispatched to ascertain anew the causes and to order remedial action."[30] As Pratt indicated, the Cottonbalers of World War II were now living in the era of modern medicine, a time when more soldiers died from combat than from disease. The Army Medical Corps performed brilliantly in the war, not just in its visible role of treating wounds and saving lives with emergency surgery but also in preventive medicine—inoculations, hygiene, and the like. The typical Cottonbaler could expect to receive a dizzying array of needle-driven inoculations, and if he got hit in combat, he could be sure that the medical care he received was the very best possible in an age when medical knowledge was growing dramatically.

The Army needed every single healthy fighting man for the task of invading Sicily. This would be a joint Anglo-American invasion. Originally, Allied planners envisioned a kind of two-pronged assault concentrating on the island's best beaches, in the northwest and southeast of Sicily. However, Britain's Field Marshal Bernard Montgomery, who would command all British forces in the invasion, adamantly opposed this plan. He argued that Axis resistance would be fierce; landing on opposite sides of the island would invite disaster. Far better to invade on a continuous hundred-mile front along the southern and southeastern coast. Montgomery persuaded General Dwight Eisenhower, the Allied theater commander, of the wisdom of this approach. The final plans called for the British to assault the southeastern portion of the island, from Pozzallo through Siracusa (often called Syracuse) and a bit beyond. From there the British 8th Army would push northeast in the direction of Mount Etna, which dominates the island, and Messina, the major port city at the extreme northeastern tip of Sicily. The American 7th Army, in the meantime, would land in a broad front along the southern coast, from west of Pozzallo all the way to Licata, an area comprising at least half of Sicily's southern coast. The Yanks would cover the flanks of Montgomery's forces and drive to the north coast (exactly how they would go about doing this became a matter of intense dispute and high command rivalry, since the plans left this matter unaddressed). D-Day would be July 10.

The planners picked three American divisions for this job: the 45th Infantry Division would assault in the east and link up with the British, the veteran 1st Infantry Division would land in the middle at Gela, and the 3rd Division in the west near Licata. In the 3rd Division sector, the 7th Regiment would assault beaches six miles west of Licata (codenamed Beach Red) and comprise the extreme western flank, not just of the division but of Lieutenant General George Patton's entire 7th Army.

Colonel Sherman decided that Moore's 1st Battalion would lead the invasion. His troops, augmented by engineers and chemical mortarmen (who could lay down smoke screens if need be) would go in at H hour. Half an hour later the 2nd Battalion would follow, and then, half an hour after them, the 3rd Battalion. Each battalion received the mission of defeating enemy beach defenses and pushing inland to cut highways and railroads. According to the regimental history, the terrain in the Cottonbalers' sector was "the western third of the Licata plain and the western portion of the broken hill mass which rims the plain in an arc about Licata. The plain is undulating, has an extensive road net and stream net, which is dry in summer, and is largely cultivated with wheat, vine and orchard farmland. In the left of the zone the plain ends and mountains rise to the north and west to average heights of one thousand feet. Beach Red . . . extends from Punta di Ciotta on the west to Punta San Nicola four thousand yards east. Width of the beach is from five to twenty yards. Most of the beach is backed by a steep bluff varying from two to sixty feet high but several breaks occur which could be used for vehicles." Intelligence anticipated a garrison of 208,500 Italian troops and about 30,000 German troops on the island.[31]

Back in Tunisia, the regiment began loading up and boarding ships between July 5 and 8. This time they rode on specially built and modified vessels designed for short ocean trips and amphibious landings. There were three types: the Landing Craft Tank (LCT), the Landing Ship Tank (LST), and the Landing Craft Infantry (LCI), the crudest of the three kinds. All of these landing craft had gangplanks and could carry various loads of troops, vehicles, or equipment. They were not exactly pretty or comfortable, but they helped win the war.

The loading and boarding process was tedious, boring, and hot. Sergeant Pratt and his buddies waited and sweltered for what seemed like an eternity. "Flies swarmed. Sweat ran. Sergeants barked and swore. Troops read, played cards, or dozed. All suffered under the blazing sun in an open field without shade in Africa in July." Bored, hot, and thirsty, Pratt decided to prepare a special treat for himself. He poured water from his canteen into his canteen cup until the cup was half-full. Then he crumpled pieces of his packed and hardened chocolate drink mix into the water and stirred the contents into a lumpy stew of modified hot chocolate. He watched the loading operations and drank his hot chocolate mix, chewing on the chocolate lumps. As he was distracted, it took him a few seconds to realize that some of the lumps were squishy and did not taste at all like chocolate. He decided to investigate. "Curiously, I pushed some fragments onto my finger . . . and . . . recognized, to my horror . . . a large, green insect eye. Next came out a piece of wing. Then a leg. Sick! And Yuk, yuk!" He spit out the fly and rinsed his mouth several times, but he was thoroughly "grossed out," as a later generation would say. He could never bring himself to consume the chocolate mix again.[32]

BY JULY 9 THE ENTIRE ALLIED INVASION ARMADA WAS UNder way. This was the greatest invasion force assembled in history up to that time. It included fleets of ships ranging from from small minesweepers, destroyer escorts, and landing craft to enormous battleships and aircraft carriers. This fleet enjoyed air support from clouds of airplanes flying from the carriers, the British-controlled island of Malta, and North African bases. The night before D-Day a windstorm hit most of the Allied fleet, causing ships to pitch and roll dangerously.

Aboard their crude landing craft vessels, the troops were absolutely miserable. Jostled around on the pitching waves, they became so seasick they could hardly move. One Cottonbaler remembered the agony of this part of the voyage: "Holds were flooded, radios were under water; it was a mess. Everybody was seasick. They almost stopped the whole operation because we had so much damage. Our tanks were jostled around; it was terrible. I thought they were going to sink. There was three feet of water in the hold. Everybody didn't care whether they lived or died; they were so seasick."[33]

In some cases the storm caused more serious danger than seasickness. Captain Rosson, still the regimental operations officer, watched in terror as the winds pitched his LCI like a toy in a bathtub: "On my own LCI . . . we had an officer washed overboard and only by a miracle was he saved by being picked up by the next ship to the rear. Fortunately as we came into the assembly areas off the coast [of Sicily] at night, the winds calmed and we were in no trouble whatsoever as we prepared to move in."[34]

After this frightening and nauseating interlude, the landings began at 0400 on the tenth. Two navy destroyers, USS *Roe* and USS *Swanson,* fired shells into the bluffs and hills beyond the beach. Their guns flashed like lightning in the night. Allied aircraft patrolled overhead. In the darkness the soldiers could not really see the hundreds of ships of the armada, but they could detect the flashes of the naval guns and sometimes detect the silhouettes of navy vessels farther out to sea. Moore's assault troops splashed their way ashore in water that varied from shoe-top to shoulder height. The waves crashed against their backs, and some men could taste the salty seawater in the backs of their

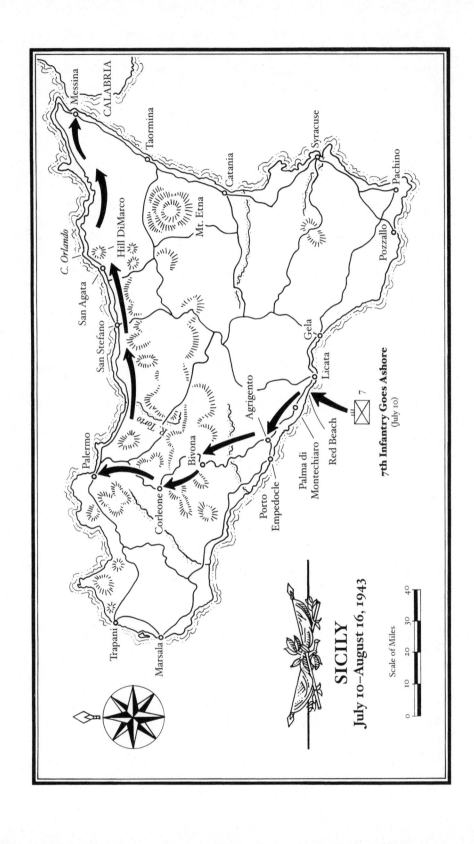

SICILY
July 10–August 16, 1943

CALABRIA

Messina

Taormina

Catania

Syracuse

Pachino

Pozzallo

Mt. Etna

Hill DiMarco

C. Orlando

San Agata

San Stefano

Gela

Licata

Palermo

R. Torto

Agrigento

Bivona

Corleone

Porto
Empedocle

Palma di
Montechiaro

Red Beach

Trapani

Marsala

7

7th Infantry Goes Ashore
(July 10)

Scale of Miles

0   10   20   30   40

throats or feel it seeping into their underwear and packs. But they had little time to worry about such things. Their orders were to move inland—fast.

A scattered array of poorly trained and motivated Italian soldiers defended Red Beach. The 1st Battalion caught them by surprise, which allowed the American soldiers to run across their beaches and find the cover of bluffs and ridges against random and mostly ineffective enemy fire. One of the troops in this first wave was a twenty-two-year-old replacement officer from Tennessee named Joe Martin. Martin had earned his commission through ROTC and joined the regiment in March 1943 in North Africa. On July 10, he led a platoon of C Company troops whose mission was to secure the left flank of the entire 7th Regiment landing area: "There was a pillbox on a point down to the left. It fired tracers . . . that came right over our LCI and they hit the water between us and the next one. There was an antitank weapon of some kind [a 47mm gun] that went through . . . the LCI next to ours. They had a few casualties. But the fire was mostly scattered. There was a sandbar offshore. The LCI has a tendency to hang up on it and you step off of it into ankle or knee deep water and by the time you get to shore you're lucky you're not in water over your head. One of our ramps . . . got flipped so we all had to go off on one side and we all got scattered." Martin assembled his troops as best he could when they reached the beach and, along with the rest of battalion, pressed inland, dodging fire from the flanks. The brush and gullies just in from the beach afforded good cover, and they systematically pressed on, killing off any resistance with grenades and rifles, reaching the sandstone bluff overlooking the beach within half an hour.[35]

Moore's men spread out along the plains beyond the beach even as the 2nd and 3rd Battalions landed and rapidly worked their way off the beach, fanning out in various directions, cutting the main road from Licata (Highway 115). The 3rd Battalion commander, Lieutenant Colonel John Heintges, had studied Red Beach reconnaissance photographs intensively. Heintges was quite an interesting character. He was born in Koblenz, Germany, in 1912, the son of a German infantry officer. Heintges barely knew his father because he was killed on the eastern front in 1915. Young Heintges experienced the privation and suffering of the war years in Germany, along with postwar occupation by Moroccans (very severe) and Americans (very lax and friendly). In 1920, his mother took his sister and him to America, where, with the help of relatives, they started a new life for themselves. Obviously attracted to military men, Heintges's mother married an American army officer who himself served for a long time with the 7th Infantry Regiment. So, Heintges grew up in the culture of the Army, among soldiers, and he loved it. He sold newspapers to the soldiers, drank sodas with them, and befriended them. He really had only one desire in life—to become a soldier like his father and his stepfather (whom he revered). Heintges entered West Point in 1932 and took to it magnificently, graduating in 1936. He served in the Philippines and later did a tour of duty as a company commander with the African-American 24th Infantry Regiment (an experience he loved), before moving on to the 3rd Division when war broke out.

For many months he ran a replacement training depot in North Africa, but like any combat arms officer, he wanted a field command. He got his wish on the eve of the Sicily invasion. The 3rd Battalion commander, Lieutenant Colonel Frank Izenour, came down with a severe case of malaria (the fever from it almost killed him), and General Truscott chose Heintges to take over command. Truscott knew that Heintges had been helping plan the invasion and that he knew the 3rd Battalion's mission well and its landing beaches even better. The general made a wise choice. Heintges proved to be a first-rate combat commander. He believed in an aggressive take-charge, communicative command style. His motto was "Get the word down to the man who does the work." Heintges had a great affinity for frontline combat soldiers, and he understood how to lead them properly.

What worried him most about the Sicily invasion was the possibility that his troops would be mistakenly landed under the cliffs on the western end of Beach Red, trapped, helpless under fire, with no way up the cliffs. He made sure his troops had ladders to scale their way up the cliffs if necessary. Sure enough, on D-Day the Navy landed his battalion under those cliffs: "The cliffs were wired and mined, but the bow guns of my six LCIs, which were 50 calibers with explosive bullets, just raked the top of the cliff. We raked those cliffs and knocked out all of the explosives. When my guys got ashore, I saw some of them hit the dirt and kiss the ground. They were so happy to be ashore." Much to his delight, Heintges found that the cliffs he had feared so much afforded his troops immunity from enemy artillery and machine-gun fire. "We were in a dead space. They couldn't hit us. We started climbing up those cliffs. Do you know that we did not have one single mine explode upon climbing up that cliff? And so, when we got on top, and then there was flat ground . . . we just took off."[36]

Only one obstacle remained on the beach. The assault troops were pushing inland, but a few machine guns and antitank guns were still in service on either flank. Naval gunfire blew some of these enemy crewmen away, but the 47mm that dropped some rounds in Lieutenant Martin's vicinity was still causing problems as Captain Rosson and the regimental command group came ashore: "Beach Red . . . was still receiving fire well after daylight when my own craft came in. The craft just to the left of my own was hit, as was my own, just as we rammed a sandbar about 100 or 200 feet offshore. There were casualties on both ships. In fact, a very good friend of mine, an officer on the craft to the left [Captain James Boyd], was killed at that time. However, we made it to shore through deep water with the help of lines swum in by sailors, and found that our assault elements were well inland." Rosson, Colonel Sherman, and the regimental staff moved single file up a pathway, or cleft, in the bluff and onto the plains Heintges mentioned. As they did so, one of the supporting destroyers sailed in close to the beach and pummeled the enemy gun with accurate 20mm fire. The gun shattered into pieces, as did its Italian crew.[37]

As Heintges indicated, the fact that the Navy landed his men along the extreme left flank of Beach Red, under the cliffs, proved to be a blessing in disguise. Once his soldiers reached the top of the bluffs, they spread out into skirmish formations and aggressively took on any resistance they encountered. The battalion took a left turn, deploying on either side of Highway 115, and pushed west. For the combat soldiers, this push took courage. Essentially, they spent the day sweating in the Sicilian heat, moving along the road, through woods or open fields, until the enemy opened fire on them, in the process playing a kind of grim game of truth or dare. Whenever they ran into enemy resistance, someone had to take the initiative to risk his life and destroy the enemy.

In one such instance, L Company was moving through an open field when a dug-in Italian machine gun opened fire. Everyone scrambled for cover and did his best to spot the well-camouflaged gun. Private Joseph Jojola, with his face buried in the grassy ground, realized that if he and his buddies stayed pinned down for very long, the Italian gunners would eventually zero in on them and cause casualties (no one had been hit by the first burst of fire). The enemy machine gun kept firing, but Jojola crawled forward to a little knoll he had noticed near the gun. While lying prone, he grabbed a grenade, pulled the pin, and hurled it at the gun. The grenade no sooner exploded than Jojola threw another one. This silenced the gun, and the Americans moved on.

Not far away the soldiers of K Company spotted an ugly-looking pill-box some one hundred yards in front of them. The 1st Platoon, under a staff sergeant named Carl Boone, was caught in the kill zone when the pillbox opened fire. The Italian machine gunners in the pillbox fired several bursts at the lead scout of Boone's platoon (in the nineteenth century these leading soldiers were called skirmishers; by World War II they were called lead scouts; by the Vietnam era they were called point men). Boone hollered orders with staccato efficiency, arranging his squads and fire teams for a flanking attack on the pillbox. The enemy gunners could not keep up with all this movement. They fired wildly, but Boone skillfully directed his squads into what he thought were the pillbox's blind spots. It worked. The Americans closed to within slapping distance of the pillbox, pulled the pins from their grenades, armed them, and killed the pillbox crew, leaving behind only a bloody, rotting mess.[38]

Late in the day, Sherman ordered his battalions to dig in for the night. He knew he could keep advancing westward, but he and the division hierarchy worried that the Germans' crack Hermann Göring Division, lurking somewhere out there in the Sicilian hills, might counterattack. The first day of the invasion had gone well. On all fronts Allied troops successfully captured their landing beaches and moved inland against varying degrees of resistance. Vehicles, supplies, and reinforcements were pouring ashore. The Cottonbalers represented the extreme left flank of the Allied armies. Their job in the days ahead entailed advancing west and then north in the direction of Palermo.

THE LANDING NOW ACCOMPLISHED, THE REGIMENT'S FIRST objective in its westward push was Palma di Montechiaro, a small town located about two miles northwest of Red Beach. In the early-morning hours of July 11, Sherman assigned 3rd Battalion the task of capturing the town. The sea breeze off the Mediterranean chilled the soldiers as they bumped their way through the darkness to the jump-off point, a stream called Faci di Palma. Sicily was very hot in the day and the men sweltered in their wool olive-drab trousers, shirts, and

M-1941 field jackets, but in the evenings these heavy clothes helped shield them a bit from the cold winds. Heintges and his men had difficulty crossing the shallow stream in time for Sherman's anticipated attack time of 0430.

Actually, Heintges was already having problems with straggling (the other two battalions probably had the same problem). The straggling began with the man Heintges had previously thought of as his best company commander, Captain James Steiner of L Company. On D-Day Steiner got a flesh wound in the shoulder. Heintges helped bandage the shoulder and asked the captain if he could continue. Steiner replied, "Oh, I think so, sir." But then he proceeded to go back to the battalion aid station, then to the beach, and arranged to get himself evacuated back to Africa. According to Heintges, Steiner never returned to combat. Heintges, totally dedicated to his mission and his men, could not begin to comprehend Steiner's actions. "Well, this was quite a shock to me. I know that he didn't have to quit. He shouldn't have had himself evacuated on the first day of battle when he had a superficial wound."

Nor was Steiner the only one. The haphazard, confused, almost chaotic nature of the combat zone during offensive operations afforded many chances for an anonymous exit. Dozens of enlisted men filtered away at the first opportunity. The problem persisted throughout the war. In talking with his officers and sergeants, Heintges soon discovered this chronic problem: "This was the first disappointment of my entire military career when I found out that we didn't have 100 percent fighting sons-of-bitches. We had people whose shoe laces becomes untied and they sit down along the roadside, or in the woods, to tie their shoe laces. It takes them a long time to tie it. In the meantime, the company has advanced 200–300 yards and they never seem to catch up until the battalion goes into reserve. Or you have things like where a man leaves the base plate of his mortar at the last drinking well . . . or the machine gunner leaves ammunition there and has to go back for it, or a wounded man has four people taking him back. It was a rude awakening and it meant that the company commanders had to make some arrangements to beat people on the damn butts . . . and watch them more closely."

Colonel Sherman had no patience for all this skulking. "Stragglers must be dealt with severely," he asserted. The colonel ordered his sergeants to solve the problem. This was a good and appropriate solution. "Verbal persuasion is sometimes effective; some splendid results have been obtained by direct physical means applied by a non-commissioned officer." In other words, the sergeants beat the stuffing out of anyone who even thought of straggling.

Of course, Heintges hastened to add that these stragglers were the distinct minority. "I had many brave soldiers who had scars all over the place, and never got a Purple Heart for it because they didn't even report it."[39]

Heintges had his men ready for the attack by 0600. The town was on a hill overlooking the stream. The Italians had dug trenches around the town and fortified them with hundreds of infantrymen. With the sun rising at their backs, the American infantrymen of the 3rd Battalion spread out and ran at the trenches, firing and maneuvering as they did so. The Italians opened up with everything they had. Bullets were flying everywhere. Some of them hit home, thudding through pitifully thin olive-drab uniforms. As the bullets hit these mortal men, pinkish clouds of blood sprayed from their wounds. They spun and fell, a few of them dead on the spot but most wounded. Frightened out of their minds, passing quickly into shock, they screamed, "Medic!!" at the top of their lungs. One such medic, Private First Class Lenny Macklin, heard the cry of a wounded corporal who had been shot through both legs. The corporal was lying right out in the open, with machine-gun bullets still kicking up dust around him. Macklin, with every fiber of his being, dreaded going to the corporal's aid but did it anyway. He crawled to the man and, when he got to him, crouched low to make the smallest target possible. Macklin sprinkled sulfa powder in the soldier's wounds and bound them up as best he could with pressure bandages. Then he gave the corporal a shot of morphine. Grabbing him by the lapels of his field jacket, Macklin laboriously dragged him to safety. Macklin's actions were repeated many times over by other Cottonbaler medics that day, in an anonymous display of bravery under fire.

Luckily, most of the assaulting troops were not hit by the enemy fire. They poured a lethal amount of firepower on the Italian trenches. Riflemen pumped clip after clip at the enemy, so much so that the many pings of their spent clips, jumbling together, produced a kind of xylophone effect. The rhythmic cadence of BARs combined with these pings; the BAR gunners kept screaming for more ammunition and their courageous carriers had to go back for more or crawl over to them with a new supply of twenty-round clips. The Italians had to keep their heads down in the face of this firepower. As they did, groups of Cottonbalers closed in on them, pitched grenades into the trenches, and sprayed them with submachine gun and rifle fire. The American bullets tore and shattered these enemy soldiers, turning them into bloody rag dolls.

Perhaps motivated now by desperation, or maybe by idealistic fascist resolve, the Italians began to pull a series of dirty, and foolish, tricks. "White flags would appear, and then the minute we started moving, they'd come down, and the machine gun fire would open up," Heintges related, "and I had a hell of a lot of casualties because of these ruses that they pulled on us." Indeed, several of his men were killed, their faces and throats blown apart by the point-blank fire. The others could only hit the dirt, scream in anger, and vow revenge.

Enraged now, the Cottonbalers fought with extreme ruthlessness. They shot at anything that moved. They disregarded white flags. They poured fire on the enemy trenches, ran at them, and cleaned them out with bursts of automatic fire. Once the Cottonbalers breached the main trenches, nothing could stop them. They ran up and down the enemy line and shot fleeing Italian soldiers without mercy. Somehow, this frenzied situation settled down and the surviving Italians surrendered, two hundred all told. Another sixty lay dead in the trench system. The riflemen glared at their prisoners and gestured toward the rear. American medics descended on the scene, evacuated those Yanks who had been hit, and did what they could for the enemy wounded.

The battle and the treachery were not over, though. As the 3rd Battalion moved toward Palma di Montechiaro, a civilian emerged from the town and asked to speak to Heintges. The colonel did not speak Italian (he did speak fluent German, though), so he referred the man to his radio operator, an Italian-speaking Brooklynite of Sicilian descent. Italian-American soldiers proved to be a major asset to the U.S. Army in the Italian campaign. Most of them were ordinary soldiers who, in addition to their regular duties, served as impromptu interpreters, diplomats, and humanitarians (almost everyone in Italy seemed to have a relative in America). In any case, the Sicilian civilian claimed to be the mayor of Palma di Montechiaro and expressed a desire to surrender the town to the Americans. Heintges looked at the mayor and then the town. He could see white flags fluttering in the breeze, hanging from the windows of several houses. He deliberated for a few minutes and finally decided to accept the surrender.

He sent a small patrol into the village to sniff things out and begin the surrender process. "I watched them disappear into the village. They had no sooner rounded the corner when all hell broke loose in that direction . . . a lot of machine gun fire and some explosions that sounded possibly like hand grenades or bazooka type sounds. Then all of the white flags disappeared."

Enraged and feeling personally responsible for the unfortunate men he had sent into the town, Heintges ran over to his new L Company commander, an Alabamian, First Lieutenant Ralph Yates. The two of them rounded up an improvised squad of heavily armed men. "I got a couple of bazookas, and some tommy guns, and some riflemen, about . . . 12 and I led this patrol into the town from a different direction. We got around the corner and got some machine gun fire, and we crawled through some backyards, over some fences. The houses all had shutters on them." The firing died down now. Wounded Americans from the patrol wailed in agony in the street where they had been ambushed. The others lay under cover behind walls and cars.

Heintges and his group kept working their way toward the house where the ambush had been sprung. He saw a shutter open slowly and a rifle poke out. The enemy soldier saw him too and quickly closed the shutter. Heintges then pulled a ruse of his own, and quite a bold one at that, at least for a battalion commander. "I sent my radio operator with a bazooka around to the other side of this house where he could see the window . . . where this guy was. And I said, 'Now, you go around there and wait until he opens that shutter again. As soon as you get there, wave to me. I'll step out in the road and let this guy get just far enough where he's going to pull the trigger, then you let him have it.' And, I walked over behind this house."

A moment later, the Italian sniper rolled a concussion grenade down the roof of the house, right at Heintges. He ducked for cover and the grenade exploded with no effect. Then, true to his word, Heintges walked into the street, using himself as bait, in essence putting his life into the hands of his young Italian-American radio operator. Almost on cue, the enemy sniper opened the shutter and pointed his rifle at Heintges. "I had no sooner seen the round part of the muzzle of that rifle when he let go with the bazooka, and it went right through that window, and there was a lot of commotion and moaning and groaning up there. There were six dead people . . . unfortunately they were not all soldiers." The dead soldiers wore black uniforms, emblematic of Mussolini's fascist guard.

While Heintges dueled with the sniper, the other American soldiers had demolished the other buildings where the fascists had been holed up. As they did so, two medics rescued a badly wounded sergeant from the original patrol. Under fire, they plucked him from the sidewalk where he had been shot and carried him to safety. The Americans captured twenty-one enemy soldiers and killed several others. The rest fled to the hills west of town. The 1st Battalion advanced on the right and secured Heintges's flanks. Palma di Montechiaro was safely in American hands.[40]

THE TARGET NOW FOR THE 7TH INFANTRY WAS AGRIGENTO, an ancient city located some twenty miles due west of Palma di Montechiaro. In fact, Captain Rosson claimed that the Cottonbalers could almost see the place already: "One could look westward to Agrigento over these rolling, open areas and see it situated on something of a ledge."[41] Founded by the Greeks as a Mediterranean trading center, the place had stood for two thousand years and was once the greatest city in Sicily, until its decline under the Carthaginians and then the Romans. Colonel Sherman and his officers found the history of Agrigento interesting, but of far more immediate importance was that the town was a key road and supply center.

General Patton, an even bigger student of history, knew all about Agrigento's past, but like his subordinates, he was more concerned with its future. The general was in the middle of a nasty turf squabble with his British colleagues, Montgomery and the immediate boss of both of them, Field Marshal Harold Alexander, commander of the 15th Army Group. Alexander had failed, during preinvasion planning, to enumerate specific axes of advance or zones of operation for Patton's 7th Army and Montgomery's 8th, in the process opening up a Pandora's box of rivalries, subterfuge, and ego battles. Safely ashore, Patton now lobbied Alexander for a free hand in western Sicily. Mindful of the fact that his orders called for the 7th Army to protect Monty's left flank, Alexander gave permission to Patton for a "reconnaissance in force" to the west, as long as the Americans did not become involved in a "major engagement" that might threaten the 8th Army's flank. Like a pushy salesman who only needs a slightly opened door to force his way inside,

Patton seized on Alexander's "reconnaissance in force" order as an excuse to bag all of western Sicily.[42]

To that end, Patton ordered Truscott to reconnoiter aggressively in the direction of Agrigento while avoiding, of course, a major engagement, whatever that meant. Truscott assigned the 7th Infantry the Agrigento mission. On the evening of July 12, the 1st Battalion boarded trucks and, closely supported by artillery, rolled west down Highway 115. After a bumpy all-night ride, they hopped off their trucks at 0600, spread out (five to ten yards between each man) into combat formation, and started walking. Every now and then enemy machine gunners or snipers opened fire. When they did, the Americans would dive into the rocky roadside ditches and wait for artillery or mortars to plaster the enemy. The American artillerymen and mortarmen did a terrific job, destroying or scattering the uneven resistance along Highway 115.

The battalion reached the Naro River by 1430 and halted there. They took cover and waited for nightfall. Then, they withdrew back to their assembly area. Sherman had all the information about Agrigento's defenses that he needed. The town's Italian defenders were mainly deployed along the eastern portion of the city, where they had dug in twelve artillery pieces, accompanied by a couple hundred infantry and some mortars. Sherman knew that a frontal attack would be foolish. Instead he planned an envelopment attack: the 1st Battalion would advance along high ground from the south and around the town while the 2nd Battalion, which had bloodlessly occupied the nearby town of Favara on the fifteenth, would follow high ground out of Favara and envelop Agrigento from the north. In addition, the 3rd Ranger Battalion would swing completely around the town from the north, bypass it, go for the coast, and capture Porto Empedocle, Agrigento's sister city and the most important southern port still remaining in Axis hands.

Sherman launched his attack on the evening of the fifteenth. The soldiers encountered mostly outpost opposition during the night: small groups of bewildered Italian defenders who opened fire, usually hitting nothing, and then surrendered. In the morning, the Americans ran into tougher resistance, especially C Company of the 1st Battalion. At 0900 the troops of C Company were silently and gingerly negotiating their way down a steep slope (if you didn't look down and watch each step you risked tripping over a rock and falling down) when Italian artillery shells began landing right in their midst. Some of the men could not find any cover. They hurled themselves to the ground and tried to scrunch their bodies into small targets. Each man sweated in the dust and prayed the rounds would hit somewhere (or someone) else. The commander of C Company, Captain Herman Wagner, watched his men squirm and break. He knew that his advance was losing momentum and that the longer his soldiers stayed pinned down, the greater their peril. So he left the safety of cover and ran out among the exploding shells, kicking men in the ass, yelling at them to get up and move, directing them to good cover. He rushed around like a man possessed, hollering, threatening, and imploring. The men responded, moving to positions of safety. Their eyes bulged with terror as they ran for their lives. None of them could believe the captain had not been hit; he seemed to have an invisible shield around him. But he didn't. He was only a mortal man, and like any other flesh-and-blood human being, if he was in the wrong place at the wrong time, he would be hit. Wagner's luck ran out. A round exploded near him, kicking up rocks and dust. Fragments tore through Wagner and he dropped like a sack of potatoes, dead on the spot. Shocked by the death of their captain, C Company remained immobilized.

Farther to the north, the 2nd Battalion left Favara and moved west along high ground. The battalion's artillery observers, roaming around with and ahead of the lead riflemen, spotted a large column of enemy reinforcements, far in the distance. These Italian soldiers, clearly forming up for a counterattack, were jumping off trucks and walking toward Agrigento. The American observers made good use of their handheld radios, calling in a bevy of fire missions. For a solid hour, U.S. artillery pulverized these cornered hapless enemy soldiers and their vehicles. The massed fire inflicted one hundred casualties on the enemy and destroyed fifty Italian vehicles. It also ended any possibility of a counterattack. Once again, artillery, in support of well-trained infantry, had proven to be the greatest killer on the modern battlefield. The soldiers of the 7th Infantry would see this dictum proven many times in the future as well.

Late in the afternoon of the sixteenth, Colonel Sherman pushed everything and everyone forward. Led by A Company, the 1st Battalion kept moving to the south of Agrigento. The 2nd Battalion, led by G Company, closed around the town from the north. The reserve battalion, Heintges's 3rd, walked straight up Highway 115, cleaning out any Italian defenders who had been left behind and were still in the mood to fight.

The bravery of men such as Private Robert Green of A Company kept the lead battalions moving, inexorably closing the ring around Agrigento. Operating as a lead scout somewhere south of the town, Green spotted a camouflaged pillbox forty yards to his right. The enemy soldiers in the pillbox spotted him at the same time and opened fire with a machine gun. Green acted as if they were shooting spitballs at him instead of bullets. At a half crouch he leveled his M1 at the pillbox and emptied an entire clip. He tossed his empty rifle aside, whipped out a .45-caliber pistol, and fired away, all the while walking toward the pillbox until he got within grenade range. He grabbed a grenade from his cartridge belt, yanked out the pin, and threw the grenade inside the pillbox. The explosion killed four enemy troops and forced twelve others to surrender. His company could now keep advancing without fear of flanking fire.[43]

This kind of thing went on all day long. Other Cottonbalers, ordinary dogface soldiers—the kind of decent, sturdy, Middle American men who won the war—performed numerous, anonymous acts of heroism to keep the regiment moving. Staff officers, advancing in their wake, spoke of "light resistance," but to the men in the lead, ferreting out enemy soldiers, not knowing when or where the next enemy bullet or fragment might come, the battle could not be summarized in so cavalier a fashion. Their existence boiled down to one question: am I in danger or not? During the advance to Agrigento (and for most of the rest of the war), the answer was usually yes.

After dark, Moore's troops broke into the southern outskirts of the town. They fought from street to street against any Italian die-hards who still wanted to fight. The Americans flushed these enemy soldiers out of buildings with bazookas and rifle grenades, working systematically among the buildings, taking cover whenever possible, minimizing the danger. Fortunately, the great majority of enemy soldiers preferred surrender to death. The Americans herded them together and marched them toward the town's civic center, which served as the command post for the Italian commanding general. He surrendered his command, twenty-seven hundred soldiers, to Moore.

Immediately to the west of the town, 1st Battalion reconnaissance patrols saw several Italian tanks approaching their positions. They sent back a frantic call for antitank weapons. Several B Company men, armed with antitank grenades, ran to the scene. The Italian tank crews must have detected the presence of these B Company antitank grenadiers, because they surrendered. At almost the same time, the Rangers captured Porto Empedocle. The battle was over. The 7th Regiment had added another victory to its long list, eventually capturing six thousand prisoners, fifty guns, and one hundred vehicles. In the process, they destroyed the main enemy strength in southern Sicily.[44]

The combat troops, exhausted and thirsty, dug holes around the town and caught a little sleep. The next day, they scavenged for food around the rich valleys outside of Agrigento. This sort of scavenging had actually been going on since the first day ashore. Weary of K and C rations, the troops found a rich variety of local foods that made their collective mouths water. Sergeant Pratt, combing the coast with the 3rd Battalion, found all sorts of succulent treasures: "The Sicilian farms and orchards were filled with ripening vegetables and fruits of all descriptions. We were able to generously supplement our diets with fresh tomatoes, melons, carrots, potatoes and squashes of many kinds. From the trees we picked fresh peaches, apples, apricots and plums . . . usually to the angry and vocal protests of their owners." The men sympathized with these farmers but did not necessarily heed their protests. Some soldiers traded rations in exchange for produce, but most took what they wanted, reasoning that these were enemy civilians ultimately responsible for the war, specious reasoning, but "it sufficed for infantrymen who were hungry for fresh things, and also tired and impatient with being shot at." Operating from positions west of the town, Lieutenant Martin, hot and sweaty, with several days' growth of beard, also carried out his share of "raids" against enemy food. "We ate almonds, green olives off trees and watermelons and marshmelons out of the fields, much to the farmer's disgust."[45]

THE SOLDIERS HAD LITTLE TIME TO SETTLE IN, BECAUSE Truscott ordered an immediate advance due north on Palermo. The capture of Agrigento had broken most Axis resistance in western Sicily, so Patton now had no qualms about overrunning that portion of the island or capturing Palermo, the largest city on Sicily's north coast. He told Truscott to get moving and Truscott, in turn, told his regimental commanders to do the same. At first, the 15th and 30th Regiments led the way, but on the evening of July 20 the 7th Infantry joined the fray. Sherman and his staff arranged for the regiment to be trucked to a jump-off point two miles shy of Prizzi, the Cottonbalers' first objective on this expedition to Palermo.

This began a two-day road march, against almost nonexistent resistance, in which the Truscott Trot training in North Africa paid serious dividends. The 7th Infantry, and its two sister regiments of the 3rd Division, covered nearly thirty miles per day in the heat of midsummer. Within two hours on the first day, the 3rd Battalion captured Prizzi, along with five hundred prisoners of war and two hundred horses and mules. The soldiers, to relieve their blistered feet, took to riding the horses and mules until General Truscott chanced upon the scene. The general, an old cavalryman, asked Heintges why his men were riding these animals. Heintges gave a jocular response, but Truscott cut him off: "Get your men off those horses. You know, Heintges, we are still infantry." Heintges smiled and said, "Yes, sir." Shorn of their four-legged conveyances, the 3rd Battalion nonetheless advanced thirty-four miles that day over steep mountain roads. The troops were tired, dusty, hot, and footsore, but their spirits were pretty high. After all, they obviously had the enemy on the run and Palermo beckoned.

The other battalions were not far behind and the regiment soon captured Corleone (the inspiration for the name of Mario Puzo's famous Mafia family) against almost no opposition. Second Battalion now took the lead, marching all night long, occupying Marineo and finally halting a mile north of that town. The 1st Battalion then took the lead, smashing up halfhearted enemy attempts to establish roadblocks or lay down artillery fire. By the afternoon of July 22, the Cottonbalers could see Palermo. The regiment converged on the town from every direction, the 2nd Battalion from the west, the 1st Battalion from the south, and the 3rd Battalion from the east. The latter battalion got there first, at precisely 1619 hours.

They found a carnival-like atmosphere. Enemy soldiers, both German and Italian, were surrendering in droves. Off to the east, American artillery was shooting up a German column of vehicles trying to escape down the coastal road. The population of Palermo lined the streets, cheering and waving at the Americans. They may have been citizens of an enemy country, but the Sicilians were tired of war and the Mussolini regime. Rarely in the history of warfare have two peoples had less reason to fight than the American and Italian people in 1942–43. A major wave of Italian immigration in the late nineteenth and early twentieth century had forged ties of kinship between the two nations. Quite commonly, Italian-American soldiers bumped into cousins, uncles, aunts, grandparents, even brothers and sisters. The majority of the Italian population, especially here in Sicily where Mussolini was quite unpopular, viewed the Yanks as liberators, from their own government and from their German "allies."

So, on that scorching afternoon of July 22, when Lieutenant Colonel Heintges and his troops entered the city of Palermo, the people treated them like long-lost relatives, showering them with kisses, flowers, and candy. Some of Heintges's superiors were not as thrilled, though. General Patton, wanting the 2nd Armored Division (his old unit) to receive the honor of liberating Palermo, had ordered the infantry to carry out reconnaissance around Palermo as far as a spot on the map called "The Blue Line," but nothing more. The order gave infantrymen like Heintges an excuse to enter Palermo ("We're only scouting for enemy resistance") and Patton should have known that, since he himself had taken advantage of such a loophole to get to Palermo in the first place.

At any rate, the Cottonbalers beat the "Hell on Wheels" 2nd Armored to Palermo. But not without some minor teeth grinding by the brass. Heintges barely had time to bask in the glow of his victory when an American armored column, flying a white flag, drove into the town and came to a halt at his position. "It was Hap [Hobart] Gay, Patton's deputy—General Gay. He spots me and asks, 'Who are you?' And I walk up and salute and said, 'Sir, I am Lieutenant Colonel Heintges, commanding the reconnaissance force which is here in Palermo from the 3rd Divsion.' He says, 'Well, damn it, it doesn't look like a reconnaissance force to me. Don't you know that you're not supposed to be beyond the Blue Line?' I said, 'Yes, sir, but patrolling is allowed, and that's what I have. I have a large reconnaissance patrol.'" This was hogwash and they both knew it. General Gay smirked, but Heintges managed to keep a straight face. After a few perfunctory orders about where to deploy his "reconnaissance patrol" east of Palermo, Gay and his armored column drove off.[46] Clearly, the 7th Infantry had gotten to Palermo first, but all that really mattered was that the town was in American hands.

Still, the men of the 7th were very proud of their march to Palermo and its capture. They knew that they had achieved something special, something very few infantry troops in the world could have done. "What happened was really quite an extraordinary tour-de-force in terms of a foot march," Captain Rosson asserted. "It was here that the

Truscott Trot really came into its own. The troops were in very good condition and they were pushed hard. They were on the go literally 24 hours a day from the time of the landing all the way up into Palermo. Although we had some vehicles, of course . . . it basically was a foot march on a single route."[47]

The regiment had earned a rest. While the generals planned an eastward push to Messina, the Cottonbalers stayed in reserve in and around Palermo, mostly guarding prisoners, taking it easy, and swimming. The rest lasted for about a week and a half.

ON AUGUST 1, THE 7TH REGIMENT, ALONG WITH THE REST of the 3rd Division, boarded trucks that took them about a hundred miles east to San Stefano Camastra, where the 45th Infantry Division had run into severe resistance. Patton had decided to give the 45th a rest and replace it with the 3rd. Initially Truscott held the 7th Infantry in reserve, so the Cottonbalers waited around in the vicinity of a town called Pollins while the other two regiments of the division deployed to the front lines. This went on for about five days, during which the 7th received forty-seven replacements. The men of the unit simply hunkered down in old foxholes and fighting positions and hung around in support of the unfortunate 15th, whose men were bleeding and dying on the rocky slopes ahead, in a series of futile attacks. Even worse, the enemy (now mostly German) counterattacked and forced the 15th back to the west side of the Furiano River, that regiment's original jump-off point. The Cottonbalers covered their withdrawal. The 3rd Division, like the 45th before it, was stymied.

The Germans made excellent use of the terrain and circumstances, bottlenecking the Americans in place, as Sergeant Pratt recounted: "The road to Messina along the north coast of Sicily where the mountains often drop down vertically to the seacoast waves was especially tortuous at places. The advance of thousands of troops, tanks, and other vehicles, were controlled by a single infantry squad, or engineer minesweeper, at the point of a column." Basically, the Marne division, confined to a tiny corridor of land along coastal Highway 113, had impenetrable mountains on its right and ocean on its left: "It was not possible to spread out the front in width more than about the width of the coastal highway. German troops . . . had thoroughly mined the only north coast road at numerous critical spots along almost its entire length." They also blew out entire sections of the road, "leaving sheer drops of hundreds of feet to the water below. These blowouts repeatedly slowed the . . . advance at times to a complete standstill until the ingenious engineers could build a span across the demolished sections of the road. [They] would hang like mountain climbers from suspended seats, using pneumatic drills to gouge holes in solid rock in which to insert timbers or poles for bridge supports strong enough to not buckle when tanks and heavily loaded military trucks later passed overhead."[48]

According to Colonel Sherman, the 10th Engineer Battalion did a particularly outstanding job: "Had it not been for the skill of the [battalion] in constructing by-passes over the many demolished bridges in the zone of action, the advance of this Command . . . would have been seriously impaired. The engineers constructed many by-passes while under fire, and were always to be found in advanced positions." They also did an excellent job of clearing mines.

Temperatures rose, creating dehydration problems and a water crisis. "At the peak of the day," the 3rd Division historian wrote, "the temperatures soared to between 100 and 110 F. It was muggy, sticky. The sun dawned each morning in an absolutely flawless blue sky, and before it was well into its zenith, men began sweating and cursing its relentless, burning rays. It was a common sight to approach large groups of men clustered around a small pipe cemented into the side of a rocky cliffside, from which a small trickle of cold water flowed. These men would edge their way in the attempt to fill their canteens then double-time . . . soaked with perspiration and covered with a film of dust, back in place in their rapidly-marching columns." Technically, local water sources like this were off-limits, for sanitation reasons. Heaven only knew what kind of microorganisms lived in such water. American troops were only supposed to drink halazone-treated or chlorinated water brought up from the rear, but in the stifling heat of Sicily in August 1943 such regulations gave way to expediency. You either drank what water you could find or you risked death. The choice, then, was easy.[49]

Patton now conceived of a way to break the deadlock. The mountains may have been impassable, but the sea certainly was not. He possessed the most highly trained amphibious division in the entire U.S. Army and he intended to utilize it that way. He ordered Truscott to execute a battalion-sized amphibious landing behind the German lines, seven miles away from the Furiano River, east of a coastal town called San Agata. Patton's bold concept was a bit risky. The 3rd Division had previously made no headway across the Furiano and east along the coastal road. If it could not do so now, then an entire battalion would be cut off behind German lines and annihilated. But Patton believed that the invasion would force the Germans to retreat. He knew that his armies could draw on more resources than the enemy; further, he knew that the Germans were merely fighting a delaying action in northern Sicily until they could evacuate their troops to the mainland. The "lucky" unit Truscott chose for the amphibious assault was the 2nd Battalion of the 30th Infantry. He ordered the rest of that regiment, led by the 7th Infantry along the coastal road, to link up with the invaders.

The plan worked well. First the supporting firepower plastered the area. Artillery pieces (mostly 155 mm), mortars, fighter-bombers, and navy destroyers and cruisers demolished any targets they saw, providing vital support for the assault troops. The amphibious troops came ashore at 0300 on August 8, a Sunday, and caught the Germans by surprise. These intrepid troops quickly moved into the hills beyond their landing beach and, for good measure, captured San Agata. As the sun rose, the rest of the 30th Infantry, along with the 15th, approached San Fratello, a town at the foot of a mountain peak by that same name.

At dawn, Cottonbalers from the 2nd Battalion went forward on Highway 113, where the 15th Infantry had met such terrible resistance only a few days before. Artillery laid down a protective smoke screen and a rolling barrage for the 7th infantrymen, but they did not need it. Knowing what had happened (and in many cases having seen it) at the Furiano River crossroads, many of the lead troops expected to be blown away at any second. They had spent a miserable, tense night ruminating on the future. Now, almost incredibly, they encountered no resistance. They captured a few German and Italian soldiers but found little other evidence of trouble. "It was a textbook attack," Lieutenant Martin commented. "We followed that road right up that hill and over the top just perfectly."[50] Sherman sent the 3rd Battalion up now. These liberators of Palermo passed by their Cottonbaler buddies, exchanging gibes of course, and pressed farther east until they reached the Rosamino River where the bridge had been blown. The river was so low (one advantage of the heat) that the troops crossed at 1915, fending off inaccurate mortar, machine-gun, and artillery fire, and successfully linked up with the invaders.

The next day, the regiment kept pushing east, right on the heels of the retreating Germans. At one point, a group of enemy soldiers made a stand behind a wall directly adjacent to the highway. First Battalion was in the lead now. Scouts from B Company, two abreast and several yards apart, walked slowly and warily down the road, their rifles at the ready. The enemy soldiers rose up from behind the walls and fired their burp guns and rifles at the scouts, hitting them in several places. The two men, bloody and moaning, writhed in agony. No one could get anywhere near them. Everyone in B Company took cover in the ditches. Many of these soldiers opened fire on the wall, forcing the Germans to duck their heads, preventing them from finishing off the two scouts. In the meantime, soldiers from C Company took action. They made use of the only place of maneuver available to them—the sea. Wading through chest-high water, their weapons held above their chins so as to keep them dry, the Americans charged the enemy soldiers, ripping them with accurate fire. None of the Germans behind that wall lived. Their stinking bodies were left to rot in the sun—flies were already descending on them—and the Cottonbalers moved on.

Several hundred yards to the right, the 3rd Battalion left the road and advanced along a rugged series of hills north of San Marco d'Alunzio. Their biggest peril was their own artillery. American firepower support was magnificent when it worked as it was supposed to, but inevitably sometimes it did not work so well, leading to "friendly fire" casualties, a major thorn in the side of the twentieth-century U.S. Army. Rounds fell short. Officers miscalculated range, azimuth, or windage. Communications broke down. Tired or careless individuals made mistakes. The trouble for the 3rd Battalion started when the battalion's artillery observer got hit, along with his radio. An officer back at regimental headquarters, working from a map, now directed the supporting barrage right onto the backs of the 3rd Battalion's soldiers. Heintges, crouching under cover, watching his soldiers being hit by American artillery, nearly blew his cork. Since his radio was down, he sent a runner back to regiment with a simple message: "Quit shooting." The firing stopped within a few minutes (those minutes seemed like hours to the soldiers of the 3rd Battalion) and the battalion resumed its advance, minus several of its men, some of whom had been killed.

The Germans now set up defensive positions along two terrain features: the Zappula River and the nearby Hill di Marco. Just before daylight on the morning of August 10, the 1st Battalion, led by B Company, attempted to cross the shallow Zappula. These unfortunate soldiers ran into a terrible death zone. They safely waded the river and scaled the opposite bank, but then the world seemed to explode. One of the lead riflemen set off a trip wire connected to eight powerful German Teller mines. A chain reaction of explosions turned the leading men into bloody hamburger. Some of them disintegrated into nothing recognizable as human. Others, a bit farther away, had arms and legs blown off or eyes torn out. Seven men were dead and fifteen wounded. The wounded lay on the ground and howled in pain, begging for water, for medics, or for their mothers, and not necessarily in that order. The uninjured crouched in frozen terror, unable and unwilling to move.

Sergeant Pratt described the horror of seeing these men get maimed by mines, perhaps the most impersonal weapon of modern warfare: "A crunching and ear shattering explosion. The air filled with dirt and smoke and pieces of rock and clods of soil rained down all around us. When the dust had partially cleared, I looked over and saw [a] poor wretched fellow, lying on his back, dazed and speechless. He raised his head and helplessly looked at a stump where his right leg had been just seconds before. To say it was sickening is, of course, to understate the matter. Such sights one can never forget or mentally overcome."[51]

The awful reality was that no one could do anything to help these wounded men, at least not yet. First, a path needed to be cleared through the minefield. A correspondent from *Stars and Stripes* described how that was done: "An engineer comes along and probes with a bayonet and it strikes metal. 'Take it easy, Joe,' says the guy who's working with him, 'those things are touchy.' The two get down on their knees around the mine and from a few yards off it looks like they're shooting craps. You see them dig out the dirt around the mine and then work their hands under the mine to see if it's boobied, that is, if it will explode when lifted up. Satisfied, the engineer called Joe lifts out the German Teller mine and the other guy unscrews the caps and defuses it. There are a pile of these Teller mines; they look just like an oversize discus."

In this manner, the engineers cleared a path for A and C Companies, and they cautiously resumed their crossing later in the morning: "You follow in the exact footsteps of the man in front of you. The man in the lead—perhaps he follows in the footsteps of God. Every snap of a twig, each rattle of a pebble, makes you twitch and shiver. If you think at all it is perhaps about what you said in your last letter home."[52]

The Germans now opened up on them with artillery, mortars, and machine guns. In response, the American soldiers quickened their pace. They ran forward to any cover they could find. One platoon from C Company jumped over a wall only to find that the field beyond it was mined. A Teller mine went off, killing one man and wounding several others. The platoon sergeant climbed over the wall and tried to find safe passage through the field. He tripped a mine, and it blew him into thousands of pieces. The attack was threatening to stall again. Heavy machine gunners and mortarmen from D Company, set up in positions on the west side of the river, were pouring as much supporting fire into the German positions as they could.

The surviving men of A and C Companies knew they had only two options: go forward or be killed. In the face of heavy enemy fire, the kind that cut men down like a random scythe, they ran ahead as fast as their still-intact legs could carry them. Through sheer guts and determination, they ascended Hill di Marco and shot up its German defenders. They tossed aside the dead enemy bodies and began to set up defensive positions in their fighting holes. But the enemy wanted, and needed, this hill, from which they could impede any advance over the Zappula.

At 1000 heavy concentrations of German mortar and artillery fire began to fall among the thirsty defenders of Hill di Marco. This enemy fire tested the nerves of the Cottonbalers but did not inflict any casualties. Unfortunately, the bombardment was only preparation for a counterattack by two hundred German soldiers. They came in waves, firing their burp guns, their Mauser 98K rifles and their MG-34 machine guns. The Americans shot back with everything they had, but it wasn't enough. Enemy bullets cracked and splattered skulls and throats. The Germans held the advantages of supply and numbers. The Cottonbalers on the hill ran into a terrifying problem. They were getting low on ammunition. They had to retreat from their hard-won hill. Supported by heavy weapons to the rear and even Moore's headquarters troops, the riflemen steadily retreated to the bottom of the hill. To this point, they had enjoyed no friendly artillery support, but someone to the rear finally supplied new batteries for radios that had been dead all morning. American artillery observers called in everything they could get, and this helped save the remnants of A and C Companies. The U.S. artillery devastated the exposed Germans, tearing them into bloody and fleshy corpses that, from a distance, had the look of mannequins. The Germans kept the hill for now, but they were not in good shape.

The American guns threw so many shells at them that the troops took to calling Hill di Marco the "Million Dollar Ridge."

The 1st Battalion was still intact, but it was finished for the day. The men had been through a hellish day. They needed rest. Sherman sent the 3rd Battalion up to relieve them and take back Million Dollar Ridge. They did so that night, chasing the Germans away with firepower and numbers.

The next day, August 11, as heat waves shimmered off the endless series of rocks and ridges ahead of the Cottonbalers, the 2nd Battalion now became the focus of the 7th Regiment advance. The same group from the 15th Infantry that had carried out the first amphibious landing four days before once again carried out a surprise invasion. They splashed ashore one mile west of Brolo at 0300 and got into trouble by the early afternoon, when the Germans unleashed a counterattack intended to drive them back into the sea. The enemy probed many times with tanks, half-tracks, mortars, and infantry. Only the tenacity of the 15th Infantry soldiers, combined with terrific support from army artillery, naval gunfire, and Army Air Forces A-36 fighter-bombers, kept the enemy from overrunning the invaders. The 2nd Battalion spent the entire day and night roaming hilly country to the west of Brolo, but they could not find the pinned-down assault force. The 3rd Rangers and much of the rest of the 3rd Division also frantically forced their way east in hopes of being the first to relieve their buddies. The 1st Battalion of the 30th Regiment succeeded in doing so, thus ending a terrible ordeal for their brethren.

The Sicily campaign was winding down a bit and the 7th Infantry spent several days in division reserve. The Cottonbalers resumed their advance on the morning of August 15, once again following Highway 113. Enemy resistance mainly consisted of roadblocks and sniper fire, so the unit advanced several miles during the day, until it reached Spadafora, where the enemy made a stand. The 1st Battalion took the lead in attacking the town. The men of C Company walked down Highway 113, and as they approached the town German 88mm guns (hereafter referred to as "88s") opened up on them. These devastating guns could shoot with unbelievable accuracy and killing power. Knowing the Germans had zeroed their 88s in on the road, the Americans ran and dived for cover in ditches and along curves in the road.

Still, the German fire continued with deadly accuracy. Shrapnel flew everywhere. Rocks, gravel, and dust from the road made this situation even worse. Many soldiers felt the sting of shrapnel (steel and rock) penetrating their skin. The company commander, Captain Hugh Carico, showed his men where to find cover. Those who could walk quickly hastened to Carico's enclave. Soon 88 shells started falling uncomfortably close. German observers had clearly spotted Carico's move and were adjusting their fire. The captain left his spot and ferreted out new cover. He screamed at his men and waved them toward this new position, and as he did so, an enemy shell dropped in, exploded, and killed him instantly. The circumstances of Carico's death were eerily similar to those of his predecessor, Herman Wagner, earlier in the Sicily campaign.

Carico's executive officer, First Lieutenant Edward Busby, made sure the men followed Carico's dying wish—that they move to new positions affording them better cover. Busby waited for darkness and sent a patrol of riflemen into the town. These soldiers spread out into two single files. Nervously and apprehensively they inched their way into the edges of Spadafora. They knew the enemy was still there. They could feel the enemy's presence, perhaps even smell them. A more frightening situation could hardly be imagined.

An enemy tank and four machine guns opened fire. The shell from the tank hit one of the men right in the abdomen, literally blowing him into pieces of random flesh and crimson shreds. Many of those pieces splattered his buddies, who hurled themselves with lightning quickness into adjacent buildings. One man, a sergeant, had just found cover on the floor of a ruined house when someone fell on top of him. Annoyed, he turned to chastise the clumsy man, only to see that the klutz was his dead lieutenant; a machine-gun bullet had blown off most of his head.

The unfortunate soldiers from this patrol were pinned down most of the night, along with the rest of C Company back under cover. They had run into a strong enemy roadblock, but the Germans did not have enough troops to sufficiently defend the town from American reinforcements. Colonel Moore sent the rest of his battalion on a flanking move to the south of Spadafora. They entered the town, via another route, during the dead of night, in pitch-blackness, and the Germans, clearly spooked, retreated east.

This proved to be the last major resistance the 7th Infantry faced in front of Messina. Weathering sporadic artillery and sniper fire from a few die-hard members of the Hermann Göring Division, the 7th

Infantry closed in on Messina. All three battalions had patrols sniffing around the town's approaches. These patrols generally consisted of squad-sized groups, led by lieutenants or sergeants, who skulked along the flanks of the roads leading into Messina, gauging the level and strength of any remaining enemy resistance. Other American units, in addition to the British, were closing in on the town. Patton, thirsting for glory and yearning to outshine his hated rival Montgomery, wanted to capture Messina as quickly as possible.

As at Palermo, Heintges's 3rd Battalion won the glittering prize for him. A patrol led by L Company's Lieutenant Yates, one of Heintges's favorite officers, entered the town first: "He was my best patrol leader. He was so good I just couldn't spare him. Yates came back and declared that the road was clear. There were several minefields on the road, but they were easily discernible, and my engineers would have no problem getting rid of them." Just as Heintges and his men were preparing to go into Messina, Patton himself showed up: "A whole cavalcade of automobiles, trucks and command cars came up, and here's Patton in the lead command car with his two pearl handled pistols, brown leather jacket, standing up in his command car. I had all kinds of tanks, TD's [tank destroyers] and machine guns set up. I talked to General Patton and he wanted to know whether the road was clear." Heintges replied in the affirmative and Patton "just takes off and all the other vehicles follow him."[53] The general entered Messina and basked in his moment of glory. In the meantime, most of the surviving German garrison had escaped to the mainland to fight again another day.

During the early-morning hours of August 17, the remainder of the 7th Regiment entered the town, amid vastly different circumstances than they had encountered at Palermo. Sergeant Pratt described what he saw: "We passed through a few buildings that appeared to be normal except that the people just sat and stared at us, as though they were stunned. From that spot on, every block and building we passed had been completely leveled by aerial bombardment. Down street after street we picked our way through the debris and around bomb craters and wrecked vehicles. The picture was one of desertion and desolation. Nowhere did we see any signs of life . . . not even a cat or a dog."[54] The regiment occupied Messina for two days before moving back to training areas in western Sicily.

The campaign was over. The capture of Sicily took thirty-eight days and cost the 7th Infantry 635 casualties: 149 killed, 6 missing, and 480 wounded. Combat fatigue rates, never recorded, undoubtedly claimed dozens more, as did malaria and heat-related problems.[55]

THE ALLIED STRATEGIC PLAN NOW CALLED FOR AN INVA-sion of the Italian mainland. The Allies had hoped that the Sicily invasion would topple Mussolini from power, and this came to fruition on July 24 when his own Fascist Grand Council met and voted to depose him. The new government, under Marshal Pietro Badoglio, spent most of its time trying to negotiate some kind of honorable exit from the war. Badoglio and his retinue perceived these secret talks as a peace negotiation, while the Allies perceived them as surrender proceedings. In effect, they were neither, but they were much closer to the latter than the former. The Badoglio government and Eisenhower concluded an agreement on September 3, and Italy was removed from the Axis side. This "surrender" really only meant two things: First, Italy, instead of participating as a belligerent in the war, would become a battleground. Second, the Germans, having sniffed out Badoglio's intentions, occupied Italy like any other conquered state. For American and British combat soldiers, Italy's surrender actually proved to be a grim and unwelcome development, because they were now sure to face tough, determined German opposition all the way up the Italian boot.

In early September, British troops crossed the Strait of Messina and invaded the toe of the Italian boot at Reggio di Calabria. They also came ashore in the crook of the boot, closer to Taranto in the east. The Germans, having extricated most of their troops from Sicily, had not yet forged a cohesive defensive line in Italy, so they gave ground steadily to the British veterans, many of whom had been fighting since the early days of the North African campaign three years earlier. In the meantime, the Allies organized an amphibious invasion, composed of two British infantry divisions, two American infantry divisions, plus Commandos and Rangers, to invade the southwest Italian coast at the seaside resort of Salerno, located at the very limit of the range of Allied air cover. The plan at Salerno was to capture the port, push inland, link up with the British 8th Army, and then turn north in a concentrated drive on Naples and, if things went well, Rome.[56]

The 3rd Division had led the two previous Mediterranean invasions, but not this one. The Marne soldiers stayed in Sicily in reserve. The men continued their usual training routine, going on mountain hikes, patrolling roads, policing up the battlefields, and the like. The soldiers got a chance to rest, sample the local wines, chase the local girls, and eat decent food. "I had the mess tents set up," Heintges recalled, "and we had constant hot coffee, drinks, sandwiches, and so forth. My soldiers could go to the mess hall anytime and get a sandwich, a piece of cake, or something like that."57

In the meantime, American and British soldiers went ashore at Salerno on September 8 and ended up fighting for their lives against powerful German counterattacks. The tenacity of the ordinary soldier, combined with excellent support from Allied air, naval, and armored forces, saved the beachhead at Salerno. On September 13, the high command called upon the 3rd Division to reinforce the beachhead. The troops descended on Palermo, hurriedly loading up their LCIs and LSTs. Because of their experience and training, they were well prepared for this quick call to amphibious arms. They had done this many times before and they would do it many times again. The 30th Infantry led the way for the division on September 19, and the 7th, secured aboard nine LCIs and three LSTs, followed late in the afternoon of that day. The journey took less than twenty-four hours. By now Allied troops had secured the Salerno beachhead and moved inland, so the Cotton-balers landed without incident on the twentieth and immediately hiked to an assembly area near Battiplaglia.

Troops from the 30th served as the vanguard for the 3rd Division, capturing the town of Acerno. The Cottonbalers spent several days simply following in their wake and getting used to the mountainous terrain of southern Italy. The steep hills, winding passes, and gorges common to this area made any kind of movement difficult. Tanks, trucks, jeeps, and artillery pieces jammed up on the tiny, inadequate roads. The Germans blew up bridges and parts of roads. In response, the 10th Engineers of the 3rd Division worked construction miracles, erecting new bridges, restoring roads, sweeping mines, and filling in shell holes. Their work was superb, but it wasn't enough. In this tangled logistical mess, the lead companies of the regiment quickly outpaced their supplies. Pack mules proved to be the best way to resupply them. Day and night, these sturdy animals and their handlers could be seen negotiating their way along the roads and mountains. Suffice to say, this scene would have been familiar to Cottonbalers from the frontier or Spanish-American war eras.

The Germans were conducting a fighting retreat. They wanted to delay the Allies while they set up strong defensive lines along the

Volturno River and, farther north, along the formidable mountains of the Cassino area. "Enemy resistance throughout consisted of typical delaying tactics featuring demolitions, mines, occasional booby traps, counter-patrolling, small unit counterattacks, and liberal use of machine gun, machine pistol, and mortar fire," the regimental after action report stated. For two weeks in late September and early October, the infantrymen of the 7th steadily, and arduously, worked their way north against this harassing opposition. Captain Rosson explained the way the unit would advance: "For the most part, we had two battalions advancing roughly abreast along high ground. We generally attempted to 'crown the heights' as our basic scheme of maneuver, taking advantage of observation we could gain [in] this fashion. And, the enemy, in addition to interdicting the trails and small roads, also operated on the heights so there wasn't any area in which we could flow easily."[58]

The division's advance was relentless, giving the Germans no opportunity to rest or set up strong defensive positions in the division's area. "We moved day and night," Heintges said. "We either had two regiments attacking during the day and one at night, or one during the day and two at night. And, most of the time . . . it was through mountainous terrain and you'd be surprised how we moved at night. We moved single file." Heintges often walked with the lead company, "about the middle of the company with the company commander. We would be in single file, and everybody holding on to everybody else all the way back through the battalion. That was the only possible way you could move a battalion at night through this rugged terrain. We had to find little trails, and sometimes we had to make our own trails. And this, of course, was good because this confused the Germans so much."[59]

More than anything, the advance to the Volturno that fall was an endurance test. Eating nothing but K and C rations, supplied with very little drinking water, clad in wool olive-drab uniforms that were hot in the day and nowhere near warm enough at night, carrying heavy packs, extra ammunition, and their weapons, the soldiers trudged along trails and tiny mountain roads, usually uphill, in the face of a determined enemy. The typical 7th infantryman also participated in patrols two or three times a week.

The very concept of a patrol was quite simple, and quite discomfiting for those who carried them out. Rather than risk sending the entire unit into an area the commanding officer wished to know more about, he sent a smaller, more expendable group to gather information or carry out specific missions. Unspoken, but always lurking beneath the surface, was that expendability; the few could be sacrificed for the good of the many. During the advance to the Volturno, most patrols were of the reconnaissance variety; in other words, you left your unit with about a dozen other men and humped around in enemy territory, trying to ascertain where the enemy was or what they might be planning. This kind of duty tested the nerves of even the most stouthearted soldiers. If they didn't come back, or if they returned with casualties, commanders, in a sense, had found out what they wanted to know, namely, that the enemy was strong in a particular area. Naturally, that proved small comfort to the men who did the patrolling.

In late September, the rains came, adding immeasurable misery to the life of the dogface Cottonbalers in the mountains and valleys of Italy. "The nights became colder," Sergeant Pratt wrote, "and the miserable Italian rainy season set in with all its cruelty. Troops stayed wet much of the time. Illnesses associated with cold and damp exposures skyrocketed. The already bad road conditions worsened as heavy military vehicles turned the thin asphalt or dirt road ways into soupy and deep quagmires of bottomless mud."[60]

The very notion of staying dry seemed like something out of a distant dream. Electrical storms crackled and boomed, pouring rain on the already drenched soldiers. Muddy boots and clothing became a way of life. Soldiers struggled to keep their weapons clean in this messy atmosphere. A man would no sooner finish oiling and cleaning his Garand when a truck would drive by and splash muddy water on it, or the rifle would brush against someone's muddy fatigue jacket. The men had no choice but to resign themselves to a filthy existence. Everywhere they walked they dealt with mud and soggy earth. Their uniforms smelled musty and they could feel lice crawling around their armpits and heads. They grew mud-spattered shadow beards and spit out pieces of earth every time they had to take cover. Many of them struggled with trench foot. Whenever they took their boots off, they could see their feet flaking away, dying before their very eyes. Dry socks helped somewhat, but they were a rare commodity. Nor did they last for long. A soldier would experience the pleasure of dry socks for all of five minutes until the next puddle or mud hole turned the socks into nothing more than slimy abettors of trench foot.[61]

After two weeks of this Italian endurance test, the 7th Regiment caught a break. On October 4, the men climbed aboard trucks and motored to Montesarchio. German planes strafed the convoy, shooting up two trucks and wounding several men, but most men were too exhausted to care. The trucks dropped them off and the infantrymen slogged to a hidden assembly area east of Caserta. They pitched tents, under careful camouflage, and ate hot food for the first time in two weeks. The rain continued, but at least now the soldiers had the benefits of the meager shelter their tents provided. They also received new uniforms, field jackets, and raincoats. For one week, the bulk of the 7th Infantry laid low in this assembly area. The rest was only a prelude, though, to the regiment's biggest mission in the war so far—spearheading the Allied crossing of the Volturno River.

By October 6, the Allies had forged a continuous front from the Tyrrhenian Sea in the west to the Adriatic Sea in the east. They now controlled the toe, heel, and ankle of the Italian boot, including the port city of Naples. The Germans had made them pay in blood and time for these gains. Now the enemy set up a strong line along the natural barrier of the Volturno and its accompanying mountains. The Germans planned to hold this line as long as they could. Alexander, still in command of the 15th Army Group, ordered an offensive across the Volturno. His armies were divided into two major sectors: the British 8th Army in the east and the 5th Army commanded by Lieutenant General Mark Clark. The 5th Army consisted of the British X Corps and the American VI Corps, under Major General John Lucas. The 3rd Division, along with the 36th and 45th, belonged to the VI Corps. The 36th and 45th were both fine units, but Clark knew that the 3rd was his best and most experienced. Besides, the river crossing amounted to an amphibious invasion and the Marne division certainly fit the bill for that mission.[62]

Truscott met with his regimental commanders on October 8 and assigned the 7th Infantry the mission of leading the crossing. One of the company commanders, Captain Orrin A. Tracy, described the terrain challenges the Volturno area posed: "The Volturno River['s] intensely cultivated farm valley is from two to seven miles wide with the exception of Triflisco Gap, just above the city of Capua. Triflisco Gap is . . . narrow. The Volturno is from 150 to 200 feet wide in a well defined and winding channel. The depth of the river along this section varies from 4 to 8 feet in depth. At this time of the year . . . it was the rainy season and the river was close to its flood peak with a heavy, swift current." Hills ranging in height from four to six hundred meters flanked either side of the river, but mostly open fields and farms dominated the southern and northern approaches to the Volturno. "The . . . river winds between highly cultivated fields. In the center of this area the river makes a hairpin loop to the north. The loop is nearly a mile in length. The distance between the river channels at its neck is 300 yards. With the exception of a few small dips in the ground and the stream beds, the valley offers no cover of any kind. Two hard surfaced highways run through the center of the valley from Triflisco toward the north."[63]

Naturally, the Germans blew every intact bridge across the river. They mined and booby-trapped the natural approaches to the Volturno, zeroed their artillery in on natural crossing sites, and dug machine-gun and infantry positions all along the riverbank. Self-propelled guns and tanks moved from place to place. When the Americans attempted their crossing, these tanks and guns would rake them over with shells. The troops opposing the 7th Infantry were none other than their old antagonists, the superbly equipped Hermann Göring Division. This unit had been replenished and reconstituted with high-quality replacements after the Sicilian campaign.

Immediately the 7th Infantry's battalion commanders began intensive patrolling along the Volturno. The problem was that the south bank was not entirely in American hands. Instead, it was a kind of no-man's-land in which German and American patrols searched around, mostly at night, attempting to ascertain the intentions of each other. In order to scout and gather information on the approaches, depth, and banks of the river, the Americans had to pass through open, partially mined areas that were crawling with enemy patrols.

But the job needed to be done and it needed to be done well. Truscott even ordered the battalion commanders to lead patrols themselves so that they knew the terrain and the river firsthand. Lieutenant Colonel Heintges spent some time hidden in the mountains overlooking the river, scouting his attack zone below. Then he led a group of more than twenty soldiers on a night patrol: "We went down to the river bank, and we snooped around and fortunately, we didn't run into any enemy fire. There were Germans on our side of the river. We knew that, but we managed to avoid them until at one point where we got very close to a hairpin curve in the river which was in my zone. They made the mistake of firing at us. Well, we had artillery fire. We had mortar fire. We had everything ready to go. We had pre-registered concentrations all along the river, and all we had to do was call for . . . whatever we had." His artillery observer called in the coordinates he wanted, and the shells soon blasted away at the Germans. Heintges said that this great fire support gave him a "terrifically good feeling."

This was the fruition of the American twentieth-century combat philosophy: expend bullets, not bodies. In an overall cultural sense, human life—individual Americans—meant far more to American policy makers than matériel. The latter could be expended to protect and aid the former. This philosophy proved its wisdom many times over, both in the saving of casualties and in its contribution to victories. The combination of well-trained American infantrymen, fighting with the help of a lethal retinue of supporting firepower, proved to be quite a potent team.

Thanks to his artillery support, Heintges and his patrol worked their way down into the river and gathered vital information. "We knew where the shallow places were across the river, where we could wade across. And, we determined . . . that there were three crossing places and all we needed were long ropes and some guy to go across with a rope and tie it to a tree. Then . . . we would just walk across the water." Heintges even sampled the water himself. "In the place where I crossed the water came up to my neck, but by holding on to the rope for just a few feet, it dipped down and then you went back up again." They exited the river and walked back to the bivouac area, where Heintges broke out four bottles of rum. They enjoyed a few drinks, changed clothes, ate a decent meal, and finalized their plans.[64]

The 2nd Battalion patrols did not go quite as smoothly. The battalion commander, Major Everett Duvall, had recently been promoted and given this command. His patrol ran into real problems. He took his staff, his company commanders, and a rifle squad with him. They assembled in the early afternoon on the forward slopes of Mount Castellone, a 405-meter peak that sloped almost into the river. Soldiers on observation duty, concealed in the brush of Mount Castellone, warned Duvall's group that enemy patrols were operating close to the river. For an hour they stayed on well-worn trails leading in the direction of the Volturno. This kept them under cover, but it also obscured any view of their river-crossing zone. They kept pressing on until they got to the bottom of the hill. Duvall sent the rifle squad to the right to provide flanking security for his officers and him. The riflemen crept away, taking care to stay low in the brush.

Duvall peeked through the underbrush and realized that he had underestimated the distance to the river. They still needed to cover several hundred yards to get to the river. The major glanced around at his officers and pointed ahead: "Let's go." They pressed ahead, out of the underbrush and into a stand of woods. Seconds later, Duvall noticed movement. He glanced in the direction of the movement and his stomach did somersaults. There, only a few yards away, three German soldiers stood staring, their weapons pointing right at his officers and him. The Germans had set a trap and Duvall had led his men right into it. The Americans had no choice but to surrender. The Germans stripped them of their weapons and began marching them toward the river and captivity. They entered more underbrush and one of Duvall's officers began to study the uniform of the guard he was following. He wore the standard field gray tunic, with suspenders, coal scuttle helmet, and knee-high boots, but something else caught the American officer's attention. The enemy soldier had a potato masher grenade wedged in his belt, roughly parallel to his hip. The officer sidled up to the German and, in one quick motion, pulled the string in the grenade, arming it. Stunned and terrified, the German soldier fumbled with the grenade, but to no avail. It blew up and ripped open his abdomen. He bled to death in seconds.

Meanwhile the other Americans turned around and took off running as fast as they could. The Germans screamed and opened fire. All of the American officers got away except the F Company commander, an engineer platoon leader, and the battalion intelligence officer. Those three officers either got killed or passed into captivity.

After this disaster, Duvall sent another small patrol out (manned entirely by enlisted men this time) that night. They ran into a strong enemy patrol a mile short of the river. The two sides spent much of the night shooting at each other and then went their separate ways. Duvall still did not have the information he so badly needed.

Second Lieutenant Harold Sandler, a young, very brave, antitank platoon leader, helped change that situation. A German-speaking Jew with a serious grudge against the Nazis, Sandler volunteered to lead a patrol to find a crossing site. On October 9 he took two good swimmers and a platoon from F Company to Mount Tifata. In total, he had twenty-two men. They spent the entire day on the mountain, in pouring rain, studying the terrain. At nightfall, they set out for the river, using the same route the battalion commander had taken. Three men carried BARs and the rest had Thompson submachine guns. The Thompsons gave them nice, body-stopping firepower especially effective at close range, in case they bumped into a German patrol.

The rain had not stopped. It came down in torrents, drenching the patrol members, making it even more difficult to see in a pitch-black night. This situation, in a sense, summed up the brutal and awful reality of American twentieth-century war. Each man was far away from home, in a country he knew little about, and each man was scared to death, soaked to the skin, cold, shivering, trying to stay alert and not give in to self-pity. Most likely each one of them, with the possible exception of Sandler, wished he were somewhere else—anywhere else.

They safely negotiated their way to the horseshoe of the river, but then a German patrol opened fire. They returned fire and kept moving. This happened several times, but they finally reached the south bank of the Volturno. The soldiers took up covering positions and kept watch in the direction of the German fire. Sandler handed his weapon to one of his men, stripped down to his shorts and T-shirt, and plunged into the river. He splashed about twenty feet into the water until the swift current swept him away. But Sandler was a fine swimmer, and in the middle of this nasty, rainy night and dark river he found his bearings and swam to the opposite bank about fifty yards downstream. The bank was fifteen feet high and covered with blackberry bushes and vines. Somehow he managed to hoist himself up the bank and onto the opposite side. He encountered no enemy soldiers and scouted in several directions. Then he returned to the river and took several soundings, discovering that, with the aid of a rope, a normal man could cross the river. He swam back across the river and the patrol made its way safely back to the American lines.

Amazingly, Sandler did not believe he had accomplished his mission and requested permission to take another patrol out the next night. The weather cleared, removing the discomfort of rain, but the men discovered a new peril—moonlight. The moonlight reflected off men and silhouetted them for over one hundred yards. They crawled through drainage ditches and made their way to the horseshoe. Sandler and two picked swimmers left the main group and slithered toward the river. The earth smelled rich and musty beneath them. They could hear the river rushing past, splashing and squishing. They could also hear German voices on this quiet night. The three American swimmers quietly slid into the river. Sandler took soundings while the two enlisted men, Private First Class Russell Brannon and Private Olegario Valenzuela, swam to the north bank. They had just ascended the bank when German voices challenged them. They froze and the Germans opened fire. Brannon was hit and fell back into the river, never to be seen again. Valenzuela dived into the river and swam back to the south bank, along with Sandler. They rejoined their patrol and, in a harrowing retreat, fought their way back to the American lines, incurring several more casualties from enemy small-arms fire.

This happened on the night of October 10 and, originally, the attack was scheduled for the next day, but it was delayed for twenty-four hours because the heavy rains had impeded necessary troop movements in the British X Corps sector. This gave the 2nd Battalion an opportunity for another night of reconnaissance. Once again, Sandler swam the river and gleaned useful information about its depth and current. Then he did something absolutely astounding. He led his men to the exact spot on the horseshoe where the Americans had exchanged shots with Germans the night before. He told them to take cover some fifty yards shy of the riverbank. Then he crept forward at a crouch, with one hand scuffling along the ground, apelike, and the other clutching his Thompson. His men watched in stunned silence as he stood up, in full view of the Germans, and started taunting them in their own language. "I can lick half of the German Army myself!!" he roared. To punctuate his bravado, he fired a burst from his tommy gun. Enemy machine guns opened fire, but by then Sandler had hit the dirt and crawled back to his men. He led them back to their bivouac. They ate a pancake breakfast together and a kind of collective shocked silence prevailed. Finally, one of the men got up the nerve to ask, "Lieutenant, why in hell did you do such a damn fool thing?" The slightest hint of a grin crossed Sandler's face. "Now I know where all of the enemy guns are located."[65]

Thanks to the efforts of courageous men such as Sandler, Valenzuela, Brannon, and many others, the regiment formulated detailed, informed attack plans for the crossing, now scheduled for the evening of October 12–13. Indeed, Truscott later wrote a tribute to that effect, referring to these men as the "real heroes of the Volturno crossings. Men who waded alone across a flood-swollen river two hundred feet wide, never knowing when they might sink over their heads in the icy water or when the crack of an enemy rifle would spell sudden death; men who had to lie helpless and shivering on a muddy bank and watch a comrade be shot as he struggled with the current. It was grim work." He estimated that each man who lost his life on these patrols saved the lives of hundreds of others.[66]

Colonel Sherman knew that the Germans had to be kept guessing as to where his regiment would cross the river. His final plan called for elements of the 15th and 30th Infantry Regiments to open fire on the left, at the Triflisco Gap, fixing German attention over there while the 1st and 2nd Battalions of his 7th Infantry crossed the river at the horseshoe, followed by the 3rd in reserve. Tanks and tank destroyers would provide fire support at the banks of the river (the commanders were deeply worried about counterattacks by German armor), as would various mortar units. The infantrymen planned to cross the river mainly by the rope method Heintges mentioned. But they also received orders to bring along rubber pontoon boats borrowed from the engineers and rafts borrowed from the Navy. These craft would be used mainly for resupplying the men once they forded the river. Secrecy and surprise were of paramount importance. In a general sense, the enemy knew a river crossing was imminent, of course, but did not know—and must not know—the time and location of the actual crossing.[67]

As the sun set on October 12 and the moon rose, a tense silence pervaded the Volturno River in the 3rd Division's area. Back in their bivouacs, the men of the 7th Infantry left their tents, grabbed their weapons, and moved out, just after midnight. Many of them had to carry the pontoon boats and rafts several miles to the river, because the senior officers did not want to take the slightest chance that the Germans might spot the boats in daylight. This meant that the infantrymen, already burdened with too much ammunition and equipment, had to drag and haul these heavy boats through soft, muddy, plowed fields all the way to the river. This would never work. Orders or no orders, they abandoned the boats in the fields. No matter how strong and well-conditioned, they could not drag these awkward things to the river and still have any energy left for an attack; just walking through these sticky fields was bad enough.

At midnight they heard the 15th and 30th Regiments, along with the division's artillery, open up with everything they had. Tracers streaked through the air and 155mm shells exploded all over the place on the opposite bank. The mortar teams laid down smoke rounds to further confuse the Germans. The Germans fired back, but as yet, they had no targets.

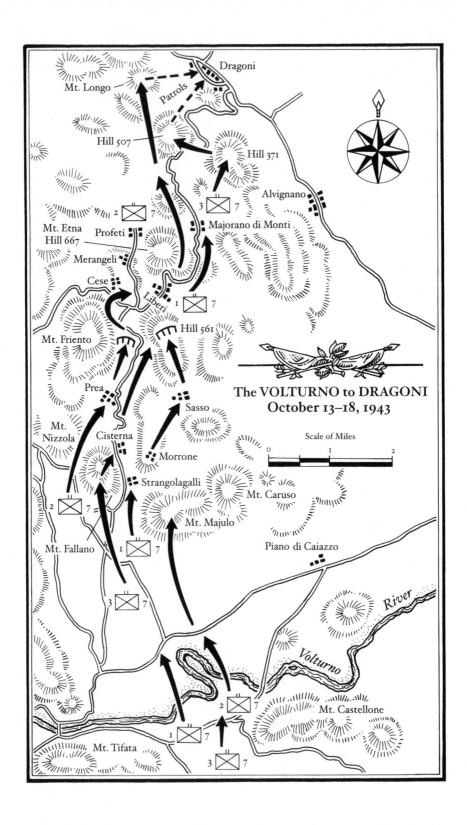

Dragoni

Mt. Longo

Patrols

Hill 507

Hill 371

Alvignano

2 ☒ 7

3 ☒ 7

Mt. Etna
Hill 667

Profeti

Majorano di Monti

Merangeli

Cese

Liberi   I ☒ 7

Mt. Friento

Hill 561

Prea

Sasso

Mt.
Nizzola

Cisterna

Morrone

2 ☒ 7

Strangolagalli

Mt. Caruso

Mt. Fallano   I ☒ 7

Mt. Majulo

Piano di Caiazzo

3 ☒ 7

River

Volturno

2 ☒ 7

Mt. Castellone

I ☒ 7

3 ☒ 7

Mt. Tifata

The **VOLTURNO** to **DRAGONI**
October 13–18, 1943

Scale of Miles

0   1   2

Soon they did. The operation, as always, came down to the infantry moving forward and capturing ground. The Cottonbalers trotted and slithered their way forward, taking cover in drainage ditches (slimy and smelly as can be) and furrows in the ground. Reaching the river, the lead assault troops boarded what few boats had been successfully carried this far and set up rope lines, fastening them into thick trees or muddy embankments. There were a few problems getting these ropes secured, but within minutes both attacking battalions succeeded in doing so. "The ropes were placed about twenty-five yards apart, and each platoon was assigned a rope," one soldier in C Company, the lead unit, recalled. "The men all had kapok life belts to assist in the crossing, and by using the ropes, they were able to cross in the swift current at this point. We lost no men by drowning on the crossing by the ropes." In columns, company by company, the soldiers of both battalions plunged into the river, fended off the chill of the water, and forded their way to the opposite bank. Machine guns from the heavy-weapons companies, dug into positions on the south bank, covered them with intermittent fire. This forced enemy troops to duck their heads. Covered by their comrades and the darkness, the soldiers of the assault companies crossed the river with relative speed.

In spite of the quick crossing, the scene on the northern riverbank was borderline chaotic. Flinching from enemy machine-gun fire (spitting out white and green tracers with terrifying frequency), the soldiers clustered along small sandbars and huddled beneath the bank of the river. Unfortunately, the enemy had mined the banks and the men found this out the hard way. Muffled explosions erupted along the riverbank as mines detonated. The sounds of the explosions mixed with the screams of the wounded and dying. The mines shredded torsos, blew off feet and hands. Thankfully, some of the mines did little damage. The recent rains had sunk these mines deep into the muck, and when they exploded they did nothing more harmful than kick up geysers of mud and sediment. German artillery shells began to drop into the river, splashing fountains of water, creating the feel of a thunderstorm. Wrecked and overturned boats littered the water and the banks. Tracers, American and German, flew crazily in the night. Scared groups of men huddled together under cover of the banks. Some of them got hit by shrapnel from German artillery. Cottonbalers were screaming and cursing, for no apparent reason, perhaps only because they could do so in the vulgar, out-of-control world of combat.

In the words of one 7th infantryman, the men knew that they had to get out of the river, up the bank, and inland as soon as possible: "The men waded the river holding their rifles over their heads with one hand and clinging tightly to the guide ropes with the other to keep from being swept off their feet by the current. Scrambling up the muddy bank, they went after the enemy machine gunners."

The enemy gunners laid down a wall of fire. Their MG-42 machine guns could spew out as many as twelve hundred rounds per minute. Many of the American soldiers ran afoul of these awful weapons. When hit, they fell down, clutched at their wounds, and screamed for medics. German mortar shells added to their misery. In this kind of murderous situation, soldiers only have three options. They can run away, surrender, or go forward and kill the enemy. Led by courageous sergeants, the Cottonbalers that night chose the third option. One sergeant in C Company led his men, at a trot, within grenade distance of an enemy machine gun. Suddenly a German potato masher grenade came spinning out of the darkness and landed at the feet of two soldiers. It exploded, wounding both of them. The sergeant immediately charged into the brush, firing his rifle, and killed the enemy grenadier. He then led the remnants of his squad to within spitting distance of the gun. They unleashed a hail of rifle fire at the gun crew, killing several Germans and prompting the rest to surrender.

Another C Company sergeant saw his platoon leader shot into mincemeat by a German machine gun. The sergeant had tripped a mine that sent shrapnel into his legs and hands, but he kept going. Acting as the platoon leader, he cajoled and threatened his men enough that they moved away from the riverbank and closed with the enemy gun. A mortar shell landed near the sergeant, adding to his wounds. He was bleeding profusely now but screamed at the men, "Come on! We've still got a machine gun to knock out up there!" The soldiers shot up the enemy gun, and the sergeant collapsed from loss of blood. Medics hauled him back to the south side of the river and evacuated him.[68]

On that desperate, confusing night, this kind of on-the-spot leadership provided the margin of victory. It went on everywhere, among lieutenants, sergeants, and privates too. Before the sun had even risen, soldiers from the 2nd Battalion pushed north and captured their unit's key objective, Mount Majulo. Only friendly artillery stopped them from advancing any farther. Most of the 3rd Battalion crossed the river and showed up just to the left of Mount Majulo, making contact with the 2nd Battalion troops. They knocked out everything that was in their path and bypassed what wasn't. By daylight, the 7th Regiment was across the river, engineers were busily working on a bridge (under intense enemy artillery fire), and tank destroyers had pulled up to the south bank of the Volturno to support the infantry on the other side.

All of this was good, but could the tired infantrymen hold off the inevitable German counterattack? The answer to that question came at midday on the thirteenth when six German tanks attacked a mixed group of F Company (2nd Battalion) and K Company (3rd Battalion) troops just to the left of Mount Majulo. Few things could be more terrifying to infantrymen than facing enemy tanks at close range, but these troops found themselves doing just that, and with no tank support of their own, since the tank destroyers and tanks on the south side of the river were out of range.

The German tanks, unaccompanied by infantry, rumbled ever closer; five hundred yards away, three hundred yards away, one hundred yards away. They fired their main guns at the Americans and then advanced. Thundering explosions shook the Cottonbaler positions as the tank shells slammed home, spraying dirt, rocks, and steel fragments in every direction. Several men were killed and wounded. No one shot at the tanks. It would have been futile and would only have attracted the Germans' vengeance.

In high-pitched, terror-driven screams, soldiers called for bazookas, but between the two companies they had only one. The rest had been lost in the crossing. The lone bazooka team, belonging to K Company, scuttled to within range of the lead enemy tank. The bazooka was actually a bit of an awkward weapon. Five feet long and weighing twenty pounds, it fired a 2.36-inch rocket and required a two-man crew. The loader shoved the projectile into the back of the tube, armed it, tapped the gunner on the shoulder, and then got out of the way of the ensuing back blast when the gunner pulled the trigger. The weapon could penetrate German armor but only from close, exceedingly dangerous range. By and large, it proved to be a better pillbox and urban assault weapon than an antitank weapon. But, right now, K Company's lone bazooka was the best hope of survival for 250 scared and desperate men.

The K Company bazooka team unleashed a shot that penetrated the lead tank's armor and blew up, lighting the tank on fire. The crew either burned to death or abandoned the tank. The K Company men displaced to a new position, but as they did so, the Germans exacted their revenge. Another tank fired a shell at the bazooka team and scored a direct hit. The two men, flesh-and-blood human beings with hopes and dreams, in a matter of a nanosecond turned into nothing more than bloody particles scattered on the Italian landscape. Their bazooka also was ripped to shreds.

The infantry now had nothing left with which to fend off the tanks. Now they could only hope to attack the steel monsters on their sides (away from their machine guns) and drop grenades into portholes, hatches, or treads. Of course, the German tankers did not know they had knocked out the only bazooka in front of them. With no supporting infantry, they had to proceed very carefully and remain wary of other bazooka teams. Minute by minute, they edged closer, firing their cannons and machine guns and exacting a terrible toll of casualties. Then, almost as if out of a dream, U.S. artillery began dropping around the tanks. If a shell hit a tank at the right angle, it could blow the tank up, and the tank crews knew this. After several minutes of shelling, they threw their gears into reverse and retreated. Once again, artillery had proven to be a savior for embattled infantrymen.[69]

The failure of the German tank counterattack figuratively ended any hope they had of destroying the 7th Infantry's Volturno River crossing. The engineers finished their bridge and by the late afternoon tanks, trucks, and troops were pouring across the river. By evening the bulk of the 3rd Division was across. The 34th Infantry Division, to the right of the 3rd, also successfully crossed, as did the British 46th Infantry Division along the sea. The Germans now had little choice but to lapse back into the "fighting retreat" mode.

GENERAL CLARK WAS SO HAPPY WITH THE 7TH REGIment's work in crossing the Volturno that he personally called Colonel Sherman to congratulate him. However, the Cottonbalers still had a lot of fighting ahead of them. On October 14, just one day after the crossing, Truscott called Sherman and gave him orders for a new axis of advance, due north, along a dirt track road to Liberi and then to the ultimate objective, Dragoni. Once again, the terrain would be hilly and rough. Sherman moved his regiment out in columns, the 3rd Battalion in the lead, followed by the 2nd and the 1st. He hoped to nab Liberi that night.

At 1645, the 3rd Battalion, supported by tank destroyers, moved out. They immediately ran into enemy machine-gun, small-arms, and anti-tank fire, but this problem was quickly solved when a squad leader and his men ran off the road, under fire, and maneuvered close to the enemy positions. With grenades, rifles, and BARs they killed five enemy troops and wounded two others. This opened the way for the column to continue.

Within a mile, the 3rd Battalion ran into more serious resistance at a stone village called Cisterna, located at the foot of Mount Fallano. Enemy troops and tanks, holed up in the town, protected by the stone buildings, unleashed terrific fire on the men of the 3rd. These men took cover while their supporting tanks and tank destroyers came up and traded shots with the enemy. The stalemate lasted all night. Sherman realized that only flanking attacks would break this deadlock, so at midnight he sent the 2nd Battalion to the left and then the 1st Battalion to the right the next morning. The troops of these units edged their way north over mountains, ridges, and ledges. Troops from the 2nd Battalion ran into enemy armor and had to expend many rounds of bazooka ammunition to persuade the German tanks to withdraw.

These enveloping attacks over forbidding ground succeeded in threatening to surround the Germans in Cisterna. Even so, the enemy was still firmly ensconced in the town on the morning of the fifteenth. Peeking from second-floor windows, German artillery observers called in accurate fire on the 3rd Battalion soldiers and the tankers still spread out around the road in front of the town. Lieutenant Colonel Heintges was standing in the sunken, muddy road, with rocks on his right and a field to his left. He heard German shells approaching and saw them explode fifty yards to his left. The rounds wiped out the better part of a mortar team. Dismembered, some of them convulsed violently for a few seconds until they lay still, dead. Several other men were wounded, hollering for medics.

Before Heintges could even react, more shells screamed in, right on top of the position where he stood talking with his communications lieutenant. "We hit the ground and . . . this shell hit—a couple of shells, boom, boom—just like that. And when those shells hit one of them knocked a wall of rock which came down, and one piece of rock hit me on the back, a pretty big rock. I'd say it weighed 30 to 40 pounds. Phillips [the communications lieutenant] and I were just raised off the ground and then dropped again. Well, when the smoke cleared, I looked over at Phillips and he was bleeding like a stuck pig from the neck." The wound looked worse than it was. Heintges gave Phillips his handkerchief and the junior officer held it to his neck. "And, then I felt a little funny, and I looked down at my leg and there was blood coming through. I had gotten a couple of little fragments in my leg."

Heintges refused evacuation, requesting instead that a smoke round be dropped on Cisterna. Later, after this was done and the Germans withdrew from the town, he went back to the battalion aid station. The battalion surgeon removed the fragments and told Heintges he had a severely bruised back. The colonel walked around on crutches for a couple days and fought stiffness in his back.[70]

During the envelopment of Cisterna, the 1st Battalion on the morning of October 16 had captured a key piece of high ground known as Hill 561. Hill 561 commanded the approaches to Liberi. If the Americans controlled the hill, the Germans would have to abandon the town. Twice that morning the Germans counterattacked. The Americans drove them off the first time, but they came back half an hour later in greater strength. Heavily armed German infantrymen, supported by artillery, hurled themselves at the hill. They swarmed up the slope, right at the American foxholes. American bullets ripped through the summer field gray uniforms of some of them, but still they kept coming. An irresistibly violent force, they swept over the crest of the hill and slaughtered many of the Americans in their foxholes. Some Cottonbalers broke and ran away as fast as they could. Others played dead. Others kept fighting from positions the Germans could not master.

Within a few minutes, the enemy overran the forward positions of all three rifle companies. Enemy infantrymen could be seen working their way down the reverse slope of the hill. But the Cottonbalers had one more asset—D Company. This heavy-weapons company, commanded by Captain William Athas, fought as if possession of this hill would decide not just their own fate but also that of their families and homes. Athas and his people were dug into supporting positions just off the hill when the German attack hit. He watched as the enemy overran the hill and outflanked his prepared positions. He knew he had to displace his men as quickly as he could. He organized them into an improvised rifle team and led them to new positions right in the path of the German advance.

With nothing more than rifles and grenades they shot at the attackers. The enemy soldiers (often called "Landsers" in their own army) took cover and fired back, hitting several Americans. German shells were also falling in the area, sometimes within thirty yards of the captain, who kept screaming at his troops to displace and lay down fire. When a rifleman fell wounded, Athas grabbed his BAR and emptied a clip in the direction of the Germans. Three enemy soldiers went down.

Meanwhile, other men in Athas's company, on their own initiative, repositioned their machine guns and mortars. The gunners spewed deadly fire into the German attackers who could not locate the source of their tormentors. Many of them died trying to do so. The 81mm mortar team adjusted their tubes for the closest range possible and laid down fire almost on top of themselves. When they ran out of ammunition, they found German shells lying around and used them. When those ran out, they fought as riflemen.

The fight for Hill 561 lasted about an hour. Having absorbed terrible casualties, the Germans broke and withdrew, leaving many dead bodies in their wake. In fact, the hill was littered with the dead and dying of both sides. The 7th Infantry Regiment on that costly October 16 lost forty-five men killed and eighty-five wounded, a steep price for a chunk of Italian real estate. At least the hill remained in American hands. The next morning, the Germans withdrew from Liberi. The regiment captured Dragoni the following day.[71]

FOR THE REST OF OCTOBER, THE SLOW, STEADY, BLOODY advance continued, even as the conditions worsened. "Rain increased and temperatures dropped," Sergeant Pratt wrote, perhaps with an involuntary shudder at the memory. "Troops caught colds and flus and were . . . miserable. Hills got higher and frozen ground got harder. Digging for bunkers and foxholes was all but impossible." The postcard, travel-brochure notions of sunny Italy had given way to the everyday reality of a raw, unforgiving climate. The typical day featured temperatures in the midforties with overcast skies and rain. Sickness and combat fatigue eroded the ranks of the 7th, as did the rifleman's great enemy, trench foot.

Pratt did not get a bad case of trench foot, but several of his friends did. He visited them in the hospital one day and witnessed the true horror and tragedy of this malady of modern war: "Even if one could withstand the nauseating odor of dead flesh, the sight of long rows of hospital cots occupied by troops with exposed feet and legs in various stages of decomposition was enough to put most souls to instant flight. One of the fellows I visited . . . had his foot amputated and the stub of his lower leg lay unbandaged and in full view. Several patients . . . had thus far retained their feet, the toes were being treated with much of the flesh rotted away, leaving toe bones exposed and protruding from what flesh remained. The toe bones pointed to the ceiling of the tent like several short straws sticking in a wad of stale hamburger meat."[72]

The voracious machinery of war continued firing on all cylinders. The Allies kept pressing north, steadily pushing the Germans back to the Cassino, or Gustav Line, they planned to maintain all winter. There was nothing fancy about this Allied campaign. The British and Americans simply lined up their troops shoulder to shoulder and moved north, in bad weather, over mountainous terrain, against whatever opposition the Germans decided to pose. The 3rd Division's assignment in the continuation of this meat-grinder campaign was to press northwest against an enemy defensive system called the Barbara Line and seize the town of Presenzano and then a mountain gap called Mignano.

In early November, the 15th Infantry captured Presenzano. Truscott lined his regiments three abreast and sent them into the Mignano Gap, a valley honeycombed with several mountains. The 7th Regiment operated on the left, or western, side of the division. The Cottonbalers began their advance on November 5 and their battle with the Germans quickly degenerated into a brawl for control of the mountains. The 3rd Battalion planned a night attack on one such peak, Mount Friello, but then an Italian-speaking GI got talking to some of the local civilians. They told him that the Germans had heavily mined Friello. Sure enough, they had planted over three thousand S-mines, generally known to the troops as "Bouncing Betties" because, when tripped, they popped out of the ground and exploded crotch or chest high. Engineers came up and ferreted out the mines (a nerve-wracking, bloodcurdling job carried out in cold rain). The Cottonbalers promptly dubbed Friello "Mount Mine." The extensive mining of Friello demonstrated the resolve and resourcefulness of the Germans. The Cottonbalers were facing some of the best soldiers in the German Army.

The proof of that statement came during the fight for Mount La Difensa, a craggy ridge-and-ravine-strewn peak located just to the west of the Mignano Gap. Once again, the low ground could only be controlled by capturing the high ground. German troops on Mount La Difensa and its neighbor, Mount Camino, commanded the entire Mignano Gap and could rake the 3rd Division's advance with accurate artillery fire. The 2nd Battalion spent the better part of a week trying to wrest control of Mount La Difesa from ferocious, determined Hermann Göring Division troops.

On November 7 the 2nd Battalion attacked the two mountains and began a bitter struggle. The troops literally had to attack straight up steep, rocky slopes. In many cases, they had to hold on to ledges or boulders with two hands to keep from falling, all in the face of German mortar and small-arms fire. Coordinating with one another, the Cottonbalers picked their spots. Some men would concentrate on climbing, using rocks for cover, while others shot at the enemy. The Germans responded with mortar and machine-gun fire. The bullets sparked off rocks, and the mortar shells exploded along ledges, multiplying the shrapnel they produced.

Company F concentrated on La Difesa itself while G and E Companies struggled to control the saddle between Camino and its taller neighbor. The fighting was beyond belief, ledge to ledge, ravine to ravine, straight uphill for the Americans, straight downhill for the Germans. Entire squads were chewed up in a matter of seconds. Dead and wounded men lay everywhere. The blood from those who had been hit seeped into the rocky soil and stained boulders. At times, the enemy was close enough to touch.

For several days, the men clung to whatever ledges they could on the mountain, dealing with rain, cold, and the close proximity of the enemy. With the exception of some supporting mortar and antitank fire, they were on their own. American artillery could not risk shooting rounds so close to U.S. soldiers, in such hazy conditions. Those wounded men who could not walk had to be carried, laboriously, off the mountain, a process that took six hours. Nor could the troops be resupplied properly. At first, Sherman arranged for planes to drop supplies, but this did not work. The supplies dropped into gorges or into German lines and only alerted the enemy as to the location of the American positions. Any supplies going to Mount La Difesa had to be hand carried, an exhausting and demoralizing job, made very frustrating by the fact that the average man could not carry much, since he needed both hands to scale the ledges. So the riflemen subsisted on one meal per day, with almost no water, and hoped for the best.

On November 11 the Germans tried to push the 2nd Battalion off its tenuous perch. In the morning, just after sunrise, they opened fire with everything they had—mortars, machine guns, and rifles. Several Americans were hit. They cried and moaned as their comrades (brothers by now) clenched their jaws tight and angled for shelter from the fire. Du-vall saw that the German attack was succeeding and that his battalion might disintegrate at any moment. He left the relative safety of his battalion observation post and rushed around the ledges, leading men to cover and steeling their resolve by showing a command presence on this lonely, desolate battlefield. A German machine-gun round slashed through his leg, but still he kept going.

Duvall's actions stabilized the situation somewhat, but the Germans kept on coming. From only two hundred yards away, forty German sol-diers launched an attack against the left flank of Duvall's position, con-sisting of the remnants of E Company and one platoon of H Company, his heavy-weapons people. Under terrific fire that smashed many of the soldiers into pulp, many of the E Company riflemen and H Company machine gunners, terrified of what might happen next, retreated about 150 yards to safer positions. One of the gunners, Private First Class Floyd Lindstrom, refused to yield any ground and, in so doing, won an immortal place for himself in the history of the 7th Regiment.

One of Lindstrom's buddies, Private Marvin Crone, crouched behind a rock and watched Lindstrom behave like a man possessed: "Even though he saw the rifle company withdraw . . . Lindstrom . . . instantly and without orders . . . set up a defensive position and opened fire with his machine gun. The enemy fire became intense. Lindstrom insisted on moving forward alone another ten yards for a better field of fire. He picked up the machine gun bodily and moved up hill over the rocky ground with his one hundred twelve pound load. In doing this he be-came the direct target of machine gun and small arms fire from some of the enemy who weren't more than fifteen or twenty yards away. At least thirty-five hand grenades of the concussion variety were thrown at [him]. I could hear the Jerries yelling at him in pidgin English, 'American soldier—you give up—we treat you fine—you no surrender, plenty trou-ble.' Lindstrom answered, 'Go to hell!' and gave them another burst."

Lindstrom soon determined that the German attack would only suc-ceed if its supporting machine gun stayed intact. "He yelled at me to cover him with my rifle, that he was going to 'get that machine gun,' and armed only with [a] .45 caliber pistol . . . he frontally assaulted the ma-chine gun in a mad up-hill dash. The Germans saw him coming and let go a continuous stream of fire which kicked up dirt inches behind his heels as he ran at them. Somehow he miraculously escaped being hit by the continuous chain of automatic fire from the machine gun, got right on top of the gunners and shot them to death with his pistol." After killing the crew, he dragged their machine gun back to the American positions and then, for good measure, braved enemy fire once more to bring back two boxes of German ammo.

Turning the captured gun over to another American soldier, he went back to his own machine gun and kept laying down fire on the attacking Germans. In the memory of Corporal Nicholas Alfier, the enemy soon decided to quit: "Lindstrom's spectacular action and withering machine gun fire completely demoralized the Germans and their counter-attack seemed to disintegrate." Those members of E and H Companies who had originally fallen back in the face of this counterattack soon worked their way forward and offered to help, but there was nothing more to do. The Germans were gone.

Only maimed bodies, both American and German, strewn about the rocky face of the mountain bore testimony to the fight that had taken place. Lindstrom received the Medal of Honor for his exploits. He was the first Cottonbaler in World War II to earn the nation's highest medal. Most of his buddies thought it was a miracle that he survived the battle on Mount La Difensa that day. His officers later offered him a rear-area job while Congress considered his medal citation, but he declined, in the belief that he belonged with his unit. He stayed with H Company and paid the ultimate price for that choice. On February 3, 1944, he was killed in action while fighting off a German attack at Anzio.

The Cottonbalers spent a few more days on that hellish mountain and even tried one more attack. In spite of extensive artillery and mortar support, they got nowhere. The filthy, fatigued, hungry infantrymen could not scale a perpendicular sixty-foot-high cliff to get at the Germans. They were neither equipped nor trained for this kind of mission. They retreated back to their own positions. Truthfully, few of them cared much anymore. They had reached the limit of human mental and physical endurance. They had seen too much horror, too much death, too much agonizing suffering, and they were spent.

Perhaps sensing this, the brass ordered the 7th Regiment off the line in mid-November. The welcome news spread through the ranks with lightning speed. For many of them the relief was an answer to their prayers for deliverance. "The weeks we had been in Italy seemed like years," Pratt explained. "Sicily and Salerno were faint and distant memories. We were totally exhausted and ready for a break." By the seventeenth of November the entire regiment had been removed from the line. The arduous campaign in southern Italy cost the 7th Regiment 278 soldiers killed in action, 33 missing in action (most of whom were dead), 672 wounded, and 41 men who became prisoners of war. Mount La Difensa alone cost the unit 63 killed, 160 wounded, and several others missing or taken prisoner.[73] The only significant accomplishment that might begin to offset these losses was the breaching of the Volturno River.

By and large, the Italian campaign of 1943 accomplished little in relation to its terrible cost. The Allies captured Sicily, toppled Mussolini, and removed Italy from the war, but those were low-yield achievements. Italy contributed little to the Axis war effort. Defeating Germany was all that mattered in the European theater, and Italy's surrender contributed little in that regard. In addition, the Allies found themselves bogged down in the Italian mud and mountains as 1943 came to a close. The Germans gave ground, but they did so grudgingly and at great cost. They firmly held Rome, and the Allies could not even begin to think about a breakout from the Italian peninsula. In the end, the most significant accomplishment of the Italian campaign in 1943 was the capture of the Foggia airfields. These airfields provided the Allies with excellent bases from which to bomb German-held Europe. So, the experiences of the Cottonbalers largely served as a microcosm of the frustrating Allied experience in Italy. The men fought hard and demonstrated great bravery, amid miserable, soul-trying circumstances and, ultimately, for little overall advantage.

THE REGIMENT MOVED TO THE NAPLES AREA AND RESTED for several days. Men enjoyed shelter, decent meals, warm clothes, showers, and mail. They tried to feel like human beings again, but letting go of the awful memories compiled over the last four months could be difficult. Replacements arrived and this helped a bit. The veterans had to indoctrinate and prepare these new men, quite a few of whom were only eighteen, for combat. This job, combined with the fresh energy of the replacements, helped give life a semblance of normality again.

The close proximity of Naples afforded men plenty of opportunity for "rest and recreation." In other words, they could find plenty of trouble if they so desired. Naples had been partially destroyed by Allied bombing earlier in the war, but now it served as a major port, a key logistical and administrative center for the Allied war effort in Italy. Never the kind of place for the faint of heart, wartime Naples under the Allies grew into one big bawdy house.

The war had been terribly unkind to the Italian people. Many of them were homeless, dispossessed, hungry, and desperate, especially here in southern Italy where so much fighting had taken place and where poverty was a way of life for much of the population. They scratched out a living any way they could, and that often meant illicit activity, selling booze, pirating supplies on the black market, running gambling and kickback rackets, robbing Allied soldiers, and, especially, women selling their bodies. Young boys acted as pimps for their teenage sisters or, in many cases, their mothers. The streets of the town were filthy and the place smacked of low-grade decadence and human de-pravity. In this underworld, American soldiers, comparatively well fed, wealthy, and strong, were like royal personages. Any GI with a little money in his pocket could get anything he wanted, and more likely than not, he usually wanted sex. If a dogface wanted a cheap whore, Naples was the place to go.

The Neopolitan whores carried and spread venereal disease like mosquitoes spread malaria, and soon the U.S. Army had a staggering problem with sexually transmitted diseases. This problem was made worse by the fact that the local strain of VD was sometimes resistant to sulfa drugs; penicillin was scarce and could only be spared for combat wounds. The GIs had been cautioned to watch out for venereal disease (color films of VD, shown during basic training, left quite an impression on some); they had been instructed on the use of condoms and had, at times, been forced to make use of extensive prophylactic stations. The Army had even gone as far as to operate its own brothels with properly inspected women. Some air units arranged for beautiful but diseased women to display the ravages of their disease to airmen. In the final analysis, none of this really worked. Soldiers did what they wanted to do and often suffered the consequences.

Not far away from the 7th Regiment's bivouac area, Sergeant Pratt witnessed an entire field hospital devoted to VD cases that amounted to a division's worth of manpower. He went over there and visited a stricken Cottonbaler buddy who had an advanced case. The man was not shy about showing Pratt exactly what the disease had done. "The hideous sight before me was both revolting and nauseating. His penis had a sickening color to it, and its head was enlarged almost to the

[size] of a large lemon." Pratt almost vomited on the spot, but his friend informed him that other men in the next row had even worse cases. Their penises had swollen to the size of grapefruits. Infection treatment for all these men, including Pratt's friend, consisted of running a bladed probe up the urinary tract and ripping up the scabbing, forcing the pus to drain, or simply hammering the penis with a rubber mallet, again in hopes of breaking up the scabs and draining the infection. "I wondered if ever again I would use my equipment for anything other than the natural act of relieving oneself," Pratt plaintively commented.[74]

For those Cottonbalers who managed to avoid the dangers posed by VD, intensive training soon began. The brass had something big planned for the 7th Regiment and its 3rd Division comrades. In an effort to break the stalemate along the Gustav Line, Churchill proposed an amphibious landing at Anzio-Nettuno, thirty-five miles southwest of Rome and probably twice that distance behind the enemy defensive line. Two divisions would assault Anzio in late January 1944, push inland, cut the main German supply roads along the coast, and then push toward Rome. In order to draw German reserves away from the beaches, the Allies would attack all along the Gustav Line at the Rapido River and capture Cassino, the key position of the Gustav Line. Churchill hoped that the Anzio invasion would destabilize the entire German position in Italy and lead to the capture of Rome, a vital political objective. The only trouble was that the Allies were finally scheduled to unleash their cross-Channel attack on France in 1944 and many American commanders felt that nothing should interfere with that climactic operation. The British and Americans only had so many landing craft to go around, and many generals opposed using these precious resources for an amphibious swipe in a dead-end theater of war.

After extensive debate, Churchill got what he wanted. Anzio would proceed. General Clark chose his best amphibious division, obviously the 3rd, to lead the assault, so the Marne soldiers spent much of December and January preparing for this invasion. The training, as usual, was thorough, tough, physically challenging, and extensive. Truscott had not changed. He wanted his men in the finest shape possible, and he wanted them prepared for any combat eventuality. Through field problems, dress rehearsals, and twelve-hour training days, he sharpened his soldiers for the daunting task ahead.[75] Truscott knew that he

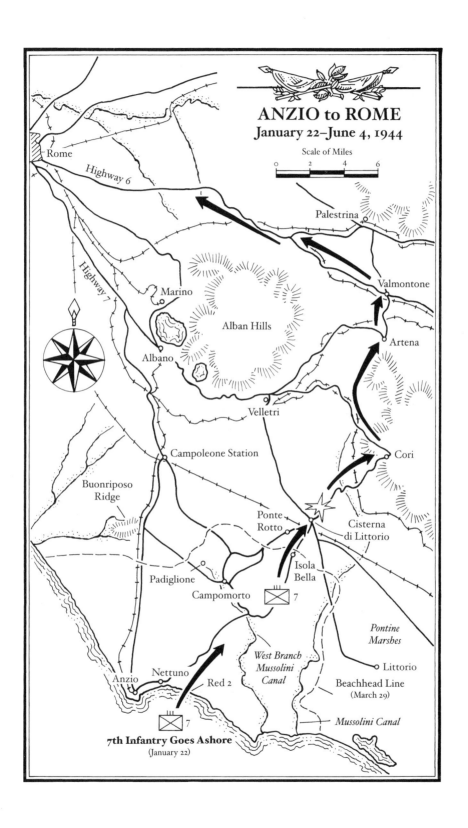

ANZIO to ROME
January 22–June 4, 1944

Scale of Miles

0   2   4   6

Rome

Highway 6

Palestrina

Marino

Highway 7

Alban Hills

Valmontone

Albano

Artena

Velletri

Cori

Campoleone Station

Buonriposo
Ridge

Cisterna
di Littorio

Ponte
Rotto

Padiglione

Isola
Bella

Campomorto

7

Pontine
Marshes

Anzio   Nettuno

West Branch
Mussolini
Canal

Littorio

Red 2

Beachhead Line
(March 29)

Mussolini Canal

7

7th Infantry Goes Ashore
(January 22)

commanded one of the best combat divisions in the entire U.S. armed forces and he aimed to keep it that way.

ON THE AFTERNOON OF JANUARY 21, 1944, TRUSCOTT'S division loaded onto transports in Naples Harbor. From there, they sailed uneventfully to the landing area and prepared to hit the beaches in the early-morning hours of the twenty-second. The targeted coast-line for the 3rd Division consisted mainly of a gentle cove with Anzio located on a small peninsula to the north and Nettuno a mile to the south. Gradually these towns gave way to sandy, rocky terrain that stretched for several miles. The landing beaches were about twenty-five to thirty yards deep. Beyond them lay flat ground for many miles, stopped only by a series of ridges known as the Alban Hills.

The plan called for a two-division assault. The British 1st Infantry Division would invade north of Anzio and push two miles inland. To their right, U.S. Rangers would splash ashore and seize Anzio. In the meantime, the 3rd Division would come ashore three miles south of Nettuno, with all three of its regiments abreast, the 7th on the left at Red 2 Beach, the 30th in the middle at Red 1, and the 15th on the extreme right at Green Beach. The mission was to land, overwhelm any resistance, push to the low ground, capture the Mussolini Canal, and then cut the north–south roads beyond the canal. The 1st Battalion would lead the way for the 7th Infantry, followed by the 2nd and 3rd Battalions. Once the two assault divisions and the Rangers were ashore, Allied reinforcements would be landed.

For the first time in the European theater, an amphibious invasion took place with almost flawless precision. The sea and weather were calm; the ships ferried troops to the right beaches; the planners achieved the complete surprise they so coveted; the landings took place on schedule and without any serious mishaps. In the calm, cool night, crowded together on their respective landing craft, the Cottonbalers watched the night sky lit up by rockets pounding the enemy shore. The landing craft sailed into the beaches, just like they were supposed to, and disgorged their loads. The infantrymen ran off their craft and trot-ted ashore, against no enemy opposition. The Germans had, at most, one thousand troops in the immediate area, and most of them had no idea what was going on. Random mines posed the only real peril to the assault troops. These impersonal killers claimed eight Cottonbalers on the twenty-second of January.

These losses aside, the invasion could not have gone much better. The lead companies accomplished all their D-Day objectives. William Rosson had been promoted to major near the end of the southern Italy campaign. Still shy of his twenty-sixth birthday, he took over command of the 3rd Battalion when Heintges, exhausted by his bad back and his wounds, succumbed to jaundice in November. Heintges needed two months in the hospital to recuperate, and in the meantime 3rd Battalion went to young Rosson.

The newly minted major was thrilled to receive this opportunity as a battalion commanding officer and even more thrilled at the ease with which his troops came ashore and captured their objectives: "We landed without any difficulty, with no fire immediately across the beaches, nor along the coast road, which was our first phase line. The only difficulty we had, really, in moving inland to our assigned beachhead line was getting through some stubborn industrial-type fences. Happily, we arrived at what we considered to be our first objective just about daylight. We then received orders to continue on to a second pre-planned line, and this proved to be no problem for us. We advanced on a fairly broad front without receiving any fire and, in fact, without observing any enemy at all."[76]

After this promising start, the Anzio operation began to unravel. Having achieved surprise and having forced the Germans to reinforce the Anzio area with troops scraped up from the Gustav Line, northern Italy, the Balkans, and France, the Allied commanders, most notably Lucas and 5th Army commander Clark, lost their nerve. Instead of immediately pushing inland, controlling the Mussolini Canal, seizing Highway 6 (the main road into Rome) and the Alban Hills, they sat and did nothing. They were worried about the possibility of German counterattacks and thought that if their troops advanced too far, they would be annihilated by strong enemy reinforcements. Maybe so, but if they were not willing to take that chance, why attempt the operation in the first place? At an absolute, bare minimum Lucas should have taken the Alban Hills. He failed to do so and, as a result, his soldiers suffered mightily in the months ahead.

The American and British troops who came ashore against such light opposition were obviously thrilled that they had achieved such surprise, but they knew the operation would not, and could not, be quite this easy. Most of them were experienced troops who knew that the Germans were far too tough, too resourceful and determined, to allow the Allies an easy victory. The old cliché "it's quiet . . . too quiet" comes readily to mind. A low murmur to the effect of "we'd better take advantage of this" rippled among the ranks of the combat troops. So, naturally, most of them were surprised and bewildered when their commanders did not order them to keep moving inland. They sensed what their senior commanders did not: the Germans rarely gave you any openings, so when they did, you'd better take advantage of it and make it count.

Lieutenant Martin sat around with his platoon and kept waiting for orders to move. They never came. For the life of him, he could not understand what the senior commanders were thinking. "We could have been at Highway 6 by dark that night [of the twenty-second]. We were sort of wondering, 'what are we doing sitting here?' We sat there a week before we decided to move."[77] Major Rosson also seethed with apprehension. "We . . . anticipated receipt of orders to strike toward . . . the logical final objectives—the hill mass directly in from the beachhead [the Alban Hills]. Highway 6, the main German supply axis . . . lay between them and Valmontone. So we expected orders to move out, and it seemed logical that they would be coming rather early because there was no opposition of consequence. Strangely, nothing was received. I would say only that we expected to drive inland, and my feeling at the time was that we should have done so."[78]

Of course they should have. The fact that they did not is, quite simply, inexcusable. By its very nature, the Anzio operation was a risky proposition, one that could only succeed if the Allies took advantage of surprise, poured troops and supplies ashore, and captured key objectives such as Highway 6 and the Alban Hills in the face of inevitable German reinforcements. The Allied commanders were not unlike a poker player who impulsively decides to risk most of his chips on the next hand, only to lose his resolve and fold, thus forfeiting most of his chips in a worthless gambit. Unfortunately, the "chips" in this case were American and British soldiers. Churchill, bitterly disappointed, later wrote: "I had hoped that we were hurling a wildcat onto the shore, but all we . . . got was a stranded whale."[79]

Lack of aggressiveness and imagination on the part of Lucas and Clark, not lack of fighting resolve among the combat soldiers, stranded that whale. When the enormity of this mistake began to sink in, Clark fired Lucas, who, in the end, was the wrong man for the job but was also serving under a man about whom the same thing could be said. A cagy, personally brave man with an extensive network of friends in high places, Clark survived the Anzio fiasco. This allowed him to preside over other disasters, the first of which was a series of poorly conceived, stilted, butcherlike attacks on the Rapido and against Cassino. These attacks failed to break the German defensive line in southern Italy; nor did they relieve any pressure on Anzio. In the days following the invasion, as the Cottonbalers and their comrades sat around waiting for orders, the Germans filtered powerful forces into the Anzio area. These reinforcements effectively penned the invaders into the low ground just beyond the beaches and created a situation that bordered on the disastrous.[80]

By late January, the 7th Regiment had dug in along the left flank of the division, a few miles east of their invasion beaches, with the Mussolini Canal at their backs. To their left they could see British troops; and to their right, a mix of Rangers and 15th infantrymen. For several days, patrols had fought small skirmishes with strengthening German forces, little brawls that inflicted a casualty or two on either side. The men had come under German artillery and mortar fire from time to time. They knew the enemy was out there in growing numbers but did not, as yet, know exactly where.

On January 30, Sherman received attack orders. Lucas and company were finally ready to push out of the beachhead. Mistakenly believing that only scattered strongpoints and roadblocks would impede his troops, the general ordered a frontwide attack. In this offensive, he ordered the 3rd Division, along with two Ranger battalions, to push forward, capture Cisterna di Littoria (not to be confused with the Cisterna near the Volturno where Heintges got wounded), and then, from there, seize the high ground around Cori and Velletri. The 7th Regiment, on the left flank, was supposed to capture the main road out of Cisterna di Littoria (Highway 7) and either envelop that town from the north or go in the other direction, toward Villetri. The Rangers would capture the town; the 15th Infantry would move on the town from the right and cut the road there. Truscott scheduled 0200 as H hour. Sherman, as usual, assigned the leading role to the 1st Battalion, commanded now by a recovered Lieutenant Colonel Frank Izenour (Moore moved up to regimental executive officer). The 1st Battalion troops were to advance along Le Mole Creek five miles to cut the road and then the 2nd Battalion would reinforce them, followed later by the 3rd if necessary.

True to their motto, the Rangers led the way. At 0100, their 1st and 3rd Battalions advanced along the main road and all the way into Cisterna. It was a trap. The Germans had sniffed out the Allied attack and brought in strong forces within the last twenty-four hours. They let the Rangers walk into the town, swung in behind them, cut them off, and annihilated them. In the course of the early-morning hours, the Germans systematically destroyed these two battalions of highly trained assault troops, forcing most of them to surrender.[81]

The fate of the Rangers proved to be a harbinger of the outcome of this ill-fated and poorly planned attack. The Cottonbalers' old enemies, the men of the Hermann Göring Division, were lying in wait for them. The soldiers of the 1st Battalion lined up in column formation, with B and A Companies in the lead, followed immediately by C and D Companies. The night was dark, cool, and quiet. They moved as silently as they could, but the occasional cough and the sounds of their boots squishing in the soft, moist soil seemed to echo for miles. Each man carried only field packs, extra ammunition, and weapons, and each man concentrated on trying to keep sight of the soldier ahead of him in the dark night. Every now and then a gust of wind swirled or a dog barked in the distance, giving nervous men a start. The air smelled musty, yet it betrayed the slightest salty hint of the nearby sea.

The lead soldiers were doing nothing more than feeling their way through the night. They did not know the terrain in front of them very well, and for good reason—their officers didn't either. They had had no time to properly reconnoiter the area. Captain Nicholas Grunzweig, the C Company executive officer, later wrote that the officers were forced to make attack plans based mainly on aerial photographs: "Owing to the lack of any high features from which to gain observation, close scrutiny of the ground over which the Battalion was to attack could not be had. The terrain was unbelievably open, with very gently rolling fields reaching toward Cisterna. Stone farmhouses were neatly spaced about 800 yards apart extending along unimproved roads. These farmhouses were to become key points in the struggle ahead. To augment the reconnaissance a study was made of the area using aerial photographs. What appeared to be minor lines of evenly spaced hedgerows, were actually deep ditches with brush growing in them. Enemy strength and dispositions were practically unknown."[82]

As Grunzweig indicated, the terrain soon presented some real problems. The lead scouts slowly negotiated their way through wire fences that the photographs had not picked up. Then, they led the battalion another eight hundred yards until they detected a drainage ditch some twenty-five feet deep. They squatted in front of this deep ditch and whispered consultations about what to do. Some of them searched around the area, in hopes of finding a way around the ditch, but to no avail. They had no choice but to go through the ditch. The entire battalion of soldiers carefully negotiated their way down the steep sides of the ditch, through its ankle-high water, and up the other side.

This consumed thirty minutes. Not much later, as they pressed on, they heard a tremendous explosion. Artillery had apparently hit a fuel dump somewhere in the distance. The burning fuel made it easier to see where they were going, but it also revealed their location to the Germans, a revelation that had terrible consequences. The Cottonbalers pressed on until a German burp gun opened up. The riflemen of the lead companies maneuvered around, rolling and taking cover as they ran and dived, trying to flank the German soldier: Whoever he was, he fled, firing all the way, most likely reporting the Americans' location to his officers.

By now, the 1st Battalion officers did not really know where they were. The wire fences, the ditch, and the enemy outpost had confused and disoriented many of the soldiers. The units were overstrength and had a nice mixture of veterans and new men; collectively they formed an excellent combat outfit, but asking them to carry out a blind attack, in the dead of night, with little reconnaissance or support, was expecting a bit too much. The men had no idea that, in effect, they were slipping their heads into a noose.

Soon after their encounter with the enemy burp gunner, flares spiraled into the air on both flanks. They burst and lit up the night. Terrified, the Cottonbalers sprawled for cover and looked around. Now they found out for sure where they were—in a pocket of low ground, smack in the middle of higher ground on both sides! "An extremely flat piece of ground with low rises on either side to the front took shape," Grunzweig wrote. "The flat area was like an immense football field. Long deep ditches at the base of east and west hills took the place of the sidelines. Deep V cut drainage ditches running parallel to each other much like 10 yard markers were spaced evenly the length of the open flat area."[83] In an instant, German machine guns opened up on the left. Luckily, they did not hit anybody. Some of the riflemen thought the machine-gun fire originated from nothing more than another enemy outpost. Determined that the enemy would not escape this time, they opened fire at the enemy guns, a difficult chore because the enemy guns did not fire any tracers. In confused clumps, they tried to close on the guns, firing, yelling, and running for about three hundred yards. This only made their situation worse.

All of a sudden, the Germans opened fire, seemingly from everywhere. Captain Harold Haines, a battalion officer, remembered: "By this time it was almost daylight. Machine guns and machine pistols [burp guns] opened up on us from the right front, right flank, and right rear. The German fire was effective and inflicted heavy casualties. The troops all got into the irrigation ditches, but each one of these was covered by some German weapon."[84] In fact, the situation was awful. No place was safe from German fire. The bullets swept everywhere, snapping in the air, thumping into the muddy ditches, tearing through flesh and cloth. The fire tore up Cottonbalers, peppering their hapless forms, shredding them into bloody, dismembered corpses. Izenour and his executive officer were both hit and wounded seriously. Enemy bullets clanked around and off helmets. Sometimes the bullets went right through the helmets and tore up the brains and skulls of cowering infantrymen. Some of the Americans tried to fire back, but it only drew more intense German return fire. The awful, tearing sound of German MG-42s (a spine-tingling *rrrrrrrrrrrp*) filled the air.

Pairs of riflemen on the left assaulted some of the enemy guns, pitching grenades. The grenades blew up and killed several enemy gunners, but enemy fire soon swept in, killing these brave grenadiers. Their bodies lay sprawled in contorted, macabre positions along the ditch. The sun continued to rise, making the Americans even more vulnerable. Basically, the Americans now had two choices: surrender or keep fighting and risk total destruction. A lesser unit would have chosen the first option, but the Cottonbalers never really contemplated it. Instead, Captain Athas, the hero of Hill 561, directed his D Company men to set up their four heavy machine guns along the irrigation ditch on the right. "As soon as these opened up on the three remaining German machine guns to our left rear," Haines related, "they pulled out. [Athas] also started riflemen moving individually toward the hill to our right rear. They knocked out the two machine pistols and apparently there weren't any more Germans on that hill because they were able to take position there without any more interference." Throughout the morning, the Germans filtered away and the Americans gradually moved men, under sniper fire, to positions of cover on the hill. Athas counted forty American bodies in the right ditch, though.[85] One group of forty survivors was caught behind enemy lines, skulking around, killing off isolated machine-gun and mortar teams, stolidly looking for a way back to the American lines.

The remaining troops of the 1st Battalion, 246 in all, peeked over the crest of the hill at the terrain in front of them. Captain Grunzweig was one of these fortunate few. Tired and filthy, he did not exactly like the look of what lay before them: "The terrain . . . was bare level fields. Extending toward Highway No. 7 was a line of evenly spaced stone farmhouses with attendant outside brick ovens, haystacks and shade trees. Further to the front about 3000 yards lay the old railroad embankment, the enemy's main line of resistance. The battalion continued to dig in."[86]

They were wise to do so, because the Germans launched a counterattack in the afternoon. Under cover of mortar and machine-gun fire, the enemy soldiers ran at the American positions. The Cottonbalers fired back with their machine guns. This fire was too much for the Germans. Many of them fell dead in the flat fields. Others got hit and tried to crawl to cover. The mortar fire increased in intensity, causing many of the Americans to crouch deeper in their small foxholes. The machine gunners kept shooting, though, and soon they ran out of targets. Having underestimated the amount of fight left in 1st Battalion, the Germans retreated.

The enemy now collected in barns and huts and behind haystacks, from which they called in mortar and artillery fire on the Cottonbaler positions. The American machine gunners shot up any position that looked suspicious. The artillery forward observers were missing, but various officers called for fire missions on their radios and this U.S. artillery helped keep the Germans at bay for a while. Eventually they came back, though, late in the afternoon with another attack. Again, American firepower broke up this attack.

As night fell, help was on the way for the embattled men of the 1st Battalion. One of the C Company platoons had previously been assigned the mission of escorting the unit's vehicles. These unscathed soldiers brought up food, water, and ammunition for their buddies. Also, Colonel Sherman sent up several tanks and tank destroyers (they had a terrible time negotiating their way over the soft ground) and threw the 2nd and 3rd Battalions into diversionary attacks to the right.

They met heavy resistance from enemy machine-gun and mortar fire and did not make much headway, but they did divert the attention of German troops who might otherwise have been able to keep pressure on the 1st Battalion.

Sherman also sent up a new commander, Major Frank Sinsel, the regimental S-4, or supply officer. "We repelled three small counterattacks during the night. Our losses during the night were about 10 men. The Germans were in houses around us to the northwest, north, and northeast so I ordered two tanks to move up to the crest of the hill at daylight and clean out the area. They shot up all the houses and haystacks in the vicinity, and 20 prisoners came in."[87]

It had been a long, desperate night. The men did not sleep. They hunkered down in their holes and, aided by flares, watched for the Germans. During the attacks, they poured as much fire as they could at the enemy. No one wanted to fight hand to hand in their holes. If they could keep the enemy at bay, they could maul the Germans with firepower, the same way they had been mauled in the morning, which seemed like weeks ago.

The worst attack came near dawn, and it hit a vulnerable, slightly elevated portion of the line the men had begun to call the horseshoe. Company B manned the horseshoe, the lead and most exposed positions of the entire battalion. The commander of this outfit, First Lieutenant Jon Capron, had one machine gun left, and he dug it in at the center and most advanced portion of his line. This spot afforded nice fields of fire, but it also placed the machine-gun team in a very exposed position, slightly forward of the rest of the company.

Sergeant Truman Olson, the commander of the six-man gun crew, who had been a milkman in Wisconsin before the war, demonstrated incredible resolve during this terrible night of January 30–31. All night long, Sergeant Olson and his men dealt with sporadic German attacks. For about half an hour, Private Bob Appel was on the gun, but he gladly yielded to Olson who spent the rest of the night in the gunner's position. A couple of Olson's men were hit. He watched in horror as German small-arms fire killed them, ripping out their eyes, their chests, and their abdomens. He sometimes touched their perforated, dead guts as he moved around during the night. He, Appel, and a couple of other survivors successfully repelled the attacks. Olson remained at his gun, out in a veritable no-man's-land, wounded in the leg, scared, shivering and waiting with dread for another German attack.

Sure enough, just before dawn, they came again. Supported by mortars, two hundred German infantrymen left their houses and haystacks and trotted across the fields, right at his machine gun. Surrounded by boxes of .30-caliber ammunition and supported by the riflemen behind him, he opened fire. Rows of enemy soldiers went down, but still they came at him. He glimpsed their shadows and fired at them. They returned fire with burp guns and rifles. Olson could hear the bullets snapping, at supersonic speeds, all around him. He kept firing and reloading his machine gun. The fight became almost monotonous, a drudging, no-holds-barred contest for survival. He knew instinctively, in his bones, that if he retreated, the Germans would break through B Company's lines and threaten the entire battalion. Almost like a robot, he kept shooting and shooting, as enemy troops fell and screamed everywhere. A mortar shell landed a few yards behind him and he could feel shrapnel tear through his back and his left leg. Warm blood dripped and ran down his back. He felt weak and tired. Still he kept shooting. The Germans were no more than twenty or thirty yards away now. The fighting had gone on for over an hour. They could not take this anymore. Their survivors dragged away what wounded they could and returned to their positions.

Sergeant Olson slumped over his gun, half-dead. He had fired thirteen boxes of ammunition (250 rounds per box) and only 50 rounds remained for his gun. He felt light-headed and weak. Capron screamed for a medic. One of them, Technical Sergeant John Earl, described Olson's condition: "He had serious shell fragment wounds in his back and left leg and was just about done for when we arrived to evacuate him. His wounds were so severe that he died while being carried to the rear. It is only because he carried on when he knew that his life was slowly ebbing away from his grievous wounds that others of us are alive today." Olson was posthumously awarded the Medal of Honor.[88]

As the sun rose on the thirty-first, Grunzweig and the other haggard dogfaces beheld the terrible landscape of destruction Olson had reaped: "Dawn found the enemy withdrawn with bodies of the dead and the positions of weapons mute evidence of the attempt of enemy machine gunners to drag automatic weapons to the lip of the horseshoe, set them up to unleash a hail of close range fire inside the horseshoe at dawn." The men could smell the stench of decomposing bodies, both German and their own. The rotting flesh smelled sweet and noxious at the same time, almost beyond description.

The men had been fighting for thirty hours, but their ordeal was nowhere near finished. Carrying parties, under mortar fire, removed the wounded and dead and, on their return trips, brought up a rudimentary resupply of food and ammunition. The soldiers munched silently on tasteless K rations while German mortar rounds exploded around them. An hour or two after daylight, they watched as the friendly tanks finally came up. "They appeared—maneuvering, backing off, attempting again, weaving around the soft mud areas until they were in the midst of the horseshoe defenders," Grunzweig recalled.

One of the tanks started firing shells into the nearest building. They crashed into the wall of the house, punching through, exploding, spouting up masonry and dust. The riflemen rose up slightly in their holes and fired at the house. A moment later, a white flag appeared in the door of the house. Eleven German soldiers, clad in bulky overcoats, emerged with their hands up. The infantrymen waved them over, disarmed them, and sent them to the rear.

The tanks changed positions and shot up a few more houses that showed no signs of life. Their firing had begun to taper off when Grunzweig, spotting very carefully with his binoculars, saw movement near a haystack in the distance. He ran to one of the tanks and shouted at the tank commander until he had his attention. Grunzweig pointed at the haystack. "There are krauts in that position!" The tank commander nodded. "Say no more." In rapid-fire sentences, he gave the necessary commands to his crew. "The first shell grazed the top of the haystack sending hay and Germans in all directions. The heavy machine guns of Company D and the .50 caliber machine gun of the tank fired on the enemy who was in a mad scramble to get away." German fire soon slackened noticeably.[89]

Incredibly, after all the 1st Battalion had been through, Truscott and Sherman ordered them to attack at 1400 and reach Highway 7. The men wanted nothing more than to rest and mourn the loss of so many of their brothers but knew they had to press on. American artillery screamed into the German lines, clobbering the buildings, the railroad, and the surrounding area. Sinsel planned to attack from the western ditches. At the appointed hour, the remnants of 1st Battalion, probably about two hundred men at the most, left their foxholes and began their attack. The Germans had been waiting for them to leave cover and made the most of it. The enemy fire was so intense that the soldiers immediately turned around and dived back into their foxholes. They panted and hugged the earth, hoping against hope they would not be ordered out there again. The tanks and heavy machine guns, covering the attackers, belched ordnance at the Germans.

Sinsel now changed his plans. He knew that German machine-gun fire was too heavy in the west, so he decided to attack straight ahead, right out of the horseshoe, over the open fields: "My orders to the tanks and TD's were to follow us closely and to fire on every building and haystack in our zone of action, whether we received fire from it or not."[90] At his command, the men went forward once more, this time with far better results, even though resistance was fierce.

Crouched over, firing as they ran, the Cottonbalers ran through the mushy fields, right at their enemies. The tanks and machine guns poured fire at the Germans, but the enemy was still shooting back with everything they had. In essence, this assault was not much different from those carried out by Cottonbalers one hundred years before at places such as Cerro Gordo and Chapultepec. The fire they braved was deadlier, but the assault still came down to courageous infantrymen moving forward to destroy their enemies and control ground. One Cottonbaler spoke of the German fire as "withering." Speaking in the third person, he marveled that "it is impossible to understand how anything that moved could survive through that fire. Firing their weapons while running in a half-crouched manner, at times creeping and crawling in the slimy ooze that made them blend indistinguishably with the surrounding terrain, the advance elements overran two enemy 105s [artillery pieces]."[91]

The frenzy of combat possessed them. They felt nothing, thought of nothing, except to move forward and kill. They existed in a kind of robotic state, or at least as close as human beings can get to that kind of mind-set. Anywhere they saw German machine guns, usually behind haystacks, they blew the enemy gunners away. Howling and snarling, the Cottonbalers ran about twelve hundred yards until they entered a small orchard, where the Germans evidently never expected them. The Cottonbalers ran right at the enemy positions in the orchard and began shooting up the surprised and stunned enemy soldiers.

Captain Grunzweig, right alongside a group of B and C Company soldiers, blazed away with his M1 carbine, a light rifle that fired fifteen-round clips of .30-caliber ammunition. "At one enemy machine gun position, the bewildered Germans started to rise to flee and were cut down by small arms fire from several directions. The enemy unit broke and ran. Hindered by overcoats and equipment, the enemy made excellent targets as they tried to step through evenly spaced rows of smooth wire across their line of retreat. Very few of this group of approximately 150 Germans were . . . captured or ever reached their own lines."[92]

The turkey shoot was sweet revenge for the day before, when the German had slaughtered the Cottonbalers in their ditches. The Americans gave no quarter, blasting the enemy soldiers into lifeless lumps. Some of the Germans tried to put their hands up and scream, *"Kamerad!"* (a gesture of surrender). They died with that word on their lips. In the heat of such close combat, with such powerful emotions churning through them, the Americans could not make the difficult transition from killers to jailers.

They pressed on and made it all the way to the railroad embankment, where the attack lost momentum. Adrenaline began to wear off, the tanks could not keep up, and many soldiers had been hit during this furious assault. German artillery and mortar fire began dropping in the area. One such shell exploded very close to Lieutenant Martin, one of the few surviving officers in the battalion: "It got me and . . . my weapons platoon leader and my weapons platoon sergeant, mortar section leader. There were five of us. I was the lucky one. I just had a scratch. The mortar section leader . . . lost a part of his lower jaw." Martin had more than a scratch. His wounds necessitated three weeks of painful recovery at a field hospital on Anzio Beach.[93]

The men of the 1st Battalion dug in along the railroad. Sinsel fully expected a German counterattack. He knew that, in spite of his successful attack, he and his men were in a vulnerable spot. They were the lead point of the entire regiment, the entire division in fact. Their positions constituted little more than a tiny fingerlike protrusion into the German lines: "There were only about 100 men left in the Bn by this time and we were practically out of ammunition—not over two to three clips in any man's possession. The tanks and TD's were also running short of ammunition." The expected counterattack did not materialize, but the Germans still put as much pressure as they could on the exposed 1st Battalion troops: "Throughout the remainder of the afternoon, and all during the night, the Germans put down heavy artillery concentrations. Some fell on the battalion positions but most of it fell in the olive grove near the house where we had knocked out [a] 77mm gun. During the night the Germans constantly tried to work machine guns close in our flanks and rear. Several times they tried to set up within 100 yards or less of our position. As soon as we would hear the Germans moving in, the nearest company commander would send out a patrol of 4 or 5 men. These patrols knocked out every enemy machine gun before it could be set up and open fire." At daylight, the pressure continued: "Throughout the day, we were continuously harassed by snipers on our flanks. The Germans also had 2 or 3 self-propelled guns which harassed us." American artillery responded in kind.[94]

The men spent the entire day dodging shells and sweating out enemy machine-gun incursions. Grunzweig, on the verge of complete physical and mental collapse, knew his men could not keep this up much longer: "Almost out of ammunition, weary from endless fighting and shelling, the rifle and other companies torn to shreds, the battalion barely existed as a fighting force." Out of 800 men who had launched the attack in the early-morning hours of the thirtieth only 127 now remained, a mere sixty hours later. Truscott, fearing they would be surrounded and cut off, ordered them pulled back. The day before, the 2nd Battalion had slowly worked its way into the rear areas of the 1st, and now these "White" battalion soldiers (commanders sometime referred to the three battalions, in order, as Red, White, and Blue) covered their exhausted buddies as they pulled back.[95]

The first Battle of Cisterna di Littoria was over. By any measure, the Allies had been defeated. They failed to push out of their beachhead, and that failure, in effect, doomed them to months of siege warfare. However, the failure at Cisterna, like the failure in the Anzio campaign, happened because of the poor leadership of Allied commanders and not any lack of fighting effectiveness or spirit on the part of the combat soldiers, British and American. The Cottonbalers, especially the 1st Battalion, fought as well as troops can fight. One of them later said, "Hollywood would have paid five million dollars to have had that on film. Here we were, *walking* in on the enemy and he had every weapon from machine guns on up zeroed in on us. Small arms and artillery were intense. Men were dropping all around. It made you wonder when you were going to get it. The rest of the men never even hesitated, just kept walking forward, only stopping to shoot. The tanks and Tds were moving right along with us, shooting hell out of houses and haystacks. When we got in on the Jerry positions they couldn't take it. They poured out of those foxholes. So then it was our turn. The fellows with their rifles and BARs and the Tds and tanks with their .30 and .50 caliber machine guns went to work on them. We knocked off a hell of a lot of krauts. In the orchard they were practically piled one on top of each other. The Marines at Tarawa had nothing on [us] at Cisterna that day."

THE 1ST BATTALION IMMEDIATELY WENT INTO REGIMENTAL reserve while the other two battalions stayed on the line and fought off strong German attacks on February 2 and 3. The front then settled into an exhausted stalemate. The 7th Infantry dug in near the Mussolini Canal, roughly along the Allies' main line of resistance. The British and Americans no longer had the option of pushing inland, unhinging the German defensive position, and moving on Rome. Their Anzio, Rapido, and Cassino operations had all failed miserably. At Anzio, the primary question now was whether or not the Allies would be pushed into the sea. A 3rd Division soldier wrote about the mind-set that prevailed among the besieged troops: "We were fighting for our lives and we knew it. There was no place to go if the Germans broke through our lines and no one was in a better position to know it than we. If the Germans made a serious penetration . . . it is hard to say what mercy we would have been shown. It was a long swim back to Naples."[96]

For almost two weeks, the 7th Regiment received replacements and consolidated its positions. Even the 1st Battalion returned to full strength. No place on the beachhead was safe, because the Germans dominated the Alban Hills and could throw ordnance at the Allied soldiers on the beaches and the smooth plains beyond. "The beachhead front line and forward positions were subjected to almost daily 'rolling barrages' from German artillery and automatic weapons," Sergeant Pratt remembered, "that would start at one end of the perimeter and continue until practically the entire front was covered. Before many days had passed, the ground around the forward troop positions was churned and rechurned by exploding shells and mortar rounds until no blade of grass or other . . . living plant could be seen. Life moved steadily underground at Anzio, especially during daylight hours. Any movements, no matter how slight, would bring almost instantaneous fire from ready and waiting German weapons." They dug in as best they could, but rainwater, seawater, and table water proved to be major headaches. The men constantly dug and improved their positions to protect themselves from the blanket of German steel that often swept the area.[97]

In spite of these struggles, the Anzio beachhead could be kept alive as long as the Allies maintained control of the sea and air. The sea was no problem and the Cottonbalers, and other units, received plenty of food, ammunition, and other supplies. German air attacks were a concern, but the Allies enjoyed air superiority.

In the meantime, Adolf Hitler personally ordered his generals to eliminate the Anzio beachhead. They unleashed their attack in the early-morning hours of February 16. The brunt of this attack hit the 45th Division sector, but it also hit the 3rd Division. The 7th Regiment was mostly in reserve when the attack started. However, two companies from the 2nd Battalion, E and G, were in the process of relieving soldiers from the 30th Infantry when the Germans came. For two days, the enemy attacked, with the support of artillery, a few tanks, and mortars. The Cottonbalers of the 2nd Battalion mainly "put out fires," rushing around to meet and defeat the Germans wherever they threatened to break through American lines or force a gap between units.

Vernon Medaugh was a rifleman and assistant BAR gunner in E Company. He and his squad rushed into one such gap to blunt a German attack. Soon a German machine gun opened up on them, killing their first scout: "I was on the left flank and someone told the B.A.R. man and myself to get to high ground on our left. We started up a little grade and got about ten yards when the machine gun turned on us, hitting the B.A.R. man in the leg. The second burst hit me and put about an eight inch wound across the my shoulder blade." The other soldiers kept screaming at them to move to safety, but every time they tried, the Germans shot at them some more. Medaugh lay frozen in place on the little embankment while his squad killed the enemy gunners. The squad moved on to some other fight and Medaugh, the BAR man, a lieutenant, and an artillery observation team hunkered down in the German fighting holes.

Soon German mortar shells dropped in, killing the artillery observer. They stayed in the hole all night exchanging small-arms fire with the enemy. In the morning, the lieutenant decided that they should make a break for the American lines. By now the wounded BAR man's legs were stiff and he needed help to get out of the hole. "I called for the Lt. to come over and help me lift him out. [The lieutenant's] hands had been burnt from the [German] machine gun and they were all swollen and blistered. It was a water cooled machine gun and the water jacket had been hit and had lost all water."

They finally made it back to the American lines and visited the aid station. A doctor bandaged Medaugh's wound, but he and Medaugh's first sergeant ordered him back to the lines. The situation was desperate and the division could not spare any men. Anyone who could walk and wield a weapon could still fight, the sergeant told Medaugh. So he went back to the front and promptly got hit again, this time by mortar fragments. "I ducked my head, but I held onto my shovel handle, and a piece of metal, about the size of the lead of a pencil and about 4 or 5 inches long, went through the back of my hand in the shovel handle." The medic bandaged him and sent him back to the battalion aid station. On the way there he ran into the sergeant, who looked at his hand and ordered him back to the front. Medaugh stayed there another thirty-one days. When he finally left the front, he could barely walk from trench foot and his hand had gotten infected. He finally got evacuated.[98]

Meanwhile, the German mid-February attack had failed. American artillery annihilated many of the enemy infantry soldiers and the dug-in firepower of American machine guns and rifle fire made it difficult for the Germans to gain much ground in the 3rd Division area. They made most of their gains against the targeted 45th Division before being stopped by massed Allied artillery, terrific air support, and, of course, the bravery and resolve of the men of the Thunderbird Division.

Again the front quieted. The Germans, foiled in their attempt to annihilate the beachhead, paused to lick their wounds. The Allies did the same. The Cottonbalers manned positions in the center of the division's area of responsibility and, in the words of the regimental historian, spent their time "improving its positions, stringing wire, laying mines and repulsing enemy patrols that showed stubborn intentions of infiltrating through the outposts to reach the rear areas. Enemy concentrations of fire were severe and caused most of the casualties."[99]

This situation lasted the rest of the month, as the Germans prepared for another major attack. That did not mean they let the combat soldiers at Anzio enjoy a vacation. One soldier from the regiment who joined the unit at this time described in detail what the soldiers experienced in late February: "All through the night there were flares going up from the Jerry lines. Once Jerry threw in a terrific artillery barrage which landed about five hundred yards behind us. I was scared. It was just plain hell all through the day, and the nights were worse. We had five days of rain. The hole got about six inches of water, and you couldn't do anything but try to bail it out with your helmet. We wrapped shelter halves and blankets around us but they didn't do much good. If you 'had to go' you had to think about it before daylight because you couldn't get out of that hole once the sun came up, or ever show the top of your head.

"At night we got canned 'C' rations. Toward the last they brought them up warmed up a little, and coffee, only a little warm by the time it got to us, and once in a while a beef sandwich or some doughnuts. Those did more to help our morale than anything else, except mail. You had to get out of the hole when it got dark for several reasons, one of which was to get some circulation back into your feet. A lot of the boys went to the medics with bad cases of trench foot, but I wasn't that lucky. Jerry threw in a lot of artillery and mortars. The best thing to do was pull in your head and pray. If you got it at night, you were lucky, because they could get you out right away. God help you if you got hit in the daytime, because you might have to lay there all day before somebody could get to you."[100]

JUST BEFORE DAWN ON THE LEAP YEAR DAY OF FEBRUARY 29, the situation got much worse. The Germans selected this day for their last big effort to push the Allies into the sea. This time, they decided to focus their attack on the 3rd Division. Parts of at least five divisions hurled themselves at the 3rd that morning. The 2nd and 3rd Battalions of the 7th Regiment were deployed in the middle of the division, right in the way of the German attack. To cover their advance, the Germans began laying down smoke in front of the U.S. lines. Naturally this tipped their hand a bit. Reacting to the smoke reports, Brigadier General John (Iron Mike) O'Daniel, the new division commander, called Sherman and warned him that he believed an attack was imminent. Clark's relief of Lucas in mid-February produced a ripple effect in the 3rd Division. Truscott moved up to command of the VI Corps, while O'Daniel took over the Marne division. Truscott took Rosson with him to corps to serve as his operations officer. Heintges, recovered sufficiently from his wounds and jaundice, reassumed command of the 3rd Battalion.

As the smoke cleared and the sun rose, the combat troops, peering cautiously from their holes, could see German troops in the distance, clearing paths through the minefields and barbed wire that the Cottonbalers had recently laid. The Americans waited for them to enter the kill zone in front of their lines and unleashed a massive array of firepower on them. Artillery and mortar shells exploded seemingly on top of one another. Machine guns sent multicolored tracers flying in every direction. Many of the tracers, and other bullets, abruptly stopped when they hit the German attackers. The enemy tried to spread out and return fire, but the fire swept through their ranks. Their blood ran into the mud and ditches. Some of them tripped mines as they tried to evade American fire. The Germans retreated and the front quieted for a time.

Later they came back and tried to force their way through the 2nd Battalion, but to no avail. American firepower shredded them into ribbons. They came back again, wheeling up six-barreled nebelwerfer mortars (the dogfaces called them "screaming meemies") to pound the Yank positions. These terrible weapons blasted men and soil alike, in a brown and red cacophony of death. The enemy could not break through in any Cottonbaler sector, but they penetrated American lines on the left of the 7th, in the sector covered by the understrength 509th Parachute Infantry Battalion.

This put the 2nd Battalion in a difficult situation. Before they knew it, the German attackers were within grenade distance. Then they were within bayoneting distance, right in the holes of the Cottonbaler soldiers. The enemies stabbed and punched each other. Anyone who could shoot a weapon killed his enemy at close range. For one of the tiny few times in modern war, soldiers used bayonets. The killing was close in, eye to eye. Men could see the expressions on their victims' faces as they snuffed out their lives. For the most part, the Americans held, although in some companies German soldiers overran U.S. foxholes, only to be killed off in rear areas by machine guns and mortars. Artillery and strafing American planes also ripped through waves of German reinforcements, causing them to take cover even as their comrades fought for their lives several hundred yards away.

Later in the day, on the right of the regiment in the 3rd Battalion area, the Germans experienced more success, mainly because they liberally supported their infantry with Mark VI Tiger tanks. The enemy dumped wave after wave of screaming-meemie volleys in the Blue battalion area. Then they dropped smoke, obscuring the vision of the American infantrymen. These troops could only catch glimpses of the German tanks but could certainly hear them, and the sounds of the grinding gears and clanking treads were terrifying. In minutes the tanks were right on top of the Cottonbalers. At point-blank range, many of the steel monsters fired their main guns into the holes, atomizing the cowering, muddy riflemen. Machine guns hosed down those Americans who tried to run for their lives. Only the onset of darkness slowed down the enemy tanks. Small groups of Americans tried to creep near the tanks and disable them with grenades. Machine guns from the tanks shot up some of these men. The rest fled. The whole scene was surreal. "Flames threw a lurid glow over the area," the regimental historian wrote, "and the skirmish lines of the German infantry closely supported by their tanks could be discerned making their way toward the battalion lines. Only by the most determined efforts . . . were the attacks beaten off." Mortars, tank destroyers, and bazooka teams, appearing like manna from heaven, destroyed many of the German tanks. The crews of these tanks screamed in agony as flames engulfed them. Their bodies soon burned to a crisp and the ammunition inside their tanks cooked off, sending flames shooting into the night.[101]

Somehow, the Cottonbalers managed to hold off the Germans for the rest of the night and the next day. The fighting continued with the same ferocity, but the 7th Regiment held on. The Germans kept trying to press their attack and unhinge the American lines. The enemy kept scraping together more troops and throwing them into battle. At 0105 on March 3, they tried one last push in hopes of buckling the bloodied 3rd Battalion. The Americans could hear the tanks rumbling toward them and across a key bridge that everyone simply called "Bridge 5." Two tanks ground their way through L Company's positions. Many of the soldiers from this outfit withdrew, but others evaded the tanks and found new positions. One man, Staff Sergeant Harry Lawlor, took a buddy with him and ran five hundred yards through mortar fire until he came upon one of the tanks, a Mark VI. German infantry opened up on him at close range, but somehow they missed him. While Lawlor acted as bait, the other man threw Molotov cocktails onto the hull of the tank. They exploded but failed to ignite the tank. Lawlor, still under fire, crawled up to the tank and fixed several "sticky grenades" (whose effectiveness was memorably shown in the film *Saving Private Ryan*) onto its treads. The grenades exploded and the tank stopped shooting. Meanwhile, Lawlor covered his buddy as he ran back to American lines. Eventually, the law of averages caught up with him. German riflemen peppered him with bullets, and he bled to death at the scene. The Army awarded him a posthumous Distinguished Service Cross.

BY THE EARLY AFTERNOON OF MARCH 3, THE REGIMENT had successfully held off some of the strongest German attacks

Americans had so far seen in this war, but not without cost. To this point, 110 men had been killed and another 254 wounded. The nerves of the unhit, the so-called "lucky ones," were completely frayed. Such was the case for Heintges. Over the last several days, he had seen too many of his men killed; he had seen them reduced to nothing more than dead sacks of dismembered flesh and rotting organs. He had seen his men wounded, crying, gasping, moaning, raging. His command post, located in a wine cellar cave, took a direct hit from heavy German artillery (called "Anzio Annie") and buried one of his men alive.

The stress of repelling furious enemy attacks, even for such an excellent combat leader, began to tell. Early in the afternoon that day, something Colonel Sherman did sent Heintges over the edge. In spite of the fact that Heintges had known Sherman for years, he did not have much respect for him. Heintges had dated Sherman's daughters. The colonel was a good friend of Heintges's stepfather. But, in Heintges's view, Sherman was not much of a regimental commander: "[He] never, and I mean never, visited our regimental front lines in Anzio . . . never." This failing of courage had consequences. For one thing, the combat men could not respect a commander who did not share their dangers, at least some of the time. For another, Sherman did not have a solid understanding of the frontline terrain because he had never actually seen it.

On March 3 he called Heintges and told him he was reinforcing the 3rd Battalion with A and B Companies that very afternoon. Heintges knew this was madness: "I told him over the telephone . . . 'Colonel, you can't do that because the Germans are registered with every damn piece of artillery they have, right on this road and my battalion sector. As soon as they come over that hill, all hell is going to break loose and we're going to lose a battalion, perhaps more.'"

Heintges was absolutely right. Plain and simple, troops could not safely move in daylight in the Anzio beachhead. He had no patience with his superior's ridiculous decision. This was not a question of parade formations or Saturday inspections; people's lives were at stake. Colonel Sherman did not seem to care. "You son of a bitch," he obdurately replied. "I know what I'm doing." Heintges did not yield an inch. "I said, 'Well, sir, I hate to hear you talk like that. You have never been up here and you don't realize how flat the terrain is.'" Sherman hung up.

Sure enough, when the unfortunate soldiers of A and B Companies tried to march straight up the road leading to the 3rd Battalion, in broad daylight at 1330, the Germans clobbered them. Enemy artillery fire laced them, cutting jugular veins and tearing off arms and legs. The men couldn't find any cover. The ground was completely flat. These unfortunate men, American soldiers with homes and families, bled to death in the Italian mud. Captain Athas, hero of Hill 561 and Cisterna, was one of them. Most of the unscathed ran back to their original positions. Some made it as far as the 3rd Battalion foxholes and breathlessly took cover anywhere they could, no doubt shaking their heads at the abject foolishness of their colonel.

In his command post, Heintges seethed at the terrible waste of American lives. "I don't know how many casualties . . . we had, dead bodies lying all over the place." Later the colonel called him and said his executive officer, Lieutenant Colonel Wiley H. O'Mohundro, was in the process of reorganizing the 1st Battalion for another movement to the front. Sherman then ordered Heintges to send his executive officer and another officer to the road as guides. Heintges muttered, "Yes, sir," but he had no intention of carrying out this order, because he knew it would mean sure death for these two men. Sherman, perhaps sensing this reluctance, called back half an hour later to see if the two officers were on the road. "I said, 'No, sir, they're sitting right here beside me.' Then he cussed me out and called me a son-of-a-bitch again and said, 'When are you going to learn to carry out my orders?'" Heintges claimed that he was following orders, that he would only send the two men to the road when the 1st Battalion made it over the ridge where the Germans had butchered them earlier that day. Sherman blew up and cussed him out again. Every bit as angry, Heintges could feel the blood rushing to his head. "I said, 'Colonel, I don't like being talked to like that. It looks to me like you're losing confidence in me.' And he said, 'You're damn right I'm losing confidence in you.' I said, 'Well, in that case, you'd better get yourself a new battalion commander.' And there was a dead silence."

Sherman told Heintges to put his executive officer on the line and he did so. Sherman tried to order this man, a solid, well-respected major from Idaho named Clayton Thobro, to leave the command post and guide the 1st Battalion. Heintges figured this out and grabbed the phone from Thobro. "'Sir, I refuse to comply with this, and I will not have Thobro go up there at the present time until that battalion gets up here because it's suicide.'" Heintges had reached the breaking point. This was the last straw. "'I'm sick and tired of . . . you getting my people killed, and I quit.' There was a dead silence again, and he finally said, 'All right, report back to the regimental headquarters.' I hadn't had any sleep for 72 hours or more. I was emotionally finished, really."

Heintges went back to regiment a day or two later when the German attack had died down. By the time he got there he and Sherman had both cooled down and the colonel gave him a fatherly talk. Heintges wanted to make sure that his record did not state that he had been re-lieved in combat. He got what he wanted and the new division com-mander, O'Daniel, assigned him to a post as his operations officer, a plum assignment. O'Daniel and his senior officers clearly held Heint-ges in high esteem. Another commander might not have profitably sur-vived such a confrontation with a superior officer.[102] In fact, Sherman's days with the regiment were numbered. He got promoted to brigadier general and bumped up to Clark's staff at the 5th Army. O'Mohundro took over the 7th Infantry.

THE GERMAN ATTEMPT TO PUSH THE ALLIES INTO THE SEA had failed and now the front settled back into another stalemate. This one lasted for over two months, until the initiative passed to the Allies. Throughout the rest of March, the 7th Infantry remained at the front lines, covering the same sector. The ferocious, personal combat of mid-February and early March now gave way to another war of patrolling, digging, outposting, and shivering in deep foxholes and bunkers. Cor-poral Wallace Bassett wrote of the episodic nature of combat that March: "Sometimes we could hear small arms fire. Other days it was so quiet, we wondered if the war was over, but when a shell hit nearby, we knew we should get to our foxholes. When we were attacked by air, we jumped into a ditch, or hugged a building very tightly."[103]

William Blanckenburg, a twenty-seven-year-old lieutenant in the regiment, chronicled frontline duty experienced by the regiment dur-ing these bleak, rainy days, cornered into a beachhead like trapped rats: "We were within . . . 300 yards of the German lines. Lots of rain meant cold, wet feet. To avoid trench foot I tried to wring out my socks to hold my feet up to dry in the sun. Almost nothing moved in daytime. Shades of WWI. At night . . . details were assigned to go for water. Pa-trolling was another night only activity. Soldiers were assigned to that duty, perhaps 6 or 8 per patrol. I had that task about 3 times in 33 days. Lines were in strong points with large uncovered areas in between. Krauts and we were constantly probing each other's . . . blank areas."

About a week after he joined the unit, Blanckenburg got assigned to a combat patrol, the kind designed to bag a prisoner: "We met after dark—about 10 . . . EM [enlisted men] and a 2d lt. leader. We never did *see* each other or know each other at all. The lt. gathered us together, said our mission was to go into the area between our lines & the Krauts, 'listen,' go to a road where they were moving around, and capture a prisoner. He then said, 'We'll go out as directed, find a couple of nice shell holes, rest all night and return to our lines before dawn. Forget that take a prisoner stuff.' We did as he said. We were close enough to see shapes walking on the road & hear them talking. We kept very quiet. Came back to our lines as scheduled. No casualties. Such a misbegotten mission. *No* preparation with an untrained patrol & a bunch of strangers. Smart lt."[104] In the real world of combat, such rule bending went on all the time.

Day after day, the Cottonbalers lived their molelike existence and endured enemy shelling. Sergeant Pratt had, over the course of many months in combat, escaped many barrages, but on March 15 his luck ran out. Shortly before this, he got promoted to first sergeant of the antitank company. On the fateful day, he was at the company command post, a series of dugouts situated around demolished buildings out of the range of small-arms fire but often under shell fire. Pratt and many others were resting in the buildings when German artillery began exploding outside and against the walls of the stone buildings. He heard a groan outside and ventured out. Two men had been hit. "One guy had been neatly decapitated and the other seemed to be bleeding heavily from numerous wounds. Crouching low, I eased up to him to see if I could help but as I reached him I could see he was breathing his last breath. His twitching stopped, his mouth dropped open and his open and glassy eyes stared out at me."

Pratt went back into the building, and more rounds landed, too close for comfort. He and the other soldiers decided to make a run for their dugouts. "Suddenly I heard a whistle from a shell, vaguely heard an explosion almost under me, and I blacked out." He regained consciousness a few minutes later, with a terrific ringing in his ears. He could not see from his left eye. "I put my hand up to the left side of my head and felt warm liquid. Lowering my hand I saw it all covered with blood. I raised myself up and started to run but immediately fell flat down. I . . . could not control my left leg. I saw that the trouser leg around the knee was tattered and red with blood."

He crawled to cover and his men dragged him inside a dugout. A medic gave him a morphine shot and loaded him onto a jeep that drove him to the 94th Evacuation Field Hospital, where he had surgery and woke the next day. He felt around and realized his head was bandaged and his leg was throbbing. A nurse soon arrived. "'You are a very lucky young fellow,' she told me. 'Your leg was severely shattered, but you still have it. At least for now, and the prognosis is hopeful you will keep it.'" The shell had torn away much of Pratt's thigh. The surgeons, seeing this, had believed that the leg could not be repaired. They were actually in the process of amputating with an electric saw when a batch of more seriously wounded casualties, in danger of immediate death, arrived at the hospital, requiring their attention. They left Pratt's leg amputation for later, but when they had more time to look at it, they decided to try to save it. The surgeons operated most of the night, painstakingly putting the leg back together. They also saved his eye, but he could barely see out of it the rest of his life. He was evacuated to Naples and spent almost two full months recuperating before being sent back to the regiment.[105]

On the evening of March 26–27, the 135th Infantry Regiment of the 34th Infantry Division relieved the 7th Regiment and they went into an underground "rest" area of sorts, a torn-up forest of spindly pine trees in the Nettuno area that the men soon began calling "The Pines." Only half the men who had landed on January 22 were still with the unit. A total of 428 Cottonbalers had been killed since then. Obviously, the soldiers badly needed rest. They spent twelve days at "The Pines," eating, sleeping, digging, and learning new military tactics pertinent to the Anzio situation.

Between April 12 and 14 the regiment left "The Pines" and went back on the line. The weather was warmer now, but other than that, the job was the same as before: stay under cover in holes and bunkers all day, keep watch for the enemy, dodge shells, and patrol from time to time. The new commanding officer, Colonel O'Mohundro, set up his command post in a small stucco farmhouse: "The Italian family, plus cow, pig, rabbit and chickens, occupied the ground floor, while my staff and I used the upstairs rooms. Normally, this would have been too vulnerable to enemy shelling, but the terrain had a small ridge in front of the house which apparently prevented them [from] getting a hit on the house."

Born the youngest of seven children in 1894, O'Mohundro grew up in rural Missouri. He was a poor farm boy, with little education but plenty of dreams about a better life: exactly the kind of young man for whom the Army represented great opportunity and a gateway to that better life. He enlisted in 1914, quickly ascended to sergeant, and then received a commission. Although he did not see combat in World War I, he found a home and a career in the Army. A loyal, decent, honest but unspectacular professional, he served in numerous posts during the interwar years. When the United States entered World War II, he became a kind of "'tweener": too old for field command, too out of the loop for senior command, but still too young and too useful to be retired off. Promoted to lieutenant colonel, he rotated around the 5th Army as a kind of field-grade errand boy, filling in wherever he might help, biding his time for a command. Over his long career, he had amassed a nice network of friends and cronies, who promised to accommodate him when the opportunity arose. So, when Sherman was promoted to brigadier general, O'Mohundro finally, after thirty years in the Army, got his chance to command troops in combat. A few weeks later, he got promoted to full colonel.

Although Heintges dismissively referred to O'Mohundro as "a doddering old man," the new colonel was still a few months shy of fifty, a bit on the old side for a regimental commander, but not by any great measure. O'Mohundro was no great commander, but he did bring a new kind of vigor and integrity, along with a deep respect for the combat soldiers, to the regiment's command group. In stark contrast to Sherman, he visited the dogfaces at the front as much as he could. "I made it a practice to visit one front line unit each night. As I would go from one foxhole to another—where the lonely soldier lived in mud and water, I would say, 'We can expect the Germans to attack us at anytime [*sic*]. Do you think you can stop them?' The answer was always to the effect of 'No one is going through here, Sir.' I thought of them as 'Sentinels of Democracy'—the real heroes."

He also presided over the creation of the Battle Patrol. The Battle Patrol consisted of volunteers from all over the regiment who operated as part of five-man cohesive patrolling groups (to alleviate the kind of ridiculous situations encountered by men like Blanckenburg) led by one of the outfit's best soldiers, First Lieutenant William Dieleman. Dieleman began World War II as a noncommissioned officer in the regiment, and through the attrition of combat and numerous instances of brave, skillful leadership he acquired a commission. Dieleman made sure that his Battle Patrol troops had "hot meals, dry clothing and a comfortable place to rest and sleep so their mental and physical condition would be greatly enhanced. All personnel were to be equipped and trained in the use of knives, grenades, bayonets, and the latest combat weapons. Nearly all missions were to be known at least thirty-six hours in advance, to allow plenty of time for briefing, planning, discussion and study of maps and aerial photographs."[106]

In late April, the Battle Patrol soldiers engaged in many dangerous missions, the kind that saw them capture a small objective and fight at very close range with German patrols. The most notable mission was the capture of the Windmill, a key observation post the Allies had been trying to take for weeks. The Germans used the battered remnants of this windmill to call in accurate artillery fire on their enemies. In a nicely coordinated assault on April 23, the Battle Patrol captured it. After that, the 7th Regiment garrisoned the place with an artillery observer, a rifle team, and a machine-gun crew, a small victory perhaps but a morale booster nonetheless.

For most of the Cottonbalers, though, frontline duty in late April conformed to the same old dismal pattern of siege warfare and daily survival. Russ Cloer was a twenty-three-year-old second lieutenant who joined the unit as a replacement infantry officer—the most perishable commodity of all—in late February. In 1943, after four years of ROTC training at Rutgers University, Cloer graduated and entered the Army. The next day he and twenty-nine other Rutgers ROTC classmates reported to Officer Candidate School at Fort Benning. Twenty-one of them made it through the challenging thirteen-week course. Of those twenty-one, only ten survived World War II.

Well-trained, eager, fresh, young, and imbued with the infantry officer's famous motto "Follow Me," Cloer took command of the regiment's intelligence and reconnaissance platoon. He found a starkly different kind of war from what he had expected: "At night, the constant rumble and flutter of artillery overhead, theirs and ours. The rattle of machine gun fire, ours slow, theirs rapid. The ricochet of brilliant tracers skyward; ours red, theirs green or white. The wavering light of a parachute flare, lighting the flat and desolate landscape. The solid mass of white searchlight beams and red antiaircraft tracers over the harbor during air attack. The sheer terror of incoming 88 mm fire from a German Tiger tank. The haunting cry of 'Medic!' echoing through the night. And on a rare quiet night, the sound of the Krauts singing "*Lili Marlene*." Bloated corpses and black flies. The sickening odor of death. Cold C or K rations. No sleep. Rain. Mud. Trench Foot. Malaria. The incredible loneliness. The joy of a letter from home!"[107]

Cloer and the others stayed in their positions until the end of the month, when the regiment once again left the front line and rested at "The Pines." This stand-down lasted for three weeks. During those three weeks, the men trained intensively in offensive tactics (assaulting pillboxes and machine-gun emplacements, dealing with minefields and barbed wire), a sure tip-off that the high command was planning a breakout from the Anzio beachhead. Rumors to that effect swept through the regiment.

The soldiers were right. Clark and Alexander planned a monumental offensive for May. In the first phase Allied soldiers were to break through the Gustav Line (capturing the vexing stronghold of Cassino), and in the second phase the besieged British and Americans at Anzio would unleash an attack on all fronts, break out of the beachhead, link up with their comrades from the south, cut off the German avenue of retreat, and push on Rome. As VI Corps commander, Truscott ordered the 3rd Division to attack straight forward and capture Cisterna, then Highway 7, and then a series of towns along the route to Rome. The 7th Regiment, located in the middle of the 3rd Division's positions, received the task of attacking in a straight line to Cisterna. Once they controlled the town, they were supposed to cut the road and push inland to the high ground beyond Cisterna. O'Mohundro drew up a plan for a standard two-battalion attack, 3rd Battalion on the left, 2nd Battalion on the right, both supported by tank destroyers, with the 1st Battalion in reserve.

After a final round of prayer services on May 20, the regiment moved to the lines the next couple days, entrenching themselves in concealed bivouacs just behind the forward American positions. On the night of the twenty-second, O'Daniel sent a message to O'Mohundro and told him the attack was set for the morning, H hour at 0630. O'Mohundro passed the attack message on to his battalions. In the stillness of the warm spring night, they left their bivouacs and moved to their attack positions, either right on the front lines or just ahead of them. Many of them thought of home and family. Many of them wondered if this night would be their last on earth. They waited in silence, alone in their thoughts, tense, preoccupied, resigned to their collective fate. As they did so, clocks ticked off the final moments before dawn.

AT 0545, THE COTTONBALERS' OLD FRIENDS THE 10TH Field Artillery Battalion, in tandem with division and corps artillery, as well as fighter-bombers overhead, unleashed an earsplitting bombardment on the German positions. Actually, they unmercifully blasted the positions apart. The long months of siege warfare produced a negative and positive factor for any prospective attack. On the downside, the Germans had had time to construct formidable fortifications, concentric rings of mutually supporting machine-gun and artillery positions, barbed wire, minefields, pillboxes, dug-in tanks, entrenched infantrymen, and many other perils. On the upside, the Allies had been able to ascertain the location of most of these positions and could now rain the usual devastating array of firepower upon them. In the final analysis, that was the greatest value of the pre-attack bombardment. It destroyed many of the forward positions of the Germans or persuaded German soldiers to take cover or flight.

Of course, when H hour rolled around and the bombardment lifted, the success or failure of the offensive came down to the essential element of most military operations—infantry moving into the kill zone to destroy the enemy and control ground. A misty rain had started to fall as the assault troops warily walked forward into enemy country. The Cottonbalers could barely see anything through the rain, the smoke, and the dust kicked up by the barrage.

The barrage had hurt the enemy but, unfortunately, nowhere near enough. The advance on Cisterna that day was, in actuality, little more than a disorganized, bloody brawl. The Cottonbalers negotiated their way through minefields as German artillery and mortars dropped around them. Step-by-step, in systematic fashion, they found (the hard way) German dugouts, pillboxes, fortified houses, and machine-gun posts and destroyed them. Tanks helped as much as they could, but they could not be everywhere at once. More often than not, the advance depended on the individual initiative and valor of small groups of soldiers.

For instance, E Company came upon a strongly fortified German dugout late in the morning. The enemy dugout spit fire at the lead troops of the company. A few men were hit, but most took cover in the grass or in small dips and swales. Private First Class Emery Brooks, a BAR gunner, rallied three of his buddies and charged the dugout. Enemy machine-gun bullets shredded his friends, splashing their blood and tissue on him, but he somehow remained unscathed and kept running at the dugout. For a moment he dived to the ground and checked his weapon to make sure he had loaded a fresh clip. He could hear MG-42 bullets snapping around him. A couple even grazed him. He stood up, ran at the dugout, and fired his BAR on full automatic, killing the enemy gunners and eliminating the dugout.

This kind of kill or be killed combat went on all day long, as the two battalions slowly slugged their way forward against tremendous resistance. With every passing second, men were killed and wounded. Some of the unwounded straggled back to the rear. Some soldiers broke down mentally and had to be evacuated with combat fatigue; they shook violently, broke down weeping, or froze in terror, unable to make their limbs move.

Most of the troops, though, remained with their outfits, scattered around somewhere in anonymous nooks and crannies of the Italian landscape, and did their part to help the unit advance. Usually that meant providing fire support for men like Brooks, or perhaps taking the lead scout position, or maybe patching up a wounded buddy—under fire of course—and seeing that he got sent back. All in all, the day was terrible, interminable, a symphony of horrible sights, smells, and sounds, a grassy, muddy maze of sudden, violent death.

On this day alone, the regiment suffered 54 dead and 150 wounded. The 3rd Division had already lost 1,000 men. The Cottonbalers had not yet captured Cisterna. They still had about a mile to go.

Because of the terrible losses and the bitterness of the fighting, O'Mohundro ordered 1st Battalion into the fray on the twenty-fourth. The added manpower of the "Red" battalion helped the situation, but the day unfolded just like the previous one. Supported by artillery and tanks, the troops moved slowly along the road to Cisterna, taking casualties every step of the way, as they killed off stubborn German defenders. It was a mess, a free-for-all, a slaughter.

By evening the regiment was finally in a position to attack Cisterna. The 3rd Battalion had captured a key objective (called "J") to the northwest of the town, along the road, and prepared to attack from there. The 2nd Battalion was in position just to the west of the town, preparing to go right into the mess of ruined, collapsed, destroyed buildings that now constituted Cisterna. The 1st Battalion was farther to the rear, destroying any bypassed opposition and rounding up prisoners.

During the night the 3rd and 2nd Battalions attacked. The men of the 3rd got nowhere, mainly because of friendly fire. American artillery dropped rounds on these unfortunate troops. Then, for good measure, American planes strafed them, killing and wounding dozens, demoralizing everyone, killing any momentum the attack might have enjoyed. The officers of this battalion spent most of the night rallying and reorganizing their shattered companies.

The 2nd Battalion advanced right into a minefield of antitank and antipersonnel mines. O'Daniel had invented ingenious ways to thwart the minefields he knew his troops would face. He fit many of his light tanks with special four-hundred-foot-long steel pipes filled with explosives. In tandem with machine-gun fire, these tanks blew nice, manageable swaths through minefields.[108] In this manner, the 2nd Battalion slowly worked its way through the minefields.

Freed of this impediment, they poured over a railroad embankment adjacent to the town and surprised at least two hundred German soldiers, shooting them mercilessly at close range. The enemy soldiers ran into the town, surrendered, or died. The 2nd Battalion soldiers, mainly men from E and G Companies, with a few F Company exiles mixed in, pursued them into the town itself. Here the fighting raged amid piles of rubble and the remnants of buildings. The combat was close range, man-to-man, as the Americans worked their way from house to house. The Cottonbalers used rifle grenades, bazookas, machine guns, submachine guns, hand grenades, and whatever else would work in this close-quarter fight. "We fought our way through the battered town of Cisterna that night," Lieutenant Cloer recalled. "Fires were everywhere from artillery and white phosphorous mortar fire. We choked on smoke, cordite, and cement dust from the shattered concrete buildings. A Sherman tank supported us, obliterating enemy strong points with its 75mm cannon at point blank range. The streets were littered with corpses lying where they fell, abandoned weapons, destroyed vehicles and collapsed buildings. This was what Hell must be like."[109]

The second Battle of Cisterna now reached a climax. The American soldiers fought with berserk courage, spreading death and bloodshed from house to house. One sergeant, leading a platoon, charged into a basement full of a hundred German troops. He chucked several grenades at them and screamed for them to surrender. The grenades exploded and he heard bloodcurdling screams. Through the dust and bloody timbers of the basement, he then saw a whole column of German soldiers, hands up, ready to surrender.

The sun rose and still the fighting raged. The 3rd Battalion now swung around from the south and was slowly mauling its way into the town, joined shortly by the 1st Battalion. The Germans holed up in a castle in the center of the town and, protected by an antitank gun that covered the only entrance to the castle, attempted to make a last stand. A machine-gun team from F Company set up in a building opposite the castle and kept up a steady fire on the enemy antitank gun, forcing the crew to take cover. In the meantime, troops from G Company, along with a tank, maneuvered to firing positions. The tank blew a hole in the castle and roared past the antitank gun and into the main grounds within the castle. Cottonbalers poured into the grounds, right behind the tank, ready to shoot anything that moved. The Germans inside, 250 in all, including the command group of an enemy regiment, threw down their weapons and surrendered.

By nightfall on the twenty-fifth, the Americans had eliminated the last enemy resistance. The men were absolutely filthy and dusty. Many of them had nasty-looking bloody scrapes or scabs on their arms and legs from diving and crawling in the rubble. Sweat on their foreheads mixed with dirt, giving their faces a streaked appearance; their eyes were dull and their faces betrayed little expression except fatigue. They looked old and haggard even though most of them were several years shy of their twenty-fifth birthday. They could hardly comprehend that three days of bitter fighting were finally over.

The regiment had incurred horrible losses: 116 men killed and 556 wounded, along with an undetermined number of missing, combat fatigued, and captured. In exchange for this harvest of death and suffering, the 7th Regiment successfully conquered Cisterna, an objective that had eluded the Allies since January, when the awful town swallowed up two battalions of Rangers. In addition, the Cottonbalers captured 931 German prisoners, most in Cisterna, and eliminated an entire enemy division, the 715th; impressive achievements, won at terrible cost.[110]

Eric Sevareid, the famous war correspondent, entered Cisterna soon after the Cottonbalers took it. He compared the scene there to the destruction at Ypres in the First World War. He could not even tell where streets had once been: "The ruins had the stillness of ancient ruins but without their dignity. A dust cloud drifted away to reveal a buggyload of old men in what had been the central square. They said nothing. They did nothing. They merely sat there and stared with unbelieving eyes. In the little park the palm trees lay blackened and uprooted."[111]

THANKFULLY, THE CAPTURE OF CISTERNA, IN CONJUNC-
tion with the 1st Armored Division's capture of nearby Cori, un-hinged the German lines at Anzio and broke the stalemate that had existed there for five months. The way was now clear for the 3rd Division to advance rapidly inland, subdue the Alban Hills, and follow the main roads, seizing many key towns along the way to Rome. The division, and the 7th Regiment, now focused on pushing for the key town of Valmontone, some twelve miles away. Valmontone sat astride Highway 6, a road that ran south to Cassino and north to Rome. Control of Valmontone would allow the Americans to cut off a natural axis of retreat for the Germans and would, obviously, provide a route into Rome.

During the bitter fight for Cisterna, the 7th Regiment had fallen behind the rest of the division. O'Mohundro let the men rest a day or so, and then he lined up all three of his rifle battalions and advanced them northeast along the main road to Valmontone. "We left a scene of desolation behind us," Cloer wrote, "burning tanks and vehicles, dead men and horses bloated in the Italian sun, their eyes and wounds covered with swarms of huge black flies, the odor indescribable. Fire, smoke and collapsed buildings destroyed by tanks, artillery and fire. Abandoned weapons, helmets, ammo and equipment of every description littered the landscape. Columns of Kraut POWs trudged to our rear in shock, helmets and weapons gone, hands clasped above heads bowed in submission. The residue of war."[112]

German resistance sharpened noticeably near Artena, where the regiment set up positions just west of the 15th Infantry, whose soldiers were on the verge of taking the town. The 1st Battalion of the 7th pressed forward and overwhelmed dug-in troops from the ubiquitous Hermann Göring Division. The Americans used two-foot-high wheat as concealment and worked closely with tanks to blast out the Germans along a hillside. The battalion commander, Lieutenant Colonel Izenour, explained why his lead assault company prevailed against such tough opposition: "Company A was able to reach its objective only because my boys wanted that ground worse than Goering's did." The successful attack won Izenour's boys a vital road and rail junction leading to Valmontone.[113]

The regiment now braced itself for the final push on Valmontone. On May 31 some of the Cottonbalers were dug into positions, dodging enemy sniper and mortar fire, not far from the town. At that time, a medic named Isadore Valenti joined K Company. The son of an Italian immigrant, Valenti hailed from Cadogan, Pennsylvania. He dropped out of school in the ninth grade to take a job in a coal mine. The draft snagged him in 1941, and he ended up being trained as a medic, serving with the 51st Medical Battalion all through North Africa, Sicily, and Italy. In late May 1944, as casualties piled up during the big push, Sergeant Valenti got assigned to K Company as a frontline medic. He met a few of the men and found a foxhole. Lonely and scared, he sat morosely in his foxhole and listened to the sounds of a limited attack by two other companies. One of his new buddies, Private First Class John Harrington, came to his hole and shared a rumor that K Company would join the attack.

Soon four tanks rumbled up to their positions and that confirmed the truth of Harrington's rumor. At 1830 hours, they went forward: "We climbed out of our foxholes and, with grim expressions, advanced through knee-high brush in half-crouched positions. It was a frontal attack. Our immediate front blazed into action. The rattle of machine guns and the crash of mortar shells blanketed the whole area. Suddenly, the Germans began blasting us with Screaming Meemies. The four tanks just up ahead were firing both cannon and machine guns." Men began screaming for medics and Valenti rushed around trying to find them. In the meantime, the Americans captured some of the German infantry and the tanks maneuvered for a good shot at the nebelwerfers. Three of the tanks got hit and began burning fiercely. The crewmen of these tanks tried frantically to exit their tank. They howled in agony as flames consumed them. A few popped out of hatches and rolled around on the ground trying to douse the flames." Darkness had begun to descend over the chaotic battlefield when Valenti heard cries coming from the direction of the burning tanks. He crawled around trying to find the source of the sounds. At first he found only dead bodies, but the cries persisted: "The stench of burning flesh was heavy. One tank, in its last throes of flickering flames, was caught in the eerie shadows it cast." In the partial light, he finally found the wounded soldier. It was his friend Harrington, moaning and in shock. "I felt for his wound, an ugly open rent in his side. I turned him over, quickly staunched the bleeding, broke out a first-aid packet, saturated his wound with sulfa powder, and covered it with a heavy dressing. He had lost much blood. Harrington cried out, 'Get me out of here!'" Valenti gave him a shot of morphine and told him to calm down.

Valenti crawled back to the company command post and rustled up four litter bearers to remove Harrington. German soldiers, hiding in a wheat field, were probably no more than forty or fifty yards away from Harrington. Valenti's little group worked its way toward Harrington, but suddenly the Germans opened up on them with burp guns. Terrified, they all dived for cover. The litter team viciously cursed Valenti: "What the hell you trying to do? Get us killed? You son of a bitch!" They left. Valenti lay flat on the ground, almost wanting to cry in frustration. He had to get Harrington out. He just had to: "I could feel the heavy throbbing of my pounding heart. Out of the night came the sound of clashing gears as a German tank was munching the ground about a hundred yards somewhere out there beyond the grain field."

He started crawling back to the command post and heard movement and German voices in the grain field. They shot at him and he ran as fast he could to the next hole and jumped in, sharing it with a dead American soldier. Finally he made it back to the command post. He had no trouble enlisting three riflemen to help remove Harrington. They took a different approach and found Harrington still alive. They hoisted him onto the stretcher and painstakingly hauled him out of there and back to the battalion aid station. Still conscious, Harrington gave Valenti a small token of his appreciation—a can of candy his girl-friend had sent him. Harrington had a million-dollar wound: the kind that did not maim you but got you out of combat. Totally spent, Valenti went back to his foxhole: "I felt lonely in the foxhole, yet I sensed a feeling of well-being, an inner satisfaction from a small measure of ac-complishment. Then I fell into an exhausted sleep."[114]

The battle reached its climax during the first few days of June, as the 7th Infantry kept pushing to Valmontone and its surrounding high ground and roads. The Germans were retreating, but they were still fighting stubbornly as they withdrew. On June 1, a nineteen-year-old rifleman replacement named Earl Reitan saw his first combat with F Company of the 2nd Battalion. Reitan was an upper midwesterner of Norwegian descent. His father was a banker in Grove City, Minnesota. In 1935 he lost his job because of the depression and the family moved on to tiny Alberta, Minnesota, where he found a job as a bank cashier. Young Earl graduated from high school in 1942 and attended Concordia College for a year before being drafted in 1943. By then the Army had a voracious appetite for young infantrymen, and Reitan was prime meat. He became a rifleman and joined the 7th Infantry as a replacement at the end of May, when the unit badly needed an infusion of new men.

Quite often in World War II, the Army threw replacements into their units with little indoctrination or orientation. The bewildered men joined their outfits as individuals, strangers, experiencing the worst stress of their young lives.[115] The 3rd Division, even in the middle of its horrendous battles of late May and early June 1944, tried to ease its new men into combat with some semblance of a welcome and orientation. Reitan remembered that General O'Daniel himself spoke to his group of replacements when they arrived in late May. The general told them all about the impressive history of the division and carefully enumerated what was expected of them as Marne division soldiers. From there the group moved on to the 7th Infantry command post, where an officer regaled them with a quick overview of the history of the regiment, dating all the way back to the Battle of New Orleans. The pep talk boosted Reitan's morale a bit: "I was impressed and stood a little taller when we marched off to join our units."

Reitan reached his unit on May 31 and met his company commander, none other than Joe Martin, along with many other members of the company. Reitan's platoon leader, Second Lieutenant William Wolever, also a new man, told him and the other replacements to dig in. The next day Reitan's platoon marched forward to support the battalion's attack for that morning: "American tanks were running back and forth behind a ridge. It was exciting; I felt like I was in a movie." The excitement soon wore off when German shells began pounding their positions: "Shells came screaming in, tearing huge holes in the ground and ripping up trees. Cries of 'Medic' . . . came from all sides. I hugged the ground as hard as I could. Never had I felt so close to Mother Earth." Mercifully the shelling soon stopped, but it took its toll. Seven men had been killed and another nineteen wounded: "I realized that I was not in a movie—this was the real thing!" In fact, Reitan had been among fifteen replacements to join the company that day. Three were already dead and another four wounded.

They continued moving through rugged, hilly terrain that night. The 2nd Battalion was now leading the way for the 7th Regiment. The soldiers saw American shells streaking overhead, exploding in the hills and valleys beyond. In the morning, F Company reached a thick stand of woods overlooking Valmontone. They braved sniper fire, and, unopposed, seized Highway 6 and the hills west of town. They dug in and watched for Germans all night on the second: "Sitting on the edge of a foxhole and peering into the darkness while reacting to every sound is nerve-wracking. Despite the tension, one must always fight sleep. After two strenuous days, I was exhausted. I think the veteran who was my foxhole buddy did most of the watching that night." Meanwhile, other soldiers from the battalion cleared out Valmontone and set up positions along high ground beyond the town.[116]

German resistance was collapsing, but the enemy still had enough strength to cause problems for 3rd Battalion the next day. The rifle companies from the so-called "Blue" battalion were in the process of advancing toward a crossroads near Palestrina. Their goal was to cut off a German avenue of retreat. Sergeant Valenti was moving with the advance elements of the battalion, near Palestrina, a small group of thirteen men, tromping around the Italian countryside on a reconnaissance mission that day. They entered a wheat field and halted for a few minutes while the patrol leader, Lieutenant Tom Scully, figured out where they were and what kind of resistance might lie ahead. The men hid in the two-foot-high wheat, sweltered under the hot sun, and chatted. One of the riflemen, a midwestern farmer, told Valenti about his farm and showed him a picture of the girl he hoped to marry. Another man, carrying a Thompson submachine gun, crawled over and asked for water. Valenti gave him a pull from his canteen. Insects buzzed around them, and when the wind blew, the wheat tickled their throats and nostrils. The whole scene seemed very peaceful.

It wasn't. A retreating group of German soldiers spotted them and opened fire. The enemy had tanks, flak wagons, and machine guns. "I felt myself being rolled over and lifted off the ground. I recall vividly the deafening sounds of exploding shells and machine-gun fire just before losing consciousness." Valenti awoke sometime later and heard nothing but silence. "The air reeked of burned flesh. The stillness was penetrated by the cry of 'Medic!' It was Carmen DeFilippo." Valenti crawled over to him. "His rifle stock was splintered. DeFilippo was in shock, with a severe hand wound. Two fingers were almost gone from his hand. I gave him a shot of morphine and dressed his wounds; later I gave him sulfa pills in case of infection."

Valenti had also been hit in the hand, although not as severely. He felt groggy from concussion. "I cleaned my wound; sprinkled it with sulfa powder and wrapped it." The Thompson gunner was still alive. He and Valenti peeked through the wheat at the nearby Palestrina road. They saw German soldiers rushing around and hollering to one another. For an hour and a half, as the sun got hotter and higher in the sky, they watched the Germans scramble around and then retreat. Soon two Sherman tanks rumbled into the wheat field and shot at the Germans. The American tanks almost ran over Valenti and the Thompson man, before moving on. Two sergeants from the patrol, visibly shaken, materialized from within the maze of wheat stalks, plopped down, and told Valenti that the rest of the patrol needed help.

Valenti crawled over to them and recoiled in horror. They were all dead, eight of them, including the farmer and the lieutenant, lying lifeless and torn in the bloody wheat: "The sight was frightening and unnerving. Already the bugs . . . were gathering for their gruesome work. I reacted with shock and disbelief." He took some water and food from the dead bodies and went back to the sergeants. Along the way, he saw the dead bodies of the regimental executive officer, Lieutenant Colonel John Toffey III, a beloved figure in the outfit, and red-haired First Lieutenant John Raney, the M Company commander.

Valenti could hardly maintain control of himself. He was emotionally spent. "My mind could barely comprehend this sort of thing happening so suddenly. Men who this day . . . talked about their plans for a new life after the war . . . lay lifeless in an Italian wheatfield." He collected himself and escorted DeFilippo to the battalion aid station.[117]

VALENTI WOULD NOT HAVE KNOWN IT FROM HIS EXPERIences that scorching day, but the Germans were now in full, headlong retreat and the road to Rome lay wide open. Clark, meanwhile, had made the worst of many bad decisions in his tenure as 5th Army commander. Instead of pushing east and cutting off most of the retreating German Army in Italy, as Alexander had ordered him to do in the original planning for this offensive, Clark ordered an immediate left turn north, in essence, choosing Rome over the destruction of most of the German forces in Italy, an incredibly dumb thing to do. The Allies were going to liberate Rome anyway; the tactical situation now dictated that eventuality. Far better to keep moving east, thus encircling the hard-pressed, retreating Germans. Once they were dealt with, everyone could then party in Rome and have a great time, secure in the knowledge that the Germans had been kicked out of Italy.

Churchill's original strategic vision might possibly have been realized. Italy could have been the gateway to the Balkans or even Austria. Such a scenario would have presented the Germans with one more unwelcome crisis at a time when they were dealing with a massive Soviet offensive in the east and the Normandy invasion in the west (an event that ultimately upstaged Clark's liberation of Rome, making his selfish decision even more foolish). In fact, Churchill saw the fruits of the breakout slipping away as early as late May and he sent pleading messages, ultimately in vain, to Alexander to make sure this did not happen. Like a prospector mesmerized by fool's gold, Clark fixated on Rome. A vain man, he wanted to enter Rome as a conquering hero. By June 4, all that really mattered to him was getting to Rome first and cruising through the city at the head of a victory parade. His shortsighted push for Rome allowed thousands of German troops to escape, set up a new defensive line in northern Italy, and inflict terrible casualties on Allied soldiers later in the war.[118]

The Cottonbalers knew nothing about such high-command machinations. They only knew that German resistance was crumbling, that the enemy did not intend to defend Rome, and that the race was on to see who could get there first. During the night of June 3–4, Colonel O'Mohundro called Lieutenant Cloer to his command post and ordered him to take a reconnaissance patrol into Rome. The colonel had heard that the Germans had declared Rome an open city and he wanted Cloer to check it out. If that was true, he could then load the 2nd and 3rd Battalions on trucks and, he hoped, make the 7th Regiment the first to enter the city.

Cloer took four jeeps and fifteen men and set off for Rome: "It was pitch dark. Smoke made visibility even worse. We passed burning American tanks and recon vehicles, and dead soldiers along the Appian Way. We met no resistance. We saw nothing alive. After five miles, we entered the city which was ominously silent. No trace of light anywhere. We saw no Krauts, no Americans, no civilians. In the total darkness, we expected to be ambushed at every corner. It was deathly quiet. Spooky." They soon got lost among the narrow, winding maze of streets, but Cloer's driver, who possessed a keen sense of direction, soon found the way to the city center: "We rounded a bend, entered a huge cobblestone piazza and there before us stood the Colosseum, silhouetted against the first blush of pink light in the eastern sky! It was a sight I'll never forget! The thrill of a lifetime!" They found their way back to O'Mohundro's command post and gave him the good news. He grinned and ordered the men to board their trucks.[119]

By the time he did so, the 1st Battalion, in tandem with members of the 1st Armored Division, had already entered the city. These Cottonbalers were serving as part of Task Force Howze (named for its commander, Colonel Hamilton Howze), a detached battle group of tankers and infantrymen whose mission was to patrol the vulnerable gap between the 3rd Division and its nearest neighbor, the 88th Division, and then press on to Rome. In this capacity, the Cottonbalers of the 1st Battalion were, most likely, the first Allied troops to enter the great city. Of course, Cloer's group may well have gotten there first, or reconnaissance patrols from the 1st Special Services Battalion, operating with Task Force Howze. It is impossible to say for sure. However, there is little question that the Cottonbalers were at the vanguard of this great moment in history, when one of Western civilization's greatest cities was liberated from an unspeakable tyranny.[120]

In the afternoon on that sunny June 4, 1944, the dirty, tired survivors of the 7th Infantry Regiment received their reward for so many months of terrible fighting. They entered Rome not as conquerors, but as liberators. Riding along in trucks and jeeps, walking in columns of twos, they basked in the moment, savoring this rare opportunity to forget death and terror, enjoy themselves, and feel good for a change. First Sergeant Pratt, the kid from North Little Rock, Arkansas, rode with his antitank company through the streets of the Eternal City: "Our motor column entered the city streets amongst some of the wildest cheering and well wishes of a rejoicing Italian population. Rome's residents were beside themselves with joy upon being liberated and especially by Americans, so many of [whom] were Italian-Americans who spoke their own language and shared their culture. The young ladies threw flowers, and young and old alike were openly weeping . . . freely and unashamedly. For us the entry into Rome was like a return to civilization. There were clean and orderly streets, beautiful buildings and pretty parks."[121]

Not far away from Pratt, Private Reitan beamed as he took in the adulation of the Roman civilians: "The route of our march took us past the Colosseum, the Forum, and other monuments of ancient Rome — the route of the victorious armies of the past. Our route was lined with civilians, dressed in their holiday best and eager to see the Americans. Italians had enormous admiration and affection for the United States, and many of them had relatives there."

When the parade was over, the regiment bivouacked in Rome and enjoyed the pleasure of garrisoning the city for a week. The men showered, shaved, got clean clothes, and immediately set about looking for women and alcohol while squeezing in some sightseeing. Private Reitan even went to Mussolini's great office and sat in his chair.[122]

The vacation was too good to last. Unbeknownst to the Cotton-balers, the generals had one last amphibious invasion in the works, and they needed an experienced unit to lead it.

9

The Greatest War, World War II

Riviera to Berchtesgaden

As far back as 1943 the Allies contemplated not just one amphibious invasion of France but two. American planners proposed the idea of two complementary landings, one in the north and one in the south. The two concurrent attacks would put intolerable pressure on the Germans in France and, the Americans hoped, would secure vital Mediterranean seaports like Marseille as supply bases for the Allied army in Europe. The British, reluctant and gun-shy about the invasion in the north, adamantly opposed the notion of a southern strike, especially as the moment for the southern attack approached in the summer of 1944. Churchill, in particular, argued vociferously against Operation Anvil/Dragoon, as the southern France invasion became known. Fixated on the situation in Italy and the Balkans, and with an ever-present eye on the impact Soviet advances would have on the postwar future of Europe, Churchill believed that an invasion of southern France was redundant and unnecessary. Far better to exploit the capture of Rome with an all-out push into northern Italy and the Balkans. Churchill lost this argument, and planning for Anvil/Dragoon proceeded.

Originally, the southern invasion, to be carried out on the beaches of the Riviera, was supposed to take place before the one in Normandy. But the demands of Anzio, Normandy, and several Pacific theater invasions soaked up most of the Allied amphibious capability, particularly landing craft. So, the generals indefinitely postponed Anvil/Dragoon. Planning continued, though, and when the Allies stalled north of Rome and Eisenhower's successful invasion in Normandy deadlocked in the hedgerows of that province, the Americans once again came to view the Riviera invasion as essential.[1]

For the Cottonbalers this meant being earmarked for one last amphibious invasion. After their all too brief Rome vacation, they trucked back to the Anzio beaches, boarded ships, and sailed back to their old training area in Pozzuoli near Naples. They spent much of the summer there training intensively. General O'Daniel believed just as strongly as Truscott in sharpening his troops to a razor edge. O'Daniel wanted them to be tougher, stronger, smarter, more physically fit, and more ruthless than their German enemies. The soldiers spent their days in mock assaults on leftover pillboxes from the Italian campaign, laying and cutting barbed wire, integrating replacements, learning how to use bangalore torpedoes (explosive-charged torpedo tubes designed to blow holes through barbed wire and minefields), coordinating with tanks, breaking in new weapons, such as flamethrowers. They also received the Army's new combat boots that replaced the old World War I–style brogan boots and leggings (an uncomfortable, annoying piece of equipment). The new boots featured a leather strap on top that fastened around the pant leg with two simple buckles. The division endlessly drilled in embarkation and debarkation, carrying out several mock invasions. In addition to all this specialized training, the Truscott Trot–style mountain hikes continued.

The men had plenty of water and food. They even had the opportunity to take regular showers. Life settled into a routine. "We slept in tents, washed in outdoor showers and ate hot food in an outdoor chow line," Lieutenant Cloer wrote. According to Private Reitan, the food was good and plentiful: "We now had cooked meals. The food was served from large kettles into mess kits. Second helpings were available. When you were finished, you took your mess kits to tubs of hot soapy water and clear water to wash and rinse. Before you got there, however, you passed a line of little Italian kids holding buckets to collect your scraps. Most of us managed to have something left to put into their buckets. A few years ago I read an article about Sophia Loren, who grew up in Pozzuli [sic] and recalled being one of those children. It was gratifying to think that I may have contributed some of the nutrition which went into building that magnificent body!"[2]

In spite of the intensive training, the troops had plenty of free time, and, naturally, Naples beckoned. Private Valenti thought the town was even seedier than the last time he had been there several months before: "Same old place, same old stink. One exception—the prostitutes [were] younger and the pimps more aggressive." In fact, these flesh peddlers were so aggressive that they plied their services just outside the regiment's bivouac area: "Ringing our bivouac area, pimps with their prostitutes set up shop. Each day girls, some scarcely in their teens, were brought in to the medics as suspected VD carriers, for . . . VD tests." In dealing with these women, one of the doctors used Valenti as a translator. As best he could, he explained to the women why they must submit to testing.

The Army could not hope to regulate or control the rampant sexual activity that went on among the regiment, and other units, that summer. If a soldier wanted a whore, he only needed money and a suitable love nest. "One day I bumped into several clusters of G.I.'s," Valenti wrote. "There, in the shadows of some thickets, I saw a half dozen pup tents, each occupied by a girl. Two sets of feet protruded from each pup tent. Other soldiers were waiting in line for their turn. Outside of each tent . . . stood a G.I. sharpie who collected the fee before permitting the pleasure-seeking G.I. to crawl in."[3]

While the soldiers trained hard and played hard, senior officers planned the particulars of the invasion. Augmented by French commandos, as well as British and American paratroopers, three veteran American infantry divisions, supported by tanks, were to assault the beaches. The 36th Infantry Division's sector was in the east, on the extreme right, near Saint-Raphael. In the center the 45th Division would hit Saint-Sardineaux, opposite a cove from Saint-Tropez. The 3rd Division drew the job of assaulting on the left (west) flank at Cape Cavalaire. As usual, the 7th Regiment would lead the way, attacking yet another code-named Beach Red. O'Mohundro chose the 2nd and 3rd Battalions to lead the assault: the 3rd on the left and the 2nd on the right. These troops were supposed to fan out left and right, link up with French commandos or Allied paratroopers, capture key road junctions and towns, and generally push as far north as possible.

In terms of suitability for an amphibious invasion, Beach Red was about as good as it got. "[It] consisted of a soft fine sand beach flanked by a narrow belt of tree covered dunes behind which is the coast road and railroad," Major John D. Foulk, the regimental operations officer, said. "Exits were adequate initially for a limited amount of personnel and heavy motor transportation after which minor preparations would be necessary. One principal hard surfaced road, Route 98, existed, however, several other good roads formed a suitable network for transportation." The beaches gradually gave way to plains of cultivated fields and slopes "covered with scattered woods, however the lower slopes are usually terraced and cultivated. Good anchorage for craft could be obtained 400 yards off shore in six fathoms of water. [Beach Red] is 3900 yards long and from 20 to 50 yards wide; the southwestern half of the beach is backed by wooded slopes and the outskirts of the village of Cavalaire-sur-Mer. In the eastern half of [Beach Red] the hinterland consisted of cultivated fields with scattered field and farm houses."

Enemy defenses were considerable but not overwhelming: "[They] consisted of a shallow line of pillboxes, casements and strong points located inland from the landing areas. All defenses were enclosed with tactical [barbed] wire and mines. Offshore mines and obstacles were numerous in the 7th Infantry Regimental sector. Counterattacks . . . could be expected in a short time after the establishment of the initial beachhead line."[4]

Foulk and his colleagues set up a top secret "War Room," a planning tent in an olive grove, surrounded by barbed wire and guards. Inside they worked on maps, aerial photographs, and sand tables. Even many of those officers who worked in the War Room, like Foulk, did not know the location of the target area: "No one except selected commanders and staff officers knew the exact country where the landing was to take place." Maps and photos were unidentified. As at Normandy, the success of this invasion depended on concealing from the enemy the exact time and place it would happen. So far, security had held. The Germans, at this time, knew an invasion was imminent, but they did not know where to expect it. In early August, word of the 7th Regiment's destination gradually filtered down from the battalion commanders to the staff officers.[5] The troops knew they would soon embark on an invasion, but they did not, as yet, know where. They had an inkling, though, because many Italian civilians routinely asked them, "Hey, Joe, you go France?"

On August 3, the regiment left its training bivouac and marched to an invasion assembly area at Piano di Quarto. They got their first real tip-off regarding their destination when finance officers ordered them to exchange their lire for French francs. No one was allowed in or out of the assembly area. Security was as tight as anyone had ever seen it.

The men gathered late in the day on an open field that featured a smattering of trees for shade. Colonel O'Mohundro appeared before them and told them their general destination but few specifics. Mostly he concentrated on firing them up for battle. Valenti called this speech a "fight talk. He told us of the big operation ahead, that we wouldn't be alone in the storming of the beaches and that we would be supported by the great power of our naval and air arms." Colonel O'Mohundro never forgot the drama of the moment. "As I talked and looked into the faces browned by the hot Italian sunshine, I couldn't help wondering how many of these fine men would be lost in the landing."[6]

Everyone else wondered the same thing. Most of the men quickly forced such thoughts out of their minds, although some let fear get the best of them. "Business picked up at the Aid Stations as a rash of self inflicted gunshot wounds broke out," Cloer asserted. "Most claimed to have shot themselves in the foot while cleaning their weapon."[7] They were given only the most rudimentary medical care in the hospital and were thoroughly ostracized. Nurses hung signs saying "SIW" (self-inflicted wound) over their beds.

The overwhelming majority of soldiers attempted no such escape. Feeling a curious mixture of excitement and trepidation, they merely concentrated on preparing for the job at hand. That usually meant helping load the LSTs, LCIs, and LCTs that would carry the 7th Infantry to the Riviera. By now, the division leadership and its experienced men were quite adept at this difficult logistical task, and the loading went as smoothly as possible.

Finally, on August 9–10 the regiment left Naples Harbor and set sail for France. "After the ships were loaded with both men and equipment, and in their rendezvous areas," Foulk wrote, "the regimental S-2 [intelligence officer] personally delivered maps and data to each unit commander."[8] Junior officers now thoroughly briefed their troops on the upcoming invasion and their particular mission. Lieutenant Cloer spent a fair amount of time studying his invasion beach and rehearsing the assault in his mind. "We had excellent maps and an accurate 20 foot sand table model of [the] beach on which we would land near Cavalaire-sur-Mer. There were detailed lectures on what we could be expected to encounter and how to cope with the defenses. The chaplains were kept busy leading us in prayer and the attendance at services grew."[9]

The convoy steamed northwest, past Corsica and inexorably toward France. The seas were calm, the food was decent, and the voyage in general was not as miserable as previous forays. The men had heard all about the great naval armada that would support them, but most could not see anything beyond the next few ships.

They had only been at sea for a few days when they spotted something quite out of the ordinary. Private Reitan was belowdecks when he heard a commotion. For some reason, men were saying something like, "Churchill is coming!" Curious, Reitan hurried up to the deck and gazed at the sea. He could hardly believe his eyes: "There he was, standing in a PT boat, buzzing along the rows of ships. His arm was extended in his famous 'V for Victory' sign, his white hair flowing in the breeze. I was surprised to see how pink his cheeks were. He did not have his signature cigar in his mouth, which led some GI's to shout 'Hey, Winnie. Where's your cigar?'" The sight of this remarkable leader buoyed their morale and spirits. Most of them had no idea he had bitterly opposed these landings. "All the ships were crowded with men," Churchill later wrote, "and as we passed along their lines, they cheered enthusiastically. They did not know that if I had had my way they would be sailing in a different direction. However, I was proud to wave to these gallant soldiers."[10]

THE CONVOY SAILED ON AND ON THE NIGHT OF AUGUST 14 edged close to the French coast. D-Day was the next day and H-Hour was scheduled for 0800. For the first time in this war, the 7th Infantry would invade a hostile beach in the daytime. Five years of accumulated Allied might was about to be thrown at the Germans in southern France. Somewhere out there in the darkness, the invasion armada bristled with battleships, aircraft carriers, cruisers, submarines, destroyers, subchasers, destroyer escorts, minesweepers, oilers, and landing craft of all sizes and description. Aboard their ships, the soldiers busied themselves with a million little tasks or pastimes—checking equipment and weapons, wolfing down one last meal, dice games, card games, prayer services, sand-table study, bull sessions, writing letters home, or maybe just sitting and thinking of what lay ahead. "There is no way to describe the tension and the knot in the pit of the stomach that one experiences at a time like that," Reitan commented. Inevitably, each man wondered, in his deepest, innermost, reluctant thoughts, if he would be alive to see the sunset on the fifteenth.

The moments ticked by with relentless indifference. On the ships carrying the assault troops, commanding voices over loudspeakers told the troops to board their landing craft. It was still nighttime, but the men could make out the faintest streaks of dawn in the east. Sailors lowered rope nets over the sides of the ships. Along with the rest of F Company, 2nd Battalion, Private Reitan prepared to make the tricky crossing from the ship to the bobbing LCVP (Higgins boat) below: "Heavily laden with my rifle, rifle grenades, ammo, pack, canteen, rations, etc., I followed my buddies down the rope net. I could see that the boat was heaving up and down about six feet. A mistake in timing would be crippling. I watched the boat go down and then come rushing up toward me. At the peak of its rise, I put my foot on the edge of the rail and let go of the net. The boat was just beginning to fall away and two of my buddies caught me and steadied me. When the boat was full we circled for as much as an hour until the other landing craft were loaded."

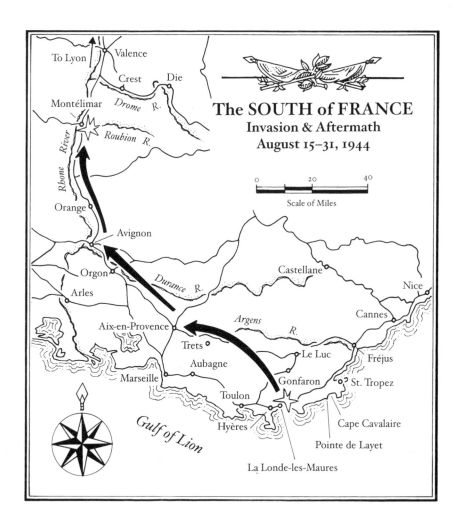

The SOUTH of FRANCE
Invasion & Aftermath
August 15–31, 1944

Even though the weather was good and the seas were relatively calm, the heaving and pitching of the uncomfortable boat, combined with the stale diesel smell of its fuel, led to terrible seasickness among the soldiers. Reitan's platoon leader, Second Lieutenant William Wolever, watched as most of his men puked their guts out. "The sides of the boat were too high to put your head over, and it was forbidden anyway. The steel deck was slick and awash with vomit. I was concerned about our fighting ability when we got to shore."[11]

The sun was rising now and, through the early-morning haze, the soldiers could see many of the surrounding Allied ships. All of a sudden, their guns swung toward the shore and the ships began blasting away. The concussion from the big guns sent shock waves shimmering through the area. The men could feel these shock waves in their chest and on their faces. The noise was thunderous. The vast Allied armada was booming away, almost as one, battering prearranged targets—successfully, the soldiers hoped. The Cottonbalers could just barely make out the sound of planes overhead. These were heavy bombers. Seconds later, they showered the landing beaches with five-hundred-pound bombs. Fighter planes followed up with sorties of their own, diving and strafing, unleashing .50-caliber rounds, rockets, and belly bombs.

The LCVPs, carrying their precious cargo, seemed like little more than vulnerable toys sailing under the noses of angry giants. On board one of those LCVPs, Isadore Valenti stood among forty helmeted heads and watched the barrage: "Thousands of swishing rockets soared over our heads toward German targets." These rockets, launched in the thousands, were designed to explode among German minefields and clear paths for the assault troops: "Shortly before H-hour, we disappeared into the morning mist. We began zigzagging toward the beach as rockets and naval gun fire still continued a steady fire overhead. It was bedlam—a scene of uproar and confusion. Ahead, through the haze and smoke, loomed the shore. As we neared it, our faces stung from the salt sprays of the water sent up by exploding shells. A German . . . shell almost swamped our craft, causing the boat to do a complete turn around. By now, the men were crouching below the gunwale."[12]

Lieutenant Martin, a staff officer with the 2nd Battalion now, sat next to the coxswain as his Higgins boat headed for shore. "B-25's [bombers] were plastering the beaches. We had a ringside seat on this beautiful sunny morning in August. I'm sitting up on the gunnel with the coxswain. I could hear machine gun bullets whizzing over my head, so I decided to get down and about that time a mortar shell landed between us and the next boat over. The shells followed us all the way in."[13]

The time was 0800 hours, the moment of truth for the 7th Infantry. The preinvasion bombardment was terrific; the sailors and airmen who carried it out did an excellent job of coordinating their fire and forcing the Germans to fall back to a second line of defenses. However, there was no escaping the fact that they and their powerful ordnance ultimately existed to support the infantry, the decisive arm of warfare, a bunch of ordinary Americans with rifles, mortars, machine guns, and grenades. The infantry could never succeed in this mission without the vast array of transportation and support the Navy and Army Air Force provided. But, eventually, the success or failure of the invasion depended upon the infantry, men such as the Cottonbalers, whose long history included many moments like these; moments when the very outcome of America's battles rested on their shoulders.

The landing craft churned closer and closer to the beach, against scattered mortar and machine-gun fire. The ugly rectangular boats skimmed the waves, hungrily searching for land. Two boats from G Company tripped floating mines and blew up. Geysers of water shot up in the air and the boats disintegrated in a mass of flame and twisted steel. Hunks of men scattered haphazardly and disappeared beneath the waves. Then the same thing happened to one of F Company's boats. The other boats, full of frightened men praying to God not to hit a mine, kept going. There was nothing they could do about underwater mines. If the demolition teams had not cleared them, then so be it. But every man on those boats had to live with the dread feeling, second by second, that a mine could explode at any moment and kill everyone aboard. Luckily, none of the other boats tripped any mines.[14]

Private Reitan's Higgins boat happened to be right next to the unfortunate one from his F Company that tripped the mine. Gory, messy debris from the destroyed boat landed on Reitan and the other men. A sailor assigned to lower the ramp of Reitan's Higgins boat panicked and forced his way back through the mass of soldiers. He kept muttering, "I gotta get outta here." Reitan and the other soldiers, more than used to this kind of carnage, kept their cool and waited to land. Reitan watched the sailor and felt a smug sense of superiority over him. "I'm tougher and more steadfast," Reitan thought.

A minute or two later, the boat rammed ashore. Someone lowered the ramp and out the soldiers went, into knee-deep surf. "When we reached the deserted beach, we fanned out and headed for the vegetation, just as we had done in practice runs. Sgt. [Earl] Swanson got us organized. There was a stucco house just back from the beach. Sergeant Swanson ordered me to fire a rifle grenade at it. I removed the pin from my grenade, inserted a blank bullet, knelt with my rifle butt on the sand . . . and fired. The rifle grenade went wobbling through the air, hit the side of the house, and exploded. No one came out, so we moved on."[15]

This experience was fairly typical for the 2nd Battalion. They received a bit of small-arms and mortar fire, but it was quite ineffective. The troops defending their portion of the beach were mostly unmotivated Hungarians and Romanians. They "seemed stunned in their holes," Lieutenant Wolever commented. Within half an hour, the battalion cleared out the beach defenses and pushed inland toward its D-Day objectives.[16]

A couple thousand yards to Reitan's left, in the 3rd Battalion sector, Valenti, the medic with K Company, felt a heart-bursting fear welling up in his chest as his craft approached the beach: "Panic was about to paralyze me, when suddenly I felt a heavy lurch: our boat's bottom scraped onto the sandy beach. Geysers of water shot up as the craft's ramp smacked down hard, with a sharp slap, as it hit the water. Men scrambled out over the beach. I streaked toward the protection of fallen trees thirty or forty yards beyond the beach. On solid ground . . . I felt much better and secure, for the moment. Everywhere, men disappeared into the heavy haze which was beginning to rise over the beach." The Navy was laying down a protective smoke screen so that German artillery and mortars could not spot the troops on the beaches. Inaccurate nebelwerfer and small-arms fire peppered the beach. For a time, Valenti stopped to help a couple of men who had been wounded by exploding mines. Then he and the others pressed on. "We dashed across the 40 or 50 yards of open beach, and entered a belt of tree-covered dunes which ran parallel to the beach. Behind this rise ran a coastal road, Route 98, a principal surface-treated, two-way . . . road, parallel to the coast."[17] All three companies of the 3rd Battalion drove on to set up roadblocks and capture their objectives, against mostly disinterested resistance.

The same could not be said for the Battle Patrol, which came ashore on the extreme left of the whole 7th Infantry. Dieleman's Battle Patrol drew the mission of landing at H hour immediately adjacent to the 3rd Battalion and pushing west to take Cavalaire-sur-Mer and the peninsula on which it was located. This peninsula housed German self-propelled guns, antiaircraft guns, pillboxes and machine guns, all with enfilade fire on the landing beaches. The Battle Patrol, beefed up to 154 men for this challenging task, experienced the 7th Infantry's toughest fight on D-Day. When they came ashore, they immediately ran into mines and came under enemy mortar and flak fire (the Germans used 20mm flak guns as very effective antipersonnel weapons). Crouched over and inching their way forward along the beach, the Battle Patrol soldiers could not make it to the highway that led to Cavalaire-sur-Mer.

The Navy came to the rescue by intensifying the smoke screen in the area. This diminished the accuracy of enemy fire and allowed the Battle Patrol to form up, turn left, and start moving. Of course, if the smoke obscured the vision of the Germans, it also did the same to the GIs. Consequently, they could not see German mines, as Staff Sergeant Herman Nevers recalled: "I suddenly noticed a wire just above my head. I looked back and . . . saw . . . a hanging mine explode and tear the platoon leader into small pieces. The force of the explosion blew S/Sgt James P. Connor [platoon sergeant] about ten feet and knocked him flat to the ground." Connor shook his head to clear the cobwebs. He had fragments in his neck and he did not look good. Dieleman ordered him to go back for first aid, but he refused. The advance continued.

They came to a bridge; a German popped up, and Connor shot and killed him. Then mortar rounds started dropping all around them. They spread out and took cover in confused little groups. Minutes later, a lone Mauser shot rang out. A nanosecond later, a bullet smashed through Connor's left shoulder. Blood, bone, and tissue sprayed from the awful wound. Nevers turned to his fellow noncommissioned officer and bellowed, "For Christ's sake, Connor, stop and get medical attention for yourself!" Connor looked at him and said, "No, they can hit me, but they can't stop me. I'll go until I can't go any farther. Get out there on the right flank and get those men rolling! We've got to clean out these snipers before we can advance farther!" Blood trickled in red droplets from both of his wounds. He looked at his scared men, all of whom were hugging the ground for dear life: "If there's only one of us left, we've got to get to that point [the objective] and clean it up, so the guys coming in after us can get in safely with no fire on them."

Crouching several yards away, Sergeant Edward Collins heard Connor order them to get moving and forget about their fear. Connor got up and started walking forward. In the face of this kind of example, Collins and the other men could do little else but follow. "With Sgt Connors [*sic*] leading us in spite of his two wounds we got busy and cleaned out the snipers and continued . . . toward our objective. We were out of . . . mortar fire now but were getting machine gun fire and rifle and rifle grenade fire. The men hesitated and wanted to stop and get help. Sgt Connor told them we had to get to our objective."

They passed through a quiet cluster of buildings and a small wooded area before running into enemy soldiers, who were dug in or ensconced in the shelter of more buildings. Connor was vulnerable, way out in front, as if willing his men forward. Suddenly a German rose from a hole thirty feet in front of Connor and shot him in the leg. Sergeant Nevers, walking a few feet away from Connor, pointed his rifle and fired. "As Sgt. Connor fell I fired over him and killed the German. This was Sgt. Connor's third serious wound in less than two hours." Nevers figured that Connor would pack it in now, but he was wrong. "Sergeant Connor called me over and told me to give him a hand to help him on his feet so he could go on with the fight. I helped him up but he couldn't stand on his leg and fell down again. I wanted to give him first aid, but he wouldn't even let me look at the wound, saying there wasn't time. He told me to take the rest of the men, about fifteen now, and to carry on. [He] told me that even if I had to get down and dig the bastards out with my bare hands to go ahead and dig them out."

Ferociously inspired by Connor's courage and leadership, Nevers and the other Cottonbalers did as he instructed. They ran forward, starting first around the right flank, but Connor called them back and sent them to the left. Breathing heavily, their hearts pounding, sweat pouring down their backs, they crashed through the smoke and shot the Germans out of their holes. Some of the men tripped more mines and booby traps. Private Norman Myhra, a nineteen-year-old rifleman and farm boy from Wisconsin, tripped a whole field of explosives and was lucky to escape with his life. "I ran into some prima-cord that was strung in some bushes . . . and it exploded when I ran up against it waist high with my M1 rifle." Private George Vanderkooi was nearby. He saw a mine disintegrate Myhra's hands. "[He] lost both hands leaving just a little piece of skin about four inches long holding his thumb on his hand. On his other hand, the little finger hung down . . . and that's all that was left of his wrist." Vanderkooi went to help his friend. "Myhra was crying for his mother and I shook him a little bit and slapped him a couple times before he snapped out of his shocked state." Myhra got up and "headed back for some medical help." He made his way to a landing craft and then to an LST. He remembered very little after that, although the medics told him that "I didn't bleed to death . . . because the explosion was so great that it swelled up into my arms and this stopped most of the bleeding." He had several operations to repair what was left of his shattered hands and was discharged in 1945. He moved back to central Wisconsin, got married, worked as a salesman, and an insurance executive, and even served a term in the state legislature.[18]

Back at Cape Cavalaire, even as Myhra got wounded, the fight was coming to an end. Forty German soldiers chose surrender. The rest died. The Americans went on a rampage now, rooting the Germans out of their fortified houses in Cavalaire-sur-Mer, destroying mortars, and closing on the peninsula. Dieleman dispatched a "strong patrol . . . to destroy all remaining enemy along the eastern coast of the peninsula. In about 1½ hours the self-propelled weapon was destroyed by a satchel charge and all other enemy weapons were neutralized by small arms fire and hand grenades." By 0945 the fight was over. The Battle Patrol had accomplished its difficult mission due, in great part, to the heroism of Connor. He later received the Medal of Honor.[19]

Follow-up waves now came ashore, including the 1st Battalion and the regimental command group. They mainly encountered artillery and mortar fire. Private Mack Bloom landed with the 1st Battalion Headquarters Company. He and the others quickly got off the beach and pressed inland to a wooded area. Bloom and his buddy, a mortarman named Morris, were getting situated when they heard the telltale sound of an incoming round: "Before we had an opportunity to react, the shell whistled in and landed right in our midst. It exploded short yards from Morris and me and we hit the ground and hugged it—at least I did. That's all there was, just one. Both of [Morris's] legs were blown away and I knew he was dead. A man couldn't live when the blood poured from him the way it did." Bloom was wrong. The medics tied tourniquets on Morris's stumps and evacuated him. A few months later, he wrote to Bloom: "His was a homey letter, no recriminations or anything."

Morris learned to walk on prosthetic legs and lived a long and healthy life.[20]

FIRMLY ASHORE, THE 7TH REGIMENT PRESSED INLAND AS fast as possible on that first day. At this point, sniper fire posed the biggest danger to the men. First Sergeant Pratt had come ashore with assault troops from the 2nd Battalion against very little resistance. He and the other men dodged a few mines and quickly made their way off the beach. "The assault troops of the 2nd Battalion, together with those of other battalions on their flanks, spread rapidly inland and soon were in culverts, just beyond the coastal road and the railroad bend. At that point I tarried behind and started scouting around for a likely command post."

He walked down the coastal road toward Cavalaire-sur-Mer, passing partially damaged cottages, until he reached a junction. "I thought the vicinity would make an excellent location for a CP." He soon learned otherwise. "I had gone only a few steps when I saw two bodies lying near the edge of the road and near the gate of a stone wall in front of a light grey stucco house." At first he thought the bodies were German, but he was wrong. They were Cottonbalers who had just been shot by an enemy sniper. Pratt thought they were dead. "I was about to walk on past the two troopers when suddenly one of them moved his head toward my direction and groaned. I went immediately to the fellow who groaned and he muttered something that sounded like 'snipers.' I started to check his wounds and could see he was shot in the arm and through the buttocks with a bullet that seemed to have hit him as he lay there by entering one side and passing out the other side of the two cheeks of his rear end. I could see that the other GI was . . . dead. He was still and his face was ashen. His eyes were partially open with the familiar death stare. Also I noticed blood on his neck and saw a bullet hole in his helmet."

Pratt began to help the wounded man. A second later, it dawned on Pratt that the sniper probably still had the spot under observation. That thought had barely registered when, all of a sudden, "I felt a stinging sensation in my left arm, and a tugging on my sleeve as though someone was pulling my field jacket—followed by a 'bump' report off to my left and down the road. The 'bump' report I promptly recognized as a rifle shot. I straightened up to buzz off for cover and as I did so, a second shot hit the asphalt between my shoes, kicking up a small puff of dust and ricocheting into the nearby hedge. I made a dive for the low wall along side the road and as I disappeared behind it, a third shot hit the wall with a 'zing.'"

This spot afforded him cover from the sniper. From there Pratt managed to crawl to safety, find the medics, and direct them to the wounded man. Pratt also reported the sniper to 2nd Battalion soldiers, who most likely found him and killed him. Pratt escaped from the harrowing incident with nothing more than grazed skin. "I had been lucky indeed. A few inches over and it would have hit my chest. Another close call of so countless many."[21]

The sun began to set and still the Cottonbalers pressed on. The enemy was on the run, fighting rearguard actions, setting up roadblocks, sniping, hurling mortar and artillery shells at the advancing Americans. The 3rd Battalion, including Valenti's K Company, pushed to the west along Highway 98 and ran into a fight sometime near midnight at Pointe de Layet. "The Germans put up a fierce fight with rifle grenades, bazookas and machine guns. One enemy machine gun was knocked out. Our only tank was crippled. I tended to the wounded." K Company was disorganized and reeling. Most of the fire came from the left, where the enemy had holed up on a small peninsula from which they could fire at anything on the road.

Valenti's tough and resourceful battalion commander, Lieutenant Colonel Lloyd Ramsey, decided to take I and L Companies and flank the enemy position. How? He swung them north of the road, to the right, through a minefield that the Germans had zeroed in on with mortars and artillery. Every few moments, unlucky soldiers tripped mines or went down with shell fragments in their arms, torsos, and faces. Most made it through the minefield, though. When they did, they effectively pinned the Germans into the peninsula and the enemy knew it. Shortly after daylight, the enemy tried to break out of this trap. For the Americans this was like a shooting gallery. German troops were running everywhere and the Yanks blazed away at them. Some of the Cottonbalers who had lain under cover all night still would not take a chance at getting hit. They kept their heads down and did not shoot. Others were more than happy to do so. The fighting did not last long. Ramsey's outfit took eighty frightened German prisoners.

In the aftermath of the fight, Valenti searched through the German tunnels and trenches for any survivors. "Only a few Germans succeeded in getting out of the trap. I searched through the maze of trenches, looking for signs of life—German or American. I found nothing but German soldiers, all dead, still in their firing positions. It was sickening. Some of the bodies were decapitated."[22]

Not long after this peninsula battle, the 2nd Battalion hit tough resistance as it tried to take the town of La Londe. This small, picturesque town featured three bridges over the Maravennes River. Without these bridges, the regiment's northward advance from its beachhead would be delayed significantly. Naturally, the Germans knew this and put up a stiff fight for the place.

During the night of August 17–18, troops from 2nd Battalion dispersed around the edges of La Londe and unleashed a hail of fire at the German defenders within. The firefight went on all night; artillery, mortars, tanks' shells, and machine-gun and rifle bullets battered the enemy-held buildings. In the morning, the Cottonbalers from E Company cautiously moved along the road leading to the town, carefully keeping an eye out for Germans. Most of the men hitched rides on tank destroyers and Sherman tanks. Everything was quiet. The Germans seemed to be long gone. Just as the tanks were about to round the last bend before the town, the soldiers saw a Frenchman frantically waving. They hollered at the tankers to stop, and they did so. In fairly good English, the Frenchman told the Americans that the Germans had set up a roadblock two hundred yards ahead; in addition, the town was full of enemy troops.

The Americans thanked him, jumped off the tanks, and fanned out along the flanks of the road, through fields in hopes of surprising the Germans. In spite of this subterfuge, the Germans still fired the first shot. Machine guns and antitank guns opened up on the Americans. One of the Sherman tanks exploded and burst into flames, incinerating the crew inside. The other armored vehicles immediately attempted to spread out and find the location of the enemy gun. The infantrymen hit the dirt or dived into ditches, sometimes crashing on top of one another.

Lieutenant George Franklin watched in horrified fascination as one soldier, a squad leader named Sergeant Stanley Bender, eschewed cover. "While I stood there with my mouth open wondering why he hadn't been killed, Sgt Bender climbed up on top of the knocked out tank and stood there looking around in an effort to spot the machine guns." Franklin himself remained standing, not out of courage but because of his extreme surprise at "Bender's audacious conduct." Sergeant Edward

Havrila, hugging the dirt nearby, lifted his head and kept his eyes riveted on Bender: "The crazy guy was standing up on top of the knocked-out tank, in full view of the krauts, shading his eyes and looking around trying to pick out the source of the enemy fire. Bullets were bouncing off that tank right beside him."

After two hair-raising minutes of this dangerous spotting, Bender jumped off the tank, ran to a ditch, and fetched two rifle squads. He had found the location of the enemy guns. They were off to the left, on a knoll some two hundred yards away. Now he wanted to lead these quivering men to the gun and destroy it. Without another word, he ran forward and vigorously motioned for the two squads to lay down a base of fire while his own squad followed him. "When the enemy saw him enter the ditch, followed by his squad, they trained their machine guns on it and forced S/Sgt Bender and his men to run the gauntlet of extremely heavy fire for at least 50 yards of the 200 yard approach," Sergeant Forrest Law, another squad leader, recalled. German machine-gun fire ricocheted around the ditch and off the road. Four of the riflemen went down as bullets ripped through their legs and torsos. They fell to the ground with a noisy clatter, coughed blood, and cried out in agony for medics. One of them was so badly wounded he could not move. Bender and six others made it through the kill zone and into a ditch some twenty-five yards in front of the machine gun. In another instant, a gaggle of German potato masher grenades came flying over the embankment. Most of the grenades burst beyond the ditch and did little damage.

Now Bender, brandishing only his Thompson submachine gun, decided to take care of the enemy machine gun himself. He crawled out of the ditch and set out on a one-man flanking expedition, walking one hundred yards or more, completely out in the open, around the enemy position. The whole company, including the intrepid remnants of Bender's squad, were just spectators now, watching Bender defy death. "Walking erect . . . he made a fine target and one of the kraut machine gunners picked up his gun and turned it around in an effort to get him," Law later wrote. Bullets, American and German, were flying everywhere. Bender's riflemen were laying down suppressive fire on the German machine gun even as the enemy gunners swung their weapon around and shot at the sergeant. Somehow nothing hit Bender, even as he steadily walked toward the German position. Law was seventy-five yards away, but he could clearly see Bender's resolute manner:

"Sergeant Bender continued his wide end sweep in a rapid walk. His manner looked as calm and unperturbed as a soldier on pass." Bender closed to within five yards of the machine gun crew, calmly raised his tommy gun, fired and killed the Germans. "Then, despite bursting hand grenades which some of the [enemy] were frantically throwing, Bender wheeled and, walking between the foxholes of some of the Kraut riflemen, made his way about 25 yds to the edge of the other machine gun position," Lieutenant Franklin wrote. "When they saw him coming they turned it around; however they were unable to fire more than two or three bursts before Bender was on top of them." Like an avenging angel, Bender pointed his Thompson and fired a short burst. The heavy .45 caliber bullets ripped through the enemy soldiers, snuffing out their lives in a matter of seconds. Bender turned and shouted at his squad to join him. In seconds they dashed out of their hiding places and joined him. In the meantime, Bender found an enemy sniper and killed him with his Thompson. Together they went from hole to hole, killing an entire squad of dug-in enemy riflemen.

All this time, the rest of E Company had been lying low, content to watch the exploits of Bender and his squad. Moment by moment, though, as they watched, their level of aggressiveness rose. The more courage Bender showed, the less hopeless and dangerous the situation seemed. If Bender could do it, so could they. "When the men . . . saw what Bender had done they went 'kill crazy' and rose from their positions screaming and yelling like Banshees," Lieutenant Franklin wrote. In a frenzy, they ran through the town, all over the knoll, hunting and killing the remaining Germans. They fell upon the German antitank guns and their surrounding positions, firing blindly and wildly. The Germans were almost powerless to respond. Before they knew it, the Americans were right on top of them, shooting entire clips of M-1 Garand ammunition, reloading and doing it again. Enemy soldiers went down in droves, littering the town and looking for all the world like gray clumps of butchered meat. The Cottonbalers shot the living and dead full of holes. The whole scene, messy and foul smelling, smacked of the vulgarity, waste, and tragedy of war. Spooked by the shocking, animallike aggressiveness of the Americans, not to mention Bender's calm, grim reaper death stroll, the unscathed Germans surrendered. The 7th Infantry killed thirty-seven Germans, took twenty-six prisoners, captured two antitank guns, and seized the bridges intact. Bender received the Medal of Honor for his actions that day.[23]

The battles at Pointe de Layet and La Londe represented the last formidable resistance the Cottonbalers encountered in the beach area. By the afternoon of August 18, the enemy was in full retreat north up the Rhône River valley. Many 3rd Division officers aptly compared the German defenses to a thin crust that, once broken, crumbled into nothing. In fact, the enemy had no desire to attempt a defense of the beach area and go toe-to-toe with Allied firepower. For one thing, Allied forces at Normandy had unhinged the German defensive line and were threatening to destroy an entire German army in addition to liberating Paris. For another, the German formations in the area were largely made up of third-line, manpower-filler type troops recruited from conquered nations. For instance, Lieutenant Cloer remembered herding hundreds of these types of prisoners to the beach. "Lots of older men and young boys with a large percentage of Russian and Polish volunteers who had apparently accepted this assignment in lieu of forced labor in German POW camps." Not long after Valenti searched through the detritus of the German trenches at Pointe de Layat, he encountered a group of Armenians itching to surrender. They had been recruited by the SS and served with a Russian battalion. "After parting with most of my water, I escorted them to the beach evacuation station for prisoners of war."[24]

In the final analysis, the German defensive system at Cavalaire-sur-Mer was not strong enough to fend off the might of the 7th Infantry and all of its supporting firepower. The Germans chose to block, impede, and harass the invading Americans as much as they could, but they did not make a determined stand like they had at Omaha Beach in Normandy. Even so, the invasion of the South of France was the costliest in the history of the 7th Infantry. The regiment lost 58 killed on D-Day alone and 5 more the next day in addition to 203 wounded. In fact, August 15, 1944, was the single deadliest day the regiment experienced in World War II.[25]

One of the wounded was Private Reitan, who ended up on the wrong side of a mortar shell early on the afternoon of the sixteenth as he and the rest of F Company rested and ate C rations: "Suddenly a cluster of German mortar shells came screaming in. The rifleman knows that the higher the pitch at the beginning, and the longer the scream continues, the closer the shell is coming. I flattened my tummy and butt against the ground and braced myself for the shock. The shell hit about two feet behind me. I felt myself bounce, and I knew that I had been hit."

A couple GIs, including Thobro, Reitan's battalion commander, helped him into a jeep and drove him to a field hospital at the beach. "There was a wound in my right buttock. I knew that I had been hit in the right knee too. There were about a dozen GI's in the hospital tent, some of them in bad shape. Since my wound did not appear to be serious, I was put on a cot to wait for the doctor." He glanced around and noticed a cot with an infamous "SIW" sign above it: "A young GI lay there sobbing. He had shot himself in the foot to get out of combat. I felt pity for him. He certainly would not have wounded himself if the tension had not been unbearable."

Medics soon took Reitan and moved him to a hospital ship just offshore. "On the ship everything was sparkling clean. Doctors, nurses, and orderlies were rushing about, taking care of the wounded, many of whom were horribly injured." At first the doctors thought he only had a flesh wound in his buttock, but Reitan told them he had been hit in the knee as well. Although they initially could find no evidence of a wound in the knee, they X-rayed it and found that Reitan was correct. The white-hot shrapnel had penetrated his knee, causing the flesh to swell and obscure the wound. In the meantime, he had eaten a big meal and swigged down a couple of Cokes. They operated on him immediately after looking at the X-rays. The anesthesia made him sick and he threw up the first decent meal he had eaten in several days: "The nurses said they had never seen anyone vomit so much." Reitan eventually went back to Naples and spent two months recovering before rejoining the unit.[26]

EVEN AS PRIVATE REITAN WORKED HIS WAY BACK THROUGH THE medical care pipeline, the 7th Infantry and its accompanying Allied units in southern France chased the retreating Germans up the Rhône valley against very scattered resistance. The French cleared out Marseille and Toulon while the Americans streaked north after the Germans. For the 7th Infantry this advance was fairly similar to the heady days in front of Palermo in July 1943 when the Cottonbalers moved an average of thirty miles per day. As a reconnaissance platoon leader, Lieutenant Cloer traveled at the leading edge of the regiment, sometimes miles ahead of the main body of troops. "My recon platoon was on the move almost continuously, feeling out the next defensive stand of the fleeing enemy. We were overwhelmed with Kraut POW's, many of whom seemed glad to have the opportunity to surrender to the

Americans. When one of my recon jeeps with four men was late getting back from what I thought was an easy mission, I went looking for them in another jeep. I found them eating ripe melons at the side of a road which bordered on a huge melon field. The weather was beautiful and you would think they were on a picnic!"[27]

Day after day, the regiment advanced, skirmishing here and there with stubborn Germans but mostly joyriding up the Rhône valley, liberating French towns every step of the way. "Our reception by the civilian population was intensely emotional and joyous," First Sergeant Pratt remembered fondly. "In almost every town we were greeted by patriotic and rejoicing French people who had long awaited . . . their day of liberation from Nazi occupation and mistreatment. The French citizens lined the streets, grabbing and kissing soldiers, and offering wines or fresh fruits. The occasions were touching to the utmost and enough to soften the hearts of even the most hardened of combat troops. Many Frenchmen wept openly in gratitude as they tried to embrace and thank their liberators for ridding them of their German oppressors."[28]

The 7th Infantry at this time got a new commander when O'Mohundro rotated home and Colonel Ben Harrell took over. A West Pointer who had once served as the regimental operations officer, Harrell was the kind of officer who led from up front. He commanded the 7th Infantry for the next four months.

The remnants of the German 19th Army were frantically trying to escape the Rhône valley and go north to Lyon and then northeast to Alsace-Lorraine or fortifications along their own western frontier, all this without being intercepted and annihilated from the northwest by Patton's advancing 3rd Army. Plus they had a victorious, fast-moving American army, led by the 3rd Division, nipping at their heels from the south. Needless to say, it was not an enviable position to be in. Basically, there was only one way out of this mess for the Germans in the South of France: Route 7 (known today as A7), the only viable avenue of escape from the area. This road wound all the way north out of the Rhône valley and through the mountainous terrain of southeastern France.

The town of Montélimar, located about halfway between Lyon and the sea, was like a first checkpoint on this German exodus. Highway 7, and a parallel railroad along the Rhône to the west, ran straight through Montélimar. As August came to a close, German troops, vehicles, and cargo packed the road, heading north as fast as they could possibly move. The convoy passed through Montélimar and made its way north.

Right behind them, the 15th Infantry moved into the town; the 7th Infantry swung around from the east, advanced, and quickly pinned them against the river. "The enemy convoys stretched for about thirteen miles," the regimental historian wrote. They "stopped as the enemy thought the road to the north had been cut. The convoy on the highway consisted practically of every type of enemy vehicle and hundreds of stolen French vehicles, trucks, ambulances, and passenger cars. An estimated 1200 horses, some tied to the vehicles and others pulling carts were in the convoy which became banked two and three deep. The railway convoy a few hundred yards to the left of the road consisted of an assortment of flat cars carrying four of the enemy's 280mm guns and two 380mm giants, boxcars with stolen foodstuffs and supplies and passenger cars."[29]

The German soldiers in this convoy were trapped and they knew it. They were about to experience the full fury of American firepower—artillery, mortars, airpower, and small arms. Like hunters tingling with excitement over the trapping of an unexpectedly large amount of quarry, the Cottonbalers portentously swapped rumors with one another about the existence of "something big" to the west over the next ridge.

Medic Valenti, moving with K Company that early morning of August 29, could feel the strange, almost ghoulish anticipation of the kill. "Veils of fog hung among the thickets, like thick layers of web. Something big was in the works." He could sense this, almost smell it, even without listening to the interplay of speculation and rumors among his buddies. Just after 0600 a couple of unseen scouts somewhere up ahead, at the apex of the ridge, spotted the quarry: an impossibly long column of vehicles and trains. They excitedly summoned an artillery forward observer, First Lieutenant Robert Metz, who gazed at the sight in the same way that Sioux tribesmen once gazed at vast herds of buffalo on the upper plains. Metz summoned his radio operator and called for every piece of artillery he could possibly summon. Then he settled back to watch the fireworks.

Not far away, with K Company, Valenti watched as the first American shells—terrible deadly "fireworks"—shrieked into the column. "The atmosphere was charged with great excitement. The first big shells landed at the head of the great column. This was followed by heavy concentrations up and down the convoy." The shells wreaked immediate havoc, tearing carts apart, sending men flying through the air, smashing cars to bits, punching holes through thinly armored vehicles, inundating infantrymen with deadly, hot fragments. Horses and men screamed in shock, barely audible above the deafening cacophony of terrible explosions. Metz had summoned the division's entire complement of artillery, plus the firepower of a nearby unit of self-propelled guns, to destroy this German convoy.

Soon Allied fighter-bombers joined in the feeding frenzy. Valenti watched them dive at their targets: "[They] added their support to the frightful work of destruction, killing horses, men and women. Yes—women. The Germans had their own fräuleins with them. It was a slaughter, a spectacle of death one is not apt to forget. We would never again see nor witness anything like it during the remainder of the war. Hundreds of human beings were strewn about in the wreckage and in nearby fields."[30]

For many minutes the slaughter proceeded. Hundreds of artillery shells roared into the expanse of the column and exploded, sowing death and liberally splashing blood everywhere. The planes made the kill zone even worse. Time after time, they dived at the column, shooting anything that moved. When their .50-caliber rounds struck vehicles, they burst into flames, cooking the men inside. The flames soon spread and engulfed those trying to get away on the road. Other strafing planes dropped their belly bombs, adding to the massive destruction. Some Germans who managed to escape the death meted out by American artillery and planes tried to move east, toward the ridge, only to be dismembered by the machine-gun, rifle, and mortar fire of the Cottonbalers. The Germans from the train convoy had a slight advantage over their comrades. Many of them jumped from the trains and hid in ditches and culverts next to the river or, in some cases, in the river itself. Most of the enemy troops were on Highway 7, though, and did not have access to the river enclave. They died awash in geysers of blood and fuel, their bodies burning and roasting in the French sun.

Finally, the planes flew away and the artillery barrage lifted. The aviators and artillerymen could no longer spot any worthwhile targets. Almost all of the Germans in the convoy were either dead, terribly wounded, or shaking violently with fear, their drawers soiled, their will broken. They would offer no further resistance. Their greatest and most immediate goal was to surrender.

The sweaty Cottonbalers now trotted down the slopes of the ridge and beheld the inferno-like scene firsthand. "Fires still burned," one of them later said. "Clothes had been burned from the bodies of the dead which were blackened beyond recognition. The dead horses lay in the most fantastic shapes, some with their legs in the air, others resting on their heads, some had been split wide open by shells and their guts and entrails were scattered about the area. Dead Germans could be seen dangling from the vehicles or in them. As the sun shone brightly and the heat of the August day increased, a terrible stench arose and many took sick." Another soldier remembered that the awful scene produced an "outrageous odor of burned and burning wood, scorched metal, stinking dead and singed flesh and clothing [that] assailed the nostrils."

Pratt grew pensive and philosophical as he took in the noxious sight of so many bloated bodies, buzzing with flies. He could only think about the awesome destruction and waste of war: "Burning and destroyed vehicles, tanks, guns, wagons, horses, and other types of rolling stock stretched up and down the highway as far as could be seen and beyond. I can recall, even to this day, pausing, as I gazed upon the hundreds of swollen, stinking and rotting corpses dotting the landscape . . . and thinking about the relatives and families on the home front."

Pratt managed to stave off nausea, but many other soldiers were down on their knees puking by the side of the road. Shots rang out as American soldiers put wounded horses out of their misery. The road was so littered with death and detritus that American vehicles, rumbling out of Montélimar, could not keep moving. Engineers had to come up with bulldozers and clear a path, shoving the remains of machines, humans, and horses into charred crimson piles by the side of the road. The engineers liberally sprinkled limestone powder over the sickening remains, in an effort to minimize the stench and the spread of disease, until burial teams could arrive in the area. "Montélimar was to be long remembered. That name was to be burned into our minds indelibly and whenever heard until a trooper's dying day would remind him instantly of an unparalleled scene of destruction, devastation and Division achievement," Pratt commented.

The 7th Regiment captured two thousand prisoners that day and killed many hundreds of enemy (the exact number has never been ascertained) and one thousand horses, destroyed two thousand vehicles, and captured dozens of enemy guns (including many 88s) along with thirty tanks. The troops looted a great deal of booty from the remnants of the enemy column, including food and weapons. Some of the men "liberated" French and German currency from a destroyed German finance train.[31]

Montélimar ranked as a kind of tiny Falaise, nowhere near as destructive and all encompassing as that famous charnel house, but impressive nonetheless when one considers that one regiment pulled off the encirclement and envelopment, mostly on its own and then so effectively utilized the incredible destructive power of American artillery and airpower. This modern-day mini-Cannae certainly must rank as one of the 7th Infantry's most decisive victories in its long history.

THE COTTONBALERS RESTED FOR A COUPLE DAYS IN THE environs of an old castle on the outskirts of Montélimar. The men cleaned their weapons and washed themselves up a bit. Then, on September 1 they boarded trucks and started driving. They left Highway 7 and veered northeast, joyriding through many more French towns in beautiful weather. Once again, civilians lined the roads and cheered them on. Quite often they could not stop and enjoy the revelry. If they did, the advance would lose momentum. In one town a beautiful blond woman tried to entice the soldiers by spreading her arms and hollering, "Stop! I love you!" The soldiers fell all over themselves trying to get out of their trucks, but much to their dismay, the speeding trucks kept going. The men morosely settled back onto their uncomfortable benches, cursed the Army, and told tales about how they would have romanced that blonde if only the convoy would have stopped ("Wouldn't you think they could cut us a break . . . just once?").[32]

Sometimes the love-starved Cottonbalers got a bit too frisky. Lieutenant Cloer, like any good reconnaissance man, led his platoon far ahead of the main truck column. On the one hand, this meant he and his men were first in danger if the Germans decided to make a stand. On the other hand, it also meant that they liberated towns first and basked in the unbridled excitement of the populace. One day Cloer's platoon entered a small town amid the ringing of church bells. "French civilians of every age and description lined the road, cheering, throwing flowers, offering wine and fruit, many crying with joy after four years of brutal occupation. A very pretty young woman danced up to our jeep on the driver's side. Steele [his driver, the one with the uncanny sense of direction] braked to a stop, and she gave him a big hug and a kiss. I was riding in the passenger seat. She leaned forward between Steele and the steering wheel and was about to give me a kiss too, when she suddenly

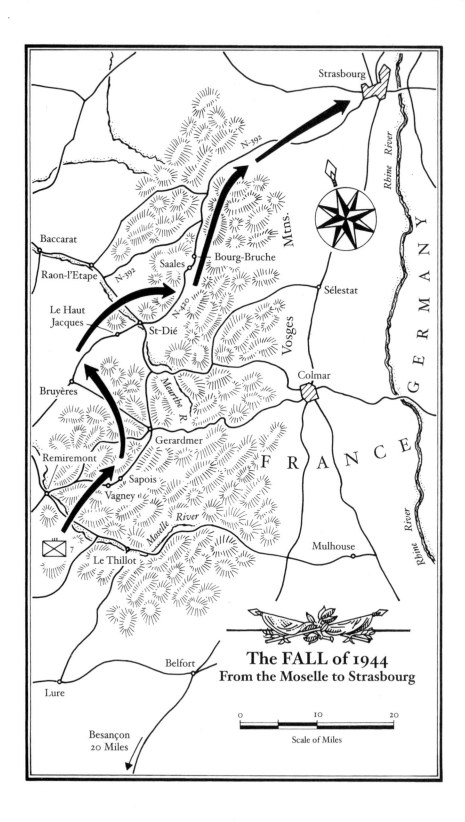

Strasbourg

Rhine River

GERMANY

N-392

Vosges Mtns.

Sélestat

Baccarat

Raon-l'Etape

N-392

Saales

Bourg-Bruche

N-420

Le Haut
Jacques

St-Dié

Colmar

Bruyères

Meurthe R.

Gerardmer

FRANCE

Remiremont

Sapois

Vagney

Moselle River

Rhine River

Mulhouse

7

Le Thillot

Belfort

The FALL of 1944
From the Moselle to Strasbourg

Lure

0   10   20

Scale of Miles

Besançon
20 Miles

recoiled and backed away into the crowd. I couldn't imagine what I had done to cause this reaction. I turned to Steele and said, 'What do you suppose that was all about?' He gave me a salacious grin and said, 'I squeezed her titty!' I said, 'Steele, you may be the best jeep driver in the company, but you're no gentleman.' To which he replied, 'You got that right, Lootenant.'"[33]

The joyride lasted several days into September. It ended when the Germans chose to make a stand at Besançon, an industrial city of eighty thousand people located on two sides of the Doubs River. Flanked north and south by formidable ridges, and honeycombed with thickly walled forts that dated back to the medieval period, Besançon was a natural fortress city. The Germans holed up in the forts (many of which were surrounded by moats) and dug in with flak, infantry, and tanks along the ridges outside of town. Their mission was to delay the Americans as long as possible while German armies to the east filtered through the Belfort Gap. Reports from the French Forces of the Interior (FFI) indicated that the Germans had thirteen thousand men in and around Besançon, an exaggeration, as there were probably about nine thousand. Still, this garrison made the most of their presence in Besançon, setting up roadblocks on all the likely approaches and blowing many of the bridges over the Doubs.

On September 5, the entire 3rd Division descended on Besançon, hitting it from all sides. The 7th Regiment mostly approached from the south and the west. The 2nd Battalion, operating with the 15th Infantry on the ridges north of town, quickly became involved in various firefights that centered around capturing key bridges. The battalion took two bridges after nasty, sharp small-arms fights like one involving Private Vernon Medaugh, who had fought so hard and had given so much at Anzio. Medaugh's squad was attempting to advance to one of the bridges when a German machine gun opened fire, pinning them down. Ever so carefully, they crawled backward on their bellies through a ditch, but the enemy gun still took a toll: "Our Sgt. got hit and a Sgt. from a machine gun section that had been wiped out took charge of our squad. The Sgt. and I gave cover fire while the others withdrew. Then I heard him say, 'cover me,' and he took off. So I decided to follow him. We ran in the ditch for about fifty yards, I was about ten yards behind him. Then we went across an open field to another ditch. The Sgt. made it. I was about ten yards from the ditch when it felt like I had run into a clothes line. A piece of shrapnel had hit me across the nose and above my left eye. The next thing I remember, I was in the ditch and the Co. medic was working on me." He passed out and did not wake up again until he reached a field hospital behind the lines.[34] The next day, the 2nd Battalion rejoined the rest of the regiment south of the town.

The Cottonbalers cautiously advanced along the main roads, company by company, supported by tanks into the environs of the town. The medieval forts proved to be the toughest part of the German defensive line to crack. Typically, the Germans defended each fort with about a company of infantry, flak wagons, and a few antitank guns. Using friendly artillery and tank fire as a shield, the Cottonbalers had to fight their way to within climbing distance of the walls of each fort. Then, supported by plenty of rifle-grenade and machine-gun fire, they climbed the walls and shot at the German garrison point-blank. Often the German flak wagons obliterated the lead assault troops. These killer flak wagons, mainly 20mm antiaircraft guns, inflicted terrible wounds on infantrymen, shredding abdomens until guts hung out and trickled halfway down walls, sawing off arms and heads too.

At one of these forts, Chaudanne, the Germans drove the riflemen away from the walls when the Cottonbalers tried a night attack. In the morning, tank destroyers rumbled up and blasted the doors of the fort, smashing them into bits, but the bridge of Chaudanne's moat would not support the weight of the tank destroyer. Only infantry could do this perilous job. An E Company officer, First Lieutenant George Stripp, led his men into the fort immediately after the tank destroyer blew down the door. In so doing, he and his men had to run across seventy-five yards of open ground, under mortar and machine-gun fire. Once Stripp and his men got into the fort, the fight quickly died out. The Germans wanted no part of a close-combat struggle. They threw down their arms and surrendered. Relieved, Stripp and his men took them prisoner, offered them cigarettes and sent them to the rear.

The 3rd Battalion, fighting north of the 2nd, also smashed its way into forts. Late in the evening of the sixth, its rifle companies had fought their way into Besançon itself. The night was foggy and slightly rainy, ideal cover for German patrols. One such patrol, platoon sized and most likely scouting around for likely exit vistas, filtered through the thinly held positions of the rifle companies, all the way to Lieutenant Colonel Ramsey's command post. The Germans, in fact, literally bumped right into the headquarters observation post. Machine-pistol and rifle fire echoed in the night. Some of the stunned headquarters troops shot back wildly. The enemy soldiers almost surrounded Ramsey's command post, a small, rickety wooden building. Closing to within ten yards of the building, they raked it with fire. The troops inside took cover, risked a few looks outside, and fired single shots at the shadowy shapes of German soldiers. One of the Americans, a wireman named Robert Maxwell, calmly peered into the darkness and kept up a steady stream of fire at the Germans, keeping them at bay. According to one of the other soldiers, Maxwell "was the coolest customer I've ever seen. Tracer bullets were just barely clearing his head, yet he didn't seem to notice."

Ramsey knew his tiny group could not survive much longer. He ordered his men to run out the back door and get away from the Germans. The Americans had no sooner left the building when a German potato masher grenade came fluttering out of the darkness. The ugly-looking stick grenade landed right in the middle of the group and clattered noisily, and ominously, on the pavement. In the blink of an eye, Maxwell, protected only by his blanket and his uniform, hurled himself on the grenade. The thing exploded, the force of it lifting him off the ground. One of the other men, Private First Class James Joyce, lay stunned on the pavement. Joyce thought they were all dead: "I lay still for a few seconds partially stunned by the concussion, then I realized that I wasn't hurt. Maxwell had deliberately drawn the full force of the explosion on himself in order to protect us." Perhaps even more amazing than Maxwell's valorous actions was the fact that he survived, albeit with a maimed foot and a shredded face. Ramsey's group grabbed Maxwell and got away. The German patrol melted into the night. Maxwell got the Medal of Honor.[35]

The next day, the division concluded its fight for Besançon. Valenti had been transferred back to the 3rd Battalion aid station, but he followed close behind the assaulting riflemen. "The fog near the ground hung like a suspended gray curtain, as the steel vise was slowly tightened on Besançon."[36] By 1930 the "steel vise" had plunged into the Germans and closed for good. Enemy resistance in the city collapsed.

The advance continued, steadily northeastward, in rougher terrain against intermittent resistance. On September 15, the 3rd Battalion experienced heavy combat when it attempted to capture the town of Vy-lès-Lure. At 1330, I and L Companies, with support from M Company machine guns and K Company in reserve, advanced across open, rolling meadows. The soldiers could see the town ahead, a collection of

wooden buildings and stone walls adjacent to a cemetery. Enemy machine guns, mortar, and artillery swept through the meadows, tearing
the flesh of many soldiers. Some fell dead instantly; others screamed in
shock and pain as enemy bullets or fragments found them. At first, the
mortars and artillery reaped a grim harvest, but soon the machine guns
became the main peril. The machine-gun bullets ate their way through
the Company I command group, felling the commanding officer and
his executive officer. Wounded and barely conscious, they looked like
nothing more than bloody lumps.

The attack lost any semblance of cohesion. The men simply tried to
crawl and roll their way out of the kill zone. The L Company commander, Captain Ralph Yates—Heintges's favorite patrol leader when
he commanded the 3rd Battalion—hugged the ground and took in the
terrible scene. His eyes darted from the town, to the cemetery, to the
meadows. He knew that he had to get the men moving in a different direction from the planned advance. He forced himself up on his elbows
and screamed at his men, "Move to the left!" The men respected him.
He was a veteran officer. He knew what he was doing. The unwounded
got to their feet and did exactly as Yates said, and this saved their lives.
The move outflanked the German outpost line and foiled their artillery
barrage. Although I Company was completely pinned down in the
meadow, Yates kept his people moving, through barbed wire and more
shell fire, until they reached the cover of ditches on the outskirts of the
town.

From their houses, the enemy now concentrated their fire on Yates
and his men. Almost involuntarily, most of the Americans slid lower in
their ditch in an effort to avoid the thick enemy fire. One of the BAR
men got hit by mortar fragments. Yates grabbed his BAR, stood up, and
sprayed German positions in the closest house. The BAR barked a staccato "da da dum!" cadence as he pulled the trigger. Spent casings cas-
caded out of the breech. Meanwhile, one of Yates's platoon leaders led
his men on a rush toward the house. One rifleman worked up enough
courage to fire in support of this bold assault. A German machine gun
opened up on him from the direction of the cemetery. The burst nearly
tore the man's arm from his body. The arm hung in crimson shreds, and
blood poured from the wounds. The man lay on his back, eyes wide, in
total shock. The platoon assault was pinned down for the moment.

Yates and his men now left their ditches and made it all the way to
the cemetery wall. Breathing heavily from exertion and adrenaline,

they rested there a second. A soldier tossed a grenade over the wall. Everyone heard an explosion and then a piercing scream. The enemy machine gun stopped shooting. A few minutes later, potato masher grenades came flying over the wall. Most of them landed beyond the men, safely out of range, but one was close enough to do damage. A sergeant picked it up and chucked it over the wall.

Taking the lead again, Yates, a tall, lanky man, raised to his full height and unleashed BAR fire into the cemetery. At the same time, he screamed at his men to assault the first house. With the classic choreography of infantry in battle, they moved in rushes—probably no more than thirty or forty men—and closed on the house. Enemy machine-gun fire stitched Yates's radio operator. Bullets ripped open his hips, groin, and stomach. He collapsed and bled furiously right at the gate of the house. A sergeant tried to pull him to safety and, for his trouble, machine-gun bullets whacked him. He got hit nine times in the legs, arms, and face, but he still dragged the wounded man to the doorstep of the house. The able-bodied burst into the house. Only three Germans were in there. One tried to resist and the Americans cut him down at close range. The other two surrendered. Yates set up his command post in the house. The place was little more than a long wooden structure, a barn really. It had animal stalls and a pigsty. The second floor featured a hayloft. The stench of animals hung everywhere.

The enemy soon put pressure on the smelly command post and the adjoining house, where Yates's platoon leader, Second Lieutenant Samuel Selvog, and eight men were holed up. A small force of Germans tried sneaking up on Yates from the rear. American fire drove them off, but the same sergeant who had been hit nine times already got hit two more times by shell fragments in the head. The two sides called to each other to surrender, with no effect. Then German shells began dropping on the two American-held houses. The shells set Selvog's house on fire, and he moved to the nearest house. Selvog and his men looked out of their new house and saw, to their abject horror, German troops wheeling up 88mm guns. The Americans sniped at the crews, but the inevitable response came. German shells blasted the two American-held houses, smashing timbers and power lines and breaking windows. Incredibly, no one was killed, even though a 170mm shell landed ten feet from a rifleman. Luckily for him, the shell did not explode.

Enemy infantry, under cover of their artillery, kept trying to infiltrate the houses, but the riflemen drove them off with aimed fire and grenades. At 1930, the Germans organized a more coordinated attempt to crush these interloping Americans. One hundred enemy infantrymen, advancing under cover from flak and mortars, attacked Selvog's house. The lieutenant and his men poked their weapons through tiny holes in the walls or through windows and blasted the Germans. Some of them saw Germans taking shelter in a ditch in front of the house; they showered the enemy with grenades. The attack faltered and the Germans could be seen dragging wounded men to safety. They left their dead where they had fallen.

Yates now did an ammo check and found that his men had run out of hand grenades and, collectively, were down to two and a half clips of ammo per man. Given this grim supply situation, he knew that he could not hold on much longer, so after dark he sent three of his men on a patrol to link up with Ramsey and tell him L Company needed help, and needed it fast. The three men ran out the back door of Yates's command post and immediately came under German small-arms fire. Somehow they did not get hit and they made it through to the meadows where I Company was still pinned down—bleeding and despairing. The tiny patrol could not find the battalion command post but they did find the regimental command post.

They would have done more good staying put, because no reinforcements came. Back at his embattled command post, Yates and his men flinched under constant mortar and artillery fire. Two German prisoners of war in the corner of the trashed main room of the house kept whimpering and begging the Americans to surrender; if not, they would all be killed. The Americans just told them to shut up. Yates glanced out the window and saw silhouettes in the streets of Vy-lès-Lure. That could only mean one thing—another German counterattack.

The enemy soon opened fire with machine pistols and rifle grenades on both American-held houses. The Cottonbalers conserved their ammunition and tried to make every shot count. They only fired when they could clearly see a target. The volume of fire was not enough. The enemy soon overran the ditches where Yates and his company had taken cover earlier that day. In so doing, they captured many wounded, or mentally shattered, Americans. Amazingly, every time the enemy tried to get near one of the houses, the Americans inside drove them off with carefully aimed shots. Once again, the Germans withdrew.

The tension inside the houses was unbearable. Most of the men had used up their last ammunition in fending off the German attack. What if they came again? Yates wondered how much more of this his soldiers could take. They were all physically spent, exhausted; the stress of being cut off and under fire for more than seven hours threatened to crack all of them, even Yates. Human beings, no matter how tough or well trained, could only take so much of this horror.

As if something out of a nightmare, the Germans launched yet another attack, not more than half an hour after the last one. Their commanders must have sensed that L Company was close to collapse. In the two houses, the Americans, most of them with shaky hands and voices, said their prayers, and prepared to fight to the last. The enemy soldiers got closer, through the ditches, into the yards, near the doors. Then, something extraordinary happened. Artillery shells started dropping among the German soldiers. The enemy troops could do nothing to shield themselves from this unexpected peril. The shells flew in and exploded, lifting enemy soldiers off their feet, tearing them into asymmetrical pieces of torn flesh, peppering them with hot fragments, cutting throats and torsos. The effect of the artillery was like insect repellent on an anthill. In a matter of seconds, the German attack withered to nothing. Their lead soldiers died in droves, many of them with grenades in their hands, most of them little more than twenty feet from the door of the command post.

In a few moments it was all over. The Germans were gone. Only their dead remained. The beleaguered survivors of L Company summoned their last reserves of energy and howled with delight, slapping one another on the back, laughing hysterically, crying tears of joy, gushing babbled sentences of unexpected salvation. The whole scene was like something out of a movie. When the joy wore off, the men shuffled back to their posts and renewed their grim watch, hoping the Germans would not be back.

A few hours later, troops from K Company and the Battle Patrol reached Yates's building. They gave the L Company men what ammo they could spare and took up positions in the houses. Throughout the night individual machine gunners and stragglers drifted in as well. Everyone pooled first-aid supplies to help the wounded, a collection of more than a dozen men, suffering and bleeding, mostly in silence. After dawn, Yates sent out a tentative patrol to see what the Germans were up to. The patrol brought back good news. The enemy had left the town. The battle was over. Company L had prevailed even though its soldiers had been outnumbered more than three to one and possessed no heavy weapons, except for the seemingly heaven-sent artillery support (just who called it in remains a mystery). The company lost seven killed, sixteen missing, and fourteen wounded in the fight for Vy-lès-Lure and it earned a rare Presidential Unit Citation.[37]

On the morning after this fierce fight, Valenti and many other medics came to the command post to help the wounded. The sights and smells were sickening: "The building was permeated by the smell of animal urine and dung, plus the strong acid smell of smoke and burnt gunpowder and the stench that emanated from the dead carcasses of cows, still in their stanchions, and swine, whose guts—some roasted—spilled out under the terrific impact and concussion of German 88s. Our clothes became permeated with the dreadful stench. The men inside, red-eyed from no sleep, and bearded, had that wild-eyed and flared-nostril look."[38]

THE BITTER FIGHTING AT VY-LÈS-LURE PROVED TO BE A grim harbinger, a signal of what lay ahead. The intoxicating days of chasing a retreating, beaten enemy were over. All along the western front, German resistance toughened. In Holland the Allies tried a major airborne operation designed to capture key bridges over the Rhine, opening the door for armored forces to overrun Germany. The operation, known as Market-Garden, failed miserably. In spite of being hard-pressed on all fronts, the German Army in the west did not disintegrate. Instead, it reorganized, set up new defensive positions extending from Holland, through portions of Belgium and France and western Germany, all the way to the Swiss border.

The 3rd Division was part of the 7th Army, commanded by Lieutenant General Alexander ("Sandy") Patch. This army, in conjunction with the French 1st Army, slowly advanced northeast in late September toward an area known as the Vosges Mountains, ideal defensive terrain for the Germans. Like nearly every other unit in the 7th Army, the 7th Regiment ran into increasingly stiff resistance as summer turned into fall.

The Cottonbalers successfully crossed the Moselle River on September 24 and kept fighting their way east, dealing mostly with enemy counterattacks and artillery fire. Even the weather got worse. "As we advanced closer to, and into, the Vosge [sic] Mountains the days cooled and became foggy and rainy," First Sergeant Pratt recalled. "The smell and feel of a hard winter was steadily surrounding us. The enemy began to defend from prepared positions and more often tenaciously held on to . . . ground. The Germans planted mines and booby traps and operated, generally, from a continuous line of resistance."

Pratt saw firsthand the increasingly deadly nature of German opposition. On the drizzly, chilly afternoon of October 1, he and his company commander, Captain Henry Goulette, set out on a mission to find the 2nd Battalion. In combat, the antitank company often split up its platoons among the various battalions so that they could have local fire support. In this case, one of the platoons had taken a few casualties as it fought alongside the riflemen and machine gunners of the 2nd Battalion, and Goulette, a hands-on, energetic, courageous officer of French and Native American descent, wanted to see if he could help his wounded men.

The captain, Pratt, and a driver hopped in a jeep and set off to find 2nd Battalion. Soon they became hopelessly lost. Pratt suggested to Goulette that they not go any farther until they knew where they were going. Goulette agreed and the driver pulled the jeep into a covered area by the side of the road. A minute or two later, two GIs emerged from the bushes and asked them, "Captain, what are you and the top kick doing here? This area hasn't been cleared. There's krauts just down the road." As it turned out, these GIs were from the 1st Battalion, and that meant Pratt's little group was even more lost than they had thought.

"We better get the hell out of here and fast," Pratt urged. The captain agreed, but first he wanted to take a look down the road to see if he could pick up any information to pass on to the intelligence section. Pratt reluctantly followed him: "We eased forward just a bit, pushed some bush limbs to one side for a view of the road ahead, and Goulette raised up on his elbows and placed his binoculars to his eyes. 'Pratt,' he whispered, 'there's movement in those trees just about a hundred yards ahead in the bend of the road. I'm sure it's German troops. Looks like a gun position of some kind. We better ease out before they see us . . .'

"At that moment it sounded as though all hell broke loose. Pine needles from the limbs overhead showered down around us as the dreaded 'quack, quack, quack' of the familiar 20mm flak shells burst all around, followed immediately with the 'bump, bump, bump' report of the cannon. I flattened myself to the ground and froze in place. I didn't dare to move even an eyelash." The slugs burst around Pratt, splashing mud on his field jacket. Finally, the shooting stopped. Still, Pratt stayed motionless, until darkness fell. He whispered to Goulette, "'Do you think we can slip out, Captain?'" The captain did not answer.

"He was about a body length ahead of me with his feet almost in my face. I reached up and shook his combat boot, but he didn't move. I tried again to talk to him, again with no success. I inched forward, still flat on the ground. I reached out and rolled him over. From his facial appearance I knew he was dead. I saw blood on his helmet and when I pushed it back I could see that one of the 20mm shells had hit him squarely in the forehead, through his helmet, and laid open his skull like a meat cleaver with a gash from front to rear. He never knew what hit him." Pratt crawled away. Later, medics evacuated Goulette's body. For the most part, Pratt kept his emotions in check during combat, but he could not help shedding a tear for his captain, especially when he thought of the man's wife and two children—fatherless now—back in Phoenix, who would soon get the terrible news.[39]

FROM OCTOBER 4 TO 11, THE REGIMENT FOUGHT ITS WAY into Vagney and Sapois, two towns located at the western edge of the Vosges. Vagney came first. All three battalions pressed forward on and around the main road into Vagney. Many of the rifle companies, especially those of the 2nd Battalion, focused on taking key hills around the northwest of the town. The Germans did the best they could to hold them up with fire from self-propelled guns and the dreaded flak wagons.

The 2nd Battalion troops seized the hills, but the Germans counterattacked. The enemy surrounded one platoon from G Company. The men of this platoon had only their weapons and a radio. They radioed to the company for help and were told to shoot their way out. They did so and escaped in harrowing fashion. For a day or so, the G Company men had subsisted on raw cabbage picked from nearby fields. They were out of rations and apparently the company mess troops had not caught up with them yet. Later, when the mess troops did, they fed the riflemen hot sandwiches, a rare commodity to the dogfaces.

The soldiers dug in and fortified their hillside positions. German artillery fire proved to be their biggest danger. The shells rained down on the hill, exploding and kicking up dirt, spraying shrapnel in every direction. The soldiers tried to crouch lower in their holes, but they could do nothing about a direct hit or a near miss. Those were the ones that killed people in holes. By the time the enemy fire finally lifted, several

G Company Cottonbalers were dead, including Private First Class
Benedict Bartkowiak, a twenty-seven-year-old rifleman from Cleveland. One of twelve children born to working-class Polish immigrants,
Bartkowiak had dreamed of becoming an engineer. His family had no
money for education, and he instead worked at the Cleveland Worm
and Gear Company until the draft snagged him in 1942. Instead of living a fulfilling life, filled with work, family, and children, Bartkowiak
died on that October day on a hillside in France outside the town of
Vagney. A random shell spewed fragments that tore his face up, killing
him instantly. He left a fiancée and a family who never forgot him, just
one more example of the terrible cost of war.[40]

While men like Bartkowiak died on the hills surrounding Vagney, the
3rd Battalion broke into the town and captured it in the face of enemy
counterattacks. Company K fought off one such counterattack along
the western edge of the town. German infantry, supported by flak wagons and self-propelled guns, advanced down a street, right at a group of
houses K Company controlled, including one containing a wine cellar
with Valenti's aid station. "Upstairs, on the first and second floors
above the aid station, Company K riflemen and machine gunners fought
desperately as they fired from open windows. Hand grenades and rifle
grenades were thrown within the shadows of the building. Wounded
were coming in."

Valenti and his commanding officer, a doctor named Captain Frank
Syladek, went upstairs at one point and spotted "through wispy veils of
fog" a lonely soldier, horribly wounded, dragging himself through mud:
"It was an American soldier, hit by German flakwagen [sic] fire. He was
brought into the aid station more dead than alive. Captain Syladek . . .
quickly saw that one leg was shattered. The leg had to come off. As I
held up the leg, Captain Syladek cut the few remaining tissues still attached. A heavy dressing was placed over the open wound. He was
given plasma and then taken to the nearest hospital. Later, I buried his
leg outside in the backyard. His foot was still inside its G.I. boot."[41]

As the sun set on October 7, the regiment controlled Vagney, but the
fighting there was not finished. That night, the Germans mounted
their men on trucks and tanks and, shielded by fog and mist, counterattacked Vagney. They hit all over town against all three battalions. The
Cottonbalers shot at them from within buildings and behind roadblocks. The German attackers went about their business deliberately,
almost cautiously, probing for weak spots. Here and there a couple of

their tanks broke through American outposts. In one such instance, an enemy tank and a group of about thirty enemy infantrymen menaced the 1st Battalion command post.

Private Mack Bloom happened to be at the command post that night. He had been assigned the job of driving a truck that towed a 57mm antitank gun for cannon company. He and his gun crew were relaxing in the house that served as the command post, watching the 1st Battalion wiremen set up the communications switchboard, when an American soldier burst in and warned, "There's a kraut [Panther] tank got through our lines, and nobody knows it but me and I'm telling you guys now—not only a tank but at least a squad of kraut soldiers and they're coming this way."

Bloom and the others looked at one another and wondered what to do. Someone suggested calling their lieutenant. Thoroughly uninterested, the lieutenant snapped, "What the hell are you guys worried about. You have antitank guns," and hung up. The lieutenant's imprecation was small comfort to the men. They knew that a 57mm gun could hardly be expected to take out a German Panther. They searched around for bazookas and found none.

An instant later, they heard the rumbling, heavy engine of the tank. Terrified, they chanced a look into the street: "There they were, 10–15 guys, dressed in those camouflage ponchos—crouched over, waving their arms slowly over their heads. A giant tank—that's the way it looked to us, close up at night." They contemplated throwing grenades at the infantrymen but feared reprisal from the tank. Bloom could hear someone "at the switchboard calling to the rear." They heard shouting from outside and saw two American tanks rolling into position. They were from the 756th Tank Battalion, a unit detailed to support the 7th Infantry. The tankers had apparently heard the emergency calls and were checking out the reports of a German tank.[42]

The commander of the tanks, Second Lieutenant James Harris, ran into the street to get a better look at the tank and see if it was really German. He quickly found out the answer to his question. "The first burst of machine-gun fire from the enemy tank caught the Lieutenant squarely," the battalion sergeant major recalled, "knocking him to the ground. The next burst killed a man beside me. We were really in a bad spot." Harris's leg was shattered, but he managed to crawl to one of his tanks and order the crew to move it to a more advantageous spot. Before they had a chance to do so, the Panther, with terrifying alacrity, pumped several shells right through the front of the tank. The Sherman exploded, sending flames and men, including Harris, shooting in all directions. The sickly sweet stench of burning flesh and hair, emanating from the roasting tank crew, permeated the street.

The shooting attracted the attention of other 1st Battalion Cottonbalers and they soon descended on the area. Soldiers threw grenades at the enemy tank and shot bazookas at it. Machine gunners and riflemen sprayed the street and the adjacent buildings where the enemy infantry took cover. By 2300 the enemy had retreated, with an untold number of casualties. A medic finally reached Harris, who had been lying in the muddy street, waiting to die. "He asked me if I had taken care of his men, and I told him I had. He seemed relieved. He told me he was done for and I saw that his right leg had been cut off at the crotch, apparently by the flying pieces of armor plate from his tank. He was in bad shape. I don't see how he lived as long as he did." The medic watched as Harris trembled, emitted a death rattle, and expired.[43]

The breakthroughs notwithstanding, the Germans failed in their quest to regain Vagney. They resumed a fighting retreat to the east and the regiment methodically pursued them into Sapois, a small town just a few miles down the road east of Vagney.

The outfit had been fighting steadily for two months now, and casualties had piled up. So many good men were dead or wounded, broken mentally, sick, or down with trench foot. The losses naturally ate away at the unit's combat effectiveness. After Vagney, most of the 7th Regiment rested or conducted limited operations ferreting out snipers or bypassed enemy soldiers who mostly wanted to surrender.

The Battle Patrol, followed by the antitank company and parts of the 3rd Battalion, closed on Sapois and took it on October 11. The situation there was confusing. The Germans were retreating slowly, and the Americans were advancing slowly too. They mixed together in the town and its rural environs and engaged in small firefights. The Germans had no desire to stand fast, so they simply tried to delay the Americans as long as possible while they got away.

Even in a comparatively benign situation like this, plenty of danger remained for the combat soldiers. First Sergeant Pratt and two other sergeants were in the process of poking around a farmhouse, assessing its usefulness as a command post, when one of the other men told the distracted Pratt to freeze. Surprised, Pratt glanced up and followed his gaze to the door. "There stood two German soldiers with their weapons pointed directly at us. I heard noise behind me and turned my head slowly around. I . . . saw two other Germans, also with weapons, at an open window on the opposite side of the room. For several more moments, no one on either side said anything." All of them, American and German, knew that this was a delicate situation. One wrong move could kill them all: the Americans, who were at the mercy of German weapons, and the Germans, enjoying an advantage in this little farmhouse but still terribly imperiled in the midst of American forces crawling all over the area. In fact, Pratt and the others could actually hear American voices out in the street.

At long last, the German squad leader ordered them to put up their hands. He and the other Landsers herded Pratt and his buddies out of the house's back door, across the clearing, and into a thick patch of woods. Pratt began to see enemy machine-gun emplacements, along with empty German ration cans. Now and again, his captors exchanged comments with small clusters of German troops. After a mile or two they reached a small village teeming with German activity. "I saw at least four . . . tanks and a pair of 88mm towed guns. Incoming American artillery rounds were landing . . . perhaps a half mile away." Their captors turned them over to a well-dressed, fairly smug German interrogation officer, who told them to wait in a barn. A guard led them to the barn, where they plopped down on piles of straw.

For hours they waited in the barn. "We looked around at each other in silence. The night cold was moving in and I started to shiver. I wasn't sure it was caused by cold or by fear. Perhaps both. I watched the guard and he watched me, and us. He appeared to be no more than 15 or 16 years old. His face seemed expressionless." The guard nodded off to sleep at times. "He looked exhausted and weather beaten. I heard vehicle engines starting up or moving through the area. German voices seemed continuously to be barking orders or yelling instructions. Under similar situations, even in combat, Americans could be expected to occasionally laugh or horse around with each other, but I heard no such [noises] that night from our German counterparts."

Pratt and the other men eventually dozed off, with their faces nuzzled in the hay and a manure pile below it. He woke up sometime around dawn. The guard was gone. Again, the men heard vehicles outside, but something about them was different. They heard voices— English-speaking voices. They apprehensively crept to the door and ventured out. The road and the field outside the barn were teeming with American GIs. One GI spotted them and almost opened fire until they yelled, "Don't shoot, we're Americans." They told the soldier and his officer about their recent prisoner-of-war experience. " 'What outfit are you with, Lieutenant?' I asked. 'Able Company, the 7th.' Our own regiment!" Giddy at their good fortune, Pratt and the other men rejoined their outfit that day.[44]

French troops relieved the 7th Infantry, and for about five days the Cottonbalers rested near Eloyes. The men showered (for many the first shower in sixty days), lived in tents or buildings, and ate decent food. The rest did not last long. General O'Daniel ordered the 7th to be ready for an attack on October 20. The goal was to capture a key road junction north of Bruyeres, a town that, for several days, had been the focus of advance for the VI Corps. So, early on the morning of the twentieth, the Cottonbalers boarded trucks and drove northeast to an assembly area just south of Grandvillers, their jump-off point for the attack.

As usual, they had to slug their way east against steady resistance: machine-gun emplacements, artillery, bunkers, counterattacks, flak wagons. The infantrymen who had to do the dirty work steeled themselves and moved forward, firing and maneuvering, using bazookas quite effectively against the bunkers, calling for artillery, coordinating with tanks. The weather was awful—rainy, miserable, foggy, chilly.

For nearly ten days the 7th Infantry fought this steadfast battle, hurling itself against the defenders, shelling them, blasting them, capturing them, doing whatever it took to root them out, defeat them, and move on. Casualties were appalling. An average of nine men, mostly in the rifle companies, died each day, a somnolent, monotonous drumbeat of daily death and dismemberment. Medic Valenti saw many of the casualties, including a number of men and civilians hurt when German artillery pounded some wooden buildings in a nameless town: "Bodies were strewn about the ground. Several Company I soldiers, dazed, in shock and muttering incoherently, just wandering around. We could hear screams for help. One G.I. was pinned beneath a heavy beam, a 12×12, pressing down on the soldier's legs. Rocks, bricks, mortar and heavy timbers added to the entanglement of the other trapped soldiers. Our efforts to free the soldier under the heavy beam were in vain. We kept trying till the heat of the nearing fire forced us to abandon him, amidst his screams, 'Shoot me! Shoot me!' "

As if that tragic scene were not enough, Valenti found something else just as horrifying in another demolished farmhouse. He spotted human hair beneath some planks. "I stopped and pulled back some of the debris. The human hair belonged to a little girl, no more than seven or eight; I had spotted her blond curls. Her angelic face was unmarked, but spattered with blood and mud. Her frail body was crushed by the heavy planks."[45]

The heaviest fighting took place on the morning of October 24 when bypassed, retreating troops from an Austrian mountain division briefly surrounded the 2nd Battalion. Lieutenant Colonel Thobro's men fought off the Germans with everything they had. At times, the antagonists could actually see the expressions on one another's faces. Luckily, Thobro's radios were functioning and he called for help. In no time, 3rd Battalion, led by the intrepid Captain Yates's L Company, came to the rescue. They brought tanks and tank destroyers with them and U.S. artillery leveled the German-controlled ring around the 2nd Battalion. The encirclement of the "White" battalion lasted about four hours. The Germans actually did not seek to annihilate the 2nd, only to immobilize them while they retreated east, but the encircled Cottonbalers did not know that. Also, the fact that the 3rd fought its way through to the 2nd did not mean the danger had passed. All day and night on the twenty-fourth, small groups of Austrians infiltrated into the fighting holes and machine-gun positions of the regiment. Again, the fighting was so close that you could spit at a man and hit him. One soldier even claimed that "fist fights" took place.[46]

The ten-day fight in late October in the Vosges saw the 7th Infantry liberate a dizzying series of towns: Brouvelieures, Vervezelle, Domfaing, Halley, Mailleufaing, Vidonchamp, Blanche Fontain. Most of the men had never heard of any of these places, nor did they ever care to see them again. Each man simply hoped to do his job and survive, nothing more, nothing less. They pressed on and endured this purgatory for one another; they shared a brotherhood of combat that would have been familiar to Cottonbalers from previous and future generations.

In any kind of sane situation, the regiment would have been rotated to reserve positions after such a tough fight, but this was the fall of 1944 in Europe, a time of absolute, all-out total war, a time when the Allies were pushing east, agonizingly, in all sectors against a desperate and resilient German Army, fighting now for its very existence. Both sides needed every available soldier. The voracious animal of war was destroying human beings at a factory-like rate. General Patch could not spare one of his best regiments from this nasty Vosges battle. The 7th Infantry would continue attacking east. This grim prospectus for the Vosges campaign added up to one stark, inescapable fact: for the Cottonbalers, the dying had only begun.

THE INDUSTRIAL, STRATEGICALLY LOCATED TOWN OF SAINT-Dié, on the Meurthe River, now became the focus of the 3rd Division's advance. For the Allies to have any hope of pushing through the northeastern portion of the Vosges and on to such political objectives as Strasbourg, they had to have Saint-Dié. For the 7th Regiment this meant attacking directly east along the road to Saint-Dié. This route inevitably led the Cottonbalers to the small crossroads town of Le Haut Jacques, located about three miles shy of the river and Saint-Dié.

The 7th Regiment left Blanche Fontain on October 30 and encountered very little resistance. By the next day, the troops were in sight of the crossroads at Le Haut Jacques. The morning mist had barely cleared on that Halloween when the combat soldiers advanced, cautiously, at ten-yard intervals, toward the crossroads. The soldiers could see their breath in the fall chill. For a few minutes they only heard the sounds of their own boots squishing in the mud along with a few twigs snapping here and there. The silence seemed strange, unearthly. It didn't last. All at once, a diverse array of enemy weapons opened fire on the riflemen: mortars, machine guns, artillery, flak wagons, rifles, mines, and machine pistols. The fire ripped up a few men as the others scrambled behind trees and into culverts. This first burst of enemy fire hit the 1st Battalion commander, Major Benjamin Boyd. He could not continue. Captain Kenneth Wallace took over for him. The 3rd Battalion lost one of its best officers when a 20mm shell caught Captain Yates. "Slammed in the head by a 20 mm shell," his battalion commander, Major Glenn Rathbun, related years later, "he lived to go home and follow a career as a teacher in Texas. We kid him about losing half his brain and still becoming a teacher."[47]

The assault companies were in disarray. The enemy fire was thick and persistent. No one in his right mind wanted to move *toward* it. The only logical course of action seemed to be to move *away* from it. But the Cottonbalers really did not have a choice. For several hours no one moved. American artillery and mortars crashed into the enemy positions, somewhere up ahead where the road led into a dark forest and a series of ridges and slopes. Most of the soldiers were more than content to stay put, but their officers and sergeants got them moving again. Company E, using the standard fire and maneuver tactics, steadily moved forward in an assault on a series of German trenches and dugouts. They took on an estimated fifty German soldiers supported by at least seven machine guns. The defenders were incredibly tenacious; E Company succeeded in closing to within a few yards of their positions, but they still did not yield. The Americans resorted to firing point-blank shots in their holes and trenches, lacing them with bullet holes. Other troops chucked grenades into the German positions and heard them explode. Sometimes the Germans were wounded but still tried to keep fighting.

The men of E Company had no sooner cleared out this German defensive line when they looked in the distance and saw something that made them rub their eyes in disbelief. "[They] found other positions behind it," wrote the regimental historian, "a third line beyond, and still others extending to the enemy's rear for a depth of approximately nine hundred yards. Enemy dugouts were approximately four feet deep, well-camouflaged and covered with logs for overhead cover. The proportion of machine guns, and other automatic weapons to rifles employed by the enemy was unusually high and gave him tremendous fire-power."[48]

Company E succeeded, with the help of a lot of rifle and hand grenades, in killing enough enemy to eject them from these elaborate positions, but in their quality and depth these positions were a kind of microcosm for their defense of the crossroads at Le Haut Jacques. The Germans had had time to prepare an extensive, and nasty, network of defenses here and, unlike in southern France, had plenty of good soldiers to man them. Approximately five to six hundred dedicated mountain infantry troops, skilled at operating in this hilly country, opposed the 7th. The terrain they defended was generally rugged, hilly, full of evergreens, and they knew how to use it to their advantage. "The enemy will allow you to advance so close, before opening fire," one officer wrote in an after action report, "that you cannot employ your own artillery." The result was a nightmarish, close-quarters, confused fight among small groups of men.

During the attack, some of the company wiremen got separated from their unit and captured while they were patching telephone wire. Dean Cannon, a runner, recounted the awful incident: "We patched the wire as we went up the hill. I was down patching wire when I heard a safety click on a Rifle. I looked up & all the Runners were standing with their hands up. It didn't take long to see 2 Burp guns behind one log and several rifles pointed at us from behind the trees. My first thought was run like H. down the hill. Then I thought of the rest of the Men they would shoot if they shot at Me. So my hands slowly went up. They lined us up and marched us back to a[n] old farm house & put us in a smoke house. There was a dead German in there." Cannon ended up in Stalag 7A at Moosburg.[49]

In fact, as the capture of the wiremen indicated, E Company's success was deceptive. By the morning of November 1, the 7th Regiment had been stopped cold in front of the crossroads at Le Haut Jacques. The troops were no more than three hundred to one thousand yards from the objective, but it might as well have been a thousand miles. The ground was so thick with mines that engineers had to work, on their hands and knees, under fire, to root them out. The weather did not cooperate at all. Cold rain poured on the men and left, in its wake, fog that did a fine job of shrouding German defenders. For three full days, the 7th Infantry attempted to inch its way toward the crossroads. Men fought soaked to the skin, slithering through mud, keeping one eye on the Germans and another on the three inches in front of them in case they tripped a German schu mine. Enemy artillery and mortars exploded in the trees, showering soldiers with a mixture of fragments and splinters. Little firefights abounded.

On November 3 alone, the regiment lost twenty men killed when the 1st and 2nd Battalions tried an envelopment attack, the 1st from the north and the 2nd from the south. Company C actually penetrated to within 150 yards of the crossroads, but the Germans counterattacked them and threatened to cut them off. These men had to fight their way out of this partial encirclement, and that meant rushing in waves at the German-held trees, shooting at anyone they saw. They captured twelve prisoners and broke out, but, needless to say, the experience took a heavy psychological toll on the C Company soldiers. The 2nd Battalion attack, meanwhile, went nowhere. The minute the men left their holes and pressed forward, they ran into such deadly enemy fire that they had to scramble back to their positions.

The next day Colonel Harrell launched an all-out attack with the entire 7th Regiment, or at least what remained of it. He made sure that his assaulting riflemen and machine gunners enjoyed every bit of support he could marshal. Tanks, tank destroyers, mortars (of many calibers), and heavy machine guns provided cover fire for the assault troops. Rain spattered the men as they went forward. No one had been dry for days. Their skin was clammy and moist. Their feet were wracked with trench foot.

The enemy opened fire with everything he had: "Every yard of ground was gained only by the most resolute fighting," one soldier recalled. "On more than one occasion . . . assault platoons were virtually surrounded." No matter, the platoons kept moving forward, leaving the bypassed resistance to be killed by follow-up troops.

Every company met bitter resistance. The Americans could only advance methodically, destroying one enemy position after another and then advancing tentatively until the enemy opened fire again, a casualty-intensive process. The rifle companies constantly needed replacements, and, ready or not, as soon as they arrived, they were fed into the maw, even in the chaotic confusion of this climactic day of the battle for "the Crossroads of Hell," as the troops were already calling it.

One such replacement was Private W. Bert Craft, a nineteen-year-old rifleman from Smith County, Mississippi. The son of a small farmer, Craft traced his heritage back to Confederate veterans of the Civil War and, further than that, to Scots-Irish immigrants. Craft had six brothers and sisters. They split the farm chores, milking cows, feeding geese, hogs, and cattle. In the winter, the family kept warm by cutting wood and burning it constantly in their fireplace. Every Sunday the whole family attended the Oak Grove Baptist Church. Craft enjoyed a healthy, normal childhood and grew to manhood imbued with an intense spirit of patriotism for the United States and the state of Mississippi.

In March 1944 he got drafted and went to Camp Shelby, Mississippi, for basic training. As the year unfolded, he progressed through the military training pipeline and, in October, went overseas as an infantry replacement. In late October, after a few days at the depressing halfway houses the Army called replacement depots, he joined the 3rd and heard O'Daniel's standard speech on the history of the division. From there Craft was assigned to C Company, 1st Battalion, 7th Infantry.

As it turned out, he joined the regiment on the afternoon of the all-out attack on the crossroads of Le Haut Jacques. Scared, cold, and bewildered, he and several other replacements dodged shell fire on the way to C Company. When they joined the company, it was in the process of attacking a machine-gun nest. "Much to our surprise we saw heavy-bearded, long-haired, dirty, filthy creatures who, upon close examination, turned out to be human (GI's)." Immediately a soldier ordered them to take care of the machine gun. They had no idea what they were doing, but they obeyed. "We . . . advanced toward the machine gun and were stopped by concertina wire. We stopped there and began firing. The machine gun quit firing as darkness had set in. We were told to dig in." This was Craft's part in the battle for the "Crossroads of Hell."[50]

By now the regiment had finally unhinged the German defensive line and captured the terribly costly objective of Le Haut Jacques and its crossroads. On the final day of the fighting alone, the regiment incurred 125 casualties, including 16 men killed. It had taken six days for the regiment to advance several hundred yards, a rate of movement reminiscent of the deadlock trench warfare of World War I. In a more immediate comparison, the 7th Regiment's hellish, dispiriting experience before Le Haut Jacques was analogous to the costly battle being fought that very moment by the U.S. 1st Army, one hundred miles to the northeast at the Huertgen Forest. One company alone suffered seventy-seven casualties in the space of these six days, a fairly representative number for the rifle companies.[51] The next day, the advance continued.

For five days after the capture of Le Haut Jacques, the Cottonbalers kept pressing east, through dense forests. The men walked up and down steep, wooded hills, and as they did so, the retreating enemy harassed them. In a typical instance, Private Craft's company was advancing along steep ground just to the right of the main road when the Germans opened fire. "We attempted to shoot it out with them, but didn't seem to be getting anywhere. The first scout from my platoon wanted to crawl up close and throw a grenade into the enemy machine gun nest but Haney, an officer, wouldn't allow it. Like any fight where bullets are flying, it was dreadful, but the most frightening were the soldiers' screams of pain when they were wounded. We retreated, carrying our wounded with us." American artillery then demolished the place. The next day, Craft's unit went back and found that the Germans had left.[52]

In this manner, the regiment advanced a few miles in the space of several days. Finally, on November 9–10, troops from the 103rd Infantry Division came up to relieve the 7th. The exhausted Cottonbalers were more than ready to leave. In the space of twenty days, the regiment had suffered a thousand casualties and gained ten miles of ground.

THE BRASS ALLOWED THE MEN TO REST FOR A FEW DAYS and then training began for the next mission, a river crossing of the Meurthe River and the ensuing push east, all the way to the Rhine. The soldiers of the 7th Infantry rode trucks to a bivouac area near Fremifontaine and enjoyed the "luxury" of tents and sleeping bags. Probably the best aspect of the Fremifontaine bivouac was the food. For the first time in weeks, the soldiers ate hot meals instead of K or C rations. Private Craft ate a huge breakfast on the first morning and savored the splendor of being warm and dry while eating good, nutritious food after spending so many days in the mud and rain: "I'm telling you, they had hot cakes, and we filled our mess kits full of them. We got six to eight in a serving. [The cooks] made their own syrup and had bacon by the bushel. The food was piping hot and delicious. They put the bacon on top of the hot cakes, then reached over and got a dipper full of syrup. We . . . devoured it like hungry dogs, then got back in the chow line again."[53]

Training consisted of the usual physical conditioning, along with small-unit "problems," such as how to spread out properly in wooded terrain, how to exploit a river crossing, how to find and disarm mines, and the like. Several inches of snow fell, blanketing the ground. The soldiers frolicked in the snow, feeling every bit like the kids they were.

Back at division headquarters, O'Daniel and his commanders meticulously planned the impending assault. As usual, he selected the 7th Infantry to lead the way. On the night of the assault, engineers would build four footbridges across the swollen river. The infantrymen would cross these bridges, capture the fortified village of La Voivre, located on a gentle slope about one thousand yards from the river, and then push through the mountains to Saales, a town situated on the main road to Strasbourg. The 1st Battalion received the job of crossing north of La Voivre, while the 2nd captured the town itself. Another unit would grab Saint-Dié, just to the south.

In the days leading up to the river crossing, engineers cleared mines from roads and paths leading to the river. Wiremen laid telephone wire. Chemical weapons specialists strategically placed smoke generators, just in case the infantry needed the protection of a smoke screen. Medium bombers and fighters pounded enemy positions on the east side of the river. Some of the bombers even dropped propaganda leaflets, designed to induce the enemy to surrender. By the afternoon of the nineteenth, everything was ready to go. The amphibious and river crossing experience of the 7th Regiment and the 3rd Division paid off through excellent planning and execution. Although the ranks of the rifle companies had turned over many times since late 1942, those of the staff officers, support troops, commanders, and specialists (who always take much lower casualties than the infantrymen) did not. These experienced men knew what they were doing and they proved it.

In their pyramidal tents at Fremifontaine, the assault troops made last-minute checks of weapons and equipment and prepared to throw themselves into danger once again. They silently boarded trucks, each one of them wondering what the chilly night ahead would yield. Their winter clothing made them look bigger than they really were. Each helmeted soldier shouldered his weapon and shuffled to the embarkation area. In the gathering darkness the men all looked pretty much alike.

Somewhere in the crowd of boots and overcoats that constituted F Company, Private Reitan shivered and waited to board his squad's truck. His shrapnel wounds had healed sufficiently for him to return to duty and only a couple days before he had rejoined his unit. His knee was still tender and sore, but that did not matter to the doctors. Their orders were to send infantrymen back to their units as soon as possible. Reitan knew that his fate pointed him in only one direction—the front. Feeling somber, morose, and even a bit depressed, he had scanned F Company for familiar faces and only found a few. Now he boarded a truck, sat on one of the hard wooden benches, packed in among his comrades, and listened to American artillery rounds shriek overhead as the truck bumped along the crude road that led to the Meurthe.

As Reitan pondered his future, two platoons of riflemen (including one from F Company), as quietly as they could, boarded small boats and paddled across the river. They spread out into combat formations on the east side of the river, keeping a sharp eye out for any enemy activity. One of them, Private First Class Ernie Boyd, recalled the experience of lying in the darkness: "[We] hid in a ploughed field for several hours, and at one point a German soldier came out into the field and fired a burst or two with his burp gun. I don't think he saw anyone but he was edgy it seemed." Aside from the German gunner, all they heard was American artillery exploding in the vicinity of La Voivre. Behind Boyd and the other riflemen, on the west of the Meurthe, engineers began building footbridges. The lone burp gunner notwithstanding, the Germans seemed to have no idea any of this was going on.

At midnight, the trucks bearing Reitan and the rest of the 2nd Battalion stopped at La Salle, a crossroads about a mile shy of the river. From there the troops slogged through mud and slush until they reached their jump-off points near the river. Reitan could see La Voivre in the distance: "La Voivre was a village of about twenty houses which the Germans had converted into a strong point. The plain between the river and the village was defended by felled trees, a mine field, barbed wire, and trenches. The stone houses of La Voivre were natural fortifications that had been strengthened by connecting the buildings with breaches in the walls or with underground tunnels." Soon it was F Company's turn to cross the river on the brand-new bridges. "These were standard floating bridges, with a three-foot gangway and attached cables for hand guides. I recall the blackened faces of the combat engineers as they steadied the footbridges while we crossed. Quietly . . . we spread out on the hard, damp, cold ground."[54]

Farther to the left (north) of Reitan, in the 1st Battalion sector, Private George Trigueros, another nineteen-year-old rifleman, crossed a floating bridge with his unit, C Company: "It was cold and clear and we were all bundled up in our heavy clothing, winter coats, and woolen underwear, with our backpacks, rifles, shovels and personal gear. One of the older members of the company instructed us to dig foxholes. Then a short time later he came back and told us not to dig in because we were in the middle of a German minefield."[55] What a feeling that must have been for poor Trigueros, lying in the darkness in the middle of a minefield!

The men of both battalions lay quietly in their uncomfortable, damp positions and waited for the sun to rise. The Germans still had no idea that two full battalions of American troops had safely crossed the river, but they did send out routine artillery, designed to inundate both banks of the Meurthe. Some of these shells fell among F Company, wounding seven men who, in spite of this, had to remain silent so as not to alert the Germans. One of the shells almost killed Reitan. "The whine began at a high pitch and continued longer than any I had heard before. I knew that it was coming for me. I prayed furiously and made my body as flat as possible. Then it hit. I bounced off the ground about three feet and fell back on my stomach with a thud, the impact knocking my breath out. The shell had landed about three feet to the right and back of my right foot, leaving a smoking black hole. Miraculously, I was un-hurt. I heard stirrings behind me, as the medics moved quietly to help the wounded."[56]

Soon after this, the American pre-attack bombardment began. The infantry soldiers watched in awe as a devastating blend of American ordnance blasted the German positions. Artillery, originating from di-vision and corps, plowed up earth and tore into buildings. Mortar shells blew up all over the place. Dive-bombers screamed downward at im-possibly steep angles, shot up targets, and dropped bombs. Antitank guns, tanks, and tank destroyers added their shells to the mix. The Bat-tle Patrol opened up with its .50-caliber machine guns, the ones they carried in the backs of their jeeps. The supporting ordnance was so close to the infantrymen that they could feel the concussion of the shells in their heads; they could feel the heat of the flames against their faces.

After half an hour, the fireworks stopped. By now La Voivre was a mass of smoke and rubble. It was hard to see anything beyond the next fifty to a hundred feet. Officers, almost in unison, hollered, "Let's go!" The men of C Company immediately got to their feet and began ad-vancing. Acting as lead scout, Private Trigueros, M1 Garand at the ready, walked about thirty yards ahead of his platoon, until barbed wire stopped him. He went to ground and fiddled with his awkward banga-lore torpedo, trying to fasten it in place so it would do the most damage to the barbed wire. Suddenly the Germans started shelling C Com-pany: "One of their shells exploded next to me and blew up my torpedo and flung me into the air. One fragment from the shell went through my steel helmet and right into my scalp. Another went into my right lung and a piece of the torpedo went into my right thigh. I was unable to move." Medics got to him and evacuated him to the battalion aid sta-tion. He never returned to combat.[57]

No more than thirty yards away from Trigeueros, Private Craft's squad walked straight into a minefield: "I stopped dead still. I froze. Al-bert from Indiana . . . said, 'Craft, we are in a mine field. What you have to do now is watch those wires and don't trip them. You watch where I step, raise your feet up high . . . and step in my footsteps.' Well, I fol-lowed Albert exactly through the mine field." The rest of the squad made it through, as well. "We came to some concertina wire on a little ridge. I helped cut the wire but we ran on to some more, which was wider. We had a [bangalore] torpedo." They blew the wire and kept going, with Craft acting as lead scout. He spotted a pillbox. Luckily, the Germans inside wanted to surrender.[58]

The rest of the battalion suffered some casualties from mines, but the 1st Battalion moved quickly and captured its objectives, including the town of Hurbache. As they did so, the 2nd Battalion closed on La Voivre with all three rifle companies in line with one another, in a textbook example of fire and maneuver. Company E attacked the town from the middle, laying down a withering base of fire on the German defenders, who were already stunned from the pre-attack barrage. Under cover of this fire, F Company worked its way to the left of town, while G Company enveloped from the right. The tactics worked very well.

The soldiers from E Company advanced in short rushes, firing and supporting one another. This soon put them right on top of the enemy trenches in front of La Voivre. BAR men fired their weapons into the trenches, while other troops threw grenades into them. The troops killed a few Germans, but most of the enemy soldiers, at the sight of the assaulting Americans, retreated into basements throughout the town.

Intense American machine gun and flak wagon fire kept the Germans pinned inside their La Voivre basements. According to one soldier, this fire "was so intense and its field of fire so close to the troops it was supporting, that it appeared to them to be too close, and they moved under it with extreme caution." But move they did. Using support-by-fire and maneuver tactics appropriate to an urban environment, the E Company Cottonbalers assaulted building after building. "The platoons worked on a mutual support principle," a sergeant later wrote, "some troops placing fire on the windows while others entered by doors or windows, grenading and machine gunning their way in, if need be, but usually finding the defenders by then huddled in the cellars and quite ready to surrender."

In F Company, two platoons led by newly commissioned Lieutenant Earl Swanson, the Minnesotan who had worked his way from private soldier in North Africa to junior officer and company commander now, attacked the north side of the town. They blasted an enemy house containing a machine-gun team. One excited man tried to fire a rifle grenade at the house, but the grenade exploded in his face, seriously wounding him. Instead of loading his M1 Garand with a dummy bullet, as required when shooting a rifle grenade, he used a live bullet—not a good idea. Swanson's people kept pressing into the town.

Reitan's 2nd Platoon, separated from Swanson's group, bumbled its way into the town through all sorts of obstacles. "We struggled through . . . felled trees and around the minefield, but our main concern was mortar shells that began dropping on the plain. When we got clear of the trees and the minefield, we rushed to the shelter of . . . fortifications, which fortunately were unmanned." They pushed into the town and hooked up with the 1st Platoon. "All I can recall is floundering through the trees, scrambling down the street with my rifle ready. That was the end of it, and I had not fired a shot."

On the right, the biggest peril for G Company was a minefield. A machine-gun team from the heavy-weapons company tripped a mine, blowing them into the air three or four feet and maiming them terribly. Still, they kept moving and, like the other companies, found the Germans in retreat. "If they had held their positions," the company commander later asserted, "it would have punched our ticket."

The battle was over by 1100 hours. In the town the 2nd Battalion captured sixty-five enemy prisoners. The sheer volume of American firepower, combined with the determination of the assault troops, overwhelmed the enemy, and they chose to surrender rather than die. By any measure the crossing of the Meurthe was a success, but a costly one. The regiment lost 167 men, mostly wounded by German mortars or mines, during the crossing. Undoubtedly the toll would have been much worse had the Germans in and around the town held firm in their positions and fought like their alpine brethren did three weeks earlier at Le Haut Jacques.[59]

The successful crossing of the Meurthe River began a weeklong advance for the 7th Infantry in the direction of Strasbourg. The Germans were retreating again, making a few firm stands where they enjoyed prepared positions. Mainly, though, they were trying to safely reach the Rhine and cross that great river to fight again another day. The regiment's fighting before Strasbourg centered mostly around the liberation of three towns: Nayemont, Saales, and Bourg-Bruche, three places the enemy had chosen to defend.

On the morning of November 22, Company A led the attack on Nayemont. The lead scouts made it safely into the town, but when their platoons attempted to advance into the town, over four hundred yards of open ground, German flak wagons opened up from a ridge overlooking the town. The two platoons ran as fast as they could for the houses where the scouts had taken shelter. Enemy flak and rifle fire snapped through the air around them. Near misses tore up muddy earth and sprayed on their trousers. Somehow they made it into the house only to discover that the Germans were right next door in a house about a hundred yards away. For an hour they exchanged shots with Germans in this house, until two Americans tanks rumbled into the open fields in front of the town. Suddenly a German artillery shell tore through the hull of one of the tanks. The tank belched smoke but did not explode. The men in the other tank had no desire to share the same fate as their dead comrades. The driver shoved the tank's gearbox into reverse, and the tank left the area.

The infantrymen in the town found a way to flank the German house. They assaulted it with rifle grenades and intense rifle fire, capturing the house and three prisoners. From their new possession, the soldiers could hear explosions outside of town. These explosions were the sounds of American tanks shooting at German artillery and flak on the ridge. The tanks knocked out a German 77mm gun, but they soon ran into a thick maze of mines on the road to Nayemont. Only their accompanying infantry could go forward, slowly, carefully, inch by inch, disarming mines all the way.

One of the tanks scored a direct hit on the German flak guns, blowing it into a pile of twisted junk, interspersed with the mangled bodies of its crew. The infantry finally got through the mines and into the town. These A Company soldiers set about the task of clearing the town house to house, blasting the enemy with grenades and rifles.

In the meantime, the battalion's two other companies snuck up on the Germans from the opposite side of the ridge. Moving across an open field, just under the ridge with C Company, Private Craft came under fire from another enemy flak gun. The gun killed one of his buddies and almost did the same to him: "I fell face down on the ground. The bullets hit the ground about six inches from my head, kicking up dirt. Then the gunner . . . shot at me again. He missed me another six inches from my feet." The shooting stopped as quickly as it began. A soldier had snuck up on the gun and, with a bazooka, blown a hole through the enemy gunner: "My shirt was pulled out of my trousers and I was disorganized, disoriented and, frankly, scared to death." One of his buddies had taken cover in a manure pile: "He was literally covered with cow manure and you know the odor of that! We shied away from him for several days." By dusk the town was in American hands, along with eighty-five prisoners.[60]

While 1st Battalion took Nayemont, the 3rd Battalion moved on Saales, the gateway town to Alsace. At 0730 on the twenty-third, K Company led the attack on Saales. The men of this outfit had encountered a tall roadblock of logs across a road, just outside the town. First Lieutenant Ralph Payne, the company commander, feared that the ground around the roadblock was mined, so he told his men to scale the ten-foot-high logs. They did so with no problems (L Company later found that the road was not mined) and slogged through mud and drizzling rain until they reached Saales.

They caught the Germans completely by surprise. This was quite fortuitous, because the Germans had fortified the place with dozens of dugouts, some of which dated back to World War I. With Americans bearing down on them, almost like ghostly apparitions in the morning fog, the Germans in front of K Company had no alternative but to surrender. The other two rifle companies soon entered the town, right on K Company's heels, surprising quite a few Germans, including the Gestapo, which had a regional headquarters in Saales. One Gestapo officer, when confronted with American soldiers bursting into his office, declared that it was impossible for them to be there. Tommy guns and Garands poking into his ribs convinced him otherwise. In one house, the Cottonbalers found roasted duck and hot coffee. The lucky soldiers quickly wolfed down these delicacies.

For many minutes it looked as if there would be no actual fight for Saales, but once the surprise wore off, the Germans rallied and put up resistance. A platoon from K Company soon began taking 88 fire from a gun concealed somewhere at the end of a winding street. The shrapnel from this hated weapon mixed with broken glass and masonry and wounded several men. They lay stunned and bleeding in the street until individual soldiers, braving enemy fire, dragged them to safety. One private, Emil Stefek, decided that he would destroy the 88 all by himself. Braving sniper fire and the 88, Stefek sprinted for the flimsy cover of a small water fountain. A German sniper bullet slashed into him, but he kept going. He skidded behind the water fountain and began shooting at the 88 crew, killing two of them. Then his M1 jammed, a real rarity for that fine rifle. He could see the Germans congregating around the 88, preparing to fire at him. Glancing around frantically, Stefek noticed a wounded BAR gunner a few yards away. Stefek ran over to him, snatched his weapon, and let loose a full clip of BAR rounds at the 88 crew. The BAR bullets sparked off the gun and ricocheted into the

German crew. They scrambled around, looking to Stefek almost like dancers, as they tried to get away from the bullets. Their evasive maneuvers were for naught. The BAR bullets punched holes in each one of them and the 88 remained unfired.

After completing this amazing feat, Stefek faded. He could feel his energy sapping. Because he had knocked out the feared 88, other K Company men left cover and advanced house to house, down the street, killing any enemy troops they saw. They also captured an entire enemy trench and pillbox system. Medics sprinted to Stefek and did what they could for him, but it was too late. He died of his bullet wound later that day.

The Americans completely controlled the town by 1535. In taking Saales, they overwhelmed and defeated four infantry companies and one engineer company. In the process, the Cottonbalers helped unhinge what remained of the German defensive line in the area. There was also a moral element to the liberation of Saales. The town had been a center of Gestapo activity. Hundreds of Frenchman and Russians had recently been forced to work on the German fortifications. The Germans worked these men as hard as they could and then moved them out of the area so that the Americans could not liberate them.

Colonel Harrell knew the Germans well enough to realize that they would certainly counterattack Saales, so he decided to launch a preemptive attack on the neighboring town of Bourg-Bruche. This was a smart move, but it guaranteed that the unit detailed to capture Bourg-Bruche, the 1st Battalion, would run into serious trouble. The battalion boarded trucks at Nayemont and rode to Saales, where they jumped off the trucks and began walking down the road to Bourg-Bruche.

The sun was setting at their backs, and in the gathering twilight of dusk they tried to spot Germans in the shadows up ahead. They moved in columns, with B Company in the lead, followed by C Company and then A Company. Private Craft was acting as a scout for C Company, trying to maintain contact with B Company: "We were going down a road, and it was dark. My boots were squashing because water was still in them. I hadn't had time to change socks or pull off my boots. It had been raining on and off all day. I was walking along, and I would drop off to sleep walking." He could hear shooting up ahead; B Company had run into roadblocks and machine guns.

Approximately a hundred yards ahead of Craft's position, B Company tried to fight its way into the town. The Germans had set up their troops along a railroad overpass. They had partially demolished the overpass and left massive concrete blocks in the road. Clearly they hoped to hold up the Cottonbalers in front of the concrete and then shoot down on them from the overpass. German machine guns peppered the area. Their ripping sounds stumbled over one another, producing an angry buzzing sound. The B Company men immediately fired back, mainly with rifles. The riflemen fired aimed shots at the Germans on the overpass and its adjacent embankments. Four enemy soldiers fell back, wounded. Quickly and with shaky hands, several Cottonbalers fitted grenades at the end of their rifles and fired into the German positions. The grenades blew up and did more damage. Then the Germans tried attacking on the right of the road. The Americans could easily see their silhouettes and laced them with deadly fire. Several enemy soldiers screamed and fell. The rest vanished into the night. They and the other Germans withdrew into Bourg-Bruche.

Tank dozers came up, pushed the concrete chunks aside, and the Americans continued into the town. They soon found themselves involved in yet another urban combat situation—a test of wills in which soldiers fought almost face-to-face, room to room, with only their rifles, their grenades, and their reflexes. The battle turned into a free-for-all as Americans and Germans fought desperately, viciously, for houses in a confused melee all over town.

In one instance, the 3rd Platoon of C Company, reduced to nine men after the Vosges fighting, holed up in a large house, ahead of the main American forces. All night long, they battled the Germans. The enemy subjected them to panzerfaust fire, machine-gun fire, grenades, and rifles. The Americans were surrounded. Led by Staff Sergeant Michael Ernst, they somehow held out. "The front and rear doors were blown apart," the regimental historian wrote. "Approximately twenty grenades and rockets exploded inside the large, ramshackle building and transformed the rooms into an inferno of flying shards of steel. One man was so deafened by the concussion from the constant explosions that he lost his hearing." The Germans massed for an assault and pitched more grenades into the house, yelling for the Americans to surrender. Refusing, they responded with rifle fire and grenades of their own.

A few houses down the street, Craft and the 1st Platoon, dealing with other enemy attacks, could hear the terrible screams of the 3rd Platoon and its German adversaries: "We could hear them fighting and we could hear Sergeant [Ernst]. He could speak German. He was yelling out to them in German. They were yelling . . . in German to surrender."

Another group of Cottonbalers barricaded the entrances to their house with furniture and held out all night against repeated assaults. The fighting went on like this all night. Small groups of men holed up in houses and fought little, almost private, battles with other groups of men.

In the morning the Germans were still contesting the town, but the Americans had succeeded in bringing up tanks and organizing their assault platoons. Company C succeeded in pushing the Germans out of the south side of the town. The enemy had mostly withdrawn from this section of the town and onto a ridge, from which they hammered the C Company troops with artillery. The Americans holed up in a tavern and used its attic as an observation post. The company commander called in artillery fire and blew up an 88, an ammo dump, and a dug-in 20mm. Germans started retreating from their trenches on the ridge. Craft and his buddies blasted away at them. "Everyone had a field day picking off Germans as they came out of the foxholes. It felt real good shooting those Krauts; it felt like killing dirty flea-infested rats."

Company A spent the day clearing out the other side of town. The fight centered, late in the day, on the ridge, and the Germans, quite simply, could not stay in place under the ferocity of American artillery and tank fire. At 1300 Cottonbalers surged up the ridge and captured eighty-five German troops. By 1630, German resistance in the town had completely collapsed. In total the 7th Regiment had now taken two hundred prisoners and had killed about seventy-five enemy soldiers. Bourg-Bruche, after a bitter all-night fight, belonged to the U.S. Army. The road to Strasbourg was now open.[61]

The French 2nd Armored Division succeeded in entering the city, and Allied commanders, concerned that the Germans might counterattack this lone Allied unit, wanted the 3rd Division to enter the city as soon as possible. O'Daniel ordered the 15th Infantry to seize the west bank of the Rhine south of Strasbourg, the 30th Infantry to remain in reserve, and two battalions of Cottonbalers, the 1st and 2nd, to board trucks and drive to an assembly area in the western suburbs of the city. The two battalions carried out this mission without incident on the night of November 26–27, followed by the 3rd Battalion the next day.

The men found the city in good condition, a welcome change from the smoking ruins to which they had become accustomed in the Vosges. Most of the Germans in the area had retreated across the Rhine, but some remained in an industrial area along the west bank of the Rhine called the Kehl bridgehead. The Kehl bridgehead was a heart-shaped stretch of lowland bordered on the west side by canals and the east side by the Rhine.

During the early-morning hours of December 1, C Company tried to cross the canal bridges and clear out the Kehl bridgehead. Enemy machine guns drove them away. After daybreak, Private Craft and his sergeant led the way on yet another attempt: "Sergeant White and I got on the bridge, one on each side. We both made a running charge. The Germans opened up with machine guns, mortars and their riflemen were shooting, but they couldn't stop us. Sergeant White and I got across the bridge and we heard some Germans talking. I hollered for them to come out, but they wouldn't budge." The Americans threw grenades into the building where the Germans were hiding: "That really brought them out. We got five or six prisoners. That seemed to demoralize the Germans and within 10 minutes, we had about 37 prisoners. We pushed on! Being first scout, I had to lead the way. We ran into a little opposition and there was heavy firing down near [some] apartment buildings. The 2nd Battalion had the job of clearing them out."[62]

In fact, Private Reitan's F Company was, at that very moment, taking the lead in attacking a cluster of apartment buildings that housed Nazi, SS, and Wehrmacht leaders. Some of the apartments were deserted, and the GIs had a wonderful time looting them. "I 'liberated' a camera and a Walther pistol." Reitan exited the building and saw other men giddily comparing their loot. "Then reality struck. As we began to rush across an open space between apartment buildings a sniper's rifle rang out. Ellis Lee, who had joined F Co. on Anzio when I did, fell dead on the pavement. I was just behind Lee and saw him fall. We skirted the buildings and eventually the sniper was trapped and surrendered. He was the most vicious-looking man I have ever seen; he had wild eyes and hair and snarled like an animal. Our guys wanted to shoot him on the spot, but Lt. Swanson insisted that he be taken back to the POW cage. The apartments were not fully cleared until 11 p.m." The enemy in the meantime had blown all the bridges across the Rhine. The 7th Infantry settled down for the second "Watch on the Rhine" in its history, the first having occurred during the occupation of German in 1919.

The troops gratefully moved into German barracks buildings and enjoyed beds, clean sheets, bathing facilities, and hot food. They spent their days patrolling the banks of the Rhine and dodging occasional German shellings. Each man spent two nights a week on outpost duty along the Rhine. The days and nights were restful compared to the horror of the Vosges. Men could get drunk, chase women, or just lie around and sleep if they so desired.

In contrast with the rest of France, the population in Strasbourg was not particularly friendly. The old city, a major political symbol, traced both German and French roots. Some of the population sympathized with Germany. The town still teemed with enemy spies. Those who were sympathetic to the Allies were not entirely convinced that the Germans were gone for good. They knew that informers and spies would exact revenge on them if they aided the Americans or behaved in a friendly way toward them. In addition to all of this baggage, many Strasbourgers were angry at the Americans over the fact that the Army Air Force had bombed and partially destroyed the city's famous cathedral the year before. According to First Sergeant Pratt, young women proved to be the friendliest segment of the population. "The [local] men were not to be seen since they had all been moved off to the war fronts. Friendships developed almost immediately between our guys and young frauleins, or mademoiselles." Some soldiers disappeared for days on their amorous adventures.[63]

During this period of light duty in Strasbourg, Colonel Harrell left the regiment to become the operations officer for the 5th Army in Italy. Izenour replaced him, but only briefly, because he got wounded by a stray German shell while inspecting positions along the Rhine on December 4. This paved the way for Lieutenant Colonel Heintges to triumphantly return to the regiment as its commander. Since his altercation with Colonel Sherman back in February, Heintges had earned more honors and proven himself, as always, to be an excellent combat commander. He served as the division's operations officer for four months and then moved over to the 30th Infantry as executive officer, earning several decorations from that unit for leadership in combat. He would command the 7th Regiment for the rest of the war.

THE COTTONBALERS SPENT THREE ENJOYABLE WEEKS IN Strasbourg, but events elsewhere conspired to end their "Watch on the Rhine." To the north, the Germans launched their all-out offensive designed to puncture American defenses in the Ardennes Forest, cross the Meuse River, split the British from the Americans, and retake

Antwerp, a valuable supply port. This unleashed a two-month-long winter campaign that became known as the Battle of the Bulge and accounted for one of America's greatest victories in this war, albeit a costly one. To the south of Strasbourg, the Germans had forged another bulge west of the Rhine in Alsace, a concentric ring of German-held territory commonly referred to as the "Colmar Pocket," after the Alsatian city that constituted the center of gravity, if not quite the center point, of the pocket. For several days, the Germans had launched strong attacks from the Colmar Pocket on the French 1st Army and an American unit under its operational control, the 36th Infantry Division (Texas National Guard).

With these crises looming north and south, the Cottonbalers, and the rest of the 3rd Division, were needed to help plug potential gaps in the Allied lines. Once again, the soldiers of the 7th hoisted themselves into trucks that drove them into danger. The truck convoy drove south and deposited the men near such tiny farming towns as Bergheim, Mittelwihr, and Ribeauvillé. From there they waited for darkness and walked the necessary one or two miles to the frontline outposts of the 36th. The Cottonbalers' new positions spanned the northern shoulder of the Colmar Pocket.

For nearly a month the 7th Infantry manned these "lines" in a defensive, stalemate situation; both sides kept a close eye on each other, patrolled, shelled, and raided, but that was the extent of the combat. In a way, the regiment was lucky. Throughout December, American soldiers in the Ardennes fought for their very lives in staving off the German offensive there. Once they had successfully contained the Germans and gone over to the offensive, Hitler launched another lesser-known offensive, Operation Nordwind in northern Alsace. Nordwind was powerful enough to cause Eisenhower to contemplate abandoning Strasbourg, but Free French leader Charles de Gaulle persuaded him, mainly through threats to remove French troops from Allied operational control, to remain in Strasbourg. The liberation of Strasbourg in December symbolized the reemergence of French sovereignty, along with French control of the long-disputed provinces of Alsace and Lorraine. Losing the city would have been an enormous blow to the legitimacy of de Gaulle's political leadership.

Thus, given the ferocious combat going on to the north, the Cottonbalers had drawn a relatively plum assignment, at least by the standards of this great war. Of course, the regiment did not exactly enjoy a vacation, though. Private Reitan described the frontline positions and the pace and nature of life in these defensive positions that winter: "If an imaginary journalist had come looking for the front line, he would first have passed through a series of wrecked French towns and villages. After stopping at the headquarters of the Third Infantry Division, he would have been escorted to the 7th Infantry Regiment. From there he would have been taken up a winding mountain road through dense forest to Second Battalion headquarters, perhaps located in a stone house or barn. There he would glimpse carefully concealed tanks, trucks, jeeps, and guns scattered among the trees. From there a guide would lead up an icy mountain trail. He and his guide would sense an eerie silence, broken perhaps by the whisper of American shells going out, or the distant whine and 'carumph' of enemy shells coming in. As he peered into the pine trees, he would begin to see the scattered helmets and faces of the riflemen in their foxholes."

More than anything else, life for the combat soldiers centered on surviving the elements. They ate basic food and tried to stay warm in the middle of one of the coldest winters in European history. "We lived mainly on C-rations. The heavy cans contained cooked food in three flavors: Stew, Ham and Beans, and Hash. Stew was the least liked; most guys preferred Hash; Ham and Beans was okay. The light cans contained biscuits, powdered lemonade, powdered coffee, two Chiclets, and toilet paper.

"The supply system worked smoothly. At night a jeep with its lights off came as quietly as possible up the snowy roads or forest trails pulling a little trailer behind it. In the trailer were ammunition, cases of C-Rations, water and sometimes mail. By twos and threes we slipped quietly out of our foxholes and through the forest to the jeep. In the darkness we took our rations and filled our canteens.

"Our basic clothing was the olive drab wool shirt and pants, and the lined field jacket [M-1941 and M-1943]. We coped with the winter cold by adding wool knit caps, wool gloves, and overcoats. Trench foot was endemic, for our feet were confined in leather combat boots that were cold and wet most of the time. At every opportunity I took my boots off and held my reddened feet in my hands. I did this primarily for comfort, but it also saved my feet."[64]

Every few days, a soldier had to go out on patrol, almost always carried out at night. A couple days before Christmas, Private Craft was selected to lead a reconnaissance patrol to ascertain German strength around a bridge roughly two miles from the frontline outposts of the regiment. "I was made first scout on the basis I was single. We had been told there was a river we could follow. We weren't on the banks . . . to prevent silhouetting ourselves. We had on a white sheet that covered our helmets down to our boots. I was going along, and all of a sudden, I had to go up an embankment. I didn't realize it was a road bed, because of the snow.

"I climbed up to the top, and I heard Germans talking and almost stepped out on the road. I heard two Germans coming down the road. I stepped back quietly and quickly and melted down in the snow face down. I watched those Germans go by. I could have reached out and touched them. We heard a machine gun click and a tank crank up and then a German ambulance came down the road and went off to the left into a little town. When we heard that we knew they had fortified [the bridge]." They went back and reported that to battalion headquarters.

Like Reitan, Craft spent most of his time trying to stay warm in a foxhole: "I shared an outpost foxhole with a fellow . . . from San Diego. It was a good foxhole. We both could lie down at one time, if we so desired. It had a good covering, with timber and dirt thrown on top of it. A deep snow had covered it. Some of the foxholes had hay in them to make it warmer. However, the hay was infested with fleas. It was real, real cold."[65] Temperatures sometimes dipped below zero, but mostly they hovered at around ten to fifteen degrees Fahrenheit.

THROUGHOUT THE DEFENSIVE PHASE OF THE 7TH REGIment's stay in the Colmar Pocket, the men knew in their hearts that eventually they would be called upon to attack and eliminate the pocket. After all, they had not come to Europe to sit and defend. They had come to Europe to liberate the continent from German domination, and that meant attacking, capturing ground, and pushing all the way into Germany. Clearly, the enemy would not surrender until their homeland was completely overrun. Everybody understood that now.

Eisenhower shared that understanding. By the middle of January both German offensives had run their course. The Allies had lost some ground, suffered many casualties, but mostly they regrouped and inflicted serious losses on the Germans. Initiative passed to the Allies. American soldiers in the Ardennes were well on their way to pushing the Germans out of the Bulge. In Alsace, Nordwind had dented the Allied lines but not breached them. The Germans were in retreat, but

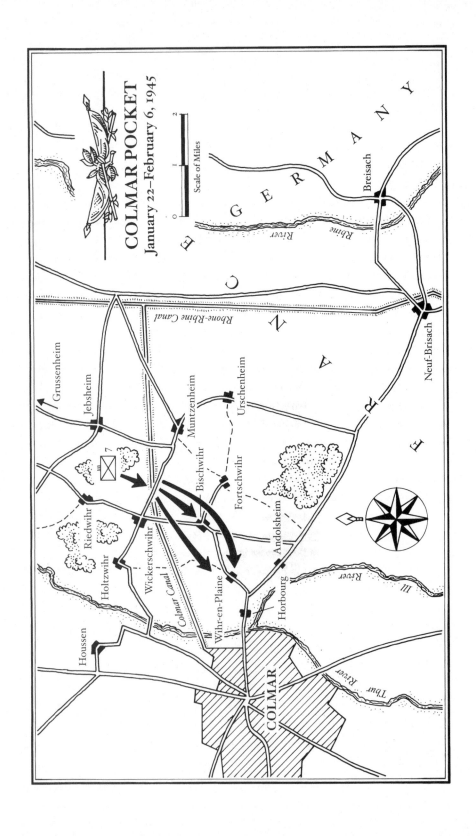

COLMAR POCKET
January 22–February 6, 1945

Scale of Miles
0   1   2

GERMANY

FRANCE

Rhine River

Breisach

Neuf-Brisach

Rhone-Rhine Canal

Grussenheim

Jebsheim

III 7

Muntzenheim

Urschenheim

Riedwihr

Bischwihr

Fortschwihr

Holtzwihr

Wickerschwihr

Andolsheim

Colmar Canal

Wihr-en-Plaine

Horbourg

Ill River

Houssen

COLMAR

Tbur River

they still controlled one last swath of territory in France—the Colmar Pocket. The supreme commander gave orders to reduce the pocket and eliminate the German presence in France.

French and American commanders planned a classic pincer-style attack on the Colmar Pocket. French troops, comprising most of the manpower for this offensive, would attack from the south and drive for Neuf-Brisach, a key supply point close to the Rhine. At the same time, the 3rd Division, along with French armor and two other U.S. divisions, would attack from the north. These troops would capture the Colmar Canal in an encircling movement, drive east, and seize key bridges, hills, and towns east of the city of Colmar before linking up with the French at Neuf-Brisach. If all went well, the Germans would be kicked out of France, most of their armies west of the Rhine would be captured, and, maybe, a bridgehead over the Rhine could be won.

The attack would begin on January 22, 1945. A few days previous to the attack, the 7th Infantry was withdrawn from the front. The men enjoyed a few days in the rear, warming up, sleeping, washing, and eating hot food. They welcomed the respite, but they knew it was only temporary. They could feel in their bones that an attack was imminent. Reitan said that the presence of Red Cross girls handing out coffee and doughnuts ("doughnut dollies") was a sure tip-off that an attack would soon begin: "They were regarded as a harbinger of bad news, because we saw them only when we were going into combat."

At 2100 hours on the twenty-second, the 1st and 3rd Battalions led the attack in frigid conditions. In total silence they crossed Bailey bridges at Geumar over the Fecht River. The Cottonbalers wore heavy overcoats, over which they draped white sheets ("spook suits") to camouflage themselves in the snowy landscape. They also replaced their helmet netting with strips of white cloth. Each rifleman carried four bandoliers of ammunition, four hand grenades, a rifle, K rations, and a pack with a blanket and extra canteens.[66]

On the right flank of the regiment, 1st Battalion soldiers moved forward as best they could through the thick snow. Their objective was Ostheim, a small village somewhere out there in the wintry distance. The night was quiet, still, almost eerie. In an effort to surprise the enemy, the Americans had not laid down a pre-attack artillery barrage.

Moving with C Company, Private Craft stumbled through the snow across an open field: "Snow was knee deep. There were high drifts hip deep. We reached the point where we made contact with the enemy, who opened up on us with machine gun fire. We took the nearest cover. There was a depression in the ground; you could tell, in spite of the snow. Everybody headed for its cover. The Germans . . . knew it was the first place that we'd head for, and they had mined the ditch. Several people jumped in, and got blown up." The battalion commander, newly promoted Major Kenneth Wallace, happened to be with them and urged them to get out of the ditch and assault the machine gun. They did so and shot up the German gun crew.[67]

Other 1st Battalion soldiers also had problems with mines. Company A began tripping them a hundred yards beyond the river. As they exploded, the mines flashed and made muffled popping sounds in the deep snow. Several men tripped them and had shattered limbs to prove it. Seeing this, some A Company Cottonbalers hit the ground, the wrong thing to do because it ensured that they too could trip mines, only with much worse effect—almost like throwing themselves on a grenade. Other men, usually veterans, froze in place and waited for scouts—ever so carefully—to find a way out of the minefield and leave tracks in the snow that could be followed.

The 2nd Platoon, led by Second Lieutenant Bernard Coday, successfully negotiated its way out of a minefield and into the Colmar Forest only to be greeted with mortar and machine-gun fire. He and his men closed on the machine gun, firing at it as they did so. Coday hurled a grenade and wounded the crew. Their anguished screams could be heard bouncing around the forest. Moving deeper into the forest, the Americans encountered more enemy fire but kept advancing, mainly by firing and maneuvering. Machine-gun bullets slammed into two men, splashing their white sheets and the blanket of snow below them with crimson blood. The wounded men moaned as steam filtered out of their belly wounds. The Americans took cover behind trees and shot back, while small groups advanced through the snow. Suddenly a bullet slashed into Coday, right into his groin. He gasped involuntarily and collapsed. He was still strong enough to gesture to his men. "Move in—fire your weapons." They did and destroyed the German position.[68]

In this kind of fighting, A and C Companies battered their way into Ostheim by the early-morning hours of the twenty-third. Working with tanks, they destroyed German resistance in Ostheim by the afternoon of the twenty-third.

The 3rd Battalion, on the left flank, pushed straight through the forest, all the way to a stand of woods east of Ostheim, known as Brunn-wald. When the soldiers of this battalion crossed the bridge and the open snowfields, they came under mortar fire near the forest. The rounds landed incredibly close, scattering fragments everywhere. Some men who were hit had a tough time finding out where because they were wearing so much clothing and equipment. Here and there, the troops found small groups of Germans, probably enemy outposts. These proved to be easy pickings. The Americans simply poured fire on them and either they surrendered or, if they didn't, two or three riflemen came up and blasted their holes. Most chose surrender. Within a couple hours, the 3rd Battalion Cottonbalers reached Brunnwald and captured twenty-five surprised enemy soldiers from their comfortable dugouts, many of which included bunks, stoves, and food.

Heintges threw 2nd Battalion into the fight last and, ironically, it ran into the toughest resistance. They had no sooner pushed through the Colmar Forest and entered a clearing when German machine guns started shooting. This time the Germans were smart. They waited until E Company walked into an enfiladed kill zone and let them have it. The terrible enemy MG-42s chattered in a continuous roar. The enemy fire tore guts open, stitched through torsos, severed arms and legs, even heads. Nor did the enemy fire let up. The machine guns kept shooting everyone who moved. Green tracers streaked crazily through the air. Wounded men emitted high-pitched primal screams; dead soldiers lay in lumps and drained still warm blood into the snow. Everyone bur-rowed into the snow, almost welcoming its moist chill, the way it infil-trated any crack in a shirt or trousers, up sleeves, down necks, into ears.

Major Jack Duncan, the battalion commander, watched all this in ab-ject horror. If this continued much longer, E Company would cease to exist. Company G was also taking some of the fire. Duncan picked up his field phone and called in artillery coordinates. Moments later he heard the welcome sound of friendly shells flying overhead. The bar-rage was perfect. The American shells landed right among the Ger-mans, exploding some of them into tatters. The enemy fire slackened. As it did, Duncan implored his men to get moving. Some of them wouldn't move a muscle, but most got up and ran straight at the enemy, right into their own shells. "The G.I.'s advanced firing rifles, tommy-guns and light 30 cal MG's from the hip," one observer reported. Amer-ican shells kept pounding the area, wounding some of the GIs. They kept moving, shooting Germans in the face and chest. Splattered blood and steam from wounds permeated the whole position. The white-clad Germans either died or surrendered. The crisis was over.[69]

Tanks and tank destroyers soon churned through the snow and caught up with the infantry in their newly won positions south of the Colmar Forest. This armor, along with artillery, helped defeat small enemy counterattacks on the 3rd and 2nd Battalions throughout the day on January 23. This development, in combination with the beating the 2nd Battalion had taken in the clearing, caused Heintges to reroute his 1st Battalion to take the Château de Schoppenwihr, originally one of Duncan's objectives.

The "Red" battalion soldiers clustered in the woods above this old château. "The Chateau was a series of large stone structures, enclosed by a stone wall, located in a wooded area," one soldier explained. The biggest challenge in taking the place would be negotiating at least four hundred yards of flat, open ground. After an artillery barrage, the men of B and C Companies moved in three waves across the flat field at 0200. Moonlight reflected off the snow and illuminated them perfectly for hostile eyes. Some of the men glanced at the sky and cursed the moon, wishing that clouds would obscure it and darken the snowy fields. The Cottonbalers made it two-thirds of the way to the château buildings and still they had not heard a peep from the enemy. Gusts of wind blew grains of snow into the soldiers' faces. Nothing stirred in the winter night.

That soon changed. Reports from enemy weapons shattered the stillness. The Germans were holed up in the château buildings and behind the embankment of a small road just ahead of the Americans. Even as bullets from enemy small-arms fire scythed through the Cottonbalers, a German tank on the road started blasting them with its main gun. The muzzle of the tank flashed orange in the wink of an eye, and a second later a shell exploded among the men, sending some of them flying, like rag dolls.

The leading troops, mostly from B Company, actually had an advantage because of their close proximity to a small area of cover afforded by the bank of the road. First Lieutenant Richard Kerr roared at his men to keep going until they reached the cover. Enemy bullets snapped and popped around them, kicking up snow, but they obeyed, firing their rifles from the hip, making it to the bank. They flopped down and caught their collective breath. Not more than twenty yards away, they could hear the Germans yelling at one another.

A little farther back, but still close to the road, C Company was taking even more of the fire. Machine guns and tank fire killed several men. Private Craft's squad was right in the middle of this mess. He had recently accepted an offer to become a BAR man, a decision he soon regretted because of the weight of the weapon (twenty pounds) and its ammunition clips (probably two pounds each). But the firepower of this terrific weapon helped him now as he and his squad ran head on into a similarly sized group of Germans. "They opened up with their burp guns. There must have been 15 or 20 of them. I threw my BAR up to my shoulder and shot down the line. I'm not sure how many of them I hit, but it didn't stop them. No sooner had I fired my clip at them, a rifle grenade hit near me. A fragment of it got . . . a guy from New York City in the eye.

"We were really in a bad way. We were disorganized, we didn't know where we were, and Colen [a buddy] had been hit and was lying down across the calves of my legs. I was lying on the ground. This German turned around and filled Colen full of bullets. Not a one struck me. There were men crying. There was a boy from Florida . . . crying and carrying on, 'Oh, Lord, we are going to be killed,' and I dressed him down. I told him we had to fight and for him to quit being a baby."

Craft's BAR jammed and he crawled to his captain. "I tried to talk to [him], and I couldn't get any response, just a grunt." He was witnessing the last moments of Captain Beverly Hayes's life. The C Company commander died quietly in the snow.

Next a German machine gun set up in a position to fire into the ditch. The bullets slammed into several men but not Craft. The enemy started closing in on the ditch, "close to where we were and throwing hand grenades on us. They would come back and say, 'Come surrender.' There was one GI, who jumped up to surrender, with his hands up, and they shot him down. I vowed then, that I wouldn't surrender. They kept on coming up, throwing grenades . . . and they threw one that exploded on my helmet. My ears were ringing. I couldn't hear anything. The concussion shook me up. There were only six of us left."

He and another man decided to make a run for it, after Craft threw his last grenade. "I pulled the grenade out, pulled the pin and peeked out over the top of the bank, and I saw three Krauts standing together in a close circle and threw the grenade and it landed in the middle of them. That grenade exploded like a cannon." The other man covered Craft with his rifle and the Mississippian ran past German soldiers and tanks. Soon they opened fire on him and he fell into the field and played dead. He wriggled free of his BAR clips and cartridge belt and made another run for it. "I could feel the bullets whizzing by me. I had only one weapon with me that night, the Lord." He played dead a few more times and finally made it back to the American rear area, where he warmed up at an aid station and got treated for concussion.[70]

Meanwhile, German tank fire and rifle grenades pounded B Company in its lonely ditch. A private tried to take out the tank with rifle grenade fire. The tank scored a direct hit on him, leaving behind nothing more than a blackened spot and bloody stumps. Other men around him were hit too, and they screamed in pain. Kerr had seen enough. He stood up and screamed, "Let's go!" The men could hardly believe his courage. Inspired in a way that only seems to happen because of good leadership in combat, they forgot their own fears and followed him. At this point, the battle turned. The B Company soldiers screamed like lunatics, shooting into the night at the vague shapes of Germans in front of them. Some of the Germans surrendered. Others died in their holes, with clean bullet holes through their foreheads, or were shredded into bloody strips of humanity by American grenades.

The Cottonbalers streamed into the small stand of woods in front of the château and killed several Germans in their holes. They soon reached the wall, which had many holes ripped into it from the earlier artillery barrage. The soldiers ran through the holes and into the château buildings. They captured a couple of enemy soldiers, but most took off into the woods.

The Cottonbaler bazooka men did not assault the buildings. Instead, they took up firing positions near the château and shot at the tank that had so tormented them moments before. Their rounds hit close enough to cause the tank to leave. Satisfied, the bazooka team joined their comrades in the houses, looting anything of value. The company spent the morning doing this, until Wallace sent up his other two companies on tanks across the fields that had seen so much American blood spilled during the night. Château de Schoppenwihr officially belonged to the 7th Infantry Regiment.[71]

The advance now focused to the east on the next objective, Houssen and its environs. Heintges lined up all three of his battalions and moved them east in yet another pincer movement. Artillerymen shelled the town and then laid down a smoke screen to cover the advance of the infantrymen and tankers across the flat ground around this objective.

The screen succeeded in confusing German artillery—it landed too far behind the dogfaces to do any damage—but machine-gun fire from German positions around the town hit several men, killing four of them. The tanks laid down a devastating barrage of fire on the German positions. This blasted the Germans out of their holes and forced others to retreat into the town. Once the Americans got into the town, they systematically went from house to house, crushing any resistance. By 0800 they had captured Houssen and fifty Germans, most of whom were rooted out of air-raid shelters. Some of them emerged from their shelters and bellowed, "Fuck Hitler!" in English.

The enemy soon tried a counterattack that failed largely because of the efforts of one man, Private First Class Jose Valdez, a BAR gunner from B Company. Valdez was part of a six-man outpost that came under fire from two companies of German infantry that were attempting to push into Station de Bennwihr near Houssen. The six men opened fire and exchanged shots with the enemy for fifteen minutes. Before long enemy fire hit four of the men. Clearly, numbers dictated they could not hold out long. Valdez took a bullet in the stomach. It tore through his abdomen and exited out of his back; he was bleeding badly. He told the other men to leave; he would stay there and call down artillery on the enemy with the help of a field phone. He called in mortar and artillery fire that sometimes landed as close as fifty yards in front of his position. The shells eviscerated many of the Germans. They tried to press forward, but it was no use. The U.S. artillery was too deadly. Valdez stayed put and kept calling it in, even as he lay dying. His actions bought time for the rest of B Company to come up, get in position, and lay fire on the Germans, completely blunting their attack.

Four soldiers, including Private Steve Kovatch, evacuated the badly wounded Valdez. "He'd been . . . paralyzed from the waist down. [We] carried him back to the railroad station. He was in bad shape then. I knew he wasn't going to live." Kovatch was right. Valdez died and was later awarded the Medal of Honor.

The next day, January 26, B Company assaulted enemy positions south of Bennwihr, near a railroad station. They crept up under cover of thick trees in battle-scarred woods. The lead scout saw a German and shot him with his Garand. The Germans started shooting and the Americans immediately began to use the torn trees as cover. Slowly but surely, they closed in on the enemy, moving from tree to tree. When the Americans were close enough, they unleashed a direct assault on the Germans.

Screaming wildly, maniacally, they plunged into the enemy holes. "Fragmentation hand grenades were tossed into the enemy holes," one soldier recalled. "German flesh and blood splattered against the dirt sides of the trenches when the grenades exploded. The wailing and moaning from the blood-soaked bodies added to the 'grimness' of the job at hand. The newer men felt 'shudders down their spine,' as they routed the enemy." Even in this environment of all-out combat, the Cotton-balers would not use their bayonets to finish off the Germans, preferring to shoot or club them instead. Bayonets seemed too vulgar, too caveman-nish, as if they belonged to another age: "[We] would rather shoot the enemy point blank or hit them with rifle butts than stick them with bay-onets."

The fighting now died down a bit and the 7th Regiment left the front lines and rested for a few days in a forest bivouac. In just four days of fighting, the Cottonbalers had driven a deep wedge into the enemy defensive system north of Colmar, captured 393 prisoners, and suffered 58 men killed, 312 wounded, and 93 "nonbattle" casualties, in other words, frostbite, trench foot, combat fatigue, and illnesses. The men certainly looked like they had been in a tough fight. "The stubble of growth on soldier's faces became frozen from the bitter cold," one sol-dier recalled. "Snow suits were rigid at grotesque angles. Rifle and ma-chine guns were chilled into uselessness."[72] It was the end of Phase One of the Colmar Pocket battle. Phase Two would soon begin.

WHILE THEY WERE IN RESERVE IN THE WOODS, THE MEN still ate K rations and lived in holes, but they had access to warming tents. Another eighty-eight men were evacuated with trench foot and frostbite, but the companies got new men to replace them.

On January 28, Heintges received orders for Operation Kraut Buster, the next phase of the campaign. Kraut Buster called for the 7th Infantry to cross the Colmar Canal, which connected Colmar to the Rhine, and push into the eastern outskirts of Colmar. To the east the 15th Infantry would also cross the canal and protect the eastern flank of the Cottonbalers. The canal itself was fifty feet wide and filled with dirty, slushy water. Eight-foot-high banks extended along both sides of the waterway. The depth of the water was about six feet.

As the sun set on the twenty-ninth, the Cottonbalers began an ardu-ous march through deep snow to the jump-off point north of the canal. The task was made worse by a traffic jam along the roads leading to the canal. There had been a foul-up in coordination between the French armor support, the U.S. engineers (carrying bridging material), and the 3rd Division command. Vehicles and bridging materials were literally parked bumper to bumper, going nowhere any time soon. The riflemen and machine gunners of the leading 7th Infantry assault companies from the 1st and 3rd Battalions had no choice but to spread out and negotiate their way through and around this mess as best they could. This cost them cohesion and delayed the attack. Finally, they made it to the jump-off area.

They watched as American artillery and mortars plastered the south side of the canal. The barrage lasted about half an hour. Then the artillerymen laid down a protective smoke screen. Meanwhile, heavy machine gunners set up their weapons along the northern edge of the canal. The infantry troops lugged their assault boats up the steep bank to the canal, bitching and cursing all the way. The boats were a real pain in the neck. They were awkward, slippery, and heavy. Soldiers slipped and fell in the snow as they tried to manipulate the boats. At last, they pushed the boats over the bank and into the water of the canal. Each boat emitted a muddy splash as it hit the water. The men quickly scrambled down the bank and into their boats. They paddled across the water, while overhead American artillery exploded on the south bank. The enemy hardly responded. The men could hear a little small-arms fire, but it was wild and inaccurate.

Within minutes the two battalions made it safely across the canal and pushed into the eastern suburbs against little or no resistance. Several Germans, dazed by the artillery bombardment, surrendered. In the suburb of Bischwihr, L Company routed a group of Germans from a cellar. Always on the alert for loot, the dogfaces ran their hands over the bodies of the enemy prisoners in hopes of finding hidden Lugers or other goodies. One Cottonbaler patted down an enemy soldier and recoiled in surprise. "For Christ sake! It's a woman!" He might as well have said that he had found a roomful of gold bars. Soldiers thronged around the German prisoners. Curiously, and lecherously, they began patting the Germans. They found fourteen women in soldiers' uniforms out of thirty prisoners of war. Someone had to escort these special prisoners to the rear, and the company commander found that he had no shortage of volunteers for this job (so much for the time-honored tradition of never volunteering for anything in the Army). Everyone gathered around the commander and furiously lobbied for the job; it was a giant game of "pick me." The commanding officer selected a few lucky GIs, and, grinning from ear to ear, they set off on their task, while everyone else scowled and made lewd remarks.

By now the 2nd Battalion had also crossed the canal, so the entire 7th Infantry was in a position to slip the noose around the Germans in Colmar. Moreover, the engineers finished building a bridge at dawn on the thirtieth and French tanks eventually rumbled across, a development that made the infantrymen feel more secure than they had before. Before the tanks crossed, the three rifle companies of the 2nd Battalion led the way for the Allied advance into the Colmar suburbs, the immediate objective being Wihr-en-Plaine.[73]

The sun had set and the weather was cold and clear as the men made their way through deep snowdrifts in the open fields in front of Wihr-en-Plaine. The Germans seemed to have vanished. "There was an eerie silence," Reitan recalled, "broken only by the crunching of boots on the snow and whispering of American shells overhead."[74]

The whole scene was too strange for Duncan. "It was too easy and quiet. I felt like we were walking into something." His instincts could not have been more correct. Companies F and G had just reached the outskirts of the town, with E Company about 350 yards behind, when the Germans let loose with a murderous barrage of fire. Enemy tank destroyers came out of nowhere and pumped rounds into the men of F and G Companies; German machine guns swept the whole area. In spite of the spook suits the Americans were wearing, the moonlight silhouetted them perfectly. The Germans slaughtered them.

Like lions ripping into cornered gazelles, the enemy tank destroyers pulverized the hapless American infantrymen. The main guns of both these monsters boomed, spitting shells that exploded almost at point-blank range. Those caught in the kill zone never knew what hit them. Their bloody shards mixed with one another. Hardly anything remained of them except bits of dog tags or helmets. Machine guns from the tank destroyers also claimed many victims, mostly by punching deep holes in them, bullets that entered in a man's stomach or chest and blew out part of his back or perhaps smashed into legs, ricocheted off bones, and ended up causing three or four wounds. In little more than a minute or two, the tank destroyers killed fifteen Cottonbalers. Several other Americans, hopelessly snared in the trap, tried to surrender. German machine gunners cut them down. Their bodies draped on top of one another, motionless in the snow.[75]

The surviving F and G Company men, including Reitan, ran as fast as they could for the cover of the town. "When I saw the German TD's I took off as fast as I could manage in deep snow with my heavy load. When I reached the village, my heart pounding and my lungs burning, I encountered a stone wall. Somehow, I got over it with my rifle and equipment and fell to the other side. As I lay there gasping, I heard other bodies plopping over the wall. Voices called quietly, 'F Company' as we tried to get reorganized." Another man, Private First Class Ernie Boyd from G Company, had a similar experience. "Running in that snow was hell, and really I went sort of like a rabbit. I was nearly done in. I felt like I was sucking in pure fire by the time I came to a low stone wall that I fell on and rolled over."[76]

Now that F and G Companies were in the town, the enemy tank destroyers turned their attention to the men of E Company, who were cowering in the snow-covered fields. The tank destroyers raked the E Company Cottonbalers with machine-gun fire, breaking bones and splashing blood everywhere. Lieutenant George Kite called back for artillery and was told to wait. Exasperated and scared, he screamed into the receiver, "I want this fire more than I've ever wanted anything in all my life!" The artillery came, but it was ineffective. The tank destroyers kept getting nearer by the second.

Major Duncan had taken cover behind a frozen manure pile. He watched the tank destroyers and screamed for bazooka teams. A two-man team crawled fifty yards to get to him. Their hands looked red and frozen. They set up their bazooka, loaded it, and fired. Duncan could hear other men praying for the bazooka team to kill the tank destroyer. They missed. A minute later, the tank destroyer scored a perfect hit on the bazooka team, blowing them into nothing but random body parts. Duncan and the other men watched this with shock and anguish. Only one bazooka remained, and it was down to one round. The tank destroyer rumbled closer.

The bazooka man, Private John Bale, turned to Duncan and said, "Well, sir, here goes the last round." Bale took careful aim. No one spoke. They simply stared at Bale, knowing that their lives probably rode on his shot. The round left the bazooka and streaked through the air. "Years seemed to pass," Duncan said. The round arched skyward and then nosed down, right into the tank destroyer. The tank destroyer burst into flames, almost blinding them with brightness. They didn't care. "The soldiers could not restrain themselves," Duncan recalled.

"They yelled at the top of their lungs. Some unashamedly wept for joy."
The German tank destroyer crew leaped from their stricken vehicle.
Some of them were on fire. They rolled around the snow in an effort to
douse the flames. The other tank destroyer drove up to these survivors,
picked them up, and left. The Americans badly wanted to shoot the
crew of the tank destroyer, but with no more bazooka rounds, they did
not dare risk attracting the attention of the other tank destroyer.

After the tank destroyers left, E Company hightailed it into the
town. Private Dale Schumacher immediately captured a German mortar crew: "The three captured Germans were very scared. They took
family pictures from their pockets and held them out to us. I'm sure
they felt we were going to kill them on the spot."

The Americans held Wihr-en-Plaine during the early-morning hours
of the thirtieth, but at daylight the Germans counterattacked from several directions. A Mark VI tank and twenty-five enemy infantrymen attacked E Company in the eastern portion of the town. Still out of
bazooka ammo, the men did the only thing they could—shower the enemy infantry with rifle fire. This worked. They killed several enemy soldiers and the tank withdrew, contenting itself with taking potshots
from a safe distance. A little later, Schumacher noticed another group
of Germans "milling around outside of the stone wall setting up a cannon of some kind. We fired at them with our rifles and they retreated."
Seconds later, the Germans responded by pumping shells into the
house. Shrapnel wounded Schumacher in the chest. The Germans retreated with their gun.

On the other side of town, another Mark VI, accompanied by sixty
infantrymen, attacked the Americans and threatened the battalion
command post. The bazooka men on this side of town had ammo and
they drove off the tank with a few shots. The infantry kept pressing, finally taking cover in sheds, only to be blasted out by the bazooka
teams. Three Germans in a Volkswagen drove up the main street. An
American machine gun opened fire and sheared the driver's head off.
The vehicle crashed into a building, killing the other two Germans.
The driver's head rolled to a stop in the street.

Duncan now ordered his men to get inside the buildings. He called
for artillery to be placed right on the town—his own position. The
"redlegs" did a devastatingly effective job. They perfectly placed 105mm
shells in the town and lobbed 155mm shells outside the town to prevent
the Germans from bringing up reinforcements. "The early morning

light was brightened by the exploding shells," one soldier recalled. "German bodies were mangled when the barrage landed. Enemy voices screamed in pain. Germans writhed on the streets in their own blood while the . . . shells continued to cut through their clothes and flesh."

Private Bale, separated from his own company, now tried a daring individual shot at the Mark VI tank on the western edge of town. Bad idea. In trying to load the bazooka himself, he tilted the tube downward. The armed rocket simply slipped through the tube and exploded on the floor at his feet, blowing off his legs. He bled to death in seconds.

The tank kept coming. Reitan could see it from his spot in a churchyard. "I took cover in a house with three or four others from my squad, but not before the tank driver saw us. We heard the clanking sound of the tank as it approached, then silence, as the tank stopped in front of the house. We heard the turret turning. We squeezed our bodies as flat as possible against the side walls. The tank fired one shot into the side of the house. The room was filled with dust and debris, and there was a hole in the stone wall about a foot above the floor. Miraculously no one was killed or wounded, apart from cuts and abrasions. I heard the tank proceed down the street and then an explosion."

A bazooka team had scored a perfect shot on the Mark VI. Private Boyd had loaded the bazooka for the gunner, Private Ernest Hallmark. "Hallmark put the round squarely into the engine, and I was stunned at the fire that occurred. One of the tankers jumped from the tank, on fire, and started running away. Someone cut him down, and the whole squad went racing out into the street firing at anyone that either managed to get out or was trying to get out. All were killed." Boyd later wondered if he and the others were right to have killed the helpless tankers. "I have often regretted that we did not take prisoners."

The engineers had by now finished their bridge allowing Allied armor to cross the canal, and around midmorning several friendly tanks rolled into Wihr-en-Plaine. The infantrymen were thrilled to see them. The tanks helped clear out the rest of the town, mostly blasting Germans into submission and taking them prisoner.[77]

The weary men of the 2nd Battalion wanted nothing more now than to rest and enjoy a hot meal and a little safety. They lounged around in the town for a few hours until General O'Daniel called and ordered them to take Horbourg, the next town, located two hundred yards away across an open field. The capture of Horbourg would deprive the

Germans of an east–west road out of Colmar. Duncan's companies were now down to about thirty men each, yet he had no choice but to comply with O'Daniel's hard-driving instructions. The 2nd Battalion commanding officer tried to enlist the help of French tankers, but their commander refused to move forward until the crossroads east of Horbourg had been taken. Duncan engaged in a chicken-and-egg argument with the French commander. Taking the crossroads would be quite difficult without armored support. If the infantry succeeded in taking it, they might not need the armor anymore. The Frenchman, concerned about the possible presence of German antitank guns at the crossroads, would not budge.

Disgusted and angry, Duncan ordered his attack, supported by one American tank, to begin at 2100 on the thirtieth. Led by E Company, the men moved out across the fields. The night was warmer than previous nights, and that had melted the snow a bit, causing some men to struggle with slush and mud. Once again moonlight silhouetted the soldiers. They got to within twenty yards of Horbourg when the Germans opened fire from the protection of trenches and buildings in the town. Five men went down. The tank blasted the buildings and a machine-gun team in the field. The infantry now got forward and burst into the leading buildings, grenading the Germans inside.

Other 2nd Battalion men soon followed. The tank fell into a tank trap and was out of the fight. A runner went back to get another tank. It came up quickly and shot into the German-held houses in the town. The Germans now held one side of the main street near the road junction and the Americans the other. They shot at each other from across the street. The stalemate situation lasted all night. Schumacher remembered holing up in a demolished house and that several times the Germans "came in after us but we were able to drive them off. We moved to a back room away from the street and finally ended up in the basement." Many others did too.

As the sun rose on January 31, exhausted Landsers and dogfaces still confronted each other from across the tattered street. O'Daniel wanted the town by noon. Duncan had reached the point of desperation. He lied to the French, telling them that the crossroads was secure. They attacked at 1300. Luckily, the French met little resistance. Once American infantrymen saw the French armor, they joined with their French counterparts and rooted the Germans out of their buildings. The Allies took seventy prisoners. They quickly cleared the rest of the town. Any surviving Germans attempted to flee east to the Rhine, but many of them were killed by American artillery. By nightfall, the German line of resistance around the town of Colmar had effectively collapsed and troops from the 75th Infantry Division relieved the hollow-eyed survivors of the 7th Regiment's 2nd Battalion.

Private Reitan, like many others, gave everything he had to give during those three horrendous days in the Colmar Pocket. He reached the point of total mental and physical exhaustion at Horbourg. "Along with eight or ten others, I was sent to the rear where they had a camp to give soldiers some rest and decent meals. While I was there, I was seen by a doctor. He examined my knee and recommended that I be sent to the rear area for limited duty." It was like salvation! "I can still hear him say, 'You've had enough of this, son.' My heart rejoiced, for I knew that I would live." He spent the rest of the war as a mail clerk in a replacement depot. After the war, he returned to college on the GI Bill, got his doctorate in history, and became a professor at Illinois State University.[78]

The three days of fighting cost the 7th Infantry thirty-nine killed, seventy-seven wounded, and sixty-two "nonbattle" casualties. Phase Two of the Colmar Pocket was now over. The regiment had a day and a half to prepare for Phase Three—the final push to the Rhine.[79]

O'DANIEL WANTED TO KEEP UP THE PRESSURE ON THE Germans, cut them off, and destroy them while he had them on the run. He ordered the 7th Infantry to move east, to Artzenheim (recently taken by the French), and attack south across the Rhône-Rhine Canal, then into the walled fortress city of Neuf-Brisach, near the Rhine. This would deny the enemy two bridges badly needed to escape across the natural barrier of the Rhine. Heintges chose the 2nd and 3rd Battalions to lead the attack. The men of these outfits rode trucks to the town of Jebsheim and then walked to Artzenheim. The 1st, in reserve, hoofed the whole way to Artzenheim. Intelligence indicated that the enemy had built up an extensive array of fortifications, including concrete pillboxes, zigzag trenches, bunkers, and foxholes. They had been working on some of these positions for years.

After an artillery preparation, the infantry went forward at 0500 on February 2. Many of the troops rode on tanks. At first they met little resistance as they rumbled into Baltzenheim and then Kunheim. They took a little sniper fire and a few prisoners. In fact, the biggest peril was short rounds from U.S. artillery. One such round wounded several soldiers. By 0900 both towns were mostly unscathed and firmly in American hands. Many of the soldiers crawled into nice warm beds throughout Kunheim and enjoyed real sheets while the engineers built a Bailey bridge over a canal south of Kunheim.

At 0200 on the third the Cottonbalers roused themselves and crossed the newly constructed bridge. The thaw had continued, making the ground slushy and muddy. Some of the men plodded through shin-deep mud. Others rode on tanks, which kicked up mud behind their tracks. Needless to say, no one walked directly behind a tank. The troops advanced about two thousand yards and began to see what they thought were empty foxholes. They were wrong. The enemy popped up and opened fire. The 3rd Battalion had actually walked past enemy outposts and into their defensive line.

Tracers and explosions lit up the night. Several Americans fell into the mud, dead or wounded. Company K found itself right in the middle of the enemy trenches. The commander, Captain Francis Kret, urged his men to move forward into the trenches. Rushing around in small groups, they followed him into the trenches. They fought close-up engagements with enemy soldiers, shooting them point-blank with their rifles. They slopped in the mud and killed any enemy they saw, not bothering to take any prisoners. Firmly ensconced in the enemy trench system, they exchanged shots with other German soldiers, who were probably no more than twenty or thirty yards away. The Americans "tossed the lifeless bodies of Germans from the trench in order to make more room," one soldier recalled. "A scream would pierce the night when a soldier was hit. First aid was administered in the muddy trenches with aid packets."

The rest of the battalion fought similar engagements and pushed into the town of Biesheim by daylight. This was the last village before Neuf-Brisach and the Germans needed it to cover their retreat across the Rhine bridges. They contested every house. The infantry needed the help of tanks and tank destroyers to overrun the town. The armor blasted the buildings, crashing in walls so that squads of infantrymen could assault the Germans within. Once again, the fighting was close, within handshake distance, eyeball-to-eyeball. The Germans either surrendered or were unceremoniously gunned down, their bodies left to rot in the rubble. Still, the fighting continued.

An operations report summed up the situation in Biesheim on the morning of February 3: "I Company had cleared the southwest section of town to 'Central Street.' Elements of K Company were located in . . .

three houses on the northwestern edge of town. L Company had cleared most of the houses north of I Company on the western side of 'Central Street' but had not made contact with K Company's three houses. The 2nd Battalion held all of the town east of 'Central Street.' "[80] The Germans, desperately trying to buy time, counterattacked, and the situation in and around Biesheim seesawed all day. The 2nd and 3rd Battalions could not claim full control of Biesheim until well into the evening.

As these two battalions fought for the town, the 1st Battalion fought a tough battle just to the northwest of Biesheim, at the Jewish Cemetery, where the Germans, ironically, chose to make a stand with tanks, mortars, and infantry. They opened fire when the battalion was about six hundred yards north of the cemetery. The men of the assault companies (most of them about sixty or seventy strong) took cover behind canals and dikes. For the better part of the day, German fire pinned down the 1st Battalion troops. Every time one of the companies would try to advance, the Germans laid down such withering fire that the men had to take cover or be slaughtered.

American artillery fired high-explosive and smoke shells on and off during the day and early-evening hours. Finally, as midnight approached, Wallace felt the time was ripe for an advance. He ordered C Company to attack the cemetery. Craft, promoted to squad leader, piled onto a tank with the members of his squad. "I was the last one to get on and had to get on the tail end of the tank, holding onto another comrade. There were three tanks abreast. I was riding the middle tank. A German tank at our right front, near the edge of town opened fire on us and missed." An American tank destroyer knocked out the German tank. A German machine gun opened fire on the right. "My tank stopped and fired three rapid shots. The noise from the big gun's blast was deafening. My ears were ringing, and I almost fell off the tank. The adrenaline of everyone was sky high; we wanted revenge." They jumped off the tank. "I spotted an enemy machine gun nest and headed straight for it. I went for the gunner, who with his two helpers, had their helmets off and their hands raised. I reached over the machine gun, grabbed him by the hair and . . . jerked him out of the foxhole. He was real small and frightened . . . trembling." Craft searched him and took his watch and pistol. The Jewish Cemetery belonged to the Americans.[81]

The final push could now begin. Aided by searchlight battalions who created artificial moonlight, along with massive artillery barrages, the regiment pushed south through the muddy fields of eastern Alsace just after midnight on February 5. Heintges did not want his men on the roads, where he believed the Germans had set up heavy defenses. Better to encircle the enemy and cut them off. Here and there, the Germans offered resistance, but they were too harried, too disorganized, to stop the Americans from seizing the approaches to Neuf-Brisach and its suburb to the east—Vogelsheim—by the afternoon of the fifth. The Germans destroyed the bridges over the Rhine, abandoning those who still remained in the rapidly collapsing Colmar Pocket, many of whom were more than happy to become prisoners.

The garrison at Neuf-Brisach did not feel that way, though. On the sixth about six hundred of them tried, in vain, to escape. The Cottonbalers, guarding every possible avenue of escape, shot them down in droves. They were like "clay pigeons in green uniforms," one soldier asserted. "Artillery and mortar concentrations began to 'find their mark.' Limbs were literally torn from bodies and strewn over the muddy terrain. Torn flesh and equipment littered the area and voices were heard screaming from the enemy locations. The Germans were running away in 'wild formations.'"

This veritable shooting gallery was a fitting end to what had been a two-week slaughter. From January 22 to February 6, the 7th Regiment suffered 134 men killed, 584 wounded, and 349 "nonbattle" (trench foot, shock, frostbite, battle fatigue) casualties in the Colmar Pocket. In turn, they had killed hundreds of Germans and captured 1,362, in addition to kicking the enemy out of France for good. No one was in much of a mood to celebrate, though. The muddy, haunted survivors slogged back to Artzenheim for a welcome rest and yet another "Watch on the Rhine."[82]

THE 7TH REGIMENT AND THE 3RD DIVISION WERE NOW shattered. Months of combat since the August invasion of the Riviera had taken a drastic toll on the fighting power of these fine units, and Colmar administered a coup de grâce of sorts. Companies were down to twenty or thirty men. Many of those who had fought so hard in North Africa, Sicily, Italy, and the Vosges were dead, maimed, or lucky enough, like Reitan, to rotate to rear-area jobs.

For its stalwart combat effectiveness, the 3rd Division received a great honor—a presidential unit citation. Only three other divisions earned such a citation: the 101st Airborne and 4th Armored for Bastogne and the 1st Marine Division for Guadalcanal. The performance of the 7th Infantry, in tandem with its sister regiments, the 15th and 30th, helped earn the division that citation.

With so many veterans gone, replacements would now have to pick up the slack if the regiment's fighting effectiveness was to continue at such a high level. These men slowly buttressed the ranks of the regiment during an extensive rest and training period in Nancy through the month of February and half of March. The Cottonbalers had the luxury of living in real buildings, with real beds and real bathing facilities. They also got plenty of entertainment. "Moving pictures and shows were provided for the men," the regimental historian wrote, "and each company held dances which were attended by the old and young 'belles' of Lorraine, who quickly learned the American 'jitterbug' steps." The training, as usual, focused on physical conditioning, coordination with tanks and artillery, and river crossings.[83]

In the middle of March, the 3rd Division, replenished and somewhat refreshed, received orders to get back in the war. The 1st Army, because of a lucky break, had captured a bridge across the Rhine on March 7 and was pouring soldiers into the other side. Even so, large areas west of the Rhine in Germany needed to be cleared out. The Allies could not hope to cross all of their armies over one bridgehead. They needed many of them, all along the north–south expanse of the Rhine, so that they could fully overrun Germany. The Rhineland, as many called the portion of Germany west of the Rhine, was where the Germans had built their Siegfried Line, or "West Wall," as they called it. The Siegfried Line was a series of fortified areas guarding the approaches to the Rhine—pillboxes, bunkers, zigzag trenches, barbed wire, machine guns, and antitank guns with interlocking fields of fire, dragon's teeth, tank traps, and minefields. General Patch planned a sizable offensive for his 7th Army with the aim of clearing out the southwestern portion of the Siegfried Line and securing the west banks of the Rhine. The 3rd Division, and 7th Infantry received the assignment of breaching the line near Zweibrücken and advancing eastward over rolling ground.

On March 13–14, trucks drove the 7th Infantry Regiment to its jump-off points on the Franco-German border. The 1st and 2nd Battalions, lining up two abreast, would lead the attack, with the 3rd following behind the 2nd. In the days leading up to the attack, Heintges wisely solicited advice from 9th Infantry Division officers on how best to breach the defenses of the Siegfried Line. Their division had spent

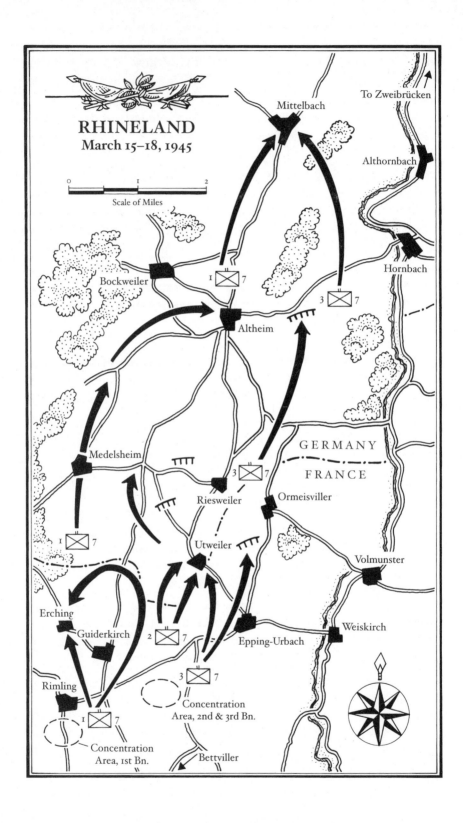

RHINELAND
March 15–18, 1945

0   1   2
Scale of Miles

To Zweibrücken

Mittelbach

Althornbach

Hornbach

Bockweiler

1 ⊠ 7

3 ⊠ 7

Altheim

GERMANY

FRANCE

Medelsheim

3 ⊠ 7

Riesweiler

Ormeisviller

1 ⊠ 7

Utweiler

Volmunster

Erching

Guiderkirch

2 ⊠ 7

Epping-Urbach

Weiskirch

Rimling

3 ⊠ 7

Concentration
Area, 2nd & 3rd Bn.

1 ⊠ 7

Concentration
Area, 1st Bn.

Bettviller

the better part of the last few months cracking the western edges of the line.[84] Thus the 7th Infantry was probably as prepared as it could be for the formidable task at hand.

Just after 0100 on the morning of the fifteenth, the Cottonbalers moved forward. The night was cool and the ground squishy. The snow had melted and been washed away by heavy rains in the last couple weeks. That meant dealing with mud. The men mushed their way forward in the muck, trying to make as little noise as possible. American artillery rumbled overhead, exploding somewhere beyond. The 1st Battalion dealt with some machine guns, but with the help of the Battle Patrol pushed fairly quickly into Guiderkirch, one of the regiment's first objectives.

The same could not be said of the 2nd Battalion. In fact, they walked into a disaster. Companies E and F were leading, with G Company right behind. The men negotiated their way, with the help of artificial moonlight from searchlights, over a road and its adjacent fields. The whole scene was eerie: the "moonlight" produced the effect of continuous heat lightning; the air and the ground smelled moist, damp, thick. The men craned their necks and strained their eyes in hopes of seeing the enemy first. They had to be out there somewhere.

The Cottonbalers had passed through the positions of the 44th Infantry Division when they moved into position for this attack. Engineers from that division had cleared paths through minefields, delineated by special white tape, for the 7th. Just to make sure that the 2nd Battalion knew where to go, an engineering officer from the 44th led F and G Companies through the paths his men had cleared. The officer walked at the head of the column with the F Company commander, the self-made Minnesotan Swanson, promoted now to captain (he rose from private at Fedala to captain in 1945).

Several yards behind the two officers, Private First Class Benjamin Loup watched the two men apprehensively. An Anzio veteran who had missed the Meurthe crossing and Colmar battle while he recuperated from wounds, he sensed impending trouble. "Everyone . . . followed Capt. Swanson down the road about 40 or 50 yards. At this point the officer who was supposed to lead us through the mine field into Utweiler [their first objective] pointed out the engineer's tape to Capt. Swanson and took off for the rear. Capt. Swanson entered the field by the engineer's tape followed by his radio operator, my squad's scout, then myself and my assistant BAR man. After traversing a short distance in the mine field, about 20 yards or so, the engineer's tape ended." Swanson looked around for more tape but found none.

Did that mean there were no more mines or did it mean that the engineers had not swept beyond this point? With his mission and his objective foremost in his mind, Swanson made a decision. He passed word back that the dearth of tape probably meant no more mines. He waved his hand forward and the men moved out again. "About 10 yards or so past the engineer's tape, Capt. Swanson's radio operator set off a mine and the explosion ripped the radio off his back. Almost simultaneously . . . there were two other explosions farther back in my squad. Capt. Swanson immediately gave us the order to stop in our tracks, do not move our feet, and gently feel around where we were standing. If we felt nothing, lay prone. The attack was stalled."

Wounded men were crying and begging for medics. Against every fiber of their being, their buddies had to ponder whether to help them. One false move could set off another mine. Swanson's decision was wrong. He and his men had blundered into an extensive minefield, causing a terrifying, heart-stopping, helpless feeling—roughly akin to being forced to play Russian roulette. The radio operator screamed for help. Fragments of his radio were burning into his back. One of the medics wanted to help him, but Swanson told the medic to stay put. He ignored the order and safely crawled to the stricken radioman.

Loup watched him, fascinated and horrified at the same time. "The medic then started toward another wounded man and was again told by Capt. Swanson not to go. He told Capt. Swanson that it was his duty and he was going. Capt. Swanson then told him to proceed to the wounded man on his hands and knees feeling the ground before him. The aid man reached the second wounded man and administered aid." He decided to press his luck and go for a third man. "On the way over he detonated a mine, and I believe he was killed." Loup felt something stinging. It was his cheek. Somewhere along the line a mine fragment had hit him and torn the cheek open. He managed to exit the minefield and make it back to the aid station.

The mine explosions had alerted the Germans to the Cottonbalers' presence. The enemy started hurling mortar, artillery, and flak rounds at the stricken men in the minefield. The other two companies of the 2nd Battalion were in a similar bind to Swanson's F Company, pinned down, disorganized, scared out of their wits. Swanson sent a runner back to the battalion command post to inform them of the company's predicament. In the meantime, his soldiers gingerly worked their way backward, to the white tape, and out of the minefield, all the while under fire. One lieutenant tripped a mine that flung him into the air. He landed on another mine. The explosion rendered him unrecognizable as a human being. A mortar round screamed in and exploded near Swanson, tearing up his arm with fragments. The captain made it back to the white tape, then the road, and had begun walking to the aid station when a shell landed near him and killed him instantly. The 7th had lost one of its best leaders. Another shell exploded close to Private Schumacher of E Company, shattering his pelvis and femur. He lay helplessly waiting for aid. It did not come until almost a day had passed.

The traumatic experience in the minefield eroded about half the battalion's combat power—an accumulation of dead, wounded, pinned-down, disoriented, straggling, and combat-fatigued men. The other half of the battalion, led primarily by Duncan (a lieutenant colonel now) and the survivors of E Company, exited the minefield and found a safe route to Utweiler. The Germans had only a small number of troops defending the town. The Cottonbalers charged them and fired from the hip; "Just like in the movies," one rifleman said. The 2nd Battalion soldiers, led by E Company, then plunged into Utweiler, where they fought the Germans at nearly point-blank range. "For almost two hours, the Company cleared building after building against bitter resistance," an officer later wrote. "The Germans fought fanatically, refusing to yield. Approximately ten of the enemy were killed and 50 overpowered and taken prisoner."

The American infantry took control of the town by 0600. The situation seemed to be under control now, but looks were deceptive. Because of the mines, the battalion's armor support had been held up at the line of departure. The tankers refused to advance without assurance that the road had been swept. The Cottonbalers in Utweiler thus had no tank support. If the enemy launched an armored counterattack, these infantrymen would be in bad shape.

Naturally, the enemy launched an armored counterattack. Upon capturing Utweiler, the 2nd Battalion Cottonbalers found comfortable spots in the houses and relaxed, content to wait for American tanks to reinforce them. Duncan had lost communications contact with Heintges but wasn't too worried. Soon the tanks would come up, followed by the 3rd Battalion. Duncan's soldiers scattered around the town. Squad leaders assigned their rawest replacements to stand watch while the rest of the men caught up on sleep or ate rations. One squad leader even found time to make it with a local fräulein.

At 0800, the Germans punctured the 2nd Battalion's nonchalant little bubble. While standing guard in the churchyard, one of F Company's replacement riflemen, Private George Corpis, felt a powerful urge to empty his bowels. He found a private spot, dropped his trousers, and did his business. When he finished he glanced upward and did a double take. There, on a slope overlooking the church, was a German tank staring down right at him. Around the tanks, German infantrymen were trotting into position. He ran for the church as the tank fired a shot that exploded against the wall of the church and wounded him in the shoulder.

Corpis did not know it, but tankers and infantrymen from the 17th, 37th, and 38th SS Panzer-grenadiers had surrounded the town. They immediately pressed forward and started knocking the hell out of the Americans, who had only bazookas with which to oppose tanks. Corpis's F Company squad holed up in the church, along with five German prisoners of war captured earlier in the day. The tank kept blasting the church, spraying mortar and dust everywhere. A tank shell smashed through the door and skidded along the floor but did not explode. The Americans knew they had to surrender. One of the German prisoners offered to facilitate the surrender. "As he stepped outside, a German opened up with a burp gun and killed him on the spot," Private John Cook recalled. This was probably an accident. German soldiers burst into the church. An SS officer wanted to kill all the Americans on the spot, but the German prisoners, in addition to a Wehrmacht officer, talked him out of it. Corpis and the others went into captivity.

Six German tanks, two self-propelled guns, supported by a company of infantrymen, closed in on the town from all sides. Private First Class Joe Englert of E Company was sleeping when he heard other men shouting about German tanks. He got up and looked out the door of his house. "There were tanks, half tracks and infantry coming at us. I stuck my BAR through the opening and fired a magazine at them." A cluster of potato masher grenades came through the doors and windows of his house. Several struck him and exploded. He heard burp gun fire. "My ears were ringing, and I started saying an Act of Contrition thinking that this was it. I was going to die." Enemy soldiers took him prisoner. "It looked like they wanted to shoot us, but thank goodness an officer stopped them and told them to take us prisoner."

Lieutenant Wes McKane, a platoon leader in G Company, was in a barnyard when the Germans overwhelmed his group. "The group I was with surrendered in a barnyard. I had memories of German officers surrendering with a real arrogant look on their faces, so I tried my best sneer on the leader of the group who captured us. Not very bright! He slugged me alongside of the head with a potato masher grenade, which didn't seem very bright of him either."[85]

The German tanks were rolling down the streets, firing into the houses, collapsing the roofs. "Shell after shell plunged into the buildings, crumpling them down over the heads of the riflemen, who tried desperately to stop the armor with their few remaining bazooka rounds," one soldier recalled. The bazooka men tried to fight back from second-floor windows. Private Richard Saffell stood next to a bazooka team and provided fire support as the team attempted to kill a tank from a second-story window. The enemy tanks were "blasting what was left of the buildings from about 25–35 yards away. It was a slaughter. The same shell from one Tiger Tank killed the bazooka man, wounded his assistant and myself. I was hit in several places and later captured with another Co. F man."

In another house, Sergeant Russell Sutton, an Anzio veteran and squad leader, led a bazooka team to a second-floor window in an effort to get a shot at one of the tanks. "We couldn't get a shot away because tree branches were in the way. We then went to the first floor. The tank fired a shot at us as we moved to the first floor. We still couldn't get a shot at the tank, so we joined the rest of the squad in the basement. A few minutes later the tank stopped in front of the basement. The tank's commander shouted to us to come out. That was the end of the fighting for us. Six of us were taken prisoner." They ended up in Stalag 5A.[86]

The Germans rounded up their prisoners and reassumed control of Utweiler. Some of the Americans eluded them, though. Most of these Americans made their escape before the Germans closed their noose around the town. Their numbers included Lieutenant Colonel Duncan, who spent many hours hiding with three other soldiers in a water-filled shell hole outside of town. A lieutenant and a sergeant managed to make it back to regimental headquarters late in the morning and tell the story of what had happened at Utweiler to Heintges, who had been frantically trying to get his tanks moving toward the town. The officer, First Lieutenant John Andanich, told Heintges, "We had the choice of giving up or making a go for it [escaping]. We did everything we could.

Outside the town I entered a pillbox where there were 15 Company 'E' men. The First Sergeant of Company 'E' lay there with one leg shot off."

Heintges now moved heaven and earth to sweep the road free of mines and counterattack Utweiler. By 1400 he had organized a powerful force of tank destroyers, tanks, and infantry to retake the town. He arranged for artillery and air strikes to blanket the place, effectively boxing the Germans into the town. The road was clear and the avenging force, led by the 3rd Battalion, quickly negotiated its way up the road and into Utweiler. This force overwhelmed the German defenders, who had expended most of their energy during their morning victory over the 2nd Battalion. The U.S. armor, along with bazooka teams, destroyed seven enemy tanks at Utweiler, mostly from a distance. German infantry in the town surrendered without much of a fight. By 1830 Utweiler was back in U.S. hands.

The 3rd Battalion troops found 2nd Battalion men who had found hiding places in nooks and crannies of Utweiler. For instance, two junior officers hid in a potato bin in a cellar. They covered their bin with straw and boards and nuzzled underneath the potatoes. All day long German soldiers had come down to the cellar and looked around. At one point an SS major sat on a board two feet away and ate captured American rations. "We remained in the bin covered over for seven hours and were badly cramped when rescued at about five o'clock," one of the officers recalled.

In a war full of meritorious battle performance, Utweiler must go down as the 7th Regiment's most ignominious moment. The 2nd Battalion began March 15 with 640 men, and in a matter of hours it was down to 184 ineffective survivors. The battalion lost 21 killed, 72 wounded, 17 missing, and 222 taken prisoner. Another 124 stragglers later rejoined the unit, but the battalion was, for the moment, destroyed as any kind of an effective combat force.[87]

The troops probably should not have pressed forward into the town without armor support, but when they did, they certainly should have been more wary of a German counterattack. When the attack came, some of the men fought hard and others did not, reflecting a lack of organization, leadership, and good training. The 7th Regiment was still a good combat formation, but it had lost many excellent soldiers, hearty veterans who might have put up a better fight at Utweiler. Still, there was probably no way that even alert and resolute soldiers could have defended the town against such powerful armored forces. In the final analysis, Utweiler showed the vulnerability of infantry without proper support, rather than any kind of major or disgraceful failing on the part of the men of the 2nd Battalion.

UTWEILER PROVED TO BE A BIT OF AN ANOMALY FOR THIS phase of the 7th Infantry's offensive into Germany. By and large, the Germans did not strongly contest the area through which the Cottonbalers advanced. The regiment, primarily led by the 1st and 3rd Battalions, steadily moved northeast into Mittelbach. The Americans could see the West Wall now, beyond Mittelbach. Heintges fully expected to attack this portion of the Siegfried Line and had, in his usual thorough way, studied a tremendous amount of intelligence (maps, photos, orders of battle, terrain) on this section of the line. Late in the afternoon on the seventeenth he was studying enemy defenses through his binoculars when O'Daniel called and told him to shift his advance radically, three thousand yards to the east, and attack the Siegfried Line at Rimschweiler early the next morning. O'Daniel wanted Zweibrücken, located about three miles behind the defenses, and the city's key bridges across the Schwarzbach River. The general also thought that if his troops could punch through the line in that sector, they could clean out the rest of the defenses from behind. He wanted a two-regiment attack. On the left the 30th Infantry would function like a dagger in the heart, puncturing the West Wall and going straight into Zweibrücken. On the right, the 7th Infantry would also breach the wall, advance to the river, and protect the 30th's flank.

Heintges was thunderstruck and not terribly pleased with the change in plan, mainly because his intense study had taught him that the Mittelbach sector was the most lightly defended in the area. Nonetheless, he followed orders and threw himself into improvising the best attack he possibly could. He arranged for trucks to take his men to the new jump-off point. Artillery harassed the German defenders all night long. Tanks rolled up to provide close support. Chemical mortar teams prepared plenty of smoke rounds in case the infantry needed a screen during its advance. Medium bombers from the Army Air Force and the French Air Force bombed the fortifications.

Still, the toughest job, as usual, came down to the infantry, especially the Cottonbalers who had to assault the most heavily defended section of the line. The regimental historian outlined, in chilling detail, the kind of defenses the Cottonbalers must soon assault: "Three rows of 'Dragon's Teeth,' with intervening pill-boxes spaced in great depth. The assault battalion had to penetrate a row of 'Dragon's Teeth,' movable blocks and concrete shelters with cupolas northeast of Rimschweiler before hitting a main dense line of 'Dragon's Teeth' backed up by an anti-tank ditch. Another line of 'Dragon's Teeth' followed the main line and in between the various lines were numerous obstacles consisting of concrete shelters, casements and overhead cables." The casements were reinforced with steel and protected by many pillboxes and gun emplacements. "Accessible terrain in front of the 'Dragon's Teeth,' such as depressions, was covered by the dreaded 'S' mines [Schu mines]. Barbed wire between pill-boxes was strung in an ingenious fashion, covering every route of approach."[88]

No one relished the job of taking on these formidable defenses, but it had to be done. The 1st Battalion, under cover of smoke, led the way at 0600 on the eighteenth of March. They had gone about eight hundred yards, bypassing several unmanned pillboxes, and penetrated three belts of dragon's teeth when the whole area erupted with fire, from in front and behind. The Germans had circled behind the lead companies, A and B, in an effort to cut them off and annihilate them. The soldiers of these two outfits hit the dirt and crawled for whatever shelter they could, but they found very little. They were taking fire from every direction. German 88s started exploding. Snipers were having a field day, pegging the trapped Americans in whatever portion of the body they could. In short, the situation was critical, a confused, bloody mess.

Company C on the right did not get it quite as badly, but enemy fire soon pinned them down too. Sergeant Craft, acting as platoon sergeant now, was advancing up a hill, toward some pillboxes, with his platoon when the Germans started shooting: "They were . . . shelling us with their 88's, mortars, and they were shooting direct with the 88's from the pill boxes, too. They pinned us down, and they kept shooting at us." The men unfastened their e-tools and dug crude foxholes. Craft looked to his left and saw a soldier with his left arm sticking out of his foxhole. "Sure enough, a sniper shot him in the elbow spraying pinkish blood and gray bone fragments all over the place."[89]

All day long, the battle continued in this fashion. Those Americans who had not been killed or wounded found some semblance of cover (foxholes, trenches, dragon's teeth primarily), aided by smoke screens, and fought back as best they could. American tanks and tank destroyers came up and drove off the Germans who had tried to encircle A and B Companies. They also took out several pillboxes. Artillery worked wonders in keeping the Germans at bay. They wanted to close in on the stricken Americans and kill them but didn't dare because of the protective ring laid down by U.S. artillery.

During the night, when artillery accuracy diminished, the Germans tried a counterattack on A Company. The fighting was fierce and violent. The soldiers of A Company stood in their German-made trenches and fought with everything they had. The enemy used grenades and machine guns to make it into the trench. The fighting was point-blank, rifle to rifle from only paces away. The Germans overran seven Cottonbalers and captured them, but that was the extent of their accomplishment. The hero on this night was Staff Sergeant Albert Haskell, who burned out three M1 Garands in fending off the enemy. When his rifles conked out, he used grenades, in spite of a painful bullet wound. The Germans fled and the attack fizzled out. Haskell killed ten of them and wounded another twenty-five. Shortly thereafter, the A Company soldiers retreated a hundred yards to another trench so that artillery could pound the Germans around their former positions. This broke up another counterattack, and A Company reassumed its place in its original trench at daybreak.[90]

The men of the 1st Battalion were fighting valiantly, but they needed help. That help came in the form of the 3rd Battalion, which attacked the Siegfried Line slightly to the right of the 1st. These men also came under fire quickly. Somewhere among them, Sherman Pratt led an L Company rifle platoon. Back in late November, as the regiment plowed its way through the Vosges, Pratt's commanding officer had offered him a field commission. Pratt pondered whether to take it. An infantry first sergeant's job was not exactly safe, but it was a damned sight safer than being a second lieutenant rifle platoon leader, which was what Pratt would become if he took the commission. He knew enough about the Army to know that the appalling casualties among junior officers, as well as the crying need for good combat leaders, opened up opportunities for men like him, who, in other circumstances, might not have had the opportunity to become officers. The Army needed experienced sergeants, but it needed experienced lieutenants even more. In the end, he decided to take it, along with a job as a rifle platoon leader. The commission had come through in February, during the regiment's time off the line.

So, today, as the 3rd Battalion sought to puncture the Siegfried Line, Pratt found himself leading them into the volcano. "As we crossed the line of departure, the first response from the enemy was an artillery barrage that knocked out more than a dozen of our men. We pushed on and by mid morning had made our way into the first belt of dragon's teeth. At that point our advance was halted. We were thoroughly 'pinned down' by enemy machine guns."

His company commander called him on the radio and asked why his platoon had stopped its advance. Three of Pratt's men were dead and several others wounded. Pratt told him they had met stiff resistance. The captain tried to call in artillery and tank support. As with the 1st Battalion, the whole attack seemed to be nothing more than mass confusion, a horrendous "FUBAR," as the soldiers would have said.

Mortars and machine guns kept firing at anyone who moved. Pratt huddled behind some dragon's teeth and pondered what to do. As he did so, he glanced back and saw a friend of his, First Lieutenant Ernest Guard, crawling forward, under withering fire, with members of his antitank platoon. Somehow he and his men made it to Pratt's position. Guard and Pratt discussed what to do. Guard said something about trying to contact his company for support, but he never finished his sentence. "Just at that moment a burst of machine gun bullets sprayed the air and dragon's teeth around us. One slug hit the holster of my pistol on my belt. I ducked instinctively, and saw that Guard was already on the ground. I peered around and saw that the fire had come from a pill box partly to our rear that I had thought was . . . unmanned." He tried to speak to Guard but got no response. "I put my hand on his shoulder, rolled him over and saw the death stare in his eyes. One of the bullets had entered the side of his neck, passed upward and exited the side of his head tearing out a hole the size of a tennis ball. The poor guy, so alive and conscientious split seconds before, had passed from this world without ever knowing what hit him. The loss of Ernest Guard was not easy for me to take."

The day wore on and still the advance was stalled. The 3rd Battalion waited for nightfall and tried a new tactic. Under cover of darkness, they simply infiltrated between and around the pillboxes. At first, they tried to blow the pillboxes up with satchel charges, but with no success. So, instead, they simply kept moving, past the pillboxes and into the rolling country beyond. Pratt and his men worried about live enemy in pillboxes behind them, but to their delight, the tactic worked. Proximity made the pillboxes and their surrounding defenses irrelevant. They were designed to defend an attack from the west, not the east. Once the Americans succeeded in getting behind them, the Germans in the West Wall could hold out and fight in isolated groups against American firepower (engineers, tanks, aircraft, artillery, flamethrowers) or they could retreat and defend their soil somewhere else. The line was not fully manned and many of the soldiers who did defend it were not terribly excited about doing so. Thus most of the German defenders filtered away, once the Americans got behind them. Germany had spent a decade building these remarkable fortifications, but they held up the 7th Regiment for only a day or two. They inflicted terrible casualties, but they did not stymie the Allied advance and that, for a Germany fighting for its life, was all that mattered.

Lieutenant Pratt's platoon had been frittered down to about ten men, but they kept pressing forward, blowing bunkers and pillboxes as best they could. In one typical instance, he and his band of survivors snuck up on an unsuspecting garrison in the dark. "We surprised a group of enemy from the rear entrance of their fortification and they promptly surrendered. Their steel door was open and some were milling around in the open and clearly did not expect to see us during the night. I sent them back to the pillbox from whence we had started but had to deplete my under strength ranks by two troops for escort."[91]

This hardly mattered. The 7th Infantry Regiment, along with much of the rest of the U.S. Army in Germany, had breached the Siegfried Line.

After cracking the Siegfried Line, the regiment breezed its way to the Rhine, setting up headquarters at Frankenthal, a small town between Mannheim and Worms. The soldiers had the opportunity to ride on the autobahn part of the way. For several days, the men stood down and enjoyed themselves while their officers planned the Rhine crossing. The plan called for the 1st and 3rd Battalions to make the assault under cover of darkness at 0230 on March 26, with the 3rd on the left and the 1st on the right. The usual bevy of weapons would support them, including massive artillery and smoke screens, and engineers would build bridges as soon as possible. Most of the assault troops would cross in motored pontoon boats, one squad of twelve per boat. Each soldier carried K rations, four bandoliers of ammunition,

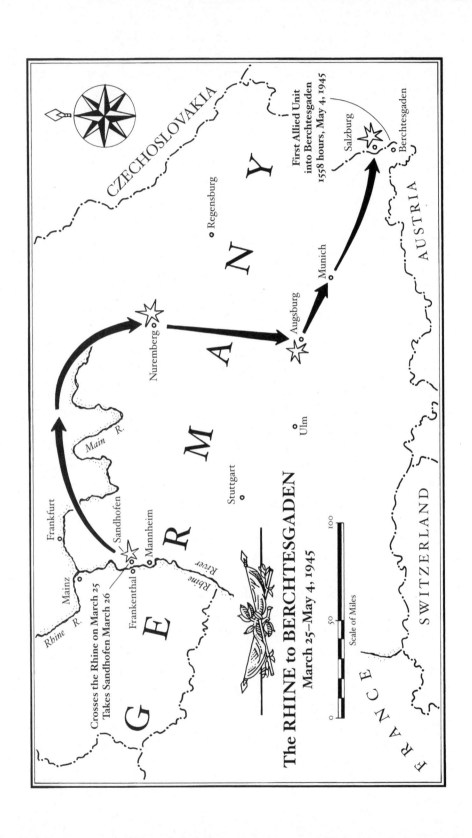

The **RHINE to BERCHTESGADEN**
March 25–May 4, 1945

Scale of Miles

Crosses the Rhine on March 25
Takes Sandhofen March 26

First Allied Unit
into Berchtesgaden
1558 hours, May 4, 1945

CZECHOSLOVAKIA

GERMANY

AUSTRIA

SWITZERLAND

FRANCE

Regensburg

Nuremberg

Augsburg

Munich

Salzburg

Berchtesgaden

Ulm

Stuttgart

Frankfurt

Sandhofen

Mannheim

Frankenthal

Mainz

Rhine R.

Rhine

Rhine River

Main R.

four hand grenades (three frags and one white phosphorous), and eight rifle grenades. Bazooka teams lugged twelve rounds per team.

The Rhine was about a thousand feet wide in the Cottonbalers' sector (Frankenthal on the west bank, Sandhofen on the east). The terrain on both sides of the river was almost completely flat: great tank country. The biggest challenge in the whole operation was to get across the river. If the Americans could do that, they had it made. The Germans had enough firepower and soldiers to defend a river crossing, but not to defend in any kind of depth beyond the river. Similar to an amphibious invasion, the Yanks would be at their most vulnerable while they were on the water. But if they made it to the east bank and moved inland, the Germans would once again be forced to run.

In the waning hours of March 25, the entire plan was set in motion, like an uncoiled spring. Major Rosson, working in a staff position at 3rd Division now, described the scene: "Our engineers were reinforced by corps engineer units brought in to ready themselves for the construction of a major pontoon bridge across the Rhine. Finally, in accordance with the plan in all its details, we moved up on a phased basis, doing so in the forward areas under cover of darkness, deployed our forces with all of their crossing materiel, and positioned the major bridging gear to carry out a very demanding undertaking scheduled to commence by stealth."[92]

The infantry who had the dangerous job of leading the assault were supposed to be supported by special duplex drive (DD) amphibious tanks, fitted with pontoons to get them across the river so they could provide direct fire support. After sunset on the twenty-fifth, Lieutenant Cloer received the mission of reconnoitering a suitable route the tanks could follow to the river. He had just returned from R & R in Paris. In fact, he barely had time to say hello before Major Duncan handed him this job. Cloer, by now, had plenty of experience at this kind of work. Like Lieutenant James Bradley and Lieutenant Harold White before him, Cloer was a born scout. He had the kind of personality that thrived on independence, information gathering, and dealing with the unknown, all vital qualities for a good reconnaissance platoon leader.

He fetched Private First Class Steele (the frisky GI who had groped the woman in southern France), hopped in a jeep, and set off for the Rhine. They drove in pitch-blackness over flat ground for about three miles until they reached the Rhine. "What I remember most is the absolute silence. The only faint sound was the soft gurgling of the water against the river bank and the muffled sound of the jeep's idling engine." To Cloer's right he could see the destroyed autobahn bridge. "I scanned the other side of the river looking for defenses but saw nothing but more flat ground with no vegetation or structures." He suspected that the enemy had antitank guns over there somewhere—maybe under the bridge ramp—but he could not spot any.

Finished with his scouting, Cloer got back in the jeep and told Steele to head back to Frankenthal, where the DD tanks were waiting. In Frankenthal, Cloer met up with the tankers and they started their drive to the river. "The tanks started their engines and the roar was deafening! I remember thinking that when we got down near the river bank, all that noise would alert every Kraut within miles. And so it was. Our jeep was about 20 feet from the river bank when the first 88mm shell came streaking across the river from beneath the bridge ramp and hit the lead tank causing it to burst into flames right behind us." He and Steele scrambled out of their jeep and took shelter in a bomb crater. More shells streamed in, but from a different direction. They burst overhead. These were American shells with new proximity fuses; much deadlier than anything seen before, they exploded in the air when they detected their targets.

Cloer and Steele abandoned their jeep and hightailed it out of there, back to the command post. Cloer noticed that his arm hurt. He took off his jacket, sweater, and wool shirt and saw "that the upper arm from shoulder to elbow was completely discolored in blues, purples, greens, reds and yellows. It was swollen and throbbing." A spent fragment had hit him, but his thick clothing prevented it from breaking the skin. Cloer found out later that in addition to the DD tank destroyed by German 88s, two others were rendered useless when shrapnel pierced their flotation gear. In the entire 7th Regiment river-crossing operation, only two DD tanks made it safely across the river to support the infantry.[93]

About an hour after midnight the assault troops reached their assembly areas on the banks of the Rhine. By now, U.S. artillery was plastering the east bank with the kind of barrage that made it seem impossible anything could live through it. The soldiers had been through briefings and prayer services. Many of them wrote last letters home. The mood was tense, apprehensive; everyone understood that soon some of them would die. They mentally coped with this awful certainty as best they could.

Lieutenant Pratt, scheduled to lead L Company across, was in the process of making final preparations to cross the river. "The boats were metal and noisy and rattled loudly as our men gathered around them and picked the boats up to carry them to the water's edge. The river banks at this spot had stone slopes that were damp and slippery and some men lost their footing and fell." They had almost made it to the water's edge when enemy artillery began dropping on them. "The whole area was saturated with the explosion of 88mm artillery shells. The shells came raining in and bursting like popcorn on a hot fire. One round hit a boat to my right squarely on the bow and blew it open, scattering the men in all directions. The shells kept coming. Troops hit the ground where they were. Some screamed, others cursed."

The fire intensified. What had been a reasonably organized scene of purpose threatened to become a chaotic mess. Pratt stole a glance at his terrified men. They were "all over the river side, mostly just lying there, hugging the ground in panic. I jumped up and moved across the river bank from boat group to boat group. 'Get your butts up and move,' I shouted. 'Get in the water and across. If you stay here you have no chance. This fire is not stopping—our only chance is to get out from under it. Move! Move!'"

All up and down the line, other lieutenants and sergeants were doing the same thing. They knew that they had to get across the river, come what may. Pratt's sergeants, like their lieutenant, screamed and raved, kicking and cursing the men into action. The platoon got into their boats and made it fairly easily across the Rhine. The farther out they got in the river "the more we put distance between us and the 88mm death and destruction." They made it to the east bank, beached their boats so the engineers could reclaim them, and scanned the terrain, "flat as a billiard table." They pushed forward against surprisingly light resistance, although enemy tanks put a scare into them. Artillery took care of the German tanks. In fact, the biggest threat to Pratt's life on the east bank was a bomb dropped by American fighters, who mistakenly thought they were attacking an enemy unit. The bomb came close to burying him alive, and it killed several men in his platoon and L Company.[94]

In the 1st Battalion area, Sergeant Craft and his C Company also experienced the terrible enemy artillery bombardment. "I've never seen anything like it! You could hear men screaming, as they were being hit; many were killed. I don't know how we survived, because it was severely intense artillery fire. The acrid powder scent would hit your nostrils, as explosions went on all around you. Men were crying out in pain, being hit. I thought we'd never survive. After we picked up our boat, all of us got under it. We carried it on our shoulders and placed it in the water.

"We started directly across, and a machine gun opened fire on us. Many more boats were getting into the water. We got to the bank. Fortunately, we didn't get hit. We all got out of the boat. We climbed the bank and it was a steep slope. It had some sort of slag or rocks. This was the city of Sandhofen." They moved into Sandhofen unmolested. German soldiers were still in the town, and enemy artillery landed throughout much of the night. They spent most of the daylight hours in a stalemate.

A wounded American lay in the street. The Cottonbalers watched in agony as German machine guns shot at any medics who tried to help the unfortunate man. Two German prisoners of war, apparently medics, volunteered to go get the wounded American. Private Donald Waller, an American medic, watched apprehensively as the courageous German medics risked their lives to save an American. "The German machine gunners allowed their medics to reach the wounded man. The German medics put him on a stretcher and both stood up. Then the Nazi gunners opened fire, killing their own medics." Incredibly, the wounded Cottonbaler survived and Waller retrieved him later when things quieted down. The Americans buried the two dead Germans with full honors.

To the soldiers, the Germans seemed to be committed to holding on to Sandhofen at all costs. In reality, most of the Germans were surrendering or withdrawing. By the night of the twenty-sixth the enemy had left the demolished town, and Craft's C Company joined up with the rest of the battalion, cleared the town, and moved out. "We had to walk through the town. It was burning! We went from house to house, building to building, through an underground trench, from cellar to cellar, almost all the way through the town. You could see German helmets, swastikas, and all kind[s] of Nazi paraphernalia."[95]

The Cottonbalers were safely across the Rhine. As anticipated, the toughest part of the operation was the crossing. The regiment lost 32 men killed, 10 missing, and 136 wounded, the vast majority of them to the German shelling at the river, or during the actual crossing. The 7th Regiment's experiences were only a microcosm. All up and down the

Rhine valley, the Allies had successfully breached the Rhine. Germany's doom was now only a matter of time.

ONCE AGAIN THE 7TH INFANTRY WENT INTO PURSUIT mode. The regiment made it all the way to the Main River against practically no opposition. The Americans advanced along the roads, on foot sometimes, on trucks or tanks other times. Every now and then they met sniper fire or a determined machine-gun nest. The tanks would blast the enemy position; the troops would dismount and shoot up any remaining live enemy soldiers. At the Main River, the Cottonbalers crossed over footbridges the engineers built.

During this chase, Lieutenant Cloer and his recon people usually traveled several miles ahead of the main body of 7th Regiment troops, scouting for any kind of enemy resistance. One day he took four jeeps on one of these types of reconnaissance missions and they drove to a small town dominated by a large, stone farmhouse. Cloer decided to investigate the farmhouse. The American jeeps skidded to a halt on an unpaved road leading to the house. Everything was quiet. Only the wind rustled. Weapon at the ready, Cloer led the way into the house. He found a deserted kitchen. "In the center of the room was a wooden kitchen table about eight feet long. The table and floor surrounding it were covered with blood! Literally gallons of it! There were footprints in the blood on the floor. The color of the blood ranged from bright red to maroon." The bloody footprints led to a cellar full of dead Germans. "One had a large bloody bandage around his chest, the other around his head. They were fully clothed except for caps or helmets. The large, snow white dressings contrasted with the dirty field gray uniforms as did the huge bright red stains in their centers." He counted twenty bodies. "Some had their eyes open. Others did not. As I looked around at those . . . young men, a great sadness came over me. They were pawns, whose lives were suddenly and painfully terminated with the War almost over. All in support of the wild ambitions of that egomaniac, Adolph Hitler."[96]

The 7th Infantry crossed the winding Main River two more times, both times in assault boats, against light opposition. "Our life for a time seemed to be one of making crossing, after crossing, after crossing of one portion of the Main River or another," Major Rosson commented.[97] After the third crossing, the 3rd Battalion ran into strong resistance at a town called Steinach in early April. Here the enemy concentrated tanks, nebelwerfers, artillery, and two companies of infantry. They set up a roadblock at the entrance to the town and opened fire on the lead American scouts, wounding both of them. The Americans outside of town took cover in roadside ditches and waited for support from tanks and artillery.

Lieutenant Pratt, because of his extensive experience, had moved up to company commander now. "The German force . . . leveled artillery fire at our platoons and even, for the first time in weeks, some nebelwerfer . . . fire was dropped on us. The fight continued all day. Particularly troubling . . . were the German tanks that seemed to be all around us." Pratt crawled over to a couple of artillery forward observers and lobbied them for fire. They were calling it in, but it was ineffective. Pratt succeeded in calling in an air strike. The fighter planes did not kill any of the tanks but drove them away. Both sides simply sat there and shot at each other all day and night. The next morning, April 8, the Americans, reinforced now, attacked the enemy tanks with bazookas, tank destroyers, and artillery, an overwhelming firepower combination. The Germans lost ten tanks and the Yanks captured the town by noon.

Later that day, Pratt's company ran into machine-gun fire as they advanced beyond the town. The spring day was clear and warm, but the sound of German machine guns shattered the calm of this seemingly idyllic day. "Instantly, all the men to my front hit the ground and, from my position in the field, most disappeared from view." The guns were lodged along higher ground immediately up ahead and the Americans were pinned down in the field. Pratt could have, and should have, called in fire support from artillery, tanks, and tank destroyers. Instead, he got up and ran to his lead soldiers, attempting to rally them, a courageous course of action but a foolish one.

He succeeded in doing nothing more than pinning himself down, in so doing cutting himself off from communication with forward observers, platoon leaders, and his commanding officer, Major Ralph Flynn. "As I dashed across the field, a machine gun fired continuously and its shells kicked the earth up around my feet all the way into the middle of the field. At least two slugs tore at my coat and pack. Another completely destroyed my canteen and cover." He dived for cover. Any time he moved, a sniper shot at him. After a few minutes Pratt realized his mistake. "I jumped up and started running to . . . my own company headquarters troopers. All the while across the field, as I zigged and zagged, crouching low, the German gunner kept up a stream of slugs around me and at my feet and over my head."

After a serious ass chewing from Flynn, Pratt called for artillery and tanks that blasted the enemy guns. The advance continued. "We had incurred about a dozen casualties in this engagement, two of which I later learned had died enroute to the mobile hospital. I remembered one of the two. He had been shot straight through the chest." The bullet "entered almost in the middle of his chest and had exited about half way down his back." Pratt and the others were surprised he even lived long enough to be evacuated.[98]

The motor march continued. Along the way, the regiment fought a series of quick engagements against scattered groups of die-hard Germans. Casualty numbers dropped dramatically. Random snipers or machine-gun fire accounted for the few casualties the regiment did suffer.

IN MID-APRIL THE ENTIRE 3RD DIVISION TURNED SOUTHEAST and converged on the northern suburbs of Nuremberg, site of so many Nazi party rallies in the 1930s. Nuremberg proved to be the last sizable fight for the 7th Infantry in World War II. A mixed force of SS, Wehrmacht, and Volksturm forces manned dugouts and bunkers all around the city, which had been pulverized into ruins by Allied planes over the course of the war. The Germans no longer worried much about air raids, now that they were defending their cities from ground troops instead of airmen. So they used their mass quantities of antiaircraft guns as antipersonnel weapons, and quite effectively, at that.

The Cottonbalers pushed into the northern suburbs of Nuremberg on April 16–17. The 2nd and 3rd Battalions ran into resistance in many areas, most notably in a cemetery to the northeast of the Nuremberg suburbs, near an industrial complex. The fighting raged with ghoulish intensity. "We came down this main boulevard with big apartment houses on the left and that big cemetery on the right," Heintges recalled. "And we got quite a bit of fire. I did not want to go through the cemetery with our armor. The infantry was already in the cemetery and we were just getting clobbered from ahead us right down the boulevard, with artillery, and from the right flank [too]." He sent his tanks through the cemetery. They blew several of the flak guns into jagged pieces and the infantry pressed forward, under the weight of this firepower.[99]

A little later in the day, Lieutenant Pratt's L Company came under intense 88 fire when they attempted to capture a small crossroads. "88mm shells began falling like raindrops. All around us they roared in at high speeds like freight trains. As the shells began passing just over my head, and hitting on the cobblestones just ahead, spraying the nearby houses with shell fragments, I promptly dived for cover in a ditch alongside the road." After half an hour the 88 fire subsided. He and another soldier cautiously took a look around. Just then, another 88 shell whizzed in and exploded near them. They both ducked back into the ditch.

A couple minutes later Pratt glanced at the other man and saw him lying still with a "large hole torn in his clothing and body which I recognized as the kind of damage done by a sizeable piece of shrapnel . . . when exiting a human body." He rolled the man over. He was dead. This man, known to the Americans only as "George," was a special Cottonbaler. He was a Czech displaced person who had befriended the men in the unit a few days earlier. He badly wanted to fight the Germans and persuaded the Cottonbalers to outfit him and arm him. Now he was dead by the side of a road leading into Nuremberg.

George's death notwithstanding, the enemy fire slackened and Pratt's unit advanced another couple miles until they hit resistance again. Once again, everyone took cover and waited. Pratt fished out his binoculars and studied the terrain ahead. Roughly four thousand yards away, clustered at the edge of a small town, he saw a concentration of enemy troops and heavy weapons. Pratt saw three tanks, several armored cars, and a couple hundred troops. The tanks were firing at the Americans. These Germans were out of range of infantry small arms, but artillery and mortars could do quite a job on them, Pratt thought. He called for artillery but was told to wait—the guns were displacing and not available. The same was true for the heavy mortars.

Frustrated and impatient, he studied the Germans some more. Now he saw flak towers shooting rapidly at some other unit (E Company, as it turned out). He called again and received a completely different response than before. Seemingly every weapon in the American firepower arsenal was now available. "Moments later we heard a rumble of artillery to our rear unlike anything I had heard since the Anzio beachhead. It sounded like distant thunder in a hurricane. So heavy and continuous that it was impossible to differentiate one gun blast from another. We could see whole batteries of guns lift in the air with the bodies of their crews and sail in every direction." Smoke soon obscured his view, but he knew the fire was still effective because the German weapons had been silenced. The shooting continued much of the night. At one time, Pratt directed fire for twenty battalions of artillery, an incredible arsenal of firepower.

The men wanted nothing more than to eat and rest, but Pratt received orders to keep moving and exploit the damage artillery had done to the Germans. That night they pushed on through the darkness clearing the suburbs of Wetzendorf, Schniegling, and Muggenhof. In the rubble of those towns, the Americans ran into small-arms fire: "From the bombed out rubble and partly standing walls of buildings along the streets, we flushed out women and young children armed with German Army rifles and with Panzerfausts. The deeper we penetrated into the outskirts of Nürnberg, the stiffer became the enemy resistance, and the closer . . . our contact with our opponents."

At around 0300 hours they ran out of energy and settled into bomb craters for the rest of the night. "The early predawn air was chilly and uncomfortable. Men shivered in their weary condition and they were hungry and drained." They dealt with pockets of machine-gun fire the next day but kept advancing.[100]

Meanwhile, the 2nd Battalion, partially reconstituted since its disaster at Utweiler a month before, took the lead, during the dark early-morning hours of April 18. They encountered the same kind of small-arms and irregular infantry opposition encountered by Pratt and his men. The SS was commandeering anyone who could hold a rifle and throwing them into the fight. All day long on the eighteenth, the men of the 2nd Battalion battled their way through the remnants of homes, apartment complexes, and businesses. In this urban wasteland, they coordinated closely with one another, working in small fire teams with bazookas and BARs, shooting up Germans mercilessly, dodging fire from flak wagons and machine guns. Sixty-millimeter mortar crews operated directly behind the riflemen and machine gunners, throwing in as much support as they could. This was an infantry fight. Artillery could not do all that much against defenders who had taken cover in ruins. Tanks helped quite a bit, but they were vulnerable to German panzerfaust fire at such close range. Only infantry could operate with the necessary effectiveness in this kind of rubble-strewn landscape.

The battle reached a climax on April 19–20 when the 7th Infantry, along with other 3rd Division troops, battered its way into the center of

Nuremberg, the walled portion of the city that dated back to medieval times. The 1st and 2nd Battalions led this final assault. Heintges, promoted to full colonel by now, was the kind of commander who led from the front, and he accompanied his men as they attacked the old city. "We were approaching the wall when we had such withering fire that we had to get off the streets. This was in a real built up area where there were apartment houses and office buildings on both sides of the street. We went off to the side . . . and we started going into the houses, breaking the walls down with shaft charges, and advancing through the houses. That wall was a fort. And, we had a hell of a time getting in there but we finally managed to put so much fire on the entrance that we wanted to go through, and we knocked down the great big [Johannis] gates that were protecting the entrance. And then finally, the Germans that were manning machine guns . . . took off. And by probing with small patrols . . . we got a foothold. And then once we got a foothold we stormed in there like the good old days when the neighboring baron would storm across the draw-bridge and knock down the gate with a big ramming rod."

Cottonbalers streamed into the old city, overwhelming and annihilating its die-hard SS defenders. The Americans quickly and ruthlessly dispatched all opposition by around noon on the twentieth. When the shooting stopped and the dust cleared, Colonel Heintges looked around and took in the landscape of unimaginable destruction. "It was nothing . . . but a flat piece of rubble except the church. The cathedral had very little damage. I'll never forget the Germans streaming out of their air raid shelters. And a little old lady that looked like my German grandmother, threw her arms around me, thanked me, and thanked God that she could smell fresh air again, and wouldn't have to worry about being bombed."[101]

Twenty more Cottonbalers were dead, but the dying would soon end.

FOR MANY MONTHS EISENHOWER AND HIS COMMANDERS had been worried about the possibility that Hitler and his Nazi retinue would hunker down in the mountains of Bavaria and hold out among the skyscraping peaks, with the benefit of enormous stocks of food, weapons, and fanatical SS soldiers. Now that the German Army had practically disintegrated and Eisenhower's armies, in tandem with the Soviets, were overrunning Germany, Eisenhower took steps to eliminate any possibility that the Nazis would set up a mountain redoubt. Instead of pushing for Berlin, the general ordered Patch's 7th Army and Patton's 3rd Army to advance southeast, into Bavaria, Austria, and Czechoslovakia.

For the Cottonbalers, this meant getting on trucks for another motor march. They rested a few days in Nuremberg and then set off for Augsburg about seventy-five miles to the south. The Germans hardly resisted at all; a few firefights here and there, some 88 and flak fire, but mostly the enemy surrendered at the first opportunity. "We had very little trouble," Heintges said. "We did get shot at a few times. We ran into a couple of ambushes, but nothing serious."[102]

Actually, the most notable occurrence at Augsburg was the liberation of fifty-two American prisoners of war, including several 3rd Division Anzio veterans. One of them, Private Frank Parco, described the joy he felt when he saw the Cottonbalers: "When I saw those guys . . . my knees started to knock and I didn't know whether to jump or fly. Everybody was out in the street hugging and slapping each other, and I even kissed the first Infantryman I saw, because I had been swearing for the last fourteen months that I would do so."[103]

Next the regiment veered southeast to Munich and took the town by April 30, the day of Hitler's death. Munich was wide-open. As they drove down the autobahn, the men saw thousands of German prisoners heading off to captivity. Ever since entering Germany, the Cottonbalers had commandeered German homes whenever they could. The men had been living in the elements long enough. Now it was time to enjoy the fruits of civilization—beds, toilets, looted food and alcohol. Sergeant Craft's C Company raced as fast as they could for Munich. "We were in a hurry and walking through little towns as if there was no enemy. There was a little shooting every now and then. I recall . . . that . . . at one place we decided to take a break. We went into a home, and commandeered it. We put a woman and her family in one of the bedrooms, and went into the kitchen." They rummaged around and found some food. "I cooked and ate 13 fried eggs with a big slice of ham and two or three pieces of toasted bread." Later they boarded trucks that took them into Munich.[104]

The Cottonbalers breezed into Munich from the west. There was hardly any fighting or resistance; no one in the regiment got killed, and only two men got slightly wounded. The soldiers did not see any combat horrors at Munich, but they did see something else stark and terrible, something that stuck with them the rest of their lives. The 42nd Division, operating near the 7th, helped liberate one of the most notorious of all concentration camps—Dachau, located ten miles to the northwest of Munich. When the Nazis took power in 1933, Dachau was the first major camp they set up (many more followed). At first it was mainly for political prisoners, but eventually the camp population expanded to include the usual array of outcasts in Nazi Europe—Jews, Gypsies, Slavs, resistance fighters, and the like. The SS starved, tortured, and neglected them over the course of many years. Some were even gassed. Dachau was home to cruel human medical experiments. The place was a living hell on earth. Word of Dachau spread quickly among the 7th infantrymen.

Most of them had no idea of the existence of such camps. Curious, they went out of their way to visit the horrible place. Lieutenant Cloer and his men drove their jeeps to the camp. "We . . . couldn't believe what we were seeing. There was a railroad siding outside the barbed wire enclosure on which stood a freight train with no place left to go. The flat cars and gondola cars were filled, layer upon layer, with the naked bodies of people who had been starved until their bones protruded through their skin. There must have been several thousand of them! A few live inmates in black and white striped suits, zombies of little more than skin and bones, wandered about in a dazed state."[105]

As a medic, Sergeant Valenti—promoted recently—had seen a lot of human anguish and tragedy in three years of war, but nothing matched the pure disgusting degradation of Dachau. "As we swung open the huge, iron door of one of the compounds—housing a crematorium—we were met by swarms of giant flies, cockroaches as big as mice and the pungent stench of decaying human flesh."[106]

Lieutenant Pratt literally could not believe what his eyes were showing him. "Everywhere we looked we saw nothing but bodies. The ground was covered with corpses of emaciated men, women and children, some recognizable, many not. Some were undressed and naked. Most were dressed in striped pajama type clothing." He walked past huge pits full of dead bodies. He saw American medical technicians working feverishly to save those who were close to death. "The stench in the air was almost unbearable and impossible to fully describe. It was nauseating and repulsive. Almost painful with its heaviness. Half alive skeletons were creeping by us like zombies. Their eyes . . . mostly showed no signs of awareness that we were there, or that the camp had been liberated.

"The inmates . . . looked like beings from another world. Eyes were protruding from sunken and shrunk facial skins, and teeth projected from mouths with drooping jaws hanging partly open." He entered a building and saw ovens. "Some had open doors and unburned bodies were inside, partly protruding from the oven entrances." After an hour of these awful sights, he and his men had seen enough. They didn't even speak on their way back to the unit. "We were too stunned, shocked and sickened by what we had seen. Memories of that day were to linger for long afterwards. To this day, they are burned in my mind like scars from a branding iron."[107]

Colonel Heintges also toured the camp and saw the gas chambers, the ovens, the trains full of dead bodies, and the half-dead prisoners. As a full-blooded ethnic German who had been born in Germany, he felt a special sense of indignation and outrage at the sight of the camp. Even so, he was glad that his soldiers did not know about these camps until after the fighting had mostly ended. "I know that whenever I got together with my commanders after that, there wasn't the usual joviality that we'd had. This was so heavy on their minds. It's a good thing . . . that we didn't know this before. Our soldiers . . . would have been ruthless with the enemy. You know the American soldier, if he knows that somebody is being mistreated he stops at nothing to get revenge from the guy who committed the crime."[108]

Over the course of their two and half years in combat, the Cotton-balers had known intellectually that the war they fought was just and necessary. They knew Hitler had to be stopped. They knew Nazi Germany represented a way of life, a way of thinking, that had to be eradicated. They knew that Germany could not be allowed to control the entire continent of Europe. They also knew that the Germans had mistreated those they ruled; the joy of thousands of liberated Italians and French certainly drove that point home. But they had never truly understood the starkly malevolent nature of the Nazi regime and its German followers until they saw Dachau. They now knew why they had fought so hard for so long, not just to survive, but to win this greatest and most just war of all time.

ON MAY 2 THE REGIMENT WAS BACK ON THE MOVE, THIS time bound for Salzburg, birthplace of the great composer Mozart. The

Germans had blown the bridges over Salzburg's surrounding rivers, so the 2nd Battalion boarded assault craft, crossed the river, and took the town against no opposition.

The easy capture of Salzburg surprised General O'Daniel because he had expected another tough fight, like the one at Nuremberg. In looking at a map, he realized that the 7th Infantry was in perfect position to make a dash for one of the great prizes of the war—Berchtesgaden and Hitler's splendid mountain home (alternately referred to as the Berghof, Obersalzburg, or the Eagle's Nest). Fears of a redoubt in this area had been quelled, but the lure of capturing this objective was well nigh irresistible. The unit that captured Berchtesgaden would go down in the annals of history, forever covered in glory, or so O'Daniel and his staff thought. "By that time the prize of Berchtesgaden was so radiant that it was obvious that considerable fame and reknown would come to the unit that was first to reach Hitler's Eagle's Nest," Rosson said. "We were resolved to be the first into Berchtesgaden."[109]

There was only one problem with that resolution. The honor of capturing Berchtesgaden had already been bestowed upon two other units, the French 2nd Armored Division and the American 101st Airborne Division. After all, the brass had expected the 3rd Division to run into a real fight in Salzburg, but of course the easy victory there changed the situation. The clincher was that the 7th Regiment controlled the only two remaining bridges over the Saalach River. One was a small wooden bridge and the other a damaged railroad bridge. Anyone wishing to get to Berchtesgaden had to cross the Saalach River.

O'Daniel had lobbied for the honor of capturing Berchtesgaden but had been denied. Now, on the morning of May 4, he decided to go for it anyway. The tactical situated dictated this course of action, but more than that, he wanted the great prize for his division. At about 1000 that morning he visited Heintges, whose engineers worked feverishly through the night to strengthen the railroad bridge so that it could now accommodate vehicles, guns, and tanks.

O'Daniel and Heintges spoke alone, overlooking the river. Although there had been a small snowstorm a couple days before, leaving a few inches of snow on the ground, this day was warm and clear. O'Daniel turned to Heintges. "Do you think you can go into Berchtesgaden?"

"Yes, sir," Heintges responded. "I have a plan all made for it, and all you have to do is give me the word and we're on our way."

O'Daniel asked him if the railroad bridge was ready. Heintges nodded. "I did not get permission to go into Berchtesgaden," O'Daniel told him. "Do you think you can do it?"

"Yes, sir."

"Well, go."

Heintges did not waste a second. He immediately spoke with his 1st and 3rd Battalion commanders and told them to move out.[110]

The troops, and their armored and artillery support, crossed the bridge and fanned out; the 1st Battalion headed west, on the most direct route, through Bad Reichenhall, while the 3rd Battalion swung east on the autobahn. The two pincers were supposed to proceed deliberately, not recklessly, and meet in Berchtesgaden. In the meantime, O'Daniel set up a roadblock and plenty of guards at the valuable bridge his men had just crossed. He left orders that no one was to cross without his express permission and immediately set about making himself difficult to contact. The great theft was on.

After cruising through Bad Reichenhall, the 1st Battalion ran into some resistance at a mountain pass. Some SS troops were defending the pass, a natural defile that could have held up the battalion indefinitely. The Cottonbalers simply backed up, set up their artillery, and fired away at the SS, who melted away into the mountains. From there the Americans hit a few roadblocks and mines but nothing really serious.

In the east, Lieutenant Pratt's L Company led the 3rd Battalion down the autobahn. "After an hour or so we had covered almost ten miles, or approximately half the distance to the objective. The going, however, was weird and scary. I was most apprehensive. The hills on both sides of the gorge were steep and we were confined in a very narrow and restricted area." In other words, the terrain was ideal for an ambush and, for all Pratt knew, SS troops waited around the next bend, ready and willing to defend their führer's shrine. But the only excitement came when a tank opened up on a German armored car and blew it up. The column proceeded unmolested all the way to Berchtesgaden, arriving there at 1640. "Berchtesgaden looked like a village from a . . . fairy tale. Its houses were of Alpine architecture and design. Some had gingerbread decorations."

Pratt's group got to Berchtesgaden shortly after a platoon from the Battle Patrol, commanded by Second Lieutenant William Miller, entered the town at the head of the 1st Battalion at 1558. The Cottonbalers captured two thousand enemy soldiers in addition to clearing out the town and Hitler's bomb-damaged home (Eagle's Nest/Berghof) at the top of some breathtaking mountains, just outside of town. "Everyone in my group was struck into silence and frozen in place by the significance of the time and place. After all the years of struggle and destruction, the killings, pain and suffering . . . here for sure was the end of it." Pratt and his men engaged in some minor looting of Hitler's home and moved on.[111]

Sergeant Valenti also explored the massive house. "We couldn't believe what we saw. The walls were covered with shelves and the shelves were stocked with all kinds of wines, champagnes and liqueurs. The food bins were well stocked with a variety of canned hams, cheese and two-gallon cans containing pickles." They sat in Hitler's great room, where he had once entertained heads of state, and drank his wine.[112]

Meanwhile, back at the bridges over the Saalach, French General Jacques-Philippe Leclerc and his 2nd Armored Division attempted to cross the bridge and head for Berchtesgaden. Cottonbaler guards would not let him cross. Lieutenant Colonel Ramsey told the French general that he had orders to let no one cross. Fuming, Leclerc demanded to speak to O'Daniel. After trying to give Leclerc the runaround, Ramsey and the officers agreed to let the persistent French general speak to O'Daniel. The two generals argued for a time. Leclerc demanded to be allowed to pass. O'Daniel refused, but he did allow Leclerc himself to cross the bridge so they could speak face-to-face. O'Daniel remained adamant in his refusals until he heard from Heintges that the 7th Infantry had captured Berchtesgaden. Only then did O'Daniel allow the French and the 101st Airborne behind them to pass. The 101st had succeeded in finding a small footbridge and sending some patrols across, but they were nowhere near Berchtesgaden and, if they wanted to cross in real strength, they needed O'Daniel's bridge. Countrymen or not, O'Daniel did not let them pass either until the race was over and the Cottonbalers had won. The Cottonbalers had captured a prize second only to Berlin.

In spite of this indisputable fact, the myth still persists that paratroopers from the 506th Parachute Infantry Regiment, 101st Airborne Division, got to Berchtesgaden first. This is largely because of a mistake made by historian Stephen Ambrose in his otherwise excellent book *Band of Brothers,* chronicling the experiences of one airborne unit—E Company of the 506th—in the war. Ambrose wrote of Berchtesgaden: "Everybody wanted to get there—French advancing side by side with the 101st, British coming up from Italy, German leaders who wanted to get their possessions, and every American in Europe. Easy Company got there first."[113] The smash success of *Band of Brothers* led Home Box Office to turn the book into a miniseries, in which the paratroopers were portrayed capturing Berchtesgaden. The continuation, on film, of this error led to an even greater proliferation of the myth.

This is quite unfortunate, perhaps even unjust. The Cottonbalers' capture of Berchtesgaden is not a negotiable historical debate. It is an incontrovertible fact and should be recognized as such.[114] Plain and simple, those who achieved such a prestigious conquest should receive its laurels. Anything else is simply not fair to those who deserve the real credit.

After little more than a day and a half at Berchtesgaden, the 7th Regiment received orders to go back to Salzburg. The men took all the wine, liquor, food, and souvenirs they could carry and hit the road, turning over control of Berchtesgaden to the French and the 101st, both of whom had entered the town several hours after the Cottonbalers.

THE SHOOTING CAME TO AN END AND THE WORLD CHANGED forever on May 8, when the war officially ended. The fighting between the 3rd Division and its immediate German opposition was already over. It was a beautiful spring day in Salzburg, and the Cottonbalers were enjoying their new billets in Salzburg, ranging from castles to apartments. Slowly but surely, word of the end spread among the men. The soldiers celebrated, but not wildly. They had been through too much. "I expected people to throw their helmets into the air and yell 'Yea' and all that business," Heintges said. "But that did not happen. Everybody was quiet. And I was really surprised at that."[115]

Perhaps the men were thinking of those who had not made it this far. In this costliest of all wars, the 7th Infantry suffered 10,244 casualties. That was more than three times the original strength of the unit! A total of 2,131 Cottonbalers lost their lives and another 468 were missing in action (most of them dead).[116] In fact, the regiment suffered more casualties, and more deaths, in World War II than in all of its previous wars *combined*. It also saw battle for a greater sustained period—two and a half years—than at any other previous time in its history. No other American regiment contributed more, or sacrificed more, in defeating one of the most monstrous tyrannies in the history of humanity.

A new world emerged from the ashes of World War II, a world that saw American military, political, cultural, and economic preeminence and the resulting international commitments that flowed from that new superpower status. The war had ushered in the nuclear age, and humanity would never be the same. The sad result was not enduring peace but enduring bloodshed and strife. World War II led to cold war–era terror, which, in turn, begat a troubling time of post-colonial Islamic terror. The new American superpower would be heavily enmeshed in all of these troubles.

Most of the surviving Cottonbalers did not want to think about such geopolitical realities. They endured several months of occupation duty, but almost all of them wanted to go home, see their families, and get back to their "real" civilian lives. Mack Bloom went back to Brooklyn. Russ Cloer rotated home in January 1946 and went back to New Jersey, where he went to work as an engineer for Curtiss-Wright. Isadore Valenti went home to Cadogan, Pennsylvania, got married, and went back to work in the coal mine. But the town seemed shabbier somehow, emptier. One day he was sipping a beer and reading a newspaper when he saw an article about the GI Bill. It changed his life. He signed up for the education benefits afforded to him by the GI Bill, finished high school, earned a degree from the University of Pittsburgh, and became a teacher and school principal. Eventually he even earned a doctorate. Bert Craft went home, got married, and resumed his rural life in Mississippi. Joe Martin returned to college, finished his degree, and became a professor at Virginia Military Institute.

A few, like Sherman Pratt, chose to stay in the Army. He had "found a home" there in 1939 and intended to stay for a while. He fought with the 2nd Division in the Korean War and retired as a lieutenant colonel in the 1960s. He married and fathered two children. He also went on to earn a law degree and pursued a legal career for many years. William Rosson and John Heintges both remained in the Army and rose to the rank of lieutenant general. Rosson even served as second in command to General Creighton Abrams in Vietnam in 1969–70.[117]

IN SEPTEMBER 1946 THE 7TH REGIMENT FINALLY, AND OFficially, returned home to the United States. It went on to a new posting at Fort Devens, Massachusetts. Those men who had fought the war had long since rotated back to America and been discharged or moved on to other army assignments. The regiment had been drastically reduced in size during the immediate postwar demobilization. Even so, the return of the regiment to the United States conclusively and forever closed the book on World War II. In many ways, this greatest war was the regiment's finest moment; the victories at such places as Palermo, Messina, Anzio, Cisterna, Rome, Cape Cavalaire, Montélimar, Colmar, and, of course, Berchtesgaden served as evidence for that assertion.

In the years ahead, new wars and different battlefields beckoned. But none of them exceeded the many Cottonbaler battles of World War II in terms of sheer magnitude or importance to the future of the world. Out of the chaos and agony of World War II, a new epoch in world history was about to begin, and the 7th Regiment would play a major role in shaping the history of that new era.

Afterword

THE 7TH INFANTRY IS A TRADITION-RICH ORGANIZATION. The regiment has carried out every combat mission its country asked it to fulfill. The remarkable story of those missions has played out in this and the other book in this series on the history of the 7th. There were defensive battles such as New Orleans, Fort Brown, the Marne, and the Chinese Offensive of April 1951; "policing" missions such as the Seminole wars, Reconstruction, the Sioux and Nez Percé wars, Vietnam, and Iraq; most commonly, there were assaults such as Monterrey, Cerro Gordo, Fredericksburg, El Caney, Argonne Forest, Sicily, the Volturno River, the Colmar Pocket, Medina Ridge, Objective Peach, and Baghdad Airport.

The Cottonbalers played a central role in all those important events in American history and so many more. In the long existence of the unit, many aspects of the 7th Infantry experience have changed. The Cottonbalers of our own time wear different uniforms, use different weapons, fight with different tactics, prepare themselves with much better training, and function with a significantly higher level of professionalism than Cottonbalers of the early years. They are black, white, Hispanic, Asian, and Native American now, where before they were always white. They are recruited more efficiently, treated way better, and fed much better than in years past. The firepower they command would be incomprehensible to their forebears of the nineteenth century. The modern-day Cottonbalers are better educated, more motivated, and better led than ever. They come from more settled backgrounds than their forerunners of the nineteenth century—they are no longer scorned, no longer outcasts from the rest of American life. Like the Army itself, the 7th Infantry Regiment and its soldiers have changed significantly over the sweep of American history.

In other ways, the regiment and its experiences have not changed and probably never will. The 7th Infantry Regiment has always been the exclusive province of men, something that may never change. The soldiers of this outfit have always been imbued with a tremendous sense of dedication, fellowship, and valor, not just to country, mission, or cause but also to one another. "It isn't friendship," one of them wrote. "We all have friends. It is something beyond regular friendship. It is the knowing that you and they have been to 'hell and back.' It is a deep rooted emotion that binds you together. It is the knowledge that when things were tough, you and your buddies stuck it out and lived through it. No one knows the feeling except those of us who were there. There is no friendship like that of combat buddies. It lasts forever."[1]

The terror, horror, and vulgarity of infantry combat never change. Generations of Cottonbalers have experienced it—the mud, the rain, the maggots, the cold rations, the primal fear, the supersonic snap of bullets, the whizzing sound of fragments, the extreme exhaustion, the disorientation, the hatred, the hopelessness, the loss of innocence, the loss of youth, the waste of life, treasure, and property, and, most of all, the constant risk of death, wounding, or mental breakdown. A World War II–era Cottonbaler best summed up the universality of the infantry combat experience. His words would be all too familiar to 7th infantrymen of all time periods: "He lived close to the earth; it was his best cover so often—a ditch by the roadside, a bomb crater, a fox hole. He lived and died in the heat and cold, in the vineyards, in the snow on the mountains, in little villages, in large cities, on patrols. He didn't know the 'big picture'—he only knew the constant dangers. He knew of fatigue so complete it completely enveloped him; of dirt it seemed would never be removed, or fear which got right into his inner self—a constant which kept him suspicious of sounds, of movement, of shadows, of being afraid of falling asleep even though he knew he couldn't stay awake."[2]

Even more than the universality of the combat experience, they would all agree on the crucial importance of the infantry's main job—controlling ground (this includes destroying the enemy and pacifying a population). Even in an age of immense firepower, satellite technology, overwhelming air power, versatile sea power, and devastating, accurate ordnance, the job of the infantry remains of central importance.[3] The view that everyone and everything military ultimately supports the infantry is still not outmoded. As long as human beings remain land creatures, those soldiers whose mission is to control ground or people are of paramount importance. In so doing, they project their nation's will over deserts, swamps, cities, plains, countryside, and continents, the very places of life on this planet.

The story of the infantry, then, is the story of the crucial agent of warfare. It is also the story of the ordinary citizen who has represented his country on the battlefield and, in the process, reshaped history. In that sense, the history of the 7th Infantry Regiment is, more than anything, the story of the ordinary American in extraordinary circumstances. Through the entire span of American history, so many of them, anonymous except to their comrades, friends, or families, contributed in some small way to the history of their country. Truly, they were, in the final analysis, willing and able.

For the amazing story of the 7th Infantry Regiment in the post–World War II era, see the other volume in this series,

The 7th Infantry Regiment:
Combat in an Age of Terror; the Korean War Through the Present

★

NOTES

1. THE BEGINNING OF THE REGIMENT: THE BATTLE OF NEW ORLEANS

1. *The Cottonbaler Newsletter: The 7th Infantry Regiment Association*, "How Old Is the 7th Infantry Regiment?" (hereafter referred to as *The Cottonbaler*), Summer 1998, p. 7; "Battle Streamers Restored," *Infantry Journal*, August 1923, pp. 130–135; U.S. Army Center of Military History Web site: Official Lineage and Honors.

2. Taylor quoted in Robert Leckie, *From Sea to Shining Sea: From the War of 1812 to the Mexican War: The Saga of America's Expansion* (New York: Harper Perennial Library, 1994), pp. 511–514.

3. National Archives, Washington, D.C., Old Army Records, Record Group 391, Entry 1254, Box 1, "Battles of the 7th Infantry Regiment."

4. Robert Remini, *The Battle of New Orleans: Andrew Jackson and America's First Military Victory* (New York: Viking, 1999), pp. 8–49; Wilburt S. Brown, *The Amphibious Campaign for West Florida and Louisiana, 1814–1815* (Tuscaloosa: University of Alabama Press, 1969), pp. 22–58; Frank Lawrence Owsley, Jr., *Struggle for the Gulf Borderlands: The Creek War and the Battle of New Orleans, 1812–1815* (Gainesville: University Presses of Florida, 1981), pp. 95–122.

5. National Archives, Old Army Records, Record Group 98, Entry 181, Volume 1, Orderly Books of Captain Richard Oldham's Company, 7th Infantry Regiment.

6. National Archives microfilm, M233, Register of Enlistments in the U.S. Army, 1798–1815, Roll 1.

7. Phone conversation with C. Steven Abolt, commanding officer of Company A, 7th Regiment, U.S.I. Living History Association, August 29, 2001.

8. National Archives, Old Army Records, Record Group 98, Entry 186, Company Book for the Company of Captain James Doherty.

9. Conversation with Abolt, August 29, 2001.

10. Register of Enlistments in the U.S. Army, Roll 1; National Archives, Old Army Records, Record Group 98, Entry 181, Volume 1, Orderly Books of Captain Oldham's Company, 7th Infantry Regiment; J. C. A. Stagg, "Enlisted Men in the United States Army, 1802–1815, a Preliminary Survey," *William and Mary Quarterly*, August 1986, pp. 615–645; and "Soldiers in Peace and War: Comparative Perspectives on the Recruitment of the United States Army, 1802–1815," *William and Mary Quarterly*, January 2000, pp. 79–120. Copies of company rosters given to author by Abolt.

11. Gene A. Smith, editor, *Historical Memoir of the War in West Florida and Louisiana in 1814–15* (Gainesville: The Historic New Orleans Collection and University Press of Florida, 1999), p. 68.

12. Remini, *The Battle of New Orleans,* pp. 69–70.

13. Ibid., p. 73.

14. National Archives, Old Army Records, Record Group 391, Entry 1254, "Battles of the 7th Infantry Regiment"; conversation with Abolt, August 29, 2001; Francis B. Heitman, *Historical Register and Dictionary of the U.S. Army, 1789–1903,* Volume 1 (Washington, D.C.: Government Printing Office, 1903), p. 656.

15. Brown, *Amphibious Campaign,* p. 104; Smith, *Historical Memoir,* pp. 242–243.

16. Heitman, *Historical Register,* p. 621; National Archives, Old Army Records, Record Group 98, Entry 181, General Orders.

17. Heitman, *Historical Register,* p. 111; Owsley, *Struggle for the Gulf Borderlands,* p. 149; Tim Pickles, *New Orleans, 1815: Andrew Jackson Crushes the British* (Oxford: Osprey Publishing, 1993), pp. 51–52.

18. Steve Abolt, Jim Parker, and Bob Wettemann, "The Uniform of the Seventh Infantry at the Battle of New Orleans," *The Cottonbale: The Official Newsletter of Company A, 7th Regiment, U.S.I. Living History Association* (hereafter referred to as *The Cottonbale*), pp. 15–16.

19. Smith, *Historical Memoir,* p. 108.

20. Remini, *The Battle of New Orleans,* p. 123.

21. This paragraph is derived from several sources: Remini, *The Battle of New Orleans,* pp. 141–142; Pickles, *New Orleans, 1815,* pp. 64–73; Smith, *Historical Memoir,* pp. 109–111; National Archives, Old Army Records, Record Group 391, Entry 1254, "Battles of the 7th Infantry Regiment"; "The Battle of New Orleans, an 1840s Account," *The Cottonbale,* January–June 2000, pp. 6–9.

22. Smith, *Historical Memoir,* p. 111.

23. Remini, *The Battle of New Orleans,* p. 167.

2. "Thirty Years of Peace": The Life of the Soldier in the Antebellum Years

1. Francis B. Heitman, *Historical Register and Dictionary of the U.S. Army, 1789–1903,* Volume 1 (Washington, D.C.: Government Printing Office, 1903), p. 976.

2. Francis Paul Prucha, *The Sword of the Republic: The United States Army on the Frontier, 1783–1846* (Bloomington and London: Indiana University Press, 1969), pp. 129–134; John K. Mahon, *History of the Second Seminole War, 1835–1842* (Gainesville: University of Florida Press, 1967), pp. 18–28.

3. Robert Paul Wettemann, "The Enlisted Soldier of the United States Army: A Study of the Seventh Regiment, U.S. Infantry, 1815–1860," MA Thesis, Texas A & M University, 1995, pp. 27–38.

4. Ibid., p. 42.

5. Charles Martin Gray, *The Old Soldier's Story: Embracing Interesting and Exciting Incidents of Army Life on the Frontier in the Early Part of the Century* (Edgefield, S.C.: Edgefield Advertising Print, 1868), pp. 13–14.

6. Ibid., p. 33; Heitman, *Historical Register,* p. 626.

7. Gray, *Old Soldier's Story,* pp. 8–63.

8. Wettemann, "Enlisted Soldier," p. 84.

9. Richard Dalzell Gamble, "Garrison Life at Frontier Military Posts, 1830–1860," Ph.D. Thesis, University of Oklahoma, 1956, p. 82.

10. Wettemann, "Enlisted Soldier," p. 85.

11. *Army and Navy Chronicle,* May 28 and June 18, 1835.

12. Edward M. Coffman, *The Old Army: A Portrait of the American Army in Peacetime, 1784–1898* (New York and Oxford: Oxford University Press, 1986), p. 172; George A. McCall, *Letters from the Frontiers* (Gainesville: University Press of Florida, 1974), pp. 372–374.

13. Heitman, *Historical Register,* p. 696; Lieutenant William Mather to Emily, May 8, 1836, original letter in archival collections of Gilcrease Museum, Tulsa, Oklahoma, copies of the originals given to the author by Mr. Kevin Young.

14. Mather to Emily, May 20, 1836, courtesy of Kevin Young.

15. Robert L. and Pauline Jones, "Occupation of Nacogdoches," *East Texas Historical Journal,* July 1963, pp. 23–41; Prucha, *Sword of the Republic,* pp. 307–311.

16. John T. Sprague, *The Origin, Progress and Conclusion of the Florida War* (New York: D. Appleton, 1848), pp. 257, 273; also partially quoted in Wettemann, "Enlisted Soldier," p. 86.

17. Sprague, *Florida War,* pp. 544–546.

18. National Archives, Register of Enlistments, Rolls 19–20; Wettemann, "Enlisted Soldier," p. 88.

19. Sprague, *Florida War,* pp. 544–545; Captain Gabriel Rains to Lieutenant Robert Asheton, April 15, 1840, copy of letter given to author by Mr. Chris Kimball.

20. Samuel G. Drake, *The Aboriginal Races of North America* (Philadelphia: Charles De-Silver & Sons, 1859), p. 492; Mahon, *History of the Second Seminole War,* pp. 275–276; *Daily National Intelligencer,* May 11, 1840; Captain Gabriel Rains to Brigadier General Roger Jones, Adjutant General, May 19, 1840, copy of letter given to author by Chris Kimball; Chris Kimball, *The Cottonbale,* March/April 1996, p. 9.

21. Drake, *Aboriginal Races,* p. 492; Sprague, *Florida War,* p. 484; *Daily National Intelligencer,* June 1, 1840; *Army and Navy Chronicle,* date unknown; Chris Kimball and Early DeBary, "Finding the Bloody Battles Along the Micanopy–Wacahoota Road during the Second Seminole War," 1996 Meeting of the Florida Anthropological Society, pp. 16–18.

22. Joe Knetch, "Fort Micanopy and the Second Seminole War," Micanopy Historical Society, January 8, 1994, pp. 13–15.

23. Correspondence of the Secretary of War, *American State Papers,* 27th Congress, 2nd Session, Captain Washington Seawell to Adjutant General, March 20, 1842.

24. Lieutenant Colonel Bennet Riley to Colonel William Worth, August 5, 1841, copy of letter given to author by Chris Kimball.

25. Lieutenant Nevil Hopson to Major Joseph Nelson, January 5, 1841, copy of letter given to author by Chris Kimball.

26. Kimball and DeBary, "Finding the Bloody Battles," pp. 18–20; Sprague, *Florida War,* p. 484; Mahon, *Second Seminole War,* p. 284; *Louisville Journal,* January 18, 1841; phone conversation with C. Steven Abolt, commanding officer of the 7th Infantry Regiment Living History Association, August 29, 2001.

3. ASSAULT TROOPS WITHOUT PEER: THE MEXICAN WAR

1. Robert Ferrell, editor, *Monterrey Is Ours! The Mexican War Letters of Lieutenant Dana, 1845–1847* (Lexington: University Press of Kentucky, 1990), pp. xiii, 7–8, 16–17, 20.

2. Thomas R. Irey, "Soldiering, Suffering and Dying in the Mexican War," *Journal of the West* (2), (1972), pp. 285–293.

3. Luther Giddings, *Sketches of the Campaign in Northern Mexico* (New York: Putnam, 1853), pp. 74–75.
4. Richard Bruce Winders, *Mr. Polk's Army: The American Military Experience in the Mexican War* (College Station: Texas A & M University Press, 1997), p. 145.
5. Robert Paul Wettemann, "The Enlisted Soldier of the United States Army: A Study of the Seventh Regiment, U.S. Infantry, 1815–1860," MA Thesis, Texas A & M University, 1995, p. 125.
6. Justin H. Smith, *The War with Mexico,* Volume 1 (New York: Macmillan, 1919), pp. 160–161.
7. Ferrell, *Monterrey Is Ours!* pp. 40–42, 45–46, 53.
8. Francis B. Heitman, *Historical Register and Dictionary of the U.S. Army, 1789–1903* (Washington, D.C.: Government Printing Office, 1903), pp. 252, 534.
9. *The Cottonbale,* May/June 1996, p. 11. Today the fort is part of a municipal golf course.
10. *Niles National Register,* August 15, 1846.
11. Ferrell, *Monterrey Is Ours!* p. 59.
12. *Niles National Register,* May 16, 1846.
13. Winders, *Mr. Polk's Army,* pp. 88–92.
14. *Niles National Register,* June 6, 1846; Ferrell, *Monterrey Is Ours!* pp. 59–60.
15. On the side of the flag not being raised, see *Niles National Register,* August 15, 1846; Earl Van Dorn, *A Soldier's Honor with Reminiscences of Major-General Earl Van Dorn* (New York: Abbey Press, 1902), p. 21; and Kevin Young, "What Happened to the 7th's Colors?" Company A, 7th Infantry Regiment Reenactors Web site. For an account of the flag being shot away, see Captain Hawkins to General Taylor, May 10, 1846, *Senate Documents,* 29th Congress, 1st Session, Document 388, p. 34.
16. E. Van Dorn, *A Soldier's Honor,* p. 23.
17. *Niles National Register,* June 6, 1846.
18. *Niles National Register,* August 15, 1846.
19. Ferrell, *Monterrey Is Ours!* p. 61; *Niles National Register,* June 6, 13, 20, 1846; C. Steven Abolt, "Jacob Brown," 7th Infantry Regiment Reenactors Web site; George Winston Smith and Charles Judah, *Chronicles of the Gringos: The U.S. Army in the Mexican War 1846–1848, Accounts of Eyewitnesses & Combatants* (Albuquerque: University of New Mexico Press, 1968), p. 63.
20. *Niles National Register,* June 6 and 20, 1846; Captain John Henshaw, diary and recollections. Henshaw was a 7th Infantry officer who had little but contempt for Hawkins. "I almost regret to soil my page with the mention of so despicable a character as he has proved himself to be," Henshaw wrote. Gary Kurutz, an archivist at the California State Library, kindly provided me with a copy of Henshaw's writings.
21. *Niles National Register,* June 6, 1846; Henshaw, diary and recollections.
22. *Niles National Register,* August 15, 1846.
23. Ferrell, *Monterrey Is Ours!* pp. 61–62.
24. *Niles National Register,* June 6, 1846.
25. *Niles National Register,* June 20, 1846.
26. Robert N. Pruyn as told to James E. Edmonds, "Campaigning Through Mexico with 'Old Rough and Ready,'" *Civil War Times Illustrated,* October 1963, p. 14.
27. Ferrell, *Monterrey Is Ours!* pp. 63–64; Henshaw, diary and recollections.
28. William Seaton Henry, *Campaign Sketches of the War with Mexico* (New York: Arno Press, 1973), p. 104. This is a reprint of a book originally published in 1847.
29. Pruyn, "Campaigning Through Mexico," p. 14.
30. Ferrell, *Monterrey Is Ours!* pp. 75, 81.

31. Ibid., pp. 98–100.
32. Pruyn, "Campaigning Through Mexico," p. 15.
33. Ferrell, *Monterrey Is Ours!* pp. 107, 114.
34. Pruyn, "Campaigning Through Mexico," p. 15.
35. Smith, *War with Mexico,* Volume 1, pp. 232–238.
36. The previous pages describing the Battle of Monterrey are derived from several sources: Ferrell, *Monterrey Is Ours!* pp. 119–139; Smith, *War with Mexico,* Volume 1, pp. 233–261; Henry, *Campaign Sketches,* pp. 189–213; Cadmus Wilcox, *History of the Mexican War* (Washington, D.C.: Church News Publishing, 1892), pp. 91–110; Smith and Judah, *Chronicles of the Gringos,* pp. 78–90; National Archives, Record Group 391, Entry 1243, "Descriptive Books of the 7th United States Infantry Regiment."
37. Ferrell, *Monterrey Is Ours!* p. 19.
38. Smith, *War with Mexico,* Volume 2, p. 26.
39. Ferrell, *Monterrey Is Ours!* pp. 190–192.
40. Smith, *War with Mexico,* Volume 2, p. 32.
41. Ferrell, *Monterrey Is Ours!* p. 196.
42. Smith and Judah, *Chronicles of the Gringos,* pp. 207–209; Henshaw diary.
43. Bob Wettemann, *The Cottonbale,* March/April 1997, p. 11.
44. Smith, *War with Mexico,* Volume 2, pp. 53–54.
45. Smith and Judah, *Chronicles of the Gringos,* p. 212; Henshaw diary.
46. William H. Goetzmann, editor, *Autobiography of an English Soldier in the United States Army* (Chicago: Lakeside Press, 1986), p. 192.
47. This information and the narrative of the battle are derived from Smith, *War with Mexico,* Volume 2, pp. 50–59; Wilcox, *History of the Mexican War,* pp. 280–300; National Archives, Record Group 391, Entry 1243, "Descriptive Books of the 7th United States Infantry Regiment," and Entry 1254, Box 1, "Battles of the 7th Infantry Regiment."
48. Ferrell, *Monterrey Is Ours!* pp. 204–211.
49. Smith and Judah, *Chronicles of the Gringos,* p. 216; Henshaw diary.
50. Wettemann, "Enlisted Soldier of the United States Army," pp. 98–123, 236; National Archives, Register of Enlistments, Rolls 21–22.
51. Smith, *War with Mexico,* Volume 2, pp. 99–111; Wilcox, *History of the Mexican War,* 358–374; Smith and Judah, *Chronicles of the Gringos,* pp. 243–244; Jeff Shaara, *Gone for Soldiers* (New York: Ballantine Books, 2000), pp. 192–220; Henshaw diary.
52. Wilcox, *History of the Mexican War,* pp. 375–376.
53. Smith and Judah, *Chronicles of the Gringos,* pp. 247–264; Wilcox, *History of the Mexican War,* pp. 378–400, 443–468; Smith, *War with Mexico,* pp. 111–119, 143–164; National Archives, Record Group 391, Entry 1243, "Descriptive Books of the 7th Infantry Regiment"; Henshaw diary.
54. The final breakdown of the regiment's casualties in the Mexican War is as follows: Fort Brown: 2 KIA, 7 WIA; Monterrey: 1 KIA, 8 WIA; Cerro Gordo: 18 KIA, 43 WIA; Contreras/Churubusco: 5 KIA, 13 WIA; Chapultepec: 10 KIA, 6 WIA.
55. Pruyn, "Campaigning Through Mexico," p. 15.

4. RECLAIMED HONOR: THE CIVIL WAR

1. Robert Paul Wettemann, "The Enlisted Soldier of the United States Army: A Study of the Seventh Regiment, U.S. Infantry, 1815–1860," MA Thesis, Texas A & M University, 1995, pp. 138–149; National Archives, Record Group 391, Entry

1243, "Descriptive Books of the 7th United States Infantry Regiment." Thirteen privates and one officer, Lieutenant Elias Potts, died of disease in Utah, most of typhoid and enteritis. Private William Bryan, probably a victim of foul play, was found dead at Fairfield, home to many grog shops. Private Benjamin Newell committed suicide for unknown reasons.

2. Robert Utley, *Frontiersmen in Blue: The United States Army and the Indian, 1848–1865* (New York: Macmillan, 1967), pp. 161–163.

3. National Archives, Record Group 391, Entry 1243, "Descriptive Books of the 7th Infantry Regiment," and Entry 1238, Box 2, General Order Number 52; 2nd Lieutenant George Bascom, no date; copy in author's possession.

4. National Archives, Record Group 391, Entry 1238, Box 1, "Proceedings of a Board of Officers Convened at Fort Buchanan, N.M."

5. Wettemann, "Enlisted Soldier of the United States Army," pp. 155–158; National Archives Microfilm, M233, Enlistments in the United States Army, Rolls 25–27.

6. Steven E. Woodworth, "The Scapegoat of an Arkansas Post," *Military History Quarterly*, Spring 2001, pp. 58–62.

7. Wettemann, "Enlisted Soldier of the United States Army," pp. 166–167.

8. *Official Records of the War of the Rebellion* (hereafter referred to as *OR*), Series I, Volume 4, pp. 16–19; A. F. H. Armstrong, "The Case of Major Isaac Lynde," *New Mexico Historical Review,* January 1961, pp. 2–9.

9. *OR,* Series I, Volume 4, p. 4.

10. Armstrong, "The Case of Major Isaac Lynde," pp. 12–15.

11. William A. Keleher, *Turmoil in New Mexico* (Albuquerque: University of New Mexico Press, 1952), p. 150.

12. Hank Smith, "With the Confederates in New Mexico During the Civil War," *Panhandle-Plains Historical Review*, Volume 1 (1968), pp. 78–79.

13. *OR,* Series I, Volume 4, pp. 5–15; National Archives, Record Group 391, Entry 1243, "Descriptive Books of the 7th Infantry Regiment."

14. Armstrong, "The Case of Major Isaac Lynde," pp. 22–34; National Archives, Record Group 391, Entry 1238, Box 1, "Charges and Specifications Preferred Against Major Isaac Lynde" and Box 2, Isaac Lynde to Assistant Adjutant General, September 17, 1861.

15. National Archives, Record Group 391, Entry 1238, Box 1, "Descriptive Books"; Captain Gurden Chapin letter, August 10, 1861.

16. Thomas Lowry, "Boys in the Bag: The 7th U.S. Infantry's Most Powerful Foe Was John Barleycorn," *Civil War Times,* August 1997, pp. 1–7.

17. *Military Order of the Loyal Legion of the United States*, Volume 46 (Wilmington, N.C.: Broadfoot Publishing, 1992), p. 60.

18. Ibid., p. 62.

19. *OR,* Series I, Volume 9, pp. 498–499.

20. Ibid., p. 491.

21. *Loyal Legion,* p. 64.

22. *OR,* Series I, Volume 9, pp. 487–503. The descriptions of the Battle of Valverde are derived from several sources in addition to the *OR:* Keleher, *Turmoil in New Mexico,* pp. 166–173; Ray C. Colton, *The Civil War in the Western Territories* (Norman: University of Oklahoma Press, 1959), pp. 26–37; *Battles and Leaders of the Civil War*, Volume 2 (Secaucus, N.J.: Castle, 1982), pp. 103–111, 699–700; National Archives, Record Group 391, Entry 1243, "Descriptive Books of the 7th Infantry Regiment."

23. *OR,* Series I, Volume 9, p. 493; National Archives, Record Group 391, Entry 1254, Box 1, "Casualties of the 7th Infantry Regiment, 1856–1865."

24. Frances B. Heitman, *Historical Register and Dictionary of the U.S. Army, 1789–1903* (Washington, D.C.: Government Printing Office, 1903), p. 496.

25. *OR,* Series I, Volume 19, Part II, pp. 133–135; Timothy J. Reese, *Sykes Regular Infantry Division, 1861–1864: A History of Regular United States Infantry Operations in the Civil War's Eastern Theater* (Jefferson, N.C.: McFarland, 1990), pp. 159–165.

26. *Battles and Leaders,* Volume 3, p. 122.

27. Ibid., pp. 124–125.

28. This account of Fredericksburg from the perspective of the 7th and its sister units is derived from: Reese, *Sykes Regular Infantry Division,* pp. 168–189; *Battles and Leaders,* Volume 3, pp. 122–125; *OR,* Series I, Volume 21, pp. 418–429; Theophilus Rodenbaugh and William Haskin, *The Army of the United States: Historical Sketches of Staff and Line with Portraits of Generals-in-Chief* (New York: University Microfilms, 1966), pp. 504–524; National Archives, Record Group 391, Entry 1243, "Descriptive Books of the 7th Infantry Regiment," and Record Group 407, Box 6357, Folder 4, "History of the Seventh U.S. Infantry Regiment."

29. Reese, *Sykes Regular Infantry,* p. 404; National Archives, Record Group 391, Entry 1254, Box 1, "Casualties of the 7th Regiment."

30. Heitman, *Historical Register,* p. 295.

31. Reese, *Sykes Regular Infantry,* pp. 191–192; National Archives, Record Group 391, Entry 1238, Box 1, "Proceedings."

32. Reese, *Sykes Regular Infantry,* p. 193.

33. *OR,* Series I, Volume 25, Part I, pp. 525–540; Rodenbaugh and Haskin, *Historical Sketches,* p. 510.

34. National Archives, Record Group 391, Entry 1254, Box 1, "Casualties of the 7th Infantry Regiment." The regiment also lost five men missing in the battle.

35. Ibid.

36. *OR,* Series I, Volume 25, Part I, pp. 536–537.

37. Reese, *Sykes Regular Infantry,* p. 234.

38. Ibid., p. 243.

39. *OR,* Series I, Volume 25, Part I, pp. 645–649.

40. Reese, *Sykes Regular Infantry,* p. 253.

41. John W. Busey, *These Honored Dead: The Union Casualties at Gettysburg* (Hightstown, N.J.: Longstreet House, 1996), pp. 314–315.

42. For descriptions of the battle I have relied on several sources: *OR,* Series I, Volume 25, Part I, pp. 644–651; Rodenbaugh and Haskins, *Historical Sketches,* pp. 510–511; Reese, *Sykes Regular Infantry,* pp. 538–559; Jay Jorgensen, *The Gettysburg Magazine,* January 1996, pp. 64–76; National Archives, Record Group 407, Box 6357, Folder 4, "History of the Seventh U.S. Infantry Regiment."

43. Reese, *Sykes Regular Infantry,* p. 404; National Archives, Record Group 391, Entry 1254, Box 1, "Casualties of the 7th Regiment."

44. Reese, *Sykes Regular Infantry,* p. 287.

45. National Archives, Record Group 391, Entry 1238, Box 2, Major Henry D. Wallen to Assistant Adjutant General, April 27, 1864.

46. *OR,* Series I, Volume 43, Part II, pp. 420–421, 519–520.

47. See, for example, the case of Frederick Lilje, a Prussian immigrant who had joined the unit in 1855. In 1859, according to his great-great-grandson, he was "seriously injured when a mule team he was driving slipped on an ice covered road. He was riding one of the wheel mules and it fell on him breaking his left leg and hip." He recuperated, went on light duty, but endured the surrender in New Mexico, the parole ignominy, and the battles of Fredericksburg and Chancellorsville before being wounded at Gettysburg. Lilje reenlisted in February 1864 in exchange for a bonus

he probably used to buy a farm in Minnesota, where he lived for forty years, having settled down and married, and raised ten children. E-mail communication, James Lilje to author, May 15, 2001.

48. National Archives, Record Group 391, Entry 1238, Box 1, Statement of Adam Horhall.

49. National Archives, Record Group 391, Entry 1238, Box 1, "Proceedings."

50. National Archives, Record Group 391, Entry 1227, Box 1, Major Henry Wallen to Lieutenant John Jackson, August 11, 1864.

51. National Archives, Record Group 391, Entry 1227, Box 1, Colonel John Sprague to Adjutant General, August 30, 1866.

5. INSTRUMENTS OF MANIFEST DESTINY: THE FINAL FRONTIER YEARS

1. National Archives, Record Group 391, Entry 1227, Colonel John Sprague to the Assistant Adjutant General, Department of the South, Atlanta, March 8, 1869.

2. George A. Schneider, editor, *The Freeman Journal: The Infantry in the Sioux Campaign of 1876* (Novato, Calif.: Presidio Press, 1977), pp. 9–13.

3. National Archives, Henry B. Freeman to Acting Assistant Adjutant General, District of Montana, November 27, 1871. I found this letter randomly included among microfilm of post returns.

4. Edward J. McClernand, "Service in Montana 1870 and 1871," *Military Affairs* 15, Issue 4 (Winter 1951), pp. 195–196.

5. William Molchert, Sworn affidavit with history of service in the 7th U.S. Infantry Regiment, Molchert pension records, Vertical files, Big Hole National Battlefield Library, Wisdom, Montana (hereafter referred to as Big Hole Library); William Molchert and Jon James, editor, "Sergeant Molchert's Perils: Soldiering in Montana," *Montana: The Magazine of Western History* 34(2) (1984), pp. 60–62.

6. Theophilus Rodenbaugh and William Haskin, *The Army of the United States: Historical Sketches of Staff and Line with Portraits of Generals-in-Chief* (New York: University Microfilms, 1966), p. 519. Molchert claimed that, of eighty-two men on the march, "all but 12 lost either both feet or both hands or parts of either." Sworn affidavit, Molchert pension file, Big Hole Library.

7. National Archives, Register of Enlistments, Rolls 38–40, and Record Group 391, Entry 1237, Description of Officers of the 7th Infantry Regiment; "Presenting the Men of Company G, 7th U.S. Infantry, August, 1877," Vertical files, Big Hole Library"; Don Rickey, *Forty Miles a Day on Beans and Hay: The Enlisted Soldier Fighting the Indian Wars* (Norman: University of Oklahoma Press, 1963), pp. 17–32, and "The Enlisted Men of the Indian Wars," *Military Affairs* 23, Issue 2 (Summer 1959), pp. 91–96.

8. Alfred W. Schulmeyer, "Presenting Company K, 7th U.S. Infantry, August 1877," *By Valor and Arms* 3 (2) (1977), pp. 42–51.

9. Journal of Private Geant, White Swan Library, Little Bighorn Battlefield National Monument, (hereafter referred to as Little Bighorn Library), LIBI-12890, Camp Folder #67, p. 1.

10. Journal of 1st Lt. William L. English, Yale University Library, Western Americana Collection, MSS-8–3, p. 1.

11. Edgar I. Stewart, editor, *The March of the Montana Column: A Prelude to the Custer Disaster* (Norman: University of Oklahoma Press, 1961), pp. 12–13. This book is a copy of the diary kept by Lieutenant James H. Bradley of the 7th Infantry Regiment.

12. Colonel John Gibbon to General Alfred Terry, March 8, 1876, Camp Folder #164, and Gibbon to Terry, March 30, 1876, Camp Folder #165, both at Little Bighorn Library.

13. Douglas Knapp, "General John Gibbon: A Half Century of Duty and Honor to His Country," unpublished article, Big Hole Library, Vertical files, pp. 1–19; Francis B. Heitman, *Historical Register and Dictionary of the U.S. Army, 1789–1903* (Washington, D.C.: Government Printing Office, 1903), p. 452.

14. Dr. Holmes Offley Paulding, Diary with Gibbon Expedition to Meet Custer, Yale University Library, Western Americana Collection, MSS-8, pp. 2, 4, 9.

15. Stewart, *Montana Column,* p. 40.

16. John Gibbon, "Last Summer's Expedition Against the Sioux," *American Catholic Quarterly Review,* April 1877, pp. 276–277.

17. "Crow Indian Scouts: Service of Push, Alias Pahtch," pension claim, and "Copy of Muster Roll of 1Lt. James H. Bradley's Company of Indian Scouts, April 30, to June 30, 1876," both in Crow files, Little Bighorn Library; Thomas W. Dunlay, *Wolves for the Blue Soldiers: Indian Scouts and Auxiliaries with the United States Army, 1860–1890* (Lincoln: University of Nebraska Press, 1982), pp. 113–114; Stewart, *Montana Column,* pp. 42–47.

18. Gibbon, "Last Summer's Expedition," p. 277.

19. Stewart, *Montana Column*, pp. 3–6, 48–49, 65–66.

20. Gibbon, "Last Summer's Expedition," p. 281.

21. Journal of Private Geant, p. 3.

22. Schneider, *Freeman Journal,* pp. 47–48.

23. Lieutenant John F. McBlain, "With Gibbon on the Sioux Campaign," Camp Folder #169; Little Bighorn Library; Paulding Diary, p. 7.

24. Journal of Private Geant, p. 3; McBlain, "With Gibbon on the Sioux Campaign."

25. Schneider, *Freeman Journal,* p. 50; Paulding Diary, p. 10. What could well have sparked this argument is the fact that Gibbon inexplicably claimed in his dispatches to General Terry that he had not found the main Indian village.

26. Schneider, *Freeman Journal,* p. 69; National Archives, Record Group 391, Entry 1227, Lieutenant Levi Burnett to Captain Sanno, July 18, 1876, and Colonel John Gibbon to Captain Henry Freeman, July 26, 1876.

27. Cyrus Townsend Brady, *Northwestern Fights and Fighters* (New York: Doubleday, Page, 1907), pp. 342–343; Gibbon, "Last Summer's Expedition," p. 293.

28. Journal of Private Geant, p. 5.

29. Stewart, *Montana Column,* p. 148.

30. Captain Henry B. Freeman, diary, Big Hole Library, Vertical files; Schneider, *Freeman Journal,* p. 57.

31. Norman Poitevin, editor, *Captain Walter Clifford: A 7th Infantry Army Officer's Career in the Indian Wars,* self-published, 2002; Freeman diary; McBlain, "With Gibbon on the Sioux Campaign"; Journal of William English, p. 69.

32. Gibbon, "Last Summer's Expedition," p. 301. It is worth noting that the Sioux were augmented by large numbers of like-minded Cheyenne and Arapaho fighters. For the sake of clarity in this narrative, though, I have mainly referred to the Sioux when referencing the Indian side of Little Bighorn.

33. Ibid., p. 300; Poitevin, *Captain Clifford,* pp. 76–77; Thomas Goodrich, *Scalp Dance: Indian Warfare on the High Plains, 1865–1879* (Mechanicsburg, Pa.: Stackpole Books, 1997), pp. 260–261; Richard C. Hardorff, *The Custer Battle Casualties: Burials, Exhumations and Reinterments* (El Segundo, Calif.: Upton and Sons, 1991), p. 97.

34. McBlain, "With Gibbon on the Sioux Campaign"; Poitevin, *Captain Clifford,* p. 102; John Gibbon, "Hunting Sitting Bull," *American Catholic Quarterly,* September 1877, p. 667.

35. Memoir of Private Homer Coon, Yale University Library, Western Americana Collection, MSS-8-4, p. 9; Poitevin, *Captain Clifford,* p. 102.

36. Journal of Private Geant, p. 6.

37. Freeman diary; Schneider, *Freeman Journal,* p. 59.

38. Journal of Private Geant, pp. 6–7.

39. For general descriptions of the Sioux campaign of 1876, I have relied on several sources: Rodenbaugh and Haskin, *Historical Sketches,* p. 523; John S. Gray, *Centennial Campaign: The Sioux War of 1876* (Fort Collins, Colo.: Old Army Press, 1976), and *Custer's Last Campaign: Mitch Boyer and the Little Bighorn Reconstructed* (Lincoln and London: University of Nebraska Press, 1991); Robert Utley, *Custer and the Great Controversy: Origin and Development of a Legend* (Pasadena, Calif.: Westernlore Press, 1980), and *Frontier Regulars: The United States Army and the Indian, 1866–1891* (Lincoln and London: University of Nebraska Press, 1973). Poitevin, *Captain Clifford,* pp. 111–113, is an excellent source for the exploits of Bell, Evans, and Stewart since these men were all in Clifford's E Company. "They are all three cool, determined men, and good shots," the captain wrote.

40. Aubrey L. Haines, *The Battle of the Big Hole: The Story of the Landmark Battle of the 1877 Nez Perce War* (Guilford, Conn.: Twodot Press, 2007, reprint of 1991 edition), p. 35; Utley, *Frontier Regulars,* pp. 296–307.

41. Charles N. Loynes, pension file, Big Hole Library, Vertical files; Charles N. Loynes, "With the Seventh U.S. Infantry in Montana," *Winners of the West,* April 1924, p. 7.

42. Jerome A. Greene, *Nez Perce Summer 1877: The U.S. Army and the Nee-Me-Poo Crisis* (Helena: Montana Historical Society Press, 2000), p. 109.

43. Haines, *Battle of the Big Hole,* pp. 21–34; Loynes, "With the Seventh U.S. Infantry," pp. 6–7, Charles Loynes to L.V. McWhorter, July 13, 1927, and January 18, 1928, Big Hole Library, Vertical files.

44. Haines, *Battle of the Big Hole,* pp. 35–41; Loynes, "With the Seventh U.S. Infantry," pp. 6–7; Coon memoir, p. 15; Colonel John Gibbon, "Report of Battle of Big Hole," September 20, 1877, Big Hole Library, Vertical files. In this report, Gibbon claimed that the Nez Percés engaged in significant amounts of plundering, theft, and destruction in the Bitterroot valley.

45. Greene, *Nez Perce Summer 1877,* p. 127.

46. Gibbon, "Report of Battle of Big Hole"; Brigadier General John Gibbon, U.S.A., "The Battle of the Big Hole," *Harper's Weekly,* December 28, 1895; Bruce Hampton, "Battle of the Big Hole," Part I, *Montana: The Magazine of Western History,* Winter 1994, pp. 6–7; Charles Loynes, "Battle of the Big Hole," *Winners of the West,* March 1925, p. 7.

47. Gibbon, "Report of Battle of Big Hole"; Gibbon, "Battle of the Big Hole"; Coon memoir, p. 16.

48. Haines, *Battle of the Big Hole,* pp. 55–58; Greene, *Nez Perce Summer 1877,* p. 131; Gibbon, "Battle of the Big Hole"; Loynes, "Battle of the Big Hole," p. 7; Charles Loynes to L.V. McWhorter, January 3, 1942, and September 9, 1942, and Captain Richard Comba, Report to Assistant Adjutant General, September 16, 1877, both at Big Hole Library, Vertical files.

49. Loynes, "Battle of the Big Hole," p. 7.

50. Ibid., p. 8; Hampton, "Battle of the Big Hole," pp. 8–10.

51. Stewart, *Montana Column,* p. 4; Haines, *Battle of the Big Hole,* p. 58; Loynes, "Battle of the Big Hole," p. 8; Charles Loynes to L.V. McWhorter, September 8, 1929, and Private Philo O. Hurlburt, pension file, both at Big Hole Library, Vertical files.

52. Haines, *Battle of the Big Hole*, p. 61; Greene, *Nez Perce Summer 1877*, p. 132; Captain William Logan, pension file, Big Hole Library, Vertical files. Logan had at least eight children and perhaps as many as thirteen. His daughter Emily was married to one of Logan's fellow officers in the 7th Infantry, Lieutenant John Van Orsdale. The couple's infant son had died in June 1877, and apparently Emily also died that year. Logan, his daughter, and his grandson are all buried in Section A, Grave 745, at the National Cemetery, Little Bighorn Battlefield.

53. Gibbon, "Report of Battle of Big Hole"; Comba report; Gibbon, "Battle of the Big Hole"; Hampton, "Battle of the Big Hole," p. 12; Thomas E. Blades and John W. Wike, "Fort Missoula," *Military Affairs* 13, Issue 1 (Spring 1949), p. 34.

54. Haines, *Battle of the Big Hole*, p. 62; Greene, *Nez Perce Summer 1877*, p. 135; Loynes, "Battle of the Big Hole," p. 8; Gibbon, "Report of Battle of Big Hole"; Charles N. Loynes to L.V. McWhorter, June 6, 1926, March, 1940, June 23, 1943, and circa 1945, and "7th Infantry: List of Killed and Wounded at the Battle of Big Hole," all at Big Hole Library, Vertical files.

55. Gibbon, "Report of Battle of Big Hole"; Loynes, "Battle of the Big Hole," p. 8; Blades and Wike, "Fort Missoula," p. 34.

56. Douglas C. McChristian, *The U.S. Army in the West, 1870–1880, Uniforms, Weapons and Equipment* (Norman and London: University of Oklahoma Press, 1995), p. 137.

57. National Archives, Record Group 391, Entry 1259, Captain Richard Comba to Board on Army Equipment, Washington, D.C., March 15, 1879; Comba report.

58. Coon memoir, p. 17.

59. Haines, *Battle of the Big Hole,* pp. 75–83; Gibbon, "Battle of the Big Hole"; Bruce Hampton, "Battle of the Big Hole," Part II, *Montana: The Magazine of Western History*, Spring 1994, pp. 20–23; Gibbon, "Report of Battle of Big Hole"; Sergeant John Frederick, pension file, and Charles N. Loynes to L.V. McWhorter, November 7, 1926, both at Big Hole Library, Vertical files. Frederick was one of the soldiers who was manning the howitzer.

60. Loynes, "Battle of the Big Hole," p. 8; Blades and Wike, "Fort Missoula," p. 34; Gibbon, "Battle of the Big Hole"; Charles N. Loynes to L.V. McWhorter, September 9, 1942, Big Hole Library, Vertical files.

61. Gibbon, "Battle of the Big Hole"; Coon memoir, pp. 17–18. That night, Gibbon sent two particularly courageous civilian volunteers, one of whom was Billy Edwards, to Deer Lodge, ninety miles away, to call for help.

62. Gibbon, "Battle of the Big Hole"; Greene, *Nez Perce Summer 1877,* p. 137.

63. Loynes, "Battle of the Big Hole," p. 8; Coon memoir, p. 18; "7th Infantry: List of Killed and Wounded at the Battle of Big Hole"; Lieutenant John Van Orsdale to Office of the Adjutant General, on the recovery and reburying of soldiers killed at Big Hole, Little Bighorn Library, Camp Folder #19. Loynes was mistaken about Sergeant Howard Clark. He was wounded, not killed.

64. "7th Infantry: List of Killed and Wounded at the Battle of Big Hole"; Haines, *Battle of the Big Hole*, p. 110; Greene, *Nez Perce Summer 1877*, pp. 364–365, 374.

65. Charles Loynes to L.V. McWhorter, June 26, 1926, and April 9, 1941, Big Hole Library, Vertical files; Hampton, "Battle of the Big Hole," Part II, p. 25; Utley, *Frontier Regulars*, pp. 310–314. One of the skirmishes, if it can even be called that, involved Sergeant Molchert, the Prussian immigrant who served in B Company. Molchert commanded a tiny guard force of a dozen men protecting an engineering project near Cow Island in Montana. The Nez Percés came his way in September. He and his men exchanged a few shots and negotiated a parley with them. Molchert and James, "Sergeant Molchert's Perils," pp. 64–65; also see Molchert, Sworn affidavit.

66. Charles Loynes to L.V. McWhorter, November 7, 1926, Big Hole Library, Vertical files; Coon memoir, p. 19.
67. Rodenbaugh and Haskin, *Historical Sketches*, p. 525.

6. First Fight on Overseas Shores: The Spanish-American War

1. For this background information, I have relied primarily on the following sources: David Trask, *The War with Spain in 1898* (New York: Macmillan, 1981), pp. 1–59; Ivan Musicant, *Empire by Default: The Spanish-American War and the Dawn of the American Century* (New York: Henry Holt, 1998), pp. 1–190; G. J. A. O'Toole, *The Spanish War: An American Epic—1898* (New York: Norton, 1984), pp. 17–89.
2. National Archives, Register of Enlistments, Rolls 48–50.
3. Herbert O. Kohr, *Around the World with Uncle Sam: Six Years in the United States Army* (Akron, Ohio: Commercial Printing, 1907), pp. 9–50.
4. Gregory J. W. Urwin, *The United States Infantry: An Illustrated History, 1775–1918* (Norman: University of Oklahoma Press, 1988), pp. 136–140.
5. Frank Friedel, *The Splendid Little War* (Boston: Little, Brown, 1958), pp. 66–68.
6. Kohr, *Around the World*, pp. 55–56.
7. Friedel, *Splendid Little War*, pp. 69–79.
8. Kohr, *Around the World*, pp. 57–59.
9. Urwin, *United States Infantry*, p. 147; Graham Cosmas, *An Army for Empire: The United States Army in the Spanish-American War* (Shippensburg, Pa.: Whitemane Publishing, 1973), pp. 3–4.
10. Friedel, *Splendid Little War*, pp. 99–107; Musicant, *Empire by Default*, pp. 377–390.
11. Kohr, *Around the World*, pp. 65–66.
12. Trask, *War with Spain*, p. 222.
13. Kohr, *Around the World*, p. 70.
14. Captain Arthur Lee, "The Regulars at El Caney," *Scribner's Magazine* 24 (1898), pp. 403–404.
15. Kohr, *Around the World*, pp. 70–71.
16. James Burton, "Photographing Under Fire," *Harper's Weekly*, August 6, 1898, pp. 773–774.
17. Kohr, *Around the World*, p. 72.
18. *The Splendid Little War*, video documentary, Kearny, N.J.: Belle Grove Publishing, 1992.
19. Lee, "Regulars at El Caney," p. 406.
20. Kohr, *Around the World*, pp. 208–209.
21. Burton, "Photographing Under Fire," p. 774; Lee, "Regulars at El Caney," p. 407.
22. Lee, "Regulars at El Caney," pp. 407–408.
23. National Archives, Record Group 391, Entry 1237, Description of Officers of the 7th Infantry Regiment, and Record Group 407, Box 6357, Folder 4, Biography of Major F. M. H. Kendrick.
24. *Headquarters: 7th U.S. Infantry Association*, March 1939, p. 4.
25. Lee, "Regulars at El Caney," p. 409.
26. Kohr, *Around the World*, p. 72.
27. Lee, "Regulars at El Caney," p. 410.
28. Musicant, *Empire by Default*, pp. 407–409.
29. National Archives, Record Group 407, Box 6357, Folder 4, "History of the Seventh U.S. Infantry Regiment."

30. Lee, "Regulars at El Caney," p. 411.

31. *The Santiago Campaign: Reminiscences of the Operations for the Capture of Santiago de Cuba in the Spanish-American War, June and July, 1898* (Richmond, Va.: Williams Printing, 1927), p. 276.

32. Kohr, *Around the World,* pp. 74–75, 83–84, 209–210; National Archives, Record Group 391, Entry 1237, Description of Officers of the 7th Infantry Regiment.

33. Kohr, *Around the World,* pp. 77–78.

34. Ibid., pp. 80–82.

35. National Archives, Record Group 391, Entry 1259, Captain Frederick Kendrick to Inspector General, February 6, 1899.

36. Kohr, *Around the World,* pp. 83–85, 221–222.

37. National Archives, Record Group 407, Box 6357, Folder 4, "History of the Seventh U.S. Infantry Regiment." With the exception of a few details in this otherwise informative history of the regiment, I found very little reference to or records of the 7th Infantry in the Philippine War.

38. Brian M. Linn, *The U.S. Army and Counterinsurgency in the Philippine War, 1899–1902* (Chapel Hill and London: University of North Carolina Press, 1989), pp. 26–27, 152, and *The Philippine War, 1899–1902* (Lawrence: University Press of Kansas, 2000), pp. 306–321.

7. THE COTTONBALERS' FIRST MODERN WAR: WORLD WAR I

1. Gregory J. W. Urwin, *The United States Infantry: An Illustrated History, 1775–1918* (Norman: University of Oklahoma Press, 1988), pp. 161–168; John S. D. Eisenhower, *Yanks: The Epic Story of the American Army in World War I* (New York: Free Press, 2001), pp. 51–61.

2. National Archives, Register of Enlistments, Rolls 66–68; Urwin, *United States Infantry,* 156–160; Edward Coffman, *The War to End All Wars: The American Military Experience in World War I* (New York: Oxford University Press, 1968), pp. 121–157.

3. National Archives, College Park, Md. (and all citations hereafter), Record Group 407, Box 6357, Folder 4, "History of the Seventh U.S. Infantry Regiment," p. 14.

4. Sandy Dechert, unpublished biography of Robert Dechert, chapter 3, p. 9, copy provided to author by Ms. Dechert.

5. Thomas Glenden Millea, personal diary, copy provided to author by his son, Mr. Thomas Millea.

6. National Archives, Record Group 407, Box 6357, Folder 4, "History of the Seventh U.S. Infantry Regiment," p. 14.

7. Urwin, *United States Infantry,* pp. 164–165.

8. John Whiteclay Chambers, editor, *The Oxford Companion to American Military History* (New York: Oxford University Press, 1999), pp. 92, 672–673; Urwin, *United States Infantry,* p. 159.

9. Urwin, *United States Infantry,* pp. 162–167.

10. Cornelia Carswell Serota, editor, "A YMCA Canteen Worker in the Great War," unpublished manuscript, p. 82, copy provided to author by Mrs. Serota.

11. Ibid., p. 94.

12. Millea Diary.

13. National Archives, Record Group 407, Box 6357, Folder 4, "History of the Seventh U.S. Infantry Regiment," p. 16; Serota, "Canteen Worker in the Great War," p. 109; Frederic V. Hemenway, *History of the Third Division, United States Army in the World*

War for the Period December 1, 1917 to January 1, 1919 (Cologne, Germany: Shauberg, 1919), pp. 86–88.

14. Francis B. Heitman, *Historical Register and Dictionary of the U.S. Army, 1789–1903* (Washington, D.C.: Government Printing Office, 1903), p. 165; National Archives, Record Group 120, Entry 1241, Box 36, Folder 14, Regimental Orders, June 13, 1918.

15. Millea Diary.

16. Hemenway, *Third Division in the World War,* p. 89.

17. Millea Diary.

18. National Archives, Record Group 120, Entry 1241, Box 39, Folder 83, "In Belleau Woods, June 15–21, 1918," After Action Report of Captain Isham R. Williams.

19. National Archives, Record Group 407, Box 6357, Folder 4, "History of the Seventh U.S. Infantry Regiment," p. 19.

20. Dechert, unpublished biography, chapter 3, pp. 23.

21. Hemenway, *Third Division in the World War,* p. 89; National Archives, Record Group 407, Box 6357, Folder 4, "History of the Seventh U.S. Infantry Regiment," p. 17, and Record Group 120, Entry 1241, Box 39, Folder 83, "In Belleau Woods."

22. National Archives, Record Group 120, Entry 1241, Box 39, Folder 83, "Report of Action of First Battalion, 7th U.S. Infantry, in Belleau Woods."

23. George B. Clark, *Devil Dogs: Fighting Marines of World War I* (Novato, Calif.: Presidio Press, 1999), p. 189.

24. National Archives, Record Group 120, Entry 1241, Box 39, Folder 83, "Report of Action of First Battalion."

25. National Archives, Record Group 120, Entry 1241, Box 39, Folder 81, After Action Report, 2nd Battalion, 7th Infantry Regiment.

26. National Archives, Record Group 120, Entry 1241, Box 36, Folder 16, First Lieutenant Carl Helm, After Action Report.

27. Hemenway, *Third Division in the World War,* p. 90; National Archives, Record Group 407, Box 6357, Folder 4, "History of the Seventh U.S. Infantry Regiment," p. 17, Record Group 120, Entry 1241, Box 39, Folder 83, "In Belleau Woods"; and Box 36, Folder 16, Helm After Action Report; Millea Diary.

28. National Archives, Record Group 120, Entry 1241, Box 39, Folder 83, "In Belleau Woods."

29. National Archives, Record Group 120, Entry 1241, Box 39, Folder 83, "Report of Operations of the 3rd Battalion, 7th Infantry, in Belleau Woods, June 17–23, 1918."

30. Clark, *Devil Dogs,* pp. 190–191.

31. National Archives, Record Group 120, Entry 1241, Box 39, Folder 83, "Operations of the 3rd Battalion in Belleau Woods."

32. Hemenway, *Third Division in the World War,* p. 91.

33. Serota, "Canteen Worker in the Great War," p. 122.

34. National Archives, Record Group 407, Box 6357, Folder 4, "History of the Seventh U.S. Infantry Regiment," p. 20.

35. Hemenway, *Third Division in the World War,* p. 92.

36. National Archives, Record Group 120, Entry 1241, Box 37, Folder 34, "3rd Battalion Plan of Defense."

37. Dechert, unpublished biography, chapter 3, pp. 19–20.

38. National Archives, Record Group 407, Box 6357, Folder 4, "History of the Seventh U.S. Infantry Regiment," p. 25.

39. National Archives, Record Group 120, Entry 1241, Box 39, Folder 100, "Extracts from Annual Report, Division Inspector, 3d Division."

40. Rod Paschall, *The Defeat of Imperial Germany, 1917–1918* (Chapel Hill, N.C.:

Algonquin Books of Chapel Hill, 1989), pp. 158–162; Byron Falwell, *The United States in the Great War, 1917–1918* (New York: Norton, 1999), p. 177–188; Frank Friedel, *Over There: The Story of America's First Great Crusade* (Boston: Little, Brown, 1964), pp. 194–198; Eisenhower, *Yanks,* pp. 168–173; Coffman, *War to End All Wars,* pp. 224–227.

41. National Archives, Record Group 407, Box 6357, Folder 4, "History of the Seventh U.S. Infantry Regiment," pp. 25–26.

42. Ibid., p. 27.

43. National Archives, Record Group 120, Entry 1241, Box 39, Folder 85, "Lieutenant H. L. White, After Action Report, July 17, 1918."

44. Homer Wilson, World War I Questionnaire, United States Army Military History Institute, Carlisle, Pennsylvania (hereafter referred to as USAMHI).

45. National Archives, Record Group 120, Entry 1241, Box 39, Folder 85, "White After Action Report."

46. Millea Diary.

47. Serota, "Canteen Worker in the Great War," pp. 180, 186, 190, 193–194.

48. National Archives, Record Group 120, Entry 1241, Box 39, Folder 84, "Operations Report of the 3rd Battalion, 18–30th July, 1918."

49. Dechert, unpublished biography, chapter 4, p. 19.

50. National Archives, Record Group 120, Entry 1241, Box 39, Folder 19, "Field Messages and Orders."

51. Serota, "Canteen Worker in the Great War," p. 251.

52. Eisenhower, *Yanks,* pp. 188–200; Coffman, *War to End All Wars,* pp. 299–306; Friedel, *Over There,* pp. 199–214, 237–242.

53. National Archives, Record Group 407, Box 6357, Folder 4, "History of the Seventh U.S. Infantry Regiment," pp. 28–31, and Record Group 120, Entry 1241, Box 36, Folder 35, "Operations Reports, 9/27/1918–9/30/1918."

54. National Archives, Record Group 407, Box 6357, Folder 4, "History of the Seventh U.S. Infantry Regiment," pp. 31–32.

55. National Archives, Record Group 407, Box 6357, Folder 4, "History of the Seventh U.S. Infantry Regiment," and Record Group 120, Entry 1241, Box 36, Folder 20, 1st Battalion War Diary, October 2, 1918; Hemenway, *Third Division in the World War,* p. 102.

56. National Archives, Record Group 120, Entry 1241, Box 36, Folder 13, "Summary of Intelligence Reports, 10/5/1918–10/8/1918."

57. Dominic Mence, World War I Questionnaire, USAMHI.

58. National Archives, Record Group 120, Entry 1241, Box 39, Folder 100, "Division Inspector Annual Report," and Record Group 407, Entry 427, Box 5608, Folder 17, Captain T.A. Harris to American Legion, Oliver Ames, Jr. Post, September 21, 1926; Hemenway, *Third Division in the World War,* pp. 102–105.

59. National Archives, Record Group 120, Entry 1241, Box 36, Folder 20, "Situation Reports, 10/13/1918–10/15/1918."

60. John Madden, *Watch on the Rhine,* April 9, 1921.

61. Henry Berry, *Make the Kaiser Dance: Living Memories of a Forgotten War. The American Experience in World War I,* (Garden City, N.J.: Doubleday & Company, Inc., 1978), pp. 147–148.

62. National Archives, Record Group 407, Box 6357, Folder 4, "Regiment" History of the Seventh U.S. Infantry, pp. 34–35; Hemenway, *Third Division in the World War,* 106–109; Infantry Journal, *Infantry in Battle* (Washington, D.C.: Infantry Journal Press, 1939), pp. 404–407.

63. Hemenway, *Third Division in the World War,* p. 109.

64. Serota, "Canteen Worker in the Great War," p. 298.
65. Dechert, unpublished biography, chapter 6, page 1.

8. THE GREATEST WAR, WORLD WAR II: OPERATION TORCH THROUGH ROME

1. Gerald Astor, *The Greatest War: Americans in Combat 1941–1945* (Novato, Calif.: Presidio Press, 1999).
2. Abner Kuperstein, *The Cottonbaler,* Winter 1996, pp. 4–6.
3. Sherman Pratt, *Autobahn to Berchtesgaden: A View of World War II from the Bottom Up by an Infantry Sergeant* (Baltimore: Gateway Press, 1992), pp. 15–22, 38–68.
4. Robert Maxwell O'Kane, *The Cottonbaler,* Summer 1995, p. 8; Russ Cloer, unpublished memoir, p. 44, memoir in author's possession. Also see John C. McManus, *The Deadly Brotherhood: The American Combat Soldier in World War II* (Novato, Calif.: Presidio Press, 1998), pp. 3–13, for an analysis and explanation of the decidedly Middle American origination and consciousness of the U.S. infantry soldier in World War II.
5. Pratt, *Autobahn to Berchtesgaden,* p. 78.
6. Paul Nelson to author, August 1, 2001.
7. Pratt, *Autobahn to Berchtesgaden,* pp. 143–144.
8. Donald Taggart, *History of the Third Infantry Division in World War II* (Washington, D.C.: Infantry Journal Press, 1947), p. 10.
9. Pratt, *Autobahn to Berchtesgaden,* pp. 152–162; *The U.S. Army Campaigns of World War II: Algeria-French Morocco,* U.S. Army Center of Military History Pamphlet, pp. 5–9; George F. Howe, *Northwest Africa: Seizing the Initiative in the West* (Washington, D.C.: Center of Military History, 1991), pp. 115–123.
10. Howe, *Northwest Africa,* pp. 121–123; Nathan W. White, *From Fedala to Berchtesgaden: A History of the 7th United States Infantry in World War II* (Brockton, Mass.: Keystone Print, 1947), pp. 2–4; Abner Kuperstein, "Notes on 7th Inf. Commanders," copy provided to author by Colonel Bill Strobridge.
11. Pratt, *Autobahn to Berchtesgaden,* pp. 168–172.
12. White, *Fedala to Berchtesgaden,* p. 5.
13. William B. Rosson, oral history transcript, USAMHI.
14. National Archives, Record Group 407, Entry 427, Box 5610, Folder 1, 7th Infantry Regiment, After Action Report, Operation Torch; White, *Fedala to Berchtesgaden,* pp. 5–8. Taggart, *Third Infantry Division in World War II,* pp. 15–19.
15. Samuel Eliot Morison, *History of United States Naval Operations in World War II: Operations in North African Waters, October 1942–June 1943* Volume 2 (Boston: Little, Brown, 1947), pp. 75–76.
16. National Archives, Record Group 407, Entry 427, 7th Infantry AAR, Operation Torch; White, *Fedala to Berchtesgaden,* pp. 8–10; Taggart, *Third Infantry Division in World War II,* pp. 24–25.
17. National Archives, Record Group 407, Entry 427, Box 6358, Folder 2, "History of Company E, 7th Infantry, Fedala-Casablanca Operations," p. 1.
18. National Archives, Record Group 407, Entry 427, Box 6358, Folder 2, "Company I, Seventh Infantry, Report of Action Observed by Captain C. H. White," p. 1. For a discussion of fire and maneuver, see Michael Doubler, *Closing with the Enemy: How G.I.'s Fought the War in Europe, 1944–1945* (Lawrence: University Press of Kansas, 1995), and Peter Mansoor, *The G.I. Offensive in Europe: The Triumph of American Infantry Divisions, 1941–1945* (Lawrence: University Press of Kansas, 1999), as well as McManus, *Deadly Brotherhood,* pp. 99–106.

19. National Archives, Record Group 407, Entry 427, Box 6358, Folder 2, "History of Company E," p. 1.

20. National Archives, Record Group 407, Entry 427, Box 6358, Folder 2, "History of Company H, Seventh Infantry, Fedala-Casablanca Operations," p. 1.

21. National Archives, Record Group 407, Entry 427, Box 6358, Folder 2, "History of Company E," p. 2, "History of Company F, Seventh Infantry, Fedala-Casablanca Operations," p. 1, and "History of Company G, Seventh Infantry, Fedala-Casablanca Operations," p. 1.

22. National Archives, Record Group 407, Entry 427, Box 6358, Folder 2, "History of Company H," pp. 1–2.

23. National Archives, Record Group 407, Entry 427, Box 6358, Folder 2, "History of Company G," p. 2.

24. National Archives, Record Group 407, Entry 427, 7th Infantry AAR, Operation Torch; Pratt, *Autobahn to Berchtesgaden,* p. 179.

25. National Archives, Record Group 407, Entry 427, Box 6358, Folder 2, "History of Company 'B,' Seventh Infantry," pp. 1–2.

26. Nelson to author.

27. Pratt, *Autobahn to Berchtesgaden,* p. 181–183.

28. National Archives, Record Group 407, Entry 427, 7th Infantry AAR, Operation Torch; White, *Fedala to Berchtesgaden,* p. 17.

29. Kuperstein, "Notes on 7th Inf Commanders," p. 2.

30. Pratt, *Autobahn to Berchtesgaden,* p. 233.

31. National Archives, Record Group 407, Entry 427, Box 5609, Folder 6, 7th Infantry, After Action Report, Sicily Operation; White, *Fedala to Berchtesgaden,* p. 23.

32. Pratt, *Autobahn to Berchtesgaden,* pp. 236–237.

33. John A. Heintges, oral history transcript, USAMHI.

34. Rosson transcript, USAMHI.

35. Joe Martin interview with Dr. Charles W. Johnson, March 11, 1986, University of Tennessee Special Collections Library (hereafter referred to as SCUTK), World War II Collection, Center for the Study of War and Society, MS 1298, Box 6, Folder 3.

36. National Archives, Record Group 407, Entry 427, 7th Infantry AAR, Sicily, and Box 5610, Folder 6, 7th Infantry Regiment Invasion Landing Diagram, Sicily; Heintges transcript, USAMHI.

37. National Archives, Record Group 407, Entry 427, 7th Infantry AAR, Sicily, and Box 5614, Folder 3, S3 Periodic Report, July 10, 1943; Rosson transcript, USAMHI.

38. White, *Fedala to Berchtesgaden,* pp. 24–26.

39. National Archives, Record Group 407, Entry 427, Box 5610, Folder 5, 7th Infantry, "Lessons Learned During Combat Action, Sicily Campaign"; Heintges transcript, USAMHI.

40. National Archives, Record Group 407, Entry 427, 7th Infantry AAR, Sicily; White, *Fedala to Berchtesgaden,* pp. 26–27; Heintges transcript, USAMHI.

41. Rosson transcript, USAMHI.

42. Carlo D'Este, *Bitter Victory: The Battle of Sicily, 1943* (New York: Dutton, 1988), pp. 412–422.

43. National Archives, Record Group 407, Entry 427, 7th Infantry AAR, Sicily; White, *Fedala to Berchtesgaden,* pp. 28–30.

44. National Archives, Record Group 407, Entry 427, 7th Infantry AAR, Sicily; White, *Fedala to Berchtesgaden,* p. 30.

45. National Archives, Record Group 407, Entry 427, "Lessons Learned During Combat Action, Sicily Campaign"; Pratt, *Autobahn to Berchtesgaden,* p. 257; Martin interview, SCUTK.

46. National Archives, Record Group 407, Entry 427, 7th Infantry AAR, Sicily, and S3 Periodic Reports, July 20–22, 1943; Heintges transcript, USAMHI.

47. Rosson transcript, USAMHI.

48. National Archives, Record Group 407, Entry 427, 7th Infantry AAR, Sicily; Pratt, *Autobahn to Berchtesgaden*, pp. 272–273.

49. National Archives, Record Group 407, Entry 427, "Lessons Learned During Combat Action, Sicily Campaign"; Taggart, *Third Infantry Division in World War II*, p. 61.

50. Martin interview, SCUTK.

51. National Archives, Record Group 407, Entry 427, 7th Infantry AAR, Sicily; Pratt, *Autobahn to Berchtesgaden*, p. 277.

52. Taggart, *Third Infantry Division in World War II*, pp. 64–65.

53. National Archives, Record Group 407, Entry 427, 7th Infantry AAR, Sicily, and S3 Periodic Reports, August 10–17, 1943; Heintges transcript, USAMHI.

54. Pratt, *Autobahn to Berchtesgaden*, pp. 281–282.

55. National Archives, Record Group 407, Entry 427, 7th Infantry AAR, Sicily, and Box 5609, Folder 8, 7th Infantry, Observation Notes, Sicily Campaign; White, *Fedala to Berchtesgaden*, pp. 34–42.

56. Martin Blumenson, *Salerno to Cassino* (Washington, D.C.: Office of the Chief of Military History, United States Army, 1969), pp. 3–118.

57. Heintges transcript, USAMHI.

58. National Archives, Record Group 407, Entry 427, Box 5610, Folder 5, 7th Infantry After Action Report, August 26–November 1, 1943; Rosson transcript, USAMHI.

59. Heintges transcript, USAMHI.

60. Pratt, *Autobahn to Berchtesgaden*, pp. 296–297.

61. For a more complete discussion of the terrible problems American soldiers experienced with trench foot in World War II, see McManus, *Deadly Brotherhood*, pp. 31–32, 54–56.

62. Blumenson, *Salerno to Cassino*, pp. 184–196.

63. Captain Orrin A. Tracy, "The Operations of the 7th Infantry (3rd Inf. Div.) Volturno River Crossing, 7–15 October, 1943," paper prepared for Advanced Infantry Officers Course, the Infantry School, Fort Benning, Georgia, copy at USAMHI; see also John C. McManus, "Crossing the Volturno: In October 1943, the 7th Infantry Regiment Led the Allied Armies Across a Major River Barrier," *World War II*, January 2005.

64. Heintges transcript, USAMHI.

65. White, *Fedala to Berchtesgaden*, pp. 51–52; Major John A. Elterich, "Patrol Actions Prior to and the Operation of the 2nd Battalion, 7th Infantry Regiment (3rd Division) in Crossing the Volturno River, 13 October 1943," paper prepared for Advanced Infantry Officers Course, the Infantry School, Fort Benning, Georgia, copy at USAMHI; "Crossing of the Volturno River by the 7th Infantry," group combat interview with Colonel Blakely, December 8, 1943, Infantry School Library, Fort Benning, Columbus, Georgia (hereafter cited as 7th Infantry combat interview).

66. White, *Fedala to Berchtesgaden*, p. 52.

67. Tracy, "Volturno River Crossing."

68. National Archives, Record Group 407, Entry 427, 7th Infantry, AAR, August 26–November 1, 1943; White, *Fedala to Berchtesgaden*, pp. 52–53; 7th Infantry combat interview.

69. Tracy, "Volturno River Crossing"; 7th Infantry combat interview.

70. National Archives, Record Group 407, Entry 427, 7th Infantry, AAR, August 26–November 1, 1943; Heintges transcript, USAMHI.

71. National Archives, Record Group 407, Entry 427, 7th Infantry, AAR, August 26–November 1, 1943; White, *Fedala to Berchtesgaden,* pp. 59–60. Blumenson, *Salerno to Cassino,* pp. 208–209.

72. Pratt, *Autobahn to Berchtesgaden,* pp. 312, 322.

73. National Archives, Record Group 407, Entry 427, Box 5610, Folder 5, 7th Infantry, After Action Report, November, 1943, and Folder 7, 7th Infantry, Unit Journal, November 5–15, 1943; White, *Fedala to Berchtesgaden,* pp. 64–68; Blumenson, *Salerno to Cassino,* pp. 228–229; Taggart, *Third Infantry Division in World War II,* pp. 98–102; Pratt, *Autobahn to Berchtesgaden,* pp. 323–324.

74. Pratt, *Autobahn to Berchtesgaden,* pp. 343–347.

75. Blumenson, *Salerno to Cassino,* pp. 293–304; Carlo D'Este, *Fatal Decision: Anzio and the Battle for Rome* (New York: HarperCollins, 1991), pp. 67–115; Taggart, *Third Infantry Division in World War II,* pp. 105–107.

76. National Archives, Record Group 407, Entry 427, Box 5609, Folder 12, 7th Infantry, After Action Report, Anzio Invasion; Rosson transcript, USAMHI.

77. Martin interview, SCUTK.

78. Rosson transcript, USAMHI.

79. Winston S. Churchill, *The Second World War: Closing the Ring* (New York: Bantam, 1962), p. 418.

80. For a full treatment of the Anzio "controversy," see Martin Blumenson, *Anzio: The Gamble That Failed* (Philadelphia and New York: Lippincott, 1963), pp. 58–105; William Allen, *Anzio: Edge of Disaster* (New York: Elsevier-Dutton, 1978), pp. 60–71; D'Este, *Fatal Decision,* pp. 124–158; and Rick Atkinson, *The Day of Battle: The War in Sicily and Italy, 1943–1944* (New York: Henry Holt, 2007).

81. Robert W. Black, *Rangers in World War II* (New York: Ballantine Books, 1992), pp. 148–168; Taggart, *Third Infantry Division in World War II,* pp. 114–115.

82. Captain Nicholas Grunzweig, "The Operations of the 1st Battalion, 7th Infantry (3rd Infantry Division) at Le Mole Creek near Cisterna, Italy, 30 January–1 February 1944, Personal Experiences of a Company Commander," paper prepared for the Advanced Infantry Officers Course, the Infantry School, Fort Benning, Georgia, copy at USAMHI. See also John C. McManus, "Bloody Cisterna: The 7th Infantry's Experience at Cisterna Sheds Light on a Staggering Allied Defeat," *World War II,* January 2004.

83. Ibid.

84. National Archives, Record Group 407, Entry 427, Box 6358, Folder 19, "Factual Account of the Attack of the 1st Bn, 7th Inf, in the Vicinity of Cisterna, Italy, 30 Jan–1 Feb, 1944," and Box 6364, Folder 1, "Action of the 1st Battalion, 7th Infantry, 29–30 January 1944."

85. Ibid.

86. Grunzweig, "Operations at Le Mole Creek, Cisterna."

87. National Archives, Record Group 407, "Factual Account," and 1st Battalion, 7th Infantry, AAR, 29–30 January 1944.

88. Bob Appel, unpublished memoir, copy in author's possession; Robert Appel, conversations with the author; Robert Appel, compiler, *The Outdoor Kids of Company B, 7th Infantry Regiment, Third Division, U.S. Army* (Kearney, Neb.: Morris Publishing, 2004), pp. 107–111, 190–195, 246–247; White, *Fedala to Berchtesgaden,* pp. 81–82; Taggart, *Third Infantry Division in World War II,* pp. 116–117. Appel was badly wounded on the afternoon of January 31, 1944, and never returned to combat. He told me that Olson was a courageous soldier and a good man who seemed to have been born to fire the machine gun. Bob believes that Olson received his fatal wounds from an incoming shell during his evacuation to the beach.

89. Grunzweig, "Operations at Le Mole Creek, Cisterna."

90. National Archives, Record Group 407, "Factual Account," and 1st Battalion, 7th Infantry, AAR, 29–30 January 1944.

91. White, *Fedala to Berchtesgaden,* p. 82.

92. Grunzweig, "Operations at Le Mole Creek, Cisterna"; Appel, *Outdoor Kids,* pp. 139–142, 246–247.

93. Martin interview, SCUTK.

94. National Archives, Record Group 407, "Factual Account," and 1st Battalion, 7th Infantry, AAR, 29–30 January 1944.

95. Grunzweig, "Operations at Le Mole Creek, Cisterna"; White, *Fedala to Berchtesgaden,* p. 83.

96. National Archives, Record Group 407, Entry 427, Box 5609, Folder 11, 7th Infantry, After Action Report, January 1944; Taggart, *Third Infantry Division in World War II,* pp. 119–120.

97. Pratt, *Autobahn to Berchtesgaden,* pp. 359–366.

98. National Archives, Record Group 407, Entry 427, Box 5609, Folder 11, 7th Infantry, After Action Report, February 1944; Vernon Medaugh, unpublished memoir, pp. 1–2, in author's possession.

99. White, *Fedala to Berchtesgaden,* p. 91.

100. Taggart, *Third Infantry Division in World War II,* pp. 125–126.

101. National Archives, Record Group 407, Entry 427, Box 5611, Folder 1, 7th Infantry, Unit Journal, February 29–March 2, 1944, and Box 5613, Folder 7, S3 Periodic Reports, February 29–March 2, 1944; White, *Fedala to Berchtesgaden,* p. 93; Captain Frank Petruzel, "Turning Jerry Back," *Infantry Journal,* February 1946, pp. 44–46.

102. Ibid., pp. 93–95; Heintges transcript, USAMHI.

103. Wallace Bassett, World War II Questionnaire, USAMHI.

104. William Blanckenburg, World War II Questionnaire, USAMHI.

105. Pratt, *Autobahn to Berchtesgaden,* pp. 370–377.

106. White, *Fedala to Berchtesgaden,* pp. 97–100; Heintges transcript; Wiley H. O'Mohundro, "From Mules to Missiles," unpublished memoir, pp. 53–55, O'Mohundro Papers, both at USAMHI; Lieutenant Colonel Roy Moore, "Battle Patrol," *Infantry Journal,* November 1944, pp. 19–21.

107. National Archives, Record Group 407, Entry 427, Box 5609, Folder 12, 7th Infantry, After Action Report, April 1944; Cloer, unpublished memoir, pp. 1–6.

108. National Archives, Record Group 407, Entry 427, Box 5609, Folder 12, 7th Infantry, After Action Report, May 1944; Box 5611, Folder 3, Unit Journal, May 22–25, 1944; and Box 5613, Folder 7, S3 Periodic Reports, May 22–25, 1944; D'Este, *Fatal Decision,* pp. 358–359.

109. Cloer, unpublished memoir, pp. 6–7.

110. National Archives, Record Group 407, 7th Infantry, AAR, May 1944; White, *Fedala to Berchtesgaden,* pp. 107–117; Taggart, *Third Infantry Division in World War II,* pp. 153–171.

111. D'Este, *Fatal Decision,* p. 361.

112. Cloer, unpublished memoir, p. 7.

113. Taggart, *Third Infantry Division in World War II,* pp. 175–176.

114. Isadore Valenti, *Combat Medic* (Tarentum, Pa.: Word Association, 1998), pp. 1–5, 44–47.

115. Francis Steckel, "Morale Problems in Combat: American Soldiers in Europe in World War II," *Army History: The Professional Bulletin of Army History,* Summer 1994, pp. 1–8; McManus, *Deadly Brotherhood,* pp. 260–272.

116. White, *Fedala to Berchtesgaden,* pp. 117–121; Earl Reitan, *Riflemen: On the Cutting Edge of World War II* (Bennington, Vt.: Merriam Press, 2001), pp. 10–14, 31–35. I am

indebted to Dr. Reitan for kindly providing me with a prepublication manuscript copy of his book.

117. Valenti, *Combat Medic*, pp. 48–55; White, *Fedala to Berchtesgaden*, pp. 121–124; Atkinson, *Day of Battle*, pp. 567–568. White's regimental history claims that Lieutenant Colonel Toffey and Lieutenant Raney were killed by an enemy artillery and tank barrage. However, some Cottonbalers believed they were killed by friendly tank fire. Toffey's son, John, recently published an excellent book entitled *Jack Toffey's War* (New York: Fordham University Press, 2008), chronicling his father's experiences and what it was like, as his son, to lose him. I served as a reviewer and commentator on the manuscript as well as an occasional sounding board for John. In spite of in-depth research, John could not definitively ascertain the cause of his father's death.

118. For a good discussion of Clark's infamous bungle, see Ernest Fisher, *The United States Army in World War II: Cassino to the Alps* (Washington, D.C.: United States Army Center of Military History, 1993), pp. 169–215; D'Este, *Fatal Decision,* pp. 366–412. Atkinson in *The Day of Battle*, pp. 521–555, is much kinder to Clark than D'Este and Fisher.

119. Cloer, unpublished memoir, p. 7.

120. National Archives, Record Group 407, Entry 427, Box 5609, Folder 11, 7th Infantry, After Action Report, June 1944, and Box 5611, Folder 3, 7th Infantry, Unit Journal, June 4, 1944; D'Este, *Fatal Decision,* pp. 383–399; White, *Fedala to Berchtesgaden*, pp. 120–124.

121. Pratt, *Autobahn to Berchtesgaden*, p. 401.

122. Reitan, *Riflemen*, pp. 35–37.

9. The Greatest War, World War II: Riviera to Berchtesgaden

1. *The U.S. Army Campaigns of World War II: Southern France,* U.S. Army Center of Military History Pamphlet, pp. 3–6; Jeffrey Clarke and Robert Ross Smith, *Riviera to the Rhine* (Washington, D.C.: Center of Military History, United States Army, 1993), pp. 3–107; Alan Wilt, *The French Riviera Campaign of August 1944* (Carbondale: Southern Illinois University Press, 1981), pp. 1–80.

2. Russ Cloer, unpublished memoir, p. 10; Earl Reitan, *Riflemen: On the Cutting Edge of World War II* (Bennington, Vt.: Merriam Press, 2001), p. 39, and unpublished memoir, MS 1764, Box 17, Folder 16, SCUTK.

3. Isadore Valenti, *Combat Medic* (Tarentum, Pa.: Word Association, 1998), pp. 61–65.

4. Major John D. Foulk, "The Amphibious Operations of the 7th Infantry Regiment (3rd Infantry Division) at Cape Cavalaire-sur-Mer, Southern France, 15 August–19 August, 1944," paper prepared for Advanced Infantry Officers Course, the Infantry School, Fort Benning, Georgia, copy at USAMHI; Nathan W. White, *Fedala to Berchtesgaden* (Brockton, Mass.: Keystone Print, 1947), pp. 128–131.

5. Foulk, "Amphibious Operations."

6. Valenti, *Combat Medic,* p. 66; Wiley H. O'Mohundro, "From Mules to Missiles," unpublished memoir, pp. 59–60, O'Muhundro papers, USAMHI.

7. Cloer, unpublished memoir, p. 11.

8. Foulk, "Amphibious Operations."

9. Cloer, unpublished memoir, pp. 10–11.

10. Reitan, *Riflemen,* p. 41; Winston S. Churchill, *The Second World War: Triumph and Tragedy* (New York: Bantam, 1962), p. 79.

11. Reitan, *Riflemen,* p. 42.

12. Valenti, *Combat Medic,* pp. 70–71.

13. Joe Martin, interview with Dr. Charles W. Johnson, March 16, 1986, SCUTK, MS1298, Box 6, Folder 3.

14. National Archives, Record Group 407, Entry 427, Box 5609, Folder 10, 7th Infantry, After Action Report, August 1944; Foulk, "Amphibious Operations."

15. Reitan, *Rifleman,* p. 43.

16. Foulk, "Amphibious Operations"; White, *From Fedala to Berchtesgaden,* pp. 133–134; Reitan, *Riflemen,* p. 43; 2nd Battalion, 7th Infantry, After Action Report, National Archives, Record Group 407, Entry 427, World War II Combat Interviews, #23 (hereafter referred to as CI).

17. National Archives, Record Group 407, 7th Infantry, AAR, August 1944; Valenti, *Combat Medic,* pp. 72–73; 3rd Battalion, 7th Infantry, After Action Report, CI-23.

18. Norman Myhra, *The Cottonbaler,* November 1993, pp. 1–2; Robert Appel, compiler, *The Outdoor Kids of Company B, 7th Infantry Regiment, Third Division, U.S. Army,* (Kearny, Neb.: Moore Publishing, 2004), p. 268.

19. Foulk, "Amphibious Operations"; Donald. G. Taggart, *History of the Third Infantry Division in World War II,* pp. 207–208; Battle Patrol, 7th Infantry, After Action Report; Sergeant Edward Collins, Personal Affidavit/account, pp. 1–3, Sergeant Herman Nevers, Personal Affidavit/account, pp. 1–3, CI-24. Aboard ship, the officers and NCOs of the Battle Patrol intensively briefed and quizzed their men on terrain and mission objectives. Perhaps this pre-invasion preparation was a factor in sparking Connor's bravery. American combat soldiers in World War II were rarely so well informed, but generally did fight better when armed with good information on unit goals and objectives.

20. Mack Bloom, *The Cottonbaler,* 1991, p. 10; 1st Battalion, 7th Infantry, After Action Report, CI-23.

21. Sherman Pratt, *Autobahn to Berchtesgaden: A View of World War II from the Bottom Up by an Infantry Sergeant* (Baltimore: Gateway Press, 1992), pp. 424–428.

22. Valenti, *Combat Medic,* pp. 73–76; White, *Fedala to Berchtesgaden,* pp. 134–135; 3rd Battalion, 7th Infantry, AAR, CI-23.

23. National Archives, Record Group 407, Entry 427, Box 5611, Folder 4, 7th Infantry, Unit Journal, August 17–18, 1944; White, *Fedala to Berchtesgaden,* pp. 136–137; Taggart, *Third Infantry Division in World War II,* pp. 213–214; Sergeant Stanley Bender, "Recommendation for Award of the Medal of Honor," Lieutenant George Franklin, personal account, pp. 1–4; Sergeant Forrest Law, personal account, pp. 1–3; Sergeant Edward Havrila, personal account, pp. 1–3, CI-24.

24. National Archives, Record Group 407, 7th Infantry, AAR, August 1944; Cloer, unpublished memoir, p. 13; Valenti, *Combat Medic,* p. 74.

25. National Archives, Record Group 407, 7th Infantry, AAR, August 1944, and Box 5616, Folder 4, S3 Periodic Report, August 15, 1944; White, *Fedala to Berchtesgaden,* p. 288; Foulk, "Amphibious Operation."

26. Reitan, *Riflemen,* pp. 44–47.

27. Cloer, unpublished memoir, p. 14.

28. Pratt, *Autobahn to Berchtesgaden,* p. 429.

29. National Archives, Record Group 407, 7th Infantry, AAR, August 1944; White, *Fedala to Berchtesgaden,* pp. 141–142.

30. Valenti, *Combat Medic,* pp. 80–81; Taggart, *Third Infantry Division in World War II,* p. 221.

31. National Archives, Record Group 407, 7th Infantry, AAR, August 1944; Box 5616, Folder 4, 7th Infantry, S3 Periodic Report, August 29, 1944, and Box 5611, Folder 4,

7th Infantry, Unit Journal, August 29, 1944; White, *Fedala to Berchtesgaden,* pp. 141–143; Taggart, *Third Infantry Division in World War II,* pp. 221–223; Pratt, *Autobahn to Berchtesgaden,* pp. 429–439; 2nd Battalion, 7th Infantry, After Action Report, 3rd Battalion, 7th Infantry, After Action Report, CI-23.

32. White, *Fedala to Berchtesgaden,* p. 143.

33. Cloer, unpublished memoir, p. 16.

34. National Archives, Record Group 407, Entry 427, Box 5609, Folder 10, 7th Infantry, After Action Report, September 1944; Vernon Medaugh, unpublished memoir, p. 2, in author's possession.

35. National Archives, Record Group 407, 7th Infantry, AAR, September 1944; White, *Fedala to Berchtesgaden,* pp. 145–148; Taggart, *Third Infantry Division in World War II,* pp. 223–229.

36. Valenti, *Combat Medic,* p. 89.

37. National Archives, Record Group 407, 7th Infantry, AAR, September 1944; White, *Fedala to Berchtesgaden,* pp. 153–157; "7th Infantry at Besançon," and 3rd Battalion, 7th Infantry, After Action Report, both at CI-24.

38. Valenti, *Combat Medic,* p. 98.

39. National Archives, Record Group 407, Entry 427, Box 5609, Folder 10, 7th Infantry, After Action Report, October 1944; Pratt, *Autobahn to Berchtesgaden,* pp. 443–447; 7th Infantry After Action Report, CI-25. This latter report is different than the one on file at the National Archives.

40. National Archives, Record Group 407, 7th Infantry, AAR, October 1944; Stephen Mazak, *Ben's Story,* pp. 2–23. I am indebted to Mr. Mazak, who sent me a copy of this fine retrospective on the life and military service of his great-uncle, Benedict Bartkowiak.

41. 3rd Battalion, 7th Infantry, "Moselle River Crossing and Vagney," CI-25; Valenti, *Combat Medic,* pp. 103–104.

42. Mack Bloom, World War II Questionnaire, USAMHI.

43. National Archives, Record Group 407, 7th Infantry, AAR, October 1944; White, *Fedala to Berchtesgaden,* pp. 162–164; Taggart, *Third Infantry Division in World War II,* pp. 250–251; 7th Infantry, AAR, CI-25.

44. Pratt, *Autobahn to Berchtesgaden,* pp. 448–455.

45. National Archives, Record Group 407, 7th Infantry, AAR, October 1944; Valenti, *Combat Medic,* pp. 115–116.

46. National Archives, Record Group 407, 7th Infantry, AAR, October 1944, and Box 5611, Folder 5, 7th Infantry, Unit Journal, October 24, 1944; White, *Fedala to Berchtesgaden,* pp. 166–170; Franz Steidl, *Lost Battalions: Going for Broke in the Vosges, Autumn 1944* (Novato, Calif.: Presidio Press, 1997), pp. 69–72; 3rd Battalion, 7th Infantry, AAR, CI-25.

47. National Archives, Record Group 407, 7th Infantry, AAR, October 1944; Steidl, *Lost Battalions,* p. 104.

48. White, *Fedala to Berchtesgaden,* pp. 170–171.

49. National Archives, Record Group 407, Box 5609, Folder 10, 7th Infantry, After Action Report, November 1944; Dean Cannon to Joe Martin, no date, MS 1764, Box 7, Folder 1, SCUTK.

50. National Archives, Record Group 407, 7th Infantry, AAR, November 1944; W. Bert Craft, *Agony of Hell* (Paducah, Ky.: Turner Publishing, 1994), pp. 7–27.

51. National Archives, Record Group 407, 7th Infantry, AAR, November 1944; White, *Fedala to Berchtesgaden,* p. 176.

52. Craft, *Agony of Hell,* pp. 30–31.

53. Ibid., p. 35.

54. National Archives, Record Group 407, Entry 427, Box 5610, Folder 2, Historical Study, "7th Infantry in the Vosges Mountains," Small Unit Study No. 4, pp. 2–9; Reitan, *Riflemen,* pp. 45–52, 57; "Powerhouse I," *The Mailing List,* Volume 59, pp. 135–144.

55. George Trigueros, *The Cottonbaler,* Fall 1999, p. 6.

56. National Archives, Record Group 407, "7th Infantry in the Vosges Mountains," pp. 11–12; Reitan, *Riflemen,* pp. 52–53.

57. National Archives, Record Group 407, "7th Infantry in the Vosges Mountains," p. 12; Trigueros, *The Cottonbaler,* Fall 1999, p. 6. The historical study claimed that the various artillery units fired fifteen hundred rounds in twenty-seven minutes.

58. Craft, *Agony of Hell,* pp. 39–41.

59. National Archives, Record Group 407, "7th Infantry in the Vosges Mountains," pp. 16–24; 7th Infantry, AAR, November 1944; and Box 5611, Folder 6, 7th Infantry, Unit Journal, November 19–20, 1944; White, *Fedala to Berchtesgaden,* pp. 180–182; Reitan, *Riflemen,* pp. 54–58.

60. National Archives, Record Group 407, 7th Infantry, AAR, November 1944; and 7th Infantry, Unit Journal, November 22, 1944; Craft, *Agony of Hell,* p. 42–45; White, *Fedala to Berchtesgaden,* pp. 182–183.

61. National Archives, Record Group 407, 7th Infantry, AAR, November 1944; and 7th Infantry, Unit Journal, November 23–24, 1944; White, *Fedala to Berchtesgaden,* pp. 182–187; Craft, *Agony of Hell,* pp. 46–51.

62. National Archives, Record Group 407, Entry 427, Box 5609, Folder 10, 7th Infantry, After Action Report, December 1944; Craft, *Agony of Hell,* p. 53.

63. National Archives, Record Group 407, 7th Infantry, AAR, December 1944; Reitan, *Riflemen,* pp. 59–60; Pratt, *Autobahn to Berchtesgaden,* pp. 473–474.

64. Reitan, *Riflemen,* pp. 62–63.

65. Craft, *Agony of Hell,* pp. 60–63.

66. National Archives, Record Group 407, Entry 427, Box 5609, Folder 14, 7th Infantry, After Action Report, January 1945; Box 5610, Folder 9, 7th Infantry, Unit Journal, January 22, 1945; and Seventh Army, "3rd Division, Seventh United States Infantry Regiment: The Colmar Pocket, 22 January–8 February, 1945," pp. 3–9, copy of paper in author's possession. This paper is a special study prepared by the historical section of Patch's Seventh Army; First Lieutenant Charles K. Blum, "The Operations of the Third Platoon, Company E, 7th Infantry Regiment (Third Infantry Division), East of Ostheim, in the Colmar Pocket, Alsace, 22–23 January 1945, Personal Experiences of a Platoon Leader," paper prepared for Advanced Infantry Officers Course, the Infantry School, Fort Benning, Georgia, pp. 6–13; Reitan, *Riflemen,* pp. 67–68; White, *Fedala to Berchtesgaden,* pp. 203–207.

67. Craft, *Agony of Hell,* pp. 70–71.

68. National Archives, Record Group 407, 7th Infantry, AAR, January 1945; Seventh Army, "The Colmar Pocket," pp. 10–11.

69. National Archives, Record Group 407, 7th Infantry, AAR, January 1945; White, *Fedala to Berchtesgaden,* pp. 208–209; Seventh Army, "The Colmar Pocket," pp. 18–19; Blum, "Operations of the Third Platoon, Company E," pp. 22–30.

70. National Archives, Record Group 407, 7th Infantry, AAR, January 1945; Craft, *Agony of Hell,* pp. 73–79.

71. National Archives, Record Group 407, 7th Infantry, AAR, January 1945; White, *Fedala to Berchtesgaden,* pp. 209–210; Seventh Army, "The Colmar Pocket," pp. 20–25.

72. National Archives, Record Group 407, 7th Infantry, AAR, January 1945; and Box 5614, Folder 5, 7th Infantry, S3 Periodic Reports, January 26–27, 1945; White,

Fedala to Berchtesgaden, pp. 211–213; Seventh Army, "The Colmar Pocket," pp. 31–48; *The Cottonbaler,* Fall 2002, pp. 10, 15; Appel, *Outdoor Kids,* pp. 64–67; Steve Kovatch, Willis Daniel, personal conversations, September 25, 2004. The same reluctance to use bayonets existed among Civil War soldiers. See James Robertson, *Soldiers Blue and Gray* (New York: Warner Books, 1988), pp. 57–58, as well as the History Channel documentary series *Civil War Combat.*

73. Seventh Army, "The Colmar Pocket," pp. 51–62.

74. Reitan, *Riflemen,* p. 70.

75. National Archives, Record Group 407, 7th Infantry, AAR, January 1945; White, *Fedala to Berchtesgaden* p. 217–218; Seventh Army, "The Colmar Pocket," pp. 62–63.

76. Reitan, *Riflemen,* pp. 70–71.

77. National Archives, Record Group 407, Entry 427, Box 5610, Folder 9, 7th Infantry, Unit Journal, January 30, 1945; and 7th Infantry, S3 Periodic Report, January 30, 1945; Seventh Army, "The Colmar Pocket," pp. 65–72; Reitan, *Riflemen,* pp. 71–74.

78. National Archives, Record Group 407, 7th Infantry, AAR, January, 1945; Seventh Army, "The Colmar Pocket," pp. 72–77; Reitan, *Riflemen,* pp. 74–78.

79. National Archives, Record Group 407, 7th Infantry, S3 Periodic Report, January 31, 1945; White, *Fedala to Berchtesgaden,* pp. 218–220; Seventh Army, "The Colmar Pocket," p. 77.

80. National Archives, Record Group 407, Entry 427, Box 5610, Folder 9, 7th Infantry, Unit Journal, February 3, 1945; White, *Fedala to Berchtesgaden,* pp. 220–222; Seventh Army, "The Colmar Pocket," pp. 78–94.

81. National Archives, Record Group 407, Entry 427, Box 5609, Folder 14, 7th Infantry, After Action Report, February 1945; Seventh Army, "The Colmar Pocket," pp. 101–105; Craft, *Agony of Hell,* pp. 84–87.

82. National Archives, Record Group 407, 7th Infantry, AAR, February 1945; White, *Fedala to Berchtesgaden,* pp. 224–225; Seventh Army, "The Colmar Pocket," pp. 105–115.

83. White, *Fedala to Berchtesgaden,* pp. 229–230.

84. National Archives, Record Group 407, Entry 427, Box 6358, Folder 18, "Observations in the Breaching of the Siegfried Line and Conclusions Drawn from the Infantry Viewpoint." This is a four-page report of carefully organized advice from 9th Division officers.

85. National Archives, Record Group 407, Entry 427, Box 5609, Folder 14, 7th Infantry, After Action Report, March 15–May 10, 1945; Box 5612, Folder 1, 7th Infantry, Unit Citation, March 1945; and Box 5610, Folder 9, 7th Infantry, Unit Journal, March 15, 1945; Reitan, *Riflemen,* pp. 83–93; White, *Fedala to Berchtesgaden,* pp. 235–239; Earl Reitan, "Disaster at Utweiler," unpublished paper, pp. 1–24. I am indebted to Sherman Pratt for sending me a copy of Professor Reitan's excellent paper.

86. National Archives, Record Group 407, 7th Infantry, AAR, March 15–May 10, 1945; Unit Citation, March 1945; Richard Saffell to Russell Sutton, February 6, 1995, copy of the letter given to the author by Mr. Sutton. Sutton's comments are derived from his unpublished memoir, a copy of which he gave to me, pp. 1–4, and a letter, Russell Sutton to Sherman Pratt, April 24, 2000. I thank Lieutenant Colonel Pratt for providing me with a copy of Mr. Sutton's letter. Oddly enough, p. 470 of Taggart, *Third Infantry Division in World War II* lists Richard Saffell as having been killed in action.

87. National Archives, Record Group 407, 7th Infantry, AAR, March 15–May 10, 1945; Unit Citation, March 1945; 7th Infantry, Unit Journal, March 15, 1945; and Box 5614, Folder 5, 7th Infantry, S3 Periodic Report, March 15, 1945; White, *Fedala to Berchtesgaden,* pp. 238–240.

88. National Archives, Record Group 407, 7th Infantry, AAR, March 15–May 10, 1945; Unit Citation, March 1945; White, *Fedala to Berchtesgaden,* pp. 241–243; Taggart, *Third Infantry Division in World War II,* pp. 331–336.

89. National Archives, Record Group 407, 7th Infantry, AAR, March 15–May 10, 1945; Unit Citation, March 1945; and Box 5610, Folder 9, 7th Infantry, Unit Journal, March 18, 1945; Craft, *Agony of Hell,* pp. 105–107.

90. National Archives, Record Group 407, 7th Infantry, AAR, March 15–May 10, 1945; and Unit Citation, March 1945; White, *Fedala to Berchtesgaden,* pp. 245–246.

91. National Archives, Record Group 407, 7th Infantry, AAR, March 15–May 10, 1945; and Unit Citation, March 1945; Pratt, *Autobahn to Berchtesgaden,* pp. 509–515.

92. National Archives, Record Group 407, 7th Infantry, AAR, March 15–May 10, 1945; William B. Rosson, oral history transcript, USAMHI.

93. Cloer, unpublished memoir, pp. 31–33; White, *Fedala to Berchtesgaden,* p. 254.

94. National Archives, Record Group 407, 7th Infantry, AAR, March 15–May 10, 1945; and Box 5610, Folder 9, 7th Infantry, Unit Journal, March 25–26, 1945; Pratt, *Autobahn to Berchtesgaden,* pp. 519–530.

95. National Archives, Record Group 407, 7th Infantry, AAR, March 15–May 10, 1945; Craft, *Agony of Hell,* pp. 110–113; White, *Fedala to Berchtesgaden,* pp. 254–255; Appel, *Outdoor Kids,* pp. 229–230.

96. Cloer, unpublished memoir, pp. 33–35.

97. Rosson transcript, USAMHI.

98. National Archives, Record Group 407, 7th Infantry, AAR, March 15–May 10, 1945; and Box 5609, Folder 14, 7th Infantry, After Action Report, April 1945; Pratt, *Autobahn to Berchtesgaden,* pp. 535–539.

99. National Archives, Record Group 407, 7th Infantry, AAR, April 1945; John A. Heintges, oral history transcript, USAMHI.

100. National Archives, Record Group 407, 7th Infantry, AAR, March 15–May 10, 1945, and April 1945; Pratt, *Autobahn to Berchtesgaden,* pp. 546–562; White, *Fedala to Berchtesgaden,* pp. 261–262.

101. National Archives, Record Group 407, 7th Infantry, AAR, March 15–May 10, 1945; 7th Infantry, AAR, April 1945; Box 5610, Folder 9, 7th Infantry, Unit Journal, April 18–20, 1945; and Box 5614, Folder 5, 7th Infantry, S3 Periodic Reports, April 18–20, 1945; Heintges transcript, USAMHI; White, *Fedala to Berchtesgaden,* pp. 264–265; Appel, *Outdoor Kids,* pp. 123–124.

102. Heintges transcript, USAMHI.

103. White, *Fedala to Berchtesgaden,* pp. 270; Taggart, *Third Infantry Division in World War II,* p. 365.

104. National Archives, Record Group 407, 7th Infantry, AAR, March 15–May 10, 1945, and April 1945; Craft, *Agony of Hell,* pp. 120–122.

105. Cloer, unpublished memoir, p. 37.

106. Valenti, *Combat Medic,* p. 217.

107. Pratt, *Autobahn to Berchtesgaden,* pp. 572–576.

108. Heintges transcript, USAMHI.

109. Rosson transcript, USAMHI.

110. National Archives, Record Group 407, Entry 427, Box 5610, Folder 9, 7th Infantry, Unit Journal, May 4, 1945; Heintges transcript, USAMHI.

111. National Archives, Record Group 407, 7th Infantry, AAR, March 15–May 10, 1945; and 7th Infantry, Unit Journal, May 4, 1945; Pratt, *Autobahn to Berchtesgaden,* pp. 592–602.

112. Valenti, *Combat Medic,* pp. 232–236.

113. Stephen Ambrose, *Band of Brothers: E Company, 506th Regiment, 101st Airborne from Normandy to Hitler's Eagle's Nest* (New York: Touchstone, 1992), p. 272.

114. Documentation that the 7th Infantry Regiment was first into Berchtesgaden (and Hitler's home) is extensive: National Archives, Record Group 407, 7th Infantry, AAR, March 15–May 10, 1945; 7th Infantry, Unit Journal, May 4, 1945; and Box 5614, Folder 5, 7th Infantry, S3 Periodic Report, May 4, 1945; White, *Fedala to Berchtesgaden,* pp. 276–281; Taggart, *Third Infantry Division in World War II,* pp. 370–371; Charles Whiting, "At Home in Hitler's Headquarters," *World War II,* Band of Brothers Special Collectors Edition, pp. 81–84; Arthur Mitchell, "The Last Prize: The Race for Berchtesgaden, May 1945," unpublished paper. I found this paper among the World War II Questionnaires at USAMHI. Heintges and Rosson transcripts, USAMHI; Dwight D. Eisenhower, *Crusade in Europe* (Garden City, N.Y.: Doubleday, 1948), p. 418; Charles B. MacDonald, *The Last Offensive,* (Washington, D.C.: Center of Military History, United States Army, 1993), p. 442; also see my article, "The Last Great Prize," in *World War II,* May 2005, pp. 51–56. Even the commander of the 101st Airborne, General Maxwell Taylor, acknowledged in his memoirs that the 7th reached Berchtesgaden first; *Swords and Plowshares* (New York: Da Capo Press, 1972), p. 106. The commander of the 506th, Colonel Robert Sink, acknowledged the same thing in his May 1945 After Action Report, located in the National Archives, Record Group 407, Entry 427, Box 14439. By emphasizing this point so vociferously, I do not mean to denigrate or dismiss the *Band of Brothers* book or miniseries. Both are excellent studies of the American combat soldier in World War II, but they propagated a myth that, in the interest of fairness and accuracy, needs to be redressed.

115. The 7th Infantry's Unit Journal for May 5 and 6, 1945, records that the unit left Berchtesgaden at 0930 on May 6. Interestingly enough, the journal also reveals that on the evening of May 5 a trooper from the 101st Airborne shot a 1st Battalion Cottonbaler; Heintges transcript, USAMHI.

116. White, *Fedala to Berchtesgaden,* p. 286.

117. Bloom Questionnaire, USAMHI; Cloer, unpublished memoir, pp. 3–4; Valenti, *Combat Medic,* pp. 244–246; Craft, *Agony of Hell,* pp. 141–142; Martin interview, SCUTK; Pratt, *Autobahn to Berchtesgaden,* pp. 608–659; Rosson and Heintges transcripts, USAMHI.

Afterword

1. *The Cottonbaler,* Spring 1995, p. 3.

2. Robert Maxwell O'Kane, *The Cottonbaler,* Summer 1995, p. 8.

3. In an age when so many Americans are tempted to view air power and technology as magical elixirs, the cure-all for every military problem, Colonel Daniel P. Bolger makes a particularly compelling case for the continuing importance of the infantry in his excellent *Death Ground: Today's American Infantry in Battle* (Novato, Calif.: Presidio Press, 1999). Bolger also makes the salient, and troubling, point that the United States Army of the present does not have enough infantry to function adequately.

SELECT BIBLIOGRAPHY

ARCHIVES AND MANUSCRIPT COLLECTIONS

Carlisle, Pa. United States Army Military History Institute.

College Park, Md. National Archives and Records Administration (II).

Columbia, Mo. Western Historical Manuscript Collection, University of Missouri, World War II Letters.

Crow Agency, Mont. White Swan Library, Little Big Horn Battlefield National Monument.

Kansas City, Mo. National Archives and Records Administration.

Knoxville, Tenn. University of Tennessee Special Collections Library, World War II Collection (repository of the Center for the Study of War and Society).

New Haven, Conn. Yale University Library, Western Americana Collection.

Tulsa, Okla. Gilcrease Museum.

Washington, D.C. National Archives and Records Administration (I).

Washington, D.C. U.S. Army Center of Military History.

Wisdom, Mont. Big Hole National Battlefield Library.

DISSERTATIONS AND THESES

Gamble, Richard Dalzell. "Garrison Life at Frontier Military Posts, 1830–1860." Ph.D. Thesis, University of Oklahoma, 1956.

Graham, Stanley. "The Life of the Enlisted Soldier, 1815–1845." Ph.D. Dissertation, North Texas State University, 1972.

Wettemann, Robert Paul. "The Enlisted Soldier of the United States Army: A Study of the Seventh Regiment, U.S. Infantry, 1815–1860." M.A. Thesis, Texas A&M University, 1995.

JOURNALS, MAGAZINES, NEWSPAPERS, AND PAMPHLETS

American Catholic Quarterly Review.
American State Papers.
Army and Navy Chronicle.
Army History.
Army Times.
By Valor and Arms.
Civil War Times.
Civil War Times Illustrated.
The Cottonbale: The Official Newsletter of Company A, 7th Regiment, U.S.I. Living History Association.
The Cottonbaler, The 7th Infantry Regiment Association newsletter.
Daily National Intelligencer.
East Texas Historical Journal.
The Gettysburg Magazine.
Harper's Weekly.
Headquarters: 7th U.S. Infantry Association.
The Huntsville Times.
Infantry Journal.
Journal of Military History.
Journal of the West.
Louisville Journal.
Military Affairs.
Military History.
Military History Quarterly.
Montana: The Magazine of Western History.
New Mexico Historical Review.
Niles National Register.
Panhandle-Plains Historical Review.
Scribner's Magazine.
St. Louis Post-Dispatch.
U.S. Army Campaigns of World War II.
Watch on the Rhine.
William and Mary Quarterly.
Winners of the West.
World War II.

Books

Allen, William. *Anzio: Edge of Disaster*. New York: Elsevier-Dutton, 1978.

Ambrose, Stephen. *Band of Brothers: E Company, 506th Regiment, 101st Airborne from Normandy to Hitler's Eagle's Nest*. New York: Touchstone, 1992.

Appel, Bob, compiler. *The Outdoor Kids of Company B, 7th Infantry Regiment, Third Division, U.S. Army*. Kearney, Neb.: Morris Publishing, 2004.

Ashcraft, W. Bert. *Agony of Hell*. Paducah, Ky.: Tuner Publishing Company, 1994.

Astor, Gerald. *The Greatest War: Americans in Combat 1941–1945*. Novato, Calif.: Presidio Press, 1999.

Berry, Henry, editor. *Make the Kaiser Dance: Living Memories of a Forgotten War. The American Experience in World War I*. Garden City, N.Y.: Doubleday & Company, 1978.

Black, Robert W. *Rangers in World War II*. New York: Ballantine Books, 1992.

Blumenson, Martin. *Anzio: The Gamble That Failed*. Philadelphia and New York: J. B. Lippincott Company, 1963.

——. *Salerno to Cassino*. United States Army in World War II: The Mediterranean Theater of Operations. Washington, D.C.: Office of the Chief of Military History, United States Army, 1969.

Bolger, Daniel. *Death Ground: Today's American Infantry in Battle*. Novato, Calif.: Presidio Press, 1999.

Bonn, Keith. *When the Odds Were Even: The Vosges Mountain Campaign, October 1944–January 1945*. Novato, Calif.: Presidio Press, 1994.

Brady, Cyrus Townsend. *Northwestern Fights and Fighters*. New York: Doubleday, Page, 1907.

Brown, Wilbert. *The Amphibious Campaign for West Florida and Louisiana, 1814–1815*. University: University of Alabama Press, 1969.

Busey, John W. *These Honored Dead: The Union Casualties at Gettysburg*. Hightstown, N.J.: Longstreet House, 1996.

Chambers, John Whiteclay, editor. *The Oxford Companion to American Military History*. New York: Oxford University Press, 1999.

Churchill, Winston S. *The Second World War: Closing the Ring*. New York: Bantam, 1962.

——. *The Second World War: Triumph and Tragedy*. New York: Bantam, 1962.

Clark, George B. *Devil Dogs: Fighting Marines in World War I*. Novato, Calif.: Presidio Press, 1999.

Clarke, Jeffrey J., and Robert Ross Smith. *Riviera to the Rhine*. United States Army in World War II: The European Theater of Operations. Washington, D.C.: Center of Military History, United States Army, 1993.

Coffman, Edward. *The War to End All Wars: The American Military Experience in World War I*. New York: Oxford University Press, 1968.

——. *The Old Army: A Portrait of the American Army in Peacetime, 1784–1898*. New York and Oxford: Oxford University Press, 1986.

Colton, Ray C. *The Civil War in the Western Territories*. Norman: University of Oklahoma Press, 1959.

Cosmas, Graham. *An Army for Empire: The United States Army in the Spanish-American War*. Shippensburg, Pa.: Whitemane Publishing Company, 1973.

D'Este, Carlo. *Bitter Victory: The Battle for Sicily, 1943*. New York: E. P. Dutton, 1988.

——. *Fatal Decision: Anzio and the Battle for Rome*. New York: HarperCollins Publishers, 1991.

Doubler, Michael. *Closing with the Enemy: How G.I.'s Fought the War in Europe, 1944–1945*. Lawrence: University Press of Kansas, 1995.

Drake, Samuel G. *The Aboriginal Races of North America*. Philadelphia: Charles DeSilver & Sons, 1859.

Dunlay, Thomas W. *Wolves for the Blue Soldiers: Indian Scouts and Auxiliaries with the United States Army, 1860–1890*. Lincoln: University of Nebraska Press, 1982.

Eisenhower, Dwight D. *Crusade in Europe*. New York: Doubleday, 1948.

Eisenhower, John S. D., with Joanne Thompson Eisenhower. *Yanks: The Epic Story of the American Army in World War I*. New York: Free Press, 2001.

Falwell, Byron. *The United States in the Great War, 1917–1918*. New York: W. W. Norton, 1999.

Ferrell, Robert, editor. *Monterrey Is Ours! The Mexican War Letters of Lieutenant Dana, 1845–1847*. Lexington: University Press of Kentucky, 1990.

Feuer, A. B. editor. *America at War: The Philippines, 1898–1913*. Westport, Conn.: Praeger, 2002.

Fisher, Ernest F., Jr. *Cassino to the Alps*. United States Army in World War II: The Mediterranean Theater of Operations. Washington, D.C.: Center of Military History, United States Army, 1993.

Friedel, Frank. *The Splendid Little War*. Boston: Little, Brown, 1958.

——. *Over There: The Story of America's First Great Crusade*. Boston: Little, Brown, 1964.

Ganoe, William Addelman. *The History of the United States Army*. New York: D. Appleton-Century, 1942.

Giddings, Luther. *Sketches of the Campaign in Northern Mexico*. New York: G. P. Putnam, 1853.

Goetzmann, William H., editor. *Autobiography of an English Soldier in the United States Army*. Chicago: Lakeside Press, 1986.

Goodrich, Thomas. *Scalp Dance: Indian Warfare on the High Plains, 1865–1879*. Mechanicsburg, Pa.: Stackpole Books, 1997.

Gray, Charles Martin. *The Old Soldier's Story: Embracing Interesting and Exciting Incidents of Army Life on the Frontier in the Early Part of the Century*. Edgefield, S.C.: Edgefield Advertising Print, 1868.

Gray, John S. *Centennial Campaign: The Sioux War of 1876*. Fort Collins, Colo.: Old Army Press, 1976.

———. *Custer's Last Campaign: Mitch Boyer and the Little Big Horn Reconstructed*. Lincoln and London: University of Nebraska Press, 1991.

Greene, Jerome A. *Nez Perce Summer, 1877: The U.S. Army and the Nee-Me-Poo Crisis*. Helena: Montana Historical Society Press, 2000.

———. *Indian War Veterans: Memories of Army Life and Campaigns in the West, 1864–1898*. El Dorado Hills, Calif.: Savas Beattie Publishers, 2007.

Haines, Aubrey L. *The Battle of the Big Hole: The Story of the Landmark Battle of the 1877 Nez Perce War*. Guilford, Conn.: Twodot Press, 2007. Reprint of 1991 edition.

Hardorff, Richard C. *The Custer Battle Casualties: Burials, Exhumations and Reinterments*. El Segundo, Calif.: Upton and Sons, 1991.

Hartzog, William. *American Military Heritage*. Washington, D.C.: Center of Military History, 2001.

Heitman, Francis B. *Historical Register and Dictionary of the U.S. Army, 1789–1903*. Washington, D.C.: Government Printing Office, 1903.

Hemenway, Frederic V. *History of the Third Division, United States Army in the World War for the Period December 1, 1917, to January 1, 1919*. Cologne, Germany: Shauberg, 1919.

Henry, William Seaton. *Campaign Sketches of the War with Mexico*. New York: Arno Press, 1973.

Howe, George F. *Northwest Africa: Seizing the Initiative in the West*. United States Army in World War II: The Mediterranean Theater of Operations. Washington, D.C.: Center of Military History, U.S. Army, 1991.

Jorgensen, Jay. *Gettysburg's Bloody Wheatfield*. Shippensburg, Pa.: White Mane Books, 2002.

Keleher, Willam A. *Turmoil in New Mexico*. Albuquerque: University of New Mexico Press, 1952.

Kohr, Herbert O. *Around the World with Uncle Sam: Six Years in the United States Army*. Akron, Ohio: Commercial Printing Company, 1907.

Leckie, Robert. *From Sea to Shining Sea: From the War of 1812 to the Mexican War; The Saga of America's Expansion*. New York: Harper Perennial Library, 1994.

Linn, Brian. *The U.S. Army and Counterinsurgency in the Philippine War, 1899–1902*. Chapel Hill and London: University of North Carolina Press, 1989.

———. *The Philippine War, 1899–1902*. Lawrence: University Press of Kansas, 2000.

MacDonald, Charles B. *The Last Offensive*. United States Army in World War II: The European Theater of Operations. Washington, D.C.: Office of the Chief of Military History, United States Army, 1993.

MacGregor, Morris, Jr. *Integration of the Armed Forces, 1940–1965*. Washington, D.C.: Center of Military History, United States Army, 1981.

Mahon, John K. *History of the Second Seminole War, 1835–1842*. Gainesville: University of Florida Press, 1967.

Mansoor, Peter. *The G.I. Offensive in Europe: The Triumph of American Infantry Divisions, 1941–1945*. Lawrence: University Press of Kansas, 1999.

Marcy, Randolph Barnes. *Thirty Years of Army Life on the Border*. New York: Harper and Brothers, 1866.

McCaffrey, James. *Army of Manifest Destiny: The American Soldier in the Mexican War, 1846–1848*. New York: New York University Press, 1992.

McCall, George. *Letters from the Frontiers*. Gainesville: University Press of Florida, 1974.

McChristian, Douglas C. *The U.S. Army in the West, 1870–1880, Uniforms, Weapons, and Equipment*. Norman and London: University of Oklahoma Press, 1995.

McManus, John C. *The Deadly Brotherhood: The American Combat Soldier in World War II*. Novato, Calif.: Presidio Press, 1998.

Military Order of the Loyal Legion of the United States. Wilmington, N.C.: Broadfoot Publishing, 1992.

Morison, Samuel Eliot. *History of United States Naval Operations in World War II: Operations in North African Waters, October 1942–June 1943*. Boston: Little, Brown, 1947.

Musicant, Ivan. *Empire by Default: The Spanish-American War and the Dawn of the American Century*. New York: Henry Holt, 1998.

O'Toole, G. J. A. *The Spanish War: An American Epic—1898*. New York: W. W. Norton, 1984.

Owsley, Frank Lawrence, Jr. *Struggle for the Gulf Borderlands: The Creek War and the Battle of New Orleans, 1812–1815*. Gainesville: University Presses of Florida, 1981.

Paschall, Rod. *The Defeat of Imperial Germany, 1917–1918*. Chapel Hill, N.C.: Algonquin Books of Chapel Hill, 1989.

Pfanz, Harry W. *Gettysburg: The Second Day*. Chapel Hill: University of North Carolina Press, 1987.

Pickles, Tim. *New Orleans, 1815: Andrew Jackson Crushes the British*. Oxford: Osprey Publishing, 1993.

Pratt, Sherman. *Autobahn to Berchtesgaden: A View of World War II from the Bottom Up by an Infantry Sergeant*. Baltimore, Md.: Gateway Press, 1992.

Prucha, Francis Paul. *The Sword of the Republic: The United States Army on the Frontier, 1783–1846*. Bloomington and London: Indiana University Press, 1969.

Rable, George. *Fredericksburg! Fredericksburg!* Chapel Hill: University of North Carolina Press, 2002.

Reese, Timothy. *Sykes Regular Infantry Division, 1861–1864: A History of Regular United States Infantry Operations in the Civil War's Eastern Theater*. Jefferson, N.C.: McFarland, 1990.

Reitan, Earl. *Riflemen: On the Cutting Edge of World War II*. Bennington, Vt.: Merriam Press, 2001.

Remini, Robert. *The Battle of New Orleans: Andrew Jackson and America's First Military Victory*. New York: Viking, 1999.

Rickey, Don. *Forty Miles a Day on Beans and Hay: The Enlisted Soldier Fighting the Indian Wars*. Norman: University of Oklahoma Press, 1963.

Robertson, James I. *Soldiers Blue and Gray*. New York: Warner Books, 1988.

Rodenbaugh, Theophilus, and William Haskin. *The Army of the United States: Historical Sketches of Staff and Line with Portraits of Generals-in-Chief*. New York: University Microfilms, 1966.

Schneider, George A., editor. *The Freeman Journal: The Infantry in the Sioux Campaign of 1876*. Novato, Calif.: Presidio Press, 1977.

Shaara, Jeff. *Gone for Soldiers*. New York: Ballantine Books, 2000.

Skelton, William B. *An American Profession of Arms: The Army Officer Corps, 1784–1861*. Lawrence: University Press of Kansas, 1992.

Smith, Gene, editor. *Historical Memoir of the War in West Florida and Louisiana in 1814–15*. Gainesville: Historic New Orleans Collection and University Press of Florida, 1999.

Smith, George Winston, and Charles Judah. *Chronicles of the Gringos: The U.S. Army in the Mexican War, 1846–1848, Accounts of Eyewitnesses & Combatants*. Albuquerque: University of New Mexico Press, 1968.

Smith, Justin H. *The War with Mexico*. Two volumes. New York: Macmillan, 1919.

Sprague, John T. *The Origin, Progress, and Conclusion of the Florida War*. New York: D. Appleton, 1848.

Steidl, Franz. *Lost Battalions: Going for Broke in the Vosges, Autumn 1944*. Novato, Calif.: Presidio Press, 1997.

Stewart, Edgar I., editor. *The March of the Montana Column: A Prelude to the Custer Disaster*. Norman: University of Oklahoma Press, 1961.

Taggart, Donald G. *History of the Third Infantry Division in World War II*. Washington, D.C.: Infantry Journal Press, 1947.

Taylor, Maxwell. *Swords and Plowshares*. New York: Da Capo Press, 1972.

Trask, David. *The War with Spain in 1898*. New York: Macmillan, 1981.

Underwood, Robert Johnson, editor. *Battles and Leaders of the Civil War*. Multiple volumes. Secaucus, N.J.: Castle Publishers, 1982.

United States War Department. *Official Records of the War of the Rebellion*. Multiple volumes. Washington, D.C.: Government Printing Office, 1890–1901.

Urwin, Gregory J. W. *The United States Infantry: An Illustrated History, 1775–1918*. Norman: University of Oklahoma Press, 1988.

Utley, Robert. *Frontiersmen in Blue: The United States Army and the Indian, 1848–1865*. New York: Macmillan, 1967.

——. *Frontier Regulars: The United States Army and the Indian, 1866–1891*. Lincoln and London: University of Nebraska Press, 1973.

——. *Custer and the Great Controversy: Origin and Development of a Legend.* Pasadena, Calif.: Westernlore Press, 1980.

Valenti, Isadore. *Combat Medic.* Tarentum, Pa.: Word Association Publishers, 1998.

Van Dorn, Earl. *A Soldier's Honor with Reminiscences of Major-General Earl Van Dorn.* New York: Abbey Press, 1902.

White, Nathan W. *From Fedala to Berchtesgaden: A History of the 7th United States Infantry in World War II.* Brockton, Mass.: Keystone Print, 1947.

Wilcox, Cadmus. *History of the Mexican War.* Washington, D.C.: Church News Publishing Company, 1892.

Williams Printing Company. *The Santiago Campaign: Reminiscences of the Operations for the Capture of Santiago de Cuba in the Spanish-American War, June and July, 1898.* Richmond, Va.: Williams Printing Company, 1927.

Wilt, Alan. *The French Riviera Campaign of August 1944.* Carbondale: Southern Illinois University Press, 1981.

Winders, Richard Bruce. *Mr. Polk's Army: The American Military Experience in the Mexican War.* College Station: Texas A&M University Press, 1997.

INDEX OF MILITARY UNITS

Military units are American unless otherwise noted.